Kiev 1941

In just four weeks in the summer of 1941 the German Wehrmacht wrought unprecedented destruction on four Soviet armies, conquering central Ukraine and killing or capturing three-quarters of a million men. This was the battle of Kiev – one of the largest and most decisive battles of World War II and, for Hitler and Stalin, a battle of crucial importance. For the first time, David Stahel charts the battle's dramatic course and aftermath, uncovering the irreplaceable losses suffered by Germany's 'panzer groups' despite their battlefield gains, and the implications of these losses for the German war effort. He illuminates the inner workings of the German army as well as the experiences of ordinary soldiers, showing that with the Russian winter looming and Soviet resistance still unbroken, victory came at huge cost and confirmed the turning point in Germany's war in the east.

David Stahel is an independent researcher based in Berlin. His previous publications include *Operation Barbarossa and Germany's Defeat in the East* (Cambridge, 2009).

Kiev 1941

Hitler's Battle for Supremacy in the East

David Stahel

Cambridge
University Press

CAMBRIDGE UNIVERSITY PRESS
Cambridge, New York, Melbourne, Madrid, Cape Town,
Singapore, São Paulo, Delhi, Mexico City

Cambridge University Press
The Edinburgh Building, Cambridge CB2 8RU, UK

Published in the United States of America by Cambridge University Press,
New York

www.cambridge.org
Information on this title: www.cambridge.org/9781107014596

First published 2012
Reprinted 2012
First paperback edition with corrections 2013

A catalogue record for this publication is available from the British Library

Library of Congress Cataloguing in Publication data
Stahel, David, 1975–
Kiev 1941 : Hitler's battle for supremacy in the East / David Stahel.
p. cm.
Includes bibliographical references and index.
ISBN 978-1-107-01459-6 (hardback)
1. Kiev (Ukraine) – History – Siege, 1941. 2. World War, 1939–1945 –
Campaigns – Ukraine – Kiev. 3. World War, 1939–1945 – Campaigns –
Ukraine. 4. World War, 1939–1945 – Campaigns – Eastern Front.
5. Germany. Heer – Armored troops – History – 20th century.
6. Germany. Heer – History – World War, 1939–1945. I. Title.
D764.3.K5S73 2011
940.5421777 – dc23 2011030300

ISBN 978-1-107-01459-6 Hardback
ISBN 978-1-107-61014-9 Paperback

CONTENTS

FIGURES

TABLES

MAPS

ACKNOWLEDGEMENTS

The process of researching and writing this book was enormously satisfying and the final product benefited from much help and advice. In the first place thanks must go to my old friend Jakob Graichen. He and his wife, Mariana, proved to be endless sources of support and inspiration for which I cannot thank them enough. Thanks also to Benjamin, Lea and Nadia for their welcome distractions. Florian Ehrendreich assisted in checking my translations, while Priscilla Pettengell helped unravel some of my more complex sentences. My numerous research trips to Freiburg for the German military archive were made both comfortable and economical by the support of Gudrun and Rainer Graichen as well as Dr Irmela Gonser.

For historical matters I have been uniquely served by some of the best minds in the field. Professor Rolf-Dieter Müller and Colonel David Glantz both gave freely of their time, reading drafts, answering questions and offering advice. Colonel Glantz also agreed to the publication of his own privately produced maps.

Dr Eleanor Hancock, Dr Jeff Rutherford, Dr Adrian Wettstein, Dr Alexander Hill and my editor, Michael Watson, all read drafts and provided invaluable feedback. Dr Alex J. Kay helped with some of the source material and proved to be a vital sounding board for many of my ideas. To all these historians I owe my deepest gratitude and heartfelt thanks.

Finally, for all his support over the years and for the wonderful person that he is, this book is lovingly dedicated to my brother Andrew.

GLOSSARY OF TERMS

BA-MA	*Bundesarchiv-Militärarchiv* (German Military Archive)
CSIR	*Corpo di Sedizione Italiano in Russia* (Italian Expeditionary Corps in Russia)
Das Reich	2nd SS Division
Einsatzgruppen	'action groups' of the SD and Security Police, used mainly for mass killings
Endkampf	final battle
FHQ	*Führerhauptquartier* (Führer Headquarters)
Gestapo	*Geheime Staatspolizei* (Secret State Police)
Grossdeutschland	Infantry Regiment (later Division)
Grosstransportraum	'large transport area', referring to the transport regiment responsible for bridging the gap between front-line divisions and railheads
Hiwis	*Hilfswilliger* (willing helpers)
KTB	*Kriegstagebuch* (War Diary)
Landser	German infantry man
Lebensraum	living space
Leibstandarte Adolf Hitler	SS Regiment (later Division)
LH	Liddell Hart Centre for Military Archives
Luftwaffe	German air force

MGFA	*Militärgeschichtliches Forschungsamt* (Military History Research Institute)
NCO	non-commissioned officer
NKVD	*Narodnyi Komissariat Vnutrennykh Del* (People's Commissariat for Internal Affairs)
OKH	Oberkommando des Heers (High Command of the Army)
OKW	Oberkommando der Wehrmacht (High Command of the Armed Forces)
Ostheer	Eastern Army
POW	prisoner of war
Pz. Div.	Panzer Division
RAF	Royal Air Force
rasputitsa	'quagmire season', refers to the biannual difficulties caused by heavy rains or melting snow in Russia, Belorussia and the Ukraine
Reichsbahn	German railways
SD	*Sicherheitsdienst* (Security Service)
Sondermeldungen	special news bulletins
SS	*Schutzstaffel* (Protection Echelon)
Stavka	Soviet High Command
UK	United Kingdom
USA	United States of America
USSR	Union of Soviet Socialist Republics
Untermensch	subhuman
Vernichtungskrieg	war of annihilation
Wehrmacht	German armed forces

TABLES OF MILITARY RANKS AND ARMY STRUCTURES

Table of equivalent ranks

German army/Luftwaffe	Translation used in this study	Equivalent US army ranks
Officer ranks		
Generalfeldmarschall	Field Marshal	General of the Army
Generaloberst	Colonel-General	General
General	General	Lieutenant General
der Infanterie	of Infantry	
der Artillerie	of Artillery	
der Flakartillerie	of Flak Artillery	
der Flieger	of Aviation	
der Kavallerie	of Cavalry	
der Luftwaffe	of the Luftwaffe	
der Panzertruppe	of Panzer Troops	
der Pioniere	of Engineers	
Generalleutnant	Lieutenant-General	Major General
Generalmajor	Major-General	Brigadier General
Oberst	Colonel	Colonel
Oberstleutnant	Lieutenant-Colonel	Lieutenant Colonel
Major	Major	Major
Hauptmann	Captain	Captain
Oberleutnant	1st Lieutenant	1st Lieutenant
Leutnant	Lieutenant	2nd Lieutenant
Enlisted ranks		
Stabsfeldwebel	Master Sergeant	Master Sergeant
Oberfeldwebel	Technical Sergeant	Technical Sergeant
Feldwebel	Staff Sergeant	Staff Sergeant
Unterfeldwebel	Sergeant	Sergeant
Unteroffizier	Corporal	Corporal
Gefreiter	Private	Private 1st Class
Soldat	Private	Private 2nd Class

Source: Karl-Heinz Frieser, *The Blitzkrieg Legend. The 1940 Campaign in the West* (Annapolis, 2005) p. 355.

Structure and size of the German army

Germany army formation	English translation	Number of subordinate units	Average number of personnel[a]
Heeresgruppe	Army Group	Two or more armies	100,000 to more than a million
Armee	Army	Two or more corps	60,000–250,000
Korps	Corps	Two or more divisions	40,000–70,000
Division	Division	Two or more brigades	12,000–18,000
Brigade	Brigade	Two or more regiments	5,000–7,000
Regiment	Regiment	Two or more battalions	2,000–6,000
Bataillon	Battalion	Two or more companies	500–1,000
Kompanie	Company	Two or more platoons	100–200
Zug	Platoon		30–40

Note: [a] Wide variations of these figures occurred especially after 1941.
Source: Author's own records.

INTRODUCTION

Nazi Germany's war against the Soviet Union began on 22 June 1941 in what was the largest military undertaking in history. Code-named Operation Barbarossa the war was to be another in a series of sweeping blitzkrieg battles, which aimed to defeat the Red Army in a matter of weeks. From the beginning the fighting proceeded with unremitting violence, which saw the German Wehrmacht undertake deep advances, while crushing numerous Soviet armies. Throughout the summer of 1941 the progress of Operation Barbarossa was reported to the German people not just as an unbroken string of battlefield successes, but as some of the greatest victories in the history of warfare. Indeed, on the surface, it may have seemed justified to categorize the battles at Belostok-Minsk, Smolensk and Uman' as a series of unsurpassed triumphs. Yet the war was not all it appeared to be in the news reels of the German cinema or the *Sondermeldungen* (special bulletins) on German radio. The Wehrmacht's *Ostheer* (eastern army) was also suffering serious losses. In June 1941, during only the first nine days of the war, some 25,000 German fatalities were sustained and in the following month no fewer than 63,000 German soldiers fell (with tens of thousands more wounded), making July the deadliest month of the war until the battle of Stalingrad in the winter of 1942/1943.[1] Even more costly to the *Ostheer*'s chances of success were the material costs resulting from the long summer advance and unceasing battles. The vital panzer and motorized divisions suffered staggering fallout rates, which there was neither the time, facilities nor the requisite spare parts to correct. By late August 1941, Operation Barbarossa was a spent exercise, incapable of achieving its central objective of ending Soviet resistance.[2]

While outright victory in a single campaign may have been beyond Germany's reach in late August 1941, the intensity of the fighting in the east had in no way abated. Nor were the German high command able to appreciate the seriousness of their strategic position. Army Group Centre, the largest of the three German army groups to invade the Soviet Union, had just completed two of the largest encirclements in military history. Not only had these netted a total of some 600,000 Soviet POWs, but the German lines were now two-thirds of the way to Moscow and the Army General Staff was determined to press on and seize the Soviet capital. Hitler, however, did not agree. The eastern front was advancing at different speeds and Army Group Centre, with the bulk of the panzer and motorized troops, was far ahead of its northern and southern counterparts. Consequently a major bulge had developed in the front, which would only be exacerbated by a further push on Moscow. Hitler was therefore reluctant to attack the Soviet capital, especially as he disputed its importance and referred to it as 'only a geographical term'.[3] More important to Hitler was the prospect of diverting Army Group Centre's renewed attack to the north and south where, in his view, much greater opportunities lay. In the north was Leningrad, which Hitler saw as the root of Bolshevism and believed to be of fundamental importance to the survival of the Soviet political system.[4] Hitler also identified opportunities in the south, which offered far more tangible benefits to the German war effort. Uppermost in Hitler's mind were the riches of the Ukraine, which, along with the oil fields of southern Russia, he saw as the key to Germany's economic autarky. On the night of 19–20 August 1941 Hitler told his inner circle:

> *It is not tolerable that the life of the peoples of the continent should depend upon England. The Ukraine, and then the Volga basin, will one day be the granaries of Europe. We shall reap much more than what actually grows from the soil... If one day Sweden declines to supply any more iron, that's alright. We'll get it from Russia.*[5]

Hitler's visions of economic independence were, however, dependent upon the defeat of the Red Army and the conquest of the Soviet Union's southern regions. There was indeed much to gain and, given the difficulties of Operation Barbarossa and the impending war of attrition that Germany now faced in the east, such economic wealth had never been more essential. Yet it was in the Ukraine that Operation Barbarossa had faced some of its most determined resistance and in spite of Army Group South's hard-fought encirclement at Uman' the total was still only 100,000 POWs. The great bulk of the Soviet South-Western Front (the main Red Army grouping in the Ukraine) was successfully withdrawn behind the Dnepr River. As Army Group South closed on the Dnepr, two months of hard fighting coupled with the great depth of the advance took a steep toll on the motorized forces. This complicated any independent action aimed at overcoming Soviet resistance along the Dnepr, especially given complications emanating from the Pripet marshes (in the northern Ukraine) from where Soviet forces where able to stage large-scale attacks into the German rear. With summer weather almost at an end and the South-Western Front entrenching itself further with every day, the prospect of destroying Soviet resistance in the Ukraine and breaking into the mineral-rich Donets Basin (in the east of the country) was looking increasingly remote.

The difficulties in the Ukraine were not, however, what interested the Army High Command (*Oberkommando des Heeres*, OKH), who were responsible for directing Germany's war in the east. For the army commanders as well as the senior generals at Army Group Centre, Moscow was the sole objective they were prepared to consider for the second phase of the campaign. The result was a standoff with Hitler as a strategic crisis paralysed the German command from the third week of July until 23 August. In the end it was Hitler who broke the deadlock by categorically overruling any further debate, denouncing the army commanders for their supposed ineptitude and insisting that Panzer Group 2, on the southern wing of Army Group Centre, turn south and strike into the Ukraine. It was the prelude to the biggest and costliest battle thus far fought in World War II.

The climactic battle of Kiev in late August and September 1941 was an epic of human endurance, strategic uncertainty and ceaseless carnage. Yet the familiar portrait of a rousing German victory, which appears to confirm the *Ostheer*'s dominance in the east, is misleading. The battle was not the seamless encounter often portrayed, but rather one typified by hard fighting, embittered command disputes and an exacerbation of the already serious decline in the *Ostheer*'s offensive strength. Indeed the scale of the German success was much less a result of the *Ostheer*'s raw military power than of the catastrophic Soviet strategic direction, which accounted in greatest measure for the one-sided outcome. Nevertheless, the battle of Kiev was a remarkable achievement, and after the bitter disputes with the OKH over the decision to strike into the Ukraine, the battle became another resounding personal triumph for Adolf Hitler. Thus the battle of Kiev was Hitler's battle not simply by the default of his being the head of the Nazi state, but more importantly because he, with almost no support within the high command, insisted upon it. Nor was the battle just one more triumph in the string of large encirclements on the eastern front in 1941. Its sheer scale exceeded any single encounter of the preceding summer and set the groundwork for the battles still to be fought on the approaches to Moscow at Viaz'ma and Briansk as well as along the Nogai Steppe on the Sea of Azov. As Army Group South's war diary stated on 1 September: 'In the opinion of the commander of the army group carrying out the annihilation battle in the Ukraine is of decisive importance for the outcome of the whole eastern campaign.'[6] Such a statement may reflect the forlorn hopes of outright victory, but it also underlines the extent of the Soviet calamity in the south. Indeed in many respects the battle of Kiev may be considered the Wehrmacht's single greatest set-piece battle of World War II and, despite attracting surprisingly little attention in the historical literature, it remains Hitler's most significant battlefield triumph.[7]

While it may be taken for granted that Nazi Germany sought to derive as much propaganda value as possible from its 1941 battles in the east, what is less explicable is the endurance of many similar depictions throughout numerous histories of the Barbarossa campaign. Accounts of the early summer period provide the best examples,[8] but even those covering the late August and September period, as the colder weather beckoned with all its ominous implications, still suggest that some form of German victory remained a realistic prospect.[9] Even more radical interpretations suggest that the German failure in 1941 occurred by only the most slender of margins.[10] Although by 1941 the Wehrmacht was the most refined and professional fighting force in the world, its battlefield superiority at the tactical and operational level did not make it infallible strategically. Indeed the defeat of the *Ostheer* did not begin with the first retreats (and at times routs) following the launch of the Soviet winter offensive in December 1941. By this time German plans to conquer the Soviet Union had long since failed and the fact that the Soviets were now pushing the Germans back only further confirmed Germany's crisis in the east. Yet post-war scholarship quickly adopted the tone set by the German generals, who were themselves simply echoing many of the triumphant phrases previously trumpeted by Goebbels.[11] More recently, the overly affirmative tone has been accepted in some otherwise first-rate works,[12] which reflect the lack of specialized operational studies conducted in the area.[13]

Far more revealing and accurate accounts of the 1941 campaign have emanated from studies on the Soviet side of the front. Unlike German historiography these works did not first have to shed the fog of distortions generated by German memoir literature, and although there were similar distortions contained within Soviet era publications these were rightfully treated from the very beginning with a far greater degree of scrutiny. Yet for all its distortions and blatant falsifications, Soviet and East German historiography did at least take a far more critical view of German operational success in 1941 and argued for Soviet successes far earlier than anyone in the west was willing to concede. At the time such views were dismissed outright as the usual self-absorbed hyperbole typical of so many eastern bloc fabrications. Although the communist view erroneously proclaimed the historical inevitability of their victory by arguing for the superiority of the Marxist/Leninist political ideology, on strictly military matters they were frequently closer to the mark than contemporary western accounts. Standard Soviet histories certainly presented the war in a typically sensationalist style with at times grossly distorted figures that helped explain Soviet setbacks, but their general conclusions about the 1941 campaign are far more consistent with the picture gained from German military files. As Soviet high school textbooks explained:

> *In the summer and autumn of 1941 the Red Army fought fierce defensive battles against the invading forces of Nazi Germany. The Smolensk battle lasted almost two months. The enemy was held at this point until the middle of September. The German invaders suffered enormous losses and were forced to postpone for more than a month their attack on Moscow... The stubborn resistance of the heroic cities of Leningrad, Kiev and Odessa and the defensive battle at Smolensk played an important role in frustrating the Hitler plan for a 'lightning war'.*[14]

In the west, the pioneering studies produced firstly by John Erickson[15] and later by David M. Glantz[16] have contributed more than any other[17] to providing a corrective remedial to the overly congenial view of German military operations.[18]

By contrast, while there has been a huge amount written on the German military campaign in the east, the standard has not always been high. In Germany much of the literature stems from the former veteran community and appears in the form of soldiers' memoirs, unit histories and campaign summaries. These typically tend to steer clear of any reference to the uglier aspects of the war in the east and project images of a gallant, long-suffering army struggling to do its duty in the east under increasingly difficult conditions. The strong interest in the Anglo-American world for perspectives of the war from the German standpoint has led to many works being translated into English, particularly German soldiers' memoirs.[19] Such books have formed a steady source of primary material within the western discourse, which tends to underline the innocence of the Wehrmacht, while at the same time drawing unfavourable, pro-German comparisons with the Red Army's professionalism (although this is somewhat less pronounced in books covering the latter stages of the war). Not only was much of this early literature uncritically accepted within the Anglo-American discourse, it helped spawn secondary works that likewise incorporated pro-German perspectives, which, especially during the cold war, audiences avidly received. Decades of such publications helped establish a flawed orthodoxy,[20] which has proved hard to break and requires a very conscientious and circumspect approach to the literature on Germany's military campaigns in the east. The prevailing taboo within German academia towards military history[21] and the relative lack of scholarly publications in the Anglo-American field have, as a result, left much room for new research to provide the requisite riposte to established popular accounts. With so little research having been done on the German side of the war in the east, and mindful of how much needs to be revisited in light of the many post-war myths, there is much fertile ground for original studies on both well-known aspects of the war and the so-called 'forgotten battles', which are regrettably numerous.[22] To that end my current study seeks to fill two important gaps in the literature: on the one hand, to provide the first intensive treatment of the battle of Kiev and, on the other, to chart the ongoing demise of Germany's operational proficiency in 1941.

When Hitler overruled his generals and diverted the most powerful panzer group on the eastern front[23] into the Ukraine, it was a decision which reflected the growing weakness of Germany's strategic position rather than the masterstroke it has occasionally been branded. Indeed the scale of the German victory in the Ukraine was highly dependent on the obstinacy of the Soviet dictator who steadfastly refused to countenance any withdrawal even after the prospects for holding Kiev had become utterly hopeless. Starting with Marshal Georgi Zhukov in late July, a string of Soviet generals had tried to warn Stalin about this, but to no avail. In addition to Stalin's unwitting complicity in Germany's success, Hitler's own commanders had fiercely opposed the operation from the beginning. To Hitler's mind the first two major encirclements in the central part of the eastern front at Belostok-Minsk and Smolensk had both failed to carve a gaping hole in Soviet defences through which a rapid, and largely unmolested, advance could be made. Yet, even more importantly, Hitler strongly emphasized the economic importance of the Ukraine, which may suggest he was beginning to doubt whether the war could be won in the rapid blitz-style campaign that had originally been conceived. In any case Hitler's interest in diverting the attack into the Ukraine was firstly economic and secondly military. Throughout August he was told time and again by his military commanders that the bulk of the Soviet reserves were being concentrated opposite Army Group Centre to defend the approaches to Moscow, and it was here they argued that a decisive blow to the Red Army should be struck. Hitler, however, was prepared to subordinate military objectives to his own sense of priorities, just as he had done by declaring Leningrad a vital objective for its political significance, rather than its military value.[24] Thus, the retrospective tendency of many histories, to suppose that the ultimate success of the Kiev battle was both obvious and apparent, was simply not the case. Hitler's interest was essentially economic and while he also recognized an attractive operational prospect, a victory on the scale that was ultimately achieved was by no means a preordained certainty. An advance into the Ukraine from the north presented significant operational hurdles, not least of which was the conduct of such an offensive with a long, exposed left flank perpendicular to the Soviet front. Serious combat losses within the spearheading XXIV[25] Panzer Corps[26] and mounting supply difficulties further hampered the offensive, while vigorous Soviet counterattacks against both Field Marshal Fedor von Bock's Army Group Centre and

Colonel-General Heinz Guderian's panzer forces produced periods of sudden crisis in the German front. There was also a new round of intense internal wrangling within the German command, this time concentrated firmly within Army Group Centre, which extended so far as to see Bock seeking Guderian's dismissal. Yet for all the complications on the German side of the front, without a doubt the most important factor in the outcome of the battle was Stalin's own role. Not only did the Soviet dictator's obstinate strategic direction benefit the Germans far more than it hindered them, but from the German perspective there could have been no accounting for this at the start of the battle.

In many ways the battle of Kiev is a misnomer. As with the so-called battles of Belostok-Minsk and Smolensk, the city itself plays a small, peripheral role in the fighting, but lends its name to the wider drama which engulfed a large segment of the eastern Ukraine. As with my preceding volume this study will concentrate predominantly on the two panzer groups that combined to enact the encirclement of the Soviet South-Western Front (Panzer Groups 1 and 2). This study can be read, therefore, as a continuation of the previous study into German operational problems on the eastern front or as a separate and distinct investigation of an all-too-neglected battle. Indeed, it is interesting to note that, although this was one of the most significant and largest-scale battles of World War II, there has been only one study written on it.[27]

First appearing in 1964, Werner Haupt's *Kiew: Die grösste Kesselschlacht der Geschichte* represented much of what is wrong with the military history of the eastern front from the German perspective. Haupt, himself a veteran of the northern sector of the eastern front, produced his study without any footnotes or bibliography, which together with his sensationalistic prose and keen use of exclamation marks, gives the study a distinct feel of historical dramatization. Research certainly went into the book (it is definitely not a fictional account), but Haupt's close affinity with both the German soldiers and the events he describes clouds too many of his judgements and conclusions. This has resulted in an all-too-benevolent picture of Germany's soldiers on the eastern front, who, according to Haupt's rendition, can be seen as both markedly superior in the art of warfare and, at the same time, long-suffering victims of the war's hardships. At the same time, the Red Army is contrasted with Haupt's duty-bound *Lansers* as a faceless and iniquitous enemy.

In the English-language literature there is very little to be found on the events taking place in the Ukraine during September 1941. For the most part the battle is subsumed within wider events of Operation Barbarossa and features in many narratives merely as a stepping-stone victory on the way to the final showdown at Moscow. Yet Kiev was a vast battle, which involved three German armies (Second, Sixth and Seventeenth), two panzer groups (1 and 2) and elements of two air fleets (2 and 4) as well as elements of six Soviet armies (Fifth, Twenty-First, Twenty-Sixth, Thirty-Seventh, Thirty-Eighth and Fortieth). In sheer numbers the battle draws few parallels even on the eastern front and yet, in spite of being one of the largest and most decisive battles of World War II, it has yet to merit its own study in English. This is a deficiency not only given its intrinsic importance as one of the great battles of the war, but because the description of events given in more general accounts has typically been coloured by the well-known outcome. Rather than highlighting the ills of Germany's campaign during the interlude before Moscow, there has been a preoccupation with the especially large numbers of Soviet POWs captured in September 1941 that has given the battle of Kiev a one-dimensional status. This interpretation neither reflects the difficulties of the battle for the Germans nor highlights the perils of overextension that were stretching the *Ostheer* to breaking point. This has helped feed the myth of the Wehrmacht's unbroken series of victories in the east, which continued, according to the popular legend, to the very gates of Moscow. There can be no question that the battle of Kiev was far more costly to the Red Army than to the Wehrmacht, but this did not alter Germany's strategic predicament in the east. Indeed even before the victory at Kiev, Germany confronted an inevitable crisis. By the end of September, without rest or spare parts the vital motorized divisions were in a terrible state. Moreover, losses throughout September had risen by another 125,000 men,[28] the flow of supplies was hopelessly inadequate, there was no winter equipment and the autumn *rasputitsa*[29] was about to begin. Even the Nazi propaganda minister, Joseph Goebbels, who was busy trumpeting the *Ostheer*'s achievements, privately betrayed an understanding of the inherent dangers now confronting Germany in the east and his increasingly awkward role in reporting it. Writing in his diary on 11 September 1941 Goebbels confided: 'In my opinion the nation now has a right to know what is and what will be, above all that the progress of the eastern operation is not what we had actually wished for and what the people had also imagined it would be.' Goebbels then alluded to his fears for the coming winter. 'To conduct propaganda when one attains victories on a conveyor belt is not difficult; but to hold a people in the palm of your hand when a crisis threatens is difficult and also shows the propagandist's actual skill.'[30] Clearly Goebbels had some idea of where things were headed and did not wish to be caught off-guard in explaining a crisis at the front.

Having already written at length in my preceding volume about Germany's ominous strategic predicament after two months of warfare against the Soviet Union, the first chapter of this study opens with a more expansive discussion of Germany's war effort and the respective strengths and contributions of the three Allied powers. Here one gains a perspective into the centrality of the eastern front and the defining role it was already playing in the demise of Nazi Germany. Far from being a mere setback, by the end of the summer Operation Barbarossa's failure left Hitler's strategy rudderless and, although scarcely recognized at the time, beyond repair. In the weeks following the invasion, the new east–west anti-Nazi coalition was rapidly taking shape and gaining in strength from week to week. Allied economic resources were being amassed on an unprecedented scale, while mobilization, especially in the United States and the Soviet Union, was proceeding by leaps and bounds. At the same time the *Ostheer* was rapidly being forced into an unsustainable war of attrition, which placed Germany at a tremendous disadvantage as the third year of the war began. Having gained a perspective from the other side of Germany's hill the second chapter further contextualizes Hitler's war against the Soviet Union by assessing the economic fragility of the Nazi empire and why the failure of the summer blitzkrieg doomed Germany's long-term outlook. From this point my discussion concentrates firmly on the fighting in the east, beginning with a brief overview of Germany's summer campaign in Army Group South and then continuing through to the main events at Kiev in late August and September 1941.

1 THE BULLDOG, THE EAGLE AND THE BEAR

Working for the Soviet theatre – Britain and America's supporting roles

The danger of assessing any one aspect of Germany's wars between 1939 and 1945 is that the process necessitates a certain degree of neglect. Without an appreciation of the bigger picture the vital tools for contextualization are absent. The proliferation of histories focused exclusively on the exploits of the Anglo-American war experience has tended to leave readers attributing an overblown significance to the contribution of the Western Allies. While the role of the west in the defeat of Nazi Germany is certainly an essential one, no other nation suffered or sacrificed more than the Soviet Union between 1941 and 1945. In order to appreciate the scale and importance of the fighting at Kiev, as well as to weigh correctly the vital role played by the Western Allies until September 1941, a certain overview is in order.

On 8 July 1940 the British Prime Minister, Winston Churchill, wrote to Lord Beaverbrook, his minister for aircraft production, about the difficulty of Britain's position in the war. In the wake of Hitler's swift conquest of France, Churchill was desperate for any means to strike back, and confided in Beaverbrook that his ministry provided the only means. As Churchill explained:

> *[W]hen I look around to see how we can win the war I see that there is only one sure path. We have no continental army which can defeat the German military power. The blockade is broken and Hitler has Asia and probably Africa*

> *to draw from. Should he be repulsed here or not try invasion, he will recoil eastward, and we have nothing to stop him. But there is one thing that will bring him back and bring him down, and that is an absolutely devastating, exterminating attack by very heavy bombers from this country upon the Nazi homeland. We must be able to overwhelm him by this means, without which I do not see a way through.*[1]

Churchill was correct. Hitler did not attempt invasion and did indeed recoil back towards the east. Yet the extent to which Churchill in July 1940 might have foreseen a future confrontation between Germany and the Soviet Union was at least as much a product of fervent hope as of any hard evidence. Churchill correctly understood that in any ensuing German–Soviet confrontation Britain's war would become a peripheral one without the means to strike at Hitler decisively. Where Churchill was wrong was in his ardent enthusiasm for the effects of strategic bombing. In spite of the optimism expressed by Bomber Command, the 'absolutely devastating, exterminating' attacks in which Churchill placed his faith were still years away. Early in the war British bombers had no radio navigation aids, no radar and only substandard bomb-sights. Crews flew into Germany navigating by the stars and located their target areas by moonlight. Such methods required good flying conditions and clear skies, which also favoured German countermeasures. Ultimately the early bombing campaign was so inaccurate that German intelligence had trouble understanding what goals the British were attempting to pursue.[2]

By 1941 Britain could still only manage to make about 400 bombers serviceable on any one night, which was well below the Luftwaffe's capacity as evidenced by the 712 German bombers that raided London on 19 April.[3] In spite of their meagre results, the British establishment maintained a strident faith in the decisive contribution of strategic bombing. One might think the British should have known better. After enduring, in the Blitz, the heaviest bombing of the war so far, they had seen only minor disruption to production, while morale, far from being broken, dramatically improved. It is not surprising, therefore, that British bombing had next to no effect on German morale or their armaments industry. Indeed, between 1940 and 1941 the

Germans more than doubled production of tanks from 2,200 to 5,200 and submarine output jumped from 40 to 196.[4]

By the summer of 1941, as Hitler's armies launched their devastating invasion of the Soviet Union, Britain could no longer deny the ineffectiveness of its bombing campaign. A statistical analysis completed in August 1941 by D. M. B Butt of the War Cabinet Secretariat revealed that a staggering 80 per cent of bombers did not reach their designated target area, which was broadly defined as seventy-five square miles around the target. The bombers were therefore dropping their loads on farmers' fields or forests, and of the small percentage of bombers that did reach the oversized target area, the margin for error was still exceedingly large.[5] Nevertheless, with the Soviet Union now bearing almost the full brunt of Germany's military might, bombing was Britain's only viable method of hitting back. The results, however, hardly justified the effort. In the ten raids Bomber Command launched against Berlin between June and November 1941, 133 Germans were killed compared with casualties in British aircrews of about three times that figure.[6] At the same time British aircraft losses in 1941 were more than double those in 1940 (1,034 versus 492).[7] Even Churchill, who had been a keen supporter of strategic bombing, began to tone down his enthusiasm and view with reservation the stoutly ambitious plans of Bomber Command for a force of 4,000 machines by the spring of 1943.[8]

With the fall of France in June 1940 Britain not only suffered the loss of its one major European ally, but also found itself at war with Italy. This essentially opened a second front against British interests in Africa and the Mediterranean – one that Britain was initially ill prepared to meet. In Italy's East African colonies of Eritrea, Somaliland and the recently conquered Ethiopian empire, Mussolini maintained a force of some 92,000 Italians and a quarter of a million locally raised troops, backed by 323 aircraft. The total British and local forces in Kenya, British Somaliland and Sudan numbered just 40,000 men with 100 aircraft. Likewise, the Italian army in Libya outnumbered British forces in Egypt by more than three to one (200,000 to 63,000).[9] The British position was further compromised by the loss of vast amounts of war materiel at Dunkirk, the priority of fighting off German aerial attacks in the battle of Britain and the need to build up home defences for a feared invasion.

The danger to British holdings in Africa was largely eased by the influx of Dominion forces. In East Africa reinforcements from South Africa, India and African colonies allowed General Alan Cunningham to contemplate an offensive aimed at expelling the Italians. The Italians, by contrast, suffered from the intractable problem of isolation from both resupply and reinforcement. Cunningham's advance drove into Italian-occupied Ethiopia and by the early spring of 1941 had largely pacified the region. This freed three divisions of South African and Indian troops for urgent redeployment to General Archibald Wavell's embattled army in the western desert.[10]

In the winter of 1940/1941 Wavell had also achieved remarkable success, largely as a result of Italian ineptitude, routing the much larger army of Marshal Rodolfo Graziani. Yet after a pursuit of some 600 kilometres ending in early February 1941 at Beda Fomm, British fortunes hit a turning point. Churchill had decided to aid Greece's stout resistance to Italian invasion and therefore Wavell lost the British 1st Armoured Brigade, the New Zealand 2nd Division and the Australian 6th Division. It was a fateful decision, provoking Hitler's intervention in Greece, but not providing anywhere near enough troops to counter it.[11] The result was a fiasco. German forces overwhelmed the Greek and Allied armies and forced the hasty evacuation of Commonwealth forces to the island of Crete. The British Expeditionary Force lost 9,000 men captured, 3,000 casualties and virtually all its heavy equipment. The battle continued on Crete, which by the end of May was also lost after fierce fighting. Commonwealth forces suffered a further 12,000 men captured and nearly 2,000 killed.[12]

Not only did the British expedition to Greece deny Wavell the ability to press his advantage, but decisions had already been taken for a German force to be sent to North Africa to aid the Italians. The first German troops landed in February 1941 as British forces were still consolidating their gains. Wavell calculated that no combined Italian/German attack would be possible before May and Ultra intelligence appeared to support this conclusion. Yet the new German commander, Lieutenant-General Erwin Rommel, had already earned a reputation for confounding his opponents (and superiors) and only forty days after landing he went on the offensive with the advanced guard of his new *Afrikakorps*. Wavell was caught off-guard with weakened forces and the result was a striking reversal. In only three weeks Wavell lost almost all the ground gained from the Italians since early December.[13]

With this coming amid the unfolding disaster in Greece, Churchill was desperate for a victory and expedited the shipment of more than three hundred tanks to Wavell's depleted army with the expectation that he move quickly to attack. Wavell complained he needed more time, but Churchill was adamant. Operation Battleaxe was launched in mid-June 1941, a week before Hitler began his invasion of the Soviet Union. It was to prove another costly defeat, with Britain's best tanks (Matildas and Crusaders) too slow and too poorly armed to cope with the German Mark IIIs and Mark IVs. Tactical employment was also dreadful as inexperienced commanders drove their tanks forward into prepared German positions without aerial or artillery support. In three days the British lost almost a hundred tanks and the offensive was called off for no gain.[14]

In the aftermath General Wavell was replaced by General Claude Auchinleck who likewise soon came under sustained pressure from Churchill for renewed action. Auchinleck was wary of being coerced into a similar mistake and resisted any premature action, preferring in fact Rommel to make the next move. Rommel might well have obliged had supply difficulties and shortages of equipment not been so acute. The consequence was stalemate, which became intolerable for Churchill as the titanic struggle on the eastern front raged. Attempting to explain this fact to Auchinleck, Churchill wrote: 'It is impossible to explain to Parliament and the nation how it is our Middle East armies had to stand for four and a half months without engaging the enemy while all the time Russia is being battered to pieces.'[15] It was not only that the British army in Africa was seen to be dragging its feet; it was also the fact that Auchinleck was facing only a small fraction of the German army at a time when the Red Army was fighting against more than 3 million German troops in a life and death struggle. In the event, Auchinleck's offensive, codenamed 'Crusader', did not commence until 18 November, almost five months after Hitler's invasion of the Soviet Union. Rommel was pushed back, but in spite of a commanding British superiority in tanks and aircraft, Auchinleck could not eliminate his army or even forestall a renewed Italian/German offensive in 1942.

With strategic bombing still in its infancy and land warfare proving such a disappointment, the British might well have hoped that the Royal Navy – the mainstay of their military might – would prove to be the decisive weapon. In World War I the Allied naval blockade not only impaired Germany's industrial output, but by the end of the war had led to widespread malnutrition, which helped produce the conditions that sparked the downfall of the Kaiser. A year into World War II the supposedly formidable Allied naval power was proving considerably less effective. The British blockade was being circumvented by means of Germany's alliance with the Soviet Union and France's naval assets were either eliminated or neutralized, while the addition of the Italian fleet bolstered the Axis position in the Mediterranean. More worrying still, the Royal Naval was finding it difficult to protect Britain from the choking grasp of Germany's own blockade.

The conquest of France, the Low Countries and Norway had provided German U-boats with new bases offering easy access to the Atlantic, while German aircraft operated at much greater depth forcing the closure of Britain's eastern ports. Congestion resulted at the remaining ports, while merchant ships were forced to undertake greatly extended journeys around Africa, owing to the extremely hazardous passage through the Mediterranean. Britain was forced to adopt a convoy system to protect shipping from U-boat attacks, but this reduced speeds to that of the slowest ship and further cut the net tonnage of imports. Above all U-boats were inflicting major damage, accounting for 70 per cent of losses to British shipping, with aircraft, mines and surface raiders making up the rest.[16] During 1940 the British lost more than a thousand ships, equivalent to some 4 million tons of merchant shipping or a quarter of British capacity. Hopes were high in the German navy that Britain could be brought to its knees by U-boats alone and on the surface this seemed a reasonable conclusion. In the first four months of 1941 a further 2 million tons of shipping were sunk and German submariners began referring to these as 'the fortunate times' (*die glückliche Zeiten*). The effects were all the more startling because the German submarine fleet was never able to send more than ten to fifteen submarines at a time to hunt in the vital North Atlantic shipping lanes. With the German navy looking to increase U-boat production significantly, the implications for Britain appeared ominous. In 1938 Britain imported 68 million tons of goods. By 1941 that figure had shrunk to 26 million tons, and in February of that year Churchill was sufficiently disturbed to declare anti-submarine warfare to be Britain's top priority.[17]

For all the danger that Germany's U-boats appeared to present, there was another side to the coin, which made the reality of Britain's defeat by U-boat alone an unlikely one. In 1941 merchant-shipping losses amounted to 3.6 million tons. In that same year new production replaced 1.2 million tons, while austere management of shipping imports and improved port management saved an estimated 3 million tons. Thus, in spite of losses the United Kingdom ended 1941 with a moderate surplus in shipping tonnage.[18] To this must be added the vast potential of American shipbuilding yards which, even in the absence of capital reserves, were becoming increasingly open to the British through Roosevelt's Lend-Lease programme. By contrast Hitler's failure to end his new war in the east by the autumn of 1941 placed enormous additional strain on the German economy and ensured renewed priority for the army. The summer of 1941 produced another boon for the British when cryptographers broke the U-boat cipher system and gained invaluable intelligence on German movements and strengths. It has been estimated that this development alone saved some 300 British ships in the second half of 1941.[19]

After shouldering the weight of the war alone for twelve months since the defeat of France, it was clear that Britain's war effort was struggling to cope with the demands placed upon it. Nevertheless, one might also conclude that Britain's success lay in Germany's failure, in both the battle of Britain and its abortive blockade. Having survived intact as a major power, Britain was freed by the advent of Hitler's colossal war in the east to concentrate its resources on offensive operations. This, however, still posed formidable challenges. Strategic bombing was an entirely new development in modern warfare without an established operational doctrine or the technology to support it fully. The British army suffered similar obstacles as it made the difficult transition from a small professional force to a mass army. Since the failure of Hitler's Barbarossa blitzkrieg gave the British time to build up and improve both, one cannot therefore underestimate the importance of the summer of 1941 in contributing to Britain's longer-term effectiveness in the war. At the same time, the battle of Kiev and the evident tenacity of the German Wehrmacht warned Britain against complacency and told of the trials yet to come.

Hitler's invasion of the Soviet Union promised to open up radical possibilities for both sides. Britain was at last to acquire another major continental ally, while Germany stood to gain economic autarky and complete dominance of the continent (which Hitler hoped would force Britain to agree to terms). In the event, the summer of 1941, while on the surface an apparently successful period of German conquest, expended so much of the Wehrmacht's offensive strength that a long drawn-out war in the east became inevitable. It was an outcome Hitler and his military commanders had not foreseen and had no contingency for. Instead of benefiting from a wealth of raw materials and new-found strategic freedom, the Germans found themselves even more limited in both. Moreover, as Germany's army became critically overextended in the Soviet Union, Britain's comparatively weak forces were able to take the initiative and prove an increasingly troublesome menace on numerous, albeit secondary, fronts. Britain's offensive strength was still, however, very limited. The great gusto of Churchill's rhetoric sought to play up the importance of Britain's military contribution in the second half of 1941, but in reality the British Prime Minister was under few illusions as to the limited significance of the British war effort in aiding the Soviet Union. Indeed, from the Soviet perspective, the whole Anglo-American war effort up until the Allied landings in France in June 1944 was significant only in terms of how many German resources it managed to siphon off from the eastern front. In the late summer of 1941 that figure was pitifully small and, it may be said, contributed to the Soviet disaster at Kiev.

In North Africa Britain faced three German divisions (numbering some 48,500 men) and some seven Italian divisions.[20] At the same time the Soviet Union engaged almost 160 German divisions with more than 3 million men,[21] supported by an additional three-quarters of a million troops supplied by Germany's Axis allies. This grossly disproportionate concentration of Axis forces on the eastern front tipped the scales decisively in favour of Britain on all its fronts. Rommel lacked the resources adequately to counter Auchinleck's advantage in Operation Crusader. The RAF's bombing campaign proceeded with the great bulk of the Luftwaffe's resources supporting ground operations in the east and the Royal Navy continued its battle against the U-boats with a commanding superiority in both naval assets and production capacity (including Lend-Lease aid). Thus, as Britain entered its third year of the war in September 1941, events on the eastern front enabled it to start throwing off the immediate fear of invasion and take the fight to Germany, with a steadily growing offensive strength and an increasing admiration for the fighting potential of its new Soviet ally.

The summer and autumn period is also significant for the change in US policy towards Germany. Under Roosevelt's shrewd direction the United States government manoeuvred itself from strict neutrality at the start of the war, to limited material support for Britain in 1940, and then to a full-blown commitment to arm Britain through the Lend-Lease programme, enacted in March 1941. Finally, by the summer and autumn of that year, Roosevelt brought his country to the very brink of war, entering into a quasi state of undeclared hostilities against Germany.[22]

Hitler's invasion of the Soviet Union proved a watershed in the urgency with which Roosevelt's administration viewed the situation in Europe. Roosevelt was sufficiently concerned to advocate extending whatever aid he could to Stalin. Only two days after the German invasion, the American President stated, 'we are going to give all the aid we can to Russia'.[23] Yet Roosevelt faced a large and hostile isolationist movement with many vocal supporters in Congress and Senate. The isolationists were opposed in principle to involvement in the war and were even more reviled at the thought of supporting the Soviet Union with its communist and atheistic regime. The view was now expressed that fascists and communists should be left to battle it out alone, providing a simple and convenient solution to American security concerns. Senator Burton Wheeler, a leading isolationist, publicly expounded this position: 'Now we can just let Joe Stalin and the other dictators fight it out.'[24] Suspicions about aiding the Soviet Union were also held on a pragmatic level, with fears expressed at the highest levels that any military or economic aid would simply end up in German hands, following the anticipated defeat of the Red Army. Yet many of the President's military and civilian advisers clearly recognized the dire urgency of the European situation and urged Roosevelt to action. Fearing the worst, Harold Ickes, the Secretary of the Interior, wrote to Roosevelt the day after the German invasion: 'It may be difficult to get into this war the right way, but if we do not do it now, we will be, when our turn comes, without an ally anywhere in the world.'[25] Likewise, the Secretary of War, Henry Stimson, viewed Germany's attack as 'an almost providential occurrence', providing a vital window of opportunity for increased US naval action in the Atlantic to meet what he described as 'our most imminent danger'.[26] While most of Roosevelt's advisers agreed on the need for stronger action against Germany, channelling precious resources to the Soviet Union was more controversial. The most ardent supporter of aiding the Soviets was Roosevelt's old friend and former US ambassador to the Soviet Union, Joseph E. Davies. He alone asserted that Soviet resistance would 'amaze and surprise the world'.[27] Roosevelt was inclined to support Davies' view, but was constrained by public opinion. According to a Gallup poll taken on 24 June 1941 only 35 per cent of Americans supported aid for the Soviet Union on the same basis as that offered to Great Britain, while 54 per cent opposed it and 11 per cent remained undecided.[28] Roosevelt could see that an extension of Lend-Lease aid to the Soviet Union was, for the time being, politically dangerous. The first appropriation of 7 billion dollars for Lend-Lease aid to Britain was nearly exhausted and Congress would soon have to approve further funding allocations. Thus, US aid to the Soviet Union initially began with a series of provisional steps calculated to achieve maximum results without instigating a political backlash. The Treasury Department released 39 million dollars in frozen Soviet assets, while the White House determined that the Neutrality Act did not apply to the German–Soviet war, allowing American ships to dock at Soviet ports.[29]

With Roosevelt willing to help his new Soviet ally in any way he could, questions were soon being asked about what exactly Stalin needed. Enquiries were almost immediately made in Moscow and the Soviets returned an enormous shopping list, far in excess of what the Americans were as yet capable of delivering either politically or materially. The list included requests for some 1.8 billion dollars in aid, which included specifics such as 6,000 planes and 20,000 anti-aircraft guns.[30] The Soviets also submitted a list to the British with requests for a further 3,000 modern fighters and 3,000 bombers as well as access to the ASDIC (sonar) system and raw materials such as aluminium and rubber.[31] The hefty Soviet demands reflect, in part, a knee-jerk reaction to the extent of the emergency they were now confronting, but they also provide a none too unrealistic insight into the immense scale of the conflict underway in the east.

In Washington a special committee was established to receive and process Soviet orders, but administration was poor and lack of co-ordination between a half-dozen agencies prevented substantial progress. Soviet aid was in any case imperilled by its exclusion from the Lend-Lease programme, forcing supplies shipped by the United States to be purchased, not donated.[32] Offering loans and credits was one option, but these presented legal problems that had to be circumvented by labelling loans 'advances' against future deliveries of Soviet raw materials.[33] Ultimately, the delays and mismanagement proved too much for Roosevelt who was appalled by the inaction. In the six weeks since the Germans launched Barbarossa a meagre 6.5 million dollars in exports had been dispatched to the Soviet Union, leaving Roosevelt to sympathize that 'the Russians feel they have been given the run-around in the United States'.[34] Roosevelt forcefully attempted to shake things up at the end of July with presidential decrees to expedite Soviet aid, but while this helped, it failed to solve the fundamental restrictions in funding or the shortage of goods.

In spite of the new-found alliance between the Soviet Union and the west, there was in practice little knowledge of, and a good many fears about, the real status of the Soviet Union's war effort. Not only did doubts persist about the ability of the Red Army to resist the German onslaught, but suspicions pervaded some diplomatic circles that Stalin, if pressed hard enough, would cut another deal with Hitler without consulting Britain or the United States. Alarmed by the pervasive atmosphere of uncertainty and apprehension in both Washington and London, the President's close confidant and Lend-Lease administrator, Harry Hopkins, abruptly determined that he should meet with Stalin during a visit to London in late July. Roosevelt willingly gave his assent and Hopkins arrived in Moscow for talks with Stalin on 30 July 1941. Although Roosevelt and Churchill had from the beginning enthusiastically supported sending aid to the Soviet Union, it was not until Hopkins returned from Moscow convinced by Stalin's defiant tone and unflagging optimism, that lingering reservations in both governments about the Soviet commitment were categorically dismissed. Stalin acknowledged to Hopkins that the Red Army had suffered setbacks, but assured his guest that Soviet forces could hold out until the winter. Indeed, Hopkins reported that Stalin exuded 'great confidence that the line during the winter months would be in front of Moscow, Kiev and Leningrad'.[35] Stalin also claimed that if his requests for anti-aircraft guns and aluminium were met, the Soviet Union would be able to hold out against Germany for three or four years. Of course Stalin was at pains to secure as much aid as possible and he probably saw the need to counter speculation about the Soviet Union's survival. Yet it was not all simply bravado calculated to impress. With the main German thrust halted east of Smolensk and vigorous Soviet counterattacks underway, there was some basis for Stalin's optimism. There can be, however, no question that early in the war there were times when Stalin exuded a dangerous overconfidence. In the discussions with Hopkins this worked to his benefit, but for the most part it resulted in some of the most calamitous military decisions of the whole war. Even as the Soviet dictator was seeking to win over Hopkins with bombastic assurances, Stalin inadvertently revealed a more desperate side to the Soviet war effort and how far he was prepared to go to sustain it. Stalin asked Hopkins to extend a personal message to Roosevelt, urging the United States to enter the war against Germany. In that event, Stalin made the astonishing offer for American troops to be deployed anywhere on the Soviet front under autonomous American command.[36] It was an almost unthinkable gesture from a man who had for so long viewed the western world with a mixture of suspicion and disdain, yet for those same reasons it proves a reliable yardstick in illuminating Stalin's unspoken fears. Even before the battle of Kiev Stalin was aware how high the stakes were.

Hopkins left Moscow to join Roosevelt and Churchill at their historic meeting off Newfoundland on board the British battleship *Prince of Wales* and the American heavy cruiser *Augusta*. It was here that the two leaders co-authored a letter to Stalin formally proposing what Hopkins had already suggested to Stalin during his visit – a Three Power Conference in Moscow to discuss strategic interests and the allocation of resources to the Soviet war effort. The letter also acknowledged the fundamental importance of the Soviet front:

> *We are at the moment cooperating to provide you with the very maximum of supplies that you most urgently need. Already many shiploads have left our shores and more will leave in the immediate future... We realise fully how vitally important to the defeat of Hitlerism is the brave and steadfast resistance of the Soviet Union, and we feel therefore that we must not in any circumstances fail to act quickly and immediately in this matter of planning the programme for the future allocation of our joint resources.*[37]

Stalin welcomed the idea and the Three Power Conference took place at the end of September attended by Lord Beaverbrook for the UK and Averell Harriman for the United States (Hopkins was too ill to attend). The Three Power Conference agreed on urgent support for the USSR, even at the expense of reinforcing other theatres. The agreement was signed on 1 October 1941 and was due to run until June 1942. In practical terms the first inter-Allied agreement, known as the First Protocol, promised the Soviets some 400 aircraft, 500 tanks and 10,000 trucks each month, as well as a wide range of other supplies.[38]

Having committed to such an extensive system of aid, the problem of funding could no longer be ignored and Roosevelt knew that Soviet access to Lend-Lease was the only long-term solution. Fortunately, as the Red Army was proving itself to be a stalwart and formidable adversary, American public opinion shifted quickly and favourably in support of the Soviet cause. Roosevelt also took practical measures, exchanging Hopkins for Edward Stettinius as the Lend-Lease administrator to make the programme more attractive to fiscal conservatives (who saw Hopkins as an irresponsible spender). For religious conservatives much was made of an apparent Nazi plan to abolish all organized religion, while Catholics were courted with a statement from Pope Pius XII distinguishing between aid to the Soviet Union and aid to communism. Clearly the administration was pushing to make the idea of Lend-Lease aid to the Soviet Union more palatable. Yet Roosevelt's masterstroke was to tie the new appropriations for an expansion of Lend-Lease aid to a bill seeking funds for the US army, navy and coast guard. Patriotic congressmen would have a harder time rejecting it and in the debates that followed Roosevelt could obscure his essential goal. When pressed on the issue Roosevelt consistently (and falsely) claimed that the Soviets could go on buying whatever they needed from the United States, but that exclusion from potential funding would be a blow to morale and limit the President's future options in the uncertainties of war. The bill passed on 24 October and four days later Roosevelt signed it into law.[39]

The groundwork was now set for what would become massive American aid to the Soviet Union, eventually totalling some 10 billion dollars by 1945. Nevertheless, by the end of autumn 1941 only 65 million dollars of American aid had been dispatched to the Soviets. With the new appropriations legislation passed, Roosevelt cabled Stalin to inform him that he could now claim 1 billion dollars in US credit (interest free and without repayment until five years after the war).[40] Although the offer was of little immediate benefit in repelling the German offensive towards Moscow, it was much more than a symbolic gesture of solidarity. The supplies would take considerable time to be manufactured and delivered into Soviet hands, but the Red Army's performance had already ensured there would be an active front waiting for the supplies when they did arrive.

While American aid was of long-term significance, British aid to the Soviet Union during the period of the First Protocol not only was more substantial in quantity but, according to recent research, also played a noteworthy role in the battle for Moscow.[41] By the end of 1941, Britain had managed to deliver to the Soviets 699 aircraft, 466 tanks,[42] 867 vehicles and 76,000 tons of other supplies.[43] It was also in the early autumn of 1941 that German military files reveal, for the first time, encounters with British war materiel. In spite of later Soviet attempts to downplay much of the Lend-Lease military aid as inferior to their own (particularly tanks and aircraft), German reports appear less concerned by the quality of the materiel than by the fact that British equipment was turning up at all on the eastern front. It indicated a new degree of co-ordination among Germany's enemies and was one more worrying implication of the failure to end the war in the summer of 1941 as planned. Whatever the tangible benefits of Lend-Lease aid in the earliest period of the war, its impact on Soviet morale cannot be discounted.

While the United States now actively armed and supported Germany's enemies, the extent of Roosevelt's undeclared war went well beyond economic and industrial assistance. Hawks in the administration had long been seeking Roosevelt's approval for the US navy to offer armed escorts for all merchant shipping in the western Atlantic. In parallel Britain had been urging the United States to relieve its garrison in Iceland, which was safeguarding the most vital position in the North Atlantic. When Roosevelt agreed to undertake the defence of Iceland and the first 4,400 marines landed in early July, Churchill hailed the decision as 'one of the most important things that has happened since the start of the war'.[44] The prospect of an 'incident' occurring in the contested areas of control between the US navy and German U-boats was now much greater. Roosevelt was not blind to the danger and in fact saw the risk as potential future leverage in securing more freedom of action from a reluctant Congress.

In the summit with Churchill off Newfoundland Roosevelt had privately agreed to armed escorts for all vessels operating across the western Atlantic, but an 'incident' in early September involving the USS *Greer* provided the right impetus for the public announcement.

Ignoring the aggressive role of the *Greer* in hunting a German U-boat, Roosevelt's administration only made reference to the U-boat firing torpedoes at the *Greer*, none of which hit. Speaking to the nation, Roosevelt described the German U-boats and surface raiders as 'the rattlesnakes of the Atlantic' from which all merchant ships would need to be protected. Yet the President went even further, issuing a direct challenge to the Axis powers: 'From now on, if German or Italian vessels of war enter the waters, the protection of which is necessary for American defence, they do so at their own peril.'[45] It was an emphatic warning, backed by ardent resolve, which saw the United States crossing the threshold between passive involvement and active belligerency. A formal declaration of war would require far more than a simple naval 'incident', but by the end of the autumn intercepts of Japanese diplomatic intelligence suggested that war with at least one of the Axis powers was imminent.[46]

By the autumn of 1941 Britain was facing a new war. Only twelve weeks before the British blockade was being circumvented through the Soviet Union and the Axis enemy greatly outnumbered Allied forces in soldiers, tanks and aircraft. Moreover, the threat of invasion, although not considered imminent, was still hanging over British heads. In the intervening summer Churchill met for the first time with Roosevelt and the two forged a firm personal commitment to work for the destruction of Nazism. In the same period the Soviet Union was thrust into the war, giving Britain the backing of two great powers, both still finding their feet, but committed nevertheless to a sustained war against fascism. No longer was Britain alone and no longer were the Axis superior in the raw indexes of soldiers, tanks and aircraft. Indeed, the trump card of the Axis – the German Wehrmacht's dynamic formula for lightning wars of conquest – had proved seriously deficient in the vital summer campaign on the eastern front. The implications were by no means small and were made worse by the failure of the German command fully to appreciate their ominous predicament. The combined economic and military potential of the Allies was enormous, while, already in the autumn of 1941, Germany faced shortages of manpower and raw materials. Hitler was now locked into a high-intensity war of immense scale, with an army incapable of either sustaining the destructive level of attrition or forcing an end to the conflict. Even the battle of Kiev, in spite of its favourable outcome, could not hope to compensate for Germany's predicament. A turning point in the war had been reached and a path to Germany's downfall, although obscured at the time, was now in place.[47]

Shouldering the load – the Soviet war effort in 1941

It has been estimated that more than a quarter of all Soviet troops killed in World War II died in 1941.[48] By another account, the first six months of the war cost the Red Army in excess of 3 million irrecoverable losses (killed, missing in action or POWs) and almost 1.5 million sick and wounded.[49] In crude terms, if one applies these losses to the 5.5 million men in the Red Army at the start of the war, roughly 80 per cent had become casualties or prisoners of war by the end of the year.[50] Such staggering figures reflect a rate of loss far in excess of any army in military history. Materiel losses were just as massive. An estimated 20,000 Soviet tanks (all types) were lost by the end of the year.[51] The extent of such losses has convinced many western historians that the Soviet Union must have been on the brink of collapse in 1941. On the other extreme, Soviet histories lauded a great defensive victory, which was won by the heroic Soviet people through an 'uncrushable faith in victory' and a determination to go on fighting until 'the last drop of blood'.[52] In fact, both interpretations are misleading. The Soviet Union was not impervious to defeat, but neither was it on the brink of destruction in 1941.

A general Soviet collapse could only have been induced under two essential conditions. The first was the destruction of the Red Army to such an extent that organized resistance ceased and a new front could not be established further east. The second was the loss of so many strategic centres (industrial regions, oil fields, mines, population centres, etc.) as to deny Soviet industry the basic requirements for continued mass production of modern armaments. Had Germany succeeded in bringing about either of these two eventualities, it would indeed have instigated a collapse. In the event, however, Soviet resilience prevailed.

Prior to Germany's invasion of the Soviet Union the Red Army had had a chequered history of success, which led many military analysts, not just those in Germany, to conclude that the Soviets possessed little genuine military might. On paper the Red Army was the largest and most lavishly equipped armed force in the world, but its recent performances in a number of small wars left many convinced that these numbers did not translate into real strength. It was well known that Stalin's purges had decimated the officer corps, forcing many to conclude that the Red Army was a paper tiger, vast in size, but without the skill or administrative framework to manage complex manoeuvres.[53] The purges were also seen to have had a stifling effect on the great bulk of officers who remained. Obedience to the party line, however absurd, overrode all other considerations, with any failings or transgressions raising questions about an officer's loyalty. In the atmosphere of fear and suspicion even orders that were known to be unrealistic or counterproductive were carried out.[54] The flaws of such a system were exacerbated in the early days of the German invasion when large sections of the Soviet front lost all command and control, forcing local commanders to act on their own initiative. Chaos reigned in the border areas and the swift-moving Germans took full advantage.[55] Some Soviet commanders resisted fanatically to the last man, while others promptly capitulated with all their troops. It was a fitting introduction for the Germans to the paradox of the Red Army. In many ways one might say the Soviets possessed an unrivalled devotion to duty, which was squandered by appalling structural and organizational failings.

The calamity suffered by the Red Army in the opening weeks of Operation Barbarossa has a complex history. The purges certainly took a great toll on the officer corps, but for all the harm they did, they may, to an extent, be credited with cutting away some of the 'dead wood' and propelling the careers of younger, progressive-thinking commanders.[56] Yet the purges did not target only the men in command of the Red Army; they also targeted their ideas. In 1937, when the purges claimed Mikhail Tukhachevsky, the famous military theorist who fathered the notion of 'deep operations', the Soviet Union also lost the progress he had made towards remodelling its foot and hoof army into a modern mechanized force. In the wake of the purges, reforms were rolled back and talk of 'deep operations' was deemed counter-revolutionary. Indeed, the Soviet newspaper *Pravda* included an editorial in February 1939 in which the author, no doubt with official sanctioning, advocated a return to the days of the Red Army in the civil war:

> *Military thought in the capitalist world has got into a blind alley. The dashing 'theories' about a lightning war, or about small, select armies of technicians, or about the air war which can replace all other military operations; all*

> *these theories arise from the bourgeoisie's deathly fear of the proletarian revolution. In its mechanical way, the imperialist bourgeoisie overrates equipment and underrates man.*[57]

The disorderly invasion of eastern Poland in September 1939 taught the Soviet high command little and a continued demodernization took place into the autumn of 1939 with mechanized corps being completely abolished. Next followed the debacles in the Winter War against Finland (1939–1940), where in spite of overwhelming numerical superiority, the Red Army suffered stunning defeats in the area near Summa and at Suomussalmi. Nevertheless Soviet authorities stubbornly avoided fundamental changes. It was not until the astonishing successes of Germany's armoured forces in the invasion of France that the Soviet high command was forced to address some of their chronic doctrinal and structural deficiencies. The result was a sweeping round of modernizing reforms that ran against the tide of changes made since 1937. Not only was this bound to result in tremendous chaos and confusion, but the Red Army had been completely purged of those officers, educated under Tukhachevsky, who might have instigated the new modifications. There could be no picking up where the Red Army had left off with 'deep operations'[58] in 1937; the whole structure of the army had regressed to primitive levels. The Red Army was now overwhelmingly staffed by party hacks and cowed yes men, with neither the training for such reforms, nor the individual competence to institute and carry out any form of independent action. There was also an undercurrent of fear about being associated with the new reforms. Engaging too quickly with them or demonstrating too much initiative might prove dangerous if the pendulum should swing again and the men now advocating the changes should suddenly become counter-revolutionary. The first nine mechanized corps reappeared in the summer of 1940 with another twenty being created in February and March 1941. The expansion was so rapid that neither equipment nor manpower could be provided to meet their requirements before the onset of war. Even the first nine mechanized corps had major deficiencies in unit training, support equipment (such as radios), logistics and basic command and control. The remaining twenty were in an even worse state, possessing, for example, only 53 per cent of their required strength in tanks. The great bulk of Soviet armour consisted of old models, with an extraordinarily high percentage (estimated at 73 per cent) in need of some form of repair.[59] Of the 23,767 Soviet tanks available on 22 June 1941, only 1,861 consisted of the newer model KV heavy tanks or the T-34 medium tanks. Yet even these were often manned by barely trained crews, without sufficient reserves of fuel or ammunition.[60] Clearly, the Soviet mechanized corps were fatally hindered in meeting the requirements of modern war, yet more worrying still, most of these problems were replicated throughout the other arms of the service. Rifle divisions were disorganized, ill equipped and suffered from poor logistics and communications. Officers in many cases filled positions one or two ranks above their level of training and experience.[61] The Soviet air force fielded 15,599 aircraft, but 80 per cent of these were of older design. On the eve of war the border military districts contained a total of 7,133 aircraft, but only 5,937 trained flight crews were available to fly them. Indeed, all elements of the Soviet armed forces suffered from pervasive problems of inadequate communications, logistics and command and control.[62]

Given the endemic problems of the Red Army, Soviet disasters that followed Germany's invasion cannot be understood simply as the product of the Barbarossa plan or the Wehrmacht's strength of arms. Indeed, the appalling incompetence of Soviet strategic direction in the first days of the war saw mechanized units having to undertake long, costly marches because of changing orders. In some cases the result was upwards of 50 per cent of vehicles breaking down without a shot being fired by the Germans. It was enough for one historian to conclude that 'the German army was not the greatest enemy of Soviet tanks; rather, the Red Army was'.[63] With such a prodigious disadvantage, one may well ask how it was possible that the Red Army survived even the first few weeks of the German invasion, let alone many months of hard fighting. The answer lies in the ardent resolve of the Soviet people to resist the invader and the unique ability of the Red Army and Soviet industry quickly to replace losses in men and materiel.

Accounts of a flood of nationalist zeal and patriotism in June 1941 sustaining the Soviet war effort have far more basis in fact than many of the other self-edifying Soviet attempts at post-war propaganda. Numerous western studies focusing on the popular mood among Soviet citizens at the outbreak of war have substantiated the basic sentiments expressed in Soviet literature. Of course there were also voices of dissent, and many in the recently annexed territories of Poland, Romania and the Baltic States expressed hope that the Germans would liberate them from Soviet occupation. Within the 1939 Soviet borders it was the Ukraine that harboured the greatest animosity towards the state, but even here responses were mixed, and in only a few places was there any form of open revolt against Soviet rule. For the most part the great bulk of the Soviet Union's 198 million citizens exhibited some form of patriotism, ranging from a simple willingness to follow the orders of the state, to a sublime fervour of dedicated, even fanatical, action. A secret police report from the start of the war concluded that '[t]he workers feel a profound patriotism', which was evident in the 'significant number of applications to join the army from young people from the cities and farms'.[64] As John Barber and Mark Harrison noted in their landmark study of the Soviet home front:

> *Ordinary people meanwhile rallied to their country's defence with a rapidity which showed that years of Stalinist controls had not destroyed their capacity for independent action. Although 22 June was a Sunday and the majority were not working, many people spontaneously went to their factory or office after hearing Molotov's broadcast. There they held meetings, pledged their loyalty to the motherland, the Soviet Union and Stalin, and in many cases worked an extra shift. Without waiting to be called up, large numbers of reservists immediately reported for military service. Many others whose age, profession or gender exempted them from conscription volunteered to go to the front none the less: 100,000 in Leningrad alone by the afternoon of 23 June, and 212,000 by the end of the first week.*[65]

In Moscow too, widespread loyalty and devotion to the regime was expressed. Many immediately volunteered for military service and when the capital was threatened in October 1941, those who fled headed east, away from the Germans, while those who remained exhibited a determination to fight for their homes.[66] Past resentments of the Bolsheviks were surprisingly quickly set aside. The nephew of the murdered Tsar Nicholas II, Prince Vsevolode, wrote a letter to *The Times* three days after the start of the war: 'We are fighting a common foe and whatever our differences in the past have been I feel that all Slav races should now unite to rid the world of Nazism.'[67] Stories exist that upon hearing the news of Germany's invasion, Russian immigrants, from as far away as Australia, returned to their former homeland to aid in its defence.[68]

A study by Gennadi Bordiugov identified two interconnected but heterogeneous forces at work in the Soviet state – the system (by which he meant the political and military leadership) and the people. According to Bordiugov, in the initial period of the war the system proved strikingly ineffective, but it was 'the force of the people' that counterbalanced the deficit and galvanized the war effort.[69] A genuine collective determination pervaded the Soviet Union's population, inspiring them to work and fight for the state in the face of many privations, uncertainties and physical risks. Alexander Werth, a British correspondent working for the BBC who was stationed in the Soviet Union throughout the war, remarked that, even in the fateful early period of the war, 'I never lost the feeling that this was a genuine People's War.'[70] Indeed, the war was soon being portrayed as 'a great patriotic war' to evoke comparisons with the victorious ejection of Napoleon's invading army by Tsar Alexander I.[71] The Soviet population felt a genuine sense of shared purpose, solidarity and determination at the advent of war, but their motives were varied and contrasting. According to John Barber and Mark Harrison, motivations included 'patriotism, political conviction, kinship, determination to liberate their native region, hatred of the enemy, desire for revenge – and simply the wish to survive'.[72]

Widespread support for the defence of the nation was also evident among the great bulk of men serving in the Red Army, including those fighting in the Ukraine in 1941. While these troops were painfully aware of the many basic inadequacies of their units, this did not fundamentally alter the desire of most to fight for their homeland. A study by Mark von Hagen, assessing the Red Army's outlook on the eve of war, concluded that in spite of some erosion of the officially propagated Soviet myths, which had previously advanced belief in a communist utopia, the majority of the Red Army met the German attack with 'some degree of Soviet patriotism and commitment to the political and social order of the Soviet state'.[73] A willingness to fight did not, however, compensate for the dreadful condition of the Red Army on the eve of war, nor was it enough to counteract the initial German superiority. The Red Army's summer crisis was inevitable but the many instances of local collapse did not constitute a general collapse: always it was possible to build a new front further east. Moreover, the disintegration of

Soviet armies left behind countless pockets of resistance, which caused havoc for the logistics of advancing German panzer groups and further delayed their slow-moving infantry support.[74] While many historical accounts seem to focus exclusively on the calamity overtaking the Red Army throughout 1941, it is worth remembering that German military records from the same period speak with alarm of their own soaring casualties and the stiff resistance of the Red Army. The Soviet soldier's initial resistance was not in response to German atrocities or the horrendous conditions of German captivity. Evidence of these tended to become generally known only in the late summer and autumn.[75] Robert Thurston's research suggests that the severe battlefield conditions, particularly for Soviet soldiers cut off in German encirclements, were the catalyst for the astonishing number of captured Soviet soldiers in 1941. Some have claimed the vast numbers of Soviet POWs resulted from mass desertion brought on by years of Stalinist terror.[76] In fact the great majority of Soviet men entered captivity unwillingly. Christian Streit's research reveals that of the 3,350,000 Soviet POWs captured by mid-December 1941, some 2,465,000 were taken in thirteen major encirclements.[77] Conditions inside these pockets quickly became unbearable as units were cut off from food and water. Attacked by the Luftwaffe, compressed by German infantry and without hope of further supply or relief, the units could not continue resistance beyond whatever stockpiles of ammunition remained. Mass surrenders, such as the hundreds of thousands captured in the battle of Kiev, were therefore a result of circumstances, not disloyalty.[78] Indeed there are countless examples of Soviet soldiers resisting to the death in hopeless circumstances. The best-known instance is the defence of the Soviet border fortress at Brest, where the undermanned and poorly resourced garrison maintained its stand for up to a month against overwhelming force.[79] Similarly, the Soviet naval base at Liepaia resisted siege for six days, while at Rava-Russkaya and Korosten Soviet forces also held on bitterly against far superior forces.[80] Countless German documents testify to this kind of resistance. In the first days of the war the German 1st Mountain Division noted that the small number of prisoners resulted from the fact that Soviet forces refused to give up and, therefore, 'most of the enemy were shot'.[81] Remarkable examples of Soviet resistance also occurred among the civilian population caught up in the maelstrom of war. Despite the inhuman deprivations endured by Leningrad's starving population in the winter of 1941/1942, civic morale did not collapse – there was no panic, no revolt and no surrender.[82] Like the soldiers dying en masse at the front, civilians worked themselves to exhaustion for the war effort. The Soviet military debacles of 1941 were caused by factors that the Soviets themselves often precipitated, yet mass desertion and dereliction of duty were not as common as is sometimes assumed. Rather, it was because of the profound *esprit de corps* shown by the Red Army that resistance was maintained and the German onslaught checked. Even during the battle of Kiev, the continued resistance of the encircled pocket delayed the release of the German armoured forces and reduced their ability to rest and refit before the next major offensive.

As news filtered back from the front of major reverses and deep enemy advances, the scale of the crisis overtaking the country could no longer be hidden and Soviet authorities, reluctant as ever to risk any loss of control, sought to uphold morale using both a carrot and a stick. While the spontaneous displays of loyalty to Stalin and the Soviet state were trumpeted, any form of dissent was punished as treason and the NKVD was quick to apprehend anyone charged with the dubious offence of 'defeatism' or serving as 'panic-mongers'. Indeed this was the more sinister side to Soviet survival in 1941 – the calculated use of terror and exemplary violence. The military purges may have reached their height over the period 1937 to 1938, but they were still in progress in 1941.[83] As the first Soviet front collapsed in June of that year (Western Front) its hapless commander, Lieutenant-General D. G. Pavlov, and some of his top lieutenants were promptly executed both as retribution and as a warning to other commanders that failure had its consequences. The principal organs of Stalin's control were the People's Commissariat of Internal Affairs (*Narodnyi Komissariat Vnutrennykh Del*, NKVD), whose chief in June 1941 was the notorious L. P. Beria, and the People's Commissariat of State Control (*Narkom Goskontrolia SSSR*), headed by the equally ruthless L. Z. Mekhlis.[84] As one former Soviet agent stated, 'you had to report glowing successes to the demanding bosses who gave you your verification assignments, in other words, your planned tasks; you had to continually find and arrest enemies, spies, and terrorists, unmask anti-Soviets and hand their cases over to the court-martials'.[85] The result was almost a million people being tried by military court-martials during the war,[86] with an unknown number whose cases were dealt with summarily. Sentences were often far in excess of what the offence would seem to merit and varied from execution to being sent to a Gulag or, more commonly for members of the Red Army, service in a disciplinary battalion.[87] Yet not everything in the Soviet state was just a reaction to offences already committed; sometimes the security organs presupposed disloyalty on the part of soldiers and citizens. So-called 'blocking detachments' were formed behind unsteady troops with orders to fire on anyone attempting to retreat, while behind the front minority peoples (Tatars, Kalmyks, Chechens, Ingermanlanders and Volga Germans) were exiled to the distant east on suspicion of being 'pro-German'.[88] The ruthlessness of the Soviet state also extended to mass killings, of which the Katyn massacre is only the most famous example.[89] While the Soviet Union was clearly responsible for its own share of war crimes,[90] for which there can be no justification, its harsh methods, while often unnecessarily brutal and frequently self-detrimental, did at times stiffen the backbone of Soviet resistance. With so many disaffected recruits from the recently occupied regions as well as the long-suffering Ukraine, the firm hand of the Soviet state may well have held together many more of these units than did patriotism alone. Yet throughout much of the Red Army popular support for the Soviet cause cannot be explained simply as a result of the fear induced by the NKVD. As Catherine Merridale observed, 'tyranny alone could not make heroes out of frightened men'.[91]

To whatever extent one may argue that Stalin's security organs served, at least in some capacities, as a necessary evil in 1941, it would be inaccurate to suggest that the Soviet state depended solely on violence to ensure its authority. The threat posed by the German invasion helped to transcend the gulf between the party elite and the Soviet people. The people looked to the state for protection and the state needed the people to achieve this. Under Stalin's direction there began an unprecedented campaign of reinvention – demanding more of the people, but offering a certain liberalization in return. The most obvious indication of this new strategy was Stalin's address on 3 July 1941. No longer did the Soviet leader appear as the lofty figure of near-divine status. Instead, he addressed his people as 'brothers and sisters' and 'friends', a previously unheard-of familiarity.

The speech went on to evoke the image of past Russian war heroes, whose deeds had not been spoken of since the revolution replaced them with more ideologically sound champions. Most importantly, Stalin admitted to his people what was becoming obvious to all – the Red Army was in retreat and the people had to prepare themselves for great sacrifice. The Soviet Union, Stalin made clear, was to wage a total war. 'This war with fascist Germany cannot be considered an ordinary war.' It was not just a war between two armies, Stalin insisted; it was a war 'of the entire Soviet people'. The increasing number of Soviet citizens falling into the German-occupied zone were extolled to form guerrilla groups and continue the war in the German rear. Meanwhile, in the remaining Soviet territories, Stalin promised, 'The masses of our people will rise up in their millions.'[92] And rise they did.

The losses being sustained at the front were enormous. However, the scale of the mobilization being undertaken within the Soviet Union was unprecedented. On 22 June the Red Army had a pool of some 14 million men who had previously received some form of military training and could be mobilized for service. The 1938 Universal Military Service Law had greatly expanded the number of males subject to military conscription and also created many new military schools to provide for the additional reservists. Their training was often rudimentary, but they provided an incredible depth to the Red Army that was almost invisible to German intelligence estimates.[93] On the first day of the invasion the Red Army comprised some 5.5 million men, yet by 1 July when the first phase of the mobilization was complete, the Soviet armed forces numbered 9,638,000 men. Only 3,533,000 of these were at the front in the committed armies and another 5,562,000 were concentrating in the military districts (a further 532,000 were designated for the navy).[94] In July the Red Army added thirteen new field armies to its order of battle and fourteen more in August. In September there was one new army, in October four and in November and December eight, making a total of forty new Soviet armies in just six months.[95] It was a staggering level of force generation and despite the new armies having even less cohesion and expertise than the forces they replaced, by the autumn of 1941 the qualitative decline in the Red Army was sufficiently matched by German exhaustion to offset the danger of exploitation. Nor was this the end of Soviet manpower reserves. The average age of the Soviet population was far lower than in Germany, with 45 per cent of the population under the age of twenty in 1941 (as opposed to only one-third in Germany). This combination of a younger and considerably larger Soviet population meant the annual number of recruits reaching military age each year was decidedly in favour of the Soviets. The class of 1923 (the birth year of men reaching eighteen in 1941) numbered 3 million, which, despite the extensive German occupation of Soviet territory, still amounted to some 2 million Red Army recruits annually between 1941 and 1943.[96]

As with manpower, the Red Army suffered a phenomenal loss of war materiel in the summer and autumn battles, which is often attributed in the secondary literature to the impressive feats of German operational superiority. In fact, owing to the haphazard organization of many Soviet units (which failed to provide adequate fuel, ammunition and support services), as well as the often poor mechanical condition of the vehicles themselves, the vast sums of captured or destroyed Soviet materiel are at least as reflective of grave Soviet deficiencies as of the German battlefield pre-eminence. It is also important to note that Soviet forces retained a good deal of their war materiel produced over the previous quarter of a century. Inventories listed numerous artillery types, some of which even pre-dated World War I. The same was true for rifle and machine gun manifests, which listed such antiquated weapons as the Degtyarev, the Lewis, the 1910 Maxim and the Colt.[97] Aircraft sometimes consisted of open-cockpit biplanes made of plywood and canvas. Thus a tremendous amount of Soviet war materiel was long since obsolete and poor maintenance had rendered much of it unusable. Of the 23,767 Soviet tanks that existed on 22 June 1941, no fewer than 15,000 consisted of the old model T-26 and BT series, the majority of which had mechanical problems.[98] Thus, as the Germans encircled one Soviet army after another and published their famous Orders of the Day, proclaiming exorbitant figures of captured or destroyed Soviet war materiel, one must bear in mind the difference between the Red Army's strength on paper and its strength in real terms. Very little could have been expected from the great bulk of the Soviet pre-war armoury, especially given the Red Army's prodigious problems in understanding and applying combined arms warfare. As Mark Harrison concluded, 'by the winter of 1941 the Soviet armed forces' equipment park had greatly diminished, but [because of new production] what was left was of a much more sophisticated technical level and far more homogeneous than before'.[99]

As the summer turned to autumn the staggering loss of so much equipment, even if old and outdated, was a major problem in outfitting the newly raised armies. It was here that Soviet industry came into its own and, like the army, it was powered by citizens who, by and large, devoted themselves tirelessly to the cause. Only in this way were the staggering equipment losses narrowly kept in check and the most basic needs of the army met. The new weaponry was not only rolling off the production line in record quantities, but much of it proved of such high quality that German soldiers often preferred Soviet weapons (such as anti-tank guns, sub-machine guns, sniper rifles and mortars) to their own.[100] The newer model Soviet tanks were also far superior to anything the Germans possessed, resulting in numerous instances where German soldiers panicked under attack by Soviet T-34s and KV-1s.[101] Soviet guns were roughly comparable to German artillery in effectiveness, but on many sectors of the front they remained vastly superior in numbers despite the repeated disasters of 1941. The Soviets also pioneered important new weaponry at the beginning of the war such as the highly effective BM-13 *Katyusha* multiple rocket launcher, known infamously to German soldiers as 'Stalin's organ'.[102] There was also the redoubtable Il-2 *Shturmovik*, a low-flying, heavily armoured ground-attack aircraft that its designer, S. V. Il'yushin, justifiably dubbed the 'flying tank' as it proved both remarkably resistant to German ground fire and highly destructive.[103] Yet in the war of attrition that had developed on the eastern front by the autumn of 1941, the composite sophistication of the weaponry employed mattered less than the quantities available. Neither side was about to be removed by a single blow, especially given the worn state of each army. In the post-blitzkrieg phase a long series of blows would now have to be traded and in this attritional style of warfare economic durability was at least as important as military prowess. The average expenditure of Soviet weaponry in 1941 testifies to the ferocity of the fighting as well as to the need for a proficient industrial effort. In a typical week towards the end of 1941 a Soviet formation could expect to be losing one-sixth of its aircraft, one-seventh of its guns and mortars, and one-tenth of its tanks.[104] Efficient economic organization and an unmitigated mobilization of the civilian sector were therefore as crucial to the Soviet Union's success as competent generals and trained men. In managing the industrial effort, the Soviet Union faced a far more severe problem than just retooling its industry for war production. Pre-war Soviet plans stipulated that the Red Army should hold any foreign invasion at the borders and then immediately advance into enemy territory.[105] Accordingly, no contingency envisaged a defensive war carried out inside Soviet borders with immense areas of the country having to be surrendered. The fact that this was now taking place had dire military and economic implications. Vast stockpiles of munitions and reserve weapons fell quickly into German hands near the borders, while an immense number of Soviet industrial assets were located in the western part of the USSR. Weapons and munitions could be replaced with time, but only if the industry could be saved. Eighty-five per cent of pre-war aircraft factories, nine large tank factories and countless peacetime enterprises vital to a wartime economy stood in the areas occupied by the Germans up until November 1941.[106]

Recognizing the danger, three days into the war, on 24 June, the Soviet government, in one of its most clear-sighted decisions, created the Council for Evacuation.[107] Headed initially by the transport commissar L. M. Kaganovich, and his deputies A. N. Kosygin and N. M. Shvernik, its task was nothing short of extraordinary: to organize the evacuation of hundreds of large industrial enterprises before the Germans could seize or destroy them.[108] Workers and their families were also evacuated en masse, as were large herds of livestock, most of which were slaughtered or died en route to the east.[109] Machinery had to be hastily loaded on to trains, shipped thousands of kilometres eastward (often as far as the Urals, Siberia or Central Asia) and there reconstructed to begin production again as soon as possible.[110] It would have been a Herculean undertaking at the best of times, but all the more so in 1941, given the crisis overtaking the country and the limitations in transport and manpower as well as the aerial attacks of German planes. Suffice to say that it remains one of the single most remarkable achievements of organization and endurance witnessed in the war. As Zhukov noted in his memoirs: 'The heroic feat of evacuation and restoration of industrial capacities during the war... meant as much for the country's destiny as the greatest battles of the war.'[111] Another depiction labelled it as an 'economic Stalingrad'.[112]

As formidable as the undertaking was, especially given the absence of any pre-war planning, in some respects it was not entirely without precedent. The ruthless Soviet drive towards industrialization, which began in earnest in the latter half of the 1920s, proceeded at a phenomenal pace and transformed the country within fifteen years from a backward, agrarian society to an industrial power. The pre-war Five-Year Plans routinely selected undeveloped, greenfield sites for major new industrial settlements, which, although the scale and urgency in 1941 was radically different, at least gave Soviet planners some idea of the difficulties involved.[113] Between June 1941 and the end of the year some 2,593 industrial sites were evacuated, of which 1,523 were classified as 'major', and of these no fewer than 1,360 were armament manufacturers.[114] As substantial as these figures were, it was later revealed that some 32,000 industrial sites of all sizes were overrun during the war.[115] Yet the colossal size of many of the evacuated Soviet factories indicates their true economic importance. To cite one example, the largest evacuated aircraft factory employed up to 30,000 workers and necessitated the removal of 5,000–10,000 pieces of machinery and equipment.[116] Estimates suggest that the whole 1941 evacuation required the use of 1.5 million railway wagonloads,[117] but managing the transportation was only the beginning.[118] Deconstruction is always easier than reconstruction and on reaching the often-desolate regions selected, the weary and sometimes undernourished workers faced the inevitable confusion of missing equipment, personnel shortages, harsh living conditions and an oppressive pressure to meet deadlines. Rudimentary shelters for the machines took priority over their own, while in the later months bonfires had to provide both light and warmth in the exposed conditions. More permanent structures required backbreaking work to smash through the stone-hard frozen earth. Improvisation and expedience dominated the new sites, and the appalling safety levels meant workers in some plants were in greater mortal danger than those exposed to German bombing in Moscow. Still, in spite of the cost, the factories were reassembled and production commenced again as quickly as possible – in one case only two weeks after relocation.[119] In the more outstanding cases evacuated factories were not only producing again, but, by the end of 1941, were exceeding their pre-war output.

Perhaps most astonishingly, given the awesome difficulties presented by both the German invasion and the industrial relocation, Soviet factories not only managed to maintain their production of essential war materiel, but in some cases, such as tanks, they actually exceeded the officially set production quotas.[120] The industrial effort was so concerted that the second half of 1941 produced a three-fold increase on key armaments manufactured in the first half of the year. The monthly averages of the first six months equalled 1,000 aircraft, 300 tanks and 4,000 guns and mortars, which jumped in the second half of the year to 3,300 aircraft, 800 tanks and 12,000 guns and mortars.[121] In fact, the USSR produced more tanks in 1941 than did Germany (6,590 to

5,200)[122] and two-thirds of these (4,322) were of the newer T-34 and KV-1 varieties.[123] Soviet industry also turned out more aircraft (15,735 to 11,776) and a great deal more artillery pieces (42,300 to 7,000) than did Germany, helping to meet the most immediate needs of the army.[124]

One may well ask how such an extraordinary achievement was possible. To begin with, Soviet weaponry tended to be of very simple construction, with numerous interchangeable parts and a high degree of redundancy. This not only made it easier to construct, a vital factor given the masses of inexperienced civilians entering the factories, but also reduced the time needed to do so. Important choices were also made at the highest levels about what to build. The USSR virtually abandoned production of large naval vessels both for strategic reasons and because their construction was so resource- and labour-intensive. Similarly, the air force was limited to short-range, low-altitude fighters and ground-attack planes, ignoring heavy bombers, night fighters or high-altitude interceptors. The Red Army did not possess any armoured troop carriers and in 1941 and 1942 lacked an equivalent of the German *Sturmgeschütz*, a self-propelled artillery gun.[125] Even truck manufacture was squeezed to an austere minimum, resulting in Soviet tanks often doubling as crowded troop transports.[126] Once a weapon was selected, judicious choices dictated its development. Unlike the Germans, the Soviets avoided a multiplicity of different makes and designs for any given weapon or vehicle.[127] Standardization was the key to cheap, fast and efficient production.

The system of building the weapons was just as important as the products themselves, and here Soviet planners applied important lessons learned from American industrialists, using the principles of mass-production assembly lines and long unit runs. Assembly lines not only resulted in the most time-efficient production yield, but had the advantage of dividing up complex jobs into individual tasks that easily accommodated a semi-skilled or unskilled workforce. The long production runs served the Soviets well throughout the war by maximizing use of resources and avoiding idleness. The Germans, by contrast, were constantly grafting improvements on to their existing weapons or retooling their production lines to initiate entirely new product runs. Improvements often came at the cost of numbers produced. Soviet soldiers, on the other hand, began and finished the war with basically the same infantry weapons, while the T-34 tank (with some refinements) was still being turned out in record numbers in 1944.[128] It was all done to ensure maximum concentration of resources and industrial capacity on a select number of weapons of decisive importance to the war effort.

While the pre-war Soviet defence industry was surprisingly large, it is important to note that the remarkable output of weaponry in 1941 could never have been achieved without the conversion of the civilian economy.[129] By early July conversion was in full swing, which resulted in important sources of new weapons. A children's bicycle factory, for example, began turning out flamethrowers and a typewriter manufacturer started producing automatic rifles and ammunition.[130] Yet pursuing conversion to provide the required materiel came at a dangerous cost. Tanks and guns are the end products of a war economy. Equally important are coal to fire the steel furnaces, electric power to run the machines and food to sustain the workers. Without one the other is not possible. In 1941 the single-minded production of military output was pursued to the detriment of all else and was only possible in the short term because of reserve stocks of essential items normally produced in the civilian economy. Neglecting secondary industries was just as detrimental as neglecting production deficiencies in the tank factories themselves. In effect the USSR was driving its economic engine at full throttle without sufficient oil or coolant and was therefore threatened with a latent crisis of economic survival.

Two fundamental problems caused the crisis and had to be resolved. The first was the German advance, which was swallowing up vital raw materials, sources of grain, industrial assets (only parts of which could be evacuated) and labour reserves. The second was the radical extent of the switch to armament production. The drive for war production was completely out of balance with the demands of the rest of the economy, effectively smothering other industries. Between the first and second half of 1941 supplies of pig iron, crude steel and rolled steel were down by as much as half, while coal and electric power were down by a third. Machine tool output fell to two-fifths, as did the grain harvest in comparison with 1940.[131] By November 1941 some 78 million people, two-fifths of the Soviet Union's population, lived in the German-occupied zone.[132] It was indeed a crisis of economic survival for the Soviet government, but not an insurmountable one. Just as the Red Army triumphed by surviving in 1941 in spite of unprecedented defeats, the Soviet economic planners managed against the odds to maintain production and avoid collapse. The halting of the German advance by the end of the autumn, as well as a renewed emphasis on the civilian economic sector (with emergency decrees and crash programmes mostly in 1942), created the conditions for both economic survival and continued high-level armament output.[133]

Despite the obstacles faced at this time, the Soviets actually sought to boost their 1941 production levels as far as possible. Later in the war the Soviet economy increasingly benefited from Lend-Lease aid, which had a much greater impact propping up the home front than it did arming the Red Army. Yet Allied aid did not flow in vast sums until 1943, meaning that, like the streamlined weapons programme turning out essential arms only, economic objectives had to focus on essential needs. Already by the end of the summer of 1941 austerity measures proliferated. These saw, for example, capital construction cut dramatically, reducing the wastage inherent in the 1938–1942 Five-Year Plan. Of some 5,700 major projects planned or in progress, only 614, deemed vital to the war effort, were continued.[134] Similarly, the Soviet pre-war economy possessed a number of 'hidden reserves', most notably in labour. Officially there was no unemployment in Soviet society, but pre-war productivity in factories was notoriously low. This often resulted from collusion between workers and managers to refrain from intense efforts so that low output would be accepted as normal. If economic planners did not know to expect more, they would not demand more.[135] With the outbreak of war this all changed.

Many workers were caught up in the surge of patriotism sweeping the country and now saw their work in light of slogans comparing their deeds to those of the heroic soldiers fighting at the front. The demographics of the workforce changed dramatically as millions of men were drafted for service in the Red Army and the acute labour shortage demanded anyone capable of work. Filling the void were women, the elderly and teenagers. The *Komsomol* youth brigades literally marched into the factories under the slogan 'Work in the factory as soldiers fight at the front.' Their patriotic energy was one of the driving forces in the new work ethos, bringing to the factories a fanatical devotion to duty and military-style organization.[136] At the same time factories issued medals for over-achievers and created new worker idols who were publicly celebrated for exceptional feats of production. A man named Bosyi won the State Prize and became a household name after producing his five-month quota in fifteen days.[137] The workers were also motivated by thoughts of relatives in the occupied areas or away at the front. Indeed the sheer proximity of many workers to the front lines provided its own stimulus, especially in light of the widely circulating stories about German atrocities.

Inducements to work harder were also imposed externally. Only days after the start of the war special decrees were issued converting the Soviet Union into Stalin's promised 'single war camp'. Martial law was declared throughout the western part of the Soviet Union and severe punishments were imposed for absenteeism or lateness for work. Holidays and leave were cancelled, the working day was extended to between twelve and sixteen hours, and managers reserved the right to expect a further three hours' compulsory overtime.[138] Unlike for the Germans, for the Soviet people it was a total war from the very beginning and worker output in the armaments industry increased almost three-fold during the course of the war.[139] Yet, as for the Germans, the Soviet war effort, at least in 1941, was sustained by a mixture of genuine patriotism and brutal coercion.

While the Soviet army and economy were being simultaneously jolted by the competing extremes of violent external destruction and massive internal support, holding the Soviet state together and providing effective direction required its own radical solutions. On 30 June 1941 Stalin assumed control of what could be described as a Soviet adaptation of the British war cabinet – the State Committee for Defence (*Gosudarstvenny Komitet Oborony* or GKO). Its authority was supreme, concentrating 'the full range of state power in [its] hands . . . All citizens and all Party, Soviet, *Komsomol* and military bodies [are to] carry out the decisions and provisions of the State Committee for Defence without question.' Stalin was installed as chairman, with the Foreign Minster, V. M. Molotov, as vice-chairman. Only three other members were initially part of the GKO – Marshal K. E. Voroshilov, Central Committee Secretary G. M. Malenkov and NKVD chief Beria – but in February 1942 it was expanded to include N. A. Voznesenski, L. M. Kaganovich and A. H. Mikoyan.[140] Decrees issued by the GKO carried the weight of law and overruled all other political and military bodies.[141] Each member was responsible for his own military, political or economic duties as well as being allocated a vital branch of the national economy. Molotov, for example, was responsible for tank production, Malenkov for aircraft assembly, Mikoyan for consumer goods and Kaganovich for railway transportation.[142]

Even before the formation of the GKO, it was immediately recognized on the outbreak of war that a supreme military command was needed to co-ordinate the activities of the People's Commissariat of Defence and the Red Army General Staff. This body, it was determined, would preside over every aspect of military policy from the inception of new armies for mobilization to the direction of the war itself. Inaugurated on 23 June, the *Stavka* of the High Command was initially chaired by the Defence Commissar, S. K. Timoshenko, but Stalin soon assumed full authority.[143] Its select membership included Molotov, Voroshilov, Marshal G. K. Zhukov, Marshal S. M. Budenny and Admiral N. G. Kuznetsov. The *Stavka*'s duties included responsibility for strategic direction, developing operational-strategic plans, creating new forces, and co-ordinating the multi-Front strategic commands, the individual fronts, field armies and the partisan movement.[144]

At the start of the war there was no command structure between the separate Fronts and the Red Army General Staff. This led to the creation of three theatre-level commands, known as the High Commands of Directions, which came into being on 10 July 1941. The first of these was the North-Western Direction, under Voroshilov, controlling the Northern and North-Western Fronts as well as the Baltic and Northern Fleets. The Western Direction was commanded initially by Timoshenko with the Western Front, and Budenny took charge of the South-Western Direction with the South-Western Front, Southern Front and the Black Sea Fleet. The purpose of these new multi-Front strategic commands was to co-ordinate the activities of the individual Fronts, yet from the beginning the *Stavka* was prone to bypassing them, issuing its orders directly to Front headquarters. Eventually they proved so ineffective that in 1942 they were disbanded.[145]

The *Stavka* was to prove significant in providing strong, centralized leadership throughout the war, but the swift collapse of field armies in the early summer created urgent demands for immediate and service-wide structural reforms. In the border areas large Soviet formations were being cut off and destroyed by German encirclements, but it was not just external German pressure that gripped these Soviet formations with a fatal paralysis. Soviet field formations were quickly recognized to be much too large and cumbersome for their grossly inadequate communication system, especially given the dreadful standards of training and experience of Soviet officers. The dynamic, organized and fast-moving Germans were taking full advantage of the rigid Soviet organization, which could never react with the required operational agility. Consequently the *Stavka* astutely reasoned that only with smaller organizations at every level of command could inexperienced officers regain effective control over their forces and provide better direction. The smaller force structures also made units more fragile and many would be consumed in the late summer and autumn fighting, but these 'lighter' formations provided a vital means of in-field education as well as battlefield flexibility.[146]

Under the new *Stavka* Directive No. 1, issued on 15 July 1941, the field armies were made smaller, and rifle and mechanized corps were eliminated altogether. The field armies now typically controlled only five or six rifle divisions, two or three tank brigades, one or two light cavalry divisions and a number of artillery regiments. The authorized strength of rifle divisions shrank from 14,500 men to 11,000, while allocations of artillery dropped 24 per cent and trucks 64 per cent. As the summer wore on and the German offensive slowed, grinding battles continued everywhere, forcing many battered Soviet rifle divisions to be redesignated as individual brigades. These brigades (typically consisting of about 4,400 men) were to prove even better suited to the inexperienced Soviet officers, and accordingly, the *Stavka* created 170 such units between the autumn of 1941 and early 1942. The surviving tank divisions also had their authorized strengths cut to 217 tanks each, allowing the excess armoured vehicles to be used in the creation of new formations. Tactical air units were reorganized from sixty aircraft into new regiments of just thirty. The new 'light' Red Army wisely abandoned many of its pre-war conceptions about force structures and organization. The *Stavka* was clearly applying the right lessons, even if these were only being learned the hard way. Ultimately, reorganization ensured the survival of the Red Army until it could again begin building 'heavier' formations in 1942.[147]

In spite of the many bitter lessons being learned at the front, the Soviet regime's learning curve was not always a positive one. Stalin still explained defeats in the most simplistic terms. Defeated Soviet commanders were accused of lacking personal courage or not showing the requisite moral fibre for hard fighting. Such factors no doubt played a role at times, but their actions were often only symptomatic of the immense problems Soviet generals faced. In any case the Stalinist regime was unsympathetic and the political commissars, attached to the field headquarters, were quickly elevated to equal status with the commanding officers. Decision-making became more difficult as military concerns became infused with political objectives. Open and frank discussion suffered in the general atmosphere of fear and suspicion. The fate of Pavlov, the Western Front commander executed in July 1941, is the most famous instance of intimidation by Stalin and the NKVD, but it is by no means the only example. Even captured Soviet soldiers who managed to escape and make their way back to Soviet lines suffered arrest and brutal interrogation on suspicion of being cowards or German spies.[148] Indeed one may well conclude that responses to the initial disasters overtaking the Red Army in 1941 reflected both the best and worst of the Soviet system. Ruthless as it was, the state forced through hasty structural changes that may well have saved the army, yet its brutal and irrational practices were never far from the surface.

For the people of the Soviet Union life after 22 June 1941 was dictated entirely by the war effort. In a total war economy there was no such thing as non-essential labour and anyone who wished to draw a ration card or steer clear of the NKVD did their duty. Their lives became a tedium of long working hours, first for the state and then for the essentials of daily life. Factory canteens did not always provide sufficient food, forcing families (especially those with non-working dependants) to tend small garden allotments or trade valuables to supplement meals. Many consumer items simply disappeared for the remainder of the war, meaning people had to make do with what they had. Clothes had to be repeatedly patched and repaired, while neighbourhood barter and trade became the staples of acquisition. The state attempted to meet only the most basic needs of the population; anything more was a distraction from the war effort.

For all the deprivations and hardships of civilian life it was still immeasurably better than what confronted soldiers at the front (although in some civilian quarters, such as in Leningrad, there was little real difference). At the front the suffering and torments of war were truly horrendous. In 1941 alone the number of Soviet soldiers who would never return to their homes numbered as many as 3 million.[149] The killing of Soviet men, sometimes in massed frontal assaults, proceeded at a ferocious rate and even in captivity the barbaric treatment of the German occupation forces, as well as the German army, ensured most captives died in the first winter of the war. The bloodshed also extended to the occupied areas where German extermination squads were hard at work killing Jews and any other suspect elements. Yet none were safe as the occupied territories soon faced alarming food shortages and the countryside became torn between the ruthless measures of partisans and occupation forces. By the end of the year disease, malnutrition and cold began taking the old, sick and very young in record numbers.

Throughout everything the Soviet people struggled on with their daily lives, working and fighting for an elusive victory in spite of all the costs and deprivations. According to Sof'ia Nikolaevna Buriakova, a housewife who lost almost all her relatives in the blockade of Leningrad, understanding the average person's capacity to endure so much was simple. 'What played the decisive role was a feeling of civic patriotism, the realization of a patriotic duty – at the cost of lives and deprivations to defend the freedom and independence of our fatherland.'[150] Clearly the unwavering dedication and conviction of the Soviet people during World War II went far beyond a mere reaction to state orders. Even so, their stubborn willingness to oppose Nazism, regardless of cost, should not blind us to the suffering such measures entailed. Indeed given its overwhelming losses the Soviet population deserves special appreciation for the calamity its war generation endured and the devastating human toll their survival demanded. The stereotyped views, often expressed in German memoirs, of Soviet soldiers seemingly oblivious to death and suffering[151] tend to denigrate the value of the many lives lost (and reflect to no small extent German wartime propaganda). The Soviet people were no better at accepting death and no more willing to die than any other people. The German invasion of the USSR demanded of them a harsh daily routine of physical hardship and psychological burden. Yet work, suffer, fight and die they did. In the end it was their remarkable commitment to a total war effort, and prodigious readiness for toil and self-sacrifice, that is the real story of Soviet survival in 1941.

2 GERMANY'S DEFEAT IN THE EAST

Going into the red – the failed economics of Operation Barbarossa

Understanding the seriousness of Germany's strategic predicament by the autumn of 1941 depends upon two essential factors, firstly, the weakness of Germany's economic base, and secondly, the failure of the *Ostheer*'s summer blitzkrieg in the Soviet Union. This chapter assesses the strategic ramifications of Hitler's failure to defeat the Soviet Union in a summer campaign and how these were set to become worse from September 1941 onwards.

There can be little doubt that together Britain and France enjoyed a superior economic position at the start of World War II. Yet in the first two years of the conflict Germany maintained the strategic initiative and effectively manoeuvred itself to offset the impact of the economic imbalance. Hitler did this by means of brief military campaigns to eliminate strategic military threats and seize vital stockpiles of foreign commodities as well as gain additional industrial capacity fundamental for the expansion of his war effort. Moreover, rather than exacting a cost militarily, most of the early campaigns yielded vast quantities of war materiel (although a good deal of it was obsolete on the modern battlefield) and proved relatively light in casualties. Nevertheless, Germany's success was limited to land warfare. In the sea and air battles against Britain, Germany was already engaged in two bitter wars of attrition, and after February 1941 the North African campaign proved a constant, albeit minor, drain on the army too. At sea the German navy was attempting to sink more tonnage than British shipyards could replace, while at the same time offsetting their own losses in U-boats by increased production. In the air campaign Germany first attempted to destroy Britain's air force, as a prelude to invasion, and then switched its priority to bombing both as a reprisal for air raids over Germany and as a means of limiting British industrial might. Yet, as costly and as indecisive as these campaigns were to prove, Germany's real hope, and overwhelming strength, rested in its army. Until the summer of 1941 the German army stood intact and unengaged, ready to reinforce North Africa, defend Western Europe, attack vital strategic possessions in the Mediterranean or possibly even launch an invasion of Britain itself.

The advent of Operation Barbarossa changed everything. The German army, which had previously been partly demobilized to provide much-needed workers for the arms industry, was now mobilized again and committed in bulk to the east, allowing very little flexibility for German strategic planning until the conclusion of the fighting. The main part of the operational plan was thought to require no longer than the summer period and, thereafter, the campaign was expected to consist of something akin to the unopposed 'railway advance' of World War I, requiring only a minimum of effort and the commitment of occupation forces.[1] The reality proved very different. Hitler expected that the concentration of nearly 160 German divisions, including the bulk of the German panzer and air arms as well as the addition of almost three-quarters of a million Axis soldiers and their allies, would simply overwhelm the Red Army. In the event, it proved insufficient for the task. As the front expanded and losses mounted, gaps appeared in the German lines, flanks became open and strength at the vital points of main concentration waned. Most worryingly, the mobility and firepower of the essential panzer groups had sunk so far by the end of the summer as to preclude the possibility of ending major operations in the year 1941.

The Soviet Union, on the other hand, with its superior production of essential war materials, its manpower reserves and its perspicacious decision to mobilize for total war in the summer of 1941, would not only survive the German onslaught, it would be an even more formidable opponent by 1942. Most importantly for the Soviets, the summer of 1941 was the only time that German operations were able to advance along the entire length of the front with rapid movement and swift conquest. Thereafter positional warfare dominated more and more of the front as the fighting became typified by slogging, pitched battles, which exacted a continuous materiel cost and constant manpower losses. It was an outcome Germany simply could not afford – a high-intensity war of attrition against a militarily and economically robust power, which was superior in both manpower and the key industrial indices of land warfare. As soon as the Wehrmacht lost its operational edge and the enormous war in the east became dominated by resources, instead of rapid manoeuvre and 'shock' tactics, the prospects for Germany's war effort were fatally altered. By the winter of 1941/1942 the Soviet counteroffensive, in spite of poor co-ordination and inept tactical leadership, was able to push the German armies back along a broad section of the front. By this point not only had Barbarossa long since failed, but Germany was now trapped in precisely the kind of war that Hitler had been trying to avoid.

Nazi Germany's economic initiatives and materiel output in the lead-up to the invasion of the Soviet Union have generated a number of differing interpretations among historians. In the 1980s Richard Overy called into question Alan Milward's long-espoused thesis that Hitler sought to pursue war production, while maintaining the civilian economy of consumer goods. Hitler, according to Milward, was seeking to provide 'guns and butter' via a 'blitzkrieg economy', which between September 1939 and December 1941 saw him repeatedly adapt Germany's production to the changing needs of the conflict.[2] Overy dismissed Milward's concept and contended that Hitler had been attempting full mobilization of the economy from the very beginning of the war. This process, however, had been thwarted by the harmful absence of an overarching administrative body with extensive powers of control to co-ordinate the competing agencies of the industrial effort and quell their fierce rivalries.[3] Although Overy became engaged in intense debate as a result of his interpretations, he was not the only one to challenge what had been prevailing wisdom. In 1988 Rolf-Dieter Müller published the first part of his seminal work on the German war economy in which he too emphasized Germany's failed attempt to pursue an efficient and co-ordinated mobilization of industry.[4]

The studies by Müller and Overy immediately established a new orthodoxy within the historiography, which, although not always in agreement, at least shared a common understanding of the stagnation in Germany's armament production between 1940 and 1941. More recently, however, a new interpretation has emerged from Adam

Tooze, who contends that there was no stagnation in the early years of Germany's wartime economy, but rather a consistent progression towards mass production. Tooze argues that the accounts of Müller and Overy are built on 'a statistical illusion'[5] implicit within the previously accepted figures of Germany's armament output.[6] Furthermore, Tooze contends that a wider analysis of the German economy, looking beyond simply armament production, reveals an extensive investment programme that provided the foundation for Albert Speer's so-called economic miracle starting in early 1942.[7] By that stage, however, the Allied lead in armament production was unassailable and Germany was doomed to fight a war of ever-increasing materiel inferiority.

While the competing fields of historical interpretations may appear to complicate our understanding of Germany's exact economic footing in the run-up to Operation Barbarossa, one thing remains clear. The German economic effort, irrespective of which interpretations one follows, was in no way equal to the coming demands of war against the Soviet Union. This is an essential factor in understanding the turning point that Barbarossa's military failure represents. Once Germany's blitzkrieg campaign had failed and been replaced by a war of resources, Germany was placed at a huge disadvantage, which the constraints on the German economy made it impossible to counter, irrespective of whether it had been consistently built for mass production or whether indeed Speer was capable of inducing miracles.

Before World War II began, the peacetime industrial output of Germany measured only some 10.7 per cent of world production, with Japan's share accounting for just 3.5 per cent and Italy's even less at 2.7 per cent. At the same time the countries that ultimately formed the alliance against Germany produced some 70 per cent of the world's industrial goods, suggesting the Axis was in an all but impossible situation once all the major powers were involved in the war by the end of 1941.[8]

When World War II began Germany's economic institutions resembled, in both operation and method, the fractured and headstrong political organizations of the Nazi state. In place of centralized direction there existed powerful competing interests, each vying with one another for access to scant resources. Walther Funk's Ministry of Economics, Herman Göring's powerful Four-Year Plan Organization and the War Economy Office (*Wirtschafts und Rüstungsamt*), headed by General of Infantry Georg Thomas, were all bitter rivals. Below this top level, adding further to the disorder, were no fewer than twenty-seven national offices (*Reichsstellen*) that became involved in the tangled planning and production process. In February 1940 Fritz Todt also entered the fray as the new minister for weapons and munitions. Against this conglomerate of competing state enterprises and notoriously corrupt officialdom, private industry struggled to preserve its entrepreneurial independence. The result was a stifling array of conflicting directives and priorities.[9] By the start of the campaign in the west in May 1940, progress towards economic mobilization had been steady, but importantly, at this stage economic planning matched strategic forecasts for a long-term ground war requiring armaments in depth. The startling success of the French campaign, however, proved a watershed. It led to a dangerous hubris in Hitler's strategic thinking (supported by Germany's political and military elites), causing him to underestimate Britain's future prospects in the war, and then to discount the danger of turning against his valuable economic ally, the Soviet Union. Not only did the prospect of war against the Soviet Union exchange a major economic lifeline for a new and unprecedented strain on the German economy, but the unexpected course of the French campaign also led to radical changes in the previous armament plans. Emboldened by the success of their seemingly unstoppable blitzkrieg strategy, Hitler and his commanders no longer feared a costly war of attrition in which the army could be forced to shed massive quantities of equipment or consume large stocks of munitions. Operation Barbarossa was to be a short and decisive campaign establishing Germany's complete dominance of the continent, and the rapid success of the intervening Balkan campaign served only to reinforce further Nazi Germany's fervent faith in the prospects of a quick victory. As a result, rather than continuing to gear up for a potentially costly war of unforeseen duration, Hitler abruptly cut production of munitions and began a complete reordering of economic priorities. Anticipating having to fight two separate wars at the same time – an ongoing aerial war against Britain and a blitzkrieg against the Soviet Union – Hitler approved a massive reorientation of priorities towards the Luftwaffe and specific weaponry for the army deemed vital for Barbarossa.[10]

Assessing the shift in focus of the German economy Rolf-Dieter Müller has been scathingly critical. The German arms industry, he argued, was being directed according to an improvised and haphazard economic formula, which the mismanaged structures of the economy did not handle well. This soon resulted in Germany forfeiting its lead in armaments over the British and the gap, once created, continued to widen as the number of Germany's enemies grew and Hitler failed for too long to address properly the internal wrangling.[11] Adam Tooze's research suggests that the reorientation of arms manufacture in the summer of 1940 was a far smoother process, which, contrastingly, points to a large degree of rationalization in economic management and an efficiency that set the basis for increased output even with the retooling of industry. What is important about Tooze's study is that, after painting a far more positive picture of German economic management in the early years of the war, which owing to the full exploitation of labour and raw materials proves there was no room for further expansion in the economy, it becomes clear that armament production had reached a maximum effort and that more could not be done. His research shows increased production between 1940 and 1941, suggesting Germany was somewhat better equipped than previously thought,[12] but even Tooze agrees it made little difference in sustaining the kind of war Hitler had undertaken in the east. Economically Nazi Germany was fatally ill-prepared for a war with the Soviet Union, especially once the campaign extended beyond the exceedingly optimistic expectations of the planned blitzkrieg.

While Germany's domestic war economy could not hope to compete with the combined strength of the Allies, it is sometimes suggested that Germany's European empire would have retained the theoretical potential to cope far better with Britain and America's vast industrial might if only it had been mobilized and managed correctly in the early phase of the war. Understanding the true nature of Europe's economic potential under the Nazis cannot be determined by recourse to pre-war statistics. Once France and the other occupied countries of Western Europe were subjected to German rule, they were also gripped by Britain's blockade. As highly developed industrialized economies with no prospect of economic autarky, these countries immediately looked to Germany for supplies of all essential raw materials. Oil was indispensable, but Germany was itself dependent on the comparatively small production emanating from Romania, which produced only 1.5 million tons of oil each year between 1940 and 1943. By contrast, Britain alone imported 10 million tons in 1942. Massive investment in synthetic fuel plants allowed Germany to avert catastrophe, but these installations, while impressive in their own right, still produced only

4 million tons of fuel in 1940. The result was a Europe-wide shortage, forcing many Western European economies to revert to something approaching pre-industrial times. France, for example, received only 8 per cent of its pre-war consumption of petrol.[13] The Italian peacetime economy, even without extensive industrialization, imported some 3–4 million tons of oil annually, and when war was declared fuel reserves were so low that the army reportedly possessed just 200,000 tons. This amount, according to the Italian minister responsible for war production, General Carlo Favagrossa, would last only eight months and that was without the high demands of an active campaign over long distances in North Africa. Germany was left to prop up its Axis ally and between June 1940 and September 1943 at least 3,572,000 tons of fuel had to be diverted to Italy.[14] The implications were clear: without access to far greater oil supplies, any kind of economic miracle in the occupied or Axis partner countries, especially one comparable to Germany's armaments drive in the latter years of the war, was a forlorn hope. As the German military commander in France, General of Infantry Otto von Stülpnagel, observed: 'If you want a cow to give milk, you have to feed it.'[15]

Despite retaining the lion's share of Europe's oil for themselves, the Germans still could not adequately meet all their vital needs. In the second half of 1941 the competing demands for fuel between Germany's industry and its army in the east led to extreme austerity measures. Yet even these could not prevent critical shortages in both. Although the shortfall at the front is often seen as a symptom of the inadequate logistics system, the fact remained that even if the transportation had existed to meet all the needs of the *Ostheer*, oil stocks were simply inadequate. Thus, whether one chooses to highlight logistics or oil stocks, the result was the same and the campaign, which had to be won quickly, was repeatedly left waiting for fuel.[16] At the same time, on the home front the inadequate fuel supplies, even in 1941, led to intermittent production halts and idle assembly lines.[17]

As fundamental as oil was to mobile armies and industrialized economies, it was not the only raw material that Germany's economic empire was desperately lacking. Coal supplied no less than 80 per cent of the energy for Western European industry and most of these countries possessed very little domestic mining or none at all. Many had relied heavily on British coal imports and the burden of supplying them would now have to be borne by Germany. As it happened, Germany did possess a large annual coal surplus and could, together with the Eastern European coal surplus countries, theoretically have covered most of the deficit. The problem, however, was one of logistics and production. The rail network was not sufficient to transport that amount of coal to the countries that required it, especially since Germany had expropriated a significant amount of rolling stock from the conquered countries to fill troubling gaps in the domestic *Reichsbahn*. As a result there were simply not enough coal supplies coming in to sustain Western European industrial demands. In France, which previously supplied 60 per cent of its annual consumption from domestic mines, authorities could no longer ensure even this amount because of the blow resulting from German rail requisitions. To make matters worse, productivity at French mines also fell dramatically, a circumstance that was exacerbated further by widespread strikes over food shortages in 1941. The decline in coal deliveries had a direct impact on industrial production and already in 1940 output in French factories fell 18 per cent.[18] This eventually dropped to just 38 per cent of the 1938 total, while only 65 per cent of pre-war coal production was maintained.[19] In Italy coal production was one of the few areas in which output actually increased during the war, but this in no way sufficed to service domestic demand, and even with German imports, industrial output (small as it was) dropped during the war.[20]

Notwithstanding the transportation difficulties, it was clear that Germany had to raise to domestic coal production to offset the disabling shortages in Western Europe and Italy. Yet this endeavour confronted German economic planners with a familiar problem, which was present in all areas of the economy. Coal mining was labour intensive and Germany was in the grip of a manpower crisis. With the army claiming so many men there could be no solution other than the drafting of foreign workers. In the meantime inadequate coal supplies meant shortages, which had a devastating impact on the occupied economies and soon also hampered German industry.[21] Far from the economies of occupied Europe growing to support Germany's new-found empire, the result of German rule was a rapid decline from their pre-war productivity,[22] a trend that was never to be reversed. Indeed Mark Mazower characterized Germany's occupation practices as 'basically organized despoliation', in which short-term exploitation led to rapid ruin. As Mazower explained:

> *Throughout occupied Europe, existing markets were broken up as civilians fled their homes and overseas trade stopped, while requisitioning depleted farmyards and stockpiles and labour conscription emptied the fields and factories of workers. Acute uncertainty about the future led to hoarding and shopping sprees, which exhausted stocks . . . The manifold partitions of France, Poland, Yugoslavia and Greece raised new barriers to trade and business and cut suppliers off from their customers. Forced deliveries, an efficient clearing system and fixed exchange rates allowed huge sums to be transferred into German hands but only at the cost of exposing the countries concerned to intense inflationary pressures. Taken together, these factors encouraged fears of imminent chaos or collapse and posed a huge challenge to wartime administrators.*[23]

The extent to which Western Europe's economies were operating efficiently in the service of Nazi Germany was a matter of widespread indifference to most of the subject populations. Yet food supplies impacted them directly and this was one of the main factors in the steadily increasing hostility felt towards German occupation. Before the war Europe had imported between 12 and 13 million tons of grain each year; however, the British blockade as well as the inevitable wartime loss of productivity in agriculture led to an estimated grain deficit of 21.5 million tons – equivalent to the food requirements of 50 million people. Germany was also not immune, having imported 17 per cent of annual food requirements before the war.[24] A solution had to be found and grain supply, like that of many other commodities in short supply, was a major factor influencing Hitler's decision to attack in the east. Already in 1940 public opinion in Germany was voicing considerable anxiety over food shortages and increased market prices.[25] At that time there was still a moderate grain reserve available for Germany, but the situation was destined to worsen the longer the war continued. Colonel-General Fritz Fromm, Chief of the Land-Force Armaments and Commander-in-Chief of the Replacement Army, reported in December 1940 that in terms of food stocks Germany could only expect to 'muddle through' 1941.[26] The situation was already considerably worse in the occupied countries where the ration allocation in Belgium and France was set at only 1,300 calories.[27] As critical as the food supply was, it was destined to become much worse and in Greece there was even famine, which by the end of the occupation was estimated to have killed some 300,000 people.[28] Clearly, although Germany was meeting its most immediate needs in 1940/1941, it was living on borrowed time and the proposed conquest of the Soviet Union was now being looked upon as *the* solution to many looming economic problems. The prospect of failing to defeat the Soviet Union in a single campaign and the colossal demands such an eventuality would place on the German economy and its military were never seriously considered.

Germany's limited access to raw materials and stubborn industrial bottlenecks were a major complication inhibiting increased industrial output, but the single greatest problem was the labour shortage, particularly that of skilled labourers.[29] The low numbers of children born during World War I meant that, once the needs of the army were met, there were very few young men left for labour. Of those between the ages of twenty and thirty physically fit for military service, no less than 85 per cent were already in the armed forces by the summer of 1941.[30] This meant that manpower reserves for the military were almost exhausted before Barbarossa even began, underlining, in the starkest terms, the danger of a drawn-out war.

Attempting to bridge the gap in armament production and the manpower shortage, an extensive leave programme was set up to send soldiers from the field armies back to the factories. Essentially they were to produce the weapons needed for the upcoming eastern campaign, yet in practice the army resisted the disruption to its training plans and the programme, which was supposed to begin in October 1940, was delayed by the army until mid-January 1941. Even then, the originally planned 300,000 men ended up being limited to just over 100,000.[31] The importance of German manpower to both industry and the army highlights another important ramification of Barbarossa's failure. Not only was industry denied vital labour to cope with the expanding dimensions of the war, but every loss in the east constituted a double blow, requiring another replacement at the front as well as denying the anticipated post-campaign dividend of a returning worker.[32]

Shortages of workers and raw materials were at the heart of Germany's stalled economic effort. Initially there was a boost received from the captured stocks of raw materials and military equipment in Western Europe, but these offered only a short-term alleviation, especially given the extra demands of administering occupied Europe and providing for future German war plans. In order to provide occupation forces, continue the war against Britain and begin building up for the invasion of the Soviet Union, the army had to be expanded to 180 divisions. Yet even this drastic measure, requiring a tremendous increase in armaments, failed to move Hitler or the OKH to press for a radical reorganization of armament priorities. The adopted solution was for military production to be determined by the capacity of existing manufacturing facilities, rather than the real requirements of the proposed army.[33] It was therefore known that German production could not cover a considerable proportion of the enlarged army's requirements and no effort was made to rectify this. This resulted in a patchwork invasion force being assembled for Barbarossa, in which shortfalls in armament production were filled by a vast array of differing weapons from all over Europe. Similarly, the motorized divisions fielded hundreds of different makes of vehicles, most of civilian origin. This led to prodigious problems of standardization. Units had to receive the correct ammunition for their guns, while repairs required a startling number of spare parts, which in the depths of the Soviet Union were often unavailable. To take one example, Major-General Walter Nehring's 18th Panzer Division fielded no fewer than 96 different types of personnel carriers, 111 types of trucks and 37 types of motorcycles.[34] Yet even after putting this makeshift force in the field, the real oversight in German economic planning was not just its inadequate provision, but the complete lack of ability to sustain it in the field once losses mounted. Accordingly, the road to demise in the east was a short one because heavy losses were not backed by an adequate replacement system. Germany would have to win the war in the east with the army at hand and, if that proved impossible, the grinding war of attrition in the east would result in what Omer Bartov identified as a 'demodernization of the front'.[35] This process not only ensured a qualitative decline in the fighting strength of the divisions, but, even before the battle of Kiev, denied the army the means to manoeuvre and rapidly engage the enemy.

The indices of German ammunition production provide a good example of how economic constraints held sway over military necessity. Although output of ammunition peaked in the third quarter of 1940 this was only the latent result of the previous policy aiming for production in depth. In the reorientation of the economy ammunition production was not a priority and, accordingly, its reduced importance was accompanied by a sharp fall in production in the fourth quarter of 1940. The trend continued throughout 1941 until a bottom was reached in October through to December, when overall production was only marginally better than it had been in the first quarter of 1940.[36] Prior to Barbarossa ammunition shortfalls were most worryingly apparent in the production of armour-piercing shells for the infantry anti-tank guns, output of which was only 50 per cent of the projected target.[37] Other calibres retained solid or even large stockpiles of shells and therefore cutting selected ammunition production to save precious stocks of copper and steel for other areas of the economy seemed a sensible course of action.[38] Yet this made sense only because the German army was convinced that a rapid campaign would decide the war in the east. For a more protracted campaign the accumulated ammunition stockpiles would soon prove insufficient, requiring a further change in economic priorities which would necessitate another halt in production and a time-consuming retooling of factory assembly lines.

The army's determination that munition stocks were ample also rested on a simple equation, which measured the inventory of shells against the corresponding number of field guns within the German army. While this appeared to offer a degree of symmetry, suggesting a cut in munitions could be made, it was only proportional to the number of guns Germany fielded, not a more objective assessment of what the Red Army could muster and hence the real needs of the campaign. The fact that Germany was seriously out-gunned by the Soviet Union mattered less in a war of rapid manoeuvre, but took on a profound significance once it came to protracted positional warfare. In such contests, which would in fact take place along hundreds of kilometres of the line by the end of the summer of 1941, the Red Army would maintain fire-supremacy, meaning it could provide far greater counter-battery fire as well as direct infantry support through creeping barrages. This translated into dominance of the static battlefield, a circumstance which not only posed an alarming military problem, but, because of economic priorities, could not be reversed in the short term. In short, German estimates for ammunition consumption proved to be completely unrealistic.[39] Unquestioning faith in the lightning war that was to be carried out in the east combined with Germany's insufficiency in armaments to reflect the fallibility of the reorientation of the economy even in areas which were identified as being in surplus.

Hitler's underestimation of Soviet arms and industry was a fatal mistake that he himself exacerbated. Speaking in October 1941 after months of the heaviest fighting, Hitler was bold enough publicly to assert, 'Today, we have taken care in advance so that, in the midst of this war of materiel, I can order further production in many spheres to cease, because I know there is no opponent whom we would not be able to defeat with the existing amounts of ammunition.'[40] Such short-sighted strategic thinking highlights the dangerous combination of limiting army production while at the same time pursuing grandiose strategic plans involving an incalculable expansion of the war. Not only did Germany wilfully blunder towards overextension, but the new war in the east involved completely different types of armaments from the ones required to fight Great Britain. Thus, Germany's already limited resources would have to be spread among numerous and diverse weapons programmes with the result being reduced production across the board.

As Germany's leaders reoriented the economy to fight two wars at once, the arms race was already being lost. The elation of crushing France in six weeks took a long time to wear off, which not only fed the myth of the Wehrmacht's invincibility, but gave many the erroneous impression that Germany now commanded the economic power of an entire continent. In fact neither was the case, and if one adds the growing armament potential of the United States to that of Britain, every month the Nazi empire was falling increasingly further behind in the arms race. Thus, while Germany produced markedly more weapons in 1940 than did each of the Allied powers individually, by 1941 the collective Allied output was far stronger than that of the Axis. Not only this, but Allied production was growing in leaps and bounds, unrestricted by lack of access to raw materials and without the same debilitating manpower shortages. Between 1940 and 1941 the United States tripled its armament output, while the UK and the USSR almost doubled theirs.[41] It was an ominous development for Germany, which only further reinforced the absolute necessity of avoiding a long, costly war of attrition in the east.

Despite major steps towards full mobilization, Germany's path to a total war economy still had its problems. In the early years of the war ambitious and highly costly civilian projects, such as the construction of the autobahn network and the Volkswagen works, were allowed to continue.[42] Examples can also be found that show armament factories were working only one shift instead of two or possibly even three.[43] The factories were in any case not well suited to the demands of mass production, nor were many of the complex weapon designs they produced.[44] Even more unfathomable was Hitler's own refusal to cancel any of the colossal building projects he had commissioned for Berlin and Nuremberg. By August 1941, as his panzer divisions on the eastern front were reporting crippling losses without the domestic production to replace them, Hitler was authorizing contracts to the value of 30 million Reichsmarks for granite to commence construction. Moreover, during the same period, Hitler was instructing his chief architect, Albert Speer, to acquire some 230 captured enemy artillery pieces as well as large Soviet tanks to line Berlin's central boulevard. Three months later, in November 1941, when Speer proposed to Hitler that the resource-intense building projects be halted until after the war, he was supposedly rebuffed with the words: 'I am not going to let the war keep me from accomplishing my [building] plans.'[45] It was a revealing statement that not only reflected Hitler's lack of appreciation for the economic imbalance inherent in the war he had initiated, but as with many of his remarks, also alluded to his flawed racial view of what mattered most in fighting and winning wars. While Allied leaders were at one in their determination to increase war production as the vital element in victory, Hitler advocated as the pre-eminent weapon the superior powers of the Nordic fighting man – his endurance, sacrifice and loyalty. The primacy of 'will' assumed fundamental importance in Hitler's conception, with weaponry viewed as subordinate to the moral qualities of the soldier.[46]

Perhaps most absurdly of all, trade negotiations with the Soviet Union had become so important in sustaining the German economy that when talks between Moscow and Berlin threatened to break down, Göring ordered that the fulfilment of Soviet orders was to be accorded equal priority with orders for the Wehrmacht. Hence, from early October 1940 to 11 May 1941, German machine tools, vital in the manufacture of high-grade weapons, were being shipped to the country that the Wehrmacht was being armed to destroy. The German war economy was paradoxically, therefore, arming both sides for the coming conflict because it could not do without oil, grain and alloy metals.[47]

The armament programme, which would have to meet the most immediate gaps in the German arsenal for Operation Barbarossa, was known as armament programme 'B' (replacing a short-lived 'A' programme). Constrained as production capacity and raw materials were, priorities had to be established, and for the army precedence was taken by the Mark III and Mark IV tanks as well as the new 50mm anti-tank guns. Additional items were divided among sub-categories, but from September 1940, when the armaments programme began, there were frequent changes to and new demands made on both production quotas, as well as the priority accorded to respective weapons. Estimates for the monthly production of tanks were already far above what could realistically be achieved, but like so many problems in the planning for Barbarossa these were quietly ignored. What could not be ignored were the new demands of Hitler's decree, published on 28 September 1940. Additional tasks now included the unlimited continuation of the U-boat programme for the navy and an increase in anti-aircraft guns and munitions for the Luftwaffe. Moreover, a new manufacturing programme known as 'Axis' was to be established to benefit Italy. This new programme was to be top priority, ahead of all other requirements including 'special category' items. In addition to this came the previously mentioned need to meet Soviet armament orders. Such excessive new demands overwhelmed the delicate equilibrium of managing armament programme 'B' which was, in any case, based on optimistic assessments of available manpower and raw materials. Nor did the interference end there. Seeking to strengthen the firepower of the infantry divisions Hitler ordered an additional 1,469 light field howitzers, the principal divisional artillery weapon. At best only 60 per cent of these could be delivered by the following spring, but, with no recourse to practical realities, a further 800 were then demanded, along with an increase in the number of 88mm anti-aircraft guns. Both weapons utilized similar production lines and the increased output of one could only be achieved at the expense of the other.[48] The result again highlights a fundamental flaw in Germany's production effort as well as the danger of juggling too many priorities between the armed services, Italian and Soviet orders, especially when Operation Barbarossa ensured the overwhelming burden of responsibility lay squarely with the army.

If the investment and allocation of resources within armament programme 'B' proved inadequate to meeting the army's needs for Operation Barbarossa, worse was still to come. At the end of 1940 the OKW established a new set of priorities in manufacturing with precedence now given to the Luftwaffe and navy, ahead of the demands of the army, for what the head of the Wehrmacht Operations Department, Colonel-General Alfred Jodl, called 'the siege of Britain'.[49] So convinced was the OKH of its ability to conduct the eastern campaign successfully that it did not even oppose its relegation. There was a firm conviction in the army's weapons department that even if armament production declined markedly in 1941, the remaining capacities, together with stockpiles, would suffice to meet '*all* future requirements of the war'.[50] Accordingly, there was no sense of surprise when Hitler's War Directive 32, the last he issued before the invasion of the Soviet Union, began with the words: '*After the destruction of the Soviet Armed Forces*, Germany and Italy will be military masters of the European Continent.'[51] The directive formalized the pre-eminence of the air force and navy in armament production and then, three weeks into the campaign, in a supplementary Directive 32a the army had all non-essential production cancelled. The new directive stated in relation to the army: 'The extension of arms and equipment and the production of new weapons, munitions, and equipment will be related, with immediate effect, to the smaller forces which are contemplated for the future.'[52]

Although armament programme 'B' partially modernized the German tank fleet it was in no way proportional to the demands of Barbarossa (nor even to a one-on-one comparison with newer Soviet model tanks). The armament programme also failed to deliver some 30 per cent of the necessary vehicles for Barbarossa, forcing highly dubious expedients,[53] which soon foundered on the Soviet roads and compromised the mobility of the crucial motorized divisions.[54] The expansion of the army by some 20 per cent, compared with 1940, also failed to produce a net gain for the army's offensive strength, as the increased numbers were swallowed up by additional tasks in the war against Britain as well as expanded occupation duties.[55] The army that was deployed for Barbarossa consisted of everything Germany could muster. There was little or no reserve and what was not included, with the exception of two panzer divisions being reconditioned following the Balkan campaign, may be considered of limited operational value. This meant that the *Ostheer* had just one chance to crush the Soviet Union. There could be little recourse to existing formations and, as we have seen, the economic backing for the army through new production was meagre.

Between July and December 1941 production of weapons for the army fell by 29 per cent, while a record 5 million men were given exemptions from military service to produce weapons mainly for the Luftwaffe and navy. Accordingly, as the *Ostheer* was being battered in the east, the home front was busy doubling the output of U-boats and preparing for a reduction of the army.[56] Thus, it was not simply the shortages of raw materials and manpower that constrained army production; it was the direction of the whole programme, from its dubious mandate to fight a war on two fronts to the ludicrous setting of priorities. It was no surprise, therefore, that the Allies were swiftly overtaking Germany in armament production – a fact Hitler attempted to downplay in a speech to old party members on 8 November 1941:

> *And when I am told, as so often lately, that the democrats are now arming, then I must say that I have also repeatedly mentioned that we are not doing nothing . . . I have merely concentrated armament in a few special spheres. When the gentlemen keep talking of figures – I do not speak of figures, but I will say one thing: They will be surprised with what we will line up one day.*[57]

It was only a few months into the war in the east and Hitler was already seeking to distract attention away from production figures. Furthermore, his implication that superior German weapons would compensate for Allied numbers was a myth. The new generation of aircraft for the Luftwaffe was proving even worse than its predecessors,[58] while Germany's Mark III and IV tanks were greatly inferior to the best Soviet tanks and the urgently ordered replacements were still only on the drawing boards and would not appear until spring 1943.

The economic foundation of Operation Barbarossa remains one of the most tenuous in military history. As Colonel-General Fritz Fromm remarked on 16 August 1941, the needs of the army demanded that the high command come 'out of the current cloud-cuckoo-land and down to reality'.[59] The economic basis of Operation Barbarossa was only suitable if the campaign could be concluded, as its planners anticipated, in a short and decisive victory. Even if the factories had had sufficient supplies of raw materials and manpower, they were neither tooled up for army production, nor endowed with the capacity to cope with the new demands of the war in the east. Considering the associated problems of mobilizing Western European economies (which, in any case, had hardly been attempted) and at the same time the escalating might of Allied military production, Germany's quagmire in the east assumes enormous significance. Hitler's previous strategic freedom to manoeuvre rapidly in short campaigns had until now sufficed to offset the threat of Allied economic dominance. By the end of the summer of 1941 that prospect was gone. The army, like the navy and air force, was tied down in a war without the prospect of a quick conclusion and the longer the conflict dragged on the worse things were bound to become for Germany. As one will see in the battle of Kiev, operational manoeuvre remained possible on the battlefield and Germany could still fight and win individual battles, but the strategic necessity of eliminating the Soviet Union had failed and with it Germany's prospects of outright victory in World War II. As Alan Milward rightly questioned, 'It is fair to ask what hopes of ultimate success could have inspired German strategy once the idea of *blitzkrieg* had been abandoned.'[60]

Iron crosses and wooden crosses – Operation Barbarossa in Army Group South

In 1812 as the crushing weight of Napoleon's *Grande Armée* crossed Russia's border, Count Simon Vorontsev wrote to Tsar Alexander I with the following advice:

> *Even if at the start we should suffer military reversals, we might win nevertheless by persisting in a defensive war and by fighting while we retreat. If the enemy pursues us, he is lost because the further he is from his stores of foodstuffs and arms, and the deeper he advances into a country which has no roads and no supplies . . . the sooner he will be reduced to a pitiful state.*[61]

Vorontsev's words proved prophetic, but even in his time they were not without precedent. A hundred years earlier the formidable Swedish army of Charles XII had foundered in its invasion of Russia in 1708 and was finally expelled in 1709. Napoleon's much greater army did not even last that long, withering on its march to Moscow and being all but destroyed in the notorious winter retreat.

The Russian theatre presented unique challenges of climate, distance and landscape, which, in spite of technical advancement, applied as much to the invading Wehrmacht in 1941 as it had to their predecessors. Nor did the Germans have to contend only with the severity of the elements and the remoteness of their objectives. The Red Army was something of a multi-headed hydra, which fought savagely in spite of heavy losses and, more worryingly for the Germans, grew itself new heads faster than the German army could cut them off. When Operation Barbarossa began on 22 June 1941 the Red Army numbered some 5,373,000 men, yet in spite of the heavy casualties, by 31 August its size had risen to 6,889,000. By the end of the year the Red Army consisted of an estimated 8 million men.[62] At the same time the size of the German army in the east was in steady decline. The commander of Army Group South, Field Marshal Gerd von Rundstedt, remarked after the war: '[T]he Russians received continual reinforcements from their back areas, as they fell back. It seemed to us that as soon as one force was wiped out, the path was blocked by the arrival of a fresh force.'[63]

Rundstedt's army group was the second largest operating on the eastern front after Bock's Army Group Centre. They were joined by Field Marshal Wilhelm Ritter von Leeb in command of Army Group North. Together these men were the field commanders of the largest military operation in history, involving more than 3 million German troops, joined by more than three-quarters of a million additional Axis and other allied soldiers.[64] The Wehrmacht's objective was the destruction of the Red Army and the elimination of Soviet power. The force assembled to achieve this – the *Ostheer* – was the most proficient and best trained in the world. Yet its power resided less in its mass than in a highly refined offensive prowess, which revolutionized combined arms warfare to exploit both new technologies and the most innovative principles of a *Bewegungskrieg* (war of movement). The result was a rapid form of mobile warfare, carried out by specialized 'panzer groups', which concentrated firepower and aggressively exploited tactical opportunities. The Wehrmacht's blitzkrieg, as it had come to be known, was seen by contemporaries as something of an operational wonder, and neither the German command nor foreign intelligence services gave the Red Army any real chance of successfully withstanding it.[65] Yet the blitzkrieg's high degree of technical sophistication, as well as its essential dependence upon resource-intensive close-arms support, was not readily adaptable to the Soviet Union's vast distances and primitive infrastructure. Accordingly, the success of the Wehrmacht's blitzkrieg in the east is best assessed through the performance of the *Ostheer*'s panzer groups, upon which the fulfilment of German plans so heavily depended.

In my preceding volume detailing the summer failure of Operation Barbarossa, my study focused principally on Army Group Centre's Panzer Groups 2 and 3 as the largest of the four panzer groups operating on the eastern front. In order briefly to revisit the problems of the summer phase of the campaign, while avoiding repetition, this section will concern itself with Rundstedt's Army Group South, and specifically Colonel-General Ewald von Kleist's Panzer Group 1.

In the latter years of World War II the British intelligence service held many of their highest-ranking German captives at Trent Park, a mansion north of London. There they secretly recorded their private conversations to identify any important disclosures. In a conversation between General of Infantry Dietrich von Choltitz and Lieutenant-General Kurt Wilhelm von Schlieben in 1944, the two eastern front veterans discussed the invasion of the Soviet Union in 1941 in the frankest of terms. Schlieben told Choltitz, 'No war was ever started or waged with as little forethought as this one, which was carried on with the slogan: "It'll be alright." It started like that in 1941.' Choltitz then replied, 'It wouldn't have been so bad if we Generals... hadn't taken part. The trouble is that we participated without a murmur.'[66] It was a startlingly candid admission that summed up not only the flawed military undertaking that Barbarossa represented, but also the wilful complicity of the German officer corps. Their failing was for a long time concealed by Hitler's principal role, but there can be no doubt that Barbarossa's flaws were greatly exacerbated by arrogant assumptions from within the officer corps about Germany's technical, military and even racial superiority over the Soviets. The reality of warfare in the east soon gave the confident German army a sobering jolt. As Rundstedt told his interrogators after the war, 'I realized soon after the attack was begun that everything that had been written about Russia was wrong.'[67] Yet Rundstedt might well have known better. His army group confronted an operational zone some 725 kilometres in length from the L'vov salient down to the Black Sea. Army Group Centre, by contrast, faced only a 320-kilometre front and possessed almost 2,000 tanks between its two panzer groups.[68] Kleist's Panzer Group 1 numbered just over 600 tanks and had to contend with the Soviet South-Western Front commanded

Fig. 1 As the Wehrmacht headed into the Soviet Union they were met by pictures of Stalin and Timoshenko who would both play key roles in the battle of Kiev. The inscription on the top of the gate reads: 'Hail our native Red Army – mighty bulwark for the peaceful labours of the peoples of the USSR!'

by Colonel-General Mikhail Kirponos. Soviet pre-war plans anticipated that in the event of an attack by Germany, the main thrust would be made through the Ukraine and therefore Kirponos commanded the single largest concentration of Soviet forces on the eastern front. Even Soviet figures, which are usually inclined to overstate Germany's numerical strength (to explain their earlier defeats), attribute to Kirponos a six to one advantage in tanks and a two to one superiority in aircraft.[69] Nor was Kirponos Rundstedt's only opponent in the south. The Southern Front, under Major-General Ivan Tyulenev, commanded an additional 320,000 men. Altogether Army Group South's 797,000 men faced some 1.2 million Soviet troops.[70]

Following Germany's attack, the Soviet Fronts were ordered to repulse the invaders with immediate counterattacks. Yet the Soviet mechanized corps were neither fully equipped nor trained and suffered from appalling standards of disrepair. Furthermore, there were critical deficiencies in fuel and ammunition.[71] Nevertheless, frantic efforts were made to carry out *Stavka* orders and Kirponos's forces were the only ones on the eastern front to enjoy a measure of success, albeit at high cost.

In the first week of operations on the eastern front the panzer forces of Bock's Army Group Centre had almost completed their first major encirclement at Minsk; further north Leeb's tanks had swept rapidly through Lithuania and secured intact bridges over the Dvina River in Latvia. Rundstedt's achievement, by contrast, was measured in the number of counterattacks by the numerically superior Soviet forces that he successfully defeated or turned back.[72] Yet the delays resulting from the June border battles meant that from the beginning Army Group South lagged well behind its northern counterparts, which would later have a decisive impact an German strategy (see maps 1–3). There was also a substantial military toll exacted from these hard-fought early battles. On 23 June at Radekhov the Soviet 10th Tank Division claimed to have knocked out twenty German panzers, for the loss of twenty-six of their own.[73] On the following day (24 June) Major-General Kiril Moskalenko, the Soviet commander of an anti-tank brigade, recalled his first encounter with the enemy: 'In this first battle, the brigade's gunners knocked out and burned almost seventy tanks and armored cars, many motorcycles, and other materiel of the 14th Panzer Division. Significant casualties were also inflicted upon the 298th Infantry Division. Our losses were heavy as well.'[74] While Moskalenko's claim of having destroyed upwards of seventy German combat vehicles in a single encounter is probably an embellishment, it nevertheless makes clear that Rundstedt's progress was not without casualties. Indeed, it was not just the destruction of precious German war materiel that Soviet commanders could take solace in, at times their forces managed to induce local setbacks and even bring about points of crisis in the German line. On 26 June, for example, the 57th Infantry

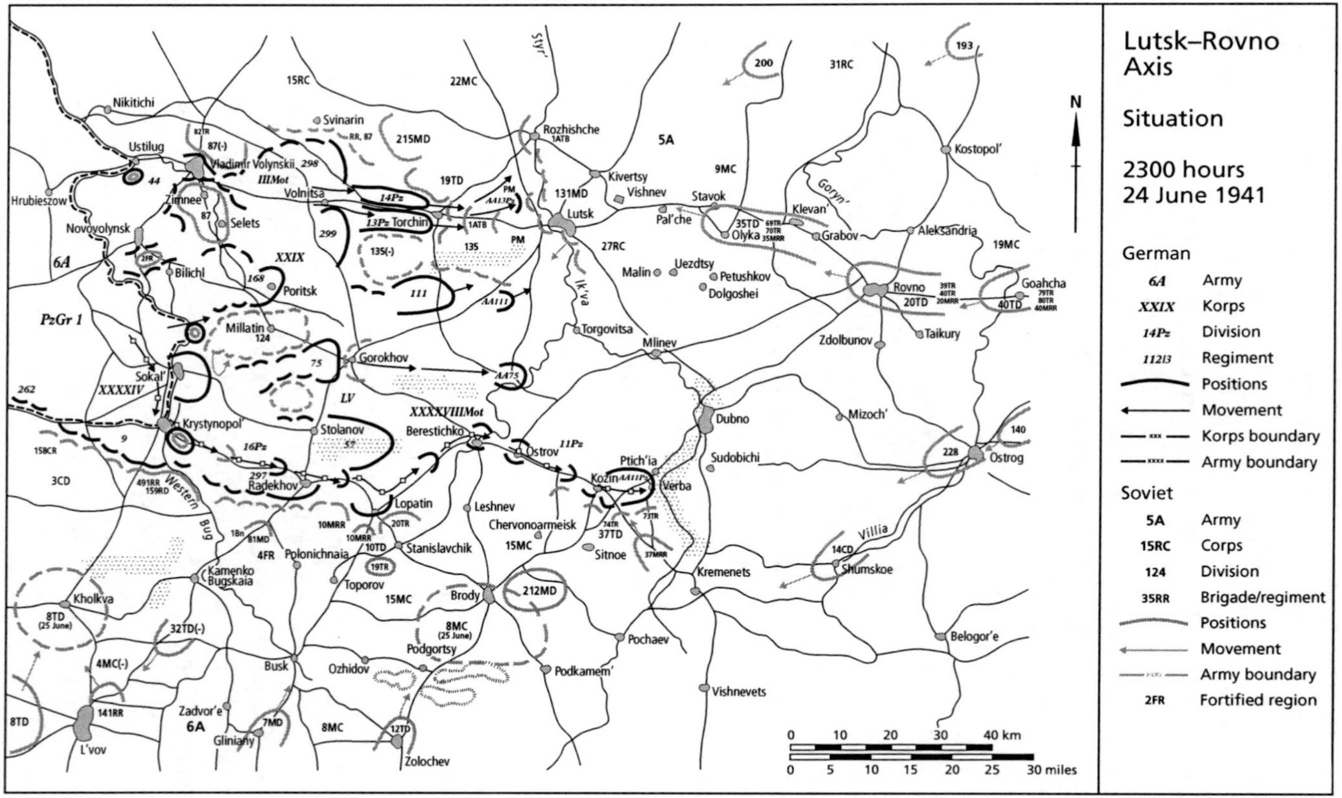

Map 1 Dispositions of Panzer Group 1 on 24 June 1941

Source: David M. Glantz, *Atlas and Operational Summary. The Border Battles 22 June–1 July 1941* (privately published).

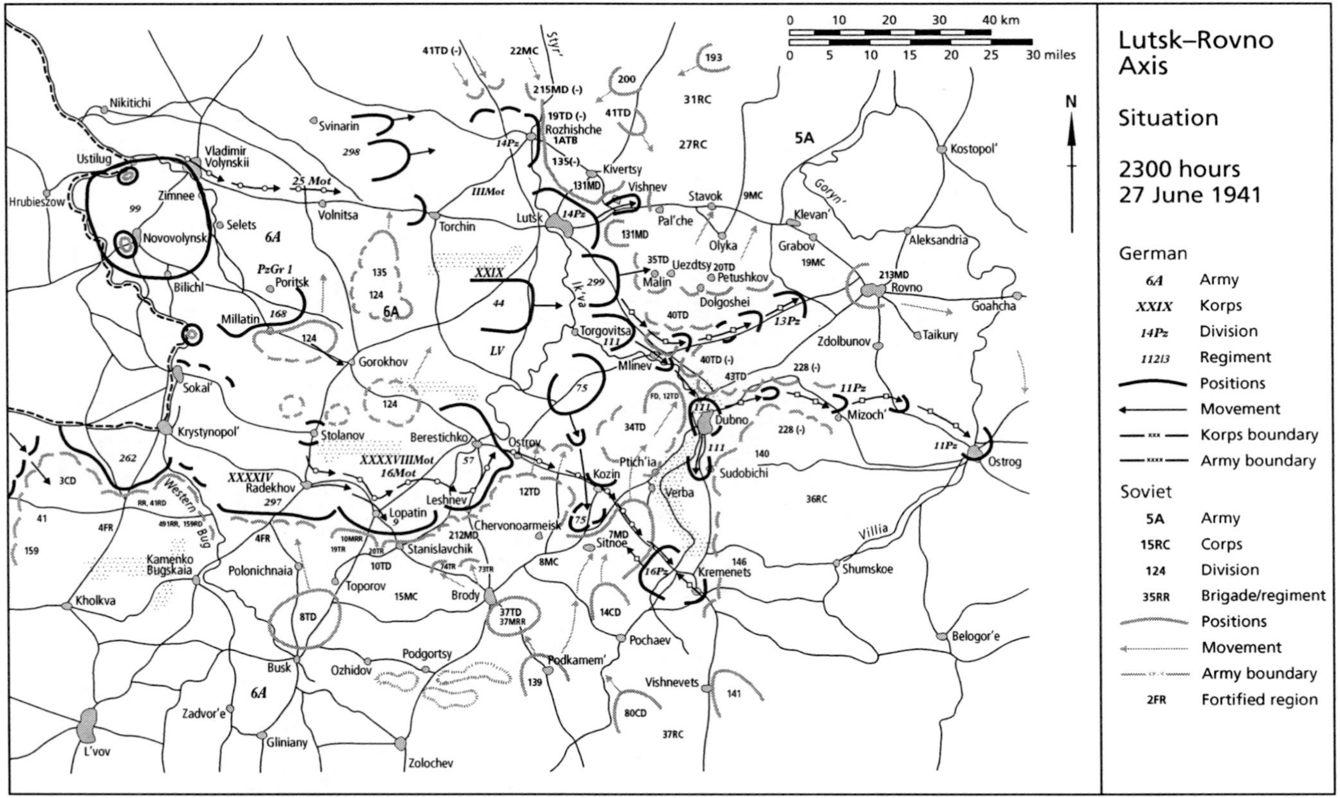

Map 2 Dispositions of Panzer Group 1 on 27 June 1941
Source: Glantz, *Atlas and Operational Summary.*

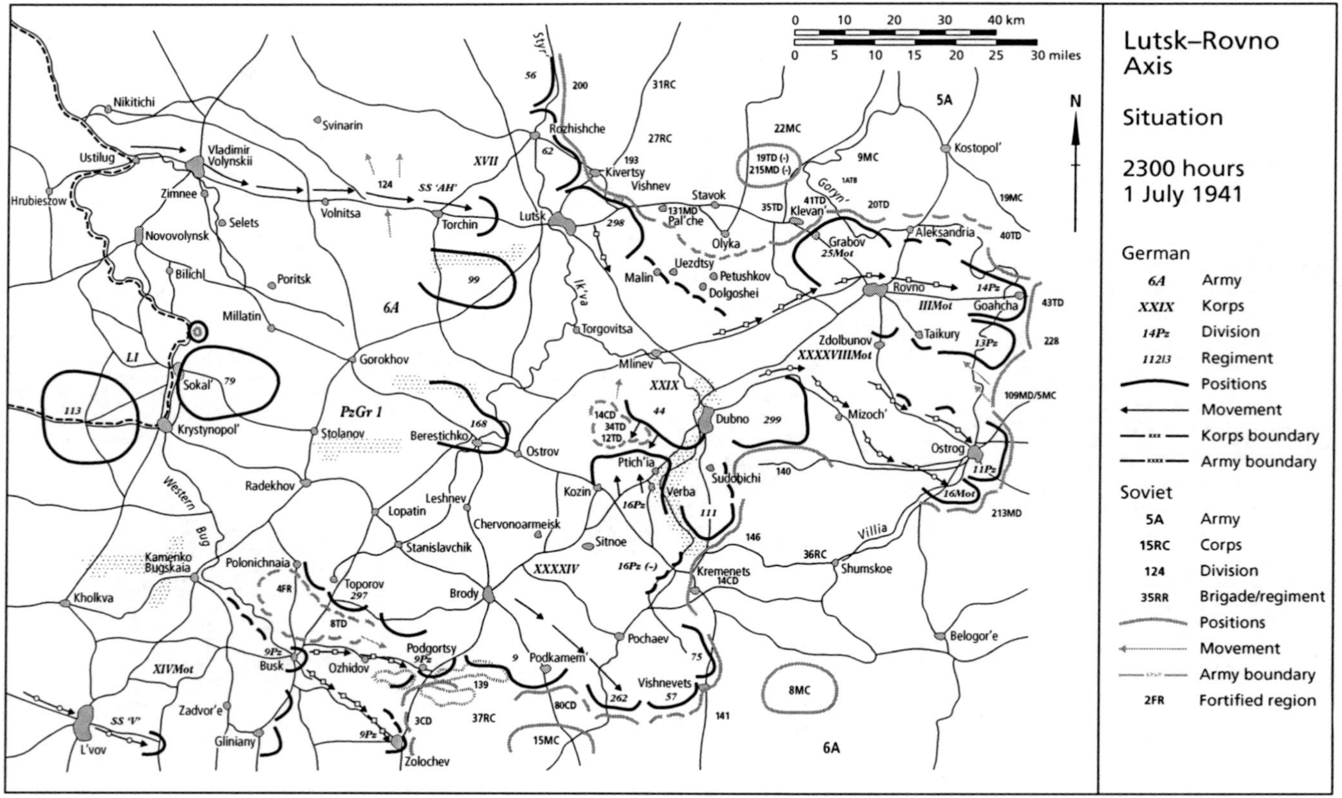

Map 3 Dispositions of Panzer Group 1 on 1 July 1941
Source: Glantz, *Atlas and Operational Summary.*

Division was forced into a 10-kilometre retreat,[75] while on the same day an unidentified German soldier from the 24th Infantry Division recounted in his diary:

> *Indescribable chaos. Motorized columns and infantry in hasty retreat. Now we had seen with our own eyes what headlong flight, what turmoil and horror are called forth by that one word: tanks! ... Their tracks crush everything, make mincemeat of motorcyclists and their bikes, ride over guns, gun-carriages, gun-crews and horses. It is said that two battalions were completely ground into the dust. Nobody can find his unit and all the guns and food supplies are lost.*[76]

The Operations Officer at the OKH responsible for Army Group South, Major Karl Thilo, noted in his diary on 26 June: 'Army has gained only very little ground. Heavy casualties on both sides... Russians are standing their ground excellently; down here there is exceptionally systematic command.'[77] Such a characterization of Soviet command in the early days of the war may be somewhat overly affirmative, but it at least reflects the impression Soviet actions were having on Army Group South's commanders. The same impression was evident from below, where after a week of constant fighting heavy casualties overwhelmed German aid stations, causing overloading and scenes of dreadful suffering. A German nurse who had already experienced warfare in 1940 recalled her earliest experiences on the eastern front:

> *I had not expected that it would be so bad! The patients all had fresh wounds and were brought in directly from the battlefield with only a simple field dressing. Some were bleeding so much that we feared they would bleed to death, which in fact happened many times. Some screamed in pain, other just whimpered. From all sides there were calls for doctors or for nurses, requests for painkilling injections, for water or just to hear that someone was taking care of them, that they were not alone... It was about life and death. None of us had a moment of rest. The doctors operated day and night...*[78]

The tremendous human cost of the war reflected the sheer numbers taking part, yet Soviet strength did not simply depend on mass: there was also the technical superiority of the Red Army's new tanks. The Soviet 4th Mechanized Corps fielded 979 tanks on 22 June and 414 of these were new models.[79] One Soviet tank commander, Lieutenant Pavel Gudz, reported that his group of five KV-1s and two T-34s destroyed a total of eight German panzers, one anti-tank gun, three armoured personnel carriers and several cars on 22 June alone.[80] A German radio message from 23 June captures the sense of shock and confusion among German officers at what they were encountering. The report stated: 'Found ourselves in combat with four enemy tanks. Type unknown, not indicated on recognition tables. Despite repeated hits, our fire had no effect. It appears as if shells are simply bouncing off. The enemy tanks disengaged without a fight and retreated. Are we to push on?'[81] By 26 June the Chief of the Army General Staff, Colonel-General Franz Halder, commented in his diary, 'Army Group South is advancing slowly, unfortunately with considerable losses.'[82] The reason for this was not lost on Kleist who was very favourably impressed by the standard of Soviet technical innovation and remarked after the war: 'Their equipment was very good even in 1941, especially the tanks... Their T-34 was the finest in the world.'[83]

Yet it was not just the raw firepower of the Red Army that proved an obstacle to the German advance. Their fanatical resolve, which at times amounted to an almost suicidal fervour, gave the combat a radicalizing edge. Wilhelm Prüller, a non-commissioned officer in the 25th Motorized Infantry Division, was astonished when he observed that Soviet soldiers, who had first survived German tanks grinding up their foxholes as well as grenades being thrown in, still somehow managed to resist. Ultimately, Prüller wrote in his diary, 'We have to creep up to each hole... and then finish the Russians with pistols or rifles. No calls of surrender.'[84] Few German soldiers had witnessed such stout zeal in their past campaigns and the frightening reality of the eastern front stimulated many private fears among the average *Landser*. Peter Bamm alluded to an 'uneasy foreboding', which he claimed everybody felt even through 'it was very rarely talked about'. The strain remained a permanent burden and, according to Bamm, 'the longer the war lasted, the more unbearable it became. In the meantime we did our best to put a brave face on it and live up to our reputations as good soldiers.'[85] Still, the heat of battle pushed German soldiers to their limits and gave them good cause for their fears. One report from the 119th Infantry Regiment of the 25th Motorized Infantry Division on 30 June illustrates the forcefulness of Soviet soldiers on the attack: 'The enemy attack could not be stopped, in spite of heavy defensive fire and serious losses. He advances upright, firing against our positions. He also launches surprise attacks with "Hurras" at the shortest range out of the camouflage of [the] cornfield against our flank. He has no fear of close combat.'[86]

As this battle continued into the following day (1 July) an entire German battalion was cut off by a new Soviet attack and the Germans had to make frantic attempts to escape the Soviet pocket. When the battlefield was eventually retaken, 153 dead Germans were found, many murdered in cold blood. 'You can imagine', commented an officer from the corps, 'that these events formed our picture of the new enemy and of the forthcoming war.'[87] Pitiless conditions and exceptionally hard fighting were the hallmarks of the new war in the east. Yet, contrary to some highly revisionist representations,[88] such harsh circumstances radicalized, but did not instigate Germany's own war of annihilation (*Vernichtungskrieg*). German soldiers sometimes prefaced their own excesses in the war by referring to Soviet atrocities; however, in many cases there was no conceivable rational or external impetus to explain German behaviour in the east, which was conspicuous by its almost unparalleled outpouring of violence. Ideological conditioning and racial propaganda motivated German soldiers to loathe and despise as well as fear their Soviet enemy. The frightful reality of day-to-day combat, as well as the not-infrequent evidence of Soviet atrocities, had a brutalizing effect, which radicalized German behaviour still further, but did not precipitate it.[89] From the very beginning the eastern battlefields tended towards a domain of anarchic brutality and wanton bloodshed. As one German soldier's diary concluded, after only a month of the war, 'For once sleep as you want, for once eat and drink your fill, for once kill to your heart's content – such are the thoughts that haunt the mind of a man who has long ceased to be a man. That's what our infantry is like at the front in the east.'[90] Another German soldier was more straightforward, describing after a hard battle how he helped shoot surrendering Red Army men. 'It isn't a fight any more that we're conducting,' he concluded, 'it's a massacre!'[91] Of course not every German soldier was personally involved in acts of murder, but war crimes on the eastern front involved a far higher ratio of 'average' men than any other war of the modern age.[92]

Without discounting the resolve of the Red Army and their impressive new equipment, these factors alone did not account for the high losses within Germany's crucial motorized divisions in the opening weeks of Operation Barbarossa. As in the north, Soviet roads in the Ukraine were of a terribly poor standard, often consisting of little more than sandy tracks. Even in the summer months, with sudden downpours these very quickly turned into impassable marshes. When the sun dried them out, the fine sand returned, to be churned up by each passing vehicle, creating thick clouds of dust. The dust overwhelmed the inadequate air filters of the vehicles, initially accounting for greatly increased oil consumption and ultimately destroying the engines altogether. According to one account, 'When the columns march grey dust clouds hang over the Russian roads that are so thick that within them a man can sometimes not see anything around him. You almost can't breathe.'[93] Another soldier referred to the accumulation of dust 'finger thick' on his uniform and face.[94] The eastern roads were also badly potted and uneven, which had a highly destructive effect on the heavily loaded trucks, many of which had been requisitioned from the civilian economy and had neither the ground clearance nor the suspension for such rough conditions. The result was a trail of wreckage behind the German advance. Willi Kubik, a tank operator with the 13th Panzer Division, noted as early as 30 June that one-third of his company's vehicles had fallen out and were awaiting repairs.[95] Yet the motor pool repair stations were quickly overwhelmed and spare parts were often extremely limited or in some cases simply unavailable.[96] Where possible, enemy vehicles were stripped, especially for easily adapted components, such as rubber tyres, of which the *Ostheer* had a crucial shortage. Nevertheless, the deficiencies within the Wehrmacht were serious and destined to become much worse. An entry on 3 July from the quartermaster's diary of Panzer Group 1 noted upon the return of one of its officers from headquarters:

> *With his return it was hoped that news would be brought of the successful assignment of replacement motors, caterpillar tracks and ten-gear gearboxes. This was not the case. The fact that many panzers are in the workshops as a result of shortages of spare parts and cannot be returned to service is extremely regrettable and greatly reduces the number of combat ready tanks. Under these circumstances roughly 50 per cent of the panzers cannot be repaired.*[97]

It has been estimated that seven out of ten repair jobs in the tank maintenance companies required the fitting of a new part, underlining the fundamental importance of spare parts in the repair process.[98] Not only were repairs proving difficult, but the heavy fighting and high fallout rate had cut the combat strength of Kleist's forces dramatically. Indeed, Panzer Group 1 had suffered a significantly higher attrition rate than Panzer Groups 2 and 3 in the same time period. Illustrating the extent of its decline is an entry in the war diary of Panzer Group 1 for 5 July:

> *After fourteen days of battle we have an estimated hundred totally lost panzers [i.e. destroyed or beyond all repair]. From experience there will be at least the same or double that amount momentarily out of action. That means that about 55 per cent are still combat ready. This percentage will fall before we reach the line Zhitomir–Berdichev.*[99]

On the same day (5 July) Rundstedt wrote to his wife that on account of the heavy fighting and 'unbelievable' roads, only slow progress was being made.[100] The continued checking of Kleist's advance resulted in part from the volume of military resources at Kirponos's disposal, but was aided by the rare exception of a *Stavka*-authorized withdrawal of Soviet forces. After the costly and increasingly futile Soviet counter-attacks, on 30 June the *Stavka* allowed Kirponos to fall back to the partially dismantled defensive positions on the so-called Stalin Line.[101] Here intense fighting continued as Kleist's three armoured corps fought and manoeuvred relentlessly to force their way through Soviet positions. By 6 July Army Group South's Operations Officer at the OKH noted bitterly in his diary, 'Operational breakthrough by Panzer Group 1 *still not* achieved.'[102] Nevertheless, Soviet resistance was in fact crumbling in front of Panzer Group 1 and by 10 July III Panzer Corps, comman-deered by General of Cavalry Eberhard von Mackensen, was in open terrain and driving towards Kiev (see map 4).

At this point strategic differences surfaced within the German command over the potential opportunity this appeared to offer for seizing Kiev and its vital crossings over the Dnepr. As recently as 9 July Army Group South and the OKH reaffirmed their primary objective of cutting off and eliminating Soviet armies west of the Dnepr. Yet emboldened by the impending collapse of Kirponos's front, the seizure of Kiev was added as a new and ostensibly secondary task.[103] Hitler had

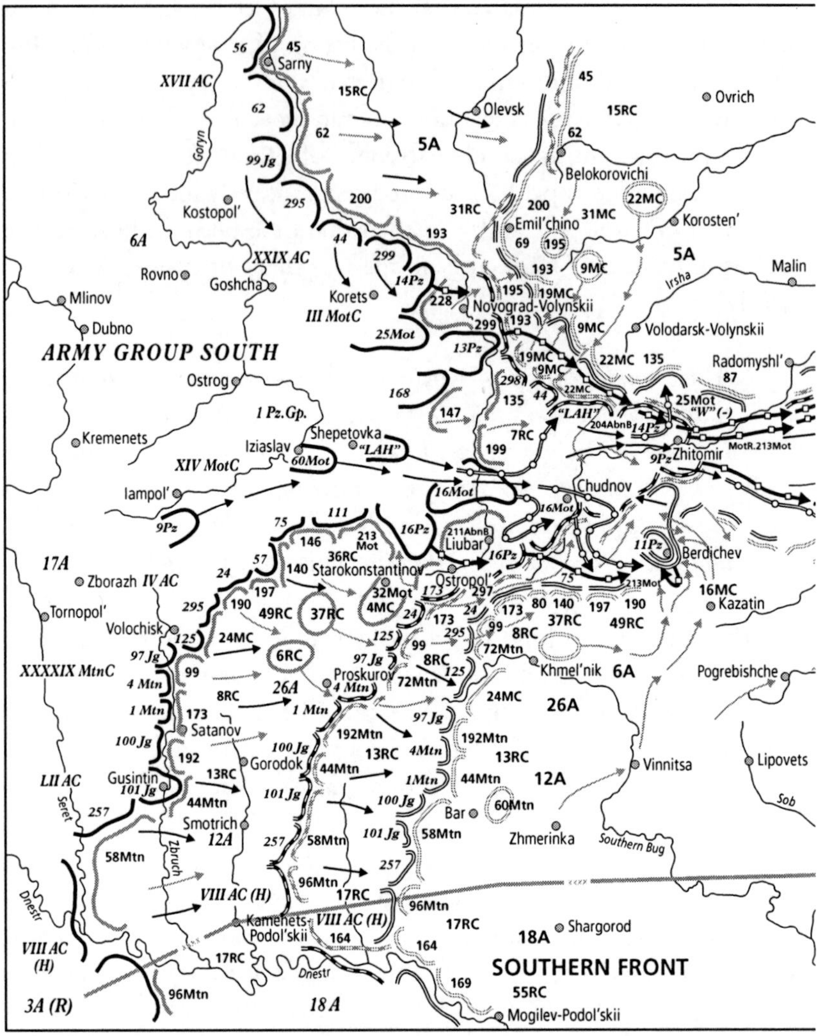

Map 4 Dispositions of Army Group South, 7–14 July 1941
Source: David M. Glantz, *Atlas of the Battle for Kiev Part I. Penetrating the*

previously shown no interest in storming Kiev and from recent discussions it was clear that securing crossings over the Dnepr was considered subordinate to destroying major enemy formations west of the river. Undeterred, the army commanders maintained their interest in Kiev. The original idea had been for elements of Field Marshal Walter von Reichenau's Sixth Army to be brought up to add assault troops and firepower to the attack. However, the aggressive actions of the Soviet Fifth

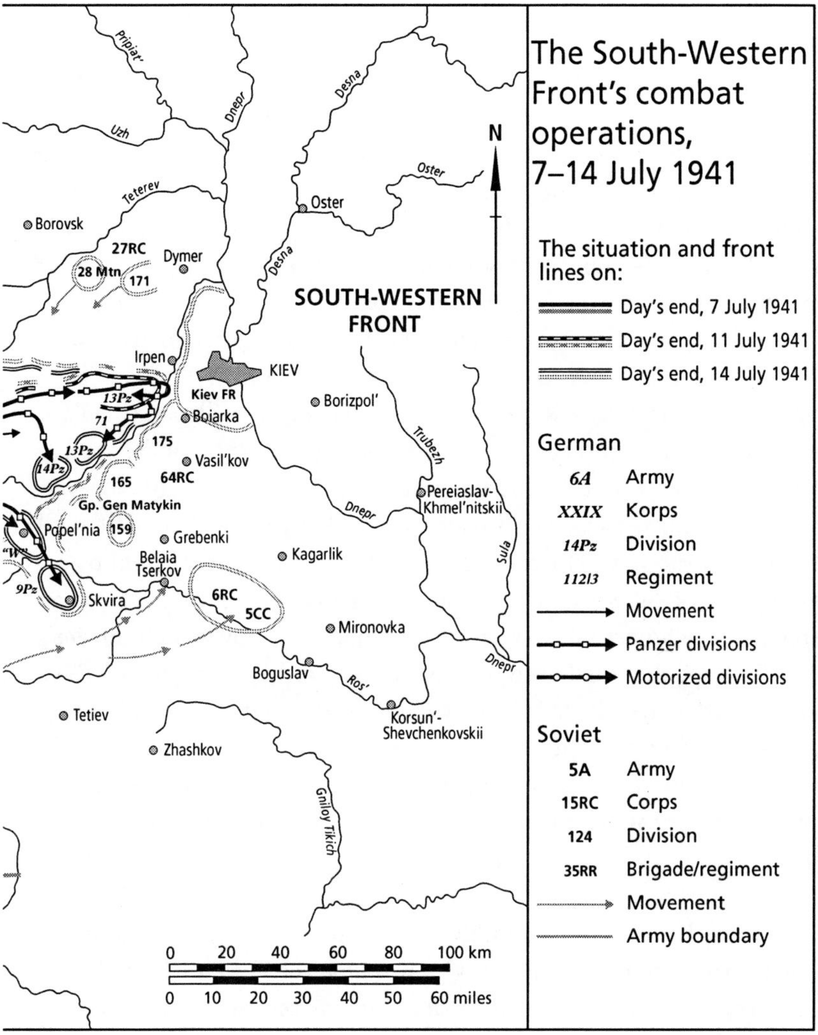

Stalin Line and the Uman' Encirclement 2 July–9 August 1941 (privately published).

Army, attacking repeatedly out of the Pripet marshes, no longer allowed for such a commitment. At this point Halder and the Commander-in-Chief of the Army, Field Marshal Walter von Brauchitsch, became pessimistic about the Kiev operation. Rundstedt, however, and his Chief of Staff, General of the Infantry Georg von Sodenstern, remained remarkably confident that Kiev could be seized directly off the march by the unfolding rapid thrust of Mackensen's III Panzer Corps. Halder agreed 'with reservations',[104] but after discussions with Brauchitsch, Hitler became greatly agitated that this would simply result in panzers being 'needlessly sacrificed'. Accordingly, at 1 a.m. on 10 July Halder telephoned Army Group South to forbid the use of armour against Kiev aside from what was deemed absolutely necessary for local reconnaissance and security.[105] Later that morning, however, as Brauchitsch arrived at Army Group South's headquarters, he was met by a teletype message from Hitler which now seemed to vacillate on the question of Kiev. Although III Panzer Corps was to guard against attacks from Kiev and 'avoid any attacks into the city', Hitler's message then continued that if the main encirclement of Soviet forces could not be achieved before the Southern Bug River,[106] 'Panzer Group 1 will be united for an advance on Kiev and the Dnepr to the southeast'.[107] Rundstedt was firm in his opinion that a close encirclement on the Southern Bug was impractical because too many Soviet units had already retreated beyond that line. According to Hitler's instructions this therefore shifted priority to an attack on Kiev, but Halder and Rundstedt still favoured an encirclement of Soviet forces west of the Dnepr and now sought Hitler's consent for a pocket further to the east of the Southern Bug, near Belaya Tserkov. Hitler acquiesced with the condition that the OKH 'make sure that nothing happens on the panzer group's northern flank'.[108] It is unclear whether this was meant to forestall any proposed attack by III Panzer Corps on Kiev or was simply a precaution to ensure the Sixth Army's security against the threatening attacks emanating from the Pripet marshes. In any case, Brauchitsch drew the conclusion that an attack on Kiev would certainly 'be in line with appropriate cover for the northern flank'.[109] Yet it was also characteristic of Brauchitsch that he avoided making any firm decision on the matter and simply left the option open to the army group's command. Here there was now also vacillation. Reichenau, who had earlier supported the attack, now opposed it and Rundstedt began to have his own doubts about a surprise seizure of the city. Ultimately Kleist was instructed that if his attacks in the north, co-ordinated together with the Sixth Army, should produce a favourable opportunity to gain the city without risk of a setback, the commander on the scene was empowered to do so. After so much concern at the highest levels, the decision was ultimately left to the lowest-ranking commander.[110] By 13 July German reconnaissance conclusively revealed that Soviet fortifications and troop concentrations offered no chance of a surprise attack, and ultimately the city would remain in Soviet hands more than two more months.

Beyond reflecting the discordant power structures that presided over German operations at the highest levels, the decisions concerning the seizure of Kiev have generated debate ever since the war as, according to some, a missed opportunity. Yet such notions, like many 'what if' scenarios of 1941, gain their credibility from the often delusional optimism expressed by the German command at the time. For example, Kiev sits astride the bend of a major river and, like Stalingrad, is mostly built on the western bank; seizing it without meeting much resistance was always going to be unlikely. Yet Kiev was also significantly larger than Stalingrad, with 850,000 inhabitants, and was linked to the east by a well-developed rail network. Local propaganda even portrayed the city at the time as a 'second Tsaritsyn', after Stalingrad's former name, when the city had proved itself an impregnable fortress in the Russian Civil War. Now Kiev's importance was growing as a key concentration point for Red Army units being rushed to Kirponos's front. To ensure the city's survival an outer defensive zone on the small Irpen River was being manned and extended, while city officials started forming People's Militia units and establishing military checkpoints and barricades across the city.[111] Initially under the command of the First Secretary of the Ukrainian Communist Party, Nikita Khrushchev, Kiev was defended by three rifle divisions, an airborne brigade, a tank regiment, an NKVD motorized force, the 1st Kiev artillery school, two anti-tank battalions and about 29,000 militia.[112] Given the subsequent experience of city fighting in the Soviet Union, even the initial German plan to combine a few divisions of the Sixth Army as well as Mackensen's panzer corps in an assault against the city would have been unlikely to succeed. The forced adaptation of the German plan and the hope that a single panzer corps might roll into the city and capture the vital Dnepr bridges was even more fanciful. Indeed at the end of July and in early August there were numerous unsuccessful attempts by Reichenau's XXIX Army Corps to seize Kiev, which again underlined the difficulty of the undertaking.[113] In many aspects of the new war in the east the German commanders would have to undergo a protracted learning curve of bitter experience where lessons were learned the hard way. City fighting, even in smaller population centres such as Odessa, Dnepropetrovsk and Sevastopol, would demonstrate both its extraordinary cost and the inadequacy of German hardware and resources.[114]

Another post-war myth, avidly discussed as perhaps the pre-eminent missed opportunity in the south, relates to the German treatment of the Ukrainian population.[115] After their long oppression under Stalin's rule, in which millions had been starved, brutalized and killed, Ukrainian towns and villages, not surprisingly, welcomed German troops as liberators.[116] Beyond Soviet tyranny, there was also the affirmative, if distant, memory of a generally benevolent German occupation dating from World War I.[117] The suggestion has also been made that the black crosses adorning the vehicles of the German army were interpreted by many Ukrainians as a sign of Christian liberation from Soviet atheism.[118] In any case Ukrainian soldiers, when granted the opportunity, appeared much more likely to surrender. Indeed, some even took it a step further and followed their surrender with requests for enlistment in the war against the Red Army.[119] Helmut Günther recalled, 'More than once Ukrainians, especially young people, requested weapons from us.'[120] Erich Kern remembered one such passionate Ukrainian rallying his countrymen against the Soviets; his message was simple: 'Just give us guns, give us ammunition.' The crowd became frantic and a cry went up: '*Pushka, Pushka*' (Rifles, Rifles).[121] Yet Hitler's war was one of *Lebensraum* (living space) for Germany, not liberation for eastern peoples, and Nazi occupation plans, drawn up before the war, left no ambiguity about this.[122] In one of the clearest examples, the planned starvation of millions in the east was purposely intended to benefit western regions of the Nazi empire.[123] Moreover, eastern Ukraine's rich supplies of raw materials would be exploited for Germany's war effort and harnessed by a local population reduced to servitude. Under German rule there would be no notion of a sovereign eastern state, not even in the historically more Germanic states of the Baltic. The military benefit of acquiring a willing ally was entirely lost on Hitler, who looked on the eastern peoples he was subjugating with a mixture of political mistrust and racial disdain.[124] Nor did Hitler believe that Barbarossa was in need of such support. Thus, those who have admonished Nazi Germany's rejection of the disaffected non-Russian minorities fail to understand Germany's own *Weltanschauung* (world-view) from which it cannot be separated.[125] Armed and organized Slavs were the problem Germany already faced in the east and, given their future plans, it was not to be encouraged or supported. Much less than a lost opportunity, the denial of any form of status for Ukrainians was seen by most in the Nazi state as the safest option. As one German soldier explained, 'these people are subhuman. God! . . . Just ask yourself; subhumans in German uniform? And that apart, there's always the little matter of granting them rights and a status we've so far denied them.'[126] Even if one sets aside the ahistorical nature of the debate and seeks to explore the strictly military implications of arming the anti-Soviet peoples, the fact remains that little could probably have been expected. This is not to doubt the ability, resolve or size of the disaffected groups, but rather it is a commentary on the weakness of Germany's economic base. The German *Ostheer* was already a patchwork army fielding equipment seized from all over Europe and still suffering notable absences. The idea of mobilizing hundreds of thousands of additional 'eastern troops' therefore raises the question of how they would have been armed, equipped and supplied. A certain number could have been provided with captured Soviet equipment, but equipping and sustaining armies in the numbers required to make a difference on the eastern front poses numerous and unresolved problems.

From the middle of July Army Group South was increasingly able to assert its dominance in the Ukraine (see map 5). Only the Soviet Fifth Army in the north was able to maintain a menacing posture, threatening Reichenau's Sixth Army with a persistent state of emergency and helping to influence German strategy across the whole of the eastern front. Hitler concerned himself greatly with the growing southern flank of Army Group Centre and the need to eliminate the troublesome Soviet formations operating from within and around the awkward stretches of the Pripet marshes. He therefore advocated a southern thrust by Guderian's Panzer Group 2, but this was bitterly resisted by the generals of the OKH who favoured a direct thrust towards Moscow, resulting in a month-long standoff. In the meantime, Kleist's motorized formations pressed their advantage, striking south-east to effect an encirclement with the hard-pressed infantry divisions of the Seventeenth Army, under General of Infantry Carl Heinrich von Stülpnagel. This was to be Rundstedt's first large-scale strategic victory, but it took until early August for the trap to be shut, and even then it ensnared only 103,000 Soviet soldiers.[127] The encirclement at Uman' eliminated the bulk of two Soviet armies (Sixth and Twelfth) and under normal circumstances would have been regarded as a crushing success, but Barbarossa aimed for nothing less than the elimination of Soviet resistance by the end of the summer period. Time was fast running out and Kirponos, for all his problems, was still in command of a cohesive fighting force, now to be anchored on the strong defensive line of the Dnepr.

In a letter to his wife on 12 August, Rundstedt wrote, 'How much longer? I have no great hope that it will be soon. The distances in

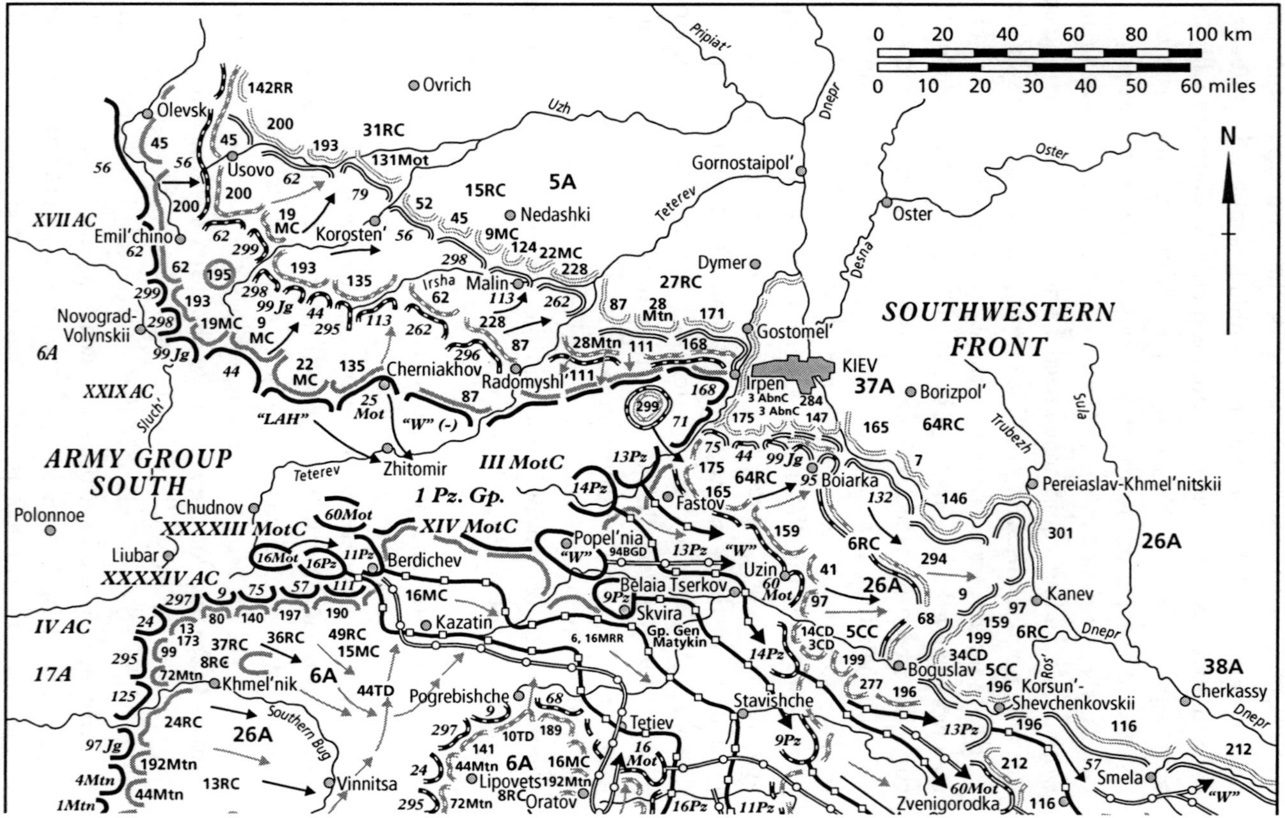
0 20 40 60 80 100 km
0 10 20 30 40 50 60 miles
N
SOUTHWESTERN FRONT
ARMY GROUP SOUTH
1 Pz. Gp.
KIEV
Zhitomir
Berdichev
Belaia Tserkov
Korosten'
Malin
Radomyshl'
Cherniakhov
Novograd-Volynskii
Emil'chino
Olevsk
Usovo
Ovrich
Nedashki
Gornostaipol'
Dymer
Gostomel'
Irpen
Oster
Borizpol'
Boiarka
Fastov
Popel'nia
Uzin
Skvira
Kazatin
Chudnov
Liubar
Polonnoe
Khmel'nik
Vinnitsa
Pogrebishche
Tetiev
Lipovets
Oratov
Stavishche
Boguslav
Kanev
Korsun'-Shevchenkovskii
Cherkassy
Smela
Zvenigorodka
Pereiaslav-Khmel'nitskii
Dnepr
Desna
Pripiat'
Uzh
Teterev
Irsha
Sluch'
Southern Bug
Oster
Sula
Trubezh
Ros'
XVII AC
XXIX AC
XXXXIII MotC
XXXXIV AC
IV AC
III MotC
XIV MotC
6A
17A
5A
37A
26A
38A
6RC
5CC
64RC
27RC
15RC
31RC
9MC
22MC
19 MC
16MC
15MC
36RC
37RC
49RC
24RC
13RC
8RC
44TD
10TD
14CD
3CD
34CD
3 AbnC
Gp. Gen Matykin
6, 16MRR
94BGD
"LAH"
"W"
"W" (-)
13Pz
14Pz
9Pz
11Pz
16Pz
16Mot
25 Mot
60Mot
60 Mot
16 Mot
99 Jg
97 Jg
4Mtn
1Mtn
28 Mtn
28Mtn
142RR
131Mot
192Mtn
44Mtn
72Mtn

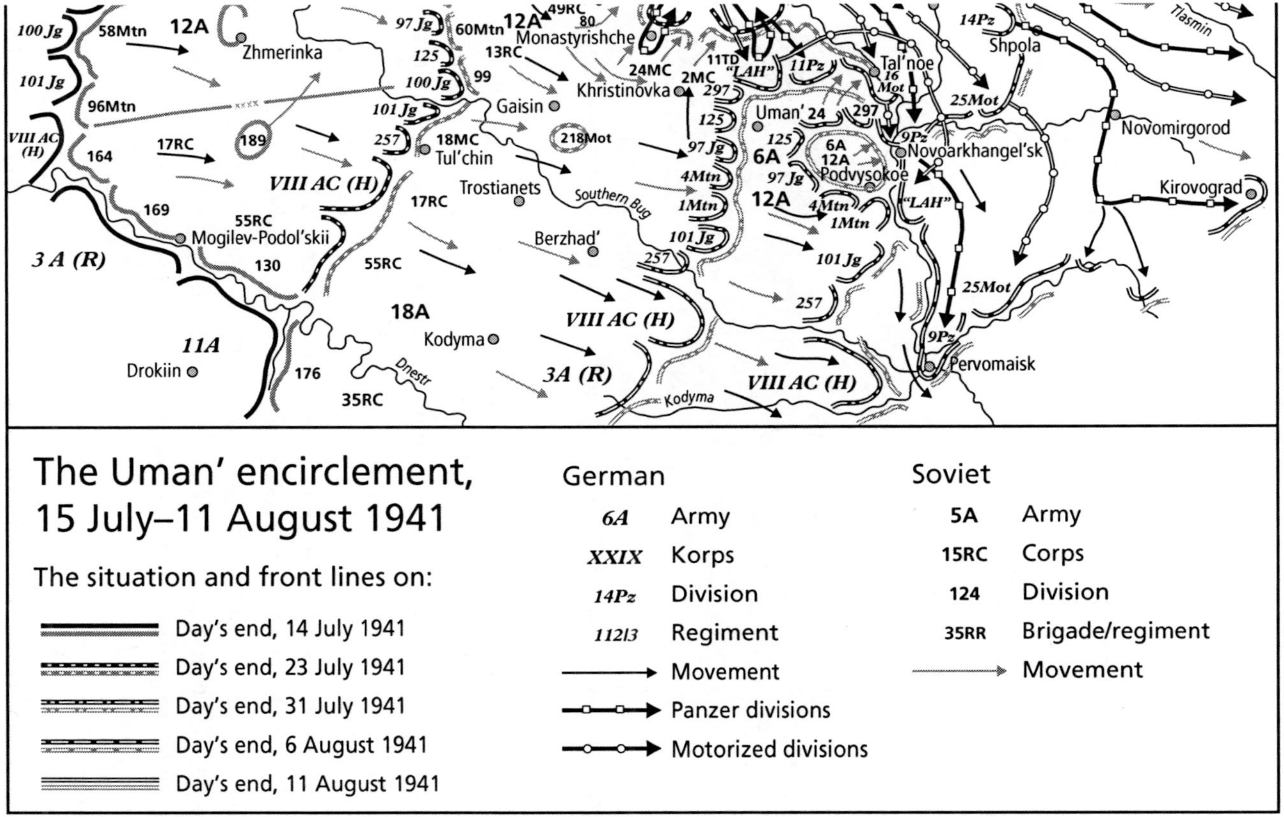

Map 5 Dispositions of Army Group South, 15 July–11 August 1941
Source: Glantz, *Atlas of the Battle for Kiev Part I*.

Fig. 2 The vast spaces of the Soviet Union hampered the *Ostheer*'s ability to concentrate forces and gave many soldiers a sense of endlessness and melancholy.

Russia devour us.'[128] It was a sentiment that his hard-pressed marching infantry knew only too well. Peter Bamm wrote of the summer advance, 'For many weeks we marched from sunrise to sunset through the endless fields of the Ukraine . . . The pace of the advance was murderous . . . The horses had grown so lean that they showed every rib. None of us had an ounce of superfluous fat.'[129] Another soldier recalled the mood the physical exertions were having on the men: 'Everybody here says; rather three wars with France than one with Russia. I fully share this opinion . . . We haven't had a single day of rest during the last six weeks, [we] have been on our feet day and night.'[130] Alois Scheuer was even more emphatic: 'I think we are marching ourselves to death, almost everyday we advance 45 kilometres.'[131] The sheer vastness of the eastern theatre, and the endless depths into which the operations extended, struck some German soldiers with justified foreboding. After hundreds of kilometres it was still impossible to see an end and the distances seemed to be swallowing up German strength. Erich Kern recalled, 'I sat in my truck looking out over the tranquil countryside, trying desperately to fight down an irrational anxiety. I hardly knew myself . . . faced with this vast expanse of country, I found myself gripped by depression – by a sense of utter desolation and fear – the fear of being trapped.'[132]

At the extreme southern end of the German advance in the Ukraine was Colonel-General Eugen Ritter von Schobert's Eleventh Army. He was advancing in tandem with the Romanian Third and Fourth Armies, but, as in the north, progress was slower than expected as Soviet forces stubbornly conducted a fighting retreat.[133] Schobert also confronted the incessant problems of bad roads and increasingly overextended supply lines. As Gottlob Bidermann, a soldier in the Eleventh Army, wrote of the early weeks of the advance:

> *Our lines of supply became more strained with each day's advance, and as our momentum slowed to a crawl we continued to experience ever-increasing sporadic shelling... The depth of our penetration into the Soviet Union began to take its toll, and ammunition rationing served as a first indication of the shortages that we were to encounter with disastrous results in future battles.*[134]

Indeed, by early August, as a good deal of Rundstedt's army group was preparing to advance into the great southern bend of the Dnepr, his forward units had just one-sixth or one-seventh of their ammunition load. There were also bitter disputes breaking out between units, accusing each other of hijacking their supplies.[135] An unknown German soldier's diary entry from 8 August reveals the desperation such shortages were causing and their impact at the front. 'The losses of the infantry are simply monstrous because they have to stick it out without artillery support. In the evening they discovered long enemy columns along one road, and the battery commander had to sit idly by and watch the enemy attack without even one of his guns being able to fire a shot. The situation is catastrophic.'[136]

Already at the end of July the quartermaster's war diary for Kleist's panzer group noted that, even in their current positions, the general supply situation, and especially the running of the trains, was 'unsatisfactory'. Moreover, it alluded to the problem of the *Grosstransportraum* (the truck-based transport fleets bridging the railheads with the armies) being unable to move in bad weather.[137] Under such circumstances almost all movement came to an end until the ground slowly absorbed the rainwater. Then the destructive dust and rutted roads returned in a vicious cycle of harmful repetition. Curzio Malaparte, an Italian journalist travelling with Army Group South, wrote in a July dispatch:

> *The road, if this species of cattle-track may be so described, is covered with a thick layer of dust, which with every breath of wind rises in dense red clouds. But in places, where the clayey soil has failed to absorb the rain-water, where a stream crosses the track, the sticky, tenacious mud grips the wheels of the lorries and the tracks of the tanks, which sink slowly into the* Buna *as into quicksand.*[138]

In the short term the effect of such inhospitable conditions was a delay in the pace of the advance, but more worrying still were the longer-term implications. A continued advance without the ability to service the demands on the vehicles or replace even a fraction of the total losses meant the army group faced an immediate and irreversible decline in motorization. With distances growing, losses mounting and, from the beginning, insufficient military resources to meet the immense demands of the theatre, Barbarossa's offensive phase had a predictable limit. The real question was whether Soviet resistance would crumble before that limit was reached; however, nothing so far indicated an imminent collapse of the Red Army. On the contrary, it was Germany's vital motorized units that were being progressively blunted, a circumstance that carried the gravest implications for Germany's overall strategic position. Highlighting the dangers, General Sodenstern, Rundstedt's Chief of Staff, warned Halder on 10 August of the mounting difficulties confronting operations in the south. As Sodenstern explained, 'the sudden change in the estimate of the situation' was based less on an evaluation of the enemy situation than on 'a revised assessment of the capabilities of our own troops. They are simply exhausted and have heavy losses.'[139] Just how heavy Germany's losses were illustrates the vast scale of the fighting in the east and the Pandora's box that Hitler, with the army's complicity, had unwittingly opened. By 2 August casualties on the eastern front amounted to roughly 180,000 men (not counting Germany's allies). From this figure Army Group South's share amounted to some 63,000 men, with only 10,000 replacements having since arrived to fill the gaps.[140] For an army group that was already poorly resourced to meet its objectives, the absence of more than 50,000 men from the ranks was clearly a significant additional strain. Within the ranks themselves the situation appeared even more foreboding. The 98th Infantry Division assigned to the Sixth Army suffered a staggering 2,300 casualties, including the loss of 78 officers, in just eleven days of fighting.[141] On 11 August Halder noted in his diary that the Sixth Army was suffering a daily loss of 1,600 casualties, of which some 380 were deaths.[142] One German soldier, in a letter to a friend, summed up the alarming rate of attrition at the front. Describing a recent attack Siegbert Stehmann wrote:

> *Eighty comrades remained [dead] on the field. It was a battle that cost us almost all the young lieutenants and was also, as on no other front, man against man, knife against knife. There is nothing worse than a bush war, especially against a numerically and materielly superior enemy. To that must be added the march, which exhausted us to death, so that we remain only as bundles of dirt and rags. That's how it is day after day... We're missing men and weapons, especially heavy guns. We have become a lost, tiny little band that has crawled into narrow foxholes and sits sleepless in rain and sun, night and day waiting for the next shell. The officers don't know what to do... Every day the dark angel comes and takes a few comrades with him. We are only half as many as in the last week and an end is nowhere in sight.*[143]

Such sentiments were echoed by Corporal Hans Efferbergen who wrote in his diary on 10 August, 'That the present engagement is bigger than any ever witnessed is proved by the number of killed and wounded alone, which is very considerable already.'[144] As company strengths dwindled and soldiers observed comrades continually falling around them, the men became more and more aware of their own mortality. Wilhelm Prüller wrote on 4 August, 'It was a terrible day. But again luck was with me. How long will it last?'[145]

There could be no denying the tremendous scale of the conflict, and the war in the air also reflected its unprecedented scale. In only the first four days of hostilities Colonel-General Alexander Löhr's Air Fleet 4, covering Army Group South, managed to attack 77 Soviet airfields

Fig. 3 While in the summer months the German advance continued relentlessly, it left behind many dead.

in 1,600 sorties, eliminating 774 planes on the ground and 136 in the air.[146] It was an unparalleled ratio of destruction, equivalent only to the carnage wrought by the other two air fleets operating to the north. The result was literally thousands of Soviet planes being destroyed in the initial period of the war, which has led some historians to conclude that the German Luftwaffe held aerial superiority over the eastern front. In the early weeks of the campaign that tended to be the case wherever the Luftwaffe was employed in strength, but its resources were hopelessly inadequate to cover the vast expanses of the front. Thus, while Soviet aerial attacks sometimes suffered heavy losses in the summer phase, they never in fact stopped and against undefended sections of the front could still operate with a good measure of success.[147] Even in the opening days of the war there were instances when the Soviet air force conducted costly attacks on the advancing German spearhead. Gustav Schrodek, who served in the 11th Panzer Division, recalled the intensity of Soviet aerial attacks on 28 June:

> *The rain stopped at daybreak, and the Soviet airplanes again emerged immediately afterwards, falling upon column after column of... units from 11th PD... Unfortunately, further personnel loses could not be avoided. It can not be denied that the Soviet opponent, here at least, had the absolute air supremacy... Never in its history did the 15th Panzer Regiment experience so many air attacks as here, in and around Ostrog.*[148]

As the German front advanced, new airfields had to be occupied in the east, which were often inadequately serviced and suffered noticeably from supply problems.[149] After the strategic air attacks against the Soviet air force in the first days of Barbarossa, Löhr's forces concentrated on their tactical role supporting the army. Working closely together with Rundstedt's staff, the two air corps of Air Fleet 4 had to be employed judiciously as there were never enough planes to meet the constant demands of the armies and this gave rise to friction. General of Aviation Robert Ritter von Greim's V Air Corps was ordered to concentrate on the elimination of the encirclement at Uman', but this necessitated ignoring desperate pleas for support coming from the hard-pressed Sixth Army. The result, according to V Air Corps's Chief of Staff, Lieutenant-Colonel Hermann Plocher, was 'friction and discord'. Nor was this an isolated instance. As Plocher noted, 'This constant appeal to the Luftwaffe for air support and the necessity to refuse it,... in favour of the concept of concentrating forces for a major effort, severely strained the mutual confidence of the command and troops between the ground forces and the Luftwaffe. Complaints became the order of the day.'[150] Thus, the Luftwaffe emulated the panzer groups in its ability to strike decisively on individual sectors of the front, but as the campaign continued, it proved incapable of providing any general aerial security or support for the infantry. As one German soldier declared in August, after repeated attacks on his sector of the front from Soviet fighters and bombers, 'The Russians have absolute aerial superiority.'[151] Nor were the tremendous losses of the Soviet air force at the start of the war a crippling impediment to future operations. The pre-war Soviet air force contained a remarkable 15,599 aircraft[152] and new production greatly surpassed Germany's output even in 1941.[153] The huge losses at the start of the war included a large number of obsolete aircraft, some dating back to the 1920s. Indeed on the eve of Barbarossa as much as 80 per cent of the Soviet air force consisted of old designs with little real value against the Luftwaffe.[154] Significantly, with so many Soviet planes destroyed on the ground, many pilots survived to man a newer generation of aircraft, promising much better results.[155] Hence the Soviet air force not only survived the Luftwaffe's initial onslaught, but retained a commanding lead in numbers. As Kleist stated after the war, 'such air superiority as we enjoyed during the opening months was local rather than general. We owed it to the superior skill of our airmen, not to a superiority in numbers.'[156]

In accordance with the Soviet Union's 'total' approach to the war, among the earliest directives was a scorched earth policy distributed in a secret order from Stalin on 27 June. The order's wording was unequivocal: 'All valuable materials, energy and agricultural stocks, and standing grain that cannot be taken away and can be used by the enemy *must*, in order to prevent such use – upon order of the Military Councils of the fronts – *be immediately made completely worthless, that is, must be destroyed, annihilated, and burned*.'[157] In the Ukraine the sheer size of the area and, at times, the resistance of local people, who feared such measures would lead to another famine, diluted the response to the order. Results varied from district to district, but generally the further east one travelled, the greater the level of Soviet destruction or the evacuation of equipment and livestock. Rail bridges over the Dnepr River at Cherkasy, Kremenchug, Dnepropetrovsk and Zaporizhzhia were all destroyed and factories in these regions were either evacuated or ruined according to plan. Explosives on the huge hydroelectric dam upstream from Zaporizhzhia were detonated, causing widespread devastation and loss of life. The destruction was often planned and conducted from above, but it was also carried out spontaneously by thousands of looters in the brief interlude between Soviet and German control. Almost every town and city experienced it.[158] The result for the advancing Germans was first felt in the realm of logistics, where greater efforts had to be made to supply the advancing armies as well as repair essential infrastructure. In the longer term it made a functioning occupation more difficult as the needs of the civil population competed unsuccessfully for resources with the ongoing needs of the German army. Ultimately, the destruction and evacuations amounted to a substantial net loss of potential resources, as well as costing the German advance precious time and demanding more and more of its overstretched materiel and manpower reserves.

Unlike the two northern army groups, Rundstedt's broad front gained substantial support from Germany's Axis partners. Romania,[159] Hungary,[160] Slovakia[161] and, towards the end of the summer, Italy[162] all provided forces in support of Army Group South. Only in Romania's case was support actively solicited by the Germans before the war and incorporated into Barbarossa's planning. Not only had that country recently been forced to cede territory to the Soviet Union, but the Romanian head of state, General Ion Antonescu, was a fervent anti-communist and even shared Hitler's anti-Semitic views.[163] For the other Axis partners there was also an unmistakable anti-Bolshevik element and participation was further encouraged by the expected prestige of a short, victorious campaign, but most centrally for all states was an avid desire to maintain Hitler's good favour. Hungary and Romania shared hotly disputed borders and both states vied for Hitler's support to ensure their claim. As a result, the two could be safely deployed on the eastern front only with a buffering of German or Italian forces between them. Antipathy between Hungarian and Slovakian units persuaded German commanders that these two forces should also be separated.[164] Indeed by the end of the summer the Hungarians revealed that they would much rather be arming for hostilities with Romania than pursuing a war against the Soviet Union. It is not surprising, therefore, that when the Hungarian regent, Admiral Miklós Horthy, and the chief of the Hungarian general staff, Lieutenant-General Ferenc Szombathelyi, tried to withdraw their Mobile Corps from the eastern front in early September, they were blocked by Hitler.[165] Beyond forestalling any renewed antagonism among his allies, Hitler was increasingly aware of his emerging vulnerabilities in the east. Moreover, according to the Chief of the High Command of the Wehrmacht, Field Marshal Wilhelm Keitel, Szombathelyi made 'a number of more than offensive remarks ... about our command and operation' of Hungarian forces. Unaccustomed to such criticism and unwilling to accept condemnation from a minor ally, Keitel quickly became very irritated. He accused Szombathelyi's men of ill-discipline, 'plundering and looting everywhere they went'. Having asserted himself and belittled Szombathelyi, Keitel noted that he 'suddenly became very amiable, oozing with flattery for our overall command of the army, and unable to express adequately how much he admired the Führer'. Clearly Szombathelyi knew what Keitel expected to hear and was no doubt aware that the favourable patronage of Hitler's regime was essential in the tense standoff with Romania. Yet the episode also highlights the closed circle of discussion that would be tolerated at the top of the German command, especially when it involved criticism.[166]

While Germany promoted the dubious façade of the Axis's common struggle against the Soviet Union, it was clearly apparent that internal fractures pervaded the alliance. The growing demands of the war in the east had a further radicalizing effect. Even before the end of July it was obvious that Soviet resistance was not abating and that Army Group South could not meet all of its military commitments. This moved Hitler to submit a request to Antonescu asking him to continue his offensive operations into the Soviet Union after the initial recovery of Bessarabia and Northern Bucovina. Together with Finland, Romania contributed by far the largest number of forces to the eastern front (325,685 troops on 22 June) and would now be asked to conduct largely independent operations at Odessa for which the Romanian army was inadequately equipped and trained.[167] Nevertheless, Antonescu willingly acceded to Hitler's request. The result was a thinly disguised catastrophe as, over the course of August, the besieging Romanian Fourth Army suffered some 27,307 casualties – more than the combined losses of the Romanian Third and Fourth Armies in the liberation of their own territories.[168] To make matters worse the August assault on Odessa failed and future attempts would prove even more costly. The attrition rate of Romanian forces was not equalled by Germany's other minor allies, but the vehicles of the Hungarian Mobile Corps and the smaller Slovakian Rapid Group suffered greatly over the course of the summer from mechanical breakdowns and combat losses.[169] By the conclusion of the summer there was still no end in sight to the war and Germany's allies had already suffered a steep decline in their operational strength. With weak economies and low levels of industrialization, war materiel was harder for them to replace and Germany committed itself to bolstering its allies, despite not possessing the capacity to do so.[170] In exchange Germany demanded fresh forces. Yet building capable armies with skilled officers and trained recruits required much more than just raw manpower reserves and here again Germany's allies operated from a significant disadvantage. The results would become plainly apparent in 1942; however, as early as the summer of 1941, Barbarossa's failure bound the minor Axis nations to Germany's war in the east and ultimately to Germany's fate.

At the conclusion of Army Group South's battle at Uman', Hitler flew to the army group to consult with Rundstedt and Antonescu. In spite of Hitler's ceremonial display, awarding the Romanian head of state the prestigious Knight's Cross, the elimination of Soviet forces west of the Dnepr had still not been achieved.[171] The Soviet Southern Front still clung to the northern shore of the Black Sea, opposing Schobert's Eleventh Army along with Antonescu's forces. Yet the conclusion of the fighting at Uman' freed Kleist's panzer group as well as elements of the Seventeenth Army for new tasks. A south-eastern thrust into the southern bend of the Dnepr could take advantage of Tyulenev's exposed northern flank and cut off his Ninth and Eighteenth Armies. Aware of the danger the *Stavka* authorized a long withdrawal to the southern reaches of the Dnepr, which Tyulenev astutely managed, saving his army and occupying a much stronger defensive position. Lieutenant-General G. P. Sofronov's Coastal Army was left behind to defend Odessa. This it would do with distinction, leading to the city being labelled one of the Soviet Union's first 'Hero Cities'.[172]

With another long advance into the southern bend of the Dnepr and Kirponos's forces still stubbornly defending their positions in front of Kiev and along the line of the great river, Rundstedt's weary forces still had much work before them. In a statement to the men of Army Group South on 15 August, Rundstedt openly addressed what he referred to as the 'extraordinary demands' of the campaign. He then continued:

> *I know that a great many divisions have been in combat every day since the start of the campaign. I also know that the tasks seem unobtainable and that the difficult combat, inclement weather and road obstacles require the greatest efforts of the troops... It is only natural that such great effort would result in fatigue, the combat strength of the troops has weakened and in many places there is a desire for rest.*[173]

The proclamation then offered the solace of reiterating the army group's successes. However, Rundstedt ultimately had to conclude, 'the campaign has not been won'. Moreover, he hinted that there were still many more toils and privations to come: 'I must demand the same devotion, the same combat readiness and the same will for victory in the future! . . . We must keep pressure on the enemy for he has many more reserves than we.'[174] Rundstedt's dubious insistence that the men maintain their previous degree of commitment may have resonated among those imbued with the Wehrmacht's fighting spirit, but it meant little in matters of logistics, the exhaustion of the horses and the panzer group's dwindling mechanical resources. Nor could it correct the army's alarming deficit in manpower. Indeed, the renewed advance into the southern Ukraine taxed Army Group South's offensive strength greatly and still there remained the formidable Soviet armies beyond the Dnepr River. Major-General Ludwig Crüwell, the commander of the 11th Panzer Division, reported on 17 August 'heavy materiel and personnel losses', which he stated rendered the division no longer fully operational and 'urgently' necessitated rest and refitting.[175] The condition of Crüwell's division was far from exceptional and Halder noted towards the end of the month that Panzer Group 1 retained only about half of its former strength.[176] More worrying still, the quartermaster's war diary for Panzer Group 1 categorized the supply situation on 20 August as 'critical'. The diary recorded that the operational demands on Kleist's motorized supply columns had resulted in a 60 per cent reduction in capacity. Notwithstanding the dramatic drop in transportation, the panzer group was nevertheless expected to supply nine motorized infantry and panzer divisions, the XXXXIV Army Corps, the newly arrived Italian Expeditionary Corps and the Hungarian Mobile Corps. The distance between the panzer group's nearest railhead and the front extended some 350 kilometres, forcing the understated conclusion: 'Under these circumstances the quartermaster can no longer guarantee a smooth supply.'[177]

While Army Group South had conquered a vast area against a numerically superior force, the expenditure of strength was prohibitively high. Rundstedt's infantry divisions were exhausted and increasingly finding themselves bound to static positions. Kleist's panzer group, like those operating further north, had proved its effectiveness through speed, manoeuvrability and firepower; however, extreme distance, dreadful roads, unceasing combat and the lack of spare parts

Fig. 4 Panzer Group 1 offered Army Group South firepower and speed, but its heavy degree of motorization proved increasingly difficult to maintain and keep supplied.

increasingly compromised its strength. The success of Army Group South was therefore a qualified one. While a relative accounting of losses sustained and ground seized suggests an imposing German triumph, such factors ignore the wider strategic context in which Operation Barbarossa was taking place. The consumption of resources necessitated by the German *Ostheer* was thoroughly unsustainable in the long term. In the planning stages the notion of a large-scale continuation of the war into the autumn had hardly been considered, mainly because of its military impracticability, but also owing to its economic cost. Operation Barbarossa was intended to be a summer campaign, striking an overwhelming blow to eliminate Soviet resistance. As it happened, by the end of August Rundstedt confronted a serious dilemma that was shared, although in no way adequately appreciated, by the whole German command. The Soviet state retained enormous powers of resistance and mobilization, while reorganization for 'total war' was already well underway. At the same time the Red Army was not only holding doggedly to an unbroken front, but it was capable of launching aggressive counterattacks against both Bock's and Leeb's army groups. The fundamental tenets of the Barbarossa plan had not been fulfilled – there was no collapse of Soviet resistance and many strategic centres still remained outside the German sphere of control. More importantly, the *Ostheer*'s offensive strength was ebbing from week to week.

The summer phase of operations had revealed the danger of becoming bogged down in the hinterlands of the Soviet Union. It also confirmed Germany's dependence upon the continued mobility and strength of the panzer groups, which by the end of the summer had become seriously compromised. A long-term campaign was now thrust upon the Wehrmacht for which it was impaired militarily and unsupported economically. The summer therefore ended badly for Germany and, although few at the time could see just how dire things were,[178] hopes were fully invested in the successful outcome of the war in the east. In late August and September 1941 that hope was focused on the Ukraine and the battle of Kiev.

3 THE ROAD TO KIEV

Subordinating the generals – the dictators dictate

On 29 July 1941 Marshal Georgi Zhukov, the Chief of the Red Army's General Staff, delivered to Stalin a detailed report on operations across the whole length of the eastern front. Zhukov was unique among Stalin's commanders for being both forthright with his opinion and uncompromising in his judgements, even when he knew these were to prove deeply unpopular. The meeting with Stalin began ominously as Zhukov noted the presence of the notorious Mekhlis, Deputy People's Commissar of Defence, who was infamous for his ruthlessness against the Soviet officer corps during the purge.[1] Zhukov commenced with a long survey of the front, beginning in the north and working his way down to the south. He orientated his audience with large maps of the front, statistics on Soviet losses and the formation of new reserve armies. Finally he came to German deployments and suggested what he believed to be their most likely future course of action. At this point Mekhlis interrupted to question how Zhukov had come by his information about the Germans, to which Zhukov defensively replied that he knew nothing of German plans, but that their disposition of forces suggested 'certain things'. Zhukov then explained:

> *On the strategic axis of Moscow the Germans are unable to mount a major offensive operation in the near future owing to their heavy losses and they lack appreciable reserves to secure the right and left wings of Army Group Centre.*

> *On the Leningrad axis it is impossible for the Germans to begin an operation to capture Leningrad and link up with the Finns without additional forces...*
>
> *The most dangerous and the weakest sector of our line is the Central Front, since the armies covering Unscha and Gomel are weak and badly equipped – the Germans can use this present weak spot to strike into the flank and rear of the South-Western Front.*[2]

The Central Front, under Colonel-General F. I. Kuznetsov, had been newly created on 23 July and consisted of the battered Thirteenth and Twenty-First Armies. Its orders were to protect Gomel and the Sozh River sector, but it was hardly in a position to do so.[3] Having identified the weakness, Zhukov recommended reinforcing Kuznetsov's front with three additional armies as well as giving it more artillery and an experienced and energetic commander (Zhukov suggested North-Western Front's Chief of Staff, N. F. Vatutin). Stalin, however, was sceptical and questioned whether the diversion of forces would weaken the vital approaches to Moscow. Zhukov was adamant it would not and explained that in two weeks nine fully equipped divisions could be transferred from the Far East to reinforce the Moscow Axis. Again Stalin was sceptical and he challenged Zhukov by suggesting that this would mean handing the Far East over to the Japanese. Zhukov ignored the comment and went on to explain that South-Western Front would also have to be pulled back behind the Dnepr. 'And what about Kiev in that case?' Stalin asked pointedly. Zhukov explained it would have to be given up, but provided a solid military rationale for such a course. Nevertheless, at the mere suggestion of abandoning Kiev, Stalin exploded.[4] As Zhukov explained, 'He cursed me in crude terms for suggesting we leave Kiev which, like Leningrad, he counted on holding at any cost.' Stalin also accused him of talking 'rubbish', which soon provoked its own outburst from Zhukov who retorted, 'If you think the Chief of the General Staff talks nonsense, then I request you relieve me of my post and send me to the front.'[5] Stalin was in no mood to back down and therefore accepted Zhukov's request. The ageing and far more amenable Marshal Boris Shaposhnikov took over as Chief of the General Staff and Zhukov was sent to command the Reserve Front.

Zhukov was without question one of the pre-eminent military commanders of World War II and his advice to Stalin on this occasion was to prove not only daringly honest, but remarkably perceptive. Still, Stalin's regime tended to emulate Hitler's Germany in its delusional tendency to reject or shun those commanders who spoke out against the officially sanctioned alternative. Germany's recent command crisis over the future employment of Army Group Centre's panzer forces did much to antagonize the already strained relations between the army and Hitler, but the dispute also soured relations within Army Group Centre itself. The roots of the dispute go back as far as December 1940 when a clear divergence emerged between the plans of the OKH, on the one hand, and those of Hitler, on the other, for the second phase of the eastern campaign. Yet nothing was openly discussed because the generals at the OKH simply hoped that the initial phase of the campaign would either prove decisive to the outcome of the war or at least convince Hitler of their strategic preference. When neither option eventuated the two sides openly clashed in the last week of July and the dispute rumbled on for a month. The climax came when Guderian, who had voiced some of the most emphatic words of defiance to Hitler's plans, met with the dictator and abruptly experienced a complete change of heart.[6] Guderian now openly adopted Hitler's proposal. Not surprisingly this transformed him into something of a pariah within Army Group Centre. He was detested for what was seen as his duplicity and indifference towards the plans of the army as well as his feeble capitulation before Hitler. Previously, the most senior field commander to support Hitler's plans within Army Group Centre had been the commander of the Fourth Army, Field Marshal Günther von Kluge, yet he was a bitter rival of Guderian and something of a pariah himself. Indeed, Kluge had such ill-feeling towards Bock that it has been suggested he supported Hitler's drive to the south, at least in part, to escape Bock's area of control. According to the Chief of Staff at Fourth Army, Major-General Günther Blumentritt, Kluge's motives were astonishingly self-centred. Writing after the war, Blumentritt stated:

> *It was his [Kluge's] idea, and desire, that his own Fourth Army should swing south to carry out this pincer movement along with Guderian's panzer forces. When setting forth the argument for this plan, he said to me, with emphasis: 'It would also mean that* we *should be under Field Marshal von Rundstedt, instead of Field Marshal von*

> *Bock.' Von Bock was a very difficult man to serve, and von Kluge would have been glad to get out of his sphere. This was an interesting example of the influence of the personal factor in strategy.*[7]

If Kluge's desire for a new commanding officer did in fact inform his strategic thinking, it is yet another example of the spiteful jealousies and egocentric behaviour of senior German commanders in the east. In any event, Fourth Army's staff was initially ordered to plan for their participation in the drive south, but this was later cancelled and Kluge was informed that he would have to remain on the central front. According to Blumentritt, Kluge became so infuriated that he took the extraordinary step of excusing himself from duty and flying home to his family estate at Bohme near Rathenau where he remained for a period of several weeks.[8]

After his meeting with Hitler Guderian flew back to Army Group Centre to prepare for his new push to the south – an operation he had only hours earlier insisted would be 'impossible'.[9] Meanwhile, as the news spread of Guderian's defection to Hitler's plan, the mood within the army command seethed with frustration and disappointment. Guderian would later claim that Halder held such a grudge again him that he failed adequately to support his impending offensive.[10] Halder, on the other hand, lamented what he later termed 'the deciding turning point of the eastern campaign'.[11] Bock was so angered that even the developing success of Ninth Army's long-delayed offensive at Velikie Luki gave him no joy. As Bock explained, 'I'm not really happy about it because the objective to which I devoted all my thought, the destruction of the main strength of the enemy army, has been dropped.'[12] Field Marshal Albrecht Kesselring, the commander of Air Fleet 2 covering Army Group Centre, voiced his regret that 'precious weeks' had been wasted with 'overlong deliberations and secondary operations'.[13] Hitler, by contrast, had emerged victorious from the dispute, yet in the days following, during a state visit by Mussolini, he was observed to be 'drawn and tired'.[14] Rochus Misch, another eye-witness, noted that the previously good mood within the 'Wolf's Lair' (*Wolfschanze*), Hitler's secluded headquarters in East Prussia, had abated somewhat towards the end of the summer.[15] The Chief of the Operations Department in the Army General Staff, Colonel Adolf Heusinger, suspected Hitler had been worn down by the weight of difficult decisions, the essence of which centred around 'when he wants to end the war and which goals he believes he has to achieve'.[16] A longer-term ramification of the protracted strategic dispute was Hitler's opinion of the desk generals at the OKH, which, already strained by fierce disputes in 1939 and 1940, had now fallen to a new low. A meeting between Brauchitsch and Hitler on 30 August produced what one participant described as a 'reconciliation'.[17] Yet it was a superficial and largely symbolic act on Hitler's part.[18] According to Major-General Walter Warlimont, Brauchitsch claimed the reconciliation negated Hitler's insulting 'study' of 22 August, which had blamed the army commanders for exhibiting poor management and a failure to provide coherent strategic direction.[19] Hitler, on the other hand, interpreted Brauchitsch's injured pride as well as his pusillanimous show of compliance in the aftermath of the dispute as yet another sign of weakness in the army's leadership. The dispute, although now reconciled on the surface, in fact reinforced Hitler's hostility towards the OKH as well as strengthening his ascendancy over those who had opposed him within the army.[20] As some in Hitler's inner circle could already see, Brauchitsch's days as the Commander-in-Chief of the Army were numbered.[21]

Although the immediacy of the strategic dispute had now passed and a measure of grudging harmony returned, the acrimony engendered by the infighting had poisoned relations and would later return, especially as conditions worsened. In spite of the outbursts of anger and frustration directed against Hitler over the loss of the much-cherished Moscow offensive, the military situation on the central part of the eastern front makes clear that Hitler's decision was not the only impediment to the OKH's plans. Indeed in the second half of August Bock's eastern front was desperately trying to hold against Timoshenko's Western Front and its sustained Dukhovshchina offensive. Opposing Timoshenko were the overstretched infantry of Colonel-General Adolf Strauss's Ninth Army. The attack launched on 17 August succeeded in forcing the Germans back across the Vop River, penetrating 10 kilometres into German positions across a 10 kilometre wide front.[22] The German 161st Infantry Division was left badly mauled and Bock noted soon afterwards that it was 'at the end of its tether'.[23] Further north, Timoshenko's forces were also able to seize crossings over the Western Dvina River and win ground against the German VII Army Corps.[24] The situation caused Bock much anguish, leading him to wonder whether the Soviet command had noticed the absence of German motorized divisions behind the Ninth Army. The following day (20 August) Strauss, citing ill health, handed over command of his embattled army to Colonel-General Hermann Hoth, the commander of Panzer Group 3. Hoth, who had been attempting to rest and refit his precious motorized divisions, saw no option other than to counterattack the Soviet spearheads. Mindful of the Soviet strength in this region Bock recommended Hoth concentrate both the 7th Panzer Division and the 14th Motorized Infantry Division, which constituted Hoth's only available reserves. Hoth, however, refused, claiming the 14th Motorized Infantry Division would take too long to arrive.[25] The result was a fiasco. The 7th Panzer Division's attack ran into two fortified Soviet lines and was swiftly stopped with a loss of thirty tanks.[26] Bock lamented not having persevered in his efforts to have stronger forces committed,[27] but Hoth's impetuousness was the real culprit. Across the whole of the eastern front German commanders were having to adjust, with limited success in many cases, to the growing limits of their offensive capacity.

At the lower levels such limits were often already very well known, as a set of reports intercepted by Soviet intelligence indicated. In early August a German battalion commander from a motorized infantry regiment reported, 'In the last few days our battalion lost 5 officers, 15 non-coms and 106 privates. Combat efficiency is dropping fast. We need men and officers. Our repairmen have no spares. Many of our vehicles are out of action, either from hits or from lack of spares. We have to replace cylinders. The shortage of fuel is acute.'[28] Days later the same commander reported that the situation was even worse: 'Due to the heavy losses of the last few days the battalion is unable to act efficiently. Battle worthiness is tragic. Personal control by the officers is in a precarious state. Tension has reached a point where the battalion can be made to attack only by coercion, that is, force of arms.'[29] In 1943 the Nazi propaganda ministry published an ideologically laden soldier's memoir of the eastern front, but even this exercise in misinformation included aspects of the difficulties in Army Group Centre during August and September 1941. As Horst Slesina wrote:

> *The days following the battle [of Smolensk] were hard for us... Weeks and weeks in rain, cold, dirt and mud, artillery battles lasting several days under mass attacks with unprecedented violence and nothing else to do but hold the*

> *positions! ... Day after day the pitiless drumming, pounding and roaring of thousands of shells in only a small space of earth – day after day the shrill screaming of the Bolshevik hordes who seem to rise up from the earth in dense masses – day after day watching the fields of bodies grow until tens of thousands lie on top of each other ... That is positional warfare! ... The time of the great defensive battles in the middle of the front begins. The hell in loam and dirt will surround us for weeks.*[30]

As Timoshenko's Western Front battered the Ninth Army on Bock's northern flank, Zhukov's Reserve Front attempted to do the same in the south, especially around the Yel'nya salient in which intense fighting had been raging since the third week of July. Zhukov's offensive was largely attritional in nature and as a result extremely bloody, yet despite Soviet losses being woefully high and meagre territorial gains, the effect on the German command was profound. Militarily holding Yel'nya demanded a constant rotation of forces as casualties in the salient became exorbitantly high, yet this also influenced strategic planning because opinions were split over whether or not the position should be given up. Ultimately the idea of a withdrawal was rejected for fear of granting the Red Army a victory, as well as the worrying signal such a move would send to German troops.[31]

As Bock struggled to hold together his front, Army Group Centre's vital panzer forces, upon which an end to the Soviet campaign depended, were split between multiple tasks. Ostensibly they were to have been husbanded in the rear, resting their weary troops and conducting desperately needed repairs to rectify their stark reduction in fighting strength. Yet the hefty demands of the defensive fighting, complicated by the shortage of infantry across Bock's extensive front, necessitated their constant reactivation to shore up endangered German positions. Compounding these demands Hitler agitated throughout August for an offensive solution to the stout resistance of Soviet forces operating along Bock's long southern flank. In addition to shortening Bock's front and freeing up more infantry from the overextended Second Army, Hitler wanted to relieve the pressure on the hard-pressed northern flank of Army Group South, where the Sixth Army was fighting desperate defensive battles. Guderian's XXIV Panzer Corps, under General of Panzer Troops Freiherr Leo Geyr von Schweppenburg, attacked

Fig. 5 Field Marshal Fedor von Bock commanded Army Group Centre in Operation Barbarossa and directed bitter defensive battles in late August and early September 1941.

(together with IX Army Corps) at the start of the month and seized Roslavl, along with 38,000 Soviet POWs.[32] It was the first major push into the most vulnerable sector of the Soviet defensive front, about which Zhukov had attempted to warn Stalin at the end of July.

On 9 August XXIV Panzer Corps was again on the offensive, attempting to cut off Soviet forces at Krasnopolye.[33] Yet Schweppenburg's forces (3rd and 4th Panzer Divisions and the 10th Motorized Infantry Division) had been in almost constant action since the beginning of the war and had suffered accordingly. Moreover, heavy rains slowed the attack and hindered movement even for the tanks, with the added consequence that the already insufficient oil stocks were being consumed at 75 per cent above normal levels.[34] Yet most worrying of all was the dwindling offensive strength of the panzer regiments. By 11 August Major-General Willibald Freiherr von Langermann-Erlancamp's 4th Panzer Division had only 64 tanks left (from a starting total of 169) and only 33 of these were the more advanced Mark IIIs (25) and Mark IVs (8).[35] Many more tanks were simply damaged or had been rendered unserviceable by the dreadful Soviet roads and long distances. Returning these to service required both an extensive period of rest and the much-promised, but so far undelivered, spare parts. As Panzer Group 2's war diary noted on 11 August, 'The technical requirements of this attack are not favourable... It is also not known whether or when the spare parts (motors, etc.) will be delivered.'[36] Ultimately, by 13 August Schweppenburg's hard-pressed corps succeeded only in eliminating a small pocket at Krichev, capturing 16,000 prisoners, 76 guns and 15 tanks.[37] In the meantime the army command, led by Brauchitsch, was insisting that Schweppenburg's corps would also have to seize both Chechersk and Gomel. Chechersk, the closer of the two objectives, had earlier been dismissed by the offensive-minded Guderian as a goal that would result in 'the end of [Schweppenburg's] corps'.[38] This assumption was reflected in the exhaustion of the fighting units within 4th Panzer Division. On 14 August the war diary noted, 'Battles on 13 and 14 [August] very costly, also in materiel. There was little benefit [in the fighting] because the enemy mass had already evacuated. Trucks in bad condition. Men tired. Division increasingly worn out.'[39]

In spite of its fatigue the rolling series of offensives by XXIV Panzer Corps continued unabated. Operational difficulties were masked by its continual ability to win ground, which resulted from the appalling state of the opposing Soviet forces and Stalin's stubborn refusal to recognize and address the seriousness of his strategic position. The battered Soviet Central Front, which had been formed as a stop-gap measure on 23 July, lacked the resources to withstand the German attacks and was persistently losing ground. On 14 August the *Stavka* again responded with an expedient measure by creating the Briansk Front, commanded by Lietenant-General A. I. Eremenko.[40] The Briansk Front was to ensure contact between the Reserve and the Central Fronts, but at Eremenko's appointment to front commander, Stalin made it clear his essential task was the defence of Moscow's southern approaches. As Stalin explained, 'We are laying a major responsibility on the Briansk Front – your main target – to cover the Moscow strategic area from the south-west and not to permit Guderian's tank group to break through the Briansk Front to Moscow.'[41] Stalin's incisiveness was supported by credible intelligence, albeit only provisionally valid, that Guderian's southward attacks represented only tactical manoeuvring before a resumption of the main offensive eastward. Stalin could not have foreseen, or guessed at, the extent of the strategic crisis consuming the German command, but the persistent risk of ignoring the danger to the South-Western Front was not lost on Zhukov. His relegation to the command of the Reserve Front did not deter Zhukov from submitting his own views to Stalin and the *Stavka* (of which he was still a member). Writing on 18 August Zhukov warned:

> *The enemy, persuaded of the concentration of powerful concentrations of our forces on the road to Moscow, having on his flanks the Central Front and the Velikie Luki grouping of our forces, has temporarily given up the blow at Moscow and, turning to active defence against the Western and the Reserve Fronts, has thrown all his mobile shock and tank units against the Central, South-Western and Southern Fronts.*
>
> *Possible enemy intentions; to destroy the Central Front, and, breaking into the area Chernigov-Konotop-Priluki, with a blow from the rear thereby to destroy the South-Western Front.*[42]

Stalin replied to Zhukov claiming that such concerns were well known to him, but that the Briansk Front had been created to deal with such an eventuality. Moreover, Stalin ambiguously assured Zhukov, 'other measures are being taken', without offering any details.[43] Zhukov's fears, however, were well founded. The Briansk Front consisted of the Soviet Third Army, the new Fiftieth Army and the former Central Front's frail Thirteenth Army, but Eremenko was fixated on stopping Guderian's expected thrust to the south-east of Moscow, not preparing for a reinforced and sustained drive to the south. The neighbouring Central Front was perilously weak and seriously lacking in cohesion, adding weight to Hitler's hope that he could attain his economic objectives in the Ukraine, while at the same time exploiting a lucrative opportunity in the south. In Hitler's gaze was the powerful, but exposed, Soviet

South-Western Front, which was defending a giant salient stretching all the way west to Kiev.

To exploit such alluring prospects in the south, Hitler looked to Guderian's already committed XXIV Panzer Corps, reinforced by the XXXXVII Panzer Corps under General of Panzer Troops Joachim Lemelsen (17th and 18th Panzer Divisions, 29th Motorized Infantry Division). In addition, Colonel-General Maximilian Freiherr von Weichs's Second Army, which had already been exerting great pressure on the Central Front in support of Schweppenburg's corps, could be concentrated for a sustained offensive south. The indications for success appeared good and certainly much better than battering against the heavy concentrations of Soviet troops assembling on the predicted Moscow Axis. The German generals who so passionately advocated this alternative were remarkably oblivious to the worn state of their panzer forces as well as the near total absence of stockpiled munitions, fuel and other provisions that would be required for such a long and hard drive east. In the south, on the other hand, a junction could conceivably be achieved with elements of Kleist's Panzer Group 1 thrusting up from the southern bend of the Dnepr. This would allow for a far more manageable advance in terms of both distance and anticipated resistance.

Of greater concern to Hitler's plan were the extremely tight logistical constraints under which the panzer groups had to operate. The current delivery of tonnage was barely adequate to meet their most pressing needs, to say nothing of refurbishing their strength or pushing the motorized divisions even further into enemy territory. Yet the disregard of logistics in German strategy was a problem that persisted throughout almost every major campaign the Wehrmacht undertook. At its root matters of supply were seen as subordinate to strategic considerations, meaning that once an objective had been decided upon it was up to lower chains of command to adapt and organize the means.[44] 'According to our opinion,' Halder told an interviewer after the war, 'the materiel has to serve the spiritual. Accordingly, our quartermaster service may never hamper the operational concept.'[45]

As XXIV Panzer Corps pushed doggedly ahead with its rolling offensives in the south, the overextended supply system had great difficulty keeping up over the terrible roads. By 18 August Soviet resistance in front of Lieutenant-General Walther Model's 3rd Panzer Division was simply melting away, as the overstretched Central Front teetered on the verge of collapse. Yet, in what would become a recurring pattern, Schweppenburg's advance was hindered as much by his lack of supplies as by the strength of Soviet resistance. On 18 August, the diary of the 3rd Panzer Division's Quartermaster-General stated: 'The forward advance of the division is so fast that the [support] columns are not able to keep pace.'[46] On the following day (19 August) fuel shortages and flagging offensive strengths caused Schweppenburg to inform Guderian's headquarters that the capture of Novozybkov, an important town to the east of Gomel, could not be achieved.[47] On 20 August Panzer Group 2 again pressed for a continuation of the attack, but this only induced an even more exasperated protest from the corps. Illustrative of the difficulties under which Schweppenburg's divisions were operating, the 4th Panzer Division's oil supplies were judged 'very tight' and the division did not expect any substantial supplies for the coming two to three days. Furthermore, the number of serviceable tanks was reported to have sunk to just 44 machines (from an initial strength of 169 tanks on 22 June) and only 26 of these were Mark IIIs (20) and Mark IVs (6).[48] Accordingly, Guderian informed Bock that he was no longer able to take Novozybkov because XXIV Panzer Corps 'was at the end of its tether'.[49]

While Schweppenburg's exhausted corps paused again, the threat of collapse on the Soviet front remained as apparent as ever. On 19 August Weichs's Second Army finally ended the battle for Gomel, taking an estimated 50,000 Soviet POWs.[50] Meanwhile, the 17th Panzer Division of Lemelsen's XXXXVII Panzer Corps was now in action at Pochep on Schweppenburg's left flank. The 29th Motorized Infantry Division was also moving south, but on 20 August Bock instructed Guderian to discontinue his operations in the south and begin concentrating his forces further north near Roslavl for the anticipated beginning of the Moscow offensive.[51] It was at this point that the final act in the long-running German strategic crisis played out, giving Hitler *carte blanche* for his southern operation.

In the north, Bock's Ninth Army was still straining under the pressure of Timoshenko's offensive, but Hoth's ill-fated counterattack with the 7th Panzer Division did not deter him from seeking another offensive solution, this time on a much more extensive scale, towards Velikie Luki. The operation had been planned for a month, ever since General of Panzer Troops Adolf Kuntzen's LVII Panzer Corps had been ejected from the city during the over-ambitious advances of mid-July.[52]

Kuntzen's panzer corps led the attack, spearheaded by the 19th and 20th Panzer Divisions and supported by the four infantry divisions of XXXX Army Corps (206th, 110th, 102nd and 256th). The attack was launched on 22 August and progressed rapidly, enveloping the Soviet Twenty-Second Army and retaking Velikie Luki.[53] Yet, as with all other major encirclements on Bock's front, large numbers of Soviet forces managed to slip through the German ring. As Halder noted on 25 August, 'At Velikie Luki it seems that noteworthy enemy elements are escaping our encirclement. Our motorized units now have such low combat strength that they do not have enough men to seal off large areas.'[54] By 26 August Kuntzen's forces had taken 34,000 prisoners and more than three hundred guns.[55] The advance then continued eastwards and ended with the capture of Toropets, 70 kilometres east of Velikie Luki, on 29 August. The offensive was an operational success similar to the achievement in the south at Gomel, but the scope and scale of German operations was clearly much reduced from those launched in June and July. The panzer groups were not at the end of their strength; however, they had been significantly reduced in machines, manpower and logistical support. Most importantly, any chance of fulfilling Operation Barbarossa's mandate and ending the war had certainly passed.

Beyond the military cost inflicted upon the Red Army by Army Group Centre's flank operations, the greatest windfall for Germany was Stalin's own strategic assessment. The Soviet dictator was convinced that these attacks were merely tactical diversions intended to distract attention or draw off resources from the vital Smolensk–Moscow axis.[56] Accordingly, the Soviet Western, Reserve and Briansk Fronts were now anticipating the wrong operation, while Bock and Rundstedt focused their plans on the Ukraine and Kirponos's vulnerable South-Western Front. Hitler, of course, could not know this; it was merely his good fortune that Soviet plans now aided his own.

It was this strategic calculation that persuaded Hitler of his opportunity in the south. He was also unconvinced of Moscow's importance and of course eager to seize valuable economic objectives in the eastern Ukraine and southern Volga. Indeed, more than at any time since late July the outlook cheered Hitler, who had previously vacillated over how the war in the east should be continued. Hitler had been under profound pressure from his army commanders to act against his own instincts, resulting in what Blumentritt described as 'endless arguments'.[57] Yet, having recovered his inner resolve and with the strategic crisis now behind him, his Luftwaffe adjutant, Nicolaus von Below, records that Hitler took a 'very positive' outlook on the war's progress. Indeed, Below continued, 'He was of the opinion that during September Stalin would be forced to bolster the front with his last reserves. If these could be bled white, the hard resistance would cease and our units would only have to march onwards.'[58] Yet Below also alluded to the questionable nature of Hitler's outlook as the gruelling reality of the fighting in the east laid bare the many difficulties of the campaign. '[Hitler's] optimism was on some days clearly justified, then, however, came reports which spoke of tough resistance and heavy fighting.'[59]

Certainly the men in the field were under far fewer illusions about the difficulties of the campaign. Indeed the further one progresses down the chain of command the grimmer the picture of the war and its prospects becomes. Bock was deeply dismayed at the loss of the Moscow operation and this had a profound impact on how he saw his 'increasingly weakened army group' being able to end the war. On 25 August he wrote in his diary, 'They apparently do not wish to exploit under any circumstances the opportunity to decisively defeat the Russians before winter! ... If, after all the successes, the campaign in the east now trickles away in dismal defensive fighting for my army group, it is not my fault.'[60] Kesselring also lamented Hitler's choice, and he not only believed that the certain capture of Moscow had been forsaken, but also what he absurdly described as the 'probability' of pushing further east to sever 'Russia in Europe' from its 'Asiatic potential'.[61]

The supposed lost opportunity at Moscow was not what bothered the lower levels of the German army; rather it was the general resilience of the enemy and the unanswered question of how the war was to be ended. In a letter on 23 August, General of Infantry Gotthard Heinrici, who commanded the XXXXIII Army Corps, wrote of his conviction that the Red Army's resistance would not end even if Moscow could be captured. Heinrici then continued, 'A change will only come with the internal collapse of the Russian system.' Heinrici, however, doubted the likelihood of such an outcome and a week later, in a second letter to his wife, he gave up any hope at all of an end in 1941: 'I am convinced that this will last a while longer. It will not be ended in this year.'[62] In similar fashion in October 1943, General of Panzer Troops Wilhelm Ritter von Thoma, who in September 1941 (at that time a major-general) commanded the 17th Panzer Division, wrote in his diary, 'When the war had not been brought to a successful conclusion by the autumn of 1941, I used every opportunity at conferences to make known my opinion that the whole situation for Germany was becoming extremely critical since time was against us and America would certainly come in on the other side.'[63]

Perhaps most revealing of all was the view from below, where a sizable number of German soldiers, in the face of unrelenting propaganda, still managed to draw their own conclusions about the progress of the war. In a letter home on 26 August, Heinz Küchler wrote:

> *The English and Russians have marched into Persia [Iran]; the fires burn on as does the murder. Still, it seems hardly anyone knows where all of this will lead. Sometimes discussions circulate among small groups about this or that incident and about the future; no one is optimistic; only each person's raw courage can prepare them for what is coming, in which deceitful ideas, false idols and fallacious wisdom will collapse and must collapse. This generation will no longer experience peace, quiet or contentment; warfare will remain for many years . . .* [64]

Many soldiers, however, did not trouble their thoughts with circumstances beyond their control; rather they preferred to concentrate on more immediate matters. In his diary on 1 September, Wilhelm Prüller wrote simply of returning home and his dashed hopes that after so many battles and weeks of advancing he could only look forward to more of the same. Prüller then alluded to his fears for the future as well as his hope that providence would preserve him, 'for then it will end well', he concluded.[65]

With the resolution of the German strategic crisis, the army command was reluctantly forced into the operation in the south, which did, however, hold two significant advantages. Firstly, the renewed German attack was to strike the Soviet lines at their weakest point and follow an axis of advance that offered the prospect of encircling the entire Soviet South-Western Front. The preconditions for such an immense battle were therefore in place, but success was by no means guaranteed. The outcome depended as much on the German direction of the operation as it did on Soviet countermoves. By late August there was almost certainly no chance of Stalin maintaining his grip on Kiev, but the fate of the Soviet South-Western Front and its five armies (Fifth, Twenty-Sixth, Thirty-Seventh, Thirty-Eighth and Fortieth[66]) was still undecided and its destruction was by no means preordained. The second important advantage for Hitler's push to the south was the size of the operational area. Unless a timely Soviet withdrawal took place, the potential pocket would be truly enormous, but the distances that German motorized forces would have to cover to close the ring were shorter than those demanded by past envelopments. This therefore offered an operation that took account of Germany's reduced combat strength as well as its threadbare logistical apparatus. Given the changed nature of the campaign in the east and the fact that a war of resources had replaced any prospect of dealing the Soviet Union a knock-out blow in 1941, Hitler's southern operation promised the greatest return for the limited number of resources available.

The spearhead of Guderian's thrust south was undertaken by Schweppenburg's XXIV Panzer Corps, with Lemelsen's XXXXVII Panzer Corps on his left flank and the infantry of Weichs's Second Army on his right. During his short visit to the Wolf's Lair, Guderian claimed to have been promised by Hitler that while undertaking his southern operation, his army group would not be split up.[67] Previously Guderian had exhibited an extreme aversion to any of his forces being removed from his command, and whenever this took place he bombarded Bock and Army Group Centre with daily, and sometimes hourly, requests for their return. In fact it was not beyond him to reinterpret a situation in whatever way was necessary to ensure the maximum chance of having his requests approved. Guderian's forcefulness was in some ways the hallmark of his success, but it also blinded him to the bigger picture. It was this lack of awareness, as well as concern, which allowed him to behave in such an obstinate manner. Now the issue of splitting his command arose again; only this time it was not just a division, but a whole panzer corps that was being subtracted from his order of battle. General of Panzer Troops Heinrich Freiherr von Vietinghoff's XXXXVI Panzer Corps was to be subordinated to the newly reinstated Fourth Army,[68] as it was thought to be too far north to participate in Guderian's offensive[69] and was in any case the only mobile reserve behind Kluge's endangered Yel'nya salient (see map 6). Guderian first learned of the order on 24 August and immediately called Bock to insist that the corps be returned to his command. Bock pointed out the threat to the Fourth Army's front, but Guderian showed no understanding of why

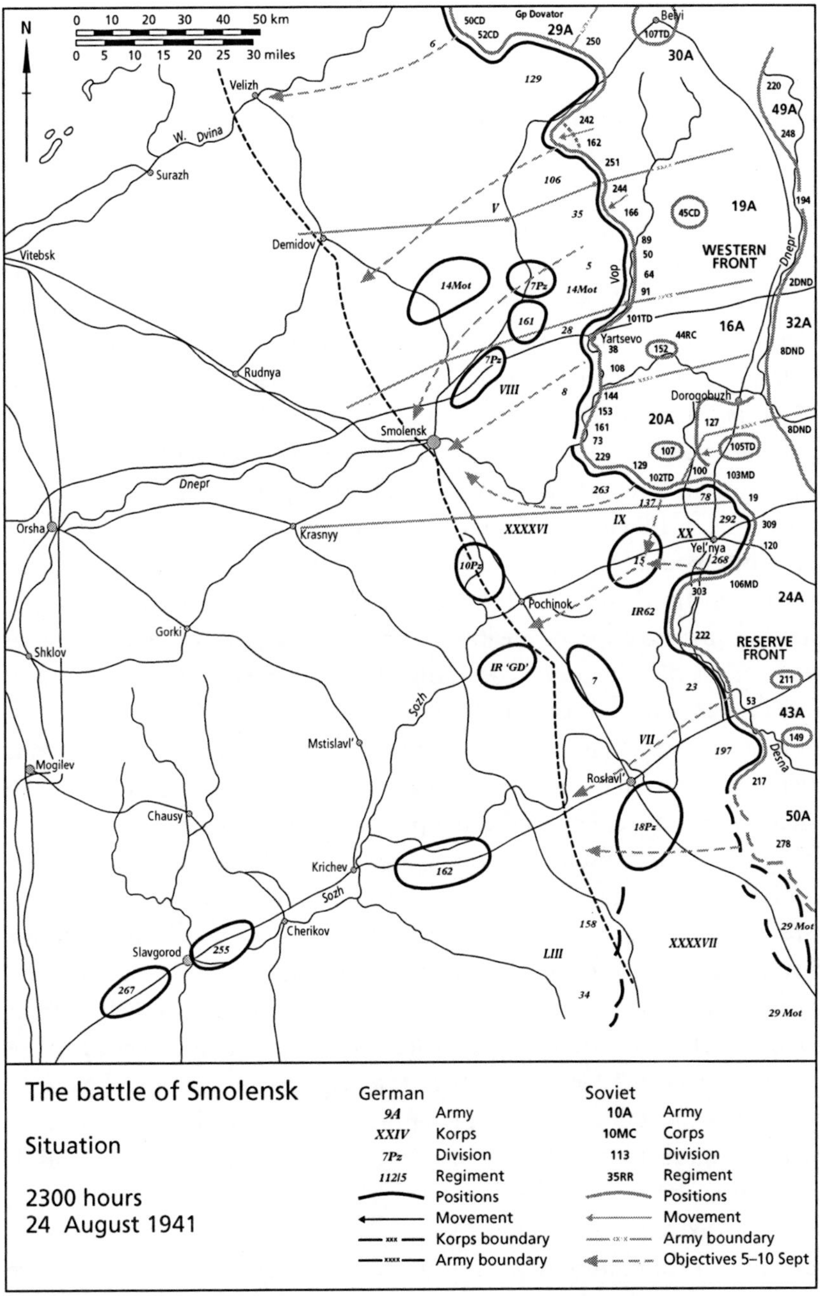

Map 6 Dispositions of Army Group Centre on 24 August 1941
Source: Glantz, *Atlas of the Battle of Smolensk.*

panzer forces should be used in a defensive battle.[70] Instead Guderian argued in his memoir that the matter was simply a petty retaliation by the army command for his perceived defection to Hitler's plan. Guderian stated that Halder 'did his best to hinder me' and thus his offensive south proceeded with 'a force which had already been recognised and described as inadequate'.[71]

Just how inadequate Guderian's forces were and the struggle they faced to enact an encirclement of the Soviet South-Western Front has found little place in the secondary literature. Rather the battle of Kiev is almost exclusively seen as yet another example of Germany's continuing dominance in mobile operations. The scale of the battle, which is renowned for its tremendous numbers of Soviet POWs and captured booty, is often discussed without any reference to German losses or the cost to the seriously faltering panzer forces. Guderian himself had argued on 23 August that the demands of the offensive in the south would 'preclude the success of *another* comprehensive operation being launched before the onset of winter'.[72] Indeed, the refitting of Bock's panzer groups, ostensibly planned for August, was at best a lacklustre series of half-measures, stunted by the critical lack of spare parts and adequate rest. Accordingly, a report from Army Group Centre on 22 August noted, 'The armoured units are so battle-weary and worn out that there can be no question of a mass operative mission until they have been completely replenished and repaired.'[73] Notwithstanding such dire forecasts, all of the senior German commanders were advocating some kind of major offensive. Schweppenburg's XXIV Panzer Corps reported on the same day (22 August), 'Every panzer is only provisionally fit for service. As a result of oil shortages no oil changes can be undertaken. If the panzers are committed to a large-scale operation in their current condition then the total loss of most must be expected.'[74] The problem stemmed from the fact that, beyond the rigours of battle, in 1941 the concept of the 'tank conveyer', the practice of moving tanks on trailers or rail wagons to avoid wear and tear, was in its infancy. As a result German tanks advanced everywhere under their own power, which, given the extreme condition of Soviet roads, produced a sharp fall-out rate. Engines, air filters, driving gears, track sprockets and grousers were rapidly overwhelmed by dust, but even secondary moving parts, such as turret traverses and gun elevators, soon succumbed.[75] In Schweppenburg's panzer corps the provisional combat readiness of the tanks was compounded by their reduced numbers. On 22 August Model's 3rd

Panzer Division, which had begun the war with 198 tanks, was now down to just 60. Langermann-Erlancamp's 4th Panzer Division, which only days earlier had been reduced to 44 machines, had managed to raise its number of serviceable tanks to 64, utilizing every provisional expedient.[76] Lemelsen's XXXXVII Panzer Corps had had much more time out of the line and was considerably stronger. The 17th Panzer Division fielded 74 tanks (down from 180 at the start of the war) and the 18th Panzer Division 114 tanks (with a starting total of 200).[77]

Given the tenuous mechanical condition of the panzer divisions and their susceptibility to breakdown, it is not surprising that the real obstacles to Guderian's advance were the Soviet roads. Moreover, it was not enough just to drive the tanks forward: they also had to be supplied. The main arterial leading south, the 60 kilometre stretch of road from Roslavl to Mglin, was described as 'very bad', with 'long stretches of sand' upon which the '*Grosstransportraum* cannot be made to move'.[78] It was hardly surprising, therefore, that vehicles and drivers were being pushed to the limit of their endurance, yet with the laborious conversion of the Soviet railroads and inadequate capacity of the German rail system, trucks had to fill the void.

On the eve of Guderian's offensive his remaining forces were certainly feeling the effects of two months' hard fighting on the eastern front. Yet their goal was now clear and the majority of his men still retained faith in some form of German victory. At 5 a.m. on 25 August Guderian's panzers, backed by the Second Army, launched their renewed offensive towards the south, this time with the resolute goal of driving into the Ukraine and encircling the Soviet South-Western Front. It was the beginning of Operation Barbarossa's single largest battle, and indeed, the largest encirclement of World War II.

Attack and parry – Bock's late August dilemma

In late August Kirponos's South-Western Front occupied a deep triangular-shaped salient with its apex fixed on Kiev. Running counterclockwise from the top, Kirponos's long flanks were under attack by Guderian's Panzer Group 2 and Weichs's Second Army; then under Army Group South came Reichenau's Sixth Army and in the southern bend of the Dnepr, Stülpnagel's Seventeenth Army and Kleist's Panzer Group 1.[79] Even before the start of German operations the Soviet position was precarious. Kirponos was in practice already half encircled and his strongest formations were not the ones opposing the dangerous German panzer groups on the outer flanks. Still, just as in the north on Bock's front, Stalin believed he understood German intentions in the south. The headlong charge of Mackensen's III Panzer Corps to Dnepropetrovsk, and the subsequent days of heavy fighting that the corps engaged in to win a bridgehead on the eastern bank of the Dnepr, deceived Stalin into thinking that, here too, the Germans intended to strike out further towards the east.[80] Kirponos was not blind to the peril he was in, but his hands were tied.

As Guderian was poised to begin his drive south, Kleist's panzer group was far from being able to offer any assistance. The hard battles of June and July, followed by the long drive into the bend of the Dnepr in August, had taken their toll. The panzer corps urgently required a period of rest and refitting, especially before another major operation. Yet, just as Hoth's and Guderian's panzer groups were forced into new operations and strenuous defensive actions, so too was Kleist denied the respite he desired. Having engaged the outer defensive zone of Dnepropetrovsk on 17 August, Mackensen's panzer corps was then forced into bitter fighting, first to cross the Dnepr River and establish a bridgehead, and then to win control of the city on the north-eastern bank.[81] In his post-war memoir Mackensen described the fighting in the bridgehead as '[l]ong, hard and difficult'.[82] In addition to denying the corps a much-needed rest, the city fighting was essentially attritional in nature, requiring enormous quantities of munitions, which the panzer group's overextended logistical apparatus could scarcely supply. Panzer Group 1's quartermaster reported that by 6 September some 40,000 tons of artillery shells had been fired in support of positions at Dnepropetrovsk.[83] This astounding figure is all the more remarkable when one considers that the participating 60th Motorized Infantry Division was transporting its supplies from dumps an average of 200 kilometres, and in extreme cases up to 500 kilometres, from the battle zone.[84] The result cast doubt over whether sufficient supplies could be brought up to replenish Kleist's remaining two corps (XXXXVIII and XIV Panzer Corps). Stülpnagel's Seventeenth Army did what it could to assist Kleist by sharing its own resources and the army group provided some extra resources for the *Grosstransportraum*, yet despite such measures the situation on 24 August remained 'precarious'.[85] The following day, as Guderian was beginning his offensive south, Kleist's panzer group was reduced to making impossible demands on

Army Group South. As the quartermaster's war diary records, 'For the intended replenishment period of ten days it is necessary that the panzer group is provided with fourteen supply trains a day.'[86] In the light of the fact that Rundstedt's whole army group had been promised twelve supply trains a day and was on some days receiving only half of these, the panzer group's request remained utterly impossible.[87] As a result the panzer group's extremely limited transport capacity had first to meet the needs of the ongoing battle at Dnepropetrovsk, 'instead of being used for the replenishment'.[88]

In spite of the difficulties and lack of supplies the refitting phase went ahead. Even if only to conduct the most provisional maintenance and permit rest for the exhausted men, the respite was a welcome one. Lieutenant-General Werner Kempf's XXXXVIII Panzer Corps began its rest and refitting on 27 August and was joined on the following day by General of Infantry Gustav von Wietersheim's XIV Panzer Corps.[89] Although the panzer corps accepted the absence of spare parts as a result of the logistical constrains, in truth the problem ran much deeper. Germany simply did not possess the means to repair, much less replace, the thousands of vehicles being lost in the east. As the Army Quartermaster-General, Major-General Eduard Wagner, explained to Halder on 26 August, 'Truck situation is beginning to become difficult. Replacements only possible in exceedingly small quantities.'[90]

Although Halder could do little about Germany's endemic shortage of vehicles, his actions did not always reflect an appropriate awareness of the problem. On 25 August as elements of the 13th Panzer Division forged their initial crossing over the Dnepr at Dnepropetrovsk, the question arose as to whether their positions should be expanded and built into a defensible bridgehead. At Army Group South, Rundstedt was of the firm opinion that such a step should not be taken, but referred the matter to the OKH for approval. According to Army Group South's war diary, 'The commander of the army group advises that the bridgehead not be held because it would lead to a disproportionately large demand on strength and munitions, which would delay the replenishment of the panzer group.'[91] Halder responded an hour and a half later that the bridgehead must be held. He was prepared to accept such a heavy burden in spite of the fact that the bridgehead had not been planned and served little immediate strategic purpose. The site chosen for the eventual thrust across the Dnepr into the South-Western Front's rear was at Kremenchug, some 130 kilometres to the northwest. Moreover when Sodenstern, Rundstedt's Chief of Staff, spoke with Halder to emphasize the limits of the panzer group's offensive strength after committing to the Dnepropetrovsk bridgehead, Halder refused to countenance any such talk. 'The Chief of the General Staff [Halder] will not allow this objection and stresses that at the deciding moment no insurmountable difficulties will be accepted and that the necessary measures must be carried out.'[92] It was typical for Halder to engage in overly optimistic operational assessments, in spite of clear evidence to the contrary – an outlook which had plagued Barbarossa since its inception. Yet he also ascribed a disproportionate value to the power of individual 'will' as if the correct frame of mind could supplant all other obstacles. It was a belief best exemplified by Hitler himself,[93] but also shared by many in the army at that time. The implications of such thinking, and its delusory power to conjure optimism in the face of the greatest peril or materiel absence, led the German army into many self-deceiving decisions, which predictably ended in disaster. Writing after the war Halder nevertheless emphasized the 'psychological values' of command as paramount. 'It becomes very clear that a strong military leader with great powers of motivation is the most important factor for success.'[94] The fallacy of this maxim is exemplified many times in World War II and the decision to seek a bridgehead at Dnepropetrovsk in late August was only one such occasion.

On 25 August Guderian's panzer group was finally set in motion to the south. While initial prospects for success appeared encouraging, the loss of the XXXXVI Panzer Corps reduced Guderian's strength by a third and the condition of the spearheading XXIV Panzer Corps was doubtful. As Guderian noted, Schweppenburg's corps was beginning a new operation 'without having had any time for rest and maintenance; and this after a long and uninterrupted sequence of heavy battles and exhausting marches'.[95] The initial advance was aided therefore by the utter disarray of the opposing forces in the Soviet Central Front which was reported to have offered only 'weak enemy resistance'.[96] Indeed, on the same day the *Stavka* agreed to disband the hapless Central Front and unify its forces under Eremenko's Briansk Front with the aim of providing centralized direction to the man charged with stopping Guderian. Thus, Eremenko now commanded the Fiftieth, Third, Thirteenth and Twenty-First Armies, but was also now solely responsible for the principal section of the endangered front.[97] To make matters worse, only the Fiftieth Army was fresh and capable of undertaking sustained offensive action; however, mistaken Soviet intelligence suggested that Eremenko was about to suffer a major blow on his northern (right) wing. Shaposhnikov, Zhukov's replacement as Chief of the General Staff, ordered Eremenko to reinforce this sector with the Fiftieth Army, which meant in practice that it was heading away from the threatened sector to meet a non-existent danger. The blunder was greatly to weaken Eremenko's counterattacks, which became an exceptionally tall order for the many battered and understrength divisions of the Briansk Front.[98]

Although organized Soviet resistance varied from haphazard to almost non-existent, a more formidable obstacle slowed Guderian's forces. According to German war diaries, the Soviet 'roads' south of Roslavl could barely be dignified by such a distinction. Typically they consisted of little more than sandy farm tracks, more accustomed to the light traffic of small horses and peasant carts. The advent of dozens of tanks and hundreds of heavily loaded trucks soon turned them into quagmires, even in the absence of rain. In the 4th Panzer Division's sector south of Unscha the trucks were constantly getting bogged down and those that could not be dug out had to be pulled out with tractors.[99] The war diary of Lemelsen's XXXXVII Panzer Corps noted that movement was 'exceedingly slow and difficult'. Indeed, the many small streams that crisscrossed the area and could not be skirted were even more of a problem than the dire state of the roads. Their bridges had to be reinforced or rebuilt as they were too weak to support the traffic, and in the worst affected areas even the deployment of all the available engineering units could not avert hours of delay.[100] Even Guderian, who was travelling in the area, got stuck so badly that he had to signal for replacement armoured command vehicles, personnel trucks and motorcycles. As he noted in his memoir, the experience 'was a grim omen for the future'.[101]

As a result of the Red Army's disorder, the best chance of halting Guderian's offensive in its earliest phase was utterly squandered. Barring Guderian's path to the Ukraine was the Desna River, which stood as a formidable natural barrier with strong defensive advantages. Not only was it an obvious place to defend, but it was vital not to allow Guderian to seize any of its large bridges intact. On 25 August, as Model's 3rd Panzer Division fought its way towards the town of Novgorod-Severskii on the Desna, Panzer Group 2 received reports that its great bridge spanning the river had been destroyed.[102] These reports, however, proved incorrect and through a combination of astounding Soviet ineptitude, good luck and swift action on the part of two German lieutenants, the bridge was seized intact on the morning of 26 August.[103] The importance of this achievement was summed up in the 3rd Panzer Division's war diary: 'Given the wide riverbed and swampy banks the bridge, with a length of 800 metres, spanned an otherwise almost impassable obstacle.'[104] As Model remarked to one of the two lieutenants involved in its capture, 'This bridge is as good as a whole division.'[105] Guderian recalled that the news was 'surprising and most gratifying',[106] while Halder, still unconvinced of the opportunity in the south, was trying to make sense of Soviet strategy. After he was informed of the captured bridge, Halder's diary hints at his enduring scepticism: 'In the Desna bend he will try to block our crossing of the river with typical Russian doggedness. It is not to be discounted that a sustained defensive position will first be encountered at the Sula–Konotop line. The future role of Kiev is not yet possible to see.'[107] Perhaps Hitler's own reluctance, evidenced later in the war, to surrender large population centres gave him an insight into his fellow dictator's frame of mind. In any case Hitler was much more convinced of the opportunity in the south and the role of Kiev. For Halder's part, the destructive lengths to which Stalin was prepared to go to try and defend Kiev would soon become startlingly apparent.

Having seized the vital bridge at Novgorod-Severskii, Model now had to ensure it was held and therefore a bridgehead was built to a depth of 8 kilometres. On the following day (27 August) strenuous Soviet efforts were made to retake the eastern bank of the river and destroy the bridge. The fragile German bridgehead came under intense Soviet pressure and was reduced in size, but the defensive lines eventually held the attack.[108] A recurring problem in holding forward sections of the line was the contracting mobility of the panzer group, which was vital for moving up infantry support. Bad roads and a chronic lack of oil resulted in many vehicles being left behind and Schweppenburg's only motorized infantry division (the 10th) was in danger of becoming a standard hoof-and-foot-based division. A report from the 10th Motorized Infantry Division on 27 August made clear the extent of its decline:

> *Aside from earlier fallouts, 30 per cent of the remaining trucks are sitting with some form of damage on the road north of Surash. As a result of the catastrophic oil shortage, from which the majority of this damage stems, there will be even more trucks lost. Consequently, the battalions in the*

Fig. 6 Even if bridges could be captured intact, they often still had to be strengthened before German tanks could attempt crossings.

> *front sometimes consist of just five platoons and are often without heavy weapons. The division will reach the Desna in some cases on foot and almost without heavy weapons.*[109]

As the 10th Motorized Infantry Division struggled to the Desna, the oil shortage became so severe that it alone threatened to halt the German offensive. The war diary of the 4th Panzer Division also reported losing trucks for lack of oil, and then on 29 August it stated that a renewed attack could only be undertaken by fifteen tanks – the only ones with any oil.[110] The quartermaster of the 3rd Panzer Division noted 'the supply routes are always getting longer', with munitions for the division having to be supplied from Mali, provisions from Roslavl and fuel from Mglin.[111] In addition to the oil shortage and the growing distances, the roads remained disastrous. The XXXXVII Panzer Corps reported 'extraordinary delays' in its march route,[112] while the subordinated 18th Panzer Division noted that at one particularly bad stretch 'almost every single vehicle must be pulled out of the sand by tractors'.[113] The wretched state of the roads on 27 August caused the Quartermaster-General of Panzer Group 2 to stress that supplies could no longer be dependably assured along the main route from Roslavl–Mglin–Starrodub. The report continued, 'Increasingly more vehicles break down and must be towed, which is time-consuming work. Assessing the fuel – and especially the oil situation – makes the worst apparent.'[114] At the OKH Halder noted on 28 August that 38,000 trucks had been lost since the start of the war, with half of all these coming from the panzer groups and the remainder from the armies and their mass of constituent infantry divisions. At the same time Halder recorded that Guderian's panzer group retained only 45 per cent of its tank strength,[115] while Kleist's panzer group had 50 per cent.[116] By the end of August the *Ostheer* had lost some 1,488 armoured fighting vehicles and received just 96 replacements from new production.[117] It was a large and unsustainable rate of loss that was made worse by the fact that the remaining tanks were, in many cases, only in a provisional state of repair, which rendered their service highly conditional.

On the afternoon of 27 August Lieutenant-General Friedrich Paulus, the Senior Quartermaster I at the OKH, arrived at Panzer Group 2. Guderian seized the opportunity to push again for additional reinforcements. Guderian claimed that Weichs's Second Army was advancing south-west in an operationally adverse direction and that it was now separated from the XXIV Panzer Corps's right flank. The result was a 75 kilometre gap. Guderian also noted that the eastern (left) flank of Schweppenburg's corps was similarly insecure and, instead of being guarded, was merely under observation. The best solution, according to Guderian, was no less than the transfer to his command of Weichs's XIII and XXXXIII Army Corps as well as the 1st Cavalry Division. Additionally, Guderian repeated his request that Vietinghoff's XXXXVI Panzer Corps reinforce his left flank.[118] Paulus agreed to support Guderian's request and his visit provided a convenient means of bypassing Army Group Centre and directing the appeal to Halder at the OKH.[119] Yet Guderian did not stop there. That evening he repeatedly called Bock's Chief of Staff, Major-General Hans von Greiffenberg, to demand reinforcements. Bock wrote in his diary that Guderian was 'very agitated' and was demanding the return of the XXXXVI Panzer Corps.[120] Bock then spoke with Halder and the two came to a quick agreement. They shared serious concerns about Army Group Centre's defensive front and were unable to see how Vietinghoff's corps could offer any real support to Guderian, owing to the distances (and roads) it would have to cover. Brauchitsch was also consulted and agreed that the release of the panzer corps could not yet be considered.[121] The only consolation for Guderian was Bock's agreement to move the 1st Cavalry Division closer to the XXIV Panzer Corps's right flank; however, that did little to placate the impetuous panzer commander.[122] Indeed, Guderian understood the decision with regard to not the strength of differing military priorities, but rather 'the general animosity towards myself that reigned in those quarters'.[123]

Headstrong and uncompromising, Guderian was not about to be deterred and, in spite of his brash manner, there was a certain justification for his requests. On the other hand, Bock's need for a reserve panzer corps to help safeguard his long and thinly held front was also justified, but with Guderian's advance already slowing and his flanks increasing in length, more strength would be needed. The problem, at its root, highlights both the dearth of military resources on the eastern front and the declining strength of those already employed. The southern offensive had been underway for just three days, against exhausted Soviet formations, and already Schweppenburg's leading corps was suggesting that the advance would have to be halted.[124]

On 28 August Paulus, true to his word, attempted to influence Bock in favour of Guderian's request. The next day (29 August) Guderian resumed his calls to Army Group Centre, making the usual claims, but, as was typical of Guderian, he went too far and depicted the situation in a manner calculated to achieve his goal, but not in line with reality. On this occasion Bock caught him out, noting in his diary, 'One of the reasons behind the request, the threat to the western flank of the panzer group, has been rendered invalid, because the panzer corps on the right wing carelessly informed Second Army that it did not feel threatened on its western flank.'[125] Nevertheless, Bock was still left to consider whether he should release at least part of Vietinghoff's corps. At heart Bock knew that the offensive must keep moving and that a sustained defensive posture was not an option for Germany. On 30 August Guderian answered a request from the army group for a further clarification of the situation. 'I wish it was less angry and clearer,' was Bock's reaction to the report, but, notwithstanding his enduring concerns, Bock now opted to release the Infantry Regiment *Grossdeutschland*.[126] For his part, Guderian was singularly unimpressed. He considered this a distinct half-measure, calling it a 'drop by drop method of reinforcement',[127] and the panzer commander would maintain his pressure on Bock for still greater support. What Guderian did not know, or could scarcely appreciate, was the extent of the pressure Army Group Centre's defensive front was under and the crisis this had created.

Since the second week of August Timoshenko's Western Front and Zhukov's Reserve Front had been engaged in vigorous offensives against Bock's eastern flank. Results varied. Little ground was seized and casualties were very high, but Bock's army group was plunged into its worst crisis to date. After the hard-fought battles at Minsk and Smolensk, which were supposed to have torn open the Soviet front and provided a clear line of advance to Moscow, the sense of shock was palpable. Not only had the Soviets continued to maintain a solid front, but they were now attacking with tremendous strength. Army Group Centre was in no way prepared for such an eventuality and the defensive front repeatedly threatened to buckle wherever motorized reserves could not be found to plug local Soviet breakthroughs. As Halder noted on 15 August, 'The front of the army group, with its forty divisions over 730 kilometres, is so strained that moving to a determined defence entails far-reaching considerations, which have not been thought through in detail. The present deposition and line organization is in no way suited for a sustained defence.'[128] Yet a sustained defence was what was required, only now the motorized forces were engaged in attacks on the extreme flanks. Hoth's Panzer Group 3 had already been forced to give up General Rudolf Schmidt's XXXIX Panzer Corps to Army Group North and Kuntzen's LVII Panzer Corps was committed to its offensive towards Velikie Luki and Toropets. Guderian was attacking towards the south with two panzer corps, leaving only Vietinghoff's corps for security south of Smolensk. Not surprisingly, Bock was averse to giving it up, especially since it consisted of only one panzer division (the 10th) as well as the battle-scarred 2nd SS Division *Das Reich* and the Infantry Regiment *Grossdeutschland*. For security north of Smolensk, there was no reserve panzer corps, but the Ninth Army retained control of the 7th Panzer Division and the 14th Motorized Infantry Division.

While Soviet attacks throughout the middle of August had been forcefully pursued, the *Stavka* now sought to counter Bock's movements on the flanks by an expanded and reinforced offensive in his centre. Indeed, there was considerable optimism in the Soviet command that Army Group Centre could be pushed back. Accordingly, on 25 August the first co-ordinated offensives were simultaneously launched between Timoshenko's, Zhukov's and Eremenko's fronts. The Western Front was ordered to capture Velizh, Demidov and Smolensk, while the Reserve Front was instructed to eliminate the Yel'nya salient and capture Roslavl. At the same time, the Briansk Front was ordered to thwart Guderian by driving towards both Roslavl and Novozybkov.[129] Although the *Stavka* remained hopeful that its lofty operational goals could be obtained, at the very least it was believed that the grand offensive would put an end to the troublesome attacks on Bock's flanks.

One of the most vulnerable sectors on Bock's front was the Yel'nya salient, which had been the scene of intense blood-letting for more than a month. General of Infantry Hermann Geyer commanded the defending IX Army Corps and reported to Army Group Centre on the first day of the Soviet attacks that the losses of the 263rd Infantry Division 'cannot be borne much longer'. In the past week alone the division had lost roughly 1,000 men and another 1,100 since the start of August.[130] The fighting resembled the trench warfare and artillery duels of World War I and Geyer noted that the same tactics proved themselves valid even after twenty-five years. Almost the same routine repeated itself over and over again: an immense Soviet bombardment followed by a massed ground assault into the German defences and concluded by local German counterattacks to repel the frequent penetrations. After the war Geyer claimed that Soviet attacks had almost been successful in achieving a total breakthrough, but were held at the last minute by the desperate commitment of every last reserve.[131] While conditions in the Yel'nya salient were bloody and unremitting, the state of affairs in the rest of the Fourth Army was not much better. Blumentritt, the Chief of Staff at Fourth Army, noted that the static warfare and persistent Soviet attacks placed almost insufferable demands on the infantry. Commenting on the ebb and flow of activity from the middle of August and into September, Blumentritt wrote:

> *Without any considerable armoured support, we were reduced to trench warfare along the Desna, which made very heavy demands on the troops. The Russians attacked violently and over and over again succeeded in breaking through our thinly held lines. Tank units had to be called in to make good the damage. This taught us that in modern*

> *warfare infantry requires armoured support not only in the attack but also in the defence.*
>
> *When I say our lines were thin, this is not an understatement. Divisions were assigned sectors almost twenty miles wide. Furthermore, in view of the heavy casualties already suffered in the course of the campaign, these divisions were usually understrength and tactical reserves were non-existent.*[132]

On the northern flank of Army Group Centre Hoth's Ninth Army was also under great pressure. On the first day of the renewed offensive (25 August) Bock wrote in his diary, 'It can't hold much longer the way things look now.'[133] On the following day, after a worrying report from Hoth, Bock agreed to commit all of his reserves, but he conceded that this was only a short-term solution. In the absence of any other troops, Bock weighed his options and reasoned that he could neither withdraw his line, owing to the fact that there was no suitable line to defend until the Dnepr, nor counterattack, which was his preference, but for which he lacked the forces.[134] In the meantime the defensive front would just have to hold – a circumstance that was aided by the outdated tactics of many Soviet officers, who senselessly directed massed frontal assaults. During many of these attacks wave after wave of men were sent forward across open fields with bayonets fixed. The attempts to break through the German lines with raw manpower were seldom very successful and for the most part ended up only grinding down the attacking Soviet rifle divisions. After one such attack the VI Army Corps estimated there were 3,000 enemy dead in front of its positions and the report concluded with incomprehension: 'unbelievable how many dead are lying in front of our lines'.[135] Fighting at the front, Günter von Scheven found it hard to comprehend the sheer scale of the killing. In a letter home he confided his revulsion: 'The last few days have placed a heavy burden on me. One cannot yet comprehend the annihilation of so much life. The desperate and wild breakthrough attempts of the Russians hit, surprisingly to us, in the middle of our front with panzers, infantry and Cossacks. I am too shattered to grasp it all.'[136] Another German soldier who endured a similar such frontal attack remembered the spectacle with a mixture of morbid fascination and sheer horror:

Expressionless, their dull eyes fixed into the distance as if, fascinated by the rattle of our guns, they would run into our hail of fire... Again and again they would come, soulless, like puppets in a dreadful marionette, with the same short and jerky movements: everything about them was mechanical, without a soul. That was perhaps the most horrible of our experiences on the eastern front, mechanical dying.[137]

While the Red Army may have been capable of mechanical dying in 1941, it was not all they were capable of and the common depiction of an inept peasant army in the early months of the war is quite inaccurate. The Red Army's mastery of combined arms warfare in the latter half of the war was not a sudden occurrence, nor simply attributable to lessons learned from the Germans. It was built on the back of countless earlier defeats as well as a share of localized victories, where successful junior commanders and their innovative ideas slowly gained in stature. In short the Red Army in 1941 was capable of mechanical dying when demanded, but also of industrial killing when adequately resourced and well directed.[138] The implications for Germany only appeared on a grand scale at the end of 1942, but smaller tactical engagements sometimes reflected remarkable Soviet aptitude as early as the summer of 1941. On 17 August Hans-Albert Giese noted how a local Soviet attack on an artillery position 5 kilometres from his post left ninety Germans dead.[139] In another attack at the end of August a German survivor recalled the speed and effectiveness of a Soviet cavalry assault:

We had no proper sentries... just a few men strolling about with their rifles slung over their shoulders, as the whole 16th Motorised was meant to be between us and the Russians... A short time afterwards there was the sound of horses, and... a dust cloud to the south. Some people said that it was a supply column for one of the Hungarian divisions. Then they were upon us... sturdy little horses at a gallop through our camp. Some of the Russians were using sub-machine guns, others were swinging sabres. I saw two men killed by the sword less than ten metres from me... think of that, eighty years after Sadowa![140] *They had*

> *towed up a number of those heavy, two-wheeled machine guns; after a few minutes whistles began to blow and the horsemen faded away; the machine gunners started blasting us at very close ranges with enfilade fire... soon tents and lorries were ablaze and through it the screams of wounded men caught in the flames...* [141]

Clearly, even considering the Red Army's many defeats and heavy losses in the 1941 summer campaign, underestimating its offensive potential could prove a fatal mistake.

Hoth's interim command of the Ninth Army had been a harrowing initiation, which suddenly worsened into a full-blown crisis on 27 and 28 August. Arduous defensive battles had been raging since he took command, and with Bock's reserves already committed, there was only the 7th Panzer Division left when the 14th Motorized Infantry Division's northern wing was overrun on 27 August.[142] Its lines were simply rolled over by the concentrated use of Soviet tanks supported by infantry. Isolated strong points remained, but without relief the situation threatened to become a major breakthrough.[143] Nor was the 14th Motorized Infantry Division the only division in desperate need of support. The 5th, 35th, 106th, 129th and 161st Infantry Divisions were all in critical need of relief, but the nearest reinforcements were five days away[144] and there was even a discussion about sending Vietinghoff's panzer corps to the Ninth Army. The exhaustion of the infantry divisions reached dangerous levels: the 161st Infantry Division, for example, was estimated to possess just 25 per cent of its combat strength and in eight days of heavy fighting had lost roughly 2,000 men and 57 officers.[145] At Army Group Centre, Bock was frantic. He had been warning since the middle of the month about the weakening of his front and the inability to hold sustained defensive positions, but now it appeared that a disintegration of the front was at hand. Speaking on the phone on the morning of 28 August, Bock told Halder, 'I must report to you that the situation on the defensive front of Ninth Army is very serious. It is such that an end to the resistance is foreseeable if the Russians remain on the offensive.' Finally, Bock asked the decisive question: 'What should I do then if as a result the front collapses?' To which Halder only offered the evasive answer: 'It was clear to me from the beginning that the mass of the Red Army was not in the south and not in the north, but rather opposite Army Group Centre.'[146] The dire situation forced Bock to consider seriously what would have been previously unthinkable. 'If Ninth Army fails to hold and Smolensk is lost, Fourth Army too will have to pull back . . . I briefed Hoth on this talk. He agrees with me on everything.'[147]

It was not only the strength of the Soviet attacks that created the crisis in Army Group Centre; it was also the cumulative effect of past battles and the growing lack of replacements for the divisions. Throughout the *Ostheer* losses far exceeded the replacements arriving from Germany. By 26 August, after just over eight weeks of warfare on the eastern front, the army had suffered the loss of a staggering 441,100 men, which equalled 11.67 per cent of the whole army on 22 June 1941.[148] In short, more than one in every ten men had now become a casualty. As Solomon Perel noted, 'In the beginning the dead were still buried in individual graves, but the closer we got to Moscow the more farm fields were turned into cemeteries.'[149] Alois Scheuer wrote home in a letter on 25 August that losses in his regiment (which was attached to the 197th Infantry Division defending Guderian's long left flank) had been so heavy that until reinforcements arrived the regiment was deemed 'in no way combat ready'.[150] Already by the middle of August Halder noted that the average fighting strength of the infantry divisions had shrunk by one-third.[151] To compensate for these losses the Replacement Army was sending just about everything to the eastern front; however, by the end of August only 217,000 men had arrived to fill the gaps. This left a deficit of 193,000 men, which was excessive for an army already attempting too much and increasingly bogged down in an enormous theatre of war. Another 100,000 replacement troops were on their way to the front,[152] but with only 46,000 men left in the Replacement Army by early September, it was clear that the *Ostheer* was in an irreversible decline.[153]

While outright casualties constituted a clear loss to the divisions, there was an additional loss of manpower often disguised in official figures. Sickness and physical ailments proliferated in the harsh conditions, especially given the demands of the advance and the continuous fighting.[154] Hygiene standards plummeted, food and water were often of a low standard and sanitation became extremely rudimentary. Wherever the front stalled for more than a few days at a time vermin, especially rats, appeared in increasing numbers and lived in close contact with the men.[155] Yet vermin were at least a familiar problem within the army; it was the vast and seemingly untouched stretches of the Soviet Union that presented the Germans with new problems. One post-war study noted that the forests and swamplands of the Soviet Union teemed with mosquitoes and isolated cases of malaria were recorded. The study also referred to a 'midsummer fly plague', which contributed to frequent cases of diarrhoea.[156] As one German soldier noted:

> *The flies and mosquitoes are a plague and I wonder what these blood-sucking pests lived on before we came along. We wear nets over our helmets but the beasts work their way up the sleeves and inside the collar. To halt is to be covered in a mass of these terrible biting insects and the inevitable flies.*[157]

Another soldier stated that the problem of mosquitoes was 'very bad' and that they were 'a lot to take'.[158] Yet probably the most common pest for the German soldiers was parasites, which became a serious hindrance in September as the night-time temperatures dropped and the men started to sleep in lice-infested peasant houses rather than in the open. Hans Pichler wrote in his diary in early September, 'For the last few days we are constantly sleeping in the unspeakably dirty Russian huts. In only these few days everyone, from the officers down to the last man, already have lice and have been bitten by bugs and fleas.'[159] A soldier from the SS *Das Reich* division recalled being sent to wake an officer in the middle of the night. Scanning the crowded hut with his torch, his account noted that 'As the light struck the wall of the stove, I dropped the flashlight in horror. A whole mass of bedbugs and other vermin marched in company files.'[160] To begin with the lice caused mild discomfort, but as they multiplied and spread around the body, the subject engaged in constant scratching and often experienced severe skin irritation. During the first year of the war the Germans did not have effective delousing powders and it was not until the end of 1942 that the front-line units received mobile delousing stations.[161] In the meantime the men began a nightly routine of picking out the lice from their clothes and bodies.[162] Such elementary cleaning actions could not rid the sufferer of lice, but it did reduce the maddening torments of constant itching. Helmut Günther explained the routine: 'Stripped to the waist, we sat around the table and killed lice. The corpses were laid out, side-by-side, nice and neatly, on a scrap of paper to see who was the champion this time. Last time, Albert had the fewest and had to forego his schnapps ration in our favour.'[163] The most serious repercussion of the lice epidemic was typhus. In some cases the disease spread so quickly that dozens of soldiers at a time became infected and whole companies had to be withdrawn from the line and placed in quarantine.[164]

Dysentery and cholera were other common illnesses on the eastern front.[165] They often stemmed from the poor standards of hygiene and especially from the consumption of unclean water or contaminated food. Blaming his illness on the supply of local water, Karl Fuchs, a tank gunner in the 7th Panzer Division, wrote home in a letter, 'The water is hardly good enough to wash with, so I guess I really shouldn't drink it.'[166] Another soldier noted, 'We are in a swamp but there is little water fit to drink. It is all brackish. Even water taken from wells tastes unpleasant and we have to boil every drop that we drink.'[167] Yet not all soldiers were so prudent. Alois Scheuer complained in his letters home about the difficulty of finding water, and when wells were located he noted that he and his comrades drank the dirty water believing they were 'hardened' and no longer sensitive to its effects. Soon his letters spoke of stomach problems.[168] The quality of the water supply varied from region to region in the European parts of the Soviet Union, but as a rule the northern areas tended to be better with the standard deteriorating as one moved south. Wells in the north were deeper, while in central and southern regions the water in the village wells was often scarce and warmer, facilitating the growth of bacteria.[169] Marching through the Ukraine, Gottlob Bidermann wrote:

> *We experienced a severe shortage of water, and the few deeply dug wells and cisterns not poisoned by the retreating enemy contained brackish water that varied from bad-tasting to undrinkable. The horses and soldiers had developed an unquenchable thirst as they laboured in the tormenting heat, and the shortage of water for the horses became so critical that even the strongest and most healthy had to be rotated in the harness often.*[170]

Hans-Albert Giese wrote that the water supply was known to be tainted, but that 'in this heat it tastes like wine or sparkling wine in France'.[171] Thirst and an ignorance of the dangers drove many men to drink contaminated water and the results were sometimes fatal, particularly given the inadequacy of medical care. Erich Kern described the ravaging effects of dysentery on his unit:

> *The hospitals were soon full and overcrowded. The first of my friends to catch it was Kaul [who subsequently died in hospital]. He complained of severe internal disorders, and when we met I saw true enough how terribly pale and thin he was... More and more cases of dysentery were reported. Some were discharged from the stomach hospital after one day, and came back to us full of ghastly stories about its horrors. Many of the sick had nothing but straw to lie on; there were no bed-pans and they had to make do with old steel helmets.*[172]

Another soldier complained that his stomach problems required hospitalization, but that there was no more room for him.[173] Given the dangers, the safest option was to obtain water directly from brooks and rivers, but even these could be dangerous as bloated bodies sometimes lingered upstream and cases of cadaveric poisoning were not unknown.[174] Nor was it just the water supply that impacted the health of the men. Livestock was routinely taken from local villages and prepared in the field by the men themselves, a practice which rarely facilitated a sound hygienic standard. The worsening September weather, replete with days of rain and cold night frosts, added further to the deteriorating health of the men, especially since it dramatically reduced their willingness to bathe and clean uniforms, which had become filthy and bug-ridden.[175] As instances of illness rose the wretchedness of conditions at the front was worsened by the growing absence of simple necessities. Razor blades, soap, toothpaste, toothbrushes, shoe-repairing materials, writing paper, needles and thread were all becoming scarce,[176] while the conquered territories offered hardly any consumer goods.[177]

Overall the general health of German troops on the eastern front during the first months of the war was maintained, but only barely. In expectation of a short campaign the men were pushed to their physical limits, lowering their immunity to ailments and providing a poor basis upon which to meet the extreme conditions that were to come. Casualty figures seldom took account of the numbers of ill soldiers who managed to remain at their post and, in any case, men had to exhibit serious symptoms of an illness before being excused from duty.[178] With already very high combat losses, the hidden costs of illness significantly added to the manpower shortage on the eastern front, which by the late summer already constituted a crisis.

4 WAR IN THE UKRAINE

The absent southern offensive – Rundstedt's intractable overextension

On 28 August Mussolini joined Hitler on a flight to Uman' in the Ukraine for an inspection of the newly arrived CSIR (*Corpo di Sedizione Italiano in Russia*; Italian Expeditionary Corps in Russia).[1] The Italian dictator had been Hitler's guest since 25 August, but little of real substance had been decided by their summit. The visit was far more important for its highly symbolic nature. The recent meeting between Churchill and Roosevelt and the subsequent publication of the Atlantic Charter necessitated a spirited show of Axis unity. There was also the current joint action by Soviet and British forces in occupying Iran, which made the entry of Italian troops on the eastern front an opportunity for convenient riposte.

Upon their arrival in Uman' the dictators were given an outline of military operations in Army Group South, where Italian troops would now be employed.[2] Rundstedt, Kleist and Löhr all gave reports. Hitler and Mussolini then set out to observe a previously arranged march-past by Italian troops. The divergent impressions of this event could not have been more contrasting. According to one witness, Mussolini took the salute and cheers of his troops 'like Caesar in person' and on the return journey he made extravagant promises to Hitler that more divisions would be sent to the eastern front 'and naturally only the best ones'.[3] While Mussolini extolled in the martial glory that he so fervently coveted, German impressions were adversely influenced by the perceived lack of professionalism and motorization within the

CSIR.[4] The OKH had initially protested against the deployment of Italian divisions owing to the additional demands they would place on the overstretched railways. Now that the Italian troops had arrived, Keitel, who accompanied Hitler on the visit to Army Group South, described what he saw as a 'boundless disappointment'. Elaborating further, Keitel wrote, 'Their officers were far too old and made a sorry sight, and could only have had a bad effect on the value of such dubious auxiliaries. How were half-solders like these supposed to stand up to the Russians'?[5] Hitler expressed a similar sentiment when he remarked to his officers that the Italians could offer very little on the eastern front. Indeed, according to his Luftwaffe adjutant, Hitler claimed they possessed no fighting strength and that their contribution was really only important for the purposes of morale.[6] Even more ominously, the former diplomat Ulrich von Hassell noted in his diary three weeks after Mussolini's visit that there was now 'great concern about Italy'.[7] Hassell was one of the few men inside Hitler's Germany who saw matters clearly. Informed by a variety of outside sources, Hassell was hostile to the Nazi party and an active figure in the resistance movement. His unclouded perspective allowed him to draw grave, if realistic, conclusions about the future. On 20 September Hassell wrote, 'Enough information about the Mussolini visit has filtered through to show clearly how vulnerable our situation is, and how every chance for a reasonable peace goes to the devil as soon as the other side sees victory ahead.'[8]

While the relatively small contingent of Italian troops was only just arriving in the east, they were of a distant importance to Hitler next to the role played by the Romanian army. Between 3 and 25 August Antonescu's Fourth Army had been engaged in a major independent action at the port city of Odessa, attempting to seize the city by direct assault. The assault soon became a siege, which Antonescu was determined to end. His forces had a six to one superiority in manpower and a five to one superiority in artillery, but the Soviet Coastal Army manned multiple defensive lines and fought with fanatical vigour.[9] The first offensive eventually foundered with heavy losses, but a renewed offensive was launched between 28 August and 5 September. The fighting around the city was a savage affair. Assaults were often conducted on the basis of a simple equation, mustering more men to throw against an enemy strong point than its defensive fire could withstand. As Hitler observed, 'Antonescu is using in front of Odessa the tactics of the First

Fig. 7 Hitler and Mussolini visiting Army Group South (28 August 1941). From left: General Ugo Cavallero, Benito Mussolini, Adolf Hitler, Field Marshal Gerd von Rundstedt, Colonel-General Alexander Löhr.

World War. Every day he advances a few kilometres, after using his artillery to pulverise the space he wishes to occupy.'[10] Even with such crude methods the offensive slowly gained ground, albeit at tremendous cost. It was here that the female Soviet sniper Mila Pavichenko soon found fame as the so-called 'Bolshevik Valkyrie' and was credited with 180 'kills'.[11] Between 28 August and 11 September the Romanians at Odessa suffered 31,552 casualties, making an incredible total of 58,859 men lost since the start of the first offensive on 5 August. To make matters worse, the second offensive narrowly failed and the Soviets were successful in landing fresh reinforcements.[12] The commander of the Romanian Fourth Army, General Nicolae Ciuperca, reported that 'nearly all our divisions have exhausted their offensive potential, both physically and morally'. Antonescu, however, saw this as defeatism and promptly dismissed him, 'because he lacked offensive spirit and confidence in the battle capacity of the Romanian army'.[13] Ciuperca's replacement was General Iosif Lacobici, who was instructed to carry out his orders without complaint or changes.[14] Lacobici soon set about organizing a third major offensive, this time with the aid of a German infantry regiment, an assault pioneer regiment and some heavy artillery. Between 9 and 20 September a desperate struggle engulfed the city as the Romanians forced the Soviets back. Again casualties were excessive, prompting one Romanian military journal later to reproach its officers with a passage printed in bold that read: 'Commanders must remember that their men are only flesh and blood.' The offensive was eventually called off when a surprise Soviet counterattack and successful amphibious landings forced the Romanian V Corps back between 8 and 10 kilometres on 22 September. The front then settled down into positional warfare until the Soviet garrison was successfully evacuated on 16 October. The Romanians claimed victory, but with an additional 39,301 casualties sustained between 12 September and 16 October, and almost 100,000 losses suffered in total over just two and a half months of siege, the 'victory' came at a staggering cost.[15] Indeed some Romanian divisions lost up to 80 per cent of their men.[16] It was not the only siege taking place in the east at that time, but it was by far the bloodiest to date.[17] It also represented the first major turning point for Romanian participation in the east. Militarily the battle for Odessa devastated the Fourth Army, but there was also a political price. Beyond the liberation of Romanian national territory, the decision to continue the fighting into the Soviet Union had been taken by Antonescu and the dramatic escalation in losses ended his fragile consensus for the extension of the war. What had in the early summer been a straightforward war of liberation against a despised enemy had already become a noticeable and growing liability.

An important factor in the emergent unpopularity of Romania's continued participation in the war was that Hungarian casualties up until this point amounted to only about 20 per cent of those sustained by Romania.[18] Given the fierce antagonism existing between the two nations, which had recently veered towards open hostilities, questions were naturally being asked about the wisdom of fighting a costly war deep inside the Soviet Union. For his part, the Hungarian leader, Admiral Horthy, did not bemoan the losses of his southern rival; indeed it was precisely these kinds of casualties that revealed the unanticipated scale and cost of the war in the east. Moreover, the Hungarians did not consider their own losses light and were sufficiently worried about the implications of a long war in the east to attempt a withdrawal of their Mobile Corps from the Soviet Union.[19] Indeed, only two days before Horthy and Szombathelyi met with Hitler and Keitel to discuss this prospect, the Hungarian Mobile Corps was facing its own crisis. Deployed to the south of the German bridgehead at Dnepropetrovsk, the Hungarians had to withstand their own local Soviet attacks, which soon proved too much. On 6 September the war diary of Kleist's panzer group records the following entry:

> *The Chief of Staff of the Hungarian Mobile Corps called the Chief of Staff of Panzer Group 1 in the early morning and depicted the situation at the front very pessimistically. The troops are exhausted, and alone are no longer capable of defending against enemy attacks. He urgently requests the support of German troops.*[20]

It was an ominous development, which followed the dire predictions of those outspoken critics who challenged Horthy's decision to enter the war in the first place. The chairman of the minority Farmers' Party, Endre Bajczy-Zsilinszky, had earlier claimed the government had to extricate itself 'in good time from this debacle, which would occur as certainly as 2 × 2 makes 4'.[21]

Throughout the summer of 1941 the problems of the eastern front were a consistent theme for the minor Axis partners fighting within Army Group South and none was exempt. The small Slovakian Rapid Group was given its baptism of fire at Lipovec, when it was sent into action against what the German command believed to be retreating Soviet forces. Although the Germans were probably hoping this would provide the Slovaks with a confidence-building early success, the result was a thinly disguised calamity. A local Soviet counterattack by two battalions of infantry, backed by artillery, split the Slovakian forces into two and destroyed six armoured fighting vehicles and damaged nine more. Only with the intervention of nearby German units was the situation restored, but the problems of the Slovak army ran much deeper.[22] The German liaison officers regarded the Slovakian officers as infected with a 'bad spirit', while the working methods of the Slovak army staff were described as 'completely impossible'.[23]

Clearly the eastern front presented prodigious problems for Germany's poorly trained, underresourced and ill-equipped allies (although not all units were affected in the same manner or to the same extent). Yet whatever their limitations, as the war continued and the heavy fighting took its toll, Germany's growing manpower crisis made its reliance on the Axis armies all the more important. The danger of this dependence was confirmed in 1942 when the German command over-zealously co-opted its allies into independent actions far beyond their capabilities. The resulting disaster at Stalingrad was by no means preordained by the end of September 1941, but the limitations of Germany's allies were apparent for all to see.

As Guderian's offensive heaved its way south against a multitude of difficulties, Kleist's panzer group confronted a different set of challenges, the most demanding of which were induced by the OKH. Halder's insistence on holding the bridgehead at Dnepropetrovsk absorbed an inordinate degree of strength, which not only placed Mackensen's III Panzer Corps under the greatest strain, but siphoned off the lion's share of Panzer Group 1's limited supplies. In addition to Mackensen's corps, holding the bridgehead demanded supplementary support, which exacerbated the shortage of combat formations at the eastern end of the Dnepr bend. The recently arrived 198th Infantry Division was diverted to Mackensen's command to help reinforce the bridgehead,[24] but could also have been effectively used to strengthen the German line to the south of Dnepropetrovsk. It was here that only days later the hard-pressed Hungarian Mobile Corps pleaded for relief in the face of stiff Soviet attacks, and, in the absence of any other aid, had to be reinforced by the supposedly refitting 16th Motorized Infantry Division from Wietersheim's XIV Panzer Corps.[25] Likewise, elements of the 13th and 14th Panzer Divisions were ordered back into the line on the left and right of the Dnepropetrovsk bridgehead.[26] It was a repetition of the unlearned lessons from the Yel'nya salient, where the attempt to hold an exposed forward position created an inordinate drag on resources and jeopardized more immediate objectives. Nevertheless, on Halder's order, the bridgehead was to be held. Indeed, in order to ensure its security, and despite a description of the combat units in the bridgehead on 31 August as 'seriously battered', orders were issued for its expansion.[27] In a desperate attempt to combat the extreme fatigue of the men occupying the bridgehead, most of whom had been unable to rest since crossing the river, they were issued with Pervitine, a methamphetamine compound.[28] On 2 September the 60th Motorized Infantry Division and 198th Infantry Division fought to gain more ground on the eastern bank of the Dnepr, but could only do so under intense enemy artillery fire, which the deployment of Ju-87s, commonly known as 'Stukas', and German counter-battery fire, could not suppress. By the end of the day the bridgehead extended only 5 kilometres in depth and 11 kilometres in length.[29] Wilhelm Rubino, who endured a great deal of Soviet shelling in the bridgehead and was later killed in the battle of Kiev, wrote home in early September: 'When I was relieved and pulled back safely to the company I was very quiet and thoughtful. There is nothing more difficult than losing one man after the other often completely senselessly.'[30] On 3 September the 60th Motorized Infantry Division was reported to be suffering from both heavy losses and the mental and physical strains of having been in uninterrupted combat since 16 August. The divisional commander therefore deemed his forces incapable of any further attacks and able only to conduct 'limited' defensive actions.[31] As a testament to the costly nature of close-quarters urban combat, the 60th Motorized Infantry Division lost 28 officers and 1,020 men between 25 August and 2 September. Even more serious were the losses of the 198th Infantry Division, which lost 35 officers and 990 men in only three days.[32] As Helmut Schiebel wrote home in a letter from the bridgehead, 'Nothing is worse than house fighting. Everywhere there are bangs, shots, hits, ricochets. A comrade suddenly screams or keels over and you don't even know where it came from.'[33]

Beyond the demands of the fighting units, there was also the serious issue of supplying the bridgehead. All of the major bridges had been destroyed and the German army's pontoon crossing came under constant attack from Soviet planes and artillery.[34] Replacement components for the bridge were not available in the quanities required and simple wooden constructions had to compensate, but these too suffered repeated damage, while substantial casualties were also inflicted on the exposed engineers. Yet the bridge had to be maintained at all costs. As Helmut Schiebel noted as early as 27 August, 'How much blood and how much anxiety it has already cost. This bridge was the life line of a few thousand soldiers.'[35]

Transportation was the other major problem, with the panzer group's war diary noting, 'There is only a meagre quantity of vehicles left available for driving; the fallout rates in motors are large.'[36] The quartermaster for Panzer Group 1 made a tour of inspection to Dnepropetrovsk on 29 August and his conclusions underlined the urgency of the situation as well as the dire implications for the recently begun refitting of the other two panzer corps. It was noted that the demand for munitions at Dnepropetrovsk was 'very high' and that the continuous needs could hardly be met. As a result, Wietersheim's XIV Panzer Corps and Kempf's XXXXVIII Panzer Corps 'do not get anything for the time being'.[37] The solution, according to Major-General Hermann Breith, General for Panzer Troops at the OKH, was simply to amalgamate several of Kleist's divisions. In the absence of another alternative, the panzer group was in basic agreement with the proposal, but the idea came to nothing (Hitler did not favour such 'losses') and the individual divisions simply had to endure in their reduced state.[38] With the southern thrust of the anticipated Kiev encirclement still missing and the OKH's ardent determination not to give up the Dnepropetrovsk bridgehead, events in the south were off to an inauspicious beginning. To make matters worse, Kleist had no way of significantly improving the mechanical condition of his vital panzer divisions, which would eventually have to join hands with Guderian. There was also the drastically overstretched logistics network, which would again have to sustain a further advance.

In view of such difficulties the outlook at Army Group South was overshadowed by pragmatic misgivings about the coming operation. On 29 August the army group's war diary assessed the future Kiev encirclement in bleak terms. After acknowledging the 'strongly emphasized attack mentality' of the OKH to thrust northwards, Rundstedt's command expressed its own reservations:

> *[I]n light of the technical difficulties of the Dnepr crossing and the momentarily insurmountable strains on the supply situation, the desired* immediate *and* swift *attack on a wide front over the river cannot be reckoned on. Consequently, it is not to be discounted that noteworthy elements of the enemy strength can withdraw east and avoid destruction. Even the most determined will of all participating command authorities is not in a position to overcome the constraints, which are forced by the unalterable present shortages in bridging equipment and the scarcity of motorized transportation.*[39]

There could be no denying the difficulties of the task ahead, which, in addition to the halting advance of Guderian's drive and the strains on Bock's defensive front, provide a corrective to the prevailing judgement of many previous histories. Even taking into account Stalin's deleterious strategic direction, the much-lauded success of the Kiev encirclement was neither a preordained certainty, nor a faultless example of German operational proficiency. Halder and Bock had both fiercely opposed it and were now backing rival strategic alternatives at Dnepropetrovsk and along Army Group Centre's endangered defensive front, which threatened to deny the panzer groups the strength they needed to implement the encirclement of Kirponos. There could be no question that German dispositions still gave them a significant upper hand, but ultimate success was by no means a *fait accompli*.

Acting on his fears that significant elements of Kirponos's forces might escape the developing envelopment, Rundstedt ordered Kleist's panzer group as well as the Sixth and Seventeenth Armies to cross the Dnepr at as many places as possible. On 31 August the LII Army Corps of Stülpnagel's Seventeenth Army forced a crossing at Derievka just south of Kremenchug.[40] It was to become the launching pad for Kleist's drive north, which meant that the largely ineffective rest and refitting of the panzer group would shortly be over. On 1 September the panzer group's worn-down *Grosstransportraum* was ordered out of the workshops and back into action. The panzer group's quartermaster concluded, 'As a result of the short amount of time, the yield in tonnage is extremely low; however, the work done will ensure that the fallout rates in trucks are somewhat reduced in the days ahead.'[41] Indeed the condition of trucks across the whole of the eastern front was uniformly poor, which, according to one study, led to reports that by the beginning of September 1941, more than half of the *Ostheer*'s truck fleet was no longer operational.[42]

Trucks were not the only casualties of the incessant pace that the war demanded. The men were driven on relentlessly, spurred by their commander's assurances that each new success brought the war closer to its conclusion. Yet the progress of the war also placed the *Ostheer* in an incessant cycle of destructive repetition because conventional military thought dictated that every new success be rapidly followed up to exploit gains and prevent the enemy from re-establishing himself. Yet the same process was rapidly undermining the *Ostheer*'s combat strength. By early September the men could see for themselves that they were now deep inside the Soviet Union without an end in sight. Günter von Scheven wrote home on 2 September:

> *We have covered more than 2,000 kilometres. The last part on foot. From the battlefields south of Uman' to the Dnepr bend in quick march, only at night, on impossible roads, where everything got stuck. The experience of death is terrible, it is like a new baptism... Where is this endless war taking us? Spatially there is no destination, the landscape stretches continually on, melancholy is setting in, the enemy is still countless, although sacrificed like a hecatomb. Probably everything will have to be destroyed before the fighting is over.*[43]

Despite the concerns of the soldiers, an enduring sense of duty, belief in eventual victory and the Wehrmacht's harsh military discipline kept the men in line. There was also a real lack of alternatives to escape the war. Fear of the Soviets discouraged surrender, while desertion, so far from Germany, would almost certainly be doomed and risk the severest penalty.[44] As a result it was as early as the late summer of 1941 that average German *Landsers* began talking in welcoming terms about the so-called *Heimatschuss* – literally a 'home shot' – a wound which would allow repatriation to Germany.[45] For the vast majority, however, they had little other option than to place their hopes in the much-promised victory. Until then it was hoped that the summer had seen the worst of the fighting and one now only had to survive the war's final stages. As Adolf B. wrote home from Army Group South on 3 September, 'Now we only hope and wish that the remaining fighting will not be too hard and not cost us too many more casualties! After that: "Never again Russia!"'[46] Yet not all German soldiers were quite so optimistic about an end to the war. Konrad Jarausch wrote to a friend on 30 August: 'Here we often ask ourselves what will happen when the operational possibilities have been reached and then the winter comes. The annihilation of Bolshevism still seems to be a long way away. An end of the war is less and less foreseeable.'[47]

As summer came to an end, the danger of the campaign becoming bogged down should have been clear to the commanders in the east. Even if the proposed encirclement of the Soviet South-Western Front could be achieved, previous battles of annihilation suggested that there was no guarantee it would constitute an end to Soviet resistance.

Nevertheless, on 1 September Rundstedt expressed confidence that if his army group could carry out the planned encirclement, it would not only effectively end the fighting in the south, but the war as a whole. As Army Group South's war diary stated, 'In the opinion of the commander of the army group, carrying out the annihilation battle in the Ukraine is of decisive importance for the outcome of the whole eastern campaign.' With the end of Soviet resistance in the south, the war diary made clear what was to be expected: 'What then remains for Army Group South are expeditions to occupy the land.' On the other hand, if the enemy could not be eliminated in the Ukraine, Rundstedt was also clear about the implications: '[N]either Army Group South nor Army Group Centre could manage a fluid operation. Their forces would be bound to tactical battles going into the winter.'[48] Such an analysis underlines the importance of assessing battles in the full light of their strategic significance and the results they entail. A battle is not an end in itself; its relative worth extends well beyond the numbers of men killed and captured. The strategic consequences of a battle and its capacity to meet the preconditions of victory are paramount. One can, after all, go on winning battles, while losing the war. By Rundstedt's own measure, expeditions to occupy undefended land or sluggish tactical fighting into the winter would be the real determinants of his success in the September battles.

As Guderian's offensive to the south withered on bad roads, insufficient supplies and inadequate reinforcements, Bock's decision to give up the Infantry Regiment *Grossdeutschland* did little to assuage Guderian's insatiable desire for more strength. Indeed, only hours after being informed that *Grossdeutschland* was being transferred to his command, the obstreperous Guderian began insisting to Bock that he also be given Major-General Wolfgang Fischer's 10th Panzer Division. Bock, however, had his own problems holding together Army Group Centre's long defensive front and, almost immediately after relenting and giving up *Grossdeutschland*, the Field Marshal began to regret it. As Bock wrote in his diary on 30 August:

> *The penalty was not long in coming! The enemy has broken into our lines south of the Yel'nya salient. Kluge described the penetration as ten kilometres in depth with heavy tanks and asked that the 267th [Infantry Division] and elements of the 10th Panzer Division be placed at his disposal to clear up the affair. I gave him both divisions in order to*

> *clear the table quickly and thoroughly. Here is proof that I cannot give more forces to Guderian without endangering my eastern front. The Russians also attacked again in the Yel'nya salient and at various places on the Ninth Army's eastern front.*[49]

On the evening of 30 August Bock ensured that Guderian was made fully aware of the seriousness of the breakthrough south of Yel'nya in the sector of the 23rd Infantry Division. Yet Bock's concerns made little difference to Guderian, who was fixated on his goal of driving his offensive south and indifferent to all other considerations. Indeed on the following morning (31 August), as Guderian lamented the slow forward movement of Weichs's Second Army and the growing threat to his eastern flank, the panzer general presented Bock with a new and even more radical demand. As Guderian wrote in the panzer group's war diary, 'I therefore request the prompt allocation of all available mobile troops in the vicinity and the establishment of a single command structure over the 1st Cavalry Division, 11th Panzer Division [at that time attached to Army Group South], the XXXXVI Panzer Corps, the 7th Panzer Division and the 14th Motorized Infantry Division.'[50] According to Guderian all other plans and agendas were secondary to the achievement of his 'principal task', to which he attributed, like Rundstedt, a decisive importance for the outcome of the war in the east. If Guderian's request for reinforcements were not high-handed enough, the panzer general went on to request that the decision be made by Hitler himself, effectively circumventing Bock and the OKH.[51] Even within Guderian's own staff there was a recognition that such a request went well beyond the bounds of tolerance. The Chief of Staff of Panzer Group 2, Colonel Kurt Freiherr von Liebenstein, noted in his diary on 1 September, 'As can be expected this wireless message created house-high waves.'[52] To make matters worse, when the radio message reached Bock, the Field Marshal noted that it was 'unpleasantly worded'. Just prior to the message's arrival Bock had decided to transfer the 1st Cavalry Division to Panzer Group 2, but now he insisted that any future allocations would be made entirely dependent on the security of Army Group Centre's front, not Guderian's incessant badgering. The idea that Bock might refer such an important decision to Hitler was rejected outright.[53] In an ensuing telephone conversation between Bock and Guderian, the Field Marshal again attempted to placate Guderian's

Fig. 8 Colonel-General Heinz Guderian commanded Panzer Group 2 in Operation Barbarossa and proved a difficult subordinate for Kluge, Bock and Halder.

forceful demands. As Army Group Centre's war diary recorded, Bock told Guderian, 'Panzer Group 2's situation is completely clear to me, but at the moment I cannot do more, particularly as the breakthrough at the 23rd Division is tying up my last strength.' The diary then continues, 'Colonel-General Guderian responds that in his opinion a breakthrough was more bearable than the halting of Panzer Group 2's offensive. If it gets bogged down, that means positional war and an end to all operations.' Bock then reminded Guderian that if the Soviet offensives managed to force Army Group Centre to give up Smolensk, that would also mean an end to Guderian's offensive.[54] It was an emotionally charged exchange that ended without agreement or resolution. Still exasperated, Bock then spoke with Halder and related the substance of Guderian's demands, the tone he had taken and his request that Hitler be consulted for a decision. 'That is an unheard-of cheek,' was Halder's indignant reaction.[55]

Clearly Guderian's relationships with his commanding officers in the army were fraught with a mounting personal dislike. The acrimony stemmed largely from Guderian's perceived defection to Hitler's strategic alternative and now worsened as the panzer general's tone became increasingly more insolent. To Guderian's mind he was acting under the direct instructions of Hitler, which superseded all other concerns of the army. Not only did Guderian believe that his mission held Hitler's resounding personal stamp of authority, but the subsequent unwillingness of Bock and the OKH to meet his wishes was seen purely in terms of a personal vendetta against him. The defensive crisis at Army Group Centre was, for Guderian, little more than a convenient justification to deny him the forces he needed, while leaving valuable forces in the centre of the front for an eventual thrust on Moscow. As Guderian's Chief of Staff noted in his diary, 'The commander [Guderian] has the impression that the army group, as well as the Chief of Staff [Halder], still cling to the old plan for a drive to Moscow.'[56] Not one to mince words, Guderian's disgust with his immediate superiors became more and more palpable as his offensive slowed and he appeared in danger of falling short of the objective Hitler had set him.

On the opposing side, Halder and Bock harboured a thinly disguised loathing towards Guderian following his perceived perfidy before Hitler, but their rationale for withholding additional units from his command was, in fact, entirely dictated by events at the front. Army Group Centre was being shaken to its core by the ferocity of the Red Army's sustained offensive. The day after the 23rd Infantry Division's front had been overrun, Halder recorded in his diary that the attacking Soviet forces had penetrated right up to the command post of the VII Army Corps. In addition, a renewed Soviet offensive at Yel'nya threatened the hard-pressed salient with yet another defensive crisis,[57] which would shortly hand Zhukov the greatest Soviet success of the summer. Yet none of this made any impression on Guderian. He was simply fixated on his own narrow sector of the front and indifferent to any competing demands for the overstretched motorized forces. For this reason Brauchitsch had already asked Bock to 'get a grip on Guderian';[58] however, the recalcitrant Guderian was not about to be subordinated. The result would cause growing friction within the German command and soon led to calls for his dismissal.

Notwithstanding the embittered exchanges of the day, Bock was also troubled by the prospect of Guderian's offensive stalling.

The advance of the Second Army had been slowed to a crawl and the panzer group was faring little better. Supply columns to Schweppenburg's XXIV Panzer Corps, at the spearhead of Guderian's advance, were moving at an average tempo of just 12 kilometres per hour,[59] while the panzer divisions themselves were being ground down by the rigours of constant combat and movement. By 31 August Model's 3rd Panzer Division was down to just thirty-four serviceable tanks, while Langermann-Erlancamp's 4th Panzer Division possessed fifty-two.[60] This made a combined total of eighty-six tanks – less than half of 3rd Panzer Division's starting total on 22 June 1941.[61] Thus, given that Lemelsen's XXXXVII Panzer Corps was entirely directed towards protecting Guderian's long left flank, it is no exaggeration to conclude that Guderian's offensive – the most important being undertaken on the eastern front at that time – was being pushed forward by the equivalent strength in tanks of half a panzer division. Accordingly, on the evening of 31 August, with what was described as the 'heaviest of hearts', Bock agreed to assign the SS division *Das Reich* to Guderian.[62]

As the army's internal wrangling continued to plague relations, the situation was hardly better at the higher echelons of command. The supposed 'reconciliation' Hitler had had with Brauchitsch was a largely superficial act on Hitler's part, intended principally to ensure a workable relationship with the army.[63] Yet while Brauchitsch took heart from the gesture, Halder saw it for what it was and remained both cynical of Hitler's actions and bitter at the loss of the Moscow alternative. On 30 August Halder commented in his diary that after the reconciliation a pretence of artificial affection and cheerfulness prevailed. Yet in fact, Halder observed, 'Nothing has changed, aside from the fact that now we must honour not only the Führer with personal presentations about railways, supply, signal communications and army replacements, but also the Reichsmarschall [Göring].'[64] Moreover, Halder also alluded to Hitler's voracious demand for new operations and to how the dictator was now casting his eyes to the east of Army Group Centre and the need for the destruction of Timoshenko's army group. Only a week before Halder would have welcomed such news as a blessing, but now the Chief of the Army General Staff recognized that Guderian's panzers could no longer be recalled.[65] They were the linchpin of the new German strategy south of Smolensk and the main hope of encircling the Soviet South-Western Front, seizing the Ukraine and freeing up the German Second, Sixth and Seventeenth Armies. Even for Halder, Moscow had now become the secondary objective, which may simply reflect his resignation at having fought so hard for an ultimately forlorn hope, but it is also not beyond the realm of possibilities that the Chief of the Army General Staff had warmed to the operational opportunities now offered in the south. What Halder found most encouraging in Hitler's new strategic deliberations was the prospect of a renewed offensive towards Moscow at the conclusion of Guderian's drive to the south. Such stout faith in yet another grand offensive to the east was another reflection of the unrestrained hubris rampant within the German high command. Hitler and Halder were fully consumed by such thoughts, and the many weeks of gruelling fighting and heavy losses were no deterrent to their plans for still more offensives. Similarly, although some of the senior field commanders were more tempered in their views, continuing notions of future large-scale victories at Moscow, Leningrad and in the Caucasus still fired the imaginations of many.

On 31 August Bock was told by Kesselring of Hitler's renewed interest in attacking towards Moscow.[66] In both Bock's and Halder's diaries Hitler's proposed offensive to the east by Army Group Centre is presented not as a future means of continuing the war, but, inexplicably, as an alternative to Guderian's current offensive towards the south. If Hitler was indeed seriously considering a complete change of plans, it would have necessitated a tremendous reversal, which may also explain Halder's contrasting determination to see the southern operation through. For his part, Bock, while keen to lead the march on Moscow, was incredulous at the apparent strategic mismanagement. Only the day before (30 August), in response to the immense length of his front, which he noted now extended to some 800 kilometres in width, Bock pronounced, 'The idea of an offensive on my front appears to be dead.'[67] In light of new developments, however, Bock again had to confront the prospect of an attack. In disbelief Bock contacted the OKH to confirm what Kesselring was reporting. The Field Marshal was told that nothing was yet certain, but that Hitler was indeed considering the idea of halting Guderian and attacking east. Bock must have marvelled at how such an absurd and altogether infuriating circumstance could come to pass after the embittered disputes of barely more than a week before. Hitler was considering halting Guderian and Weichs at the Nezhin–Konotop railway line and attacking east with Bock's entire army group, supported by elements of Leeb's forces. Meanwhile, Halder, the former firebrand advocate of attacking towards Moscow, was now committed to first completing the drive south. It was an incredible reversal, even for the haphazard leadership that typified the German command. The alarming prospect of an abrupt change in orders, should it be confirmed, was now apparent to Bock and added to his unease. 'I fear that the Supreme Command's sudden change of opinion has come too late to force a decision against the main body of the Russian Army which I so desperately desired. Just concentrating my widely scattered forces will be very difficult and time consuming.'[68]

At the OKH the bewildering picture of Hitler's shifting strategic deliberations soon began to crystallize. On the afternoon of 31 August Halder called Jodl at Hitler's headquarters and learned that the dictator was now intending to strike against Timoshenko after what Jodl referred to as the 'intermezzo' in the south.[69] From Halder's point of view this avoided the danger of an abrupt reversal in plans and costly redeployments, but if Bock feared it might already be too late to force a decision against Timoshenko's concentrations, the additional delay could only add to his concerns.[70] Nevertheless, Halder related the news to Greiffenberg, Bock's Chief of Staff, that in the south Guderian's group was 'again free for involvement'.[71] While the development of operations in the Ukraine was still far from certain, the German command placed Moscow firmly back on the agenda. Preliminary planning within the OKH and Army Group Centre now began in earnest, and following a familiar pattern, assumed the objective to be obtainable from the very beginning and took far too little account of operational strengths, logistical considerations, Soviet countermeasures or the coming seasonal difficulties. A new war directive from Hitler would follow shortly, and passed smoothly into the new attack plan, ensuring many of the lessons from Operation Barbarossa remained unlearned. The reincarnation of Barbarossa, in what would soon be known as Operation Typhoon,[72] was then charged with achieving all that the summer campaign had so far failed to accomplish. With much less motorization, the spiralling manpower crisis, less than half of the original panzer force, worsening weather and a hopelessly overstretched logistical system, the German command still firmly believed that the final act in the destruction of the Soviet state was within their grasp. The answer to how this might be possible was, to their minds, plainly apparent. Army Group Centre had to defeat Moscow's numerous defending armies decisively and capture the city. In reality, however, neither the objective itself, nor the decisive consequence that was expected to result, was realistic by early September and the start of the operation was still weeks away with much heavy fighting still to come.

Guderian and Eremenko – the linchpins to success

As the combined Soviet offensives from Timoshenko's Western Front, Zhukov's Reserve Front and Eremenko's Briansk Front hammered away at the German lines, they appeared to achieve little success either in their lofty operational goals or even in local territorial gains. Hence, while most histories have chosen to ignore these battles altogether, those that have dealt with them have tended to emphasize their appalling waste in men and materiel. Yet the dogged attritional fighting, while excessively costly to the Soviets, also led to severe bloodletting for the German infantry divisions. In dozens of nameless battles, lasting from the second half of August into early September, the fighting raged on, often for days on end. The commander of the LIII Army Corps, General of Infantry Karl Weisenberger, noted on 3 September, 'We are fighting the war of the poor man. We must manage on less so that other positions can advance rapidly.'[73] Similarly, the diary of a German doctor, Hans Pichler, noted towards the end of August, 'In the last twelve days our division has lost a thousand men dead ... In every regiment the III battalion has been dissolved to provide replacements for the others.'[74] Berndt Tessen von Heydebreck, who arrived on the eastern front at the start of September as a replacement for the 7th Infantry Division (belonging to Kluge's Fourth Army), described what he found upon reaching his unit: 'Found out that of a whole company only twenty men were left. Among the wounded was the company commander ... Static warfare, just like in the World War ... The men are covered with dirt from head to foot. Their clothes are in tatters and their faces unshaven. Immense casualties.'[75] Yet such depictions were not the only indications of Soviet success. The fact that so much of the eastern front had now settled down to positional warfare clearly indicated that the German blitzkrieg had seriously waned. Moreover, the vivid scenes of anguish and disharmony within the highest echelons of Army Group Centre were a direct reaction to the difficulties and unanticipated strength of the Red Army's offensive. Nor was it the case that all the Soviet armies failed to achieve their operational goals. Zhukov withheld his Twenty-Fourth Army long enough both to provide it with substantial reinforcements and to allow the other offensives to absorb Bock's limited reserves. Then on 30 August he launched his renewed attack against the Yel'nya salient (see map 7). With its forces concentrated into two shock groups north and south of the salient, the Soviet Twenty-Fourth Army opened its offensive with a barrage by 800 guns, mortars and multiple-rocket launchers.[76] The following assault immediately penetrated German defences, which were then counterattacked, beginning days of gruelling and costly close-quarters fighting.

By 2 September Bock noted in his diary, 'Today the enemy attacked the extreme southern wing of Fourth Army . . . If he keeps at it, we could end up in a fine mess.'[77] By the end of that day (2 September) Bock could no longer see any point in holding on to the salient. Already in mid-August there had been a discussion about whether holding the position was worth the casualties it necessitated, but at that time, with the prospect of an offensive towards Moscow still considered likely, Bock opted to continue defending Yel'nya. Now he had had enough. 'The divisions deployed there are being bled white as time passes. After several conversations with Kluge, I decided to order the salient abandoned.'[78] On that same day Halder visited Army Group Centre to be informed by Bock of the 'heavy losses among the troops' as well as his decision regarding Yel'nya.[79] In spite of having strongly supported Bock's decision in mid-August to hold the salient, Halder now recognized the futility of pouring in further reserves and did not object. Yet the episode stands as an appalling indictment of the whole German command. It was Guderian who first captured the position in the third week of July by thrusting further to the east than required with his XXXXVI Panzer Corps, instead of swinging to his left and closing the southern side of the Smolensk pocket. The result was a hole, which Hoth could not close on his own (in spite of attempts to do so) and through which countless Soviet units escaped. Guderian, however, stubbornly maintained that Yel'nya would be invaluable for the assumed continuation of the offensive towards Moscow. For the same reasons Soviet strategy favoured eliminating the corpulent bulge in their line and weeks of intense fighting were the result. In the static conditions of positional warfare the Red Army, with its preponderant advantage in artillery pieces as well as its enhanced ability to supply its guns with shells, proved superior. German divisions suffered such heavy casualties that they had to be constantly rotated through Yel'nya and then transferred to quieter sections of the front. The 137th Infantry Division,

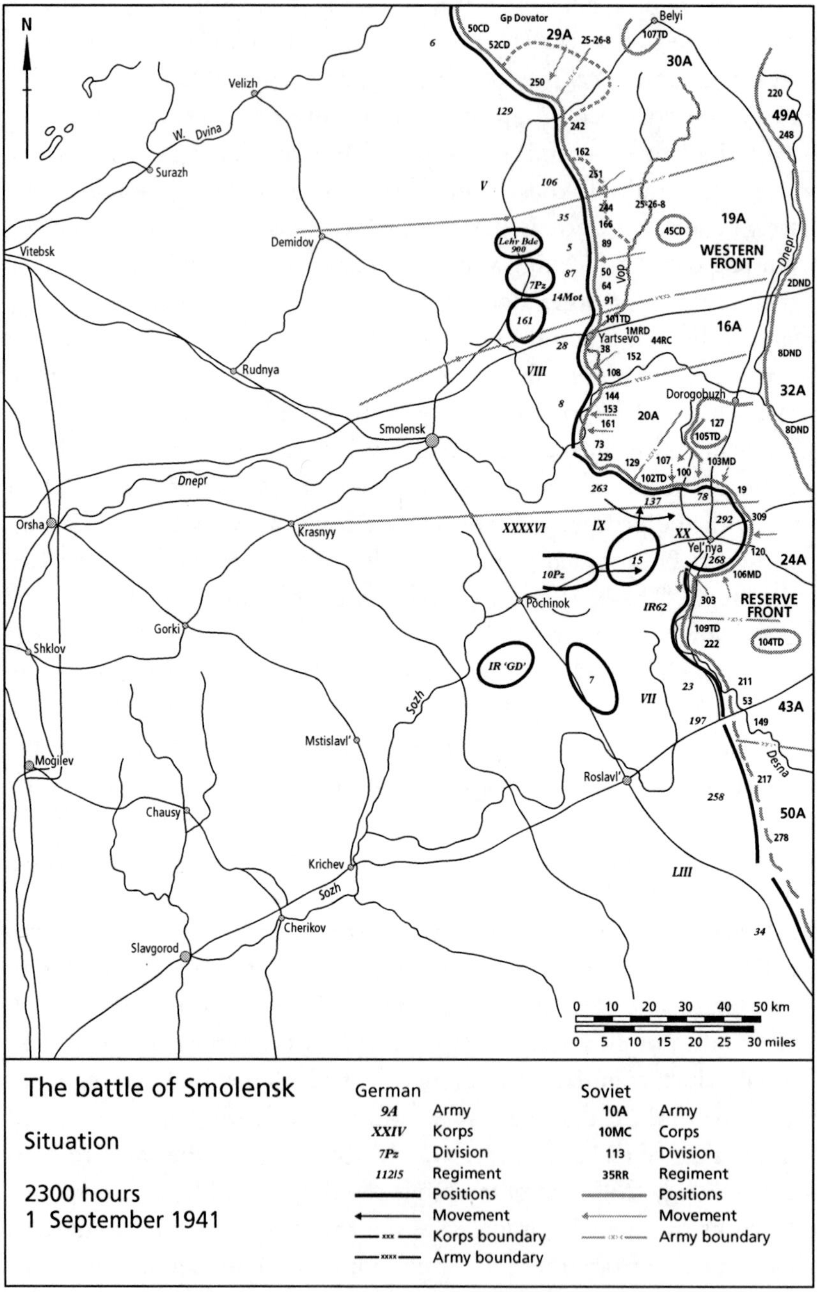

Map 7 Dispositions of Army Group Centre on 1 September 1941
Source: David M. Glantz, *Atlas of the Battle of Smolensk 7 July–10 September 1941* (privately published, 2001).

for example, suffered almost 2,000 casualties at Yel'nya between 18 August and 5 September, while the 263rd Infantry Division lost 1,200 men in only a single week in the salient. By 5 September these two divisions had sustained more than 8,000 casualties between them since the start of the war.[80] Nor were these divisions outstanding exceptions. By early September 1941 there were fourteen German divisions on the eastern front that had sustained more than 4,000 casualties, a further forty had losses in excess of 3,000 men and another thirty divisions counted over 2,000 dead and wounded each.[81]

Ultimately, in spite of German attempts to depict the retreat as a mere 'tactical withdrawal' or a 'straightening of the front', the outcome of the battle for Yel'nya was clearly the result of a sustained Soviet offensive that eventually ousted them. The implications for the Germans were not as positive as they had hoped. Bock's line was indeed shorter and he had freed some more formations, but the same was also true for the Red Army. On the other hand, Hermann Geyer, commander of the IX Army Corps, which had been defending the salient, noted that the withdrawal illustrated the growing credibility gap in Germany's war in the east: 'The broadcast propaganda, which spoke a lot about the end of the war, had to have a bad effect. Because it was not consistent with the situation as the soldiers experienced it.'[82] Franz Frisch, who fought at Yel'nya, was a case in point. In his memoir he recalled with bitterness:

> *Officially it was called a 'planned withdrawal', and a 'correction of the front lines'... But to me it was so much bullshit. The Russians were kicking us badly and we had to regroup... The next day – or maybe a few days later – we heard on the radio, in the 'news from the front'* (Wehrmachtsbericht) *about the 'successful front correction' in our Yel'nya defensive line, which was east of Smolensk, and the enormous losses we had inflicted on the enemy. But no single word was heard about a retreat, about the hopelessness of the situation, about the mental and emotional stagnation and numbness of the German soldiers. In short, it was again a 'victory.' But we on the front line were running back like rabbits in front of the fox. This metamorphosis of the truth from 'all shit' to 'it was a victory' baffled me, and those of my comrades who dared to think.*[83]

Not only was the retreat itself an obvious setback for the German troops who had endured so much, but according to Frisch its conduct was more in line with a rout than a planned withdrawal.

> *I remember well the retreat from the Yel'nya line. We had nearly exhausted our supplies of artillery ammunition, and did not provide the proper counter-battery support of infantry. As such our battery received a constant amount of Soviet artillery fire, and casualties... I remember we did not receive a re-supply of shells until days later when the front settled. It was pitch dark and we tried to make it back to the main front line. Every truck, every tractor with its gun, every soldier was on his own... But nobody knew where the battery commander was, and I guess he did not know where his guns were. [The retreat proceeded] without organization, without communication and without command.*[84]

As Bock now sanctioned a major withdrawal to generate reserves and relieve the pressure on his line, it also reflected how serious the manpower crisis was becoming. Not only were there an insufficient number of divisions available for the length of the front, but the constant fighting was rapidly eroding the strength of those deployed. One soldier from the 268th Infantry Division wrote in a letter on 2 September, 'We have hard times and heavy losses. We have been at the same place for five weeks and are constantly hit hard by Russian artillery. I don't know how long our nerves can stand it... I believe the quantity of our tremendous sacrifices is already enough. It is constantly promised that we will soon be home, but always to no avail.'[85] Examining the casualty figures at the OKH on 3 September, Heusinger wrote to his wife, 'this struggle costs us heavy losses', which he worried would consume Germany's human resources 'after the bloodletting of the last war'.[86] Days later, on 5 September, Halder noted in his diary that officer casualties were running at an average of 200 a day and that by November no fewer than 11,000 replacements would be necessary.[87] At the front Colonel Erhard Raus alluded to the worrying manpower shortages and the absence of reserves: 'Losses in our combat units made themselves felt more and more, especially among the officers, because a replacement crisis had arisen for the first time since the beginning of the

Russian campaign. No replacements were arriving.'[88] Likewise, Geyer noted that after his weakened corps had evacuated Yel'nya, the arriving replacements were '[n]ot much, we could not by any means fully replenish'.[89] With losses running so high and the replacement army almost devoid of men, reserves were sought from Germany's occupation forces in France. Many of these divisions were not equipped or adequately trained for front-line service, but the demands of the war in the east necessitated immediate solutions. Accordingly, in the course of September, the 339th Infantry Division was transferred to Army Group Centre's rear area, while ten battalions from the remaining infantry divisions were disbanded to provide immediate reserves. As a longer-term solution five divisions in the west were earmarked to be made '*ostfähig*' (ready for the east) by reorganizing their personnel and re-equipping them from new production.[90] Nevertheless, such schemes were a distinct stop-gap measure and could not compensate in any adequate manner for the haemorrhaging depletion of manpower in the east.

While German casualties were a prohibitive factor in the attempt to sustain their offensive success, they remained, nevertheless, inferior to Soviet losses. In the battle for Yel'nya, Zhukov lost 31,853 men or one-third of the total force committed to the offensive.[91] On other sectors of the front, Soviet casualties were considerably higher and achieved less. Remarkably poor tactical leadership as well as senseless frontal attacks ensured that many German positions gained a disproportionate advantage even when overwhelmingly outnumbered. The outdated Soviet principle of blind headlong assaults into German defensive positions was repeated so often that it prompted one historian to note that Soviet armies were 'ground to dust, not so much by the Germans as by their own commanders'.[92] It was a staggeringly costly method of wearing down the German infantry divisions, yet it was at least effective in that regard.[93] The price was paid in blood and the utter exhaustion of the Soviet armies opposite Army Group Centre, which helped presage their subsequent defeat in the earliest phase of Operation Typhoon.[94]

For the time being the Soviets had their first major offensive success against Army Group Centre, prompting the unusual pronouncement of a Soviet victory (see map 8). On 7 September Zhukov issued an order to his troops, which read, 'After unrelenting and bitter battles, brave units of our Twenty-Fourth Army have achieved a great

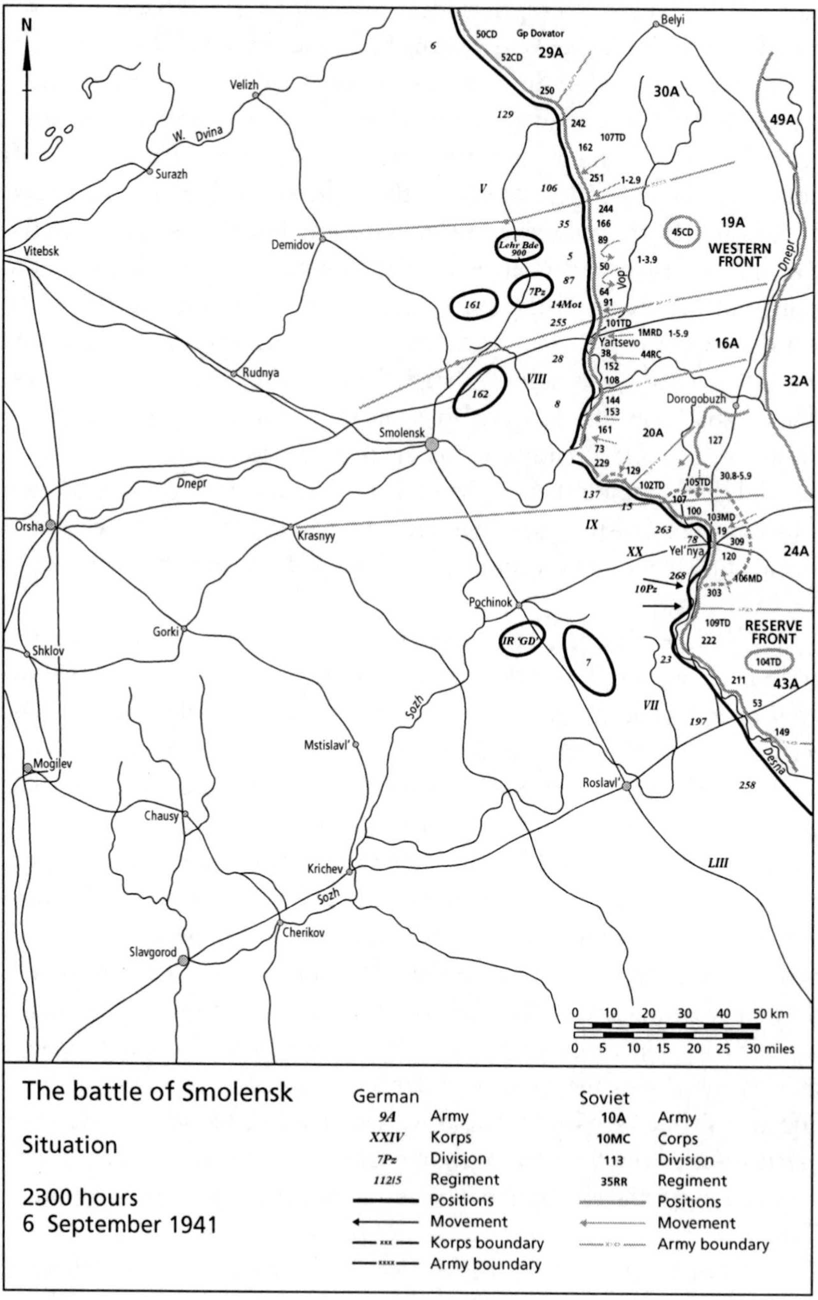

Map 8 Dispositions of Army Group Centre on 6 September 1941
Source: Glantz, *Atlas of the Battle of Smolensk 7 July–10 September 1941.*

victory. In the Yel'nya region German forces have been dealt a crushing blow.'[95] For their outstanding role in the battle, four of Zhukov's divisions received the exalted distinction of becoming the Red Army's first 'Guards' divisions, a new designation denoting exceptional service in combat and carrying the status of an elite formation.[96]

While Zhukov's Reserve Front battered its way to a victory in the centre of Bock's elongated front, Timoshenko's Western Front was attempting the same in the north with its Dukhovshchina offensive. The results were less impressive because Bock and Hoth were always able to scrape together just enough reserves to plug gaps in the line and counterattack local Soviet breakthroughs. After numerous emergencies, which included concerns in late August that the whole defensive line might collapse, the prevailing sense of desperation carried on into early September as Timoshenko's attacks continued unabated. By 3 September Bock wrote of Hoth's urgent request for yet another division (the 162nd Infantry Division) to bolster his faltering defences. Bock was sympathetic, but unable to acquiesce. The 162nd Infantry Division was committed in what Bock described as 'the dangerous Smolensk sector' and could only be relieved by a division coming up from Yel'nya in another three days.[97] Timoshenko's offensive may not have been making any process on the ground, but it was having a decidedly adverse impact on Hoth's Ninth Army, which had sustained significantly more casualties than either of Bock's other two armies.

Of all the Soviet Fronts battering away at Bock's army group, the one tasked with the most important, and most ambitious, assignment was Eremenko's Briansk Front. Eremenko was charged with breaking through, cutting off and 'smashing' Guderian's panzer group, thereby protecting the vulnerable northern approaches to Kirponos's South-Western Front. In doing so Eremenko would also occupy a line extending from Petrovichi in the north, to Kilmovichi and down to Shchors. For a force made up of reconstituted dregs from formerly defeated armies, fused together with raw, barely trained recruits and complicated by critical shortages in equipment, Eremenko's orders were a consummate impossibility. Worse still, the command staffs of both the front and its constituent armies were, for the most part, grossly inexperienced in their roles. Furthermore, there existed a serious gap between Eremenko's original force and those added to his front by the amalgamation of the former Central Front. It was not surprising, therefore, that Eremenko's first counterstroke in late August had utterly failed.

The Briansk Front was straining at the limits just to slow down Guderian's march south, to say nothing of completely halting his advance or the absurd idea of encircling and destroying the panzer group. Nevertheless, the *Stavka* was adamant and Eremenko, affectionately known by the sobriquet 'the Soviet Guderian', was not about to refuse. To assist in his renewed effort, the *Stavka* authorized reinforcement of Eremenko's front by the aviation of the high command reserve, which could attack Guderian with no fewer than 450 aircraft,[98] including the new Il-2 *Shturmovik* ground-attack aircraft.[99]

On 26 August Halder had noted ominously in his diary that despite two months of war, Soviet aircraft strengths were estimated 'in the area under observation' at around 3,700 planes.[100] Even at the start of Operation Barbarossa the Luftwaffe's total strength amounted to only 2,995 planes[101] and German production was already being surpassed by Soviet factories.[102] Given the additional fact that the Luftwaffe's inadequate resources were being split to meet the continuing requirements of its war against Britain, the danger of a resurgent Soviet air force over the eastern front was already a reality in the late summer of 1941. Events on the ground reflect the menace this caused to German operations. Between 29 August and 4 September Soviet planes flew more than four thousand sorties against Panzer Group 2, destroying, according to one source, dozens of German tanks and twenty armoured vehicles. Moreover, the Germans were said to have had fifty-five planes shot down and another fifty-seven destroyed on the ground in raids on eight airfields.[103] On 30 August the war diary of Nehring's 18th Panzer Division noted, 'Throughout the whole day lively [enemy] aerial activity with numerous bombing missions whereby losses were also sustained.'[104] The war diary of Lemelsen's XXXXVII Panzer Corps was even more explicit. It referred to Soviet aerial attacks interfering in the ground battle in an 'extremely uncomfortable manner'. In the area of the 29th Motorized Infantry Division alone, sixty-nine enemy sorties were counted before midday on 30 August. At its height up to eighteen enemy planes, both ground-attack aircraft and bombers, were attacking the division at the same time.[105] In his post-war memoir Eremenko claimed that his massive air offensive was 'highly effective' and matched by an intense ground assault with everything he could muster.[106] Even if Eremenko stood no chance of fulfilling his orders and enveloping Guderian, he did at least force Panzer Group 2 to halt in order to meet the fierce Soviet counterattacks. As the OKW war diary observed, 'The [panzer] group must cease the advance and go over to the defensive in the west, south, south-east and to some extent in the east.'[107]

Nor was it only at Briansk Front that the resurgence of Soviet air power was felt. In the south on 31 August there were twelve aerial attacks by a total of sixty-six aircraft at Dnepropetrovsk. On the same day there were twenty-nine aerial attacks on the Seventeenth Army, seven against the Hungarian Mobile Corps and an undisclosed number of bombing missions in the area of the Sixth Army.[108] Protecting Army Group South was Löhr's Air Fleet 4, but by the end of August his forces had shrunk to an operational strength of 320 bombers, 100 fighters and 35 reconnaissance aircraft. The opposing aircraft in the Soviet South-Western and Southern Fronts numbered 493 bombers, 473 fighters and 20 reconnaissance aircraft. There was still a qualitative gap in the training and experience of the German and Soviet aircrews, but the relentlessness of the air war in the east was soon claiming even Germany's top fighter aces. Erich Hohagen, with thirty 'victories', was shot down and severely wounded on 8 September.[109] Of more importance were those with the highest public profile. When Heinrich Hoffmann was killed in his Bf-109 south of Yel'nya he was the fourth highest ranked German fighter ace, with sixty-three 'victories'. Above him in third place was Hermann-Friedrich Joppien with seventy 'victories' (twenty-eight of them in the east), but he was killed in action on 25 August. Heinz Bär was in second place with eighty 'victories'; however, he was shot down on 30 August and would spend two months in hospital recovering. At the top of the table was Werner Mölders with 101 'victories', yet the celebrated pilot would also be dead before the end of the year in a non-combat-related plane crash.[110]

Soviet aircraft and tactics were also adapting to the unique aerial combat in the east, which was proving very different from the war the Luftwaffe had waged against Britain. Although on the eve of Barbarossa some 80 per cent of Soviet combat aircraft consisted of obsolete models, the newer generation of fighters (IaK-1, LaGG-2 and MiG-3), light bombers (Pe-2 and Pe-8) and ground-assault aircraft (Il-2) were more than capable of standing up to or even outclassing their German equivalents.[111] Tactical aviation was the essential feature of the air war in the east and the Soviets were uniquely served by the introduction of the Il-2 *Shturmovik*, a heavily armoured plane built to sustain the heavy fire of infantry weapons for low-flying raids. German fighters often arrived too late to intercept its raids on front-line positions, but even if they came in time, staying low to the ground, the Il-2 exposed German planes to the heavy fire of Soviet ground forces.[112] Additional changes in Soviet tactics reversed the suicidal raids of older model bombers, which suffered horrendous losses in the early summer of 1941, frequently with entire squadrons failing to return. More and more, Soviet bombers were switched to night-time raids and tended to operate in smaller numbers in a co-ordinated shuttle service that repeatedly bombed German front-line positions, often for hours at a time. Typically these raids inflicted little physical damage, but they added to the fatigue and psychological stress of the German troops who began referring to the constant nightly drone as the 'duty sergeant' or the 'sewing machine'.[113] Erich Kern remembered the relentless Soviet bombing attacks, which he noted, 'hammered against our ears'. He then continued, 'Every few minutes during the night, bombs were tipped, as [if] from a giant shovel on our resting columns, . . . its effect in [the] course of time was very heavy on our nerves.'[114] Simially, Hans-Albert Giese noted the nightly attacks by Soviet bombers, but their frequency and the disruption caused to his sleep finally outweighed the danger and he could no longer be bothered to get up and find cover.[115]

While Eremenko's front was heavily supported by airpower to stop Panzer Group 2, Guderian was afforded the backing of Bruno Loerzer's II Air Corps, which provided vital ground support both to defend his long flanks and to assist local counterattacks. Already on 27 August Loerzer's forces were able to fly 220 aircraft in support of Thoma's 17th Panzer Division (180 Stukas and 40 Destroyers).[116] On the afternoon of 30 August more than ninety Soviet tanks belonging to the Soviet 108th Tank Division attacked Thoma's panzer division. More troubling than the sheer number of Soviet tanks was the fact that many of these were the heavy 52 ton KV-1s, which were invulnerable to German anti-tank weapons and could only be destroyed by armour-piercing shells, fired from 88mm anti-aircraft guns. German intelligence about Soviet strength in the area had been very poor and the sudden appearance of so many Soviet tanks caused great alarm within Lemelsen's XXXXVII Panzer Corps. There were fears that the corps, operating on the eastern bank of the Desna River, might be split into two[117] as the Soviet attack drove 2 kilometres into the German line.[118] On 31 August Thoma's 17th Panzer Division organized a failed counterattack, the cause of which was recounted in the panzer corps war diary: 'Numerous tanks of the heaviest variety, which our guns cannot penetrate, shoot with superior weapons from well-camouflaged positions at our advancing panzers. This causes considerable losses, among them eleven destroyed [German tanks].'[119] On the following day (1 September) Lemelsen's second panzer division (the 18th) was brought into the attack, but had to contend with the Soviet 4th Cavalry Division, which was supporting the 108th Tank Division. The war diary of Nehring's 18th Panzer Division referred to well-placed Soviet artillery fire and machine gun positions, which led to a 'very critical situation'.[120] Yet, as Lemelsen's attack developed and his panzer divisions were able to concentrate their firepower together with aerial support, Eremenko's thrust was beaten back with serious losses. On the German side losses were also heavy, with Thoma's 17th Panzer Division alone suffering twenty destroyed and an undisclosed number of damaged tanks in only two days of fighting.[121] Once again the heavy model Soviet tanks reflected their superiority, even in the absence of adequate supporting arms. Indeed all along the eastern front these colossal machines had developed a fearsome reputation within both the German panzer and infantry divisions. The 7th Panzer Division noted on 3 September that, despite all the efforts of anti-tank crews, an attack by just two KV-1s could not be stopped. Days later the same division noted that the appearance of four KV-1s caused the nearby infantry immediately to retreat in spite of the fact that the tanks did not attack.[122] The helplessness of the German troops against this unparalleled weapon was summed up by a battle report from the 4th Panzer Division: 'Now one field gun opens fire and fires to the last shell. Then it is run over and crushed by a 52-ton tank.'[123]

The war was clearly not all going Germany's way, and even minor setbacks, when taken as a whole across the length and breadth of the eastern front, were proving costly enough to compromise the cutting edge of Germany's offensive strength. Even once a crisis at the front had been surmounted and the situation restored, losses in both manpower and equipment were increasingly difficult to replace, meaning that many divisions found themselves in a steady process of irreparable decline. The implications were already evident in Guderian's sluggish advance to the south, and the situation was even worse in some of the infantry divisions, especially from the battered Ninth and Sixth Armies.

While Lemelsen's panzer corps fought desperately to defend Guderian's left flank, elements of Schweppenburg's XXIV Panzer Corps were struggling to maintain their position in the south. In addition to the vital bridge seized by the 3rd Panzer Division at Novgorod-Severskii, the 10th Motorized Infantry Division had forced another crossing over the Desna further south near Korop. On 30 August the motorized division attempted to thrust further south from the river, but was caught in the teeth of Eremenko's offensive and, operating alone, was beaten back. By 2 September Bock's diary recorded that the division had 'lost its bridgehead south of the Desna'.[124] According to Guderian's memoir, four Soviet divisions as well as a tank brigade attacked the 10th Motorized Infantry Division. When Guderian visited the division on 3 September, he noted that the heavy engagements of the past few days had elicited 'tragically high casualties'.[125] The difficulties of his panzer group again gave Guderian cause to request further reinforcements from Bock's critically depleted reserves. Guderian had already received the 1st Cavalry Division, the Infantry Regiment *Grossdeutschland* and, most recently, the 2nd SS Division *Das Reich*. Yet Guderian's forces were still bottled up in northern Ukraine and it was unknown how much more strength Eremenko could bring to bear. As Guderian wrote after the war, 'XXIV Panzer Corps was insistent about the growing threat to its ever lengthening southern flank and the increasing weakness of its spearhead.'[126] A report by Guderian on 2 September depicted the panzer group's situation as, according to Bock, 'so pessimistic' that the Field Marshal proposed seeking Brauchitsch's approval for a tactical withdrawal of Guderian's forces. Specifically, Bock suggested that Guderian's units currently on the eastern bank of the Desna be withdrawn to support the Second Army's struggling left flank. Yet, upon hearing of the idea Guderian immediately rejected it, assuring Bock that his panzer group would be able to fulfil the task it had been given, provided additional forces were supplied.[127] More than likely, although his situation was indeed very difficult, Guderian took advantage of his predicament to compel Bock to surrender units, which the panzer commander believed had been unfairly denied to him from the beginning. On the other hand, assuming the circumstances reported by Guderian were not a ploy calculated for effect, the need for so many reinforcements to maintain the advance says much about the degree to which the panzer group had been weakened by Soviet counterattacks. In any case, with Guderian reporting the worst and the absolute necessity of keeping the attack south moving, on 2 September Bock released Vietinghoff's XXXXVI Panzer Corps to Guderian's command.[128]

In spite of this gesture, the bitter acrimony stemming from the outcome of the July–August strategic crisis still complicated relations within Army Group Centre. Guderian not only took great exception to the dismemberment of his panzer group, but he also bitterly rejected having his strategic judgement called into question. The issue at stake was Guderian's employment of Lemelsen's panzer corps and its protection of the panzer group's long right flank. The Desna River flows south on a parallel course with Guderian's advance until it cuts sharply to the west, requiring that the panzer group cross the formidable river to cut off the Soviet South-Western Front. As discussed earlier, Schweppenburg's 3rd Panzer Division had already won an important crossing at Novgorod-Severskii, which forced the advance to continue south on the eastern bank of the river. North of Novgorod-Severskii, Lemelsen's panzer corps supposedly had the benefit of the river to assist in providing flank security. Yet Guderian also controlled river crossings further north of Novgorod-Severskii, and at the easiest stage of the offensive he ordered the 17th and 18th Panzer Divisions on to the eastern bank to engage Soviet forces. This detracted from Lemelsen's ability to concentrate more forces in the south, where the spearhead was supposed to be driving forward. It also engaged Guderian's strength unnecessarily on his left when he was already having difficulty maintaining contact with Weichs's Second Army on his right.

On 29 August Bock inquired of the panzer group as to why Lemelsen had not advanced south using the safety of the river, to which Guderian replied that he had directed the corps to engage and destroy an enemy group massing in the east.[129] That same day Bock discussed the matter with Halder, at which the Chief of the General Staff commented disparagingly, 'If one plays with fire, it is not surprising that as a result he gets burned.'[130] Halder's concerns proved justified. With the commencement of Eremenko's late August offensive, Lemelsen suddenly found himself engaged by the above-mentioned KV-1s on the eastern bank of the river. Lemelsen was, therefore, unable either to close the harmful gap with Weichs or to assist Schweppenburg's stalled advance in the south. By 31 August this circumstance induced Halder sharply to criticize Guderian's strategic sense. Writing in his diary Halder vented his frustration:

> *The morning situation is dominated by a decidedly uncomfortable situation within Guderian's [panzer] group. Caused by the fact that he made his advance as a flank movement along the enemy front, and, naturally as a result, was under heavy enemy attack on his eastern side, as well as the fact that his long advance to the east separated him from the Second Army, and that the enemy exploited this opening to attack him from the west, Guderian's offensive strength in the south is so weakened that he is stalled. Now he is blaming the whole world for this objectionable circumstance and hurls accusations and obscenities in all directions. He can only be helped by infantry support relieving his 18th Panzer Division and later the elements further south (17th Pz.Div.), as well as by forces from Weichs's left wing closing the gap to Pz.Gr.2. This will all take a few days and meanwhile Guderian is stuck, the result of his mistaken approach.*[131]

Halder was not the only one to assert that Guderian's strategy was false. On 2 September Hitler became equally displeased with the 'unnecessary fighting by Guderian's group on the eastern bank of the Desna'.[132] To Guderian and his staff, however, the issue was a matter not of how the available units had been deployed, but rather of the withholding of forces by higher echelons of command which prohibited the advance from moving forward. Liebenstein, Guderian's Chief of Staff, noted in his diary on 1 September: 'It is a major mistake . . . that insufficient forces have been committed to achieve success quickly, to reach our goals before the onset of winter.'[133] Likewise, Lieutenant-Colonel Walter Nagel, the panzer group's liaison officer to the OKH, attended a conference at Army Group Centre on 3 September at which both Halder and Brauchitsch were present. Apparently in the course of discussions Nagel went too far in arguing the case for Guderian and, according to the panzer commander's account, 'he [Nagel] was, therefore, described as a "loudspeaker and propagandist" and immediately relieved of his appointment'.[134] The following day (4 September) Hitler voiced exasperation that Lemelsen's panzer corps was still tied up fighting east of the Desna. Given that Hitler was now casting his gaze towards Moscow (the OKW was preparing a new war directive on the subject), the slow progress of Guderian's offensive and the added complication of

Eremenko's counterattacks were now causing Hitler the same trepidation that had been disturbing Bock for some time. The whole of Belorussia had been overrun in the first nine days of Barbarossa, but since 25 August the most advanced units of Guderian's spearhead were only 100 kilometres from their starting positions and most of his units were further back defending the endangered flanks. Thus, incensed at Guderian's imprudence, and dismayed by the irresolute actions of the OKH and Army Group Centre in not correcting the matter, Hitler insisted on action. As Halder noted, 'The Führer is very angry with Guderian, who cannot give up his intention to push south with the XXXXVII Panzer Corps east of the Desna.'[135]

Bypassing the OKH, Army Group Centre was then instructed by the OKW to have Guderian explain himself and his lack of progress. This they dutifully did, informing Guderian that Hitler was 'not satisfied with the development of the situation'.[136] Guderian immediately drafted his response. He cited the great length of his flanks, the bad deployment of Weichs's Second Army, the need to attack enemy groupings east of the Desna and finally the weakness of his forces and the repeated denials of reinforcements.[137] When Bock saw what Guderian had submitted for transmission to the OKW he became irate. He felt he had already been exceedingly generous to Guderian, in spite of the dire threat to the rest of his army group, and now the panzer commander was effectively blaming Bock, at least in part, for his difficulties. It was the last straw for Bock, who now approached Brauchitsch seeking that Guderian be relieved of his command. Brauchitsch, however, persuaded Bock to think the matter over. In the meantime, Bock included his own attachment to Guderian's report, asserting, as he noted in his diary, the dreadful status of the army group's defensive front: '[T]he army group was strained to the point of ripping apart (the divisions on the Fourth Army's southern wing are manning fronts 40 km wide), ... consequently a further release of forces to Guderian was out of the question, and ... indeed it might even become necessary to turn the Guderian group around in response to a breakthrough on the Fourth Army's southern wing.'[138]

Hitler's decision reached the panzer group just after midnight on 5 September.[139] As Halder noted, 'Orders were issued for Guderian [that is, Lemelsen's divisions] to return to the western bank.'[140] Halder also alluded to the antagonism within Army Group Centre: 'Tension between Bock and Guderian. The former approached Brauchitsch

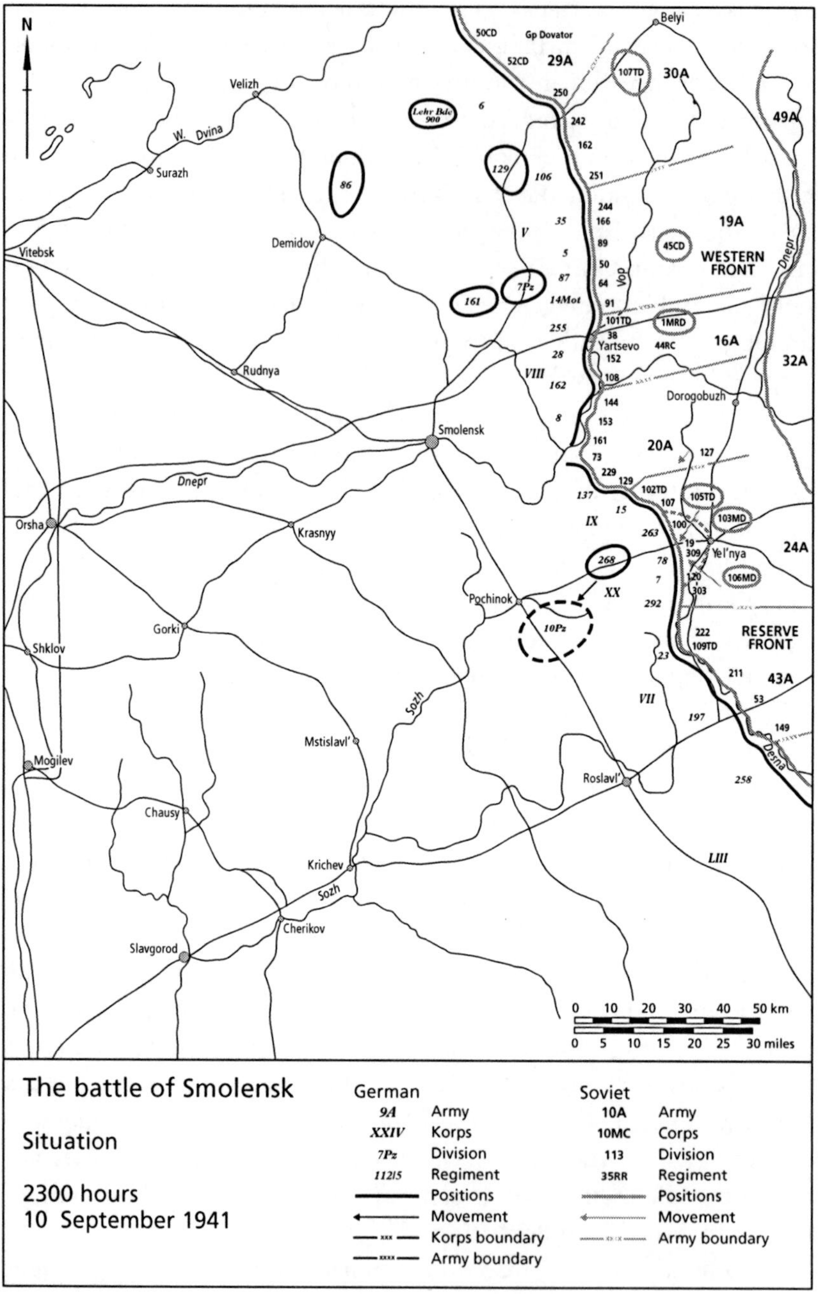

Map 9 Dispositions of Army Group Centre on 10 September 1941
Source: Glantz, *Atlas of the Battle of Smolensk 7 July–10 September 1941.*

for Guderian's relief from command.'[141] When Guderian received the transmission with his new instructions he was disgusted. He noted bitterly in his memoir that the OKH's orders 'were cast in an uncouth language which offended me'. He lamented the fact that the redeployment would take days to implement, which he believed could have been saved by the continuation of Lemelsen's attack towards the south. Yet on this occasion even the cantankerous Guderian knew he would have to accept his orders and, accordingly, he instructed Lemelsen to abandon the eastern bank of the Desna. Not only did Guderian fail to accept the universal condemnation of his actions, but he in fact felt slighted that his achievements up until this point had received 'no word of recognition'.[142] Liebenstein felt the same way and complained in his diary on 5 September, 'When can we expect orders, not criticisms?'[143] Just as Guderian had overextended himself in July by striving for Yel'nya, instead of closing the pocket at Smolensk, his attempt to push south, as well as engage Eremenko east of the Desna, ended in spiteful recriminations and bitter accusations of blame. As fate would have it, at the same time as Lemelsen was retreating back across the Desna, the final evacuation of the Yel'nya salient was also taking place (see map 9). This was an event the panzer commander also alluded to in his memoir, reproaching his superiors for the casualties at Yel'nya, which Guderian audaciously claimed, 'I had sought to avoid'.[144]

As in the preceding month of the strategic crisis, the German command still seemed to be expending as much energy fighting among themselves over operational deployments and the placement of reserves, as they did worrying about the Red Army. The post-crisis pretence of harmony between Hitler and the OKH was replaced by fiery disputes within Army Group Centre itself. Underlying it all was a palpable sense of frustration at the growing limitations of the *Ostheer* and the frightful implications of its diminishing strength. Even for the most powerful army group on the eastern front the ability to repel Soviet attacks, while remaining on the offensive, was proving too much. Two months before, the whole of Bock's army group was moving forward in one fluid motion; yet now it could barely manage a flanking manoeuvre with an entire panzer group in one of the weakest sectors of the Soviet front. To put it another way, in the first ten days of Operation Barbarossa some 300,000 Soviet troops were surrounded in the battle of Minsk. By contrast, in the first ten days of Guderian's drive to the south in the battle of Kiev, Panzer Group 2, advancing against many previously shattered Soviet units, reported just 30,000 Soviet POWs.[145]

Available histories largely ignore the operational difficulties of Guderian's advance to the south, with the whole operation typically evaluated through the narrow prism of its well-known outcome. In truth, however, the early stages of the operation were, from the German perspective, by no means a foregone conclusion guaranteeing ultimate success. Guderian's offensive managed to push forward only under great strain, while Kleist's panzer group was still nowhere to be seen in the south. From the Soviet perspective, despite the inauspicious beginnings of the German offensive, the danger of encirclement for Kirponos's South-Western Front was very real and there was little time left to avert disaster. Eremenko's front was barely restraining Guderian's spearhead and his strength was almost exhausted. Meanwhile, in the south, the Seventeenth Army had just secured bridgeheads near Kremenchug, which would facilitate Kleist's eventual advance north of the Dnepr. If the Soviet Union were to ward off, or at least ameliorate, the effects of Stalin's inaction up to this point, the coming days would have to prove decisive.

5 OMINOUS HORIZONS

September strategic dilemmas – Hitler and Stalin invite disaster

If by early September the enduring hope for Germany's success in the Ukraine rested largely on Guderian's shoulders, the hopes of the Soviet Union rested with equal gravity on Eremenko's success in stopping him. Although the fighting along the eastern front raged across more than 2,700 kilometres, from the Barents Sea in the north down to the Black Sea in the south, there was no position of more fundamental importance than Eremenko's Briansk Front. More specifically, his Twenty-First and Thirteenth Armies had to defend Kirponos's exposed rear, but they were ill disposed to do so and were soon split apart despite Panzer Group 2's sluggish advance. Anticipating the danger, yet utterly failing to appreciate its magnitude, the *Stavka* endeavoured to deploy the newly raised Fortieth Army (under Kirponos's command) to plug the gap. It was an expedient measure of little real substance since the Fortieth Army consisted of two rifle divisions and one airborne corps, which had all been severely weakened in earlier fighting on the Dnepr.[1] In any case, Guderian was not supposed to pose a serious problem for the Fortieth Army because Eremenko's offensive was theoretically intended to dismember Panzer Group 2. By 2 September Eremenko's lack of success placed him in a similar boat to Guderian and he too suffered the ire of his superiors, not least of all Stalin himself. Acting on Stalin's instructions, Shaposhnikov, the Chief of the General Staff, informed Eremenko in a coarsely worded communiqué:

> *The* Stavka *is much displeased with your work. In spite of the efforts of aviation and ground units, Pochep and Starodub remain in enemy hands... Guderian and the whole of his group must be smashed into smithereens. Until this happens, all your statements about success are worthless. I await your reports on the destruction of Guderian's group.*[2]

The commander of the Soviet South-Western Direction, Marshal S. M. Budenny, was not ignorant of the danger, but he was extremely cautious in his dealings with the *Stavka* and sought approval for virtually all decisions of any substance.[3] On 4 September he submitted to Stalin a report detailing the emergent threat to his flanks and requesting immediate reinforcement. If this was not possible, Budenny asked permission to create his own reserve by transferring four divisions from Kirponos's Thirty-Seventh and Twenty-Sixth Armies. On Stalin's order Shaposhnikov rejected Budenny's request for reinforcements and also forbade the makeshift solution of internally reorganizing divisions to support the flanks.[4]

Time was running out, but Stalin could still not accept what Kirponos and Budenny recognized as the inevitable consequence of attempting to hold out at Kiev. Not only was Eremenko's front breaking apart, but Kirponos correctly foresaw the potential danger emanating from the German bridgehead in the south near Kremenchug. Accordingly, he ordered a special command group to the Thirty-Eighth Army with instructions to eliminate the German crossings.[5] Meanwhile, Eremenko's desperation was driving him to extreme measures. On 5 September he requested and received permission from the *Stavka* to form 'blocking detachments' in order to prevent frightened and demoralized troops from retreating without orders. The idea of such formations reflects the ruthlessness of the Soviet state and its willingness to use lethal force as an instrument of control even against its own troops. Unauthorized withdrawals within Briansk Front were henceforth to be halted 'using all necessary weaponry'.[6]

While Soviet field commanders had been fearing the worst for some time, the higher echelons of the Soviet command, with the notable exception of Stalin, were also growing increasingly anxious at what appeared to be the impending collapse of Kirponos's northern flank. Guderian, in tandem with Weichs's Second and Reichenau's

Sixth Army, was making slow but steady headway and Shaposhnikov could no longer ignore what Stalin refused to accept. Late on 7 September Shaposhnikov, together with the head of the Operations Staff and Deputy Chief of the General Staff, Lieutenant-General A. M. Vasilevsky, resolved to confront Stalin directly. Although such a move may be seen as a rather belated action given Zhukov's perceptive warning in late July, the Soviet dictator's temper, as well as his ardent objection to opinions that contradicted his own, was most likely the reason for Shaposhnikov's and Vasilevsky's hesitance and trepidation. By the same token, Zhukov's ignominious demotion for suggesting Kiev could not be held no doubt also influenced Shaposhnikov's vacillation. In any case, Shaposhnikov and Vasilevsky tried to persuade Stalin of the necessity for withdrawing the South-Western Front and of the dangers inherent in further delay. As Vasilevsky later recalled, 'The conversation was tough and uncompromising. Stalin reproached us, saying that like Budenny we took the line of least resistance – retreating instead of beating the enemy.'[7] Ultimately, Shaposhnikov and Vasilevsky extracted permission for tactical withdrawals of the Fifth and Thirty-Seventh Armies to better defensive lines, but nothing substantive. As Vasilevsky concluded:

> *In other words, this was a half-way measure. The mere mention of the urgent need to abandon Kiev threw Stalin into a rage and he momentarily lost his self-control. We evidently did not have sufficient will power to withstand these outbursts of uncontrollable rage or a proper appreciation of our responsibility for the impending catastrophe in the South-Western Direction.*[8]

If the Soviet generals shared a degree of responsibility for the more immediate catastrophe their forces were to suffer, the German generals were at the same time becoming complicit in a later one. On 6 September Hitler signed War Directive 35 ordering yet another major offensive operation to commence at the end of September. Without mentioning the staggering losses of the campaign or the run-down condition of the motorized and panzer divisions, Hitler now imposed a tremendous new undertaking on the overstretched *Ostheer*. Even sustaining the current operation, which was only a week and a half old, placed a barely manageable strain on the Wehrmacht, and there was still the elimination of multiple Soviet armies to be achieved as well as a vast area of the eastern Ukraine to be occupied. Nevertheless, Hitler's War Directive 35 commanded that renewed operations from Army Group Centre be directed against what it called 'Army Group Timoshenko', which had to be 'annihilated in the limited time which remains before the onset of winter'.[9] Even if this grand objective could be achieved within the short time frame, Hitler envisaged a second and far more ambitious goal for the *Ostheer*. As the war directive stated, 'Only when Army Group Timoshenko has been defeated in . . . encircling operations of annihilation will our central army be able to begin the advance on Moscow with its right flank on the Oka and its left on the Upper Volga.'[10] It was an operation so audacious in scope and so bereft of understanding of the capabilities of the forces that would have to carry it out that it suggests nothing had been learned since the first days of Operation Barbarossa's planning. The only tangible reinforcement for such an extensive new operation was the intended release of the two panzer divisions not so far committed to action (the 2nd and 5th Panzer Divisions)[11] and a consignment of previously withheld panzer production. The war directive also alluded to a regrouping of support from the flanking army groups to provide additional units from the army and Luftwaffe for Army Group Centre. Yet, in the meantime, the war directive insisted upon simultaneous offensives on the flanks. Army Group South was tasked with providing 'a flank guard' involving an advance 'in a general north-easterly direction'. At the same time, Army Group North 'should be moved forward on both sides of Lake Ilmen to cover the northern flank [of Army Group Centre] and to maintain contact with the Finnish Karelian Army'. Not since July had the three army groups been able to maintain simultaneous advances, and the shortage of resources as well as the fatigue of the German combat units had been growing steadily worse from week to week. Yet it was not just Hitler and the generals of the OKW who accepted War Directive 35 without reservation. At the OKH and Army Group Centre there was relief that Hitler now supported what Bock referred to as 'my old wish'.[12] As with Barbarossa, problems were clearly apparent, but these were once again ignored. Instead there was a strident faith in the ability of the troops to meet whatever objectives they were set and an astonishing refusal to consider the intervention of practical matters such as the shortage of manpower, logistics or the plummeting level of motorization. Indeed none of these factors found any mention at all in War Directive 35.

Beyond the obvious dichotomy between the weakness of German forces and the profligacy of German plans, a new factor was slowly coming into the mix, which would impact with ever worsening consequences for the *Ostheer*. On 25 August, the first day of Guderian's offensive into the Ukraine, Ernst Guicking, a soldier from the 52nd Infantry Division, wrote home to his wife: 'Here the Russian autumn is gradually becoming noticeable. The wind already blusters through the branches.'[13] Days later, on 1 September, Hans Pichler complained in his diary, 'In recent days it has become noticeably cold and, as a result, there is no chance to properly dry the damp blankets, boots and clothes.'[14] The following day (2 September) Guicking wrote home in another letter, 'At the moment we have terrible weather. It rained the whole night long and it does not look as though it is going to stop. It really seems as though it is gradually becoming winter.'[15] The implications of such seasonal changes were not lost on the men. Solomon Perel noted that as the colder weather was setting in, the soldiers of the 12th Panzer Division began drawing ominous parallels with Napoleon's fate.[16] By contrast, at the highest echelons of the Nazi state concerns about the changing weather were not permitted to alter belief in the final victory. On 27 August, after having been informed about the poor weather conditions on the eastern front, Joseph Goebbels noted in his diary, 'It will not make it easy for us to win this war. Yet once we have won it, then the difficulties we are now experiencing, which are causing the greatest concerns, will appear as only pleasant memories.'[17] In a similar fashion, the chief of the operations department of the Luftwaffe, Major-General Hoffman von Waldau, commented in his diary on 9 September, 'We are heading for a winter campaign. The real trial of this war has begun, the belief in final victory remains.'[18]

On 30 August Halder conceded that the winter was likely to 'necessitate operations against limited objectives' and he therefore ordered a report from the Operations Department on providing winter clothing for this purpose. Far from the envisaged occupation duties of an inactive and scaled-down army, adequately maintaining the entire *Ostheer* in the east throughout the winter would be vastly more demanding than anything previously conceived of and necessitated certain prerequisites well beyond Germany's capabilities. Nevertheless, in a stark reminder of Halder's remarkably flawed strategic conception during the planning phase of Barbarossa, he accepted this momentous new undertaking with an indifference indicative of his blindness.[19] With little real understanding of the prodigious problems a winter campaign would entail, in either the production of so many uniforms or their distribution to the front, Halder simply instructed that a report on the measures be 'passed to the Organization Department for the necessary action'.[20] One might conclude that it was a blindness born of ignorance, but there were others in the German army, including some considerably lower in rank, who were under no illusions as to the severity of what was coming. Hans Meier-Welcker, an officer in the Ninth Army, wrote home in a letter on 6 September: 'It is already often really cold. Thoughts are directed towards the winter, which will, in effect, mean for us a life cut off from Europe. I myself observe the whole development in silence and wonder sometimes how naive men can be.'[21] Even as early as August the British press enjoyed stoking the issue. A cartoon in the *Daily Mail* depicted a German soldier trudging through knee-deep mud as Hitler suddenly appeared behind him with a gift. 'Look!' Hitler says. 'I've bought you a lovely fur coat!'[22] Ironically even the scornfully mordant British press were assuming too much if they thought that the average German soldier would be adequately equipped for what was coming.

The changing weather was not the only indication that time was running against German operations in the east. Stalin was anxious to augment the Red Army with as much British and American war materiel as possible, and by early September the first large-scale deliveries of Lend-Lease materiel were at last arriving and being pressed into service. In addition to British armaments, the Royal Air Force transferred the 151st Fighter Wing to Vianga airfield 27 kilometres north-east of Murmansk on the Barents Sea.[23] Ostensibly its role was to provide training for Soviet pilots and ground crews in the newly arriving Hurricane fighters,[24] yet the proximity of Vianga airfield to Finnish and German airbases meant a combat role soon became inevitable.[25] On 12 September Wing-Commander Henry Ramsbottom-Isherwood, a New Zealander, led his men in their first action, which resulted in three German planes being shot down for one lost Hurricane. Overall Wing 151 conducted 365 sorties until its mission came to an end in November 1941. For their expert leadership and combat performance Ramsbottom-Isherwood and three of his men received the Order of Lenin – the only non-Soviet servicemen to win them during World War II.[26]

As one might expect, Ramsbottom-Isherwood and his fellow RAF pilots flying combat missions over the eastern front was of far more symbolic, than tangible, importance (just as bestowing the Order of Lenin on four foreign servicemen was), yet the symbolism was indicative of the new Anglo-Soviet relationship. Whatever ideological differences they may have previously harboured, the common threat posed by Hitler's expanding empire surpassed all outstanding grievances and allowed for an immediate concord built on co-dependency.[27] When Churchill's private secretary, John Colville, suggested to the Prime Minister that aiding the Soviets was not consistent with his many years as an arch anti-communist, Churchill is said to have explained 'that he had only one single purpose – the destruction of Hitler – and his life was much simplified thereby. If Hitler invaded hell he would at least make a favourable reference to the devil!'[28] By the same token, the ferocity and magnitude of the struggle now raging inside his own country drove Stalin to seek any assistance his new ally could provide. In a letter to Churchill on 3 September 1941 the Soviet dictator made two brash requests. Firstly, he asked that the British open a second front somewhere in Europe in 1941, and secondly, he appealed for enormous military aid in the form of 400 planes and 500 tanks to be supplied to the Soviet Union every month.[29] Three days later (6 September) Churchill responded to Stalin's letter by immediately rejecting the idea of a second front in 1941.[30] Action leading to fiascos, he told Stalin, 'would be of no help to anyone but Hitler'.[31] The supply of war materiel, however, was a different matter. In spite of the demands Stalin's request would place on British production and shipping, Churchill not only agreed in principle to the deliveries, he co-ordinated with the Americans to ensure that Stalin's figures for aircraft and tank deliveries formed the basis of the First Protocol governing Lend-Lease aid to the Soviet Union until June 1942.[32]

While some have scoffed at the initial Anglo-American military contribution to the Soviet war effort, seeing it as a whimsical gesture aimed simply at maintaining Soviet morale, or worse, a proxy exchange of western war materiel for Soviet blood, neither representation is accurate. In the course of 1941 British industry manufactured a total of 4,841 tanks,[33] and according to the terms of the First Protocol, some 4,500 tanks were due to be shipped over a nine-month period. American military aid accounted for a portion of this figure, but Britain remained the Soviet Union's main supplier of arms throughout 1941 and much of 1942. Indeed, given the scale of Britain's commitments in North Africa and the defence of the home islands as well as the wider empire, the scale of Churchill's undertaking to the Soviet Union testifies to how seriously he took the war in the east.[34] At the same time, the British leadership's public promises of aid for the Soviet Union were briskly dismissed within Nazi Germany. Goebbels stated his belief that the 'cries of help for the Soviet Union would probably remain more platonic' than tangible.[35] Yet again the German leadership underestimated the resolve of their enemies. Popular enthusiasm for the Soviet cause was at an all-time high within Britain and on 22 September 1941 Lord Beaverbrook declared 'Tanks for Russia' week in British factories. The first tank off the assembly line was dubbed 'Stalin', followed by others named 'Lenin' and 'Another for Joe'. The programme proved so popular in British factories that the frequently strained labour relations were set aside for any orders labelled 'Goods for Russia'. At Ashford in Kent a railway construction yard completed an order for a thousand railway wagons in just ten days despite seventy-six air raid warnings. Even before the First Protocol was signed (1 October) the first British convoy bound for the Soviet Union was underway on 12 August in Operation Dervish.[36] With the Anglo-American war industries still gearing up for mass production, the terms of the First Protocol claimed a significant share of Allied armament production, indicating that the early period of war on the eastern front involved the western powers to a considerably larger extent than is often recognized.[37]

With colder weather and the first shipments of Lend-Lease aid now arriving, the importance of keeping Guderian's offensive in motion was now starkly underlined. At that time the only other major offensive operation still making progress on the eastern front was Army Group North's attempt to isolate Leningrad and then link up with the Finnish army of Field Marshal Carl Gustaf Emil Mannerheim. In the meantime Guderian struggled with the fierce counterattacks of Eremenko's Briansk Front and what he viewed as the infuriating interference of his own high command. With the full backing of Hitler and the OKW, the OKH had ordered Guderian to redeploy Lemelsen's XXXXVII Panzer Corps, which the panzer commander had bitterly resisted. Such a move not only implicated Guderian for his flawed strategic approach, but, as we have seen, the dispute had grown so acrimonious that it entailed a request by Bock for the panzer commander's dismissal. By late on 5 September, with the matter now resolved to Bock's satisfaction, the commander of Army Group Centre no longer insisted upon Guderian's removal. Instead he accepted Brauchitsch's offer to talk with Guderian on his behalf. Nevertheless, the Field Marshal harboured very real doubts for the future, and after noting Brauchitsch's offer of mediation, Bock concluded, 'but I cannot hide my worries about new difficulties'.[38] Such concerns proved well founded. On the very same day that Bock was agreeing to overlook Guderian's insubordinate behaviour (5 September), a minor matter again flared into another serious confrontation. The issue concerned an order from Bock requiring that the newly freed 1st Cavalry Division, belonging to Panzer Group 2, be moved in the direction of Pochep to act as a defensive reserve or to release more mobile elements on Guderian's long flank. The following morning, on 6 September, Bock discovered that the division had still not departed and he therefore immediately instructed that the cavalry division be set in motion with conformation from the panzer group. By the afternoon still nothing had happened and Bock therefore called Liebenstein, the Chief of Staff of Panzer Group 2, and personally dictated the order to him, which now also placed the division under the direct command of Army Group Centre. When Liebenstein reported back to Bock, as he had been instructed to do once the order had been passed on, he stated that parts of the division would not be following the order because Guderian insisted they were needed south of Dolshok. Liebenstein's report made clear that Guderian had openly declared his defiance and that he would personally answer for the failure to obey Bock.[39] Bock was incredulous and once again insisted his orders be followed 'without hesitation'. The final comment on this episode in Bock's diary says much about the parallel war being waged by the commanders of Army Group Centre: the Field Marshal concluded, 'Apart from these battles with the armoured group, the front was relatively peaceful.'[40]

In the early days of September Eremenko's offensive intended both to put an end to Guderian's offensive momentum and then to fragment his panzer group before destroying the constituent pieces. The latter was certainly well beyond the strength of the Briansk Front and while Eremenko failed in the former as well, it is fair to say he came much closer to this objective. Despite the immense pressure on Bock's eastern front, the commander of Army Group Centre was careful to maintain a steady flow of reinforcements to Guderian's panzer group so that the panzer commander's vital offensive did not bog down as so much of the eastern front had done. By contrast, Eremenko's best efforts certainly slowed Guderian's advance, halted him in places and, it could be argued, forced Lemelsen's XXXXVII Panzer Corps to retreat back across the Desna, but he could not terminate the offensive. In spite of this Eremenko was still inclined to claim a significant degree of success in his post-war memoir:

> *The territorial gain made in the offensive was not very great, but the operational impact was. It was a time when the enemy held the initiative, when his panzer drives, supported by the Luftwaffe, followed in quick succession and the state of our troops, forced to retire deeper and deeper into the country, was anything but good. The determined action against the strongest and most mobile enemy force, and an action, moreover, that succeeded in pushing the enemy back, did a lot to boost morale... They gave us a better knowledge of the enemy and showed us how he could be flogged.*[41]

Despite what might be construed as Eremenko's face-saving claims there was a measure of truth to his assessment. Had Stalin not resolutely forbidden the withdrawal of the Soviet South-Western Front, the dogged efforts of the Briansk Front to hold and counterattack Guderian's thrust might well have provided the time necessary to preserve the overwhelming bulk of Kirponos's forces. As it was, Eremenko's success is probably best measured not by any boost to Red Army morale as he claimed, but rather by the extent to which his actions drew out the battle for the Ukraine and thereby delayed the subsequent German thrust on Moscow. By contrast Guderian's success, together with Weichs's Second Army and Loerzer's II Air Corps, was in keeping his drive south moving, however slowly, using every means at his disposal. Yet not all Guderian's difficulties were man-made. On the night of 3/4 September a thunderstorm hit Guderian's area of operations and, as one panzer corps war diary noted, 'with one stroke all large-scale movement became impossible'.[42] It was the beginning of bad weather that would last for two whole weeks. As Curzio Malaparte, the Italian war correspondent in the Ukraine, wrote in a September dispatch:

> *All of a sudden it starts to rain. At first it is a gentle shower, silent and almost furtive. But soon it develops into a regular hurricane, a veritable cloudburst... Around me I hear a chorus of yells and oaths. The German soldiers look up at*

> *the sky shouting and cursing. The artillery-trains come to an abrupt halt, the horses slither about in the mud that has formed as if by magic, the lorries skid on the slippery surface. 'Oh b——the rain!' yell the artillerymen and drivers, clustering around the guns and lorries, which are soon stuck fast in the mud.*[43]

Rundstedt's private correspondence also made reference to the deterioration in the weather and its impact on operations in the Ukraine. In a letter to his wife the commander of Army Group South wrote on 4 September, 'The mail seems to be functioning badly. Today is a viciously cold autumn day with rain. In view of the bad roads all our communications are cut, even the air courier is not operating regularly. We are already heating with wood. I hope the situation is better with you. Otherwise I am well, only things are not going fast enough, and patience is not one of my virtues.'[44] On the following day (5 September), Rundstedt added in another letter, 'The weather is bad and exercises a paralysing influence on everything . . . Otherwise I am well, of course one wonders about the future.'[45] Clearly Rundstedt was starting to have his own doubts about the progress of operations, and the difficulty of movement in poor weather brought these into sharp focus as the autumn beckoned. Keeping the roads open was paramount for continuing the advance and Lemelsen's XXXXVII Panzer Corps press-ganged local Soviet civilians and captured POWs into doing the work.[46] Yet unlike earlier storms, which had turned the roads to mud and then dried almost as quickly once the hot summer sun came out, in the days following the initial storm the rain was almost unceasing. On 7 September the 18th Panzer Division's war diary noted that the past few days of rain had made the roads 'bottomless' and that ten hours were required to move 20 kilometres. This became a major problem for the panzer division as it was attempting to pull back to the west and was under heavy Soviet air attack leading to 'heavy losses'.[47] To make matters worse, the flanking 167th Infantry Division was being redeployed and therefore stretching the 18th Panzer Division's line to the north. The division was desperately trying to pull back, but could not do so, and the threat of further enemy counterattacks posed the danger that the many bogged-down vehicles would be overrun by the enemy. 'With these terrible road conditions it must inevitably follow that if the enemy remains as active as he had been up until now, the destruction of a great part of the division, or at least the vehicles, will result.'[48] As the situation worsened the divisional command staff became more frantic and tried to have the orders of the 167th Infantry Division overturned. They also requested that the corps commander approach Guderian for an offensive to cover their withdrawal. The panzer division's war diary then recorded the exasperation of the commanding officer: 'One must consider the terrain and not just give orders! I report to anyone who will listen: division is cut off and will be lost if something is not done *immediately*!'[49]

The division was not lost. In fact the Briansk Front's offensive strength was seriously waning as Guderian's slow but steady advance stretched Eremenko's lines and hampered his ability to concentrate for offensives. Yet the sunken roads plagued the long motorized columns of Panzer Group 2, which even in the best of circumstances tended to grind small roads out of existence. On 5 September Bock noted that Guderian's only success was seizing the small town of Sosnitsa, and two days later he added that the panzer group's advance was 'only mediocre'. By contrast, the typically less mobile infantry of the Second and Sixth Armies was managing to force multiple bridgeheads across the Desna.[50] The implications of the changing conditions, as well as the fatigue of the German motorized units and the fanatical Soviet resistance, discredit the references to Guderian's oft-lauded, seamless blitzkrieg into the Ukraine in August and September 1941. Aided by Weichs's Second Army, Guderian's panzer group fought a tough, grinding and sluggish campaign, advancing on a broad front with a long, thinly defended left flank. Meanwhile, Kleist's Panzer Group 1 and Stülpnagel's Seventeenth Army made no progress, aside from the costly house-to-house fighting in Dnepropetrovsk and the more recent bridgehead across the Dnepr near Kremenchug. This is not to say that the offensive in the Ukraine did not enjoy a measure of success – and the potential rewards multiplied at an almost exponential rate the longer Stalin insisted on holding Kiev – but the German advance was by no means rapid, trouble free or inexpensive in blood and materiel.

The condition of the roads upon which the advance was taking place not only posed a serious problem to the movement of Guderian's combat units, they also threatened his supply apparatus.[51] Already in the planning stages of Barbarossa it was made clear that the truck-based logistic system could only operate effectively up to 500 kilometres inside the Soviet Union, which by chance coincided with the

Dvina–Dnepr line.[52] Beyond that point it was preordained that the further operations extended, the worse the supply situation would become. When one then considers the extremely limited transport capacity of the German railways in the occupied Soviet territories and the fallout rate of trucks, the supply situation was in crisis even before the intervention of bad weather. As it was the heavy rain since 4 September added another weight to the burden of maintaining operations towards the south. Already on 4 September the Quartermaster-General's war diary for Panzer Group 2 noted, 'On account of the transportation difficulties resulting from the unfavourable roads and weather conditions, the general supply situation is in question.'[53] The worst-affected formation was Schweppenburg's XXIV Panzer Corps, the spearhead of Guderian's offensive.[54] On 4 September the constituent 3rd Panzer Division reported that the roads 'could no longer be driven on' (*unbefahrbar sind*) and that along some stretches of the supply route most of the trucks remained bogged down in the mud. By 7 September the division was reporting its fuel supplies as 'tight' and by 10 September this had deteriorated to 'very critical'.[55] Guderian noted from his visit to 3rd Panzer Division on 10 September that the landscape 'was dotted with vehicles hopelessly stuck in the mud'. He then observed how the customary march discipline had become impossible and that the advancing columns 'were badly straggled out'.[56] Tractors normally intended for towing the guns now also had to tow the trucks and in places even tanks could no longer move alone.[57]

Nor was there an end in sight to the bad weather. In a preview of what was to come with even greater force in October, rain continued to flood the fields and wash away the roads. From the evening of 10 September to the morning of 11 September there was another severe thunderstorm, which lashed the front with a driving rain for most of the night. Guderian, who was attempting to return to his headquarters, took ten hours to travel 130 kilometres.[58] Meanwhile, on 13 September the Nazi propaganda minister, Joseph Goebbels, conceded in this diary that, after almost two weeks with little respite, 'the God of weather is not on our side'.[59] Such conditions not only slowed movement, but with vehicles operating in lower gears and with reduced traction, fuel consumption rates spiked, resulting in even more demand for the limited stocks. Even on good roads the German Mark III or IV tank consumed roughly 300 litres of fuel per 100 kilometres. Considering the depleted number of tanks in the panzer

Fig. 9 The September advance through the Ukraine was hampered by heavy rains, which slowed the German attack.

divisions, moving fifty tanks 100 kilometres would nevertheless require 15,000 litres of fuel and, to make matters worse, estimates suggest that during cross-country operations, consumption rates jumped by 100–200 per cent.[60]

Nor was it just fuel that the army's logistics system was failing to supply in sufficient quantities. Oil, new tyres, spare parts and replacement motors were all urgently needed. The problem was ubiquitous across the eastern front and had been plaguing attempts to maintain offensive operations since July. In desperation German units commonly searched for what they needed independently of the formal army channels. As one soldier noted, 'Despite the efforts of our engineers, spare parts became unobtainable although we searched a distance of up to one hundred kilometres throughout the army and corps rear area.'[61] On 8 September Brauchitsch visited the headquarters of Panzer Group 2 to fulfil his promise to Bock and address Guderian's unruly conduct; however, the meeting soon took on another agenda as the panzer commander used the opportunity to present a four-point list of requirements. Firstly, Guderian wanted an extension of the railways from Gomel to Bachmatsch. Secondly, he elaborated on the need for spare parts, replacement motors and new trucks. Guderian's third point involved a request for a special delivery of oil, which was in critically short supply. Lastly, and perhaps most ominously, Guderian asked for delivery of the soldier's winter kit, especially the requisite two blankets. Brauchitsch, who probably felt somewhat slighted at having Guderian so blatantly manipulate the intention of his visit, refused to agree to any of the panzer commander's requests.[62]

At its root the German supply system was a house without a foundation. Operating at such depth inside the Soviet Union the trucks of the *Grosstransportraum* could never meet the demands of the army without an extension of the railways. Generally speaking the system was predicated on the idea that at least one high-capacity railway line would be used to support the operations of a single army. Yet in the case of Barbarossa the dearth of a pre-existing, highly developed rail transportation network meant that only three main east–west railway lines were envisaged to support each army group. In early September Army Group Centre commanded three armies (Ninth, Fourth and Second) as well as Guderian's panzer group and the one remaining corps from Hoth's Panzer Group 3 (LVII Panzer Corps).[63] Not only did this clearly represent an inordinate strain on the railways, but the train tracks themselves were often of such poor quality, from either age, lack of maintenance or the damage caused by retreating Soviet forces, that speeds, and therefore carrying capacity, remained low. The German railways operating in the east were clearly overburdened and too slow, yet at the start of the war they suffered from an even greater hindrance. The Soviet rail gauge was wider than that in the rest of Europe and therefore it had to be reset to accommodate German trains (as well as many requisitioned from occupied Europe). This process took weeks and placed far greater strain on the *Grosstransportraum* as it was the only means of rapidly moving supplies forward, aside from the use of a very limited number of captured Soviet locomotives and rolling stock.[64] Goebbels, who received daily military briefings and was therefore very well informed about the military situation in the east, recorded in his diary on 8 September, '[A]lmost without exception the Bolsheviks managed to evacuate all their railroad material so that almost nothing fell into our hands.'[65] The results had a very telling effect on Army Group Centre's motorized transportation.

In the first two months of the war one panzer division recorded the distances its supply vehicles travelled to secure supplies.

In total 303,982 kilometres were covered hauling ammunition, another 199,385 kilometres were driven transporting fuel and 63,073 kilometres were travelled carrying spare parts.[66] Considering the corrosive effects of moving such enormous distances on Soviet roads, with their notoriously uneven surfaces as well as the all-pervasive clouds of dust that overwhelmed air filters and ruined engines, it is not surprising that by early September Panzer Group 2 was experiencing shortages in trucks and supplies. Indeed supplies were being ferried hundreds of kilometres for an individual load. It was around 350 kilometres from the Soviet border town of Brest to Minsk, 500 kilometres to the Dnepr River and some 700 kilometres to Smolensk.[67] Not only did the trucks have to bridge the ever-growing distance between the railheads and the spearhead of the attack, but with the capacity of the railways proving grossly inadequate, there were more than a few instances in which the Quartermaster-General was bypassed altogether and the panzer groups independently dispatched trucks back to Germany to obtain what was required. This ensured that the trucks endured enormous wear and tear for a comparatively diminutive yield in supplies.[68] Under such circumstances there was a manifest difference between what the statisticians were projecting in the distant army headquarters and the reality of conducting operations at the front. A German officer assigned to the OKH, who also had the opportunity to tour Army Group Centre's rear area in the early months of the war, remarked, 'The inherent antagonism between the theorist from the OKH and the supply realist from the panzer group, who both viewed the operation of the *Grosstransportraum* from different perspectives, also impacted the atmosphere.'[69] Guderian confirmed the increasing discrepancy between the means at the panzer group's disposal and conditions they were forced to operate under. Describing events up to 11 September Guderian wrote:

> *Only a man who has personally experienced what life on those canals of mud we called roads was like can form any picture of what the troops and their equipment had to put up with and can truly judge the situation at the front and the consequent effect on our operations. The fact that our military leaders made no attempt to see these conditions for themselves and, initially at least, refused to believe the reports of those who did, was to lead to bitter results, unspeakable suffering and many avoidable misfortunes.*[70]

By the beginning of September studies suggest anywhere between a quarter and a half of all trucks supplying the *Ostheer* had been lost,[71] and even more worryingly for the army, the inability to conduct more than emergency repairs led to projections that suggested many of the remaining vehicles would be lost after an additional 300–400 kilometres.[72]

Bereft of adequate supply and in accordance with the OKH's planning to supplement the needs of the troops, German soldiers plundered their way across the eastern territories. Not only do accounts attest to the thoroughness of the German pillaging, which often left nothing for the impoverished inhabitants, there was also a maliciousness to their actions that led to much unnecessary hardship for the local population. A report from Army Group Centre's rear area on 31 August stated:

> *The population not only in Orsha, but also in Mogilev and other localities, has repeatedly made complaints concerning the taking of their belongings by individual German soldiers, who themselves could have no possible use for such items. I was told, amongst others, by a woman in Orscha, who was in tears of despair, that a German soldier had taken the coat of her three-year-old child whom she was carrying in her arms. She said that her entire dwelling had been burnt; and she would never have thought that German soldiers could be so pitiless . . .* [73]

Most commonly, German soldiers seized foodstuffs from the Soviet peasantry, which they largely justified in their letters and diaries as a simple necessity of war. Yet recent case studies have shown how such practices led directly to the widespread starvation of thousands of Soviet citizens.[74] Helmut Pabst wrote about how he and his comrades looted onions and turnips from people's gardens and took milk from their churns. 'Most of them part with it amiably,' he wrote home in a letter, but he also made clear his indifference to the suffering of the local people: 'Willingly or unwillingly, the country feeds us.'[75] Konrad Jarausch wrote home that 'Everyone is constantly looking for "booty".' He then noted that even in such a poor country it was still possible to obtain honey and kilos of butter.[76] The looting was ubiquitous and endemic to all levels of command. In Witebsk the occupying authorities removed almost all of the town's two hundred head of cattle (paying for just twelve), requisitioned a million sheets of plyboard from the local timberyard and seized 15 tons of salt from a storehouse.[77] Such arbitrary actions, especially when committed by individual soldiers, had been strictly regulated during the 1940 campaign in France. The radical change in policy reflected both the Wehrmacht's complicity in the war of annihilation in the east and also the great difficulty of managing the *Ostheer*'s supply.

Holding together the house of cards – the home front and the eastern front

On 11 September Goebbels noted in his diary that Hitler had not spoken to the German people in almost three months.[78] In fact Hitler had not even left his secluded Wolf's Lair headquarters in East Prussia since the start of Operation Barbarossa. The business of government now came secondary to the direction of the campaign, but unlike Hitler's past blitzkriegs the war against the Soviet Union offered no clear end in sight. In fact by late August there were already numerous acknowledgements within the German high command that the war in the east would run into 1942.[79] During the western campaign in 1940 Hitler had stayed at his *Felsennest* headquarters near Bad Münstereifel for less than a month.[80] By the time Goebbels was contemplating Hitler's growing removal from public life the German dictator had already been absent from Berlin for more than two and a half months. Nazi Germany had suddenly become the Führer state without a Führer and there was no indication that this was about to end.[81] In practice this led to an exacerbation of the already chronic diffusion of co-ordinated administration within the Nazi state because, even by comparison with other dictatorships, Hitler had placed himself in too many roles and acted in each as the sole arbiter of power and decision-making.[82] The result was a hopeless overconcentration of power, which, even without Hitler's long absence from Berlin, could never be effectively managed by one man. The fact that Hitler was now so removed from his government only propagated the independence of the Nazi state's many economic, military and party fiefdoms that, in the absence of sufficient direction, feuded with each other for resources and influence. Thus the persistence of the war in the east was not only swallowing up Germany's limited manpower and resources, it was also effectively denying the Nazi state its leader.[83]

If Hitler's public absence was detrimental to German morale, as Goebbels had noted, it was, however, overshadowed by the question of how much longer the war in the east would last. None of the past campaigns had lasted so long and the initial jubilation inspired by Goebbels's grandiose victory proclamations was soon being tempered by the heavy losses that were increasingly becoming known from the thousands of official death notices as well as the harsh realities reported in soldiers' letters. Only two weeks after the start of Operation Barbarossa Erich W., a soldier home on leave, heard at his Sunday church service about those who had lost their lives. As he noted in his diary, 'There were read out – in a very matter-of-fact tone – the name, year of birth, date and place of death of the dead and fallen, and precisely these cold facts had a doubly moving effect. The widows sobbed throughout the church.'[84] Hildegard Gratz noted that after Barbarossa had begun, '[s]uddenly everything changed. The radio carried on broadcasting news of victories. But the daily papers carried endless columns of death notices.'[85] Classified SD reports (the SD or *Sicherheitsdienst* was a sub-element of Heinrich Himmler's SS) undertaken to gauge the public mood detected a rising apprehension about the costs of the war in the east. One report from 4 August read:

> *It is often said that the campaign has not been proceeding as might have been assumed from reports at the start of the operation... Since then, we have had the impression that the Soviets have plenty of materiel and that there has been* increasing resistance... *From the number of reported deaths... the panzer corps reports and front reports, one can safely assume* that casualties really are higher than in previous campaigns.[86]

While there were certainly those elements within the Nazi state willing to pay any price for Hitler's promise of *Lebensraum*, by the summer of 1941 there was also a distinct war-weariness among other elements of the German population and the burdens of the new eastern campaign, demanding ever more sacrifice, were observed with much private trepidation. Indeed Operation Barbarossa had a polarizing effect in which dissenters were bold enough at times to risk open objection.[87] A local *Landrat* (chief administrator of a rural district) in northern Franconia reported on 1 July, 'Overworked and exhausted men and women do not see why the war must be carried still further into Asia and Africa.'[88] He then continued, at the end of August:

> *I have only one wish, that one of the officials in Berlin or Munich . . . should be in my office some time when, for example, a worn-out old peasant beseechingly requests allocation of labourers or other assistance, and as proof of his need shows two letters, in one of which the company commander of the elder son answers that leave for the harvest cannot be granted, and in the other of which the company commander of the younger son informs of his heroic death in an encounter near Propoiszk.*[89]

By 8 September the classified SD reports were reporting the circulation of disturbing rumours, which, in the face of the unremitting victory pronouncements, reflected a surprising degree of pessimism. Many people were talking about a 'freezing' of the front or a 'positional war' as being inevitable.[90] The next SD report, from 11 September, went even further, referring to a 'fundamental change in the attitude of the population'. Many people, it was reported, had begun to draw their own conclusions about the almost unchanged fronts and the weeks of inactivity in both the central and southern parts of the front. The report then went on to state, 'The "increasingly more modest prisoner and booty reports" as well as the absence of "news about newly captured territory" gives the impression that on all fronts intense battles are taking place.'[91] As an example the report cited the sieges at Kiev and Odessa. It stated that people had begun questioning why these two cities had not been captured after both had been so directly threatened by besieging forces for such a long time. It was also noted that soldiers' letters were having a decidedly detrimental effect on the home front. They talked of 'increasing difficulties in the provisions', the 'unimaginably large reserves of the Soviet army in men and materials' and 'the loss of hope in a [war-ending] decision in the foreseeable future'.[92]

Nor did the growing sense of melancholy go unnoticed at the top. On 12 September Goebbels noted in his diary that the people had become 'sceptical' about the military situation in the east and that they held fears for what the coming winter would bring.[93] Indeed, the Nazi propaganda minister had been concerned for some time that the victory reports from the eastern front were no longer having the desired effect. In late August he noted how the quoted figures for Soviet prisoners of war were 'having almost no impact on the German people'.[94] Hauls of 30,000–40,000 captured Red Army men and even groupings of up to 80,000 or 100,000 Soviet POWs were no longer enough to stir emotions and Goebbels knew it was his ministry's overenthusiastic reporting of the war that was in large part to blame. Writing on 5 September, Goebbels acknowledged:

> *Our victory reports are no longer able to make a strong impression. This is for the most part because in the first weeks of the eastern campaign we showed off a little too much. We have destroyed the Bolshevik attack armies too often or claimed that the Bolsheviks were no longer capable of grand operational manoeuvres. The people demand that we finally deliver on our prognoses and promises. The system of news in the eastern campaign has been exceptionally difficult, which at its root comes back to the fact that we incorrectly assessed the Bolshevik powers of resistance, that we had mistaken figures [for the Red Army] which we used as the basis for our whole news system.*[95]

It was a frank admission, but an accurate one. For weeks the German people had been bombarded with special news bulletins (*Sondermeldungen*) declaring one victory after another, which allowed only one conclusion to be drawn – that final victory was close at hand.[96] Likewise, the weekly newsreel footage became a veritable victory parade of triumphant German soldiers, fields of destroyed Red Army equipment and swastikas rising over Soviet towns and cities. From the earliest days and weeks of the campaign everything reflected the coming victory, yet from one week to the next the war stubbornly rumbled on, with one 'decisive' battle after another, until increasingly, every day, Germans began to wonder where final victory lay. Suddenly the emphatic declarations of success following each new advance were taking on a monotonous repetition that seemed less commentary on the war's progress than a reminder of the still unfulfilled promise to end it. In short a credibility gap was arising between what the regime was saying and what people were inferring for themselves. Private doubts, fuelled sometimes by soldiers' field post and sometimes by what were denounced as 'Jewish rumours', gave people an uneasy sense that there was much more hardship in the war in the east than they were being led to believe.[97] The growing suspicion surrounding the official accounts led more and more people to seek alternative sources of information and these tended to confirm their fears or at the very least offer substantiation for their doubts. Naturally enough British radio was broadcasting a very pessimistic view of Germany's progress in the Soviet Union, but so also were the media in neutral countries and it infuriated Goebbels. In Sweden the press were particularly negative, which Goebbels complained about in his diary on 9 September: 'They believe that the German Wehrmacht has become bogged down in the east and that they no longer possess the chance to secure victory.'[98] Such pronouncements echoed the tone of *Pravda*, the Soviet daily newspaper, suggesting that not all the bombastic claims of the Soviet information bureau were just the usual self-serving hyperbole typical of Stalin's propaganda machinery. Nor was Sweden the only example. Reporting on the Red Army in the summer fighting, Swiss radio presented a very different picture from the German view: 'There are no signs of waning morale or materiel in the Russian Army. In spite of the enemy's gigantic assault and gain in territory, the soldiers are fighting with an equanimity peculiar to the Russian people, which even heavy losses and reverses cannot easily break.'[99]

Seeing that his attempts to maintain an exceedingly optimistic portrayal of Operation Barbarossa had become a liability, Goebbels now sought to change course. The new face of the war in the east was supposed to be more in line with the reality, as Goebbels explained on 10 September:

> *As it stands I am also of the opinion that the people must gradually be prepared for a longer lasting war. They must be told and be made familiar with the difficulties of the war. Creating illusions is now at an end. After it has become known that the campaign in the east cannot be brought to an end in the time we had actually expected to do so, the people should also be made aware of what difficulties we confront…* [100]

Two days later on 12 September Goebbels offered a more perceptive interpretation of the fighting than that given by many of the army's own commanding officers. Summing up the transformation of the campaign from a blitzkrieg to a war of resources, Goebbels stated, 'It now depends on who can endure this the longest.' The Nazi propaganda minister then added his concern about another looming danger: 'and in addition to that, whether or not we will be surprised prematurely by the winter'.[101] The following day (13 September) Goebbels made what was probably his most insightful commentary to date on the war in the east. Summing up Germany's predicament by mid-September, he concluded, 'Indeed, we are now fighting with our backs against the wall.'[102]

What becomes clear from the summer reporting of the campaign is that Germany's successes were exaggerated and that this was even being acknowledged within the Nazi state at the time. Only two weeks into the war Hans-Albert Gises wrote home to his mother, 'The war here is certainly a bit different from what is on the radio at home.'[103] Likewise, Albert Neuhaus wrote to his wife on 20 August, 'No propaganda company can convey the impressions we have here and what we go through to the homeland.'[104] Yet even on the German home front the people could see for themselves from the scores of black crosses adorning the *Todesanzeigen* (death notices) in the newspapers that the conquests in the east were not always as effortless or as one-sided as the official propaganda maintained. Added to this were the stories which circulated about the dreaded 'black letters', officially notifying families of deaths at the front. Hildegard Gratz recalled, 'There were these terrible letters, and the postmen told stories of pitiful scenes of grief... It wasn't just a question of witnessing grief and suffering. The official line was that women were bearing their news "with proud grief" but many of the women in their despair screamed out curses on this "damned war".'[105] The changing fortunes of war were a principal reason behind the rising undercurrent of anti-Nazi sentiment within Germany and the multiplying numbers of people who were prepared to involve themselves in resistance activities.[106]

While the German population would soon be introduced to a new, more difficult war in the east, without what Goebbels termed the creation of 'illusions', the realities of the day-to-day fighting had long since dispelled any such delusions for the German soldiers. The notion that Bolshevism would 'collapse like a house of cards'[107] was almost immediately refuted by the vigour of Soviet resistance and the direct impact this had on German casualties. At the beginning of the campaign opinions on the Soviet population and what the soldiers might expect were heavily influenced by years of Nazi propaganda. The Soviet people had been portrayed as racially inferior Slavs, led by a hostile Jewish clique that conspired to foment revolution and impose Bolshevism on the world.[108] As the soldiers began their advance into the Soviet Union they were confronted by a new world of extreme poverty, which seemed a self-evident repudiation of the Soviet Union's much-touted depiction as the 'worker's paradise'. Not only was it the backwardness of village life that caught the soldier's attention, but also the peasants themselves, who were easily categorized according to Nazi propaganda as simpleminded Slavs. The proliferation of this view confirmed the indoctrination of the Wehrmacht and the widespread embrace of Nazi dogma.[109] By the same token, the primitive conditions in the rural areas acted as a form of substantiation for Hitler's many denunciations of Soviet communism, which also fortified the portrayal of the Soviet people as racially inferior.[110] An OKW directive to the *Ostheer* (*Mitteilungen für die Truppe*) in June 1941 plainly sought to dehumanize the enemy: 'Anyone who has ever looked at the face of a red commissar knows what the Bolsheviks are like . . . We would be insulting animals if we were to describe these men, who are mostly Jewish, as beasts.'[111] Not surprisingly, such expressions flowed seamlessly into the perceptions of the men. Wilhelm Prüller wrote in his diary on 4 July, 'It's not people we're fighting against here, but simply animals.'[112] Similarly, Karl Fuchs wrote home early in the war, 'Let me tell you that Russia is nothing but misery, poverty and depravity! This is Bolshevism!'[113] Later he added, 'Hardly ever do you see the face of a person who seems rational and intelligent . . . And these scoundrels, led by Jews and criminals, wanted to imprint their stamp on Europe, indeed on the world.'[114] Hans Becker, a German tank commander in the battle of Kiev, later wrote, 'My first impressions were of a uniformly brutish and impoverished people, nearer to beasts than men.'[115] Yet after months of hard fighting followed by years in Soviet captivity, Becker qualified this view: 'it took me some time to appreciate that, in common with other nations, all Russians do not fall into a single category'.[116] Yet for the overwhelming mass of the German soldiers entering the Soviet Union racial stereotypes informed their observations and, as a result, radicalized many of their actions towards the population.[117] Indeed, beyond the mere representation of the Soviet people as racially

Fig. 10 Germany's war of annihilation in the Soviet Union resulted in millions of civilian deaths. Here six supposed partisans are executed in September 1941.

inferior, their treatment by the German army was governed by Hitler's well-known criminal orders.[118] The first of these was titled the 'Decree on the Exercise of Martial Jurisdiction in the Area "Barbarossa" and Special Measures of the Troops' (*Erlaß über die Ausübung der Kriegsgerichtsbarkeit im Gebiet 'Barbarossa' und über besondere Maßnahmen der Truppe*). This effectively permitted *carte blanche* within the eastern territories by absolving German soldiers of all ranks from prosecution for war crimes.[119] This was followed by the 'Guidelines for the Treatment of Political Commissars' (*Richtlinien für die Behandlung politischer Kommissare*), which demanded that the army immediately execute all captured Soviet political commissars without recourse to any form of legal procedure.[120] It was all part of the coming war of annihilation, which the army and the SS were to prosecute with such brutal effectiveness from the very beginning of the conflict.[121]

While there was an undeniable ideological bias governing German actions in the east that would in many respects never be expunged, there was, nevertheless, a certain qualification to Nazi propaganda that took place on the battlefield. Countless German documents and individual records make reference to the surprising, and wholly unexpected, fighting resolve of the Red Army. All of a sudden the supposedly inferior Slavs were proving more than a match for their German counterparts in sheer bravery and willingness for sacrifice. It was the most obvious and effective form of discrediting the Nazi racial myth and, for many in the *Ostheer*, a jolting awakening to the vicious realities of life on the eastern front. The fighting also contrasted baldly with official propaganda which presented a picture of effortless victories and a rapid end to the war. Indeed the commander of the IX Army Corps recalled that, by the beginning of September, 'The official propaganda, which spoke at length about an end to the war, had to have had a negative effect because it did not relate to the situation as experienced by the soldiers.'[122]

Examples of the Soviet proclivity for toil and endurance at the front had been evident since the first days of the campaign, but even in September German soldiers were still reacting with a mixture of wonderment and trepidation at what they were witnessing. Adolf B., a soldier fighting in the Ukraine, wrote home in early September, 'The Russian war is much more difficult and bitter than the French! No one would have thought that our Soviet brothers were capable of such fervent resistance!'[123] Erich Kern, another veteran of Army Group South, wrote after the war, 'We had often wondered at the almost inhuman tenacity with which the Red Army was fighting, the terrible obstinacy with which even the youngest *Komsomol* youths, boys of fifteen, defended their pillboxes, their tanks and their own selves.'[124] Hans Pichler served with the 4th SS *Polizei* Division and was subjected to no small degree of National Socialist indoctrination, yet after only two months of fighting, his opinion of the enemy seemed to have surpassed his opinion even of the much-vaunted Waffen-SS: 'It has already occurred to me many times just how much harder, resilient and tougher these eastern peoples are than we Europeans.'[125] The notion that Soviet soldiers possessed special powers of resilience that constituted something extraordinary, or even something unnatural, is found in many German letters and diaries. Some of the more brazen examples stem from observation of captured Soviet wounded. Curzio Malaparte noted that 'They do not cry out, they do not groan, they do not curse. Undoubtedly there is something mysterious, something inscrutable about their stern, stubborn silence.'[126] Another more graphic account suggests a certain inexplicable quality to the behaviour of the Soviet men, which the observer recorded with a combination of awe, dread and horror:

> *Several of them burnt by flamethrowers, had no longer the semblance of a human face. They were blistered shapeless bundles of flesh. A bullet had taken away the lower jaw of one man. The scrap of flesh, which sealed the wound, did not hide the view of the trachea through which the breath escaped in bubbles accompanied by a kind of snoring. Five machine-gun bullets had threshed into pulp the shoulder and arm of another man, who was also without any dressing. His blood seemed to be running out through several pipes ... I have five campaigns to my credit, but I have never seen anything to equal this. Not a cry not a moan escaped the lips of these wounded, who were almost all seated on the grass ... Hardly had the distribution of supplies begun than the Russians, even the dying, rose and flung themselves forward ... the man without a jaw could scarcely stand upright. The one-armed man clung with his arm to a tree trunk, the shapeless burnt bundles advanced as rapidly as possible. Some half a dozen of them, who were lying down also rose, holding in their entrails with one hand and stretching out the other with a gesture of supplication ... Each of them left behind a flow of blood, which spread in an ever increasing stream.*[127]

Given the German predisposition towards racial categorization, it is hardly surprising that such remarkable scenes were commonly drawn upon as evidence of a unique Slavic racial peculiarity, which presented them as less subject to physical suffering. This in turn informed the rapid role-reversal in how the Soviet adversary was being perceived, from an inferior, second-rate foe to a fierce, hardy and bitter enemy. Not surprisingly there are accounts that speak of badly wounded Red Army men, who had been bypassed, suddenly assailing German troops from behind.[128] In other instances Soviet pilots whose planes were hit sometimes directed their aircraft into suicidal attacks on German positions.[129] Such stamina in battle and willingness for sacrifice shocked the Germans and harked back to Frederick the Great's ominous aphorism: 'Every Russian soldier has to be shot dead twice, and even then he has to be pushed to make him fall.'[130] Accordingly, the men of the *Ostheer* were no longer able to take comfort in their supposed 'natural' superiority. Indeed, from the fanatical resolve of the Red Army, to the appearance of superior Soviet weapons such as the T-34 tank, the Il-2 *Shturmovik* ground-attack plane and the *Katyusha* multiple-rocket launcher, there were many indications that the enemy in the east was much more than the unsophisticated brute commonly depicted. As one German soldier from the 24th Infantry Division concluded in his diary, 'Impressions [of the Soviet Union] are so contradictory that they do not furnish a basis for a comprehensive picture. You often see things that do not fit into the frame of the Russia that has been depicted to you . . . for instance, in almost every inhabited place you come across new schools with modern equipment.'[131] Similarly, a German lieutenant stated bluntly in a letter to a public official, 'This country is full of contradictions.'[132] By the late summer of 1941 the men of the *Ostheer*, and to a lesser degree the German population, were discovering just how flawed their image of the Soviet enemy had been. The era of the rapid advances had passed and the bitter struggle that remained would absorb far more men in gritty positional warfare than the supposedly seamless operational manoeuvres frequently depicted. The stagnation of the front was the most obvious symptom of the paralysis that had already ruined Operation Barbarossa's chances for success. It left the eastern campaign a wayward venture, incapable of securing its objectives, devoid of a strategic purpose and without an end in sight.

Given the dire circumstances, the stakes in the battle of Kiev were extremely high for both Hitler and Stalin. The Red Army stood to lose four complete field armies with hundreds of thousands of men, while the *Ostheer* desperately needed to finish off the South-Western Front in order to kept their offensive going and gain time for the planned attack on Moscow. As Guderian struggled south against Kirponos's forces, his panzer group was still acting alone. The envisaged second arm of the offensive by Kleist's Panzer Group 1 had so far failed to materialize as its forces were split between competing objectives. Mackensen's III Panzer Corps was still heavily engaged in the Dnepropetrovsk bridgehead, while Kempf's XXXXVIII Panzer Corps and Wietersheim's XIV Panzer Corps were attempting to refit and stockpile reserves for the push north of the Dnepr. The problem they all shared was a lack of supplies and Army Group South's logistical constraints represented an intractable bottleneck. Mackensen's extremely costly battle at Dnepropetrovsk had priority, and even then was underresourced, leaving precious little for Kempf and Wietersheim. The planned crossings at

Kremenchug also had to be secured by expanding the bridgehead and reinforcing the bridges. In the meantime the same inclement weather plaguing Guderian's operations in the north was also hampering Kleist's resupply. This was such a problem that after the war the commander of Army Group South cited it as the chief reason, second only to the Russian winter, for the failure of German operations in 1941. As Rundstedt explained,

> *But long before winter came the chances had been diminished owing to the repeated delays in the advance that were caused by bad roads, and mud. The 'black earth' of the Ukraine could be turned into mud by ten minutes' rain – stopping all movement until it dried. That was a heavy handicap in a race with time. It was increased by the lack of railways in Russia – for bringing up supplies to our advancing troops.*[133]

While time was a constant concern for all the German army groups in the east, Army Group South had been delayed much longer in the initial border battles and therefore began its advance into the vast expanses of the Ukraine considerably later. As in Bock's area of operations, compounding the problem was the shortage of east–west railway lines. Army Group South operated two such lines with which it had to supply three German armies (Sixth, Seventeenth and Eleventh), two Romanian armies (Third and Fourth), Kleist's panzer group and the contingent forces of the other Axis partners. In September both railway lines became blocked, the southern line because of flooding and the northern one owing to congestion, meaning that in the course of the month the daily quota of trains was met on only twelve days. Even more frustrating for the field commanders was that some of the trains arrived at the front only partially loaded.[134] With the inefficiency of rail transportation, trucks became the only alternative for moving supplies long distances. Here Rundstedt suffered as much as Bock owing to the alternate ills of dust and mud, which placed exorbitant demands on his vehicles. As one witness summarized, 'Such is war on the steppes of the Ukraine: dust, mud, dust, mud.'[135] Yet, by the first half of September the dust clouds were replaced by a late summer preview of what the autumn would become. Indeed Major-General Hoffman von Waldau claimed that by 11 September the rainfall in the Ukraine was the worst

Fig. 11 As the periodic downpours and heavy traffic reduced roads to quagmires, the Germans build corduroy roads, which restored movement, but were often difficult to construct on the treeless plains of the Ukraine.

since 1874.[136] After days of rain, the flat landscape began to transform into an inescapable bog, which stretched on as far as the eye could see. 'The war is being fought in the midst of a sea of sticky, clinging mud,' concluded Curzio Malaparte at the time.[137] Kleist's trucks suffered accordingly. Kleist's *Grosstransportraum* had taken such a battering during the summer advance that, after a brief pause for refitting at the end of August, it could only be raised to 60 per cent of establishment before being pressed back into action to help address the panzer group's critical supply shortage. By early October, despite absorbing countless Soviet trucks from the spoils of the Kiev pocket, the number of Kleist's trucks was still in decline, with less than half of establishment available (48 per cent).[138]

Although the dreadful Soviet roads and early September rains exacerbated the shortage of supplies within Panzer Group 1, and the Dnepropetrovsk bridgehead tied down an entire Panzer Corps,[139] there was a still an urgent need to send a force to meet Guderian's two-week-old drive south. For this reason a meeting was held on 8 September, which was attended by Brauchitsch, Rundstedt, Sodenstern, Colonel Friedrich-August Weinknecht and Kleist's Chief of Staff at Panzer Group 1, Colonel Kurt Zeitzler.[140] At the opening Zeitzler provided Brauchitsch with an overview of the situation at the Dnepropetrovsk bridgehead. It was not an encouraging picture. Zeitzler stated that the sole bridge supplying the three German divisions was constantly under attack and had already been damaged and repaired fifteen times (ten times by Soviet artillery, three times by bombers, once by a shot-down plane crashing into it and another time by the stormy weather). The engineers working there had already lost 450 men, while in the bridgehead itself losses were averaging more than 300 men a day.[141] In one of five Soviet attacks led by heavy tanks on 6 September, the forward positions of the 198th Infantry Division were overrun, resulting in heavy German casualties. By the end of the day one company of the 308th Infantry Regiment was reduced to just twenty men.[142] Meanwhile, even as the commanders of Army Group South were meeting with Brauchitsch, Soviet planes were engaged in heavy aerial attacks against the vital bridge across the Dnepr as well as forward German positions. By the end of the day no fewer than twenty-two attacks had been recorded, each undertaken by six to eight bombers or fighters.[143] To relieve Mackensen's beleaguered corps in the bridgehead, the panzer group had been hoping to advance a panzer division from Kempf's or Wietersheim's corps across the Dnepr at Kremenchug and assault directly into the rear of the Soviet positions downstream at Dnepropetrovsk. Yet the necessity of effecting a junction with Panzer Group 2 had absolute priority and nothing was to be spared for secondary operations towards Dnepropetrovsk. Zeitzler therefore suggested that elements of the Seventeenth Army's right wing be dispatched in the same manner to relieve the pressure on III Panzer Corps; otherwise, he warned, 'given the daily losses the bridgehead will gradually burn itself out'. Brauchitsch would make no firm commitment and merely promised to refer the matter to Hitler.[144] Clearly, if the bridgehead could in fact be relieved by striking the Soviet forces from behind, in other words from the eastern bank of the river, the whole point of forcing a crossing at Dnepropetrovsk had become pointless. It was precisely this point, in addition to the heavy German losses, that persuaded Zeitzler to make repeated pleas to Army Group South, first on 5 September and then again the following day, to abandon the bridgehead. Yet his arguments had been rejected by Rundstedt who was under direct orders from Halder to hold the bridgehead.[145]

In discussions about the coming offensive by Panzer Group 1, it was determined that the junction point for the two panzer groups was to be at Romny,[146] almost 200 kilometres north of the Dnepr at Kremenchug. Zeitzler then reported on the strength of the panzer group. Although its wheeled transport had received only a few days' respite at the end of August, the tanks within Kleist's four panzer divisions had been granted a relatively long period of rest and refitting. Accordingly on 8 September Zeitzler was able to report that three of the panzer divisions could again field a hundred tanks each and the last seventy-nine.[147] Yet, as was the case all along the eastern front, the absence of spare parts and replacement motors made most repairs highly provisional and Zeitzler emphasized this point to Brauchitsch: 'Soon after operations are set in motion the fallout of machines will again begin and this time in even greater numbers than in the first part of the campaign.'[148] Fuel stocks sufficient for the offensive were in the process of being collected and did not appear to represent a problem; however, the same could not be said for munitions. Owing to the enormous demands of III Panzer Corps very little was left for the other two panzer corps, and thus they would have to be committed to battle with very limited reserves of ammunition. Zeitzler also addressed personnel losses within Panzer Group 1, reporting that since the start of operations some 22,000 men had been lost, for which only 13,000 replacements had been received. Most ominous was Zeitzler's conclusion: 'In summary one can say that in comparison to the beginning of the campaign the materiel and personnel stand of the panzer group is weaker by about a third. A further third has been lost due to the handing over of the 11th Panzer Division [to the Sixth Army], the SS AH[149] [to the Eleventh Army] and the 60th Motorized Infantry Division, which, battered from the [Dnepropetrovsk] bridgehead, will not be available for fourteen days.'[150] Consequently, after Kleist's comparatively long refit and before his panzer group had even commenced its vital offensive to forge a union with Guderian, Panzer Group 1, according to Zeitzler, was only one-third of its starting strength. Rundstedt, however, did not share Zeitzler's appraisal of the panzer group's waning strength, and without offering any explanation, simply labelled his assessment 'exaggerated'.[151]

On the same day (8 September) another meeting took place at the headquarters of Army Group South, attended by Brauchitsch, Rundstedt, Sodenstern, Halder, Heusinger and Zeitzler. Here Sodenstern set out the operational objectives for the coming offensive. Panzer Group 1 would have to advance as far as Romny and then hold a line extending south as far as Lubny, through which resurging Soviet forces could be expected to launch strong breakout attempts. South of Lubny, Sodenstern indicated that four infantry divisions of Stülpnagel's Seventeenth Army would be deployed to hold the line, while a further six divisions were to take advantage of the much hoped-for operational freedom to the east and advance on the industrial city of Khar'kov.[152] The date set for the launch of Army Group South's new offensive was 11 September. Before the chiefs of the OKH departed, Rundstedt expressed his desire to unite all German forces taking part in the battle under one command, and therefore asked for the transfer of Guderian's Panzer Group 2 and Weichs's Second Army to Army Group South. Halder, however, rejected the idea.[153]

Two days later, on 10 September, the issue of abandoning the Dnepropetrovsk bridgehead again came up for discussion, only this time it was Sodenstern who contacted Zeitzler. The Chief of Staff for Army Group South was clearly seeking advice on the best method of dealing with the problem and, unlike the army group's previously inflexible position, it now seemed that all options were on the table.[154] Sodenstern asked whether the bridgehead should be held, reinforced or given up. Zeitzler was incredulous. In his opinion that matter should have been dealt with days ago and, although he had earlier advocated a withdrawal, he now elaborated on the difficulties of pulling back. There were thirteen artillery detachments operating inside the bridgehead and the time required to ferry just one detachment across the river amounted to about ten hours. Accordingly, removing the whole artillery component would take some five and a half days. It was for precisely such practical issues that an early decision had been required, not only to effect a timely withdrawal, but to prevent the panzer group from reinforcing the position in accordance with the army group's instruction to expand (in order to secure) the bridgehead. Now, after so many casualties and with the offensive about to begin from Kremenchug, it no longer made sense to Zeitzler to attempt a withdrawal. Rather he again requested that elements of the Seventeenth Army be used to relieve III Panzer Corps as part of their drive to Khar'kov. Sodenstern ultimately discussed the matter with Rundstedt and agreed to support Zeitzler's recommendation.[155]

In many ways the German decision to undertake the bridgehead at Dnepropetrovsk was a fiasco with many parallels to the Yel'nya salient and should have led to some hard questioning within the army. Both had proved costly battles, demanding constant supplies of men and materials, but ultimately serving no real strategic purpose. Yet in many ways these were only symptoms of a wider problem within the German high command. From its very inception Operation Barbarossa was attempting too much,[156] and even if that was painfully obvious by September, as Goebbels's diary and German public opinion would suggest, there was hardly any acknowledgement of this fact within the highest ranks of the army. There was no process of enquiry, no change in personnel and no reappraisal of methods. Accordingly nothing changed and nothing was learned, allowing men like Halder, who was so directly implicated in Germany's overextension in the east, to go on advocating ideas and operations which were simply beyond the capabilities of the *Ostheer*. Clausewitz[157] had written about the diminishing stages of an attack and the need for a strategist to be wary of the potential for overextension.[158] In an expansive theatre such as the Soviet Union this was especially true, but in World War II the German Wehrmacht had reforged itself with a powerful new cult of the offensive, which tended to justify every new territorial gain without the requisite consideration for either the cost of an objective or its overall importance to the wider aims of the war. Understanding how the Wehrmacht's commanders came to such illogical and ultimately self-deceiving conclusions about the war in the east involves many precepts of the Nazi world-view, which they so brazenly shared. There was an utterly irreconcilable differentiation made between the strength of German arms and the qualities of the Nordic fighting man and the Bolshevik foe. The long summer campaign, although hard fought and bloody, was nevertheless viewed as an outstanding string of German victories and, however ominously the strategic implications may have loomed, it must be remembered that most commanders even at the highest levels only concerned themselves with the operational level of command. To the extent that problems impacted their continuing operations there was the ardent belief in the power of individual 'will', which counted as much for a general as for a soldier in the field. Meanwhile, on the other side of the hill the Red Army was repeatedly characterized as being near the end of its strength, and there was the feeling that one last push, however desperate for the Germans, could at last produce the final result. Soviets were after all Slavs, and their strength was believed to stem more from mass than from any aptitude for warfare comparable to that of the Wehrmacht or the German General Staff. Thus, while the fighting was recognized to be hard, the progress of the war was typically still viewed optimistically and warnings about the future remained in the minority. Nevertheless such warnings did exist. As one panzer commander stated in July 1941, the relentless onward march into the Soviet Union and its associated casualties held the potential for Germany 'to be destroyed by winning'.[159] In the summer of 1941 this was precisely what was happening.

6 THE BATTLE OF KIEV

'The biggest battle in the history of the world' (Adolf Hitler)

Even before Hitler's new War Directive 35 was issued, authorizing a renewed offensive from Army Group Centre in the direction of Moscow, Halder was already busily working out the details. In order to concentrate the maximum strength for the coming operation, Halder sought a removal of panzer and infantry divisions from Army Groups North and South in favour of Bock's command. In the north Colonel-General Erich Hoepner's Panzer Group 4 would have first to transfer the 1st Panzer Division as well as the 2nd Motorized Infantry Division, while Leningrad, after much debate within the German high command, was now to become a 'secondary theatre'.[1] In the south Rundstedt was sent a more complete list of what he would have to relinquish to Bock after the conclusion of the current battle: in total, three infantry divisions from Reichenau's Sixth Army, two panzer divisions (to include the 11th Panzer Division, the other was as yet undecided) and two motorized infantry divisions.[2]

At Army Group Centre Bock was delighted that his 'old wish', to attack the main grouping of enemy forces and then to proceed to Moscow, was back on the agenda and this time with Hitler's blessing. Yet upon inspection of the attack plan Bock had considerable reservations. In essence he was concerned that the opening encirclement was too tight and needed to be screened to the east by a secondary force pushing much deeper into Russian territory. 'I asked [Lieutenant-Colonel Helmuth von] Grolman[3] [of the Operations Department at the OKH] to make it clear from the start that the planned tight turn by both of the attack's offensive wings does not correspond to my view in this case ... this has to be screened to the east.'[4] Yet Bock's criticism touched on a major of point contention from July. At that time Hitler had expressed serious misgivings about the practice of large encirclements that, in his opinion, did not allow for decisive results.[5] Not only did Bock have reservations about the strategic approach to the offensive, but he also wanted more forces to carry it out. In the north he requested 'the strongest possible forces' from Colonel-General Ernst Busch's Sixteenth Army, operating as part of Leeb's Army Group North. Bock claimed that, without such support, the attack by Strauss's Ninth Army would be too weak and that 'outflanking the enemy will be out of the question'. He approached Brauchitsch about this, but in the aftermath of the recent strategic crisis the Commander-in-Chief of the Army proved 'evasive' and was unwilling to make any promises that did not already have the approval of Hitler or the OKW.[6] At the same time Bock complained that Army Group South was 'causing difficulties' because Reichenau's Sixth Army had built bridges that could not support tanks and consequently the transfer of the 11th Panzer Division could not take place. As Bock concluded in frustration, 'I'm not getting much help in putting the new operation together and yet everything depends on it!'[7]

The following day (11 September) the new OKH directive for Operation Typhoon arrived at Army Group Centre's headquarters, but its content only infuriated Bock further. 'Nothing of what I recently said to the Commander-in Chief of the Army was taken into consideration,' Bock complained in his diary. The support of the Sixteenth Army was 'vaguely worded' and while Guderian was being sent to Orel, which Bock considered too far to the east, the other attack wing was to concentrate 'in the area of Viaz'ma, a town in the middle of the enemy system of positions'. Thus, in Bock's opinion, one of the attacking wings was closing too soon and the other too late.[8] Bock set out his concerns in a letter to Brauchitsch, but after two days without a response, the commander of Army Group Centre phoned Halder and at least secured an agreement regarding Viaz'ma. While the inner wing of the attacking forces would still close near Viaz'ma, the outer wing would continue east to Gzhatsk.[9] If Bock thought he had made some progress towards resolving the strategic complications dogging his upcoming offensive, the following day (14 September) was to leave him dumbfounded. The OKH informed Army Group Centre that all panzer forces – inner and outer wings – would have to concentrate at Viaz'ma. Bock was incredulous. He complained first to Heusinger about turning his tanks 'in front of the Russian anti-tank ditches' and then to Halder. In the case of the latter Bock was merely told that he should not take the new directive 'too seriously'. Yet after having received no understanding from the OKH for his concerns, and indeed having had Halder go back on his word from only the day before, Bock was not about to be mollified by placatory words with no substantive meaning. As it was Bock remarked bitterly, 'As at Belostok and Minsk and at Smolensk, those "above" are now once again showing a tendency towards very limited action and thus throwing away sweeping strategic success.'[10] It was a harsh rendering of events, and the suggestion that attempting even larger encirclements at the earlier battles could have led to greater success ignores the profound problems Bock's army group confronted just closing and eliminating those attempted. Accordingly, Bock's charge that 'limited action' in Operation Typhoon was preventing grander-scale operations from producing 'sweeping' successes does not appear consistent with either past battles or the manifest state of the *Ostheer*. At no point did Bock discuss the depletion of the panzer forces, nor the worn-out condition of the troops. Moreover, considering the long and costly experience of supplying the encirclement at the eastern edge of the Smolensk pocket, the prospect of another far-reaching operation in October appears optimistic to the point of folly. Beyond Bock's own weaknesses in troops, panzers and logistics, there were also numerous Soviet armies opposing Army Group Centre, which could not be eliminated without costly fighting. While the prospect of another embittered dispute within the German command must have appeared tiresome to those involved, the uncertainty it introduced into the planning process did have one benefit – the exact plan could not be known by the British cryptologists working at Bletchley Park, despite their having decrypted the German orders for Operation Typhoon on 9 September.[11]

Whatever the virtues of the strategic plan for Operation Typhoon, the German command still faced the more immediate issue of successfully cutting off Kirponos's vulnerable South-Western Front in the Ukraine. To this end the most important formation was Guderian's Panzer Group 2, which in spite of every effort was still making slow progress on account of bad weather, weakened forces, limited supplies, terrible roads and incessant Soviet counterattacks from Eremenko's Briansk Front. Certainly the soldiers under Guderian's command were under no illusions about the ease of their advance, and the observations of a Jewish boy metaphorically captured the sense of adversity they faced:

> *[E]ven though the advance of the German army units was slowed, they continued to push forward, crushing everything that stood in their way. I remember watching sadly as the half-trucks rolled through the golden fields of ripe wheat. And then, with delight, I saw the stalks trying to right themselves. Some succeeded, as if to say, 'We, too, are not ready to bend before the conqueror; we won't make it easy for the occupying forces.'*[12]

The boy's words echoed the thoughts of a German soldier who wrote home in mid-September, 'It's going even slower, the difficulties are increasing, the land stands defiantly in our way.'[13] Nevertheless the advance was still continuing and with it the danger to Soviet forces in the Ukraine was rising with each passing day. Yet nothing would make Stalin see reason, and in spite of the desperate pleas of his commanders and the threat of collapse now gripping the entire northern wing of the South-Western Front, the Soviet dictator would brook no talk of withdrawal from Kiev.

During the second week of September, as Eremenko's bloodied and exhausted forces began to break up and lose cohesion, Guderian's advanced forces at last gained some operational freedom (see map 10). On 8 September the 4th and 3rd Panzer Divisions seized a crossing over the Seim River and on 9 September Konotop fell.[14] Guderian was on hand to observe these battles, but even as he noted their successful outcome, he also underlined the cumulative effect of constant operations. According to the panzer group commander, 'the limited combat strength of all units showed how badly they needed rest and recuperation after two and a half months of exhausting fighting and heavy casualties'.[15] Notwithstanding Guderian's difficulties, Eremenko was in an even worse state after weeks of draining battles and nonsensical orders for offensives with completely impractical objectives. As a result dangerous gaps began to appear in his lines,[16] and on 9 September Bock took great satisfaction from Second Army's 'very good progress'

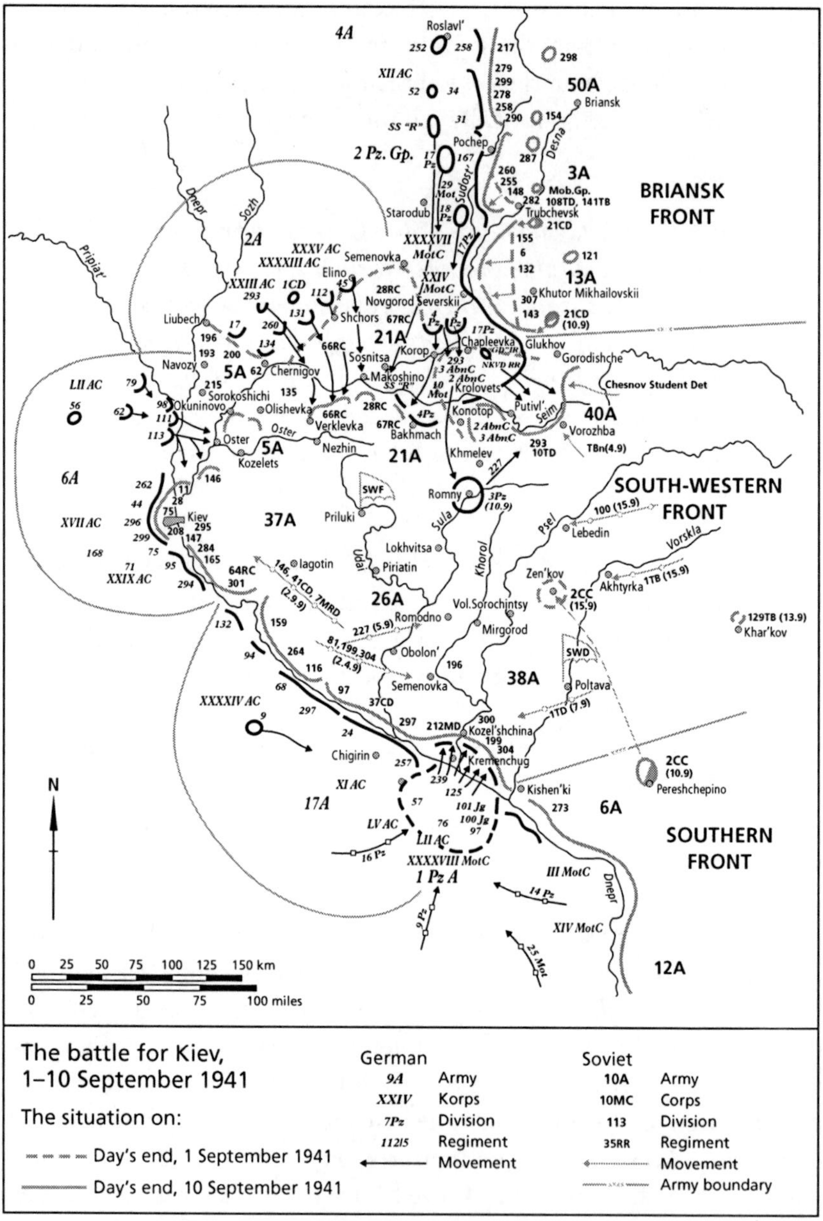

Map 10 The battle for Kiev, 1–10 September 1941
Source: Glantz, *Atlas of the Battle for Kiev Part III.*

in seizing Chernigov and Guderian's 'significant progress in the direction of Romny'.[17] The German successes exacerbated the crisis within the Soviet lines and on 10 September, in spite of pouring rain, the 3rd Panzer Division seized its opportunity and undertook a bold thrust deep into enemy territory to capture the crucial town of Romny directly off the march.[18] Fuel supplies barely sufficed for this operation, yet the small number of serviceable panzers in Model's division made it possible. Once in Romny fuel stocks were described as 'very critical' and as a result of the sunken roads new supplies were moving 'very slowly'.[19] Nevertheless the rewards of having captured Romny were immediately apparent. The town was supposed to have been shielded to the north by a new defensive line built along the Roman River; however, the elements of speed and surprise allowed the 3rd Panzer Division to bypass these fortifications almost without a fight.[20] Moreover, Romny itself was a major staging area for the Red Army and contained vast stocks of food and munitions, as well as a consignment of eighty cubic metres of fuel.[21] All of this was captured intact and acted as a vital source of forward supply. Yet for all these benefits, the real significance of the thrust to Romny was the alarming speed at which the trap now appeared to be closing on Kirponos's South-Western Front.

On the same day (10 September) Langermann-Erlancamp's 4th Panzer Division captured Bakhmach, about 60 kilometres north-west of Romny, and the Infantry Regiment *Grossdeutschland* reached Putivl, about the same distance to the north-east of Romny. While the wretched conditions hampered all movement by road, they also dramatically cut the ability of Loerzer's II Air Corps to provide air cover to Guderian's attacking forces. Soviet aircraft, on the other hand, were operating from dry airfields and made heavy attacks on Schweppenburg's XXIV Panzer Corps.[22] On 9 September the 4th Panzer Division endured repeated enemy attacks with only weak fighter support, and on the following day there was no cover at all from the Luftwaffe. Given the state of the roads and the bottleneck at bridges, this resulted in what the divisional war diary termed 'heavy losses'. Indeed on 10 September the division's panzer regiment numbered just thirty-four tanks, consisting of twelve obsolete Mark IIs, thirteen Mark IIIs and nine Mark IVs.[23]

As the offensive now pushed forward at a rapid pace Guderian had to extend his already elongated flanks to the south. Nehring's 18th Panzer Division, freshly extracted from its entanglement on the eastern bank of the Desna River, now proceeded to extend itself towards the south, taking responsibility for a defensive zone no less than 60 kilometres in length. On the following day (11 September) this was extended to 70 kilometres, which posed a serious problem when aerial intelligence reported on 12 September the approach of eighty Soviet tanks, with at least twenty of these confirmed as being heavy tanks. The divisional staff endured an anxious night of waiting as it was considered 'questionable' whether such a strong enemy attack could be held, but in the event the Soviet force continued to move south and did not seek an engagement.[24] Not surprisingly, attempting to defend such long sections of the front placed paramount importance on having long-range intelligence capable of identifying enemy groupings, knowing what forces were arrayed against them and having some idea where they were likely to strike. Yet the state of aerial intelligence of the XXXXVII Panzer Corps, to which the 18th Panzer Division belonged, says much about the process of 'demodernization' at the front. Lemelsen's panzer corps was responsible for overseeing 150 kilometres of front, but on the evening of 13 September it lost its last observation plane to an enemy fighter and no replacements were available. In the absence of the necessary aircraft, the corps's aerial intelligence staff was transferred to Vietinghoff's XXXXVI Panzer Corps. Along with them were sent the aerial intelligence staff from Thoma's 17th Panzer Division which, likewise, had no planes left.[25] Nehring's 18th Panzer Division retained its staff, although they themselves were down to their last aircraft, which now had to act as the eyes of the whole corps along an overextended front and without fighter cover.[26]

With Bock's eastern front now extending as far down as Romny in the Ukraine, his previous concerns about maintaining his defensive positions in the north were not unjustified. Since the surrender of the Yel'nya salient the Soviet attacks against the defensive fronts of Strauss's Ninth and Kluge's Fourth Army had slackened, but not stopped. On 8 September Bock noted, 'The Russians continue to assail the defensive front with major and minor assaults. Their air superiority is especially uncomfortable; the bulk of our aircraft are deployed on the attack flanks.'[27] Two days later on 10 September, Halder noted that the Fourth Army was being subjected to three separate offensives along its line with 'limited local successes'.[28] The following day (11 September) Bock noted '[h]eavier Russian attacks' against Kluge's army and, while Strauss's front was quieter, the Field Marshal wrote, 'there are indications of an attack'.[29] Such slogging battles all along the eastern front belong to a largely unknown history of the campaign, subsumed by the wider and seemingly more dramatic events taking place at Leningrad and Kiev. Yet it was the nameless battles set among the long stretches of barren front that consumed thousands of German lives and gave real meaning to the dangers of a drawn-out war. To cite just one example, the 14th Motorized Infantry Division serving in Hoth's Panzer Group 3, which was subordinated to Strauss's Ninth Army during the defensive battles, suffered 2,200 losses in just over two weeks between 23 August and 8 September.[30] Indeed for the *Ostheer* the attritional battles were already becoming routine. On 12 September Bock commented in his diary, 'On the defensive front the usual picture. The enemy is organised for attack opposite the familiar sectors of the Fourth and Ninth Armies and here and there attacks, sometimes with tanks.'[31] Among the lower ranks the same daily battles elicited a different response that was anything but routine and better characterized by the torments of anguish they endured. Horst Slesina wrote of his experiences within Army Group Centre during the September defensive battles:

> *One battalion commander spoke about Flanders in the world war. The features of our current situation have many similarities with that time. Wet and dirt, the sodden ground, the heavy artillery battles, the fighting in trenches and positions – it is the worst form of war! . . . Hard days are coming. The last man is forward in the position and fights against the suffocating masses that are thrown against us. The Bolsheviks will be sacrificed hecatomb by the stubborn hate of their leaders . . . But it is masses, always new units repeat the attacks that will often be prepared by hours of pounding fire. Not infrequently they manage to break into our positions.*[32]

As the defensive battles rumbled on along Army Group Centre's front the attacking infantry divisions of Weichs's Second Army were in an analogous state to those of the Ninth and Fourth Armies. Weeks of heavy fighting without relief had left the constituent combat units exhausted to the point of collapse. Even senior officers now recognized the limitations of their men and pleaded for a respite, which Bock would not permit. General Heinrici, the commander of the XXXXIII Army Corps, commented bitterly in his diary that the state of his forces was not commensurate with the ongoing demands of the offensive into the Ukraine. He described his troops as 'dead tired, battle weary [and] weakened'. Nor did he mince words when it came to Bock's insistence on attack. Heinrici attributed this to 'short-sighted people who think only about their own operations'. As for his fellow officers in the XXXXIII Army Corps, Heinrici noted, 'Everyone concerned is speechless.' In his opinion the men desperately needed a few days' rest, but Weichs was under strict orders to continue. Resigned to doing his duty Heinrici concluded in disgust, 'One must shake one's head.'[33]

While the situation within Army Group Centre was fraught with constant pressure, internal tensions and the heavy toll of consecutive operations, the contrasting picture within the opposing Soviet fronts, especially in the south, was considerably worse. Kirponos's armies were overstretched, undermanned and increasingly lacking in essential supplies. Not that this in itself preordained their defeat. Soviet forces had been operating at a severe disadvantage to the Wehrmacht since the first days of the war and while there can be no doubt that the general quality of the Red Army had suffered over the course of the summer, German losses, combined with the rapid process of demodernization within the *Ostheer*, meant that by September the gap between the rival forces was marked far more by professionalism than by materiel. Indeed already by the late summer Germany was fighting a poor man's war in the east, with shortages in many key indices that could not be made good; in fact most would remain for the rest of the war. Notwithstanding the stark decline in Germany's formerly lethal system of rapid operational manoeuvre, the real problem for Kirponos's South-Western Front was strategic. His front had been slowly undergoing encirclement since late August and yet he was strictly forbidden to conduct a withdrawal of his forces or even to redeploy them in such a way as to mitigate the danger. Zhukov, Vasilevsky and Shaposhnikov had all, to varying degrees, attempted to intercede with Stalin and avert the looming disaster, but the Soviet dictator was determined he would hold Kiev at any cost. From Kirponos's point of view the slow strangulation of his armies was the failure not simply of Stalin's astonishingly inept judgement, but also of the men within the *Stavka*, who, in spite of well-founded fears for their personal well-being, were nevertheless prepared to prioritize their obedience to Stalin over the loss of hundreds of thousands of men in a calamity without precedent. With Guderian's panzer forces suddenly advancing unchecked as far as Romny, Kirponos felt he could wait no longer. On 10 September, the same day 3rd Panzer Division took Romny, Kirponos sent a communiqué to the *Stavka* reporting the presence of German panzers deep in his rear and warning that the responsible Twenty-First and Fortieth Armies could no longer stand their ground, or restore the situation. Accordingly, the front commander called for an immediate transfer of forces from the Kiev region to shore up defences along the path of Guderian's advance, but he then went further and boldly requested 'a general withdrawal of front forces', which he knew directly contradicted Stalin's orders.[34]

As recently as 7 September Shaposhnikov had been shamed and censured by Stalin for advancing this same course of action,[35] and the obsequious Chief of the General Staff was not about to repeat his mistake, or risk exciting Stalin's temper. Thus he replied to Kirponos's communiqué with a repudiation of the facts, which he himself knew to be fallacious. Shaposhnikov insisted that the armies of the South-Western Front should maintain their current positions and labelled Guderian's thrust into the rear a mere 'sortie'.[36] It was a fraudulent action, which suggests that blame for the impending Soviet crisis, so often attributed squarely to Stalin's incompetence, deserves to be shared, at least in part, by his closest cronies. While Shaposhnikov's reply absurdly tried to assuage Kirponos's fears by altering the facts, Stalin took a more direct approach when he phoned the commander of the South-Western Front and told him, 'your proposal to withdraw forces . . . we consider dangerous . . . Stop looking for lines of retreat and start looking for lines of resistance and only resistance.'[37]

Emboldened by Kirponos's brash action and wary of the impending disaster, on the following day (11 September) Budenny, the commander of the South-Western Direction, also signalled Shaposhnikov requesting decisive action:

> *For my part I suggest, that at the present moment an enemy intention to outflank and to encircle the South-Western Front from the direction of Novgorod-Severskii and Kremenchug is perfectly apparent. To circumvent this a powerful concentration of troops must be established. In its present state the South-Western Front cannot do this.*

> *If the* Stavka *for its part cannot concentrate at this time such a powerful concentration, then withdrawal for the South-Western Front appears to be absolutely ripe.*
>
> *Delay with the withdrawal of the South-Western Front will lead to losses in men and a large quantity of equipment.*[38]

When Stalin was shown Budenny's communiqué, which he considered evidence of a defeatist attitude, he promptly relieved the Marshal of his command and once again categorically forbade Kirponos from undertaking any form of retreat. For his part Shaposhnikov repeated his confidence that Eremenko's front would deal with Guderian, a claim which none of the relevant commanders had any faith in.[39] As for the rest of the South-Western Front, on 12 September Stalin and Shaposhnikov signed a new directive ordering every division in Kirponos's front to form a 'blocking detachment' consisting of 'reliable fighters' to ensure the 'order and discipline' of all units.[40] Yet it was no longer a case of just ensuring discipline or rooting out the defeatist elements; events had progressed too far for such simplistic solutions. Stalin and the *Stavka* had crossed the Rubicon and were now tied to a major defeat. The only question was: on what scale?

With Guderian's forces so deep in Kirponos's rear there could not be any ambiguity about Germany's strategic intention and this made Bock impatient to see some form of movement from Kleist's panzer group, lest the Soviets began escaping through the still considerably sized breach between Romny and Kremenchug. By 10 September Bock had obtained his objective in the south (Romny); however, with the absence of Rundstedt's own offensive, he shrewdly began to fear that more would be expected of him. This Bock resented because he knew it would draw Guderian's strength still further away from his centre where the latter attack towards Moscow would have to proceed. Indeed on 10 September Bock sought an early start to Kleist's breakout from the Kremenchug bridgehead, but he was told it was not possible on account of the rain in the south.[41] Thus the long-awaited southern offensive was due to begin as planned on 11 September. The appalling conditions and unceasing rain, however, hindered the movement of Kleist's divisions into their staging areas for the attack and consequently the breakout from the bridgehead was postponed until 12 September. Bock received the news with no small measure of frustration and may have felt inclined to point out that his own forces had been pursuing an offensive in the same conditions for more than a week.[42] Yet before Kleist could break out from the Kremenchug bridgehead it was the Soviets who went on the offensive in the south. On 10 September Soviet forces from the Thirty-Eighth Army launched a heavy counterattack, which, Halder noted, enjoyed some success.[43] By 11 September the fighting had become extremely fierce. The Soviets attacked with up to a hundred tanks and, although sixty-eight of these were reportedly destroyed in the fighting, the German line was forced back.[44] Meanwhile Kleist's failure to attack confirmed Bock's fears about having to extend himself further to the south,[45] especially since German aerial intelligence was now starting to detect the movement of large enemy columns acting independently and moving east towards three towns – Romny and its southerly neighbours Lokhvitsa and Lubny.[46] Connecting the three towns was the Sula River, which ran from north to south and made control of the vital bridges centred around each town vital. Model, the commander of the 3rd Panzer Division, put together a small battle group (*Kampfgruppe*[47]) that could strike out from Romny. It consisted of just three tanks, eight armoured reconnaissance vehicles, one anti-tank company, six artillery pieces and some motorized infantry.[48] The battle group's diminutive size reflected both the end of Model's strength and his overextended supply lines, which made the expedition an especially dangerous one. In spite of the sizeable stock of Soviet supplies captured at Romny, Model's battle group was still desperately short of fuel and reinforcements. The rain was almost unrelenting and on those occasions when it did stop, the roads did not dry as quickly as they had in the summer. Thus the forward movement of Guderian's supply trucks was reported to be 'hardly possible' and Model's tiny battle group was all that remained to deliver the *coup de main* from the north.[49]

While Guderian had done everything he could to secure the ring around the Soviet South-Western Front, from 12 September it was largely up to Kleist's Panzer Group 1 to finish the job. The spearhead of Kleist's attack was entrusted to Kempf's XXXXVIII Panzer Corps and more directly to the tough, one-armed Major-General Hans Hube who commanded the 16th Panzer Division.[50] Following Hube was the 9th Panzer Division under one of the relatively few high-ranking Austrian officers in the Wehrmacht, Lieutenant-General Alfred Ritter von Hubicki. The attack began at nine o'clock in the morning on 12 September. According to German reports, Soviet forces were

Fig. 12 Colonel-General Ewald von Kleist commanded Panzer Group 1 in Operation Barbarossa and provided the southern arm of the Kiev encirclement.

'visibly surprised' and after just over half an hour of 'intense fighting', Hube's lead elements were in open country. Driving hard towards his first major objective, Hube's panzers encountered little serious resistance and reached the town of Semenovka by the late afternoon. Yet Hube's advanced units were running very low on fuel and, instead of pausing to await resupply, he made the tactically dangerous decision to continue the advance until the tanks literally stopped dead. This they did in the late evening, 15 kilometres short of Khorol.[51]

While the 16th Panzer Division enjoyed rapid success on the first day of the offensive, Hubicki's 9th Panzer Division was less fortunate. The approach roads to the Dnepr crossing consisted of the now familiar sea of mud, which halted most movement and meant that the majority of the division could only be moved with the aid of tractors. Hubicki had done the best he could, but by the end of the day his division was only partly across the Dnepr, leaving Hube's immobilized division a long way to the north and operating in total exclusion.[52] As precarious as Hube's position appeared, the fact remained that there was no Soviet force in the vicinity with either the strength or mobility to take advantage of his predicament. The Germans' position also benefited from the fact that they had built two 16 ton bridges over the Dnepr, which, unlike the pontoon bridge at Dnepropetrovsk, allowed for far smoother movement and supply across the river.[53] Indeed on 12 September it was not just Kempf's panzer corps that was filing into the bridgehead; Wietersheim's XIV Panzer Corps was utilizing the southerly bridge to concentrate Major-General Friedrich Kuehn's 14th Panzer Division into staging positions north of the Dnepr.[54] While Kempf's corps had the vital task of making contact with Schweppenburg's corps in the north, Wietersheim's corps was charged with first advancing to Mirgorod and then helping to safeguard the eastern perimeter of the pocket.[55] As Wietersheim himself noted, 'In this situation we must risk a great deal, susceptibility in the flanks is of no consequence.'[56] Similarly at Army Group South Rundstedt alluded to both the potential of the new operation and its uncertainty. On the first day of the offensive (12 September), he wrote to his wife, 'I'm very anxious to find out how our new operation will work out, it *could* be a very big thing.'[57]

On the morning of 13 September Model's small battle group advancing south of Romny took the important town of Lokhvitsa as well as its bridge over the Sula River (see map 11).[58] Yet with dense enemy concentrations headed for the town, the battle group desperately needed further reinforcement and Model opted to send everything that remained of his panzer regiment, which in any case amounted to only a handful of tanks with some infantry. In the meantime the battle group requested and received aerial support from Loerzer's II Air Corps to slow the approach of enemy columns.[59] As Guderian followed events at the spearhead of his attack, he became convinced that more strength was needed in the south, especially given the prospect of Soviet attacks from the east as well as the west. He requested that the northerly stationed 18th Panzer Division, guarding 80 kilometres of the panzer group's long eastern flank, be relieved by infantry and set in motion towards Romny. Bock, however, wanted this division for his upcoming offensive to the east and he held well-founded fears that the march south would entail a great deal of wear and tear as well as mean it

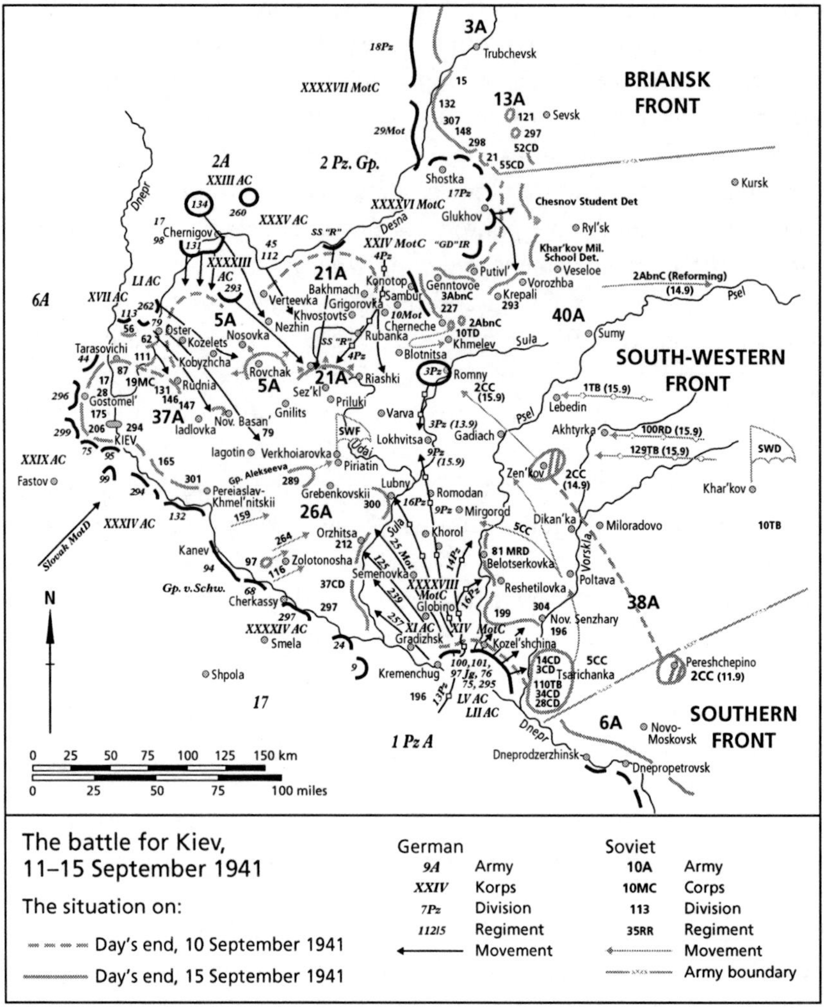

Map 11 The battle for Kiev, 11–15 September 1941
Source: Glantz, *Atlas of the Battle for Kiev Part III.*

would arrive too late to address Guderian's immediate concerns. Halder agreed with Bock and Guderian's request was refused.[60] As one may expect the panzer commander did not take this decision well and with nothing left available to move south, Guderian later complained, 'No consideration was given to the confused situation on our eastern flank or to the potential dangers that threatened from that quarter'.[61] Even if Guderian's concern were legitimate enough to warrant even more reinforcements, it only demonstrates that, despite the one-sided nature

Fig. 13 During mid-September Kleist's panzers broke out of the bridgehead at Kremenchug and raced north to link up with Guderian.

of the encounter playing out in the Ukraine, German forces were still judged as insufficient for the purpose.

While Model's units were preparing for their first defensive battles against the fleeing Soviet troops, on 13 September Hube's division, having been refuelled during the night, was able to press on to the town of Lubny. At this point the forward elements of the 16th Panzer Division were only 40 kilometres from Model's men at Lokhvitsa and seemingly on the verge of closing the ring, but from here they would advance no further. On the first day of Hube's offensive they had fought their way across 70 kilometres of enemy territory, and by the time they reached Lubny they had been on the march for two days and two nights. In this time they had blazed a strip across the Soviet supply lines, seizing 1,500 Soviet POWs, 600 trucks, 70 guns, 20 tractors and 3 planes.[62] Yet in Lubny they were to meet fanatical resistance. The town was defended by some formations of the NKVD, an anti-aircraft unit and a hastily organized workers' militia.[63] German reports also speak of many civilians, specifically women, taking part in the fighting. They were armed and took up positions on roofs, from cellar windows and behind makeshift barricades. German tanks were engaged at close range by Molotov cocktails.[64] The fighting was to continue into the night and following day, tying down Hube's forces and preventing their further advance.

The OKH had expected the link-up of Guderian and Kleist's panzer groups on 13 September[65] and even if that hope had now been dashed, with Kleist's other panzer divisions surging northward, it was only a matter of time. It was also discovered that the movement of large enemy concentrations in the area of Lokhvitsa consisted mainly of rear area troops without heavy equipment or even much combat training.[66] With knowledge of German tanks behind their positions causing scenes of panic, there were desperate attempts to flee eastwards, sparking the first signs of disintegration in Kirponos's South-Western Front. At the same time in the north the slower-moving offensives of the German Sixth and Second Armies were also making progress as Kirponos's whole northern wing steadily fell apart.[67] To the south elements of Stülpnagel's Seventeenth Army, which had been holding open the Kremenchug bridgehead, also began filing out of the breach towards the north. The XI Army Corps (with the 125th, 239th and 257th Infantry Divisions) was subordinated to Kleist's panzer group on 13 September and deployed to help ensure a strong eastern perimeter of the pocket.[68] Meanwhile Hubicki's 9th Panzer Division superseded Wietersheim's XIV Panzer Corps by capturing Mirgorod ahead of Kuehn's 14th Panzer Division.

Even without having sealed the encirclement front by 13 September, the progress of the battle in the Ukraine had rapidly reached a point of no return for Kirponos's forces. The largest battle of encirclement up to that point on the eastern front had been the battle of Smolensk in July and August, but the particulars of the Soviet predicament in the Ukraine were markedly different and not just in terms of scale. At Smolensk there were numerous Soviet reserve armies within striking distance of the German pocket and they exerted enormous pressure on Bock's motorized formations to keep open a narrow escape route for the almost cut-off Soviet forces. At the same time the retreating armies, who operated as one of the first mobile pockets on the eastern front, were not impeded by any higher orders expecting them to maintain untenable positions to the west. At Kiev there were no substantial Soviet forces to be brought to bear against the eastern flank of the pocket and the armies that had been hammering Bock's eastern front were now exhausted and drained of manpower. More importantly, they could not be moved south for fear of exposing Moscow. Not only was there to be no substantial relief force to assist Kirponos, but his armies were tied to their positions by the *Stavka*'s unyielding insistence. With no further prospect of resupply, a retreat up to 200 kilometres to the east over awful roads and a major battle to be fought at the end of it in order to break out, every day wasted before ordering the retreat doomed literally tens of thousands of Soviet men. The debacle so obvious to many in the Soviet high command had now occurred. Germany had been handed a triumph far in excess of what its exhausted armoured forces could have achieved without Stalin's obduracy and incompetence. To make matters worse there was still a wanton lack of comprehension as to the extent of the crisis; indeed Stalin still hoped the situation could somehow be salvaged and Kiev held. It was a forlorn hope, ensuring that what Hitler dubbed 'the biggest battle in the history of the world' would also be his greatest triumph.[69]

Running rings around the Red Army – Guderian and Kleist join hands

Having dismissed Budenny from command of the strife-ridden South-Western Direction, Stalin sought a replacement who was both militarily capable and satisfactorily compliant. In July the halting of Bock's surging advance had been credited to Timoshenko's astute command of the Western Front and now Stalin hoped he could repeat this feat by saving Kiev. On the same day that Budenny was relieved of command (11 September), Timoshenko was summoned to Moscow and given his instructions. At midnight he and his immediate staff boarded a train and headed for their new command in the symbolic town of Poltava. It was here in 1709 that the Russian Tsar, Peter the Great, ended the invasion of King Charles XII of Sweden by decisively defeating his army. Timoshenko was initially convinced he could restore the situation, and at the *Stavka*'s behest he ordered a renewed attack by Eremenko's overwhelmed Briansk Front against Guderian's panzer group.[70] Eremenko was ordered to transfer all available forces to the Thirteenth Army and then to push through Guderian's panzer group to re-establish contact with the South-Western Front. This was to be achieved, according to the *Stavka*, 'not later than 18 September'. As if Eremenko's success was simply a matter of encouragement, he was also promoted to

Colonel-General, but his offensive predictably failed. In fact German military files make almost no reference to a renewed attack by the Briansk Front. After weeks of hard fighting Eremenko's forces were spent. Throughout late August and September the Briansk Front's so-called Roslavl–Novozybkov operation committed more than a quarter of a million men and 259 tanks to battle, sustaining roughly 100,000 casualties and losing 140 tanks. Despite not reaching its objectives, the Briansk Front's offensive need not have been in vain if the time Eremenko had won by slowing Guderian's advance had been used for a withdrawal of the South-Western Front, but as it was the fighting only delayed the inevitable. Moreover, the cost of Eremenko's frantic attacks was a dramatic weakening of his front so that fewer than 200,000 men were left to oppose the start of Operation Typhoon.[71]

While Timoshenko invested his hopes in Eremenko's success against Guderian, on the night of 13/14 September Kirponos's Chief of Staff, Major-General V. I. Tupikov, took matters into his own hands and sent a blunt telegram to Shaposhnikov, which ended with the words, 'This is the beginning, as you know, of catastrophe – a matter of a couple of days.'[72] When Stalin was shown the message he refused to accept the severity of the situation and, after condemning Tupikov's report as 'panicky', he told Shaposhnikov:

> *On the contrary, the situation requires the maintenance of extreme coolness and steadfastness on the part of commanders at all levels. Avoiding panic, it is necessary to take all measures to hold occupied positions and especially to hold on to the flanks. You must compel [Lieutenant-General V. I.] Kuznetsov [commander of the Twenty-First Army] and [Lieutenant-General M. I.] Potapov [commander of the Fifth Army] to cease their withdrawal.*[73]

Although Stalin may have sought to appear undaunted by events and fully composed in his response, there are indications that he was feeling the pressure. On 13 September he sent another letter to Churchill again pressing for the idea of opening a second front against Hitler in Europe. Failing to do so, Stalin told Churchill, 'is playing into the hands of our common enemies'.[74] He then went on to make a most extraordinary proposal by the standards of the notoriously insular and secretive Soviet state. After two decades of almost paranoid fear of the western world, Stalin's letter continued:

> *If at the moment the opening of a second front in the west seems unfeasible to the British government, then perhaps some other means could be found of rendering the Soviet Union active military aid against the common enemy. It seems to me that Britain could safely land 25–30 divisions at Archangel or ship them to the southern areas of the USSR via Iran for military cooperation with the Soviet troops on Soviet soil in the same way as was done during the last war in France.*[75]

It was an astounding offer that went far beyond the current deployment of a single RAF fighter wing in the distant north. Stalin's offer to invite hundreds of thousands of foreign troops into his country perhaps therefore reveals a good deal about the Soviet dictator's hidden fears at the height of the battle of Kiev. Obviously Stalin was under a great deal of pressure as the warnings he had repeatedly rejected seemed to be playing out just as he had been advised they would. Whatever Churchill's response,[76] nothing could avert the loss of Kiev and indeed a large part of Kirponos's South-Western Front. It was now only a matter of saving what could be saved, and for this Stalin would have to accept the fallacy of his strategic conceptions and allow an immediate breakout from the rapidly closing pocket. This, however, would not be forthcoming and in the days ahead the German command would be more than ready to capitalize on their good fortune.

While the fighting in the Ukraine progressed favourably for Germany, Bock's defensive front also gained a reprieve with a near total cessation of Soviet attacks from the east.[77] The crisis that had gripped his front in late August and early September had now fully abated, allowing Army Group Centre a free hand to plan and organize for Operation Typhoon. To the south, however, Guderian still held grave concerns for his eastern flank, which now extended more than 200 kilometres in length. Although the halting of attacks against Bock's Ninth and Fourth Armies was noted to be 'conspicuous', the OKH could not identify any large-scale transfer of forces to the south.[78] This, however, was of little comfort to Guderian who on 14 September noted that, as a result of the ongoing bad weather, aerial reconnaissance was 'impossible' and ground reconnaissance was 'stuck in the mud'.[79] After almost two weeks of such conditions, and well before the advent of the much worse autumn rains, the bad weather had already played a persistent role in impeding German operations. Nor was Guderian's concern for his southern flank unjustified. He had no way of knowing the appalling losses sustained by Eremenko's forces, and the two corps detailed to protect his eastern flank (XXXXVI and XXXXVII Panzer Corps) were stretched to a dangerous degree. Moreover, after his recent experiences at the battle of Smolensk, as well as the heavy attacks by the Briansk Front during his drive south, the absence of sustained pressure from the east probably seemed too good to be true. Indeed from the perspective of the defending divisions, the length of their respective fronts forced even routine actions to be viewed as especially serious. Between 14 and 18 September Nehring's 18th Panzer Division was stretched across more than 90 kilometres of front and the divisional diary made it clear that enemy activity 'did not allow for one second the thought that the division was deployed to a "quiet" sector. Everything is deployed forward and fully engaged.'[80] It was also difficult to shift reserves to flashpoints in the line owing to the dreadful road conditions, which rendered the panzer corps, according to Guderian, 'almost immobilized'.[81] This exerted additional strain on the men at the front; as one soldier lamented in a letter home on 13 September, 'here in this damned Russia one must have nerves of iron'.[82] The absence of intelligence also meant that Guderian's headquarters had little idea of what was happening beyond their eastern perimeter and the uncertainly this created 'increased from day to day'.[83]

Uncertainly also reigned with regard to the coming winter; this stemmed largely from the high command's stubborn unwillingness to recognize the gravity of the problem. The post-war memoirs of many high-ranking German officers refer to the winter of 1941/1942 as either arriving early or being exceptionally cold. The argument typically advanced is that uncontrollable natural forces, commonly referred to as the fabled Russian ally 'General Winter', presented the *Ostheer* with an exceptional set of circumstances that could not have been foreseen.[84] Despite its acceptance in many early histories of the 1941 campaign, this rendering of events was greatly embellished and became a convenient crutch for many former commanders in explaining their otherwise wanton lack of preparation for the winter.[85] Already on 5 September Goebbels, who headed the annual German Winter Aid programme, noted in his diary, 'Above all in the large, empty areas of the front the coming winter in the east will probably mean very heavy losses.'[86] Indeed the very idea of a so-called 'General Winter' was ridiculous, as one former German officer in the OKH noted after the war: 'That it is cold in Russia at this time belongs to the ABC of an eastern campaign.'[87] In July expectations of an early victory led the OKH to plan for just fifty-six German divisions remaining in the east during the winter period.[88] By early September the base figure for the winter occupation force had been revised upwards, but only by 50 per cent, even though it was now generally recognized that the war would continue well into 1942. Inexplicitly, winter planning was still being conducted only for a force of some 750,000 men, although the *Ostheer* currently numbered some 3 million soldiers.[89] Even for this much lower figure German preparations would prove inadequate, reflecting the totality of the OKH's failure.

By 14 September Model had moved his divisional headquarters forward to Lokhvitsa where his weakened panzer regiment was now holding the town against what was reported to be strong enemy concentrations moving eastwards. However, it soon transpired that these large formations consisted primarily of supply troops who lacked heavy weapons and did not appear to operate with a cohesive command structure.[90] Thus, in spite of their superior numbers, these units proved woefully ineffectual in forcing a breakout even against Model's small force at Lokhvitsa. While larger towns guarding strategically important crossings over the Sula River were now in German hands, the pocket's cordon was not always hermetically sealed. Indeed on 14 September the forward command post of Schweppenburg's XXIV Panzer Corps suddenly found itself under attack from a Soviet column fighting its way eastwards. The command post was in danger of being overrun and was only narrowly saved by the timely arrival of a German relief force.[91] On another section of the front the 1st Cavalry Division was holding the line when it was suddenly attacked by powerful enemy forces, including Soviet T-34s and KV-1s. The only defence against these heavily armoured tanks was the powerful 88mm anti-aircraft gun, but as one soldier who participated in the battle explained:

> *The problem was that the [88mm] batteries were not always in the right place and our 14 Company could not, with its smaller cannons, always pierce the Russian armour... We*

> *were utterly helpless in those situations. Warfare against tanks we had hardly practised because it was not our job on horseback. The best we could do was get out of the way, seeking cover in the wooded areas, and hope for the best.*[92]

Yet fleeing before an enemy attack was strictly forbidden and the men of the 1st Cavalry Division were soon ordered to stand their ground. With the vital support of Stukas the fighting went on for twenty-four hours, after which the soldier's report continued:

> *We were simply exhausted and also had many casualties, not only in the way of men, but horses as well . . . On my way to my horse I could not avoid seeing the truckful of young corpses. It was just ghastly, and those were only a few from our immediate area. Blood was literally running down the side from the floodboards of the truck, and the driver was, despite the heat, white as a sheet. Shells were still flying about, but we were ordered to get ready to march, not for retreat, but en route to Kiev. So it looked as if the Russian counterattack had been stopped, but at what cost? We marched on, leading our horses, looking constantly to the skies for attackers and wondering how long this senseless slaughter could go on.*[93]

With Model now in Lokhvitsa and still no contact with Panzer Group 1, the wily commander of the 3rd Panzer Division, who within two and a half years would rise to become the Wehrmacht's youngest Field Marshal,[94] sent a small detachment south towards Lubny and union with Hube's 16th Panzer Division.[95] The force ran a gauntlet of disparate Soviet units until it arrived just north of Lubny and made contact with a company of engineers from Hube's division. A signal was sent and Model's headquarters received the instruction, '14 September 1941, 18:20 hours: link-up of 1st and 2nd Panzer Groups.'[96] Anticipating success, Model instructed that the password for his forces on 14 September be 'Tannenberg'.[97] In fact Model's supposed link-up was more symbolic than real given that wide open spaces were still being freely traversed by Soviet forces. Yet on the following day (15 September) major units of Hubicki's 9th Panzer Division pushed north to make firm contact with Model's division just south of Lokhvitsa.[98] That evening Halder noted in his diary, 'The encirclement ring is closed.'[99] The battle that he had fought so hard to avoid in July and August was now entering its final phase and already it promised to deliver an unprecedented windfall in men and materiel. Indeed observing the scale of events Halder may well have privately reconsidered his former opposition to Hitler's southern alternative, especially given the renewal of optimism within the OKH that Operation Typhoon could still capture Moscow before the end of the year. For Bock the achievement in the south was still a tremendous gamble and he was certainly not prepared to rescind his previously bitter denunciation of Hitler's decision to divert the attack away from Moscow. Commenting on the closure of the encirclement front, Bock rejoiced that 'The "Battle at Kiev" has thus become a dazzling success.'[100] Yet the commander of Army Group Centre then sounded a far more demurring tone, questioning the cost of Hitler's battle in the south and what it meant for, as Bock saw it, the essential goal of the campaign. As Bock prudently cautioned, 'But the main Russian force stands unbroken before my front and – as before – the question is open as to whether we can smash it quickly and so exploit this victory before winter comes [ensuring] that Russia cannot rise again in this war.'[101] Clearly the magnitude of events in the south had not distracted Bock from the fact that the Soviet Union still commanded vast forces and might yet still 'rise again in this war'.

With the union of Panzer Groups 1 and 2 the ring around the Soviet South-Western Front had at last closed, trapping four whole armies (the Fifth, Thirty-Seventh, Twenty-Sixth and Twenty-First) with a total of forty-three divisions.[102] It was an immense pocket extending 200 kilometres from the point at which Guderian and Kleist joined hands to the city of Kiev and encompassed a total area of about 20,000 square kilometres, making it about as big as the German state of Saxony or present-day Slovenia.[103] At Hitler's headquarters there was jubilation and no small sense of vindication for Hitler after his uncompromising stand against the generals. Goebbels noted on 16 September that Hitler was in the best of moods and looked towards the future with optimism and certainty.[104] Indeed after Hitler's last great clash with the OKH over plans for the invasion of France, the dictator once again found himself with cause to doubt the expert advice of his military professionals. Indeed it was not only Hitler who was now more inclined to trust his inner convictions irrespective of outside circumstances or advice. The small inner circle of generals belonging to the OKW was also positively influenced in this direction. It was after all Jodl who had told Heusinger in August, while the two were debating Hitler's preference for the turn to the south, 'One must not try to compel him [Hitler] to do something which goes against his inner convictions. His intuition has generally been right. You can't deny that!'[105] Thus the encirclement at Kiev was another major step in solidifying the absolute loyalty of the men who would, in future years, time and again trust the dictator's judgement against all odds.

As Hitler revelled in the impending calamity about to overtake the Soviet forces in the south, he cast his mind forward to the anticipated end of Stalin's rule, in which his war of annihilation, currently in progress, would lay the foundation for Germany's future *Lebensraum*. While the *Ostheer* concentrated on the battle against the Red Army, the SS and SD, together with the necessary support of the German army, were directed towards a campaign of genocide without precedent in history. By the late summer there were daily mass executions of Soviet Jews performed by special 'task forces' (*Einsatzgruppen*).[106] On any given day the number of victims could easily reach into the thousands and occasionally the tens of thousands.[107] Nor could non-Jewish Soviet civilians feel safe as random acts of extreme violence spread throughout the occupied territories and starvation threatened certain communities as a result of German food seizures. It was a truly apocalyptic picture that ultimately claimed more Soviet lives during the course of the war than did the staggering losses of the Red Army.[108] Indeed the war was only the start of the German genocide in the east as post-war plans aimed to reduce the Soviet population by up to 30 million through a deliberate policy of starvation.[109] As Hitler considered his future empire in the wake of his latest successes in the Ukraine, he told his inner circle, 'The struggle for the hegemony of the world will be decided in favour of Europe by the possession of the Russian space . . . The essential thing, for the moment, is to conquer. After that everything will be simply a question of organization.'[110] It was precisely what this process of 'organization' meant for the occupied peoples of Europe, especially those in the east, that made the Soviet Union's war effort, however desperate at times, so important. Already in September news of widespread German war crimes was being broadcast openly,[111] offering a palpable inducement for resistance, even in the most desperate circumstances. Such stout resistance manifested itself in many bitter examples as the pocket east of Kiev constricted. From a strictly military point of view the German command failed utterly to recognize their own role in the radicalization of Soviet resistance, particularly in potentially anti-Soviet regions such as the Ukraine. Indeed the German leadership became so enamoured with the scale of their achievement that numerous high-level officials, not just Hitler, rejoiced in premature visions of an end to the war in the east. The secretary of state in the foreign office, Ernst Freiherr von Weizsäcker, noted in his diary on 15 September, 'An autobahn is being planned to the Crimean peninsula. There is speculation as to the probable manner of Stalin's departure. If he withdraws into Asia, he might even be granted a peace treaty.'[112] In defiance of the view from above, many soldiers at the front were growing increasingly sceptical of any hopes for a foreseeable end to the war in the east. One soldier wrote home in a letter on 19 September, 'In the future I want to stay away from all these "prophecies" about the length of the Russian campaign or the whole war.'[113] At the end of September another soldier commented on the successes at Kiev and then concluded, 'but there is, however, only one [form of success in war] and that is called "finished"!!'[114] Even senior officers at the front had grown increasingly doubtful about the progress of the war. The commander of the XXXXIII Army Corps, who was taking part in the battle of Kiev, wrote in a letter to his wife on same day that Guderian and Kleist linked up:

> *The last great blow, that hopefully will decisively deplete the enemy, has yet to be struck. Even so I scarcely believe that Russia will give up before the winter, even if this blow is a great success. The country is too big and the populace too numerous, there is also the present hope of help from England and America. Both will do anything to sustain their ally, who is providing them with decisive support. The Soviets absorb the whole German Wehrmacht and cause us heavy casualties – from our best. You should see how tired and battle weary our troops are. Three months of such unheard of fighting and forced marches leave their mark on the men. Thus an end to this campaign and leave in autumn is not to be expected.*[115]

Not only was there no end in sight to the war, but as General Heinrici noted, the continuing toils of the troops were compounding their fatigue. One soldier from the SS division *Das Reich* who was marching south as part of Guderian's panzer group kept a diary relating his experiences. On 12 September he noted, 'We march along a railway embankment. It is very tiring walking on the sleepers ... Our feet are suffering from being continually wet from the rain and the swamp.' Two days later on 14 September he continued:

> *On roads that have been washed away, in pouring rain, carrying all our weapons and equipment, we fight our way against enemy resistance. We are at the end of our strength. We have been marching for days and with only poor rations. The supply trucks are stuck fast in the mud 30 or more kilometres away. Many of the comrades have only socks to cover their feet. Their boots have fallen to pieces. Others go bare-foot and their feet are torn as a result of the marches ... Soaked to the skin we dig in and our slit trenches fill quickly with water. The rain continues to pour down ... We are lying in water and yet we are thirsty.*[116]

Nor was it just the rigours of the march that the men were forced to endure: on the same day the soldier's company was attacked, sustaining serious casualties. As the diary stated, 'We come under fire ... everywhere there are calls for stretcher-bearers ... Our Company suffered 14 killed and 17 wounded.'[117]

German casualties on the eastern front were the most tangible indicators of Soviet success, despite their own setbacks and substantially larger losses. However, the tendency of some historians simply to set forth baseline figures and make clear-cut comparisons favouring Germany is deceiving. One must not forget that Germany and the Soviet Union operated in different strategic circumstances, which bore a direct correlation to their ability to absorb and sustain losses. The Soviet Union's far larger population, as well as its lower time and capital investment in training its soldiers, meant an individual loss was of lower aggregate cost than the same result would entail for Germany. Moreover, while Germany had to deploy soldiers to all corners of Europe as well as fight a small but draining war in North Africa, the Red Army was almost completely free to concentrate on one front. Thus German losses took on a heightened and disproportionate significance, especially given the rapidly rising potential and belligerency of the western powers.

Overall figures for German casualties in the east until 16 September were approaching half a million men and constituted 14 per cent of the entire *Ostheer*. In total some 460,169 soldiers and non-commissioned officers had been killed or wounded, while another 16,383 officers had been lost.[118] These figures, however, do not include those listed as sick. If an example may be extrapolated from the two divisions of IX Army Corps, which had together sustained 8,000 casualties up to 5 September, but counted another 2,000 as ill, then real losses within the *Ostheer* were around 20 per cent higher.[119] This would have raised the total number of German troops deemed unfit for service to well over half a million, constituting a sizeable portion of the initial 3.4 million strong invasion force. At Army Group Centre the ever-growing list of casualties boded ill for the renewal of the offensive, especially as replacements had not sufficed to cover all of the preceding losses. By 15 September Weichs's Second Army had suffered the least of Bock's armies, having avoided the gruelling defensive battles of August and early September. Nevertheless Weichs had sustained a total of 23,000 losses. Kluge's Fourth Army and Strauss's Ninth Army were considerably worse off, having suffered 38,000 and 48,000 losses respectively. Hoth's Panzer Group 3 had been stripped of some of its divisions in August, distinctly cutting its overall tally of casualties. In total it registered 17,000 losses by mid-September. Finally came Guderian's Panzer Group 2, which after almost three months of constant attacking had by far the highest rate of losses of the four panzer groups on the eastern front. Altogether it had lost 32,000 men.[120]

For each of Army Group Centre's major formations, losses in the tens of thousands had a perceptible impact on the combat strength of their units. As Eremenko noted in his memoir, 'Prisoners from the 10th and 11th companies of the Nazi 107th Infantry Regiment [34th Infantry Division] testified that their companies had consisted of 160 soldiers and 5 officers each before the fighting broke out. On September 8 and 9 the prisoners said the companies had no more than 60 soldiers each and some officers, and as little as 30 soldiers and no officers by September 12.'[121] Nor was Eremenko's claim simply the product of Soviet propaganda. On 16 September Halder noted the good progress of the battle in the Ukraine, but then added simply, 'Unfortunately losses!'[122] On 9 September Ernst Guicking, a soldier from the 52nd Infantry Division in Weichs's Second Army, noted with some alarm that the second company in his battalion had only sixty-eight men left.[123] Another soldier from the 98th Infantry Division in Reichenau's

Sixth Army wrote in a letter that casualties in his company had reached 75 per cent.[124] Meanwhile on 15 September Goebbels reviewed the cost of the defensive battles on Bock's front and concluded that losses there had been 'extensive'. This, he explained, was a result of the massive concentrations of Soviet artillery as well as the fact that the troops had been fighting on the defensive for weeks and could not be pulled out of the line. He concluded, 'There are companies there that have only sixteen men left.'[125] One soldier travelling behind the front saw numerous German cemeteries 'with twenty, thirty, forty graves following one after another'.[126] Hans Schäufler, a tanker in Langermann-Erlancamp's 4th Panzer Division, noted that the road south leading to the link-up with Kleist's panzer group was littered with innumerable quantities of destroyed Soviet weapons, but next to these 'were also the reminders provided by the graves of fallen comrades'.[127] Indeed, even without access to official figures the men could see for themselves what the war in the Soviet Union was costing the Wehrmacht. Already in August one soldier perceptively noted, 'In Russia alone more will have fallen than in all other countries together. By that of course I mean only our fallen.'[128] The frightening number of fatalities and the constant loss of comrades led to a morbid fatalism about the prospect of death. Konrad Jarausch wrote in a letter on 21 September, 'I too am very burdened by the many reports of dead young men . . . One often has to pull oneself together in order not to fall into unthinkable thoughts.'[129] While it may have been natural for the men to avert their thoughts from their ever-present proximity to death, one German chaplain summed up their predicament in the most direct terms: 'Yes, many of us won't see our families any more, [and] are doomed to spend our eternal rest far from the fatherland.'[130]

Four days after the chaplain had written his letter (on 12 September) Colonel-General Eugen Ritter von Schobert, the commander of the Eleventh Army operating on Rundstedt's southern flank, was killed near the front.[131] He was in a Fieseler *Storch* aircraft[132] on a visit to the front when his pilot unknowingly landed on a Soviet minefield, killing both men. Schobert was buried in the city of Nikolayev on 16 September.[133] Yet Schobert was not just another casualty. He was one of Germany's highest-ranking officers, a public figure featured in reports from the front and the most senior German officer to be killed in the war so far.[134] Goebbels lamented the loss of one of the Wehrmacht's 'most competent army commanders' as well as an outstanding member of the Nazi party who was 'a political general and a soldierly politician'.[135] SD reports showed that there was also a strong public interest in Schobert's death, which led to people asking uncomfortable questions. As the report framed the public's concern, 'how large must the losses in officers and men be when even an army commander dies'?[136] Nor was this a long way from the truth. There is evidence that numerous other senior German commanders either narrowly escaped death during the course of the summer or felt compelled to involve themselves directly in engagements with the enemy.

When General Heinrici wrote to his family in August he alluded to the many dangers that even a corps commander faced in the east. Heinrici noted the uncomfortable feeling he had driving through kilometres of forest, 'always with the possibility of running into Russians'. In another instance he wrote about having taken over command of a battalion at the front, which had 'descended into chaos'. More recently he noted an artillery bombardment of his headquarters in which seven men were wounded. He was thankful it was not worse because '[t]he possibility that things could have turned out differently has appeared often enough before.'[137] Guderian also noted close calls with Soviet artillery and cited one instance in which five officers sitting near him were wounded. As Guderian concluded, 'It was a wonder that I remained unhurt.'[138] The panzer commander was also no stranger to the battlefield and sometimes during his visits to the front he proceeded right up to the forward positions and even took part in attacks.[139] Perhaps the most revealing instance of this kind is found in a letter from Field Marshal von Reichenau to Paulus at the OKH, in which the commander of the Sixth Army related his role in an attack on Soviet positions during the battle of Kiev. As Reichenau explained, 'I did not lead this assault out of any lust for adventure', rather there was the urgent need to plug a gap in the line, which Reichenau personally undertook at the head of a regiment in the 44th Infantry Division. Recounting his experiences he told Paulus, 'I led the assault for three kilometres, quite literally not only with the first wave, but as the leading man in it. Enemy resistance was very stubborn, their mortar fire being particularly severe, and the only way we could avoid it was to advance just as fast as we could.' Rendering a final judgement Reichenau acknowledged, 'The fighting has been really fierce, literally to the last drop of blood.'[140] The idea of a corps commander leading a battalion or a Field Marshal leading a regiment might say something about the élan of the

German officer corps (and perhaps equally the imprudence of the protagonists), but underlying it all was the absence of officers at the lower levels, which given the danger experienced even at the higher levels of command is hardly surprising.

As gaps increasingly appeared within front-line formations, the ongoing demands of the war forced German commanders continually to ask more from fewer and fewer men. A stop-gap measure adopted as early as the summer of 1941 to address the critical manpower shortage in the east was the recruitment of local auxiliaries. These forces became known as '*Hiwis*', which stemmed from the German *Hilfswilliger* (literally 'willing helpers'). Local commanders typically instigated their recruitment without any official sanctioning owing to the fact that Nazi policy at the start of Operation Barbarossa was opposed to any form of collaboration with the subjugated peoples of the east. Nevertheless, as the situation became desperate even pro-Nazi officers relented in favour of alleviating the strain on their men. The *Hiwis* were employed in a variety of roles, mainly involving some form of manual labour such as building bunkers, working at aid stations, preparing food, driving trucks or acting as translators.[141] On 31 August Albert Neuhaus noted that Soviet POWs were not sent away to camps, but immediately put to work improving the state of the roads and building bridges. This, he stated, they did willingly, having not received enough to eat in the weeks before their capture or defection.[142] Goebbels also commented on the enthusiasm of some Soviet POWs to work for the Germans and added that they were being used to carry ammunition for the troops.[143] Only very rarely in 1941 were *Hiwis* allowed to participate as combatants within German units, but even this is hard to determine with any accuracy given the official restriction, which prevented commanders from reporting on the incorporation of anti-Soviet elements. In one concrete example, a defecting Soviet regiment with an indeterminate number of Cossacks was re-employed in anti-partisan operations as 'Cossack Detachment 600' behind Army Group Centre.[144]

The unofficial use of *Hiwis* in the late summer of 1941 was a clear sign of the progressive radicalization in military policy on the eastern front. The practice was forced on the army by the desperate need to reduce the inordinate strain on the *Ostheer*. Nevertheless, the number of *Hiwis* in 1941 constituted only a small fraction of the *Ostheer* and although their numbers would grow dramatically in the years to come, it was never adequately proportionate to the scale of Germany's manpower deficiency on the eastern front. By the middle of September 1941, the battle of Kiev may have appeared to be heading towards a grand operational success, but it was also an outstanding symptom of the intractable problem Germany confronted in the east. With each new advance and conquest, the *Ostheer* was shedding men at an alarming rate, while at the same time the depth and length of the front grew owing to the expanding funnel of Soviet geography. Thus more ground was continually having to be held by fewer men, increasing the demands on the armies and limiting the ability of the *Ostheer* to concentrate forces for new operations. With already more than half a million casualties in less than three months of fighting and no possibility of ending the war, Operation Barbarossa had doomed Germany to a colossal bloodletting in the east.

7 SLAUGHTER IN THE UKRAINE

'We will break them soon, it is only a question of time' (Adolf Hitler)

With the ring around the Soviet South-Western Front now closed German intelligence estimated that they had cut off up to sixty Soviet divisions, but that under the prevailing circumstances they would collectively possess a battle strength of only about twenty divisions.[1] In many respects Kirponos now found himself in the eye of the storm as German forces prepared to press the South-Western Front from all sides. In spite of all his warnings and desperate pleas to shore up the flanks Kirponos had been surrounded, and yet still he could not secure permission to order a breakout to the east. Meanwhile his front was already in an advanced state of disintegration. The northern flanks had largely collapsed and his strongest army (the Thirty-Seventh) remained meaninglessly tied to Kiev, some 200 kilometres from the new Soviet line. With his hands firmly tied from above, Kirponos faced an excruciating choice – either risk sharing Pavlov's fate[2] by openly defying Stalin and ordering a retreat or go on rejecting the pleas of his subordinates and accepting the steady suffocation of his entire front. The war diary of Army Group South anticipated that the coming reduction of the Kiev pocket would be a 'difficult battle', in which the enemy would have to be 'smashed' by 'strong forces'. There was also a degree of wonderment expressed at the static nature of the Soviet response, which the German command could only guess resulted from 'complete surprise' on the part of the Soviets as well as a lack of orders about what to do next.[3] General Heinrici expressed his utter incredulity at Soviet actions: 'In an incomprehensible manner the Russian has left his troops to remain in a situation in the Ukraine which must result in their capture . . . In eight days there will be a special announcement that another very far-reaching victory has been won.'[4] Even so the one-sided battle still remained to be won and Army Group South cautioned, 'Without a doubt in the next few days one must expect the beginning of large breakthrough attempts.'[5]

On 14 September as the immense battle approached its climax, Halder rejoiced at the 'classic succession of events'[6] in the south and two days later depicted the fighting as 'running according to a programme'. Indeed already on 16 September Halder anticipated being able to redirect most of the Second Army away from the encirclement front and subordinating the remaining divisions to the Sixth Army.[7] As confusion and panic began to take hold inside the Soviet pocket, the Luftwaffe took full advantage. Greim's V Air Corps (from Löhr's Air Fleet 4) combined with Loerzer's II Air Corps (Kesselring's Air Fleet 2) to strafe and bomb at will. German dominance of the air was absolute. The few available Soviet aircraft were thrown into battle against the German armoured ring, but the results were extremely meagre. On 13 September as Kempf's XXXXVIII Panzer Corps raced north of Kremenchug, it registered only eight enemy attacks by a total of twenty-three aircraft.[8] Over the pocket itself German aircraft hounded Soviet movement on the roads, resulting in devastating losses. Already by 14 September Greim's V Air Corps listed 560 enemy trucks, 3 tanks and 44 Soviet planes as destroyed. In the same period a further 267 trucks were estimated to have been damaged and 17 trains were attacked with total or significant degrees of destruction.[9] Loerzer's II Air Corps also played a key role in the battle, as Kesselring noted in his memoir: 'I would not be doing justice to the Luftwaffe if I omitted to mention the decisive performance of II Air Group . . . The skill of our crews was evident from the fact that railway lines in the battle zone were permanently cut. In one short section of the line twenty or thirty trains were held up which were subsequently smashed to pieces by destroyer attacks.' Moreover, when enemy formations appeared on the roads, Kesselring noted, 'they were relentlessly attacked with devastating results'.[10]

While aerial operations proceeded apace in the early days of Army Group South's breakout from the Kremenchug bridgehead, the frantic tempo of operations could not be maintained. As was so often the case in Operation Barbarossa logistics proved a greater obstacle than actual Soviet resistance and Greim's air corps suddenly ground to a halt with only a handful of bomber sorties flown on 16 and 17 September. As V Air Corps's Chief of Staff, Lieutenant-Colonel Hermann Plocher, noted, 'Repeated requests to the air fleet by the V Air Corps, asking for timely and sufficient fuel supplies, were futile; even after the air fleet had begun to exert its influence in the matter, the tremendous distances and inadequate available transport space did not allow a smoothly functioning supply system.'[11] Likewise, Kesselring also cited the absence of supplies as a key factor hampering the operation of his air fleet at the battle of Kiev. Yet the Field Marshal suggested that in Army Group Centre it was more than just long distances and limited transportation space which was causing the problem. Kesselring referred to an absence of rear combat formations, which he stated had become necessary because 'the Russians had learnt the lesson of previous engagements and almost completely throttled our communications'.[12] In principle Kesselring was correct. The partisan war was a significant threat even as early as the summer of 1941, but suggesting that the Soviet leadership had learned the value of partisan operations and was already equipped to direct forces in a serious campaign was incorrect. The overwhelming bulk of what were described as 'partisan' attacks in the summer and early autumn of 1941 were instigated by soldiers of the Red Army who had simply become trapped behind German lines and remained determined to carry on the fight. In any case the result was clear: with the already faltering railway timetables, an alarming shortage of trucks and bad weather, the partisan menace was a further serious complication to maintaining German operations.

On 18 September Greim's V Air Corps was able to resume operations and concentrated significant forces on the city of Kiev with the stated aim of reducing the city to 'rubble and ashes' and doing 'half the work' of the army.[13] With Soviet airbases inside the pocket inoperable and the city so far from those that were, Kiev was effectively abandoned, allowing the Luftwaffe to operate with impunity. Inside the Ukrainian capital German Stuka attacks led to panic and despair.[14] Although Kiev had become a focal point of the German aerial assault, the remainder of Greim's corps together with Loerzer's air corps went on harrying Soviet forces inside the pocket, inducing turmoil and heavy losses among the scattered and increasingly leaderless formations. In total Plocher stated that between 12 and 21 September the V Air Corps alone flew 1,422 sorties and dropped 567,560 kilograms of bombs and

96 Type-36 incendiary bomb clusters, inflicting 'extraordinarily heavy' destruction on the ground.[15] Gabriel Temkin, a Jewish man assigned to a Russian labour battalion, observed, 'The Luftwaffe's favourite places for dropping bombs, especially incendiary ones, were forested areas close to main roads. Not seeing, but expecting, and rightly so, that the woods were providing resting places for army units and their horses, German planes were bombing them, particularly at night.' As forest fires swept the region Temkin added, 'For the first time I smelled burnt flesh.'[16] In addition to an unknown human toll, Plocher stated that his corps destroyed 2,171 motor vehicles, 107 planes, 52 trains, 28 locomotives, 23 tanks, 6 anti-aircraft batteries and one bridge between 12 and 21 September. In addition, hundreds more motor vehicles, horse-drawn wagons and rolling stock were reportedly damaged. Losses to the V Air Corps amounted to just seven officers and twenty men killed or missing. Seventeen German planes were shot down, another nine received damage to more than 30 per cent of the aircraft and five suffered less than 30 per cent damage.[17]

Such comparatively light losses need to be viewed in perspective. Air Fleets 2 and 4 certainly capitalized on the Soviet disaster in the Ukraine and repeated many of the successes from the early days of Operation Barbarossa when the Luftwaffe performed with such unprecedented destructiveness. Yet after weeks of unremitting operations, in which the Luftwaffe could only satisfy a select number of the demands made on it, the effects were beginning to show. At the start of Operation Barbarossa the Luftwaffe deployed a combined total of 2,995 aircraft on the eastern front, but by 6 September the number of these still operational had shrunk to just 1,005 planes.[18] In addition, personnel losses by the end of August amounted to 1,600 dead, 1,500 missing and 3,200 wounded.[19] Crews were exhausted, vast numbers of planes were in need of repairs and the forward bases were typically poorly serviced or had been badly damaged (in part by previous German aerial attacks). As Kesselring acknowledged, 'Our divisions, including the Luftwaffe, were simply overtaxed, at the end of their tether and far from their supply centres.'[20] On 21 August Field Marshal Erhard Milch, the Inspector-General of the Luftwaffe, conducted a tour of airfields in the east and noted that they were littered with scores, sometimes hundreds, of damaged aircraft.[21] The damage to so many German aircraft was, however, not simply attributable to Soviet aerial attacks or damage sustained while flying combat missions. In fact, estimates suggest that most damage to German aircraft resulted from pilot error. The Luftwaffe had been engaged in a war of attrition against the RAF since the spring of the previous year and heavy pilot losses demanded replacements from the training schools before the men were fully qualified. These young pilots were supposed to complete their training in their new squadrons by being eased into their roles with only progressive exposure to hazardous missions. Yet the heavy demands placed on the overextended Luftwaffe did not allow much time for training flights or exposure to non-hazardous missions. The flying conditions on the primitive eastern airfields also significantly added to the dangers, and with air safety standards within the Luftwaffe already dangerously lax, new pilots damaged and destroyed aircraft at an astonishing rate. Estimates suggest that for every four German aircraft destroyed in combat, another three were lost in non-combat-related accidents.[22] For example, 225 Stukas were lost in 1941 as a result of enemy action, but another 141 were destroyed in non-combat-related incidents.[23] The number of Stukas listed as damaged in combat was 56, but a further 130 were damaged in non-combat-related accidents. Even more revealing were the figures for German single-engine fighters. A total of 622 were destroyed in combat, but an additional 705 were written off as 'not due to enemy action'. The number of single-engine fighters damaged in action came to 246; however, an incredible 813 more fighters were damaged in non-combat-related activities.[24] As one might expect, the combined impact on aircrews from both combat and accident-related losses took a steep toll on the Luftwaffe's personnel. The average monthly crew strength for bombers operating on the eastern front[25] was 901 men and they suffered an average monthly loss of 126 men, equalling 14 per cent of the total each month. Single-engine fighter and Stuka pilots suffered average monthly losses of 9 and 7 per cent respectively, which after four months of warfare totalled 36 and 28 per cent of their starting totals.[26] Clearly without the ability to end the war in the east and given the growing demands on the Luftwaffe in other theatres, an improvement in the overall experience and skill of the pilots and crews was impossible to achieve. Accordingly, the high rate of attrition among German aircrews and the steady demise of the Luftwaffe in World War II began irrevocably in the summer of 1941.

Just as the Luftwaffe's destructive role in the battle of Kiev belied its growing weakness, so too did the closing of the encirclement front conceal the ruinous state of Guderian's panzer group. Halder

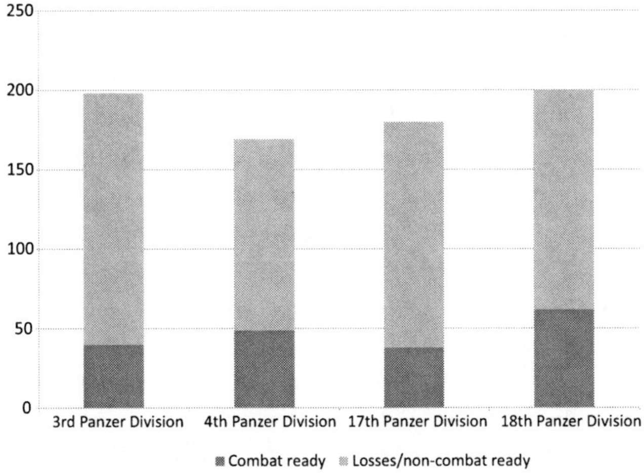

Fig. 14 Combat strength of Panzer Group 2 on 14 September 1941
Source: Halder, KTB III, p. 231 (14 September 1941).

noted in his diary on 14 September that just 20 per cent of the tanks in Model's 3rd Panzer Division were operational.[27] Given the division's initial strength of 198 tanks at the onset of Operation Barbarossa,[28] Halder's figure would have indicated a remaining strength of about 40 serviceable tanks (Figure 14). Yet Halder's 20 per cent figure probably took some time to work its way up to his desk because the following day (15 September) Lieutenant-Colonel Oskar Munzel, the commander of Model's Panzer Regiment 6, reported to Guderian an even more alarming figure. According to Munzel the entire division possessed just one Mark IV, three Mark IIIs and six Mark IIs, making a total of ten operational tanks for the entire division. As Guderian noted, 'These figures show how badly the troops needed a rest and a period for maintenance. They show that these brave men had given of their last in order to reach the objectives assigned them.'[29] Yet just reaching their set objective no longer sufficed; there were also the inevitable breakout attempts by countless Soviet troops that would have to be repelled and after that Army Group Centre was already planning a major role for Panzer Group 2 in Operation Typhoon. In fact the underlying reason for why there were so few tanks in Model's division was because there was no rest on the eastern front and that even after almost three months of continuous action there was always a new 'decisive' goal that had to be obtained.

Beyond the relentless forward motion of the offensive, the German maintenance system for tanks was highly centralized in Germany and required that most major repairs be undertaken back at the home depots or one of the original production plants. Such a system had proved sufficient for the Wehrmacht's preceding campaigns, but the Soviet Union presented a vastly different challenge, and although some minor modifications to the system could be adapted, it was still an overwhelmingly centralized system. As one post-war study conducted by former German officers in the *Ostheer* noted:

> *Once the Russian campaign got under way, the need for tank maintenance installations and the demand for spare parts increased by leaps and bounds... The tank maintenance services were handicapped because only the larger towns contained buildings that provided even minimum shop and billeting facilities. Despite strenuous efforts, the maintenance personnel were unable to cope with the ever-increasing volume of repair work. The German army's requirements for all types of supplies, particularly ammunition, fuel and medical supplies, exceeded all expectations. The inadequate road and rail nets made it impossible to support the rapidly advancing armored columns... The unsatisfactory rail transportation situation had a disastrous effect on the tank maintenance system at a time when the number of disabled tanks reached an all time high.*[30]

Although the deficiencies of the system soon became apparent, it took until the summer of 1942 before the maintenance system could be extensively decentralized, rendering the *Ostheer*'s heavy losses irreversible in the pivotal year of 1941.

While the heavy fallout rate in Model's panzer division was the worst in Panzer Group 2 it was hardly an outstanding exception. According to Halder's diary on 14 September, Lieutenant-General Hans-Jürgen von Arnim's 17th Panzer Division[31] operated with a near identical 21 per cent serviceability rate. While Model's and Arnim's panzer divisions were numerically the weakest, Guderian's remaining forces, according to Halder's information, were in only marginally better shape. Langermann-Erlancamp's 4th Panzer Division retained just

29 per cent of its starting strength and Nehring's 18th Panzer Division 31 per cent.[32] Given the discrepancy in Model's numerical strength it is hard to know whether Halder's information was not somewhat out of date, but even if one accepts his figures as current, it still highlights an alarming reduction in serviceability. Indeed if one totals the numerical strength of Guderian's entire tank fleet, by mid-September Panzer Group 2 possessed the equivalent strength of just one panzer division and that was before the end of the battle of Kiev. However much a lame duck the Soviet South-Western Front had become, the prospect of Guderian's panzer group gaining any kind of substantive rest and refit before the next big offensive was highly doubtful and in that sense Kirponos's desperate last stand still served a wider purpose.

To the south of Panzer Group 2, Kleist's panzer group was already taking its first large hauls of prisoners. On 17 September Kempf's XXXXVIII Panzer Corps reported capturing 7,000 Soviet POWs, 35 guns and countless trucks.[33] At the OKH Halder observed the situation within the Soviet pocket and noted how 'enemy formations are bounding off the encirclement ring like billiard balls'.[34] Yet Kempf's divisions were not simply holding the eastern perimeter of the pocket and waiting; they were now attacking westward, compressing the pocket. Against the increasing tide of Soviet units seeking to escape captivity, this was no easy task. Indeed as Hubicki's 9th Panzer Division attempted to take the town of Gorodischtsche it was met on the approaching roads by heavy resistance, which included dug-in anti-aircraft guns used in an anti-tank role. After three German tanks had been destroyed the attack was called off until the following day.[35] Nor was it just the panzer divisions that were seeking to force their way into the Soviet pocket. Kleist's XI Army Corps, which had been subordinated to him from Stülpnagel's Seventeenth Army, was pushing westward between the southern flank of Kempf's panzer corps and the Dnepr River. To maximize the pressure, Reichenau's Sixth Army, together with significant elements of the Luftwaffe, was ordered to assult Kiev with all available forces. The city was seen as the nerve centre of Soviet resistance within the pocket and had the highest density of Soviet troop concentrations.[36] At the same time, having utterly shattered Kirponos's northern flank, Lieutenant-Colonel Walter von Seydlitz-Kurzbach's LI Army Corps (belonging to the Sixth Army) was making remarkable progress towards the south against scattered enemy resistance. Indeed on 18 September the corps linked up with elements of General of Infantry Alfred Wäger's XXXIV Army Corps (also of the Sixth Army), which had forged a new bridgehead over the Dnepr at Rzhishchev.[37] The great pocket was now split into two distinct hemispheres and was continuing to shrink fast.

At Kirponos's headquarters there was consternation. There was no longer any need to threaten the *Stavka* with what would happen; to convey the scale of the catastrophe confronting the South-Western Front they only need inform them of what was actually taking place. By 18 September, however, even sending and receiving messages had become difficult as communications broke down along with the command and control of the armies. Redeployed Soviet units became cut off from their parent organizations, became lost, could not receive new orders and had no idea of where the Germans were operating. It was chaos and the more the turmoil spread the greater the panic became. Watching events unfold, it was no surprise that Timoshenko, the new commander of the Soviet South-West Direction, quickly lost his initial faith in restoring the situation. As he correctly assessed soon after taking command, 'Each fresh day of delay only increases the scale of the catastrophe.'[38] On 16 September during a discussion with Major-General I. Kh. Bagramian, the Chief of Operations for the South-Western Front, Timoshenko orally gave permission to withdraw Kirponos's forces to a new defensive position on the Psel River.[39] In actual fact forces from Stülpnagel's Seventeenth Army, which had originally been deployed in the bridgehead at Kremenchug, had meanwhile undertaken another offensive towards the east and had already crossed the proposed defensive line on the Psel. Even so Timoshenko's order for retreat was stillborn. When Bagramian returned to the pocket it took him most of the day to find Kirponos, and when he finally did the commander of the South-Western Front balked. Kirponos had received his instructions directly from Stalin and, fearing the consequences of defying him, he could not bring himself to order a retreat without at least some kind of written order from a higher authority.[40] At the same time, Stülpnagel's eastward-marching infantry divisions were approaching Timoshenko's headquarters at Poltava and thus the command of the South-Western Direction was out of contact while it was being evacuated to Khar'kov. Kirponos therefore sent a signal directly to the *Stavka* repeating Timoshenko's oral instructions and requesting clarification. Kirponos ended his transmission, 'I consider that pulling troops back to the Psel is correct, which means immediate and complete withdrawal from Kiev and the River Dnepr. Urgently request your instructions.' It took an entire day, until 2340 hours on 17 September, for a reply from Shaposhnikov to be sent. It was as ambiguous as it was blunt: 'The Supreme Commander authorized withdrawal from Kiev.' Yet nothing was said about authorizing a retreat over 200 kilometres to the Psel River. As the Secretary of the Ukrainian Communist Party Central Committee, M. A. Burmistenko, commented on Shaposhnikov's reply, 'He says "a" without wishing to say "b".'[41] In any case the matter had become redundant. A few hours before Shaposhnikov's communiqué arrived, Kirponos, despairing at the procrastination in the high command and the plight of his forces, finally decided to act on his own volition and authorized all his forces to attack eastwards to escape the pocket.[42] Yet Kirponos's belated order came too late to make any substantive difference. His forces were under attack from all sides as well as from the air, there was no possibility of obtaining new supplies and communications everywhere were failing. Indeed even before Kirponos had resolved to act on his own, scores of subordinate commanders, many in far more desperate circumstances, had already begun their own precarious attempts to flee the pocket with as many men as possible. By late on 17 September, as Kirponos's order went out to every unit with a functioning radio, the chaos within the remnants of the South-Western Front became complete. The supposed retreat became the inevitable rout, in which the confusion was only surpassed by the level of destruction. For the men of the South-Western Front the battle of Kiev was hardly a battle anymore, but rather a desperate attempt to survive against overwhelming odds.

At the Wolf's Lair in East Prussia, Hitler was in a triumphant mood. When SS-*Sturmbannführer*[43] Otto Günsche, who had served as a member of Hitler's bodyguard from 1936 to 1941 and was now fighting on the eastern front in the *Leibstandarte Adolf Hitler*, visited his former comrades at the Wolf's Lair in mid-September, Hitler granted him a personal audience. Günsche noted Hitler's affable demeanour and polite interest in the activities of the *Leibstandarte*. When Günsche reported on the stubborn resistance of the Red Army, Hitler's reply evinced an unshakeable faith in victory: 'We will break them soon, it is only a question of time. I have ordered panzer armies with over two thousand tanks to group before Moscow. Moscow will be attacked and will fall, then we will have won the war.'[44] Yet Günsche's account also provides evidence for Hitler's increasing departure from the strategic reality of the eastern front. According to Günsche, after the conquest of Moscow Hitler told him that the advance would only be halted when the *Ostheer* had reached the Ural mountains; the remainder of the Soviet Union could starve to death. 'As the reformer of Europe,' Hitler concluded, 'I shall make sure that a new order is imposed on this land according to my laws!'[45]

As the German command observed events in the Ukraine with great satisfaction, attention within Army Group Centre turned more and more to the preparations for Operation Typhoon. Planning had been under way since mid-July when Army Group Centre and the rest of the German command had believed they were on the last lap of their conquest of the Soviet Union. The long postponement, so often attributed to a self-imposed halt while the strategic dispute played out between Hitler and the generals, was actually an inevitable delay brought on by supply shortages, the need for an extension of the railroads and the almost unceasing Soviet counteroffensives. When Hitler decided on striking first towards Kiev, Army Group Centre gained even more time to stockpile essential supplies, which still proved inadequate. There were also a number of outstanding strategic concerns. Bock was already deeply frustrated with the OKH's limited proposal and argued for a grand operation, promising 'sweeping strategic success'. To that end, on 14 September Bock sent a proposed map to the army command outlining his conception for the upcoming operation, which he claimed 'left all doors open'.[46] On the following day (15 September) Halder studied Bock's proposition together with Heusinger and came to the conclusion that Bock was 'still projecting himself too far to the east'.[47] Indeed Halder wanted an even tighter encirclement of the opposing Soviet forces than the one he had previously proposed and this only deepened the rift between them. As Bock wrote in his diary, 'Halder gave me a verbal response to the map of the new operation submitted to the Army High Command. The essence of it is that the battle is to be "even more limited" in scope! Narrow-mindedness is becoming an art! And after the battle we will again be facing the enemy's reserves!'[48] Bock was correct in his assessment that without a larger-scale operation Army Group Centre would again have to deal with the Red Army's reserves, but what he failed to grasp was the limitation of his own forces, not to mention the seasonal difficulties, which, given the already heavy rainfalls of September, could only be expected to worsen in October. There was simply no possibility that Army Group Centre could launch another operation of the depth initially achieved in June towards Minsk or in July towards Smolensk. The insufficient number of available motor vehicles, the diminutive stockpiles of fuel and munitions, the unreliability of the railways, which were persistently falling short of their promised daily quotas, and the stark decline in the fighting strength of all combat units – infantry, panzer and Luftwaffe – predetermined the failure of Bock's grand solution. The war diary for Hoth's Panzer Group 3 also rejected the idea of a deep penetration, arguing, 'Given past experience it seems inadvisable to attempt an encirclement with an objective too far to the rear because the Russian does not react to threats to the flanks and only holds a longer time at the front.'[49] In comparison with Bock's proposal for a deep thrust, Halder's more modest plan, therefore, appears the more rational choice, but it actually contained the same fatal flaw. The dispute between Bock and Halder was largely confined to the first phase of the operation – the destruction of the Soviet Western and Briansk Fronts. Yet after this anticipated victory, Halder had lost none of his heedless ambition and intended to push Army Group Centre well beyond its capabilities in a second phase of the campaign aiming for the capture of Moscow. Indeed, given all the unlearned lessons of Operation Barbarossa's failure, Operation Typhoon was essentially preordained to miscarry. The ratio of space, time and force was incongruent with the preconditions for operational success.[50] The weakness of the available forces, the proliferation of obstacles constituting 'friction' and the distances involved were all utterly misunderstood by both Bock and Halder. A so-called 'battle of destruction' opposite Army Group Centre constituted a realizable plan, but raw firepower was no longer matched by mobility and the fortress of Moscow was still another 300 kilometres from German lines. Simply getting there would consume an inordinate amount of Bock's strength, especially given the major battle to be fought in the first phase of the operation. Seizing Moscow therefore constituted a prohibitive delusion, logistically unworkable, wilfully ignorant of the seasonal conditions and inexcusably dismissive of Soviet strength.

Not only was Bock frustrated by the operational plans for his upcoming offensive, he was also angered by the protracted redeployment of forces to his front. As he wrote on 17 September, 'Kesselring came and was shocked that the gathering of forces for the attack is taking so long. I am too. In fact, of all the panzer divisions that Army Group North is to release to me, not one is yet on the march today.'[51] This was especially disturbing news given that the offensive was supposed to begin before the end of the month (soon to be postponed to 2 October) and that the redeployment south would undoubtedly prove especially costly to the motorized vehicles. Panzer Group 3, which was due to incorporate three panzer divisions (1st, 6th and 8th) currently operating within Army Group North (as well as the 7th Panzer Division), noted on 18 September that 'the advanced time of year' necessitated the earliest possible beginning to the next offensive. The diary then continued, 'For Panzer Group 3 this depends entirely on the arrival of the divisions coming from the northern front, which as a result of the march will probably also require a number of days for refitting and repairs.'[52]

Panzer Group 3 was not the only one anticipating problems with mobility in the upcoming offensive. While Guderian's panzer force had shrunk to precarious levels, his fleet of trucks, vital for moving forward fuel, munitions and infantry, was in no condition to sustain another long advance. Even with most of the panzer group in static positions and with large quantities of captured supplies at Romny, the trucks were still struggling to deliver enough fuel to the front. The 3rd Panzer Division was worst affected and the quartermaster's diary for 15 September stated that its supply dumps were simply too far away,[53] forcing the trucks to endure long journeys for comparatively little yield.[54] By the same token, the supply of Guderian's XXXXVI and XXXXVII Panzer Corps was entirely unsatisfactory owing to the unpredictability of the railways. The war diary of the panzer group's quartermaster described the line between Gomel and Novgorod-Severskii as 'completely insufficient and unreliable'. As a result the supply of the two panzer corps was 'not guaranteed' and relief was deemed 'urgently necessary'.[55] In such cases there was little choice other than to pick up the slack by placing even greater demands on the trucks of the *Grosstransportraum*. The result was predictably destructive. As the war diary for the XXXXVII Panzer Corps noted on 18 September:

> *The status report submitted to the [panzer] group on 18.9, for the period August to September, showed that as a result of the heavy demands over the last weeks on outrageously bad roads the state of the trucks has worsened. Owing to*

> *the failure to deliver spare parts innumerable instances of damage, often only relatively minor, cannot be repaired. This in part, therefore, explains the high percentage of conditional and non-serviceable trucks.*[56]

The shortage of trucks within the panzer group was well known to Guderian, as was the lack of replacements and spare parts, but weeks of desperate pleas for relief had yielded very little help. Thus the impetuous Guderian hit on a new idea that once again reflected his obstinate determination to service his own needs irrespective of any other concerns. The main source for replacement trucks in many German units was captured Soviet war booty, which as Gottlob Bidermann explained, not only provided vital replacements, but proved far easier to maintain. 'The Russians possessed large numbers of robust Ford heavy trucks[57] as well as those of "Sis" manufacture. Those two types seemed to make up the entire inventory of trucks possessed by the enemy, and we always chose the American-manufactured Ford whenever possible, as many replacement parts seemed to be always available.'[58] Yet incorporating Soviet and American model trucks into the *Ostheer* only added another element to the already chronic problem of standardization within the army. As Bidermann continued:

> *Due to this method of salvage and use, our army appeared to consist of vehicles of every type and description from half of Europe, sometimes making it impossible to obtain even the most simple replacement parts. We found ourselves growing envious of the uncomplicated Russian supply system. Although their inventory of weapons and equipment might not have been as varied or as specialized as our own, what they did have was reliable and could be logistically supported almost anywhere.*[59]

Thus, in the absence of any meaningful replacements from Germany, securing captured Soviet trucks became a priority for German commanders and Guderian was determined to have the lion's share of the booty in the Kiev pocket. Previously, in the aftermath of the battle of Smolensk, the competition for the seizure of Soviet trucks became so intense that Guderian's requisition squads actually engaged in firefights with elements of the German VIII Army Corps.[60]

Fig. 15 In order to make up for the loss of motorization within the army German units attempted to requisition as many captured Soviet vehicles as possible.

Now, with the need for replacement trucks as urgent as ever, Guderian's panzer group requested that Army Group Centre intercede on its behalf and secure from Army Group South an order granting Guderian priority for all captured vehicles throughout the entire area of the Kiev pocket. The communiqué to Army Group Centre first underlined the heavy losses of Schweppenburg's XXIV Panzer Corps while closing the Kiev encirclement and then continued, 'Panzer Group 2 urgently requests, therefore, an order from Army Group South allowing for the requisition squads from the divisions of Panzer Group 2 to secure and drive away captured vehicles from within the whole of the Kiev pocket . . . '[61] It is not certain what happened to this request, as no further details could be located, but more than likely Bock reacted with the same circumspection that greeted many of Guderian's requests and, perhaps foreseeing a pointless furore with Army Group South, rejected the idea outright.

While Guderian had no problem surreptitiously attempting to undercut Kleist's share of the captured motorized transport, he nevertheless wanted Panzer Group 1 to aid him in holding his long eastern flank.[62] Even in his relations with his fellow panzer group commanders Guderian proved a difficult personality. He had enjoyed a generally favourable relationship with Hoth during the encirclement at Minsk; however, this soured considerably during the battle of Smolensk. Kleist and Guderian, on the other hand, began Operation Barbarossa with a turbulent past, which had come to a head during the French campaign when Kleist, as Guderian's superior, tried to have him dismissed from his command for disobeying orders.

On 18 September a Soviet thrust towards Romny from the east ruptured German defences and approached to within only a kilometre of the town. Not only was Romny a vital storage and communication centre, but it had since become the command centre for Panzer Group 2, which now found itself thrust on to the front line. Having observed the attacking Soviet forces converging on the town in three separate columns, Guderian later noted 'we found ourselves in the midst of a crisis'.[63] Recently seized Soviet POWs reported that two panzer brigades (each with forty tanks), two infantry divisions and one or two cavalry divisions were driving the Soviet attack.[64] Against this Guderian could muster only two battalions of the 10th Motorized Infantry Division and a few anti-aircraft batteries. The Soviet air force also had local air superiority and subjected Romny to a raid by heavy bombers.[65]. Desperate for relief Guderian urgently requested aid from the closest of Kleist's formations, the 14th Panzer Division, but even if this was authorized, it would still take some time to arrive.[66] In the meantime Guderian ordered a partial withdrawal of *Das Reich* and the 4th Panzer Division from the encirclement front. *Das Reich* arrived at Romny on 19 September and sufficed to hold the town, while the 4th Panzer Division concentrated for a counterattack from the south. On the same day Guderian's headquarters were evacuated to the relative safety of Konotop.[67] While the Soviets did not succeed in retaking Romny the episode remains an instructive lesson in the regenerative qualities of the Red Army. Although the Soviet front had been shattered in the Ukraine there were already new formations appearing in the east, which were capable of causing serious problems for the Germans even in the midst of their most triumphant battle to date.

Biting the bullet – the Soviet South-Western Front's destruction

With the remnants of the Soviet South-Western Front now split into two pockets the collapse of organized resistance proceeded apace. On 18 September most of the command staff of the Soviet Twenty-First Army, including three generals, were captured by elements of Langermann-Erlancamp's 4th Panzer Division.[68] On the following day (19 September) intelligence gathered by the 3rd Panzer Division indicated the whereabouts of Kirponos and his command staff, which was said to include some 15 generals and 400 officers.[69] There were also the first significant reports of Soviet POWs captured by Guderian's panzer group. In the period between 13 and 19 September Schweppenburg's XXIV Panzer Corps alone reported the capture of 31,000 POWs, 190 guns, 23 panzers and a further 23 anti-tank guns.[70] Similarly, in just one day (19 September) Kleist's panzer group took 12,000 Soviet POWs, while destroying or capturing 277 guns and 44 tanks.[71] On the inside of the pockets Soviet soldiers were granted little opportunity for rest, having constantly to keep moving east, all the while repelling or fleeing German attacks. One letter written on 19 September by a Soviet major, who had not slept in four days, captures the nervous tension of their situation: 'All around, wherever you look there are German tanks, sub-machine guns or machine gun nests. Our unit has already been defending on all sides for four days within this circle of fire. At night the surrounding ring is clear to see, illuminated by fire that lights up the horizon, which here and there gives the sky a wondrous pink hue.'[72] Yet the final days of the battle were by no means a simple case of corralling the great mass of Soviet soldiers into German captivity. Soviet resistance was as tenacious as ever. 'The Russians' behaviour in action is simply incomprehensible,' noted a letter found on a German corpse killed amidst the September fighting. The writer then continued, 'They are incredibly stubborn, and refuse to budge even under the most powerful gunfire.'[73] Nor were the men of the South-Western Front fighting simply to defend themselves from German attacks; these men knew that their only chance of escape was to break through the German ring and they fought tooth and nail to do so. Soviet losses were consequently exorbitant, but against the tide of manpower surging eastwards even major German formations suffered heavily, a fact made clear by German accounts:

> *Whether they come in with tanks or whether the infantry comes in without support, whether their Cossacks charge in on horses or whether they come rolling forward in motor lorries, the end is always the same. They are driven back with such losses that one wonders how they can find the courage and the men to keep coming on... Do they have any feeling of fear? It certainly seems not for they attack regularly and charge forward without hesitation. Some of my comrades think that the Bolsheviks must be either drugged or drunk to keep coming in like that... The [Soviet] dead stretched for miles. Here there would be one or two. Farther away a small group, some piled upon each other. We lost men too, for it must not be believed that this was an easy victory. But their dead, particularly where there had been a fierce battle, formed a carpet.*[74]

East of Piriatin, in the area of Major-General Heinrich Clössner's 25th Motorized Infantry Division, Soviet forces fought fanatically on the offensive and by 19 September had overwhelmed the positions of the 35th Infantry Regiment and temporarily effected a breakthrough.[75] The nearby 9th Panzer Division rushed its panzer regiment to the area and retook the small town of Melechi on 20 September, but German bodies lay everywhere. Unwilling to take prisoners Soviet soldiers not only killed every German they came across, but many of their captives were gruesomely mutilated. As the war diary of the 9th Panzer Division recorded, 'This regiment had countless losses and time and again one comes across German soldiers horribly mutilated...'[76] The same ghastly treatment was also administered to the captured German wounded,[77] but atrocities on the eastern front were by no means an exceptional occurrence and neither side shrank from the worsening cycle of retributive violence. Around the same time, on another battlefield in the Ukraine, a group of just over one hundred German soldiers were found hung by their hands from trees, while their feet had been doused with petrol and burnt until the victim was dead. It was a slow, tortuous method of killing known to German soldiers as 'Stalin's socks'. Yet such gruesome Soviet atrocities also revealed the Wehrmacht's own potential for ruthless mass murder. The discovery of the hundred burned Germans prompted a swift response:

> *At noon next day an order was received by division to the effect that all prisoners captured during the last three days were to be shot as a reprisal for the inhuman atrocities which the Red Army had committed in our sector. It so happened that we had taken very many prisoners during those fatal days and so the lives of four thousand men were forfeit…*
>
> *They lined up eight at a time, by the side of a large anti-tank ditch. As the first volley crashed, eight men were hurled forward into the depths of the ditch, as if hit by a giant fist. Already the next file was lining up.*[78]

As untold numbers of defenceless people were being ruthlessly slain by German murder squads in the rear areas (details of which had become common knowledge in the unoccupied parts of the Soviet Union),[79] it was hardly surprising that many men in the Red Army were reluctant to surrender themselves. As one member of the 25th Motorized Infantry Division noted on 20 September, 'We take a few prisoners: most of them have to be dragged out from under haystacks or flushed out of the furrows. Shy, unbelieving, filled with terror, they come. Many a Bolshevik has laid down his life here – his stupid pig-headedness and his fear (drilled into him) have to be paid for by his death.'[80]

With Kirponos's order for his entire front to flee eastwards and attempt to escape the encirclement, the pivotal hour had struck for the city of Kiev.[81] The Ukrainian capital had been under siege since the second week of July and, after days of relentless attacks by Reichenau's Sixth Army, the *coup de grâce* finally fell shortly before midday on 19 September when German troops broke into the city.[82] By noon the swastika was flying over Kiev's citadel,[83] but the German conquest had not come without cost. In the course of the siege the 71st Infantry

Fig. 16 A German soldier stands guard on the newly captured Kiev citadel, 19 September 1941. Beyond can be seen the Dnepr River.

Division had lost 46 officers and 916 men killed, with a further 108 officers and 3,150 men wounded.[84] As one German soldier noted in his diary, 'On 19 September our division took the citadel of Kiev . . . I thank the Lord God for my life. I cannot express how much luck and chance helped me to survive everything; . . . Oh, you good old IV company, you no longer exist. H.H., the best comp[any] leader, fell and so many, many comrades.'[85] Yet the NKVD had a latent plan for Kiev, which meant that the killing of Germans in the city was not quite over.

Throughout the summer of 1941 the Soviets implemented a strict scorched earth policy, in which anything of value that might be put to use by the Germans was to be systematically destroyed. Yet Kiev was captured largely intact, its inner city had been spared the destruction of city fighting and none of the most prominent buildings were burned or blown up.[86] The German command and administrative staffs quickly set about occupying the best buildings, just as the retreating Soviets had anticipated they would. The NKVD had hidden hundreds of explosive devices set to detonate by remote control or time-delayed fuses. The same tactic had been utilized against Finnish forces in Vyborg only days before and the Germans had in fact been warned by their allies about this kind of attack.[87] Another anonymous tip, possibly by anti-Soviet Ukrainian nationalists, led to the discovery and removal of some explosives; however, the Germans were utterly unsuspecting of what was to come.[88] The first detonation took place on 20 September in a former arsenal next to the Monastery of the Caves, killing the occupying complement of German artillery officers and men. Jews were immediately implicated in the bombing, but the explosion proved only a prelude to the main attack.[89] On 24 September, five days after the Germans had captured the city and firmly established themselves in its many buildings, a huge explosion ripped through a depot for captured equipment and ammunition located next to the main post office.[90] Nearby thousands of Ukrainians were following orders to register themselves and hand in any prohibited equipment such as hunting rifles and radios. They were all gathered at a German administrative centre located on Prorizna Street. Suddenly the first floor exploded, followed by an even bigger blast on the third floor. Fifteen minutes later the Grand Hotel, where numerous high-ranking German officers were quartered, blew up. This was followed by explosions at the Arcade and Hotel Continental. More blasts would rock the city that night and the following day, but even more dangerous was the raging fire that had been started by the initial explosions. With no functioning water mains in the city, almost no fire-fighting equipment and high winds to fan the flames, the fires spread uncontrollably.[91] In desperation German military engineers demolished more buildings to create firebreaks,[92] but at the same time Soviet agents were surreptitiously throwing Molotov cocktails to spur the blaze. An estimated two hundred Germans were killed in either the initial explosions or the resulting fires,[93] including Colonel Freiherr von Seidlitz und Gohlau of the Army General Staff.[94] Civilian losses were much harder to estimate as tens of thousands of people had fled the city with the Red Army,[95] but anywhere between 10,000 and 25,000 people were left homeless.[96]

It was only on 29 September, five days after the fires had begun, that the last blaze was finally extinguished. In the aftermath both Germans and Ukrainians were outraged at the scale of the destruction. The indignation grew when even more unexploded devices were found in the Opera House, the former building of the Central Rada, the central bank and the headquarters of the Communist party and NKVD. In total another 670 explosive devices were removed from around the city, but in October still more buildings were to explode (the former Duma and

Fig. 17 At the end of September fires set off by hidden explosives around the centre of Kiev destroyed whole city blocks.

the Supreme Soviet). For the incensed German occupation authorities the city's large Jewish population was the obvious culprit, which they concluded despite the fact that many Jews had also been victims of the fires.[97] Posters were plastered all around the city. At eight o'clock in the morning on 29 September all Jews in the city and its environs were to report to the corners of Mielnikovskaja and Dokhturovskaja streets. Any Jews failing to appear would be shot.[98] More than 33,000 Jews crammed into the streets near the assembly point and from there were led to the Babi Yar ravine just outside the city. Here the Jews were made to undress in groups and leave behind all their belongings. They were then channelled in small groups to the unseen ravine, where they could finally witness what awaited them. Kurt Werner, one of the German executioners, described what happened next:

> *I still recall today the complete terror of the Jews when they first caught sight of the bodies as they reached the top edge of the ravine. Many Jews cried out in terror... There were three groups of marksmen down at the bottom of the ravine, each made up of about twelve men. Groups of Jews*

> *were sent down to each of these execution squads simultaneously. Each successive group of Jews had to lie down on top of the bodies of those that had already been shot. The marksmen stood behind the Jews and killed them with a shot in the neck.*[99]

The killing of Kiev's Jews continued for two days until 33,771 men, women and children were dead.[100] It was Germany's largest single massacre to date and an unmistakable symbol of what the new era of Nazi rule would mean for the Ukraine.[101] Yet in spite of the NKVD's bombing campaign in Kiev, it is important to note that the mass murder of Soviet Jews required no pretext, however feeble, for German action. By the late summer of 1941 the *Einsatzgruppen* were already roaming the rear areas of the eastern front with instructions to wipe out whole Jewish communities simply because they were Jewish.[102] Long before the gas chambers industrialized the whole process, the Holocaust was underway in the east using crude but effective means.

Not only did Kiev fall on 19 September, but on that same day the remnants of the South-Western Front were broken up into a third pocket.[103] The most powerful of the three Soviet pockets was concentrated around Borispol to the south-east of Kiev.[104] It was predominantly made up of the Soviet Thirty-Seventh Army and had an almost impossibly long journey to reach the safety of Soviet lines, especially as the German Seventeenth Army was now pressing further eastwards. Indeed Poltava, which had hosted the former headquarters of Timoshenko's South-Western Direction, was also captured on 19 September.[105] The other two major groupings of Soviet forces were located further east (see maps 12 and 13). One extended in a bubble to the west of Orzhitsa near the Sula River and contained the remainder of the Soviet Twenty-Sixth Army. It was being compressed by the German XI Army Crops, while attempting to break through towards the north-east against Hube's 16th Panzer Division. On 21 September the *Stavka* received a frantic appeal from the Twenty-Sixth Army's commander, Lieutenant-General F. Kostenko: 'All efforts to cross the [Sula] river are futile. No ammunition left. Help required from the air force!'[106] The third grouping, comprising the remaining forces of the Soviet Fifth and Twenty-First Armies, was concentrated to the south of the road between Piriatin and Lokhvitsa. It was noted to have already suffered tremendous losses attempting to break out to the east.[107] Indeed the destruction

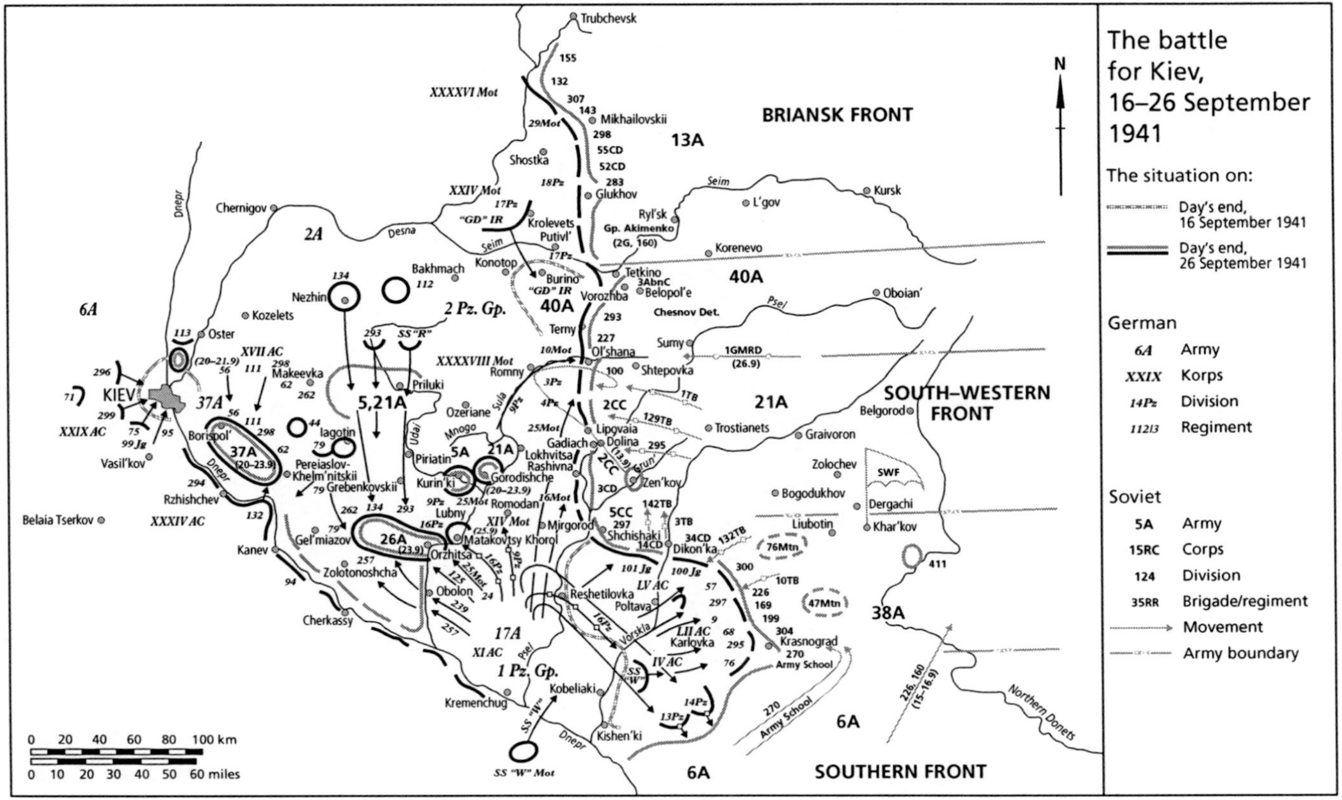

Map 12 The battle for Kiev, 16–26 September 1941
Source: Glantz, *Atlas of the Battle for Kiev Part III*.

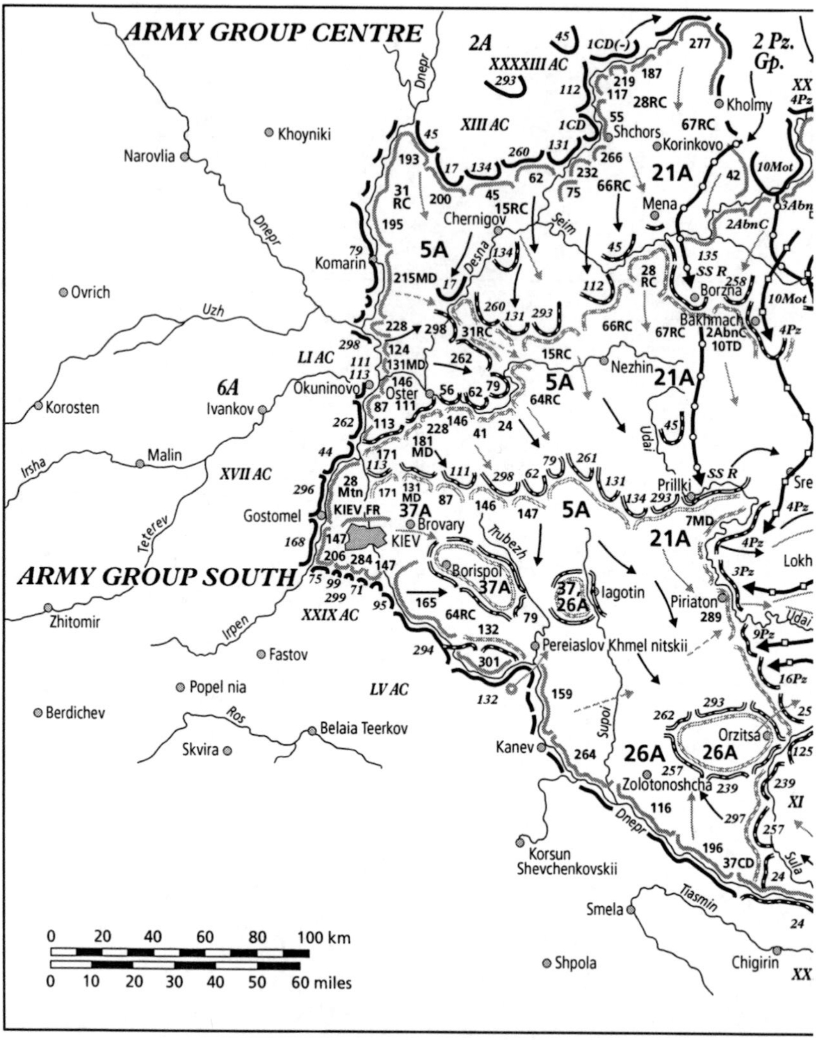

Map 13 The battle for Kiev (summary), 31 July–26 September 1941
Source: Glantz, *Atlas of the Battle for Kiev Part III.*

in the town of Piriatin shocked even battle-hardened German soldiers. Wilhelm Prüller wrote in his diary on 19 September, 'I can't describe how the enemy vehicles in the town look, and how many there are – at least 2,000. In a curve they were standing four abreast, apparently knocked out by our Stukas. Hundreds of skeleton vehicles were sitting there, burned out right down to the iron frame.'[108] Similarly, the war diary of Kempf's XXXXVIII Panzer Corps noted that the masses

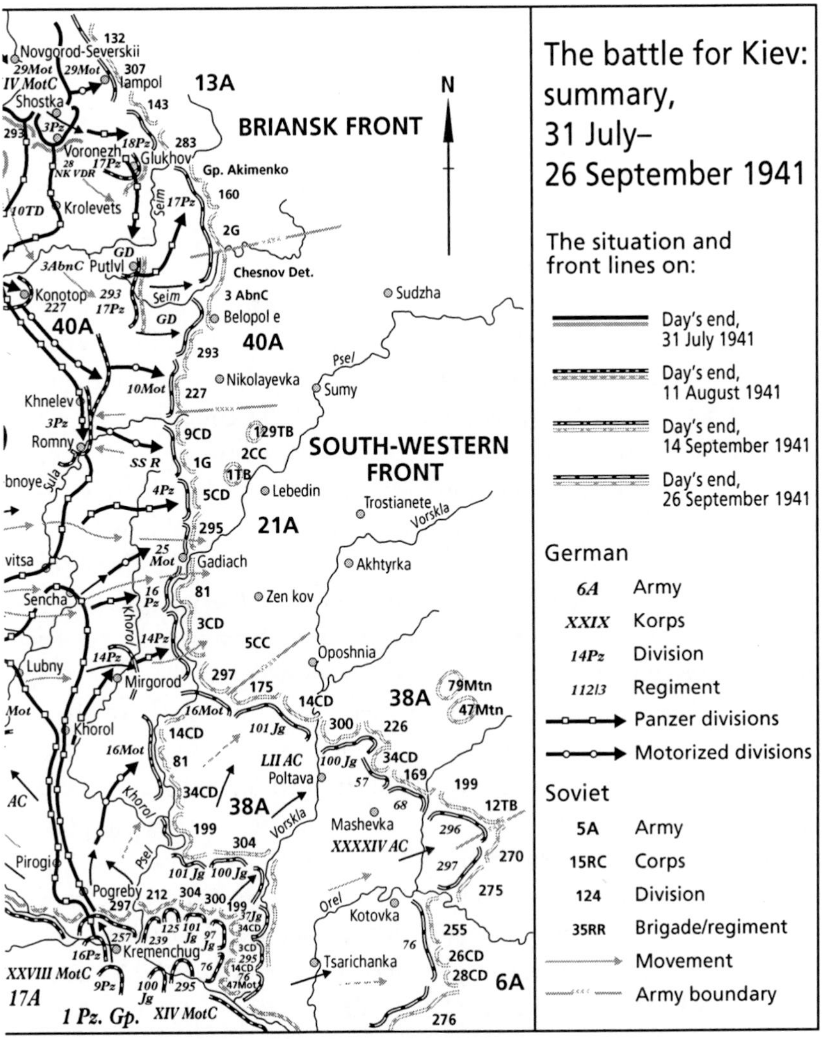

The battle for Kiev: summary, 31 July– 26 September 1941

of Soviet equipment found in and around Piriatin brought to mind the picture of Dunkirk at the conclusion of the British withdrawal.[109] Another account from a medical officer in the 3rd Panzer Division noted on 21 September, 'It is a picture of horror. Corpses of men and horses scattered among vehicles and equipment of all types. Ambulances are turned over. Heavy air defence guns, cannons, howitzers, tanks, trucks, some are stuck in the marshes, some were driven into the houses or trees. It is chaos.'[110]

Amidst the chaos, hiding out in a small wood near the Shumeikovo State Farm, about 11 kilometres south-west of Lokhvitsa, was Kirponos, together with 800 of his men. He had started out from his command post in the village of Verkhoyarovka near Piriatin with some 3,000 men. On 19 September Bagramian, Kirponos's Chief of Operations, led an advanced combat group to force a breakthrough in the German lines. This, it was intended, would clear the way for Kirponos and his staff. Bagramian's attack was initially successfully in breaking through the German positions; however, reinforcements quickly sealed the breach before Kirponos and his men could join the combat group. Cut off from his main force and on the wrong side of the German encirclement, Kirponos led his 800 strong force into a small wood. It was dawn on 20 September and with little natural cover there was no hope of avoiding the Germans until nightfall. In addition to their small arms and machine guns, Kirponos's force included four anti-tank guns and six or seven armoured cars.[111] The Germans soon became aware of the group and, acting on intelligence (probably gathered from the many POWs taken in the area), they were alerted to Kirponos's presence.[112] The wood was surrounded and the Germans prepared to close in. Kirponos led his men on the perimeter of their defensive line until he was seriously wounded in the left leg. He was carried deeper into the wood, but a mortar shell landed nearby and shrapnel struck him in the head and chest. He died within minutes. Tupikov, the South-Western Front's Chief of Staff, was also killed in the fighting, as was Major-General D. S. Pisarevsky, the Chief of Staff of the Fifth Army.[113] Lieutenant-General M. I. Potapov, the commander of the Soviet Fifth Army, was badly wounded and captured by elements of Model's 3rd Panzer Division.[114] Few Soviet prisoners were taken; those who had thus far survived the fighting elected to use their last cartridge on themselves.[115] Completely surrounded and without hope of reinforcement or relief, Kirponos's hapless group became symbolic of the whole Soviet South-Western Front. By the same token, Kirponos's death represented its fate. Stalin's insistence on holding Kiev and overruling all military counsel was now being paid for by the blood of tens of thousands. It was a military calamity with few parallels in history, which handed Hitler his greatest battlefield victory of the war.

Although Kirponos's small group was extinguished, the main pockets continued their abject struggle towards the safety of Soviet lines. A Soviet major, Jurij Krymow, who was trapped in one of the pockets, noted how the men continued to form new combat groups to throw against the tightening German noose. 'The pocket', Krymow wrote, 'is constricted to an appalling degree. There is nowhere for one to move.' Under such conditions it is easy to see how destructive German aircraft and artillery could be and, by the same token, why Krymow and his men knew that breaking out of the pocket was their only chance of survival. 'But how?' Krymow wondered as he wrote. 'At what price? This is what consumes the thoughts of the unit commanders.'[116] While the Germans could clearly identify the three main enemy pockets that accounted for the bulk of the Soviet South-Western Front, the countryside beyond these was nonetheless alive with countless bands of fugitive Soviet soldiers. Larger bands typically hid by day and moved by night, but there were also many smaller groups, even individual soldiers, who could hide themselves quickly at short notice. The war diary of Kempf's XXXXVIII Panzer Corps noted on 20 September, 'As in the last few days and again today, aerial reconnaissance and ground troops constantly find new enemy groups in areas that have already been cleared many times.' The diary then went on to explain the diverse tactics employed by these groups: 'The enemy attempts to escape using every means, in plain clothes or uniform, with or without weapons, in groups or alone and in battle most flee using the vast terrain and various streambeds. As a result of the wide area that has to be covered it is simply impossible to seal it against individual people.'[117]

Soviet troops who threw away their uniforms and tried to pass out of the contested areas as civilians undertook a dangerous gamble. The war diary of Kuehn's 14th Panzer Division noted a report from the divisional commander in which he reported that everywhere in the forward positions they were seizing 'Russian soldiers in civilian clothes'. On the same day the war diary also noted, 'Clearing actions against reported, or suspected, partisan detachments throughout the whole area of the division.'[118] Here the difference in dress blurred the line between partisans and regular soldiers of the Red Army. The distinction was important because partisans were put to death, while Soviet soldiers were interned as captives. Yet even without a difference in dress the distinction between men of the Red Army and bona fide partisans had been blurred since the first days of the war when large Soviet formations were cut off behind the rapidly advancing German front. In the battle of Kiev this now also became manifest as a serious problem for the Germans, which in practice meant there was little security in the rear areas. On 20 September a transport of captured Soviet soldiers under guard by men of the 3rd Panzer Division was attacked by forty 'Russians' with machines guns and rifles. As a result all the captives were able to escape.[119] Part of the problem was what to do with the enormous numbers of Soviet POWs. German units that needed every man at the front could not repeatedly dispatch guard details for the hundreds, and sometimes thousands, of captives arriving every few hours. It was therefore not exceptional for groups of Soviet POWs to be dispatched along the road in the direction of rear area assembly points completely unguarded. As Gottlob Bidermann recalled:

> *During the attack on Kanev prisoners were simply sent to the rear unguarded, as every available man was desperately needed at the front. However, I maintain the belief that from the masses of prisoners sent to the rear in this manner, many communists and Russian patriots used the opportunity to slip into the undergrowth and eventually make contact with the ever-growing bands of partisans. The well-organized partisans units would become an increasing menace to our rear areas. As the war continued, the people came to trust and support the partisans to a great extent, and they were able to find shelter and protection everywhere.*[120]

Of course the trust and support given to the partisans was in no small part a result of Germany's draconian occupation methods.[121] Indeed the same problem the Germans had of distinguishing between soldiers and partisans also extended to the wider Soviet population. The Germans could not tell who were peaceable civilians and who were partisans, but because the Slavic peoples of the east were considered untrustworthy and viewed as little better than *Untermensch* (subhuman), widespread reprisals against the civilian populace for partisan activity were deemed completely justified.[122] If the assailants of an attack were discovered they were typically hanged in public places and left there for days as a warning to the rest of the population.[123] Yet in 1941 the Soviet partisan movement was still finding its feet.

Soviet propaganda both at the time and after the war attempted to draw parallels between the so-called 'partisan warfare' conducted

Fig. 18 Even in the summer of 1941 Soviet partisans constituted a danger in the German rear areas, especially in the regions where large Soviet armies were encircled. The sign reads, 'Partisan danger from Welish to Ukwjati. Individual vehicles stop! Continuation *only* with two vehicles or more. Hold weapons ready. The commanding general.'

against Napoleon's army in 1812 and the war being waged behind the German lines in 1941. While both wars utilized the term 'partisan warfare', in fact there were appreciable differences. In 1812 the core Russian forces conducting 'partisan raids' on the French rear were squadrons of regular light cavalry (together with Cossacks) detached from larger Russian armies.[124] A more genuine 'people's war', in which civilians organized together to fight regular forces, was in fact a much less common phenomenon for civilians in 1812 than in 1941. Thus not only was the nature of partisan warfare different, but 1941 was in many ways a more aggressive form of a 'people's war' than the historical parallel held up by Soviet propaganda. While studies suggest that the number of Germans killed and wounded by partisan attacks in 1941 was low, the already profound shortages of men in the *Ostheer* rendered this additional burden hardly inconsiderable. Of far greater effect were the materiel and transport losses caused by Soviet partisan attacks, which exacerbated one of Germany's most serious problems.[125] Indeed already in September 1941 partisan strikes had become so widespread that in some areas trucks were no longer allowed to drive at night.[126] Less direct methods of attack saw the partisans target bridges, railway tracks and other vital sources of infrastructure, which cost the Germans time and resources to repair. The problem was already so pronounced that some divisions were already undertaking large-scale operations to clear their surrounding area of clandestine enemy activity. These were the precursors to the murderous anti-partisan sweeps typically associated with the later years of the German occupation. Yet as the commander of the 31st Infantry Division informed higher command in September, 'large-scale actions have delivered no discernible success'.[127] In most of the regions conquered by the Wehrmacht the rapid onward advance of the main German formations granted surviving Soviet forces the opportunity to conduct sabotage or commence renewed action against vulnerable German targets.[128] This was also a problem in the aftermath of the battle of Kiev, when many hostile elements remained hidden throughout the countryside. As Max Kuhnert recalled, 'My first assignment after the terrible days of Kiev was a fairly simple one. All I had to do was to keep in touch with our battalions . . . ' Yet Kuhnert was warned by his lieutenant about 'stray Russian soldiers' and 'partisans', who he was told would show no mercy. 'Now that was the first time I had heard that word "partisan" . . . Not only would they kill and destroy: they were also after uniforms and documents . . . '[129]

While many Soviet soldiers were prepared to make any sacrifice to avoid German captivity, there were also a large number for whom the war no longer mattered as much as preserving their own lives. Others actively despised the Soviet state, particularly a high percentage of Ukrainians, and were glad of the opportunity to abandon the brutal discipline and deprivations of the Red Army. Fedir Pihido, a Ukrainian native, observed a group of recently captured POWs from the Kiev encirclement. They were guarded by Slovakian soldiers who allowed civilians to fraternize freely with the men. As Pihido recalled, 'All of them complained about a terrible chaos in the army. The Red Army soldiers were always hungry and had to beg or steal. There was no underwear, no soap, many had lice. Footwear was mostly broken; they had to fight barefoot or with rags wrapped around. There were no blankets.'[130] Under such conditions Pihido saw how low morale had sunk; many now spoke out openly against Stalin's regime. 'They want us to die for them – no, we are not as stupid as they think,' said one; another added, 'They left our children without bread, to starve to death, but force us to defend Stalin and his commissars.'[131] There was even a more extraordinary tale from a Siberian soldier who told Pihido about joining a group of about two hundred men who took up arms against their Soviet commanders and fought their way to German lines in order to hand over their weapons and surrender. Twice the group had to fight pitched battles against loyal members of the Red Army. Nor was this the only case of open defiance. In another recorded instance a divisional commissar spoke at a regimental assembly, telling the men that they would have to fight their way to the east. 'He assured us that there were very few Germans and that it would be very easy . . . The Red Army soldiers became agitated.' At that moment the regimental commander openly rebelled. 'Who do you obey? Away with the damned Chekist!' The commissar immediately shot him, but was then set upon and 'torn to pieces' by some of the men.[132]

While dissent progressed at times into open revolt during the battle of Kiev, instances of this must be considered the exception rather than the rule. Clearly the September fighting had weakened the morale of the Soviet soldiers, but in the prevailing chaos those who wished to escape the clutches of the Red Army had ample opportunity. German propaganda companies also attempted to encourage this process by promising Soviet soldiers rations of bread and cigarettes. On 21 September the war diary of the 14th Panzer Division noted that signs in Russian had been posted throughout the area, which read: 'Soldiers of the Red Army, follow the example of your comrades and come over to us, we will give you bread!' The divisional war diary noted that this method had had 'very good success' with 'masses' of enemy troops giving themselves up.[133] In another instance German aircraft dropped fliers to Soviet troops encouraging them to surrender, whereupon they were promised cigarettes. A nearby German regiment was then inundated with Soviet POWs until all of their cigarettes had been handed out.[134] On other sections of the front propaganda vehicles were employed, which were fitted with large speakers that attempted to persuade Soviet soldiers to come over to the Germans. This method also reportedly met with success.[135]

With the enormous Soviet South-Western Front rapidly disintegrating and the capture of so much new territory, Goebbels had a great deal of new material to reinvigorate the propaganda war and try to address the waning public mood, especially in relation to the war in the east. The most recent SD reports suggested that the negative trends in public opinion were continuing in spite of the recent announcement that Leningrad had been cut off.[136] That for 18 September reported that many Germans now believed the Soviet people were fighting out of their own profound belief in communism and not just for fear of the commissar's pistol. The German population also feared the vastness of Soviet territory and its seemingly inexhaustible reserves of men and materiel.[137] Goebbels may have been inclined to view this as part of the German population's tough new introduction to the war in the east, a 'hardening' process by which he would groom them for the longer and costlier than anticipated struggle. Yet Hitler wanted the new successes celebrated with the full fanfare of triumphant victory announcements. Dutiful as ever, Goebbels immediately discarded any reservations he may have had about raising expectations too high and set about planning daily announcements, peaking on 20 September with three new *Sondermeldungen* to be broadcast over the course of the day. The first of these outlined the great success in effecting the encirclement of Soviet forces in the Ukraine. The second declared the capture of Poltava and the third, in the evening, announced that Kiev was now in German hands.[138] The effect was immediate, giving many Germans fresh hope of an end to the war in the east. Goebbels noted on the following day (21 September) 'a complete change' in the mood: 'Everyone feels as if he has been born again.'[139] In Romania the jubilation of expectant victory was also in evidence. On 21 September *Universul* led with the headline 'Collapse of Soviet Armies Inevitable'.[140] At the same time a German woman writing a letter to her husband in the east noted, 'Maybe the war against Russia is in fact soon to be over, because our [forces] are advancing faster, for three days *Sondermeldungen* have been reported. So and so many divisions or armies encircled, that must surely soon mean the end of the Russian soldiers. Yet the best *Sondermeldung* would be that Russia is finished.'[141]

This, however, was precisely the danger. German morale was not improving simply because another battle had been won, but rather because there was a deliberate intimation that the elusive end to the war was again suddenly within reach. It was exactly what Goebbels had earlier criticized and wanted to avoid in the future, but in his slavish devotion to Hitler's infallibility all this was now forgotten. The next SD report appeared on 22 September and noted the 'considerable improvement in morale'. It also specifically alluded to the renewed hope many now had for an end to the war in 1941, some even suggesting it would come in only 'four to six weeks'. Many people also believed that Leningrad would be the next major triumph and predicted its fall in the coming days.[142] Yet Goebbels did not desist and in fact continued the stream of special announcements, which, because he read the SD reports, he should have known were actively propagating an untenable degree of optimism. On 22 September two new *Sondermeldungen* were broadcast: the first reported the current total of 150,000 Soviet POWs captured so far in the battle of Kiev. The second announced the capture of Ösel[143] and Moon,[144] two Estonian islands in the Baltic Sea.[145] The second announcement was hardly of such great significance as to warrant another *Sondermeldung*, but in the fever-pitched atmosphere it is doubtful many people even noticed. What mattered was the sense of victory, which had become palpable and would be concluded with a final drive to Moscow. After following the announcements of the past few days, one soldier wrote home on 24 September, 'The war here in the east will also one day be over – maybe much sooner than we think. I personally do not believe that this will be stretched out into the winter – it is not part of the plan – and apart from that *we* have the strength at the moment to be victorious.'[146] Yet more discerning and better-informed elements within the *Ostheer* were not so easily swayed; indeed, they saw Goebbels's ruse for what it was and knew it was the German leadership who had been deluded, largely by themselves, about the Soviet Union. On 24 September General Heinrici wrote in his diary, 'The decisive success has not yet been achieved. With regard to Russia those above were greatly deceived.'[147] At the same time others within the Nazi state were drawing a very different conclusion from Germany's strategic circumstances. The well-connected former diplomat Ulrich von Hassell poignantly wrote in his diary on 20 September:

> *The last weeks have brought a very low barometer reading, not only among the people but also, according to news from headquarters, in high places: there is strong Russian resistance; meagre success in the battle of the Atlantic; Iran is occupied by the English and the Russians; considerable*

> *English success in the Mediterranean against the supply lines to North Africa; open rebellion in Serbia; grotesque conditions in Croatia; hunger and poor morale in Greece; high tension in occupied France – also in Norway...*[148]

Hassell also added that the USA was 'looming more and more as an actual military opponent' and that there was 'great concern about Italy'.[149] Nor was Hassell alone in his view. Later in September his diary mentions a Bulgarian minister for whom Hassell noted, 'It is quite obvious that he sees no prospect of a German victory...'[150] Yet it was not only in Germany that self-deception had reached such incongruous heights. The Italian foreign minister, Galeazzo Ciano, noted Mussolini's detached understanding of events. On 22 September Ciano wrote in his diary, 'He [Mussolini] says that the uneasiness of the Italian people is due to the fact that they are not participating in the war on the Russian front on a larger scale. I cannot agree with him. The people are not interested in this Russian war, and the real misery of our people is due to [the] lack of food, fats, eggs, etc. But this aspect of the situation is not the one that disturbs the Duce.'[151]

As the battle of Kiev drew to a close Goebbels made sure that no one underestimated Germany's achievement in the Ukraine. The battle's scale shared very few precedents in history and, having had to overrule almost all his senior generals to fight it, Hitler now wanted the appropriate recognition of what had been accomplished. The battle was not only Hitler's own resounding personal triumph; it also acted as an important symbol to the wider world, showing that Germany's much-maligned campaign in the east was not in fact bogged down and that the Wehrmacht was still capable of great successes. Most importantly, the German people were able to balance out their toils and sacrifices with the pride of more great conquests as well as the future promise of a rich *Lebensraum*. Yet all of this was of course predicated on the idea that the immense war in the east would soon be over, which Germany was propagating as though belief alone could instil the end result. The Nazi mythology of 'will' was therefore raising expectations that the *Ostheer* could simply not deliver. However, for the time being Germany basked in its own delusional visions of battlefield glory and future victory. Operation Typhoon would simply have to deliver what Operation Barbarossa had not and, with all the ignorance and oversight that plagued the initial invasion, final victory was still judged entirely feasible. With winter looming, massive losses, reduced motorization and powerful enemies remaining in both the east and the west, Germany's faith in victory was a bubble destined to burst. What remains remarkable is not that it did burst, but that much of the historiography charting Germany's first failure in the east dates only from the battle of Moscow in late 1941.

8 VISIONS OF VICTORY

Circling the wagons – the siege of Leningrad begins

While the battle of Kiev proceeded with the bulk of Army Group Centre and Army Group South's motorized forces, it was not the only German offensive under way in September. The thrust towards Leningrad had earlier attained precedence over Moscow as one of the supposedly decisive objectives in deciding the eastern campaign. Yet, just as the battle of Kiev was not the effortless blitzkrieg sometimes portrayed, so too achieving the blockade of Leningrad was no pushover. Indeed much of the historical argument about whether the Germans should have pressed for the capture of Leningrad in September 1941 seems devoid of an understanding of the difficulties involved, which had to be considered on top of what the two and a half month drive to the city had cost Army Group North. The difficulties of Guderian's long drive to Romny or Kleist's far-flung battle at Dnepropetrovsk were by no means exceptional, and with Hoepner's Panzer Group 4 assigned a vital role in Operation Typhoon, its condition by the end of September was vital to Bock's much anticipated success.

Leeb's underresourced Army Group North had been struggling to reach Leningrad since the beginning of the campaign. After advancing 450 kilometres in only the first two weeks of the campaign, there seemed little doubt that the remaining 250 kilometres to Leningrad could be covered in a roughly similar time. Yet the same problems hampering operations further south also plagued Leeb's advance. Roads, when available, were potholed and sandy, there were not enough forces to fill the expanding area of operations, supplies at the spearheads ran short, combat losses mounted and Soviet resistance stiffened. Already by early July Leeb's army group was overextended. After the rapid gains of the first two weeks the next month of operations saw an advance of only 120 kilometres.[1] Even so Leeb's forces had to be propped up by the transfer of major units from Army Group Centre. Colonel-General Wolfram von Richthofen's VIII Air Corps was dispatched at the end of July[2] and that was followed by General of Panzer Troops Rudolf Schmidt's XXXIX Panzer Corps in mid-August.[3] Only with such strong reinforcements could Leeb's army group penetrate successive Soviet defensive lines and continue closing in on Leningrad. Nevertheless the fighting was taking its toll on the combat units, for which there were not enough replacements to keep pace with losses. At the beginning of August Army Group North had already sustained 42,000 casualties, but received only 14,000 replacements.[4] Nor did the situation improve, and by the end of the month Leeb wrote in his diary, 'Unfortunately the replacement situation reveals itself to be more and more catastrophic'.[5] For those who had survived the fighting unscathed the strain was becoming all too apparent. Albert Neuhaus wrote home on 20 August, 'The first four weeks of the advance seemed to us almost like a Strength through Joy trip,[6] until we arrived up here and met horrendous resistance. And what the next four weeks meant for us only we know, we who have experienced it . . . I was a few days at the end of my nerves, so that my heart was in my throat when I only heard a grenade whistle.'[7]

It was at this point towards the end of August that Leeb's forces at last managed to penetrate the Soviet Luga Line and open the road to Leningrad. Colonel-General Erich Hoepner's Panzer Group 4 led the attack and on 8 September Leningrad's last land link was cut when Shlisselburg on Lake Ladoga was seized.[8] It was a momentous day, which was to herald the beginning of the deadliest siege in history. Yet even after closing the last road and rail exits to the beleaguered city, Leeb complained in his diary about having to fight a 'poor man's war'.[9] The problem was that to cut the city off effectively Leeb needed to link up with Finnish forces to the east of Lake Ladoga, otherwise the effects of the blockade could be somewhat circumvented by boat. Reaching the Finnish lines, however, meant scraping together fresh forces from his already overtaxed and depleted army group, while in the meantime the Soviets could be expected to prepare new defensive lines and gather their own reinforcements. The Finnish forces had reached the Svir River in Eastern Karelia on 7 September, but from here they refused to advance any further.[10] It was against this backdrop that Bock lamented the delay in the transfer of panzer forces back to his army group for Operation Typhoon. Yet even before the difficulties of linking up with the Finnish army became fully apparent, the weaknesses of Army Group North had already persuaded Hitler to instruct Leeb not to attempt to seize Leningrad in a direct assault. 'The Führer is not concerned with occupying particular cities,' Goebbels recorded after a visit to the Wolf's Lair in August. 'He wants to avoid casualties among our soldiers. Therefore he no longer intends to take Petersburg by force of arms, but rather to starve it into submission.'[11]

Hitler's decision evoked much hostility among the field commanders, who believed they were being denied victory at the last possible moment. On 12 September the commander of the Eighteenth Army, Colonel-General Georg von Küchler, referred to 'the bitter feeling a commander must have after leading troops, who gave their all, until their long-desired goal was before their eyes and then telling them – now you may go no further'.[12] On the same day (12 September) Hoepner wrote to his wife that his panzer group had 'once again been fobbed off at the appearance of victory'.[13] Similarly, General of Panzer Troops Georg-Hans Reinhardt, who commanded the XXXXI Panzer Corps, wrote to his wife expressing his 'bitter disappointment'.[14] Much in the same way as Hitler's decision to attack into the Ukraine was later portrayed as the decisive factor in the failure to seize Moscow, the decision not to attack into Leningrad has likewise been misconstrued as one of the pre-eminent lost opportunities of the war.[15] Blumentritt even told Liddell Hart after the war, 'Leningrad could have been taken, probably with little difficulty. But after his experience at Warsaw in 1939 Hitler was always nervous about tackling big cities, because of the losses he had suffered there. The tanks had already started on the last lap of the advance when Hitler ordered them to stop – as he had done at Dunkirk in 1940.'[16] In fact seizing Leningrad was in no way analogous to the halt before Dunkirk and Hitler was wise to take heed of the debacle at Warsaw. More recent examples at Odessa and Dnepropetrovsk should only have confirmed Hitler's caution and warned against quick victories in large urban areas. Indeed for all the ineptitude of Marshal Voroshilov's command of the Soviet North-Western Direction,[17] there was at least a concerted effort made to fortify the environs of the city with earthworks, trenches and gun emplacements. By the time the German siege had begun Leningrad was shielded behind 640 kilometres of anti-tank ditches, 600 kilometres of barbed-wire entanglements, 1,000 kilometres of earthworks and 5,000 pillboxes. It was a remarkable effort carried out over many weeks by half a million people mobilized from the Young Communist League as well as ordinary civilians.[18] On 16 September Georgi Kniazev, a citizen of Leningrad, recorded in his diary, 'The whole city is bristling with bayonets, machine guns, firing points, obstructions. In some streets, in the approaches to the city, barricades are being erected. Leningrad has been got ready for fighting in the streets, in the squares, in the houses. What are we to be witnesses of?'[19] In addition to the fortification of the city, there was also a renewed sense of purpose when Marshal Zhukov arrived, fresh from his conquest of the Yel'nya salient, to replace the inept Voroshilov. He immediately suspended Voroshilov's plan to demolish Leningrad and scuttle the Baltic fleet, and on 17 September he signalled his ruthless commitment to holding the city by ordering under pain of death: 'Not a step back! Do not give up a single verst of land on the immediate approaches to Leningrad!'[20]

While Soviet forces were clearly fighting with their backs to the wall, it does not follow that Leeb's forces were, by sheer proximity, on the brink of a major victory. Hitler's assumption that assaulting the city would result in heavy casualties was not only accurate, it begged the question of how such a battle could be sustained given the already stark depletion of the combat units.[21] As Walter Broschei, a German infantryman taking part in the siege, wrote:

> *In the middle of September we reached a chain of hills about five miles from the Gulf of Finland and ten miles south-west of Leningrad city centre. In the distance the city pulsed with life. It was bewildering – trains ran, chimneys smoked and busy maritime traffic ran on the Neva river. But we now had only 28 soldiers left from 120 normally in the company and had now been gathered into so-called 'combat' battalions – totally unsuitable, in view of our reduced strength, to attack Leningrad.*[22]

Another soldier, William Lubbeck, offered a similarly bleak picture of the regular German infantry in mid-September. Lubbeck stated, 'While our heavy weapons company of about 300 personnel had lost perhaps 10 to 15 men over the preceding three months, the toll of almost daily combat had been far more costly for most of our regular infantry companies. From their initial strength of about 180 troops they had typically been reduced to a force of between 50 to 75 men.'[23] On 20 September Küchler informed Leeb that his infantry fighting at Leningrad were 'already very worn out', while the commander of the XXVIII Army Corps, General of Infantry Mauritz von Wiktorin, bluntly informed Leeb 'it [the offensive] is not possible anymore'.[24] While the close proximity of the Wehrmacht to Leningrad's city centre has often been used as a crude measure for gauging how close Leeb came to seizing the city, in truth both sides were exhausted by mid-September. Not only was Leeb's infantry numerically weak, but he had already received orders to transfer the bulk of his motorized forces to Army Group Centre as of 15 September.[25] Indeed, even without attacking into the teeth of well-prepared and heavily defended positions, Leeb's attempt to continue his offensive and link up with the Finnish army would consume more strength than he possessed. Thus the decision not to continue the assault towards Leningrad was a bittersweet salvation for the German troops. As Hans Mauermann observed, 'Then suddenly it was halt – which was actually met with some satisfaction. Everyday it had been attack, with all its uncertainties and not knowing what might happen. From the perspective of even more hardship this was very much welcome. The emotion swung between shame that we had not pulled it off to thanking God we did not have to go in there.'[26]

Utilizing the so-called 'hunger strategy', Hitler believed he could still force Leningrad into submission, while sparing the blood of his troops. It was a strategy which again blurred the line between 'legitimate' military operations and the war of annihilation. The achievement of victory at Leningrad now depended upon the starvation of the Soviet Union's second largest city with a population of two and half million people. There was now no difference between the soldiers of the Red Army defending the city and its women and children. All were targets under the new German plan for a city-wide atrocity and, as with the criminal orders and the mass killing of Soviet Jews, the army leadership were more than willing to oversee its implementation.[27] As Halder noted on 18 September after Leeb's final assault was blunted by Soviet defences:

> *The ring around Leningrad has not yet been drawn as tightly as might be desired, and further progress after the departure of the 1st Panzer Division and the 36th Motorized Division from that front is doubtful. Considering the drain on our force before Leningrad, where the enemy is concentrating large forces and great quantities of materiel, the situation will remain tight until such time when hunger takes effect as our ally.*[28]

Unhindered by any moral misgivings Goebbels too was excited by the prospect of a bloodless victory and noted in his diary on 10 September, 'Furthermore we shall continue not to trouble ourselves with demanding Leningrad's capitulation. It has to be destroyed by an almost scientific method.'[29] Indeed the Germans evinced a penchant for systematic mass killing following an exacting premeditated procedure and here at Leningrad it was no different. An expert from the Munich Institute of Nutrition, Professor Ernst Ziegelmeyer, was engaged to advise on all aspects of the hunger strategy, leading to his pitiless conclusion: 'It is essential not to let a single person through our front line. The more of them that stay there, the sooner they will die, and then we will enter the city without trouble, without losing a single German soldier.'[30] Inside the isolated city starvation rations were soon being issued. The Badaev warehouses, which had been used to store most of the city's supply of grain, sugar, meat, lard and butter, had been bombed on the same day Shlisselburg fell (8 September) and completely burned out.[31] The loss of so much food was not the only factor in the starvation of the city, but it definitely quickened the process. As Liubov Shaporina wrote in her diary on 16 September, 'Rations are being cut once again. Now I receive two hundred grams of bread instead of six hundred, and that is certainly not enough. Two hundred grams of bread for an entire fourteen hour day in the hospital is rather difficult, to say the least.'[32] Such meagre rations prolonged life, but could not prevent the onset of a major famine, which would soon grip the whole city. German soldiers blockading the city differed in their expectations of what was to come. Albert Neuhaus expected the city to surrender soon and expressed excitement at knowing the number of Soviet POWs.[33] Franz Fenne, on the other hand, foresaw events developing in a darker, if more accurate light. The Soviets, he believed, would 'never give up', at least, that is, 'not before they turn to ash'.[34]

The siege transformed the war on the northern sector of the front as the army switched from presiding over a major battle to taking a leading role in the application of the starvation policy. Hundreds of thousands were calculated to die in Leningrad, while in the interim Leeb employed heavy guns and air raids to further batter the city into submission. The strategy employed at Leningrad formed an outstanding example of the ruthless lengths to which the German army was prepared to go in the service of the Nazi state. As with the other agencies of the regime there really was no limit to the murderous excesses the army was prepared to tolerate. On 29 September a letter of instruction relating Hitler's macabre intentions for Leningrad reached Army Group North. It read:

> *After the defeat of the Soviet Union, no one will be interested in the continued existence of this population centre ... It is intended to encircle the city tightly and to level it to the ground with artillery fire of all calibres and continuous air raids. Requests for a surrender resulting from the situation of the city will be declined, since the problems of housing and feeding the population cannot and should not be solved by us. We are not interested in sustaining in existence even a part of the population of this metropolis in this war.*[35]

Not a word of protest was raised by the army command; indeed they dutifully implemented Hitler's orders to the best of their ability and in the months ahead Leningrad did indeed starve. The only concern expressed at Army Group North was whether the troops would be able to gun down masses of women and children in the event of a mass breakout by starving civilians. The matter was ultimately resolved by determining that the artillery would be employed, 'preferably by opening fire on the civilians at an early stage [of their departure from the city] so that the infantry is spared the task of having to shoot the civilians themselves'.[36] Ultimately Leningrad became a battleground in Hitler's war both against an enemy state and against an enemy people whom he felt no compulsion to spare. Summing up the symbiotic merger of German military and racial policy Dr Werner Koeppen, a senior liaison officer at Alfred Rosenberg's Ministry for the Occupied Eastern Territories, reported to his chief on 10 September:

> *For three days now our 240mm guns have been firing into Leningrad. Luftwaffe bombing has already destroyed the largest waterworks. The Russians have only evacuated top-grade workers – and the population has been swollen by evacuees from the surrounding countryside. Already it is impossible to get bread, sugar or meat in the city. Leningrad is to be shut in – shot to pieces – and starved out.*[37]

While the *Ostheer*'s focus in September was centred on the battles in the Ukraine and at Leningrad, it was at Army Group Centre that, according to Halder and Bock, the key to the eastern campaign lay. Even with Leningrad blockaded and assured success in the battle of Kiev, it was more and more apparent that the Soviet Union had still not been subdued and that another great effort would have to be made. Increasingly the importance of Operation Typhoon grew in stature. Yet it was no longer enough to aim just for the elimination of the heavy Soviet force concentrations opposite Army Group Centre. Moscow was now the unambiguous goal and that was, erroneously, ascribed a decisive importance for ending the war. As had so often been the case in German planning, the desired objective was assumed from the outset to be obtainable and was therefore not affected by questions surrounding its viability. The available units would simply have to 'take whatever measures are necessary' to reach their goal. In September 1941 it was not just Hitler and the OKW who were at fault in this distorted methodology, but also the OKH and many of the field commanders, including Bock.

Any offensive by Army Group Centre depended upon the strength of the constituent panzer groups, which, given the fact that these had all been in almost uninterrupted combat since the start of the war, weakened their contribution. Their deployment also posed a major obstacle to the commencement of Typhoon. In the third week of September two of the three panzer groups allotted to Bock's upcoming offensive were split between the Leningrad front in the north and the central plains of the Ukraine. What was worse, they were still actively engaged and at the end of long and tiring campaigns. Achieving concentration therefore necessitated wide-ranging strategic redeployments, destined to tax their strength even more and cut the already limited time required for rest and refitting. Indeed for much of Guderian's panzer group a major redeployment was deemed too demanding, given the limited time remaining before the beginning of the offensive, and therefore the bulk of his forces were left to operate from the south in a degree of exclusion. By contrast, Hoepner's panzer group had to redeploy to the area of Kluge's Fourth Army (operating south of Smolensk) and this required a relocation of some 700 kilometres. Most of Hoepner's units, however, did not follow all the way to the Fourth Army (the exception was the 3rd Motorized Infantry Division). Hoepner's units instead transferred to Hoth's more northerly Panzer Group 3 operating in the area of Strauss's Ninth Army, but this still required a transfer of about 600 kilometres for the XXXXI Panzer Corps (it was much less for the LVI Panzer Corps).[38] One of Hoth's panzer divisions (the 20th) was then in turn transferred to Hoepner's new staging area, while another division came up from Guderian's panzer group (*Das Reich*). Given the paucity of north–south rail connections along the eastern front, the transfer of so many vehicles had largely to be completed under their own power over appalling roads with predictable results. Even before this regrouping could begin Leeb had to release Hoepner's panzer group, which he was proving reluctant to do as he was still engaged in achieving the close encirclement of Leningrad.[39] Indeed this in itself proved a rather high-handed action on Leeb's part as he only initiated the offensive after he had received instructions ordering the discharge of Hoepner's forces to Bock. Yet such casual instances of insubordination were certainly not an uncommon feature of high-level command in the east.[40]

Leeb was allowed to retain Schmidt's XXXIX Panzer Corps with the 12th Panzer Division and two motorized infantry divisions (the 18th and 20th). However, on 13 September Major-General Josef Harpe's 12th Panzer Division reported fielding only twenty-seven operational tanks[41] (with no Mark IIIs and only three Mark IVs) and subsequent reports made clear the division's lack of suitability for major offensive action.[42] Leeb decried the removal of so much offensive strength, which also included the loss of Richthofen's VIII Air Corps, and in his diary he equated the decision to the loss of a battle.[43] Yet Leeb was not just blustering for the sake of prestige; in addition to manning Leningrad's siege lines with Küchler's Eighteenth Army, Busch's Sixteenth Army had to defend a long section of front facing east. If Leeb feared he would be pressed for a further advance to link up with the Finnish army east of Lake Ladoga, as had been foreseen in Hitler's War Direction 35,[44] he was wise to doubt his strength. Indeed there was already particularly heavy fighting to the south of Lake Ladoga and to the east of Mga as the Soviet Fifty-Fourth Army counterattacked in desperate attempts to relieve the blockade of Leningrad.[45] Schmidt's XXXIX Panzer Corps was deployed here, but had to be reinforced by Major-General Erich Brandenberger's 8th Panzer Division.[46] This division had been earmarked for transfer to Army Group Centre, but ultimately would have to remain with Leeb, denying Bock's already ambitious offensive another crucial formation.

Just as Guderian's panzer group was a mere shadow of its former self, many of the divisions coming down from the north were likewise in a sorry state. Among the worst was Colonel Georg von Bismarck's 20th Panzer Division,[47] which had served as part of Hoth's Panzer Group 3, but now, together with Kuntzen's LVII Panzer Corps, was transferred to Hoepner's Panzer Group 4 and ordered to march south to its new staging grounds. Already on 8 September a report from the LVII Panzer Corps condemned the 20th Panzer Division for being unfit for service as a panzer division. Even before the campaign the corps complained that the division was grossly inadequate in the training of both its drivers and commanders. The division was also criticized for its inferior French vehicles, which not only proved mechanically unreliable, but by September were burning oil at six times their normal rate of consumption. Oil supplies could not cover such an exorbitant expenditure and thus, devoid of adequate supplies, the motors were grating and grinding to a rapid demise.[48] By 22 September, as the redeployment towards the south was under way, the leading march group (consisting of the 112th Motorized Infantry Regiment) had already sustained a fallout rate of 50 per cent of all vehicles that had set out only a few days earlier.[49] Beyond the increasingly compromised mobility of the division, Bismarck's strike power, concentrated mainly in the 21st Panzer Regiment, was seriously diminished. Although records do not indicate how many tanks were lost on the march, they do tell us that by 20 September (as the march was getting under way) the division was down to just 40 operational tanks from a starting total of 245.[50] There were 105 inoperable tanks within the division (presumably the others had been destroyed) and it was estimated that 20 per cent of these could be repaired and a further 35 per cent could be brought back into service if the necessary spare parts were made available.[51] While Bismarck's 20th Panzer Division was certainly one of the weakest overall panzer divisions being transferred down from the north, its migration from Hoth's Panzer Group 3 to Hoepner's Panzer Group 4 was only about 120 kilometres. The more robustly equipped and better-trained 1st and 6th Panzer Divisions, as well as the 3rd and 36th Motorized Infantry Divisions,[52] would have to endure far longer advances of up to 600 kilometres.

In addition to the exacting demands of the summer campaign the required redeployment of the panzer and motorized divisions before Operation Typhoon was yet another encumbrance to Bock's already precarious plans. He was still not happy about the strategic plans being drawn up for his operation, and on 17 September he wrote to Halder again to complain about the 'very narrow scope of attack imposed on me'. Bock again set out the case for a larger-scale operation seeking to bite deeper into the Soviet front and carve out an irremediable hole. Yet Bock also ignored pertinent questions pertaining to the weaknesses of his attacking armies as well as their overburdened logistics system. Indeed it was perhaps with these questions in mind that Bock concluded, 'The bigger solution involves having to ride out crises, which is now part and parcel of big decisions.'[53] Hoepner agreed with Bock and on the same day (17 September) noted how once again the German command seemed to be at odds: 'Tomorrow I am flying over to see Bock, to discuss my new role. This is a large task. Unfortunately we are not united in the way we envisage the attack, and quarrels and disagreements are breaking out.'[54] Kluge, Hoepner's new superior and commander of the Fourth Army, favoured a tighter encirclement, in line with the proposals of the OKH.[55] The dispute had all the hallmarks of another bitter command dispute, with the important difference that Hitler allowed the matter to be resolved within the army and here the OKH held sway. When Halder read Bock's letter he made light of the strategic differences (perhaps because on this occasion he knew they posed no threat to his own plans), but he did see eye to eye with Bock on one important point.[56] The movement of Hoepner's forces had still not begun, which raised serious questions about their ability to concentrate and refit in time for Typhoon. Indeed any further delay threatened a postponement of the whole operation, a fact which Bock alluded to on 20 September when the promised forces had still not crossed into the area of Army Group Centre.[57]

As the daylight hours grew perceptibly shorter during the course of September, Operation Typhoon loomed more and more as Germany's last hope for a solution to the war in the east. It was enough to entice Hitler to reverse one of his earlier decisions concerning the equipping and supply of the *Ostheer*. Throughout the summer Hitler had repeatedly forbidden the reinforcement of the *Ostheer* from stocks of newly produced tanks. These he instructed were to be held back for future campaigns extending, according to Hitler, 'over thousands of kilometres'.[58] Yet the greatly diminished offensive strength of Bock's designated panzer divisions necessitated some kind of boost, which not even the indefatigable optimism of the German high command could fail to see. Accordingly, on 15 September Halder received word that Hitler had authorized the release of 60 Czech-designed 38(t)s, 150 Mark IIIs and 96 Mark IVs.[59] This was barely 300 tanks from a new production total of some 815 units (all models) turned out in the three-month period between June and August.[60] Nevertheless, it was further supplemented by the transfer of Germany's last two panzer divisions (the 2nd and the 5th) to Hoepner's Panzer Group 4. These two divisions had spearheaded German operations in the Balkans during the invasions of Yugoslavia and Greece (April 1941), but owing to their worn-out condition at the conclusion of the campaign, could not partake in Operation Barbarossa. Between them these two formations fielded some 450 tanks, raising Bock's total of panzer reinforcements to 750 tanks. Yet two fresh panzer divisions and 300 replacement tanks, while certainly beneficial, were not able to alter the *Ostheer*'s ominous strategic circumstances. Bock's army group was lavishly endowed with most of Germany's elite formations on the eastern front. He would soon command three of the four panzer groups as well as receiving an additional panzer corps from Kleist (the XXXXVIII); however, the German high command (as well as some subsequent historians) placed too much weight on the paper strengths of these formations without sufficient understanding of their strength in real terms. The fact was that the panzer divisions were no longer a quantifiable whole because they all operated at varying levels of their former establishment. As the examples of the 3rd and 20th Panzer Divisions have illustrated, there were radical differences between the formations, and the mere fact that Bock ultimately commanded an impressive total of fourteen panzer divisions in Operation Typhoon cannot be equated to commanding anything approaching their strength on 22 June 1941.

Indeed although there is a somewhat natural tendency to evaluate offensive strength predominately through the prism of tanks and aircraft, these formations do not of course operate in a vacuum and any assessment of their capabilities must also include a discussion of the strategic circumstances in which they operated. It is in this wider context that Typhoon receives its most damning indictment. An army is the sum of hundreds of constituent departments and specialized commands, each dependent on the others for overall success. While Army Group Centre was receiving hundreds of replacement tanks, which in any case amounted to an average of just twenty-five new tanks for each of the panzer divisions taking part in Typhoon, other elements of Bock's command were seriously deficient. The *Ostheer* invaded the Soviet Union with some 600,000 motor vehicles,[61] concentrated heavily within the four panzer groups. Although an exact figure for overall losses by late September is not available, Panzer Group 2 reported a loss of 30–40 per cent of its wheeled transport by 20 September.[62] If that figure may be extrapolated to the whole *Ostheer*, then anywhere between 180,000 and 240,000 vehicles had been written off during the summer campaign and a sizeable number of those remaining may be considered functional, but in a highly provisional state of repair. To view this level of attrition in perspective, at the same time that Hitler was releasing tanks for Operation Typhoon he also authorized a consignment of replacement trucks numbering 3,500 vehicles.[63] The disparity in the figures reflects the yawning discrepancy between the *Ostheer*'s rate of loss and access to resupply. Nor was this attributable simply to Hitler's fanciful notion of withholding supply for future campaigns. The fact remains that German industrial capacity, as well as access to raw materials, was in no way equal to the staggering losses of the eastern front (not to mention the additional losses of the other theatres). Across the board, from the highly technical panzer groups and air fleets to the more rudimentary infantry divisions, there was an appreciable and rapid demodernization of the army, which new supplies could ameliorate, but never rectify. As Halder noted after the war, 'When the battle of Kiev ended, after ruthless demands on the already seriously worn motors, Hitler ordered the attack in the direction of Moscow, which first required that strong elements be pulled back out of the Ukraine. Now it was too late. The motors were at the end of their strength.'[64] Yet this was not the tone sounded by Halder in September 1941 and while much of the German command were hedging their bets on Typhoon's success, their actions reflected none of the lessons of the preceding summer. They appeared to have no idea how high the stakes for victory had risen, or how weak their hand had become. Emboldened by the blockade of Leningrad and the impending victory in the Ukraine, the preconditions for the final showdown at Moscow seemed at hand. The last push would have to decide the war in Germany's favour and under no circumstances could the myriad problems be allowed to distract anyone from that outcome.

Triumph in the Ukraine – Hitler's pyrrhic victory

Even with Leeb's forces closing in on Leningrad, the battle of Kiev remained the focal point of German operations in September. All over the Soviet Union the desperate defence of Kiev was being closely followed, which may in part explain Stalin's utter refusal to accept its loss. Even amidst the tumultuous events at Leningrad the besieged citizens were also following the news from the Ukraine. On 22 September Georgi Zim remarked in his diary on newspaper reports from the preceding days that told of very heavy fighting. He then noted with thinly disguised trepidation the news, just broadcast over the radio, that Kiev had been abandoned.[65] This had in fact taken place three days earlier, but the situation in the Ukraine had spiralled so far out of control that even the Soviet command had little idea of what was actually taking place. On 21 September, with Kirponos already dead, Shaposhnikov sent an urgent communiqué to the South-Western Front demanding answers to three questions. Firstly, he wanted to know whether Kiev had in fact been abandoned and, secondly, if so, whether the bridges over the Dnepr River had been destroyed. His third question reflected both the *Stavka*'s obsessive paranoia and their complete inability to grasp the scale of the military catastrophe taking place. This third question asked, 'If the bridges have been blown up, who will vouch for the fact that the bridges have been blown up?'[66]

As the *Stavka* was still trying to figure out exactly what was happening on their southern front, local German commanders were impressed by the scale of the Soviet disaster. First-hand accounts speak in mystified terms of whole fields strewn as far as the eye could see with charred bodies and mangled wreckage, the discarded remains of whole armies. Even at the higher levels of the German command the figures being reported evoked a sense of bewilderment. On 21 September the war diary for Kleist's Panzer Group 1 recorded that the number of prisoners taken during the course of the day was 'tremendous' and had almost doubled their total figure of POWs taken since the beginning of the battle. In the preceding twenty-four-hour period the panzer group had taken some 50,000 Soviet POWs, and destroyed or captured 17 tanks, 34 guns, 10 anti-aircraft guns and a staggering 1,257 trucks. This brought the panzer group's total number of Soviet prisoners taken since the start of operations to 110,404 (and 322,000 POWs since 22 June 1941).[67] Guderian's Panzer Group 2 was not quite so successful. After almost a month of heavy fighting during its long journey into the Ukraine, Guderian's forces had by 21 September taken 82,000 POWs. Yet, having managed to maintain the advance, however slow at times, and having successfully beaten off Eremenko's repeated counterattacks, Panzer Group 2 had done more than any other German formation to shape the outcome of the battle of Kiev. In addition to his tally of POWs Guderian also counted some 220 enemy tanks and 850 guns destroyed or captured.[68]

As large as the figures from the panzer groups were by 21 September, the fighting in the fragmented pockets of the now defunct South-Western Front had by no means ceased. Indeed the Germans had compressed the Soviet pockets so tightly that there was now no alternative than to break out – whatever the cost. Many of these attempts were chaotic, haphazard affairs, brought on by crude necessity rather than any premeditated plan. Often the breakouts proceeded without any semblance of organization and were therefore unrestrained by what might otherwise be considered unacceptable losses. The fervour of the Soviet soldier was well known to the Germans, but at the battle of Kiev the sacrifices of the Red Army, now trapped in the hundreds of thousands, led to unparalleled scenes of carnage.

In the pocket to the west of Orzhitsa near the Sula River the remainder of the Soviet Twenty-Sixth Army was being driven by General of Infantry Joachim von Kortzfleisch's XI Army Corps into the teeth of Hube's 16th Panzer Division. Caught between the hammer and the anvil, Soviet forces sought to evade capture by driving straight through the German lines in vehicles crowded with shooting soldiers. Although noticeably weaker, the remaining Soviet artillery still managed to offer supporting fire, yet the backbone of the breakouts lay with the mass of Soviet infantry.[69] At appalling cost wave after wave of Soviet men charged into the German lines following a seldom co-ordinated pattern of attack that rarely concentrated on one sector. Still Soviet forces often hit the German lines with vastly superior numerical strength and

Fig. 19 A burning Soviet BT-7 tank and dead crewman attest to the heavy Soviet losses in the Ukraine during the summer months of 1941.

their efforts were not always without effect. The war diary of Panzer Group 1 noted on 21 September, 'In the Orzhitsa sector the 16th Panzer Division has repelled continued heavy breakout attempts at great cost to the enemy; our own losses have not been small either.'[70] Nor were the Soviet breakout attempts always unsuccessful. Kortzfleisch's XI Army Corps consisted of three infantry divisions, the 24th, 125th and 239th. In the late morning of 21 September Soviet attacks against the centre of Lieutenant-General Ferdinand Neuling's 239th Infantry Division not only broke through his lines, but encircled his 372nd Infantry Regiment. Kortzfleisch feared that the breaches in Neuling's lines might rapidly widen if not immediately sealed and he therefore ordered the 'transfer of all available rear area units from south, from west and east to dam the breach'.[71] By the early afternoon Kortzfleisch was also informed that the Soviets had broken through the left flank of Major-General Willi Schneckenburger's 125th Infantry Division.[72] Here there were reports that Soviet prisoners included armed women and, as pressure from the Red Army was reaching crisis point, the divisional war diary noted, 'The front is broken up into hundreds of individual fronts. Everywhere there is fighting... Soon the last soldier in the division will be committed with a weapon in his hand.'[73] With the division's front dismembered and broken it would quickly prove impossible to ensure a secure cordon against enemy breakouts. Indeed Germany's encirclement fronts were seldom as clear cut as they appeared on the staff maps and, with events changing by the hour, opposing forces constantly ran into each other in confused and bloody encounters. Thus the view of the battle from the front was a far more harrowing experience for the German forces involved than the outcome might suggest. As one German soldier from the 24th Infantry Division wrote in his diary after a day fighting to reduce the Orzhitsa pocket, 'Yesterday we were again gripped by fear. To show fear no longer embarrasses people. Fear is no longer an unmentionable word.'[74] Another soldier wrote home to his family on 23/24 September, 'Hard days of battle and many fearful hours lay behind us! We took part in the great battle of Kiev! That was a crack and a thunder of cannons and other weapons from every nook and cranny. Often one did not know who was encircled, the Bolsheviks or us! ... The losses on our side are also quite high.'[75]

On 22 September the fighting in the Orzhitsa sector continued with bloody results. Schneckenburger's 125th Infantry Division again found itself in the thick of the action, with the divisional war diary reporting hours of intense fighting, which the enemy directed 'with a great commitment of men and materiel'.[76] Indeed in only two days (21 and 22 September) Schneckenburger's division alone took the astonishing total of 18,795 Soviet POWs.[77] The bitter fighting continued on 23 September as the Germans made a final effort to eliminate the Orzhitsa pocket. At the same time the remaining Soviet forces desperately attempted to escape and, once again, the war diary of the 125th Infantry Division recorded the enemy breaking into German positions, which they 'apparently succeeded in breaking through'.[78] Of course a Soviet breakthrough was no guarantee of security for those fortunate enough to escape the pockets. The men typically found themselves in makeshift bands of varying size, weakened from their toils and scattered over a vast area. More importantly, they were still well behind German lines, which were now determined by the formation of a new German–Soviet front far to the east. Yet most of the South-Western Front's men were not so lucky. They were either killed while attempting to break out or taken prisoner in the process. Of those who remained in the Orzhitsa pocket as the Germans closed in on the last Soviet concentrations, many opted to be killed rather than give themselves up. Kortzfleisch's XI Army Corps noted that in these final battles on

23 and 24 September the enemy put up 'the toughest resistance' and 'led by officers and commissars, sought to hold out to the last man'.[79] The last Soviet positions were finally extinguished around evening on 24 September by the 24th and 125th Infantry Divisions, leaving behind further scenes of unparalleled destruction. In the town of Orzhitsa itself one report stated, 'Masses of trucks and vehicles of every kind, reaching all the way to the riverbank in countless numbers, were partially set on fire and destroyed at the last moment by the enemy.'[80] Another account from 25 September stated:

> *The defeat of the enemy is huge. Anyone who has seen Denysivka confirms that.[81] This place is a giant arsenal of abandoned vehicles, wagons, weapons of all kinds including heavy guns. Moreover thousands of deserted horses graze in the nearby area.*
>
> *The narrow causeway between Denysivka and Savyntsi has become the scene of a human tragedy. In the attempt to break out towards the north hundreds of Russians were mown down by the machine guns of the 419th and 420th Infantry Regiments[82] and the 16th Panzer Division which were aiming at the northern bank of the Orzhitsa.[83] Left and right [are] swamps. Without enough cover on the causeway lay man against man pressed together – dead.[84]*

To the north of the Orzhitsa pocket another grouping of Soviet forces, comprising the remaining vestiges of the Soviet Fifth and Twenty-First Armies, was concentrated to the south of the Piriatin–Lokhvitsa road. It was here that Kirponos and Tupikov had been killed and many of their men were soon to follow. Once again a familiar pattern repeated itself as trapped Soviet forces sought desperately to flee encirclement, while German forces struggled to collapse the pocket from all sides. Here Hubicki's 9th Panzer Division and Clössner's 25th Motorized Infantry Division played the principal roles, along with some weak forces from Model's 3rd Panzer Division. In many instances the fighting was by no means an even affair. The Germans dominated the skies above, bombing and strafing at will, while also directing their motorized units towards the main enemy concentrations. At times this led to slogging pitched battles, but in other instances the German advantage was pressed home in one-sided battles bordering on massacres. A soldier from the 3rd Panzer Division wrote after one encounter, 'We advanced further. It was the Soviets already. This time it was an enormous column of batteries, supply trains, construction battalions, guns, horse carts, and tractors, with Cossacks and two combat vehicles riding in between. The machine guns howled anew, shooting a passage through the Russian column, and the tanks raged with great speed into the middle of the stream.'[85] Similarly, Wilhelm Prüller, a German soldier from the 25th Motorized Infantry Division, wrote with great satisfaction in his diary about a battle on 20 September:

> *After passing through the first village, we spread out over the fields. Beforehand we are assigned some tanks, and now we've spread out the tanks and other vehicles in a broad formation over the fields and are charging into the fleeing Russians . . . There ought to be some newsreel men here; there would be incomparable picture material! Tanks and armoured cars, the men sitting on them, encrusted with a thick coating of dirt, heady with the excitement of the attack – haystacks set on fire by our tank cannons, running Russians, hiding, surrendering! It's a marvellous sight!*[86]

Yet the fighting was not always so one-sided, or even successful. On the same day that Prüller was relishing his unit's success, Guderian notes that in another sector of the 25th Motorized Infantry Division the Soviets appeared to have forced a breakthrough.[87] Reports from Hubicki's 9th Panzer Division spoke of vast hauls of POWs and captured materiel, but also fanatical Soviet resistance, which continued 'in spite of the hopeless situation'.[88] Hans Becker, who commanded a German Mark IV tank, wrote that he lost his first tank in the fighting and then, after being issued with a replacement, lost that too the following day in a direct hit, which also killed two of his men. Nor were Becker's men the only casualties. On that same day he stated that two complete crews were reported as 'missing' and his squadron commander was badly wounded. Becker was subsequently awarded the Iron Cross (First Class) and the Close Combat Clasp, but, while he expressed pride in being recognized, he added he was 'not exhilarated'. The raw emotions of his ordeal and the sense of loss were still overpowering. In conclusion he added, 'Glory grows with the passing of time and the best battles are battles long ago.'[89] Max Kuhnert's unit also experienced heavy casualties at the battle of Kiev, leaving him to recall a similar sentiment:

> *We saw so many corpses lying there at the roadside. And pieces of bodies, some of them scorched or charred from the heat of guns or exploding shells.*
>
> *Pain, hunger and thirst took second place now, with the ice-cold breath of death brushing our cheeks and sending shivers down our spines. The dream of glory diminished as survival became the only thing that mattered. One could actually become jealous of others who got wounded, not badly mind you, but just enough to get them home or away from this place of slaughter, stench and utter destruction.*
>
> *The punching of bullets into flesh, the screams, however short, of agony from man and beast. Truckfuls of young corpses – 'cannon fodder' our mothers used to say when young men were called up or mustered . . . We had all changed our minds a long time ago, but it was too late to turn back, and where could one turn to in any case?*[90]

By 23 September the pocket containing the remnants of the Soviet Fifth and Twenty-First Armies had been extinguished, freeing the panzer and motorized units for redeployment to their new staging grounds. It was essentially the end of the battle against major Soviet formations for both Kleist and Guderian, although there still remained countless enemy bands scattered throughout their rear area. There was also another major battle of encirclement taking place nearer to Kiev, which was being fought by the infantry divisions of Reichenau's Sixth Army. For the motorized forces the immense battle of Kiev was now over, yet as the divisions redeployed across the vast expanses of the central Ukraine, everywhere there was evidence of the fury and horror of the preceding weeks. On 24 September a doctor serving with the 3rd Panzer Division described the macabre scenes from a former battlefield: 'A chaotic scene remained. Hundreds of lorries and troops carriers with tanks in between are strewn across the landscape. Those sitting inside were often caught by the flames as they attempted to dismount, and were burned, hanging from the turrets like black mummies. Around the vehicles lay thousands of dead.'[91]

On 24 September a major conference was hosted by Bock at Army Group Centre to discuss the renewal of the offensive towards Moscow. In attendance were the heads of the OKH (Brauchitsch and Halder), the commanders of Bock's three armies (Strauss, Kluge and Weichs), as well as the three panzer group commanders (Hoth, Hoepner and Guderian). The assembled commanders were informed of their duties according to the OKH's plan. In the north Strauss's Ninth Army together with Hoth's Panzer Group 3 were to attack from the area near Dukhovshchina and form the northern arm of the first major encirclement, closing at Viaz'ma. While Hoth's panzers would provide the striking power, Strauss's infantry would have to cover the northern wing of the whole offensive as it had proved impossible to get Leeb's army group to extend itself further to the east. Kluge's Fourth Army and Hoepner's Panzer Group 4 were to attack on both sides of the Roslavl–Moscow highway in the centre of Bock's front and head for Viaz'ma to close the pocket from the south. Further to the south Weichs's Second Army and Guderian's Panzer Group 2 were to break through the Soviet positions on the Desna River and co-operate in a strike to the north-east with an encirclement centred on Briansk. Reichenau's Sixth Army, attached to Army Group South, would also have to press forward in the direction of Oboyan to cover as much of Bock's southern flank as possible.[92]

With the OKH's plan now handed down Bock was forced to put behind him any lingering resentment towards Operation Typhoon's strategic curtailment.[93] At the conclusion of the conference it was decided that the new offensive should begin on 2 October. Hoth had argued for 3 October, but was overruled. Guderian, on the other hand, requested and received permission for his panzer group to begin two days earlier on 30 September.[94] Guderian claimed his request was motivated by two factors. First was the absence of good roads in the area in which he was going to be operating and therefore the desire to make full use of the short period remaining before the autumn *rasputitsa*. The second reason he gave was his expectation of additional air support prior to the opening of the rest of Army Group Centre's offensive.[95] These factors were not, however, what persuaded Bock to authorize Guderian's early start. He was concerned that Guderian was operating so far to the south that his offensive could not have any influence on the main attack for the first four or five days.[96]

While Bock had been forced to accept the OKH's strategic conception, he at least expected their support in securing the promised reinforcement from Army Group North. Already on the morning of the conference Bock heard from Kesselring that Richthofen's VIII Air Corps was still at Leningrad, news which Bock then took to Brauchitsch with the warning that he 'did not consider the attack by Ninth Army feasible without the support of VIII Air Corps'.[97] Two days earlier (on 22 September) Bock had learned that the 8th Panzer Division would most likely be retained by Leeb, which caused him to proclaim that Hoth's panzer group was now 'significantly weaker'.[98] The next day (23 September) Bock lamented the enduring delays in the transfer of forces from the north, which he stated 'are beginning to become uncomfortable'.[99] Yet only after Bock had heard about the postponement of the transfer of Richthofen's VIII Air Corps did the situation really deteriorate, causing Bock to fume with frustration. While Army Group Centre's command conference was taking place, Leeb was dealing with a new crisis in the sector of his II Army Corps (belonging to the Sixteenth Army). The result was that the 19th Panzer Division was redirected to deal with the situation, while Bock was forced to give up an infantry division (the 253rd) to strengthen Leeb's line. At the same time another problem for Leeb at Leningrad caused Hitler to intervene and halt the movement of the 36th Motorized Infantry Division. With the start of operations now only a week away there would be precious little time, if any, to rest and restore many of the divisions upon which Typhoon's tremendous expectations depended. As Bock summarized the situation on 24 September, 'The sum total of the day is that I, on the eve of the attack, have to do without the 8th Panzer Division, that the arrival of the 19th Panzer and 36th Motorized Divisions is unforeseeable, and that I must give up the 253rd Division to Army Group North. The arrival of VIII Air Corps is also questionable.'[100] Nor was that the end of Bock's difficulties. Early on 25 September the ongoing crisis at Army Group North led to Bock being stripped of the newly arrived Spanish 'Blue' Division.[101]

As Panzer Groups 3 and 4 sought to organize themselves on the highly provisional basis of when, and even if, their allotted forces would appear, Guderian faced a similar race against time in the south. He of course was now operating with a self-imposed two-day head start, which may have promised some tactical advantages, but also denied his weary forces another forty-eight hours of rest. Yet Guderian was hopeful he could be ready. On 19 September his panzer group was informed that 124 Mark IIIs and 25 Mark IVs would be made available for Guderian's five panzer divisions in Operation Typhoon.[102] Then on the following day (20 September) the panzer regiments of the 3rd and 4th Panzer Divisions were immediately ordered, irrespective of the combat situation, to break off from the fighting at the battle of Kiev and be ready to depart for their new staging areas no later than 21 September.[103]

While Guderian was actively seeking to disengage and use whatever time remained to him to prepare for the next great offensive, his panzer group was hampered by the repetition of Soviet attacks from the east. The battle of Kiev had not even concluded and already there was the spectre of a new eastern front with aggressive Soviet forces attacking into the German lines. This is not to suggest that the Soviet Union had not been badly crippled in the south, but once again the German command had failed to tear an irremediable hole in the Soviet front.

Although elements of Guderian's XXIV Panzer Corps fought in the closing stages of the battle of Kiev, his other two panzer corps (XXXXVI and XXXXVII) were detailed to hold his long left flank. Yet even elements of Schweppenburg's XXIV Panzer Corps had been urgently recalled eastwards to protect Romny from a concerted Soviet attack on 18 and 19 September. The town remained in German hands, but Soviet pressure remained firm up and down Guderian's line. On 20 September Lemelsen's XXXXVII Panzer Corps was heavily attacked from the air, with the war diary recording waves of up to thirty enemy aircraft (bombers and fighters) striking at the same time.[104] These were combined with ground attacks that led to costly fighting and denied many of Guderian's men a much hoped-for respite. As Guderian noted, 'What were clearly fresh enemy formations were now heavily attacking to the east of Glukhov and against the Novgorod-Severskii bridgehead. These kept us occupied during the next few days.'[105] Although Guderian mentions the attacks at Glukhov and Novgorod-Severskii these were not the only places Panzer Group 2 had to repel Soviet offensives. On 22 September Langermann-Erlancamp's 4th Panzer Division was attacked by up to twenty Soviet tanks, including four heavy KV-1s, which penetrated its front lines and pushed right up into its artillery positions, crushing guns and proving invulnerable to anti-tank fire. The division's panzer regiment was not available, having been deployed well to the rear to begin its rest and refitting. The divisional war diary concluded, 'The attack cost us heavy losses, as much by the infantry as the artillery ... For the division a hard, costly day.'[106] On the same day (22 September) Erich Hager, a soldier in Arnim's 17th Panzer Division, recorded a similar calamity in his sector:

> *The gruesome day is over. We did not get to sleep. The Russian attack started early. We were firing with all barrels ... Now all hell is breaking loose. We've really got to keep our heads down ... On the right of us 3 platoon and 1 platoon have to skedaddle, as the Russians reached the beech wood road. 5 men fell here and 5 seriously wounded. Fldw. [Staff Sergeant] Pusch, Krethner Max are dead. Shot in the back. Grossmann shot in the lung. Mäual Fritz shot in the stomach, seriously wounded ... Now we've had it! There is no one left on our right. Dare not raise our heads ... Now there is a gap 1km wide where there are no Germans ... All of a sudden a 52-ton tank attacks. Comes from the edge of the woods with a Russian assult gun. Our flamethrowers clear off. What do we do? The Russians are firing so much that the mud is flying! We run for our lives as never before. Right, left, behind us, in front of us MG [machine gun] strikes. Up down, that's how it went, always on open ground. Sweat runs down us, we run for our lives. Everyone runs. The Gef. Ltn [Lieutenant] Meyer, the whole of second platoon. Further and further, just get away from here. The tank behind us. We get out. In our village [of] Slout there are 8 of us ... What will we do?*[107]

It was these kinds of attacks, coupled with the final bloody encounters in the battle of Kiev, that denied many elements of Panzer Group 2 a desperately needed period of rest. Ultimately Guderian admitted, 'only three days could be allotted to the gallant troops for this purpose and even this short period for rehabilitation was not vouchsafed to all units'.[108] After the three long months of almost constant engagement and heavy fighting, Guderian's battered and much depleted force was now to embark on another great offensive for which they had a mere three days to prepare. Nor was Panzer Group 2 the exception. Colonel Walter Chales de Beaulieu, the Chief of Staff of Panzer Group 4, noted after the war that in the prelude to Typhoon his forces 'had little or no rest and must join the new battle directly from a tiring march'.[109]

While Germany certainly retained the strategic initiative on the eastern front, the prospect of defeating the Soviet Western, Reserve and Briansk Fronts, advancing 300 kilometres to Moscow, capturing the city and ending the war against the Soviet Union was surely impractical. Yet to Hitler as well as many of his senior commanders the will to succeed, even against the growing Allied materiel dominance, was paramount. As Hitler stated on 25 September, 'The myth of our vulnerability, in the event of the war becoming prolonged, must be resolutely discarded. It's impermissible to believe that time is working against us.'[110] Such self-deceiving ignorance of the prevailing strategic and economic circumstances provided the basis for Nazi Germany's enduring optimism in the war.[111] Before the invasion of France grave doubts had been expressed in many quarters, but Hitler's victory, supposedly born of his iron will, had defied his many detractors as well as the formidable Allied armies. Now with the *Ostheer* having just enacted the greatest encirclement battle in military history, there seemed no reason to doubt Germany's ultimate success. The finer details of how this might be achieved were not what mattered; Hitler had led Germany to one triumph after another and the German people as well as the great majority of the Wehrmacht still trusted in their leader to do the same against the Soviet Union.

On 22 September Rundstedt wrote home to his wife, 'Our battle is nearing its conclusion. We are counting on about 300,000 prisoners of war. Then the journey east starts again.'[112] Even as Army Group South's grand victory was being cemented it was clear that more – indeed a great deal more – would be required. Another letter written on the same day (22 September) by one of Rundstedt's soldiers reflected the battle of Kiev less as a mark of Germany's achievement than as a warning about Soviet potential:

> *Three months ago today the campaign against Russia began. Everybody supposed at the time that the Bolsheviks would be ripe for capitulation within no more than eight to ten weeks. That assumption, however, was based on a widespread ignorance of the Russian war materiel... Just this morning we happened to hear that, for example near Kiev, 600 guns and 150,000 men were captured. What kind of figures are those! Russia is almost inexhaustible.*[113]

Fig. 20 The aftermath of the battle of Kiev. The destruction of four Soviet armies left battlefields strewn with wreckage, animal carcases and countless bodies.

Of course the Soviet Union's capacity to manage losses was impressive, even remarkable, but, unlike the myth that would soon be accepted as dogma throughout the *Ostheer*, the Red Army did not benefit from an endless stream of men and materiel. Shortages of both were in fact ubiquitous, especially in 1941, and major defeats like the one at Kiev seriously exacerbated the situation. Yet the Red Army did manage to scrape together enough forces to restore and repair their shattered front. In some respects, as Churchill would later comment, it did not matter so much where the eastern front found itself on the map in 1941, so long as it continued to exist and devour German strength.[114]

On 26 September the last of the three major Soviet pockets was eliminated near Borispol to the east of Kiev by eight German infantry divisions. As an army chaplain from the participating 45th Infantry Division noted:

> *If it were not necessary to contribute further to the fury of the war one might have admired the countless dazzling columns of fire that made up this grandiose spectacle of illumination. In between, the infantry fanned out in wide skirmish lines and finally cleared the area of the last remnants of its defenders. Here and there the last magazine was fired off or a grenade thrown from haystacks already on fire.*[115]

A divisional report noted there were dead in 'countless masses',[116] while Goebbels wrote after a military briefing that once the final enemy group had been eliminated, 'the battlefield was covered by an unusual number of dead'.[117] These, however, were not just Soviet dead. The 45th Infantry Division's casualties included 40 officers and 1,200 men, while the neighbouring 44th Infantry Division lost 41 officers and 1,006 men.[118] The battle of Kiev was now officially over, although fugitive Soviet soldiers would continue to roam the central Ukraine for weeks to come. Most of these would be killed or captured; however, some would slip back into the civilian population, while others would keep their arms and form the nucleus of new partisan brigades. Those who successfully fled eastwards and actually managed to rejoin Soviet lines were not always welcomed back, as paranoid fears abounded within the NKVD that newly recruited German agents were attempting to infiltrate the Red Army.[119]

In Germany Goebbels did not wait for the last shot to be fired to begin trumpeting the achievement at Kiev. On 24 September the *Völkisher Beobachter* led with oversized banner headlines proclaiming the conclusion to the 'the greatest battle of annihilation of all time'.[120] On the same day Kleist issued an order of the day lauding the success of his panzer group. He stated that the battle had involved 'intense fighting' against an enemy 'numerically far superior'. Yet Kleist's order, like all the Wehrmacht's published orders, was essentially an exercise in propaganda. Kleist erroneously claimed that his panzer group had managed to prevent 'all breakout attempts' and then exhorted his troops on towards the elusive '*Endkampf*' (final battle).[121] Guderian also issued an order of the day on 23 September in which he too claimed that all enemy breakout attempts had been successfully prevented. He also listed his panzer group's total number of Soviet POWs as 86,000 together with 220 tanks and 850 guns.[122] Kleist's panzer group issued a more comprehensive list of its battle tally on 25 September. In total it had taken some 227,719 Soviet POWs and destroyed or captured 92 tanks, 784 guns, 127 anti-aircraft guns, 115 anti-tank guns, 24 planes, 6,070 wagons, 133 field kitchens, 10 trains and 1 field hospital. There were also 348 tractors and an incredible 16,500 trucks, which the war diary noted had mostly been destroyed.[123] These were remarkable figures, especially when added together with the tallies from the German Second, Sixth and Seventeenth Armies. In yet another *Sondermeldung* to the German people on 27 September, Goebbels presented a figure of 574,000 Soviet POWs,[124] yet by the following day this had risen to 665,000 POWs, together with 884 tanks and 3,718 guns captured or destroyed.[125] This remained Germany's final figure in the battle of Kiev and has been cited time and again by World War II historians to underscore the totality of Germany's September victory.[126] There can be no denying the decisive nature of Germany's victory, but Goebbels's figures may present problems, which may suggest they had simply become another tool in his propaganda campaign to shake Germany out of its melancholic war weariness and reinvigorate a sense of imminent victory in the east. On 1 September the Soviet South-Western Front fielded 850,000 men (including reserves and rear service organs) as well as 3,923 guns. Yet according to Soviet records, Kirponos's front lost some 616,000 men killed, captured or missing in the course of the battle.[127] The remainder may be accounted for as either wounded (and therefore evacuated before the ring closed), escaping the ring before the panzer groups united or being caught inside the encirclement and successfully evading capture (as partisans or 'civilians') or finding a way back to Soviet lines. One may safely assume that a significant percentage of the 616,000 men lost by Kirponos were killed or went missing, leaving a figure of Soviet POWs significantly below that claimed by the German command. The disparity in the figures is nevertheless difficult to resolve with any certainty as the accuracy of Soviet figures may also be called into question, but one may at least regard the German figure of 665,000 Soviet POWs as, at best, a high-end estimate and, at worst, a deliberate manipulation of the facts. British radio claimed the Germans were simply including the local population in their newly won areas to inflate the numbers of POWs.[128] There are, however, other explanations, which may provide more simplistic reasons for Germany's high-end figure. Counting the flood of Soviet prisoners, a system based largely on estimates, may simply have overestimated the numbers or suffered from significant duplication. It could equally be the case that the German figure included earlier tallies from other battles, which would then pose the question of when the battle of Kiev actually began for all the formations involved.[129] In any case what remains clear is that in the course of September the Soviet South-Western Front was utterly destroyed, with untold thousands killed and hundreds of thousands of Soviet POWs captured. Four Soviet armies and roughly three-quarters of a million men had been removed from the Red Army's order of battle, but at the end of it all there was still no sign of Germany's final victory, and the last month of mild weather was now drawing to a close.

9 THE CALM BEFORE THE STORM

The final roll of the dice – 'The spell is broken' (Joseph Goebbels)

As more and more details of Germany's unprecedented victory in the Ukraine streamed into Hitler's headquarters the mood at the Wolf's Lair was jubilant. On 24 September Goebbels noted that Hitler 'is exceptionally happy about this development and radiates real joy'.[1] Goebbels also voiced a smug satisfaction with Hitler's ultimate triumph over the generals of the OKH, who had opposed Hitler's proposals so bitterly. There was a sense that the war in the east had at last turned in Germany's favour. 'The spell is broken,' Goebbels wrote. 'The Führer believes that heavy fighting will last until about 15 October; after that, he believes, the Bolshevik will be on the run.'[2] Nor was Hitler the only one who saw final victory on the horizon. His rival in the July–August strategic dispute, Franz Halder, while not prepared to utter a word of acknowledgement for what was indisputably Hitler's triumph, nevertheless now envisioned rapid gains with little resistance. Referring to newspaper reports that erroneously claimed the British were applying pressure on the Soviets to surrender parts of southern Russia, Halder revealed an extraordinary naivety: 'It is possible that Stalin, even if against his will, may have to take this advice. The result for us would be that we rapidly reorient Army Group South to the pursuit and above all not wait too long to free Panzer Group 1.'[3] Indeed the sense of triumph at Kiev pervaded the German high command and not only in terms of the future outcome of the German–Soviet war. Weichs attributed to it a more profound importance alongside the greatest battles in history:

'I believe this victory was one of the most outstanding operations in the history of warfare, and for the skill in which its strategy was executed it can take proud place alongside other great encirclement battles of the past at Cannae and Tannenberg.'[4] It might well have been prudent to point out to Weichs that while Hannibal certainly won a crushing victory at Cannae, Carthage went on to lose the Second Punic War against the Romans. By the same token, Hindenburg may have humiliated the Russians at Tannenberg, but imperial Germany likewise lost World War I. Yet almost no one in Germany at the time considered the prospect of an eventual Soviet victory; instead the focus was squarely on how long Germany's own conquest in the east would take. To that end Goebbels's propaganda campaign had certainly achieved a remarkable reversal in public opinion.

Exploiting the battle of Kiev and the placing of Leningrad under siege, Goebbels won back public enthusiasm for the war by presenting the final victory as imminent. The classified SD reports gauging German public opinion reported on 25 September that fears of positional warfare in the east or the prospect of a winter campaign had now receded.[5] The next SD report on 29 September confirmed that more and more people were becoming convinced of a German victory before the onset of winter.[6] Reflecting on his success, Goebbels noted in his diary on 27 September that 'The depression is now completely gone. At times the mood of the people goes far beyond the real possibilities. Once again one hopes that this winter the war will be over and we have very much to do in the next weeks to pull back the now extreme optimism to a normal level.'[7] Even at the front hopes were buoyed by the turn of events. Ernst Guicking wrote home to his wife in a letter, 'Kiev is over. Now the [Army Group] Centre is due again. The great final chord will soon be played in the east. All our hopes are on the coming four weeks.'[8] Erdmann Schönbeck, an officer in the 11th Panzer Division,[9] stated, 'The victory at Kiev made a deep impression on me. When they said, "We've done it!" I felt an incredible sense of triumph. It was an overwhelming experience seeing the long lines of enemy prisoners going past.'[10]

Without doubt it was the sheer number of Soviet POWs that more than anything else represented the scale of Germany's victory in the Ukraine. Newsreels avidly relayed to the German public the images of endless columns of Soviet POWs, but, with rations already tight on the home front, many people, according to the SD reports, were

Fig. 21 Hundreds of thousands of Soviet prisoners of war were taken in the aftermath of the battle of Kiev, but very few would survive German captivity. ullstein bild – Arthur Grimm.

already questioning the impact of this new burden on Germany's food reserves.[11] The Nazi authorities as well as the army held the same fears, and with all manner of supplies already extremely limited in the occupied Soviet Union there was no intention of unduly burdening themselves with any notion of providing for Soviet POWs.[12] Accordingly their fate was heavily bound to Germany's concurrent war of annihilation and led to what one historian described as a 'forgotten Holocaust'.[13] Of the 3.3 million Soviet POWs who were captured in 1941 more than 60 per cent – roughly 2 million – would already be dead by February 1942.[14]

Even the ordeal of German captivity was not assured to surrendering Soviet soldiers as immediate executions were far from exceptional, especially for anyone identified as a commissar. The tremendous stress of combat as well as the heavy losses some German units suffered in combat led to many murderous rampages. Siegfried Knappe related the actions of his soldiers after some of the men lost comrades during a battle: 'Our soldiers went berserk, and from that point on during the attack they took no prisoners and left no one alive in a trench or foxhole. I did not try to stop them, nor did any other officer...' Later, in reference to the killings, Knappe's superior, Major Kreuger, assured him, 'There is nothing you or I or anyone else can do about an incident like that. The Russians took control of the situation out of our hands. "*Jawohl*, Herr Major," I agreed.'[15] Thus in the twisted logic of these army officers the Soviets were responsible for their own massacre and it goes without saying that no action was taken against the men involved. Nor was this exceptional behaviour. Omer Bartov's investigation of the 18th Panzer Division, 12th Infantry Division and Infantry Regiment *Grossdeutschland* revealed all three to have engaged in 'wild' and indiscriminate illegal shootings.[16] Fighting in the Ukraine in late September, Kurt Meissner wrote how his anti-tank unit dealt with Soviet men escaping from their crippled tanks: 'All the crews were killed as they bailed out and no prisoners were taken. That was war. There were times when such things happened. If we felt we could not collect or care for prisoners then they were killed in action.'[17]

For those Soviet soldiers who were taken into custody there was rarely any form of rest for the often exhausted captives and almost never any medical treatment available to the many wounded. Max Kuhnert noted in the aftermath of the battle of Kiev, 'The columns [of POWs] seemed not to end. Many of the poor fellows were wounded and limping. All were in tatters, their faces in utter despair.'[18] Yet it was not simply the condition of the men upon capture that the army chose to ignore. Their treatment soon instituted a new regime of suffering. Camps for the POWs were often far to the west, sometimes hundreds of kilometres from the front, and the prisoners were transported to them by forced marches.[19] In most cases little or no preparation was made to feed the prisoners and discipline was enforced by the most ruthless brutality. Christian Streit, who has authored the most authoritative study of the German treatment of Soviet POWs, stated that during the forced marches of Soviet captives after the battle of Kiev tens of thousands died.[20] Nikolai Obryn'ba, who survived a period in German captivity as well as a forced march, wrote a record of his experiences. 'The first transit camp was near the town of Belyi. We were kept there for ten days. We were not fed or given water, and we were exposed to the elements...Here for the first time, I saw young, healthy men dying of starvation.' Obryn'ba described how once the march resumed the starving men threw themselves on dead horses and tore off meat even as the German guards shot at them. After periodic rest stops those too weak to rejoin the march were murdered. His account then continued:

> *Before each new march, guards with sticks lined up on both sides of the column and the command 'All run!' would be given. The mob ran and hard blows would rain upon us. This kind of beating would last for one or two kilometres before the word 'Stop!' was announced... The exercise was repeated several times, so only the fittest would survive and march on. But many remained behind and solitary shots would ring out, as the Germans finished them off.*[21]

At Trent Park Lieutenant-General Friedrich Freiherr von Broich was secretly recorded by British intelligence telling his fellow inmates about the treatment of Soviet POWs, which he himself had witnessed. According to Broich, 'we marched down the road and a column of about 6,000 tottering figures went past, completely emaciated, helping each other along. Every 100 or 200 metres two or three of them collapsed. Soldiers of ours on bicycles rode alongside with pistols; everyone who collapsed was shot and thrown into the ditch. That happened every 100 metres.'[22]

For those who survived and reached the camps the day-to-day struggle for survival continued. Many of the camps were little more than open fields surrounded by barbed wire with the prisoners having to construct their own crude shelters, which were typically just dugouts or sod houses offering little protection from the elements, especially once the cold weather began.[23] Already by August 1941 the conditions gave rise to numerous epidemics, particularly dysentery and typhus, which soon ravaged the camps, killing thousands. One camp had only two latrines for the 11,000 prisoners, ensuring the most squalid conditions.[24] Malnutrition was another key factor in the soaring death rate as starving prisoners were reduced to eating grass, leaves and tree bark.[25] Towards the end of 1941 there would be instances of cannibalism.[26] One camp already held 74,000 men by mid-August, but its cooking facilities could only cater for 2,000. Every day dozens would be killed in the frantic scramble for food.[27] At another camp a German inspection tour concluded in its report, 'The prisoners receive nothing to drink, washing facilities are also not available. When the water carrier brings the water for the kitchen, a ferocious brawl always breaks out, which can only be ended by shooting. Hunger revolts with incessant shooting are also the order of the day.'[28] At Trent Park Broich related his experience at a camp for Soviet POWs holding about 20,000 men. 'At night they howled like wild beasts,' he told the other generals. 'They hadn't got anything to eat.'[29] Deaths in the camps soared in October as the colder weather, frequent epidemics and the weakening effects of starvation combined to decimate camp populations. A report from the Seventeenth Army at the end of November gave a stark indication of the fate suffered by the soldiers of the Soviet South-Western Front: 'During the transportation of the enormous number of prisoners from the battle eastwards of Kiev, where under the worst weather conditions only a part of the prisoners could be housed in barns, 1 per cent died daily.'[30] If one assumed a total of about half a million POWs from the battle of Kiev, then by the end of November five thousand men were dying every day. Not surprisingly the appalling conditions, which soon became known, served both to strengthen the Red Army's will to resist and to radicalize the treatment of German POWs. For the men of the Soviet South-Western Front who surrendered in September 1941 the horrors of the war did not end with their capture. In many ways they entered into a far more brutal world of torment with no possibility to defend themselves. Although no figures are available, one may surmise that only a small minority of those captured in the battle of Kiev ever lived to see liberation.

With the elimination of the large pockets east of Kiev, the danger for German soldiers in what was now a rear area, scores of kilometres from the front, remained ever present. It was simply impossible to clear such a vast area of all enemy forces and unknown thousands of Soviet soldiers remained at large, making it dangerous for isolated German outposts or individual vehicles. Schneckenburger's 125th Infantry Division noted, 'Reports constantly arrive of attacks from scattered enemy groups.' The war diary then cited numerous examples, which ranged from an individual soldier being shot dead while out searching for food to more brazen attacks involving the shooting of Germans soldiers through the window of their barracks.[31] Kuehn's 14th Panzer Division conducted sweeps through its area of operations to eliminate rogue enemy bands, yet it was not always easy to locate men hiding in the countryside and its success sometimes came from simply checking houses for groups of sleeping men.[32] Another method used by the Germans was to place non-smoking soldiers at the front of their patrols literally to sniff out hiding Soviet soldiers. Many men in the Red Army smoked the pungent *makhorka* tobacco, which gave off a powerful odour that was absorbed into their uniforms, making it possible to smell them from some distance.[33]

By contrast Soviet soldiers employed unorthodox methods of their own. In one instance a wooden bridge was found in ruins, but a next to it had been placed a convenient supply of fresh wood in the correct assumption that the Germans would use this to repair the bridge. The wood pile was laden with mines. In another instance a large bomb blast had created a sizeable crater in the road, and while rounding the edge of the pit German vehicles ran into carefully placed mines.[34] At the same time, one German report noted a 'high percentage' of Soviet troops, who were trying to evade capture in the Kiev pocket, attempting to cross back into Soviet-controlled territory by throwing away their weapons (and presumably also their uniforms) and endeavouring to pass themselves off as civilians.[35] The majority of Kirponos's men headed east in an attempt to reach the new Soviet front. In past encirclements at Minsk and Smolensk fleeing east had led to significant numbers breaking out. At Kiev, however, German mobile forces were much stronger at the eastern edge of the ring and prevented large enemy groups from forcing a way out. Nevertheless the Germans could not completely seal their front and an estimated 15,000 men from the South-Western Front made it back to Soviet lines.[36] As Blumentritt wrote after the war:

> *The barricading line was often penetrated by night; the motorised troops, especially the tanks, were then off the road at night and in forest or marsh were less capable of hermetically sealing. In such cases in the east the infantry divisions could do this better. But our old infantry divisions of that time, on foot and on horseback were not manoeuvrable enough and they also lacked materiel defensive strength, above all their own tanks for counter attacks. In all 'pockets' in 1941, therefore, it was difficult to carry out the encirclement hermetically.*[37]

Among those who escaped the encirclement was Lieutenant-General A. A. Vlasov, the commander of the Soviet Thirty-Seventh Army, which had been encircled not far to the east of Kiev. Not only was his escape over such a great distance a remarkable achievement, but it was already the second time that Vlasov had been caught in a German encirclement and successfully managed to escape (the first time being at L'vov).[38] Kostenko and Kuznetsov, the respective commanders of the Twenty-Sixth and Twenty-First Armies, also found a way out of the encirclement, as did Kirponos's Chief of Operations, Bagramian, who would go on to become a Marshal of the Soviet Union.[39]

Although the Germans clearly dominated the battlefield during the September fighting in the Ukraine and inflicted greatly disproportionate losses on the Red Army, their own losses were by no means inconsiderable. In the twelve-month period from the beginning of August 1941 to the end of July 1942, September 1941 was the costliest month on the eastern front with more than 51,000 men killed. Indeed the first three months of Operation Barbarossa proved the costliest quarter on the eastern front until the first quarter of 1943, when the Germans suffered disaster at Stalingrad. In these opening months of the war the *Ostheer* suffered an estimated 185,198 dead, which comes to 14,420 men a week or the equivalent of having one division eliminated to the last man every week, and this does not count German wounded.[40] A casualty figure just for the German armies participating in the battle of Kiev is not available and it must be remembered that a considerable percentage of the *Ostheer*'s total September fatalities stem from Bock's fierce defensive battles in the first half of the month and Leeb's fighting near Leningrad.[41] Yet firsthand accounts give some impression of the bloody nature of the encounter for the Germans. Max Kuhnert, who fought in the battle with the 1st Cavalry Division, wrote:

> *It was nearly the end of September now, and Kiev had fallen. After counting the losses in men, horses and equipment we realised that we in our rider unit had to change our arrangements. The regimental rider troop had lost not only men but also horses and had shrunk to a mere two squads that were usable. Erich Helm explained to me, with tears in his eyes, what had happened.*
>
> *'Mind you,' he said, 'our losses are nothing like the poor devils of the battalions.' Replacements were out of the question at the moment. Many motorcycles with sidecars were standing or lying on the primitive track and there were bodies everywhere.*[42]

In a similar vein, a Soviet soldier who survived the fighting recalled after the war, 'The Germans outnumbered us, their munitions were practically inexhaustible, their equipment without fault and their daring and courage beyond reproach. But German corpses strewed the ground side by side with our own. The battle was merciless on both sides.'[43]

The casualties for Guderian's Panzer Group 2 between 27 August and 30 September came to 12,239 men and increased his total casualties in Operation Barbarossa to 41,243 men.[44] Among Guderian's elite formations *Das Reich*'s '*Deutschland*' Regiment alone suffered a total of 1,519 casualties (all ranks) by the end of September and the losses of the '*Der Führer*' Regiment were comparable.[45] Such heavy losses produced a melancholic fatalism about the course of the war, which even in the Waffen-SS induced a sense of morose resignation that the war could drag on for a lot longer than many had hoped. *Sturmbannführer*[46] Otto Kumm, the commander of '*Der Führer*' Regiment, later stated, 'in spite of all our self-confidence, a feeling of isolation crept over us when we – following the army's armoured spearheads – advanced into the endless expanses of Russia. We did not share the unfounded optimism of many who hoped that they might spend Christmas 1941 at home. For us the Red Army was a big unknown ... The goal of this struggle lay in the unforeseeable future.'[47] With no end in sight and such heavy losses it becomes clear that the best elements of the *Ostheer* were being bled white on the eastern front, which, with no more reserves available from the home army, presented a clear and present danger for Germany. Hitler, however, was more focused on the victory he felt sure he was about to win. Speaking to his inner circle on 25 September he alluded to the problems of the eastern campaign, but suggested these would be forgotten upon victory: 'We've forgotten the bitter tenacity with which the Russians fought us during the First World War. In the same way, coming generations will see in the campaigns now in progress only the magnificent operation that it will have been, without giving any more thought to the numerous crises that we had to overcome by reason of this tenacity.'[48] Germany's loss of manpower in the east was indeed a crisis, but exactly how it was to be overcome Hitler did not explain. By the end of September the *Ostheer*'s total losses (including wounded) came to 551,039 men, which equalled 16 per cent of the total Barbarossa invasion force.[49] On 26 September Halder matter-of-factly noted in his diary that the *Ostheer* was short of 200,000 replacements and that these 'could no longer be replaced'.

He also noted that the average daily loss of officers was running at a disconcerting 196.[50] If this induced any alarm in Halder he did not record it. On the other hand, one did not have to be the Chief of the German General Staff to see how costly the war in the east was proving. One letter from a German civilian to the front on 27 September stated, 'One does worry about the soldiers out on the front and everyone who is still alive can speak about a particularly good guardian angel and a lot of luck.'[51]

Of course the demands on German manpower were not simply confined to the war in the east and the longer the war against the Soviet Union dragged on the more difficult it was to cope with other flash points in Hitler's European empire. By late September the security situation in Yugoslavia had deteriorated to such an extent that partisans under Josip Broz Tito had successfully seized control of an autonomous territory which included the town of Uzice with its rifle factory producing 400 guns a day.[52] With local German occupation forces unable to cope and almost every major combat formation committed against the Soviet Union, the only option was to transfer forces away from the eastern front. At a time when the *Ostheer* desperately needed reinforcement, Halder actually had to remove forces. The 113th Infantry Division was eventually dispatched from Reichenau's Sixth Army.[53] Not only did Yugoslavia draw off German manpower, but it also absorbed the lion's share of captured enemy tanks (mainly French), which were predominately used in security roles. On 8 October a total of 81 such tanks were being used in the occupied Soviet Union with another 30 being sent. At the same time there were already 184 in Yugoslavia with a further 194 on their way.[54] Nor was Yugoslavia the only security concern. The German occupation armies in Greece, France, the Low Countries and Norway tied down substantial forces defending against the prospect, however remote, of a British landing. Here too captured tanks were deployed in significant numbers with France receiving 140, Norway 100 and the island of Crete 17.[55]

Of course the greatest drain on Germany's potential reinforcements for the east came not from internal threats, but from the external role played by Britain. The war in North Africa, although marginal by comparison with the eastern front, still absorbed two vital panzer divisions (the 15th and 21st) as well as thousands of vehicles, guns and planes. Furthermore, the ongoing effects of the British bombing campaign as well as the battle of the Atlantic demanded further precious resources. Yet the British were also involving themselves directly on the eastern front. As previously noted there was a minor contribution in the form of the 151st Fighter Wing deployed near Murmansk, but their real input stemmed from Lend-Lease aid. On 23 September Halder noted the concern expressed by Hitler in his new War Directive 36 (issued 22 September), which was limited solely to Finland and Norway and spoke specifically about the new danger posed by the British presence.[56] Hitler expressed strong concern about Germany's continuing access to the Finnish nickel mines as well as the expected flow of war materiel through Murmansk. He even foresaw the prospect of the British landing Canadian and Norwegian troops in the area.[57] Yet it was the tangible contribution of British support for the Soviet Union that mattered most and the war materiel that had only recently begun to arrive at Murmansk were already being expected by Army Group Centre. On 26 September a warning was sent out to all the armies and panzer groups under Bock's command informing them that British Hurricane fighters could soon be expected before their fronts. As the war diary of Panzer Group 2 noted, 'It is the first time that English help for the Soviet side is identified.'[58] Meanwhile only days after Operation Typhoon began, Major Carl Wegener, the Ia of Panzer Group 3, reported encountering the first American-made quarter-ton army jeeps.[59]

At the end of September Lord Beaverbrook and Averell Harriman, representing Britain and the United States, flew to Moscow for what became known as the Three Power Conference. Their negotiations resulted in the First Protocol signed on 1 October 1941. This set out the vast scope of future Allied aid to the Soviet Union and, in addition to the recent co-operation in Iran, proved a major step in solidifying the Grand Alliance. At the top of the list of agreed items were 400 aircraft and 500 tanks a month,[60] but these were followed by a remarkably long list of other war supplies, many of which testified to the tremendous scale and bloody nature of the German–Soviet war. The Allies, for example, agreed to send 20,000 amputation knives, 15,000 amputation saws, 800,000 forceps, 4 tons of local anaesthetics, 100 portable x-ray sets and a million metres of oilcloth for covering wounds. Infantry weapons, trucks, ships, foodstuffs, clothing, petroleum products and raw materials were also on the list, acutely binding the Allied production effort to the eastern front.[61] It was clear to Churchill that by far the best weapon against Nazi Germany was the Red Army and he was determined to spare no effort in aiding it. Even the highly secretive

British intelligence programme at Bletchley Park, which was successfully decoding German military transmissions, was instructed to pass on all its information pertaining to Operation Typhoon to the Soviets.[62] In the summer and autumn of 1941 Britain's direct and indirect role in the war against Germany only underlined, once again, the dire implications of Hitler's failure to defeat the Soviet Union in a rapid campaign.

While Germany had no shortage of enemies in Europe, by September 1941 Hitler's network of European alliances had already entered its long but steady decline and the demands of the war in the east were providing the main cause of the difficulties. Having already unsuccessfully attempted to extract their Mobile Corps from offensive operations, the Hungarians were perhaps understandably lacking what Rundstedt referred to as the 'proper enthusiasm'.[63] Nevertheless they continued to fight on as part of Army Group South. In the ensuing advance to Izium on the Donets River the Hungarian Mobile Corps's losses increased to some 10 per cent of its total manpower and almost all its tanks and trucks were disabled or destroyed.[64] As one Hungarian soldier remarked, 'At first we made fun of the Romanians, who used oxen to pull their cannon, but not after the subzero temperatures shut down our modern motorized transport.'[65] Towards the end of 1941, when little real combat strength was left to the Hungarians, the Germans acquiesced and the Hungarian Mobile Corps began redeploying back home.

Finland was also reconsidering its contribution to the war after Mannerheim's summer campaign regained all of Finland's territory lost in the Winter War. There were also dire domestic pressures as, like Germany, Finland had only prepared for a short war. There was no labour for the economy, a critical food shortage and prices were rising sharply because the war was being funded mainly by printing money. Casualties were also high for the country's small population base (75,000 losses by the end of the 1941).[66] Under German pressure Mannerheim agreed to a limited autumn offensive,[67] but with the seizure of the Soviet naval base of Hanko on the southern coast of Finland (3 December)[68] and the capture of Medvezhyegorsk in Eastern Karelia (6 December), Finland's offensive war ended and rapid demobilization began.[69]

While the cost of contributing to Germany's war in the east caused some of Hitler's allies to work towards extracting themselves, others drew the opposite conclusion. Mussolini's Italian Expeditionary

Corps had arrived on the eastern front only in August, but its lack of full motorization delayed its arrival on the left flank of the Dnepropetrovsk bridgehead until 15 September.[70] At this point Wietersheim's XIV Panzer Corps, now operating on the northern bank of the Dnepr, thrust south-east towards the exposed rear of the Soviet positions at Dnepropetrovsk, finally relieving the pressure on Mackensen's bottled-up III Panzer Corps. As part of this developing manoeuvre the Italian Expeditionary Corps crossed the river and, in the so-called 'Petrikovka operation', encircled a Soviet force numbering in excess of 10,000 men.[71] Mussolini was euphoric as Ciano noted in his diary on 30 September: 'Mussolini is elated at the successes of the expeditionary force to Russia . . . the prisoners captured on the Eastern Front have cheered the Duce's heart, who now sees a rosy future, even from the military point of view. But this is typical of the ups and downs of his nature.'[72] As Ciano implied, Italy's military situation was far from bright. There were dangerous shortages on the home front and a serious overextension of Italy's deficient armed forces. To that end the expeditionary corps sent to the Soviet Union was a further harmful distraction, but Mussolini was not capable of seeing the danger; indeed he planned to increase his commitment greatly.[73]

Mussolini did not lack an example of the dangers that the eastern front represented to an underresourced and inadequately prepared force. Antonescu's siege of Odessa was a quintessential example. During August and September 1941 the Romanian army represented about 12 per cent of the total Axis forces on the eastern front (including German forces). Yet during the same period they suffered more than 30 per cent of all casualties. Indeed, as Mark Axworthy points out, each of the three assaults on Odessa cost the Romanian Fourth Army more men than the much-lauded final assault of the Eleventh Army at Sevastopol in 1942, which the Germans regarded as an epic of endurance and sacrifice.[74] Nor was Odessa the end for the Romanian forces. As the year wore on the Romanian Third Army was to take part in the fighting along the Nogai Steppe (often referred to as the battle on the Sea of Azov) and the Crimean campaign.[75] In addition to the staggering 98,000 Romanian casualties sustained by the Fourth Army at Odessa,[76] the Third Army lost a further 10,000 men by the beginning of November.[77] What is more, these losses were sustained during the supposedly victorious phase of the campaign when each time the Romanians found themselves on the winning side.

The minor Axis nations could not escape the consequences of the failure of Germany's blitzkrieg in the east. Having committed to Hitler's war in the east on the assumption of easy gains and political favour, they soon found they could neither hide within their borders nor make a decisive difference by increasing their commitment. As the war worsened for Germany over the winter of 1941/1942, all except for Finland (which was not part of the Axis anyway) were pressured into sending larger armies to the Soviet Union for Hitler's 1942 campaign. Far from turning the tide for Germany these new armies only encouraged Hitler towards a dangerous overextension of his southern flank that resulted in disaster near Stalingrad. It was the end of the large-scale Axis commitments to the eastern front, but the difficulties that undermined the Axis armies were already apparent in 1941.

Barbarossa reforged – Hitler's Russian roulette

In his 1812 campaign Napoleon invaded Russia two days after the date chosen by Hitler (24 June) and entered Moscow on 15 September.[78] In eighty-four days, with no motorization or railways, the French emperor had reached and taken Russia's largest city. On 26 September 1941 as the vast battle of Kiev came to an end, Hitler's campaign was on its ninety-seventh day and he was still 300 kilometres from Moscow. The nights were also growing uncomfortably cold, the days were shortening and the first morning frosts were appearing. As one Romanian Jew observed with evident satisfaction, 'Hitler is lagging behind the 1812 schedule.'[79]

Bock's Army Group Centre needed more time to gather its forces for the final offensive, but it was not just the distance and the time of year that boded ill for Germany. The Soviet capital was guarded by some of the largest concentrations of the Red Army (some 1,250,000 men), which, despite having been weakened by the recent fighting, the Germans would still require time to overcome. In spite of the unfavourable parallels with Napoleon's 1812 campaign, preparations at Army Group Centre continued with little overt concern for where the campaign seemed to be heading. The idea of Typhoon as the 'deciding battle' (*entscheidende Schlacht*) might not have appeared quite so imprudent if the notion had not already been used to preface most of the major battles in the campaign so far. Throughout Operation

Barbarossa the German generals proved exceptional at the operational level of command, but when time and again their battles failed to deliver the decisive strategic victory, they could do no more than suggest more of the same and seemingly had little concept of the difficulties their operations would encounter. Accordingly, in late September, Bock's biggest concern was the concentration of the motorized forces for Typhoon.

On 17 September Halder stated that Reinhardt's XXXXI Panzer Corps (1st and 6th Panzer Divisions plus the 36th Motorized Infantry Division) was to be transferred from the Leningrad front to Hoth's Panzer Group 3 – a distance of some 600 kilometres – in just five to seven days.[80] It was a huge undertaking given that the corps was quite literally being pulled directly out of the front lines after a long and costly advance. Not surprisingly Colonel Hans Röttiger, the Chief of Staff of the XXXXI Panzer Corps, noted that, 'this far-reaching movement placed a heavy strain on troops and materiel'. He then stated that during the preceding advance to Leningrad the corps 'had already been overtaxed', but that his men submitted to the new exertion 'with [the] utmost devotion'.[81] Röttiger's corps was not the only one to be making a long journey. Major-General Hans-Karl Freiherr von Esebeck's 11th Panzer Division,[82] which had been in reserve at Reichenau's Sixth Army, had to redeploy to Hoepner's Panzer Group 4 more than 700 kilometres away.[83] Similarly the 2nd SS Division *Das Reich* had to transfer directly from the front line near Romny to a staging area near Roslavl some 450 kilometres to the north.[84] Kuntzen's LVII Panzer Corps (19th and 20th Panzer Divisions) was also redeployed from Hoth's Panzer Group 3 to Hoepner's Panzer Group 4, a distance of 120 kilometres, which, while considerably shorter than the others, was still enough to inflict crippling damage.

The major problem for all these units was the poor state of the Soviet roads and the worn-out condition of the vehicles. Spare parts were in such short supply that once a vehicle's suspension broke or its gearbox seized up, it could just as well be written off because replacements had been unobtainable for many weeks. The Chief of Staff of Panzer Group 4, Colonel Walter Chales de Beaulieu, stated that by the end of September the equipment of the panzer forces was 'worn out' and that the availability of spare parts was 'catastrophic'.[85] Despite being outfitted with German trucks and having only a comparatively short distance to redeploy, Lieutenant-General Otto von Knobelsdorff's 19th Panzer Division noted that the fallout rate was so high that only 'a small percentage of serviceable trucks can be expected for the planned operation'.[86] The war diary for Panzer Group 4 noted on 22 September that the state of the 19th Panzer Division's trucks made refitting 'urgently necessary', yet the state of the 20th Panzer Division's French trucks was even worse. The panzer group determined that this division 'will no longer be mobile in about three or four weeks'.[87] Yet even this dire assessment may have reflected too much optimism. According to Kuntzen's LVII Panzer Corps on 28 September, the last march group of Bismarck's 20th Panzer Division had just arrived at the assembly point. The diary then observed, 'As far as one can tell only 50 per cent of all vehicles have arrived, the fallouts are exceedingly high.'[88] On the same day (28 September) it was reported that the division could transport only two-thirds of its infantry in the coming operation.[89] To make matters worse on 29 September, only two days before the start of Typhoon, a report on the 20th Panzer Division's artillery revealed that no less than 80 per cent of all its tractors were out of commission, making it impossible to tow the great majority of its guns.[90]

Hoepner's Panzer Group 4 was a good example of the disparity between what appeared on paper and what in fact actually existed. Already for some time on the eastern front a panzer division could no longer be accepted as such just because of its designation. The assembly of forces in Hoepner's panzer group was a case in point. It included both the 2nd and 5th Panzer Divisions fresh from Germany, but at the other extreme there was the 20th Panzer Division, which had already lost a good deal of its mobility and retained only a fraction of its former strength in tanks.[91] Between the competing extremes were many shades of grey, although it is not always easy to reconstruct exact strengths owing to the incomplete nature of the records. Knobelsdorff's 19th Panzer Division had only 65 tanks (from a starting total of 239) *before* it began its transfer from Hoth's to Hoepner's panzer group.[92] Given the heavy toll the redeployment took on the division's wheeled transport one may surmise that the division's combat strength was therefore only marginally better than that of the 20th Panzer Division. Indeed Knobelsdorff's division was initially not assigned a combat role in Operation Typhoon and instead held back in Bock's reserve (later it was committed in the area of the Fourth Army). Figures for Esebeck's 11th Panzer Division in late September are not available. The division saw heavy fighting in the Ukraine during the summer and was down to just 60 serviceable tanks at the start of September (from a starting total of 175),[93] but the division was granted two weeks for rest and refitting in September before undertaking the 700 kilometre redeployment to Panzer Group 4. The state of the panzer regiment and the division's vehicles upon arrival are unknown, but given previous advances over that distance it may be assumed Esebeck's division incurred significant losses.

Lieutenant-General Curt Jahn's 3rd Motorized Infantry Division was the only element of Panzer Group 4 to remain under Hoepner's command after his relocation to Army Group Centre, but this required a transfer of at least 400 kilometres from Demiansk to its staging area north of Roslavl. The redeployment exacted an enormous toll on the division's French trucks, many of which consumed so much oil (six times the normal quantity) that the quartermaster requested that these vehicles be temporally removed from service. This, however, had to be refused as otherwise 50 per cent of all remaining vehicles would be lost.[94] Even with this refusal losses were such that 20 per cent of the infantry could not be transported in the coming operation.[95] Likewise *Das Reich*'s 450 kilometre transfer to Hoepner's panzer group resulted in so many trucks being lost that only 75 per cent of the division's infantry could be transported in Operation Typhoon.[96] Indeed the only mobile division not to have been imported into the area was Fischer's 10th Panzer Division, which was well rested and retained a high percentage of its panzers, making it the strongest division after the newly arrived 2nd and 5th Panzer Divisions. Clearly it is only upon closer inspection of the component divisions that the true strength of a panzer group's order of battle can be assessed. Indeed on 29 September after finishing an inspection tour of Panzer Group 4, Bock concluded that Hoepner's forces were 'still lacking in many areas'.[97]

Hoth's Panzer Group 3 consisted of just five mobile divisions, three of which were panzer and two motorized infantry. Both of Hoth's two panzer corps (Lieutenant-General Ferdinand Schaal's LVI Panzer Corps and Reinhardt's XXXXI Panzer Corps) had transferred down from Army Group North, having previously served in Hoepner's Panzer Group 4. Schaal's corps command brought none of its divisions with it[98] and had to relocate about 250 kilometres from Demiansk to Dukhovshchina. Reinhardt's corps, on the other hand, with three divisions, had to move some 600 kilometres all the way from Leningrad. In spite of being equipped with more robust German trucks, these too had suffered greatly under the prevailing conditions, as the war diary of Major-General Walter Krüger's 1st Panzer Division makes clear. On 20 September, as many of the division's trucks were still under way, the diary recorded, 'The question of procuring replacement parts is ever more urgent. There is hardly a vehicle with intact suspension, we are lacking rubber pads and [tank] tracks, the rivets have loosened, the motors require reconditioning. To make the division combat ready in the few remaining days left available [before Typhoon] requires the full commitment of the workforce. The difficulties, which have to be overcome, are very large.'[99] Given the tremendous demands the transfer to the south would place on the trucks, all track-laying vehicles were scheduled to be shipped to the new assembly area by rail. Yet, as was so often the case, what the railways promised and what they could deliver proved two very different things. Accordingly the tanks were left waiting endlessly at Luga. As the Chief of Staff of the XXXXI Panzer Corps, Hans Röttiger, explained:

> *As a result, the majority of the track-laying vehicles, which had initially been left behind at Luga for shipment by rail had, after all, to be brought up by road. The wheeled vehicles of these units had already departed by road towards the south. Consequently, the track-laying vehicles which followed now also by road, disposed over no pertinent unified command, over no maintenance services whatsoever, and only over a limited amount of fuel trucks. Unfortunately, it took considerable time before the corps headquarters learned of the delayed departure of the track-laying vehicles. However, then corps headquarters immediately diverted again the most essential supply services towards the north, in order to furnish the incoming track-laying vehicles with adequate technical assistance. Despite all the expedients we tried out, the delayed departure of the track-laying vehicles by road resulted nevertheless in a considerable number of breakdowns of the track-laying vehicles belonging to the panzer and artillery units. However, this abortive scheme on the part of the higher echelon command greatly delayed the arrival of the troops in their new assembly area. A further disadvantage was that the maintenance units, by necessity, had been moved up to the north again, and that their services could*

> *consequently not be used in the new assembly area for a long period of time.*[100]

According to Röttiger's account not only did the tanks of the 1st and 6th Panzer Divisions have to undertake a transfer almost equal in length to their advance through the Soviet Union, but many of their trucks had to add countless extra kilometres to their own movement in order to support them. Ultimately the fault lay with higher command, which displayed a fundamental inability to recognize the shortcomings of its logistics system, especially with regard to the rail network. On 17 September Halder indicated in his diary that Krüger's 1st Panzer Division would reach its assembly area on 22 September, with Lieutenant-General Franz Landgraf's 6th Panzer Division arriving the following day.[101] Yet according to Röttiger, even by the start of Typhoon on 2 October the corps was still 'not yet fully assembled', which in practice meant 'Next to tanks, there was also a particular shortage of artillery pieces.' As Röttiger stated it was these shortages that were 'responsible for the limited *effective strength* of the corps' in Typhoon.[102] Not only did the transfer of the corps take so long, but as Bock had repeatedly complained, it was constantly delayed. Albert Neuhaus, a soldier who took part in the XXXXI Panzer Corps's redeployment to the south, wrote that his unit only began the march south on the evening of 22 September – the same evening that Halder had anticipated Krüger's 1st Panzer Division would be arriving at his designated assembly area. Neuhaus's unit began the march at night to avoid the danger of Soviet aerial attacks on their column, but this also meant driving without lights, which made it hard to distinguish between the road and the drainage ditches that had been dug in parallel. As Neuhaus recounted his experiences in a letter home to his wife:

> *So the trucks lumber along, one after the other, through the dark night. Hopefully everything goes well, that's what we still think. The truck jolts over stick and stone, we are forcefully shaken about... Then suddenly the front of the truck does a powerful hop, the driver turns sharply, but it does no good, the front left wheel no longer touches the ground. The whole weight of the truck presses and then we feel the truck lean to the left side and turn over.*[103]

Neuhaus's truck had to wait until the following day before it could be pulled upright and then, in spite of a hole in the fuel tank and broken springs, it continued on its way. In the course of its long journey Neuhaus's truck was also attacked by two Soviet planes, but neither was successful in hitting it. When at last they arrived at their assembly point Operation Typhoon had already begun. As Neuhaus concluded, 'When we were with the troops we heard that, apart from us, a host of other vehicles had difficulties on the long march and are still expected; the attack, however, has rolled on without us . . .'[104]

Mobility had always been the key to Germany's success on the battlefield, but in the Soviet Union over the course of the summer mobility had suffered significantly on account of the bad roads and the alternating spells of bad weather. By the end of September the weather had already begun to change and the autumn *rasputitsa* was not far off. The roads in the future area of operations varied from passable to downright awful, but it was the state of the vehicles that reflected one of the greatest differences between the *Ostheer* at Barbarossa and at Typhoon. Motorization had been greatly reduced both in absolute terms and in the serviceability of those vehicles that remained. With more than three months of arduous campaigning behind them, hardly any pause for repairs and a dire absence of essential spare parts, maintaining effective mobility for the 300 kilometre drive to Moscow was always going to be doubtful. Some may be tempted to conclude that if the trucks had just completed a 600 kilometre redeployment, many could surely manage a final 300 kilometre advance to reach Moscow. Yet the outright distance to Moscow is not to be compared with the actual distance the trucks would have to travel during the offensive. The vehicles of the *Grosstransportraum* would have to fill the growing gap between the panzer group's railheads and the front, which meant ferrying supplies back and forth in order to maintain the advance. At the same time, for those trucks accompanying the divisions into battle, the giant encirclement battles, necessary to defeat the defending Soviet armies, would require extended flanking manoeuvres. Here too there would be much shifting of forces as well as transporting of supplies, which would greatly add to the aggregate distances travelled. Combat losses would further cut mobility. When one then takes into account the miserable roads, the impending rains and Army Group Centre's inadequate supply of fuel, hopes of encircling Moscow and ending the war in October appear nothing short of folly.

Next to the *Ostheer*'s heavily compromised mobility, there was also room for doubt about its firepower. Guderian's Panzer Group 2 used the short time available before the start of Operation Typhoon to raise the number of tanks contained in its panzer divisions. Granted the rare opportunity of not having to move or fight, the numbers in the panzer regiments did rise appreciably, but most of the repairs were highly provisional and fallout rates were destined to spike soon after operations recommenced. By 27 September Guderian's five panzer divisions (and the specialized panzer flame detachment) fielded a total of 256 operational tanks,[105] which was still a far cry from their combined strength of 904 tanks on 22 June 1941.[106] Yet Panzer Group 2 was issued half of the new production released by Hitler, which amounted to 149 tanks (124 Mark IIIs and 25 Mark IVs), raising Guderian's combat strength to 405 tanks (Table 1). This, however, was only his strength on paper and not what was available to Guderian on 30 September, the start date for Panzer Group 2's renewed offensive. The reason for this was that some 44 per cent of the new tanks being transported from Germany were mistakenly sent via Orsha instead of Gomel. Even the 56 per cent that were correctly dispatched via Gomel were 'at best' due on the evening before the offensive, so the panzer group estimated at least a two-day delay for the remainder. Yet this was not the only complication with the new tanks. The panzer group's war diary noted that a 'large part will be inadequately equipped and [arrive] without time for maintenance'. In many tanks the radios were not yet fully installed, rendering them 'not yet operational'.[107] Although these tanks would eventually join the offensive, it is clear that Guderian's panzer group commenced Operation Typhoon with a force well below four hundred tanks.

Unfortunately comprehensive figures for Panzer Groups 3 and 4 are not reported in the files, but from what is known one may extrapolate rough estimates. Hoth's Panzer Group 3 consisted of just three panzer divisions (1st, 6th and 7th) in Operation Typhoon and while none of these divisions reported figures for operational tanks at the end of September, it may be assumed that one division was rather weak, one of moderate strength and one exceedingly strong. On 4 October, two days after the beginning of Operation Typhoon, Krüger's 1st Panzer Division reported having just forty operational tanks (thirty-three Mark IIIs and seven Mark IVs).[108] This figure would assume a sizeable share of the new Mark IIIs and IVs were issued to Hoth's

Table 1 *Strength of Panzer Group 2 and projected reinforcements on 27 September 1941*

		Mark I	Mark II	Mark III	Mark IV	Total
3rd Panzer Division	Combat ready	0	11	15	10	36
	Replacements	0	0	37	8	45
4th Panzer Division	Combat ready	0	19	29	9	57
	Replacements	0	0	35	7	42
17th Panzer Division	Combat ready	0	5	10	1	16
	Replacements	0	0	30	10	40
18th Panzer Division	Combat ready	1	22	40	16	79
	Replacements	0	0	15	0	15
9th Panzer Division	Combat ready	3	15	26	9	53
	Replacements	0	0	7	0	7
Pz. Flame Detachment	Combat ready	5	8	2	0	15
	Replacements	0	0	0	0	0
Total	Combat ready	9	80	122	45	256
	Replacements	0	0	124	25	149

Source: 'Kriegstagebuch Nr.1 Panzergruppe 2 Band II vom 21.8.1941 bis 31.10.41', BA-MA RH 21–2/931, fols.322–323 (27 September 1941); author's calculations.

panzer group, identifying the 1st Panzer Division's tank strength in the prelude to Operation Typhoon as being truly low. Part of Army Group North Major-General Franz Landgraf's 6th Panzer Division served in the same panzer corps as Krüger's 1st Panzer Division and they had both endured the costly 600 kilometre redeployment to join Hoth's panzer group. Thus one could assume that they had suffered roughly equal losses. Yet Landgraf's panzer division was numerically the second strongest on the eastern front at the beginning of Operation Barbarossa (it had possessed 254 tanks), which was exactly 100 tanks more than Krüger had.[109] When one considers a share of the 70 new tanks issued to Hoth's panzer group (50 Czech 38(t)s, 5 Mark IIIs and 15 Mark IVs)[110] it is reasonable to assume that Landgraf's 6th Panzer Division had anywhere between 100 and 150 tanks. Finally there is Major-General Freiherr Hans von Funck's 7th Panzer Division, which started the war with a hefty 299 tanks. By 7 September after weeks of fighting in the gritty defensive battles supporting Strauss's endangered Ninth Army, just 40 per cent of Funck's tanks were still operational

(121 tanks).[111] Yet the pause in the fighting during the second half of September, and not having to redeploy to new staging grounds for Operation Typhoon, allowed extensive time for repairs. By the end of September, with the addition of new panzers, Funck's 7th Panzer Division could have fielded anywhere between 150 and 200 tanks. If we then take the median average of my estimates and assume a starting figure of 50 tanks for the 1st Panzer Division on 2 October, Hoth's Panzer Group 3 fielded a total of 350 tanks at the opening of Operation Typhoon.

Hoepner's Panzer Group 4 had five panzer divisions, the weakest being Bismarck's 20th Panzer Division, which retained only a handful of operational tanks after its redeployment to the south. This division, however, received Hoepner's entire share of new tanks, gaining 55 38(t)s and 14 Mark IVs.[112] As a result Bismarck commanded around 80 tanks on 2 October, but that figure may well have been much lower, especially if Hoepner's new tanks suffered from a similar rash of technical problems to the ones that plagued Guderian's panzer group.[113] No figures are available for Esebeck's 11th Panzer Division and his panzer strength at the start of Typhoon is hard to estimate. On 4 September the division fielded 60 operational tanks (from a starting strength of 175);[114] however, the division did not take part in the last two weeks of the fighting in the battle of Kiev and would have accomplished a significant number of repairs. The division then had to conduct its 700 kilometre redeployment to reach Hoepner's staging areas, making a final figure of operational tanks difficult to deduce. One may suggest a figure anywhere between 75 and 125 tanks. Fischer's 10th Panzer Division did not have to redeploy anywhere and, like Funck's 7th Panzer Division, benefited from the relative quiet of the front from the middle of September. Accordingly, its panzer strength by the start of October was somewhere in the order of 150 tanks. Taken together these three veteran divisions fielded some 320 tanks between them, but Hoepner was also given control of Lieutenant-General Rudolf Veiel's 2nd Panzer Division and Major-General Gustav Fehn's 5th Panzer Division, which were both fresh from Germany and possessed some 450 tanks between them.[115] In total therefore Panzer Group 4 commanded some 780 tanks and as a result had double the numerical strength of the other two panzer groups taking part in Operation Typhoon.

Not surprisingly this regulation caused Guderian some irritation and he thought it 'questionable' that so much strength should be concentrated 'in a frontal attack' instead of reinforcing what he termed his 'flanking movement'. Not content with having already received half of all the new tanks distributed to the three panzer groups, Guderian also wanted the return of Vietinghoff's XXXXVI Panzer Corps as well as Fehn's 5th and Veiel's 2nd Panzer Divisions – the two strongest on the eastern front.[116] Yet if Guderian was unnerved by his numerical inferiority to Hoepner, it may also have weighed on his mind that a substantial portion of Panzer Group 2's tank fleet still consisted of the hopelessly outdated Mark II as well as a handful of Mark Is. Nehring's 18th Panzer Division, for example, contained twenty-two Mark IIs and one Mark I, Hubicki's 9th Panzer Division had fifteen Mark IIs and three Mark Is, while Langermann-Erlancamp's 4th Panzer Division fielded nineteen Mark IIs. In total 20 per cent of Guderian's total panzer force (including reinforcements) were obsolete Mark IIs (eighty) or Mark Is (nine).[117] By the same token Hoth's two numerically strongest divisions (Landgraf's 6th and Funck's 7th Panzer Divisions) contained a majority of the increasingly outdated Czech 35(t)s and 38(t)s. These were no match for the Soviet T-34s or KV-1s in either armour or firepower and those that remained after 1941 were no longer employed on the eastern front.[118]

Although Hoepner now commanded the strongest panzer force on the eastern front there is evidence that he had a decidedly pessimistic view of Operation Typhoon. Kesselring stated that Hoepner, who was an old friend from their service together in Metz, had been deeply shaken by the difficulties experienced in Leeb's army group. According to Kesselring, Hoepner had 'little confidence' in the October offensive and had to be convinced of 'the entirely different circumstances of Army Group Centre'. Kesselring claims to have slowly talked him around, in part by promising Hoepner reinforced air support in the upcoming attack. In the end Hoepner's doubts and hesitancy 'gradually waxed more confident' until, in Kesselring's judgement, he eventually joined the battle free of uncertainties.[119] Yet Hoepner was not the only one to have doubts. Richthofen, the commander of the VIII Air Corps, complained to Army Group Centre that his force was 50 per cent weaker than preliminary planning for Typhoon had foreseen. Accordingly Richthofen was not prepared to accept responsibility for the limited effectiveness of his forces and condemned the army command in his diary for their unwillingness to accept his difficulties.[120] The overestimation of strength was by no means confined to the VIII

Air Corps; indeed it pervaded the whole of Army Group Centre. After the war Rundstedt claimed to have voiced strong reservations about the attack towards Moscow and even to have advocated taking up winter positions on the Dnepr River in late September. According to the personal notes taken by Liddell Hart during his interview with Rundstedt on 26 October 1945, the commander of Army Group South stated that Brauchitsch also shared this view. Liddell Hart's notes read, 'The German army should have stopped on the Dnepr, after taking Kiev. He [Rundstedt] argued this with the General Staff. Brauchitsch agreed with him. But Hitler was insistent on continuing, and Rundstedt thought that at that time both Halder and Bock tended to concur with his view – "their noses were pointing towards Moscow".'[121] Attempting to substantiate whether the Commander-in-Chief of the German army did in fact wish to halt operations as early as the end of September, Liddell Hart interviewed Lieutenant-General Curt Siewert who had served as Brauchitsch's adjutant from 1938 until early 1941. Siewert was careful to point out that he was no longer working with Brauchitsch in September 1941, but added, 'Judging by conversations later with Brauchitsch I gathered he did not want to go on with the campaign.'[122] Whatever Brauchitsch may have said in private or to kindred spirits like Rundstedt, neither Bock's nor Halder's diary, nor any other source, offers any suggestion of such serious reservations, suggesting Brauchitsch fell into line when around more dominant personalities, which was very much in keeping with his previous behaviour.

If reservations about Typhoon were held within the German high command, there could be no better basis to doubt the outcome of what was being planned than to look at logistics. Indeed the addition of so many new tanks to Bock's army group may have improved his firepower, but this mattered little if they could not be provided with fuel. Indeed one might argue that Guderian's ability to secure Romny during the battle of Kiev was precisely because of his shortage of tanks. The town was reached with almost no fuel remaining and what fuel Guderian did receive was only achieved by Army Group Centre prioritizing Panzer Group 2 in the distribution of supplies. Now Guderian would enjoy no such preference and with two other panzer groups, three armies and all the reinforcements being mustered for Bock's army group, Typhoon was preordained to outstretch its supply lines. The later attempts by the generals to blame their logistical difficulties on the severity of the autumn *rasputitsa* are therefore fallacious.

Irrespective of the weather, Bock would have encountered crippling difficulties attempting to move such a large force all the way to Moscow. In any case the inevitable change in weather and the fact that the German command took so little account of it in their plans further exacerbated the fuel shortage.

After months of bitter experience and repeated crisis at the front, one might be inclined to think that the summer campaign had been a hard lesson for the German command in balancing logistics with operations. Yet despite all the problems of maintaining mobility and supply, the German command exhibited the steadfast conviction that they could continue major operations further eastward. Part of the problem was the unrestrained optimism of the Army Quartermaster-General, Major-General Eduard Wagner, who, in spite of being repeatedly caught out for his failed promises to deliver, continued to advise the OKH. On 11 September Halder reported in his diary a meeting with Wagner in which it was estimated that twenty-seven fuel trains a day would be needed to support the build-up for Typhoon. This request had been approved by the OKW and Wagner believed he could supply Bock with precisely this number of trains every day between 17 and 30 September. Until 17 September, however, Wagner estimated he could provide just twenty-two trains a day.[123] Six days later (17 September) Wagner confidently told Halder that the fuel supply for October was 'secure'.[124] Yet his promised deliveries were soon in arrears and on 20 September Halder was informed by Wagner of 'difficulties with the fuel supply: trains from the homeland occasionally cancelled (depots empty, fuel wagons missing, containers missing)'.[125] By 22 September Wagner again reported difficulties with the fuel supply, but this time he changed tack and instead complained to Halder about 'the assembly of so many mobile units', which made 'tremendous demands' and placed an inordinate strain on the supply system. Halder then alluded to the extent of the shortfall in fuel trains by concluding, 'Nineteen fuel trains a day are necessary!'[126] By 28 September Halder reported the transport of fuel to Bock's army group was 'somewhat better', but then cited a new problem, which would also worsen considerably during the autumn: 'Time and again partisans disrupt the railroads.'[127] On the whole the threat to German plans was profound. The amounts of fuel being delivered were barely enough to meet the daily requirements of the three armies and panzer groups, so that the stockpiling for the coming operation was in no way sufficient. Nevertheless, in a typical display of his delusory optimism Wagner boldly informed Halder on 29 September that supplies for Typhoon were 'satisfactory'.[128]

Evidence for just how unsatisfactory the fuel supplies for Typhoon really were comes from the army files. Panzer Group 2's war diary noted on 27 September that '[t]he fuel situation for the beginning of the new operation is *not* favourable'. The panzer group was to receive only one-third of its promised fuel supply, which in light of the already limited allocations assured dire consequences. Schweppenburg's XXVI Panzer Corps viewed the situation as so bad that it informed the panzer group it no longer believed it could reach its first objective. Guderian's reply to Schweppenburg was that he should simply advance as far as possible.[129] Fuel stocks were especially important given that on Soviet roads the average *Verbrauchssätze* (unit of consumption) for 100 kilometres typically lasted for only 70 kilometres.[130] The war diary of the 4th Panzer Division provides a vivid illustration of the problem. Already on the first day of operations (2 October) the division listed the exact fuel reserves for each of its units, how far this would take them and how far they had to go to reach their first objective (Orel). The 1st Battalion of the 35th Panzer Regiment would fall 40 kilometres short, while the 2nd Battalion would run out of fuel 20 kilometres before the city. Of the two motorized infantry regiments the 12th would reach the city, but the 33rd would not. One-third of the artillery would also fall short.[131] That operations were conducted in the east on the back of a threadbare logistical apparatus was nothing new, but the fact that this was only the first day of an operation destined to end in Moscow boded extremely ill for the future.

Supply problems also dogged Hoth's Panzer Group 3. As the Chief of Staff of the XXXXI Panzer Corps, Hans Röttiger, explained, 'Panzer Group 3's main supply point in the area of Ribshevo in no respect carried sufficient supplies to feed a far-reaching attack ... This shortage applied particularly to fuel and ammunition, but also to spare parts, and here again particularly to spare parts for tanks and prime movers for artillery pieces.'[132] Strauss's Ninth Army, under which Hoth's panzer group served, also reported shortages, as did Kluge's Fourth Army to which Hoepner's panzer group was subordinated. There were simply not enough supplies arriving to meet the needs of nearly 2 million men as well as provide additional stocks for a new operation in depth.[133] Part of the problem was that previously the soldiers had lived off the land by foraging for food, but while occuping static positions there was no way the local area could sustain so many men. With ominous implications for the future advance, Kluge noted in a report from 13 September, '[W]ith the growing distances the army is almost completely dependent on the railways. At the moment, the latter meet current consumption only. The transport situation did not allow the establishment of depots sufficiently large to enable the troops to receive what they need in accordance with the tactical situation. The army lives from hand to mouth, especially as regards the fuel situation.'[134] While the shortage of fuel was the most glaring deficiency confronting Operation Typhoon, it was by no means the only insufficiency. Munitions were generally adequate for the planned envelopment of the Soviet fronts, but, unless the army commanders believed that Moscow would simply capitulate, there is no conceivable way that munitions, even if the requisite transport capacity had existed, would suffice for such a distant and costly battle. In addition, shipments of replacement parts were not only inadequate, in many cases there simply were none to be had or what was delivered was utterly nonsensical. Liebenstein, Guderian's Chief of Staff, noted in his diary, 'Resupply is often senseless. For instance, sometimes we receive mortar ammunition which contains a high percentage of concrete bombs, or mudguards instead of spare parts for engines.'[135] Accordingly, although Bock's reinforced army group retained a degree of its former potency, it was once again destined to be pushed far beyond what could reasonably have been supported.

In assessing the difficulties of supplying Bock's new offensive beyond Smolensk, it is worth remembering the original constraints, dictated by logistics, under which major operations had to be conducted during Operation Barbarossa. Blumentritt, the Chief of Staff of Kluge's Fourth Army, wrote after the war to Liddell Hart, 'I must, however, clearly emphasise that at that time [prior to the invasion] it was the opinion of the Supreme Command of the Army that the military decision must be accomplished at Minsk, at the latest, that is, while still west of the Beresina and the Dnepr. It was repeatedly stressed that supplies would come to a standstill on the Dnepr at the latest.'[136] Now to the east of the Dnepr the OKH sought not only to sustain major formations, but to conduct a vast new offensive. In a warning to the high command the OKH's Army Supply Department reported on the state of the *Ostheer*'s tanks, vehicles and fuel supplies, noting that these might be 'insufficient to bring the eastern campaign to a conclusion in the autumn'. Furthermore, it stated that 'a great reduction in the fighting power and mobility of the army, perhaps at the crucial moment', might occur.[137] Indeed army files suggested, and subsequent events would prove, that operations on the main axis of the advance could not be sustained beyond Viaz'ma, some 200 kilometres short of the Soviet capital.[138] As one German soldier summed up the German predicament at the end of September, 'We still had to face many more battles and our position was not exactly hopeful; the further we went into Russia, the more difficult it became to get supplies and the summer was gone. Already the nights were getting longer and cooler.'[139]

A new phase of the war was about to begin and a new German blitzkrieg was devised to meet it. Yet in contrast to 22 June the *Ostheer* had fewer tanks, vehicles, aircraft, horses and men and these were deployed over an ever more expansive breadth of front. In many respects Germany's eastern front was already dangerously overextended, especially given the reserves of the Red Army and the time of year. Germany did, however, still hold the initiative and, in line with so much of their command of the war in the east, Hitler and the OKH were more than willing to risk the further overextension of their forces so long as there was any hope remaining of delivering the elusive 'decisive' success. The forlorn hope this represented ensured that the drive to Moscow would ultimately prove almost as costly to the *Ostheer* as to the Red Army.

10 MOSCOW IN THE CROSSHAIRS

Throwing caution to the wind – the Typhoon swells

As the days counted down to Bock's final offensive, spirits among the German soldiers were generally high. The men of the *Ostheer* had been left in no doubt about the scale of the German victory in the Ukraine, nor the tenuous state of the Red Army. Not surprisingly hopes were renewed that the war might indeed be ended in 1941 and many expressed the belief that, however bad the situation might appear in their own units, on the whole the German army was still strong and it was the Soviets who were having to stave off defeat. Yet if there was one aspect of Russian history that every German soldier knew, it was the fate that had befallen Napoleon's invading army in 1812. Indeed the French Emperor had already conquered Moscow in September and by the middle of October was withdrawing from Russia, heading back to his supply centres, when his army was so utterly ruined. Bock, by contrast, would be heading further east and further away from his supply centres. The fabled spectre of campaigning through a Russian winter thus assumed a certain foreboding prominence, which loomed in the minds of many *Landsers* as the weather began to change. Solomon Perel, who was travelling with a group of soldiers from the 12th Panzer Division, noted that the men 'had not forgotten Napoleon's defeat in 1812 and... [t]hey were scared out of their wits'.[1] Another soldier wrote home on 21 September, 'God save us from a winter campaign in the east. It is very cold here already and rains practically every day.'[2] Wilhelm Prüller wrote in his diary on 28 September that it was so cold he and his comrades had to sleep in their vehicles. He then continued, 'Terribly cold. You can't wrap yourself in too many blankets. When I think back on the July and August days, when we simply spent the nights lying in a field on the grass, I have to mourn for the summer . . . And who knows what's in front of us as far as the weather goes?'[3] It was a prudent question, which held dire implications not only for the operational aspects of the campaign, but also for the war of annihilation. With a chronic shortage of housing in the forward areas of the front, German soldiers ensured they were not the ones being left out in the cold. As Wilhelm Prüller's diary records:

> *You should see the act the civilians put on when we make it clear to them that we intend to use their sties to sleep in. A weeping and yelling begins, as if their throats were being cut, until we chuck them out. Whether young or old, man or wife, they stand in their rags and tatters on the doorstep and can't be persuaded to go . . . When we finally threaten them at pistol point, they disappear for a few minutes, only to return again yelling even more loudly.*[4]

While no one was freezing to death in September 1941, the Russian peasants knew better than anyone what was coming and knew that survival depended on shelter and stores of food for the coming winter. Without access to these the weather would soon prove fatal for countless Soviet peasants. In this indirect way Germany's war of annihilation involved average German soldiers to a far greater extent than is often acknowledged. Between seventeen and eighteen million Soviet civilians died in the war with Nazi Germany and most of these died not as a direct result of a German action (that is, by being shot), but rather from the conditions created by the German army and occupation forces (starvation, disease, exposure, overwork, etc.). Accordingly, however some historians may seek to 'interpret' the circumstances or apply restrictive definitions to what constituted a war crime, the fact remains that the *Ostheer* and its soldiers, each to varying extents, participated in and contributed to the conditions which resulted in the deaths of so many. In this sense one must keep in mind that the well-known suffering of the German army during the winter fighting had even worse results for the civilian population, especially in the areas of heavy German troop concentrations.

By the end of September 1941 the German soldiers in the east were only just beginning to feel the extent of the threat they faced from the cold. In some ways it would become a more pervasive killer than the Red Army, since the men had little winter training, inadequate access to shelter and, most importantly, very few had winter uniforms. The LIII Army Corps reported on 24 September that it had not yet received any winter clothing at all.[5] This was typical of most of the *Ostheer*'s divisions, leaving the men to manage as best they could with their worn-out summer uniforms.[6] Of course the same transport bottlenecks that prevented the supply of fuel and munitions also impacted the OKH's ability to supply winter uniforms. It was another crisis in the making, but because it did not yet have an impact on operations – the operations that were intended to deliver the decisive result – the supply of winter clothing was not of the highest priority. In any case there were not enough winter uniforms in Germany and, according to the war diary of the 19th Panzer Division, no more than 20–25 per cent of its forces could hope to receive uniforms, while the shortage of leather meant that replacement boots would no longer be issued.[7] It was a frightening prospect even for those parts of the German army which were digging into static winter positions. For those that would be pushing forward into the open it was a clear indication of the additional strain they would be expected to endure. Not surprisingly, many of the men placed their hopes in reports claiming the war would soon be over. Alois Scheuer wrote home on 24 September, 'We know that we are standing before great decisions that could end the war here in the east. It's about time too as the cold already makes everything very uncomfortable.'[8] On the northerly Finnish front the cold weather arrived even earlier, causing Franz Fenne to write on 10 September, 'I am curious when all this shit will be over, it is no fun any more. The nights are much too cold, one can hardly sleep you get so chilly and then there is also the rain.' Nine days later on 19 September Fenne reported seeing the first snow.[9] To the south on the main German–Soviet front the earliest report of snow comes from a soldier's letter on 27 September, when Leopold Schober wrote home in a letter, 'The winter is just around the corner. We already have here a little snow flurry.'[10]

While the sight of snow was the obvious harbinger of the winter to come, what was more important at this point was the rain because the dreaded *rasputitsa* would precede the freezing conditions. On 29 September Wilhelm Prüller noted, 'The summer really is finished.'

He stated that the rain was 'depressingly regular' and lamented what this would mean for the roads, which he concluded would be 'quite impassable. And what these mean for an armoured division, anyone can see.'[11] Even in the higher command there was trepidation about what was to come. Rundstedt wrote home to his wife on 30 September, 'The weather is bleak and cold. The central heating doesn't make up for it. Lousy quarters. And then one has one's thoughts about the future . . . We are all scared of the winter.'[12] No such words of foreboding can be found in either Bock's or Halder's diary and it is perhaps no coincidence that the two firebrand advocates of the attack on Moscow were proving steadfastly impervious to doubts. Halder did, however, note on 1 October that the Soviets were exchanging their divisions at the front in order to re-equip them with winter clothing.[13] In Germany Goebbels evinced a certain degree of alarm about the oncoming winter when he wrote on 27 September that it was 'high time' that the objectives of the eastern campaign be reached. 'Otherwise,' he continued, '"General Winter" will come into play and maybe achieve some of what our enemies at the moment hunger for.'[14] With so much uncertainty about the idea of a winter campaign there was an obvious need to counter the widespread apprehension stirred by comparisons with 1812. The *Völkischer Beobachter*, the Nazi party's daily newspaper, carried an article on 30 September entitled '1812 and Today', written by a colonel from the General Staff.

> *That the winter will bring our operations to a halt is inevitable. Did not our troops also spend several winters at our eastern front in Russia during the 1914–1918 World War without suffering privations? True this time our front is much further east. But then we are not fighting on two fronts and can supply our troops with whatever they require to survive the winter without harm to body and soul. A people like ours, having the organizational skills to build a network of national highways, a Siegfried Line*[15] *and powerful armaments industry and equally powerful armed forces, will have no difficulty organizing the battle against the Russian winter . . . One thing can be said without exaggerating: The German Wehrmacht will tide over the Russian winter better than their eastern foe!*[16]

Such hubris was at the very heart of Germany's difficulties in the east and reveals the stubborn persistance of derisive racial and cultural precepts within the army.[17] While in Germany such absurd notions simply fed the verbose diatribes of Nazi party hacks, in the east they directly and adversely impacted the strategic outlook. At no point in the first three months of the war was the prospect of a Soviet revival considered possible and, as the *Ostheer* became more and more depleted and overextended, estimates of the Soviet enemy were simply downgraded accordingly. Yet unlike the *Ostheer* the Red Army was not in decline[18] and its technical state in a number of key areas was actually improving as the summer losses effectively culled a great deal of obsolete Soviet equipment, which new production was slowly replacing with advanced, even superior, designs. The contrasting demodernization of the *Ostheer* placed the opposing two armies on far more even terms heading into the autumn – a fact the battlefield reflected in a way German strategic direction did not. The blitzkrieg mentality still predominated with the OKW and the OKH, but the war had irrevocably transformed into an attritional struggle.

Reflecting the changing nature of the war in the east Guderian's opening battle in the preliminary stages of Operation Typhoon proved a nasty surprise. Intending to secure better starting positions for his right flank, Guderian ordered Kempf's XXXXVIII Panzer Corps to advance north to Putivl by attacking up through a section of the Soviet front. His devoted Chief of Staff, Liebenstein, attempted to persuade Guderian that he should simply move the corps north behind the German front so that it could avoid major operations until the start of the panzer group's offensive on 30 September.[19] Guderian, however, insisted. Starting on 28 September Kempf's corps was to attack near the junction of Eremenko's Briansk Front and Timoshenko's reconstituted South-Western Front. Such junctions generally constituted weak points in the enemy lines, but on this occasion the attack was immediately stopped and Clössner's 25th Motorized Infantry Division was subjected to costly counterattacks.[20] Even the recalcitrant Guderian soon understood that the attack would have to be abandoned so as to avoid a delay to the main operation due to start in less than two days. Yet extracting Clössner's heavily committed forces required the additional commitment of Hubicki's 9th Panzer Division, which noted in its war diary that Soviet forces were much stronger than ground and air intelligence had suggested.[21] In an uncharacteristically candid admission, Guderian stated in his memoir:

> *I had underestimated the powers of resistance of the Russians who had not been engaged in the Kiev battle. XXXXVIII Panzer Corps – as will be shown – did not succeed in throwing back the enemy opposite it, but had to break off the battle and march to its assembly area behind Infantry Regiment* Grossdeutschland's *front. The 25th (Motorised) Division had a hard time shaking the enemy and unfortunately lost a number of its vehicles in the process.*[22]

Bock's account was more explicit: 'In the course of an attempt to disengage Panzer Group Guderian's southern wing from the enemy, the 25th (Motorized) Division was attacked by tanks and escaped only at the cost of abandoning the vehicles of an entire regiment, which were stuck in the mud.'[23] Yet not everyone escaped. Werner Bergholz, a German soldier caught up in the fighting, described how the anti-tank guns stood no chance against the fast-moving and heavily armoured enemy tanks. The Soviets overran the German positions, where, immobilized by the mud, there could be no retreat and panic quickly took over. Bergholz was only able to escape because his vehicle did not get bogged down in the mud. He then recounted the scene in his diary: 'An indescribable welter of horses, troops, trucks and other vehicles. I shall never forget this spectacle. The soldiers discarded whatever they could. We had to run for our bare lives. Literally run, as the machines refused to budge. Such was the sad fate of our division.'[24] Lieutenant-General Sigfrid Henrici's 16th Motorized Infantry Division also became caught up in the fighting and the result prevented Kempf's XXXXVIII Panzer Corps from joining the main attack on 30 September. Indeed while the rest of Guderian's forces were attacking, the war diary of Panzer Group 2 referred to the 'critical situation' in Kempf's corps. Fuel could not be transported to the divisions because of the terrible roads, while during the fighting on 30 September parts of Clössner's division were encircled by the Soviets.[25] Nevertheless, it was not all bad news for Guderian. The remainder of his forces had pushed up to 60 kilometres into the Soviet front by the evening of 1 October and on the following day the panzer group's offensive would be joined by the entire Army Group Centre.[26]

Clearly Germany's offensive strength, even for major operations, had not yet expired, but by the same token it is equally clear that the Red Army's powers of resistance were by no means exhausted. Indeed, Kempf's experience at the end of September, which was paralleled near Lake Ladoga in Army Group North by the costly defensive battles of Schmidt's XXXIX Panzer Corps, reflects the fact that Soviet forces could now directly challenge even motorized German formations at the corps level. It was a sign of both the declining strength of Germany's elite formations and the corresponding lessons learned by increasing numbers of Soviet officers regarding German armoured tactics. Moreover, shortly after Operation Typhoon was under way, Lieutenant-General Ernst Köstring, who was born in Russia and had been the German military attaché in Moscow from 1931 to 1933 and again from 1935 to 1941, informed an assembly of German officers from the 18th Motorized Infantry Division, 'You will all be amazed. The Russians will only now truly mobilize.'[27] At the same time the Department of Foreign Armies East (*Abteilung Fremde Heere Ost*), which gathered intelligence about the Soviet Union, reported a demographer's findings comparing Soviet manpower resources with those of Germany. The report stated that the Soviets could mobilize and maintain 469 divisions, which was 2.2 times the maximum Germany could support (213 divisions).[28]

By the eve of Operation Typhoon Bock was in command of the single largest assembly of forces any individual German commander would possess during World War II. On paper the figures are indeed imposing and have suggested to many that Typhoon could in fact only have failed by the narrowest of margins. Yet Army Group Centre, while certainly no paper tiger, was a long way from ever capturing Moscow and had no chance of ending the war in the autumn of 1941. A comparison of figures for Operation Barbarossa and Operation Typhoon was produced in Army Group Centre's war diary on 2 October, giving a deceptive impression of increased strength. According to the diary, on 22 June 1941 Bock commanded a total of nine panzer divisions,[29] six and a half motorized, one cavalry, thirty-one infantry and three security divisions, making a total of forty-nine and a half divisions. On 2 October 1941 Bock's forces had expanded to fourteen panzer, eight and a half motorized, one cavalry, forty-seven infantry and five security divisions, producing a total of seventy-five and a half divisions (Table 2). By this accounting Army Group Centre was a third stronger than it had been fourteen weeks before. Numerically, the war diary noted, Army Group Centre had increased from a starting total of 1,308,730 men to 1,929,406 men. Again Bock's strength in manpower was almost one-third stronger in October relative to June. In artillery the army group increased from 750 batteries (421 light and 329 heavy) to 1,022 batteries (624 light and 398 heavy).[30] Only the Luftwaffe appeared to be in decline as Bock started the war with 1,235 aircraft (all models), but by 2 October listed just 1,006 (all models).[31]

Such raw data can be deceptive without the appropriate context to provide a fuller accounting of Army Group Centre's real strength in Operation Typhoon. On 22 June 1941 Bock's eight panzer divisions totalled together 1,530 tanks, which was just below the total strength on 2 October.[32] Thus Bock's panzer forces were only slightly stronger in spite of the addition of a third panzer group and four panzer divisions. Yet this is not where most of Bock's increased strength came from. Half of Bock's entire panzer forces on 2 October came from the allocation of new production (300 tanks) and the deployment of the 5th and 2nd Panzer Divisions to the eastern front (450 tanks). Accordingly, after almost three and a half months of fighting on the eastern front and before the allocation of new tanks, twelve of Bock's fourteen panzer divisions contributed only half of the tanks to Operation Typhoon. Indeed a significant percentage of these had moderate to serious mechanical problems, rendering them only provisionally operational. If one were to compare the numerical strengths of Bock's twelve veteran panzer divisions on 22 June and 2 October one would record a 70 per cent drop in strength from 2,476 to 750 tanks.[33]

The increase in infantry divisions by one-third was not equalled by a one-third increase in artillery, reflecting the reduction in firepower of the individual units. More seriously, the total frontage of Army Group Centre on 22 June was 500 kilometres, but this had expanded to 760 kilometres by 2 October.[34] Hence the one-third increase in Bock's divisions also had to cover a one-third increase in frontage. Moreover, just as many panzer divisions no longer retained the combat strength their designations implied, so too many infantry divisions were well below their establishment and were no longer able to perform as full divisions. Chales de Beaulieu noted that by the end of September reserves for the divisions were so deficient that 'at the time what one

Table 2 *Army Group Centre order of battle on 2 October 1941 (Operation Typhoon)*

Army Group	Army	Corps / Panzer Group	Corps (Panzer Group)	Divisions
Army Group Centre Infantry Regiment *Grossdeutschland* 19th Panzer Division Motorized *Lehrbrigade 900* Rear Area Command (Centre) 707th Infantry Division 339th Infantry Division SS Cavalry Brigade 221st Security Division 286th Security Division 403rd Security Division 454th Security Division (in transfer)	Ninth Army 161st Infantry Division	XXIII Army Corps		251st Infantry Division 102nd Infantry Division 256th Infantry Division 206th Infantry Division
		Panzer Group 3	VI Army Corps	110th Infantry Division 26th Infantry Division
			XXXXI Panzer Corps	36th Motorized Infantry Division 1st Panzer Division 6th Infantry Division
			LVI Panzer Corps	14th Motorized Infantry Division 6th Panzer Division 7th Panzer Division 129th Infantry Division
			V Army Corps	35th Infantry Division 5th Infantry Division 106th Infantry Division
		VIII Army Corps		28th Infantry Division 8th Infantry Division 87th Infantry Division
		XXVII Army Corps		255th Infantry Division 162nd Infantry Division 86th Infantry Division
	Fourth Army	IX Army Corps		137th Infantry Division 263rd Infantry Division 183rd Infantry Division 292nd Infantry Division
		XX Army Corps		268th Infantry Division 15th Infantry Division 78th Infantry Division
		VII Army Corps		267th Infantry Division 7th Infantry Division 23rd Infantry Division 197th Infantry Division
		Panzer Group 4	LVII Panzer Corps	20th Panzer Division 3rd Motorized Infantry Division SS *Das Reich*
			XXXXVI Panzer Corps	5th Infantry Division 11th Panzer Division 252nd Infantry Division
			XXXX Panzer Corps	2nd Panzer Division 10th Panzer Division 258th Infantry Division
			XII Army Corps	98th Infantry Division 34th Infantry Division
	Second Army 112th Infantry Division	XIII Army Corps		17th Infantry Division 260th Infantry Division
		XXXXIII Army Corps		52nd Infantry Division 131st Infantry Division
		LIII Army Corps		56th Infantry Division 31st Infantry Division 167th Infantry Division
	Panzer Group 2	XXXXVII Panzer Corps		29th Motorized Infantry Division 17th Panzer Division 18th Panzer Division
		XXIV Panzer Corps		4th Panzer Division 3rd Panzer Division 10th Motorized Infantry Division
		XXXXVIII Panzer Corps		9th Panzer Division 25th Motorized Infantry Division 16th Motorized Infantry Division
		Higher Command XXXV		95th Infantry Division 296th Infantry Division 262nd Infantry Division 293rd Infantry Division 1st Cavalry Division
		Higher Command XXXIV		45th Infantry Division 134th Infantry Division

Source: Militärgeschichtlichen Forschungsamt (ed.), *Das Deutsche Reich und der Zweite Weltkrieg. Band 4. Der Angriff auf die Sowjetunion* (Stuttgart, 1983) p. 573.

referred to as a "division" was actually only half a division'.[35] On 15 September the war diary of Panzer Group 4 described their last consignment of reserves to fill the gaps in the ranks as 'almost useless'. Their shortage of infantry training as well as their high average age (thirty-five to thirty-seven) was 'especially noticeable', while supplementary training was deemed not possible owing to the constant commitment of all units.[36]

While Bock's strength in real terms was considerably lower than the total number of divisions might suggest, his reinforced army group nevertheless did present a powerful force. Leeb and Rundstedt, however, had been badly depleted to achieve this, which meant that they could not advance on the flanks of Army Group Centre and Bock would have to subtract an ever increasing number of forces from his front to guard his rear. Furthermore, the massing of 1,500 tanks, 1,000 planes, tens of thousands of other vehicles and nearly 2 million men could in no way be supplied by the army group's logistical apparatus, especially for an advance hundreds of kilometres in depth along a front 760 kilometres wide. Of course Bock's strength is also relative to Soviet opposition. As early as July the Soviets began to prepare for a German attack on the approaches to Moscow by erecting an echelon system of field fortifications. Colonel-General I. S. Konev's Western Front,[37] Budenny's Reserve Front[38] and Eremenko's Briansk Front manned the outer defensive line which ran along the Desna and Sudost Rivers to the west of Viaz'ma. Further east there were two belts of defences separated from each other by 35–45 kilometres, which together were known as the Rezhev–Viaz'ma Defensive Line. Yet the most important defensive line was the Mozhaisk Defensive Line, which was anchored on four defensive regions at Volokolamsk, Mozhaisk, Maloiaroslavets and Kaluga. Altogether the Western, Reserve and Briansk Fronts commanded eleven armies in their first strategic echelon and four armies in their second. This amounted to some 1,250,000 men, 7,600 guns, 990 tanks and 667 aircraft. While Bock's force represented about 60 per cent of the entire *Ostheer*, the combined forces of Konev, Budenny and Eremenko accounted for only 40 percent of the Soviet forces between the Baltic and the Black Sea.[39] Despite being outnumbered and outgunned on the Moscow axis, across the full breadth of the eastern front the Red Army actually had more tanks than the *Ostheer* (2,715), more guns (20,580) and roughly the same number of men (3.2 million).[40]

While Bock could clearly expect bitter opposition on the road to Moscow, Soviet forces were not without problems of their own. The average strength of a division in the defending Soviet armies was between 5,000 and 7,000 men, which was half of their usual establishment. They were short of artillery, machine guns and trained officers, while the severe shortage of motor vehicles fixed many Soviet units to their defences without the ability to manoeuvre. Yet just as in the battle of Kiev, the greatest danger to the three Soviet fronts was not the prospect that the Germans might attack their weakened forces – the *Stavka* already knew to expect a major offensive; rather the greatest danger again proved to be the strategic direction of the *Stavka* itself. Throughout the second half of September British and Soviet intelligence pointed to the build-up of German forces throughout Army Group Centre and a major offensive was all but assured. To counter this the *Stavka* deployed most of Soviet forces well forward, densely manning the 800 kilometres of front that Konev, Budenny and Eremenko collectively shared.[41] Having so often experienced the 'shock' effect of major German offensives, with the loss of command and control as well as the rapid German encirclements, the actions of the *Stavka* (and not just Stalin) were almost inviting another calamity. Screening the front with light forces while holding back the bulk until the main axes of the attack could be identified and engaged would have saved countless formations, but the *Stavka*'s rigid insistence on holding every metre of ground was a clear sign that the principles of mobile warfare were not yet fully appreciated.

By the end of September 1941 the battle of Kiev was over, Nazi Germany had won an unprecedented victory and Hitler could take most of the credit. The battle had captured record stocks of war materiel and hundreds of thousands of Soviet POWs; the Dnepr River had been crossed and central Ukraine conquered; four Soviet armies had been destroyed and Army Group Centre's exposed southern flank was now secure. Only on the eastern front could such a huge battle draw parallels. Operation Typhoon would soon yield its own extraordinary totals of war booty, but the coming battles at Viaz'ma and Briansk were made possible only by Hitler's insistence on first pursuing the battle at Kiev. For all that it accomplished Kiev was the dictator's greatest battle and yet it did not suffice to defeat the Red Army decisively, or bring the war in the east to a conclusion. Such a feat was already beyond Germany's strength.

As the German solders concentrated in their positions for what was supposed to be the last great offensive of the eastern campaign, many took the opportunity to write a last letter home before the rigours of the advance commenced again. Ernst Guicking reflected the confidence of many when he wrote to his wife at the end of September:

> *The second thrust begins ... The prisoners that we made last night come from the Ural [Mountains]. It does indeed look desperate for the other side. It seems to be his last reserves. And that is what we are going to attack.*[42] *Bobi, we are looking forward to the coming weeks. This will be a straight march through Russia. Mopping up work, you will soon hear. Much will be new. It will definitely be the best rabbit hunt.*[43]

While Guicking evinced an unshakeable optimism, he served in the relative safety of the artillery. In the combat units, which had already suffered so many casualties, the tone was decidedly less enthusiastic. Alois Scheuer, whose company had been in action at Roslavl and Gomel, wrote on 29 September, 'September is coming to an end; maybe October will bring a change because the longer this now lasts the worse everything will get. We hope for the best.'[44] For Ewald H., whose company had been almost destroyed in the fighting for the city of Kiev, there was no excitement at the prospect of a further advance, only embittered war weariness. On 27 September he wrote in his diary:

> *Haven't we earned a rest in the Kiev we have conquered? But we have to wipe the platter clean while others make themselves comfortable here ... It goes on to the north-east, where to Moscow – Khar'kov? None of my old comrades are with me any more, I am with the VIII Company. During the incessant six-hour march without a break or food something crossed my mind: they are asking too much of us ... How far away remains the good and beautiful. One has the feeling that being a solder will never end.*[45]

The physical and emotional burdens of the preceding three and a half months had left their mark on many in the *Ostheer*. None of Hitler's previous campaigns had lasted so long or cost so much. Speculation as to how much longer the war in the east could last was as much a question about the future and what was to come as it was a commentary on the past and all that the men had already endured. Remaining on the eastern front meant physical suffering, mental hardship, emotional grief and bodily harm. It was a brutalizing process from which those who survived the war often never recovered. At the time, however, all that mattered was the elusive final victory and to that end Operation Typhoon carried the hopes of all Germany. As erroneous as such faith may have been, by the end of September 1941 the alternative was simply unimaginable. That the war in the east, far from being won, was still only in its earliest stages appeared inconceivable, but it was not even the worst aspect of the German predicament. The economic and military circumstances predetermined that over time the attritional struggle would look less and less like a German victory and more and more like a probable German defeat. It was here that the Nazi 'will' to succeed, regardless of the odds, stiffened German resolve, just as it did in September 1941 when victory was mistakenly believed to be imminent. Accordingly, at the start of October Halder dubbed Operation Typhoon 'this great deciding operation' (*diese große entscheidende Operation*)[46] and, in spite of all the evidence to the contrary, evinced a steadfast belief in victory. At the front Helmut Pabst observed the build-up around him and wrote home in a letter:

> *We don't know when it will start. We only feel the veil over the calm getting thinner, the atmosphere gathering tension, the approach of the hour when it will only need a word to let loose hell, when all this concentrated force will spring forward, when the barrage will again be before us and I may be following the machine-guns again. In any case this is where we shall have to crack the nut and it will be some crack.*[47]

In the early hours of 2 October Heinrich Haape's unit moved into their forward attack positions. 'Soberly the day broke in the east, like a grey monster, spreading relentlessly and menacingly towards us, seeking to engulf us. We went out to meet it.'[48]

Operation Typhoon had begun.

CONCLUSION

Establishing the relative importance of a battle is probably a subjective undertaking, destined to evoke disagreement and debate. Yet Kiev was no ordinary battle. From its earliest inception it was fraught with controversy on both the German and the Soviet side, forcing the dictators to impose their views on their respective military commands. In the course of events Zhukov lost his position as the Chief of the Red Army's General Staff and Budenny was replaced as the commander of the South-Western Direction. On the German side Guderian's sudden reversal to support Hitler's preference earned him the enmity of the OKH, while the wider dispute further poisoned the atmosphere between Hitler and the army command. Halder in particular was extremely bitter and would later take every opportunity to blame Hitler for the failure of Operation Barbarossa, although there is no reason to believe that Halder's alternative would have been any more successful. Brauchitsch too was deeply affected. Hitler's scathing attack on the army's leadership shattered Brauchitsch's already feeble confidence, reducing him to a high-level messenger who ferried reports back and forth between commands, but was too cowed to take any independent action that might first require approval from above.

Beyond the effect the battle of Kiev had on the personal and power relationships within the Nazi and Soviet states, the battle, while unable to revive Germany's hopes for outright victory, nevertheless had a major impact on the course of the war in the east. By the end of September Soviet forces in the Ukraine were starved of resources, which gave Rundstedt the advantage in the fighting along the Nogai Steppe and led to the battle on the Sea of Azov. Here two more Soviet armies (the Ninth and Eighteenth) of Lieutenant-General D. I. Riabyshev's Southern Front were caught behind German lines by the rapid southern swing of Kleist's Panzer Group 1. German sources claimed 106,332 Soviet POWs, 212 tanks and 672 guns destroyed or captured.[1] Thereafter the road into the Donbas was open to Kleist, while Manstein's Eleventh Army, which had also played a leading role in the battle, was free to turn south and attack into the Crimea. Further north the major industrial city of Khar'kov, with 840,000 inhabitants, was now also threatened and would soon fall to Reichenau's Sixth Army.[2] Yet in the aftermath of the battle of Kiev the Germans benefited most from the strategic ramifications arising in the north. Throughout July and August Weichs's Second Army as well as major formations from Guderian's panzer group had been tied up holding Bock's long and exposed southern flank. The destruction of the South-Western Front allowed their full commitment to the east, along with the addition of reinforcements from Kleist and Reichenau. With no southern flank to guard, Bock was free to engage in what would become known as the battles of Viaz'ma and Briansk, which were fought at the same time as the battle on the Sea of Azov. At Viaz'ma and Briansk estimates suggest up to a million Soviet men were killed or captured in the first half of October, while seven more Soviet armies were completely destroyed.[3] The 'twin' encirclements produced colossal figures that together exceeded the German total at Kiev, but they belonged to a sequence of events that were not mutually exclusive. The battle of Kiev led to the battles at Viaz'ma, Briansk and on the Sea of Azov. As Evan Mawdsley observed in his history of the German–Soviet war, Kiev was the *Ostheer*'s 'greatest triumph of the war in the East and the Red Army's greatest single disaster'.[4] Similarly, Michael Jones dubbed the battle of Kiev 'the Wehrmacht's greatest victory of the war'.[5]

Without intending to aggrandize his achievement, Kiev was uniquely Hitler's triumph. It was opposed by Bock at Army Group Centre and, at Halder's urging, by Rundstedt at Army Group South. Guderian had been a bitter opponent until his eleventh-hour meeting with Hitler on 23 August resulted in a seemingly inexplicable about-face. The senior staff at the OKH was united in its opposition and even enjoyed the influential support of Jodl at the OKW. In the face of all this expert opinion, however, Hitler refused to yield. Yet before anyone attributes to Hitler a visionary prescience capable of foreseeing the sweeping calamity that would befall the Soviet Union, it must be remembered that Hitler had an important confederate. If written from the Soviet perspective, this book might just as well have been titled 'Stalin's Greatest Defeat' for it was the Soviet dictator, just as much as Hitler, who was responsible for the outcome of the September fighting. Recalling his dealing with Stalin in September 1941, Churchill observed in his memoirs, 'It is almost incredible that the head of the Russian government with all the advice of their military experts could have committed himself to such absurdities... It seemed hopeless to argue with a man thinking in terms of utter unreality.'[6] Churchill was referring to Stalin's request for a British army to be sent to fight on the Soviet front, but a better example of Stalin thinking in terms of utter unreality was the events in the Ukraine. As Geoffrey Roberts has concluded, 'There were many occasions, too, when it was Stalin's personal insistence on the policy of no retreat and of counterattack at all costs that resulted in heavy Soviet losses. The best-known example of this is the disaster at Kiev in September 1941.'[7] Certainly the men who fought under Stalin were under no illusions as to who was responsible for their defeat. Eremenko wrote after the war that the debacle at Kiev 'was one of the disastrous effects of Stalin's crude disregard for the elementary rules of military strategy'.[8] Clearly the scale of the German victory was heavily dependent on Stalin's obliging role. Even with this great advantage, the weakness of the German panzer groups still rendered the battle a hard-fought, if one-sided, encounter.

For a battle that had been spoken about in August as the last 'decisive' campaign of the year, in the aftermath of Kiev such pronouncements were inexplicably forgotten in favour of a new 'final campaign', which was also given the dubious distinction of being dubbed 'decisive'. Indeed the battles at Minsk and Smolensk from June through to August had already demonstrated the disquieting paradox between operational success and strategic consequence. The September fighting in the Ukraine could only have reinforced that view, rendering German confidence in Operation Typhoon a foolhardy conception. Understanding how and why the German command remained so single-mindedly intent on continuing the offensive in spite of all the inherent perils requires more than just an assessment of the personalities involved and rather requires a broader conceptual focus to include what Robert

Citino has termed the 'the German way of war'. According to Citino, Prussian/German military doctrine since the time of Frederick William I 'The Great Elector' (1620–1688) has been governed by the principle of attack irrespective of the force ratio or even the strategic circumstances. Attack was simply seen as the sole path to success in warfare, which Citino has argued was so ingrained in generations of officers 'that it might no longer have been conscious'.[9] Yet explaining German strategy in 1941 solely in terms of such overarching trends in Prussian/German military history would be inadequate. Citino is correct to highlight the pervasive cult of the offensive within the Prussian/German officer corps, but in 1941 one must also look to the deepseated Nazi world-view, which pervaded the Wehrmacht and both encouraged a defamatory foe-image (because they were Slavs) and promoted a delusional cult of the 'will', which prioritized the 'spiritual' fighting qualities of the German soldier over almost any competing circumstances.

While the battle of Kiev in many ways set the groundwork for the *Ostheer*'s further victories in October, the two dictators drew sharply divergent conclusions from the battle. For Hitler Kiev was one more substantiation of his own aptitude for strategic command, which would remain with him for the rest of the war and have lasting implications from 1942 onwards as the generals unsuccessfully attempted to counter his increasingly irrational decisions. Stalin, by contrast, tended to draw the opposite conclusion and after the many defeats of 1941 and more in 1942, he allowed his generals increasing autonomy, which, for the most part, they used to purposeful effect.

Ultimately, for all that the battle of Kiev achieved it was clearly still well short of what was required for Operation Barbarossa's success. While Kirponos's South-Western Front was lost, the resistance of the Red Army was far from being broken. The economic implications for the Soviets of losing Kiev and the central Ukraine were ameliorated by the evacuation of Soviet machinery and the destruction of what remained to avoid it falling to the Germans. Furthermore, the huge commitments made by the western powers during September at the Three Power Conference effectively ensured that the Soviets were no longer alone in equipping and sustaining their vast armies. Even at the time it was clear that the blow struck at Kiev, while hard, would not prove fatal. Writing in his diary on 13 September Halder acknowledged that the continuation of the eastern campaign into 1942 was a prospect the army would have to face.[10] Later, in a letter to his wife, he compared the fighting at Kiev to an arm being torn off, but commented that the back of Soviet resistance still remained to be broken.[11] Thus one can say that while the battle of Kiev achieved a great deal in operational terms, especially given the worn-out condition of the *Ostheer*'s motorized troops, it was not able to avert Germany's dangerous strategic predicament of becoming bogged down in the east. Thus, while the September fighting in the Ukraine destroyed an unprecedented amount of Soviet men and materiel, it could not change Germany's fundamental strategic dilemma. The *Ostheer* did not have the manpower or mobility to take advantage of the breach it had created. Conquering European Russia in 1941 was out of the question and enduring a winter campaign was hardly conducive to the *Ostheer*'s prospects for achieving in 1942 what it had failed to gain in 1941. Even before the declaration of war on the United States of America, Germany was fatally overextended. This is not to suggest that the Wehrmacht's coming campaigns and battles were somehow irrelevant to the course of the conflict; they certainly determined the length and cost of the war. Yet the conflict Hitler had started in the east had failed to achieve a knock-out blow and it could not be sustained in the long term. The scale of Germany's future battlefield victories in Operation Typhoon, the battle of Khar'kov, the Crimean campaign and the opening stages of Operation Blue remain unquestioned, but as with the battle of Kiev, they could not alter the intractability of Germany's strategic predicament. Indeed these successes only encouraged Hitler to risk more and advance further, spreading his increasingly limited resources still wider. The danger this posed was strikingly revealed in the battle of Stalingrad and the elimination of an entire German army as well as the armies of Hungary, Italy and Romania. Many have dated this as the beginning of the end for the Germans in the east, but even without the fateful decisions that led to Stalingrad, the gap in manpower and materiel between the Allies and the Axis had become desperately large. In the aftermath of Stalingrad Germany's operational brilliance was needed just to maintain the *Ostheer*'s position in the east, and thus Field Marshal Erich von Manstein's much-praised spring 1943 counteroffensive was trumpeted simply for restoring the German line in the south. Essentially the line Manstein had secured was the same as the one held by Germany at the end of the battle of Kiev in 1941. Yet what had changed in the intervening eighteen months? Between

October 1941 and April 1943 Germany had won many more battles and in aggregate terms had inflicted much more damage on the Red Army, yet historians agree that the *Ostheer* was now further than ever from victory. In fact the odds against a German victory in the east after Operation Barbarossa had failed were hopelessly large and, just as at Kiev in 1941, continued battlefield successes in 1942 were frequently prefaced by disastrous Soviet strategic direction (as at the Kerch peninsula in the Crimea and Timoshenko's abortive offensive at Khar'kov). To no small extent, therefore, the *Ostheer* was reliant on a degree of Soviet complicity in its victories and even these were only sufficient in maintaining a certain status quo on the eastern front. When the Red Army was well directed and adequately prepared, the *Ostheer*'s vulnerabilities were exposed, while Germany's sensitivity to major defeats was far greater than that of the Soviet Union. The Red Army's road to Berlin was not a simple straight line leading directly from the battles at Stalingrad or Kursk. The road was in fact much longer, beginning in the aftermath of Barbarossa's failure and including many twists and some brief U-turns. Even after Stalingrad it was not always a one-way highway, but the signs were at least clear. What was not always clear was that Germany had in fact been on the same road since the late summer of 1941.

Irrespective of how successful the battle of Kiev may have appeared on the surface, it was the German generals themselves who became its staunchest critics. Desperate to shield themselves from blame for the failure of the eastern campaign, they portrayed Hitler as having hijacked their well-laid plans to capture Moscow in September and presumably win the war in the east. Such counterfactual interpretations attract much popular interest because the alternative can clearly be shown to have been inadequate, while the suggested substitute enjoys the freedom of never having been attempted. Yet the claim of the generals, that an earlier drive on Moscow would have met with greater success, avoids the many complex problems pertaining to logistics, the manpower shortage, panzer strengths and Soviet reserves. Moreover, at no point did any of the generals address how Bock might have attempted such a deep advance with an exposed southern flank stretching all the way back to Gomel. Nevertheless, as numerous studies have attested, in the aftermath of the war the German generals proved extremely guarded about the truth. In a submission to the International Court of Justice at Nuremberg Brauchitsch, along with Manstein, Halder, Warlimont and General of Cavalry Siegfried Westphal, signed a document intended to exonerate the German army for any blame in the botched management and inept direction of the war. Essentially the document sought to shift responsibility for the many military blunders squarely on to Hitler, which, while true to an extent, denies, just as in the case of war crimes, the substantial role played by the army command. With regard to 1941 and the battle of Kiev, the generals asserted:

> *It diverted the German effort from the main task to a second-rate operation, which involved an irreplaceable loss in time and strength. When Hitler then ordered the attack on Moscow, it was too late for it . . . Soon after [the start of Operation Typhoon] the winter cold set in, a series of military set-backs started, the deeper causes of which were to be found in the effects of the battle of Kiev, especially in the exhaustion of the troops, in the countermeasures taken by the enemy and in local errors in the command on the German side.*[12]

The view of the German generals was subjected to little criticism at the time, but Marshal Zhukov, who commanded the Soviet forces around Moscow in the autumn of 1941, roundly dismissed any such assertion in a 1970 interview. When asked about the timing of the German attack on Moscow and whether an earlier offensive might have enjoyed greater success, Zhukov was blunt:

> *German troops failed to take Moscow by a* coup de main *in August, as some of their generals had intended. In [the] case of an offensive they would have found themselves in a tighter situation than near Moscow in November–December of 1941. You see, Army Group Centre would have come up against the stiff resistance of Soviet troops directly on the approaches to the capital, and besides [these forces] a strong counter-blow from our troops in the South-Western Direction could have been inflicted as well. That is why all attempts by the German generals and some western war historians to place the blame for the defeat near Moscow on Hitler alone are just as groundless as the entire German strategy.*[13]

The extent to which Zhukov's proposed counterstrike by the Soviet South-Western Front might have hindered Bock's drive to Moscow is hard to say; however, there seems little doubt that the open flank would at least have cost Bock a sizeable portion of his total attacking force. One must also consider that in mid- to late August, when the generals were seeking to begin their offensive, Hitler had not yet agreed to release either the 300 tanks from new production or the 2nd and 5th Panzer Divisions, which together doubled Operation Typhoon's panzer strength. Moreover, the logistics of such an operation were better in September than in August, owing to an extension of the railways, while the opposing Soviet armies would have been stronger in August because they were greatly depleted by the Dukhovshchina and Yel'nya offensives (28 August to 10 September).[14] Accordingly the battle of Kiev was almost certainly the best option for the *Ostheer* in August 1941, but in no way sufficient for the ultimate goal of Operation Barbarossa.

In my preceding volume (*Operation Barbarossa and Germany's Defeat in the East*) I argued that Germany's invasion of the Soviet Union had failed as early as the middle of August and that by implication Hitler's war effort had already reached its fatal turning point. While the book has largely received a positive reception, some critics pointed to the battle of Kiev and sought to question whether this was the piece that did not fit the puzzle.[15] How was it possible that a victory of such scale could be won if Germany's armoured forces really were so badly depleted? Given the many affirmative accounts one finds in the secondary literature referring to Germany's performance in the battle (many of which lack any archival sources), it seemed a reasonable question to ask. This book has attempted to address this question, while charting the ongoing decline in Germany's operational proficiency in the east. Hitler captured the Central Ukraine and effectively removed the huge bulge in his front. More importantly, he eliminated the powerful South-Western Front and created the conditions for further exploitation of Soviet dispositions. Yet the battle of Kiev was not the clear-cut victory many accounts have suggested. The path to Hitler's triumphant battle in the Ukraine was neither smooth nor harmonious and the outcome was certainly not preordained from the beginning. Indeed by the time the battle of Kiev was underway Germany's days of blitzkrieg victories were already over. Although Guderian's role in the battle typically dates from 25 August, in fact his principal panzer corps at Kiev (Schweppenburg's XXIV Panzer Corps) had been desperately fighting Soviet formations on Bock's southern flank since the middle of July. Once Guderian was formally tasked with the operation, his battered forces laboured their way south for another three weeks against weak, but determined resistance. The further he progressed towards his goal, the longer his left flank extended and the less strength he could commit to his pincer in spite of Bock's continual reinforcement. Only Kleist's delayed southern thrust sealed the pocket, but the battle was neither straightforward in its execution, nor painless in its result. The *Ostheer* suffered more than 50,000 fatalities in the month of September alone[16] and many of the vital panzer divisions were operating at a fraction of their former strength. Hitler may have won a great battle, but he was still losing the war. The losses of the *Ostheer* could never be replaced by German industry and all this was taking place in the period many consider to be the victorious phase of German operations in the east. With the autumn now in evidence and the worst seasonal conditions still to come, Germany's hopes for capturing Moscow in 1941, much less ending the war, were destined to be disappointed.

Summarizing the war in the east during September 1941, Curzio Malaparte, the Italian journalist travelling with Army Group South, penned a short verse which might be considered the most succinct portrayal of the dramatic events taking place and the results they were leading to. Shortly before he was sent back to Italy and placed under house arrest for expressing 'sympathy for communist Russia' in his dispatches, Malaparte wrote:

> *This is the Russian war, the eternal Russian war, the Russian war of 1941.* Nichts zu machen, nichts zu machen. *[Nothing can be done, nothing can be done.] Tomorrow the roads will be dry, then the mud will return, and everywhere there will be corpses, gutted houses, hordes of ragged prisoners with the air of sick dogs, everywhere the remains of horses and vehicles, the wreckage of tanks, of aeroplanes, of LKWs [trucks], of guns, the corpses of officers, NCOs [non-commissioned officers] and men, of women, children, old men and dogs, the remains of houses, villages, towns, rivers and forests.* Nichts zu machen, nichts zu machen. *Farther, ever farther, into the heart of the 'Russian Continent': across the Bug, across the Dnepr,*

across the Donets; towards the Don, towards the Volga, towards the Caspian. Ja, ja, jawohl. Wir kämpfen um das nackte Leben. *[Yes, yes, yes, sir. We're fighting for our very lives.] And then the winter will come – the beautiful, beautiful winter . . . Such is the war against Russia, 1941.*[17]

NOTES

Introduction

1 Rüdiger Overmans, *Deutsche militärische Verluste im Zweiten Weltkrieg* (Munich, 2000) pp.277–278.
2 For a detailed elaboration of this thesis see my earlier volume, David Stahel, *Operation Barbarossa and Germany's Defeat in the East* (Cambridge, 2009). See also David Stahel, 'Radicalizing Warfare: the German Command and the Failure of Operation Barbarossa' in Alex J. Kay, Jeff Rutherford and David Stahel (eds.), *Nazi Policy on the Eastern Front, 1941: Total War, Genocide and Radicalization* (forthcoming).
3 Hans-Adolf Jacobsen (ed.), *Kriegstagebuch des Oberkommandos der Wehrmacht (Wehrmachtfürungsstab). Band I/2. 1. August 1940–31. Dezember 1941* (Munich, 1982) p.1030, Document 77 (21 July 1941); hereafter cited as: KTB OKW, Volume II.
4 Michael Jones, *Leningrad. State of Siege* (London, 2008) pp.16–18.
5 Hugh R. Trevor-Roper (ed.), *Hitler's Table Talk, 1941–1944. His Private Conversations* (London, 2000) p.28 (19/20 August 1941).
6 'Heersgruppe Süd Kriegstagebuch II. Teil Band 3, 16 Aug.–15 Sept. 1941', BA-MA RH 19-I/254, fol.147 (1 September 1941).
7 Although Hitler's campaign in the west is sometimes referred to as 'the battle of France' it did in fact consist of many battles as well as two distinct operational phases (Case Yellow and Case Red). Karl-Heinz Frieser, *Blitzkrieg-Legende. Der Westfeldzug 1940* (Munich, 1996) pp.90–91.
8 The foremost proponent of Germany's early summer success is R. H. S. Stolfi who argues that Nazi Germany could have been victorious in World War II by October 1941. R.H.S. Stolfi, *Hitler's Panzers East. World War II Reinterpreted* (Norman, OK, 1993).

9 Andrew Nagorski claims that it was only in early October 1941 that 'For the first time, the panzer units began encountering occasional fuel shortages,' allowing Nagorski's conclusion that German forces were 'still victorious and formidable'. Andrew Nagorski, *The Greatest Battle. Stalin, Hitler, and the Desperate Struggle for Moscow that Changed the Course of World War II* (New York, 2007) p.110; Andrew Nagorski, 'Stalin's Tipping Point', *Newsweek* (US Edition, 10 September 2007) p.44.

10 John Mosier states that by the end of September 1941 the German *Ostheer* had been 'thus far victorious' and 'their basic fighting machine hardly scratched' (pp.138 and 140). With such a distorted understanding of what the eastern campaign had thus far cost the German armies it is small wonder that Mosier concludes: 'Hitler came very close to winning that war [World War II], and on the Eastern Front, his soldiers came within an ace of winning outright.' John Mosier, *Deathride. Hitler vs. Stalin: the Eastern Front, 1941–1945* (New York, 2010) p.4.

11 When Alfred W. Turney deemed Army Group Centre's summer battles 'spectacular successes', and remarked that '[t]he period saw the German blitzkrieg at its best', one might be tempted to forget that while other blitzkriegs succeeded, Barbarossa clearly failed. Alfred W. Turney, *Disaster at Moscow. Von Bock's Campaigns 1941–1942* (Albuquerque, 1970) pp.62–63. Similarly, the prominent military historian John Keegan wrote in glowing terms about Germany's achievements in 1941. 'The results of the fighting on the fronts of the three army groups were spectacular... These results not unnaturally led both OKH and OKW, in the person of Hitler, to believe that the "Battle of Russia" had been as good as finished within the first four weeks.' The assumption that the German high command had to a large extent succeeded, and was 'not unnaturally' looking forward to victory, reflects the same misplaced optimism that doomed the German armies. John Keegan, *Barbarossa. Invasion of Russia 1941* (New York, 1971) p.71. Albert Seaton, author of the popular histories of the eastern front *The Russo-German War 1941–45* and *The Battle for Moscow*, tended to see the initial stages of the war in very bleak terms for the Soviet Union. In the latter study he titled his second chapter 'The War is Virtually Won' and went on to describe the Soviet state as being 'near disintegration' as early as July. Albert Seaton, *The Battle for Moscow* (New York, 1993) p.49.

12 Richard Overy, *Why the Allies Won* (New York, 1996) p.211. See also Overy's comments in Guido Knopp's 2007 documentary 'Die Wehrmacht – Eine Bilanz', episode two: 'Wende des Krieges'; Robert M. Citino, *Death of the Wehrmacht. The German Campaigns of 1942* (Lawrence, KS, 2007) pp.34–35 and 38–39.

13 Ernst Klink's contribution to the fourth volume of *Das Deutsche Reich und der Zweite Weltkrieg*, which deals with the military campaign during Operation Barbarossa, offers a measured and dependable account. Yet while

he refrains from rash declarations forecasting the impending demise of the Soviet Union, his account neglects a sufficient discussion of the German operational problems, which stems from his dependence on the files of the OKH and High Command of the Armed Forces (*Oberkommando der Wehrmacht*, OKW) without the contrasting perspective gained from the files of the field formations. Ernst Klink, 'Die Operationsführung' in Militärgeschichtliches Forschungsamt (ed.), *Das Deutsche Reich und der Zweite Weltkrieg. Band 4. Der Angriff auf die Sowjetunion* (Stuttgart, 1983) pp.451–652. Although volume IV of *Das Deutsche Reich und der Zweite Weltkrieg* appeared in 1983 it has since appeared in a slightly updated English translation from Oxford University Press. Ernst Klink, 'The Conduct of Operations' in Militärgeschichtliches Forschungsamt (ed.), *Germany and the Second World War. Volume IV. The Attack on the Soviet Union* (Oxford, 1998) pp.525–763.

14 Graham Lyons (ed.), *The Russian Version of the Second World War. The History of the War as Taught to Soviet Schoolchildren* (New York, 1976) pp.33–34. See also: Hans-Heinrich Nolte, 'Die erste Phase des Zweiten Weltkrieges und der deutsche Überfall auf die Sowjetunion in Schulbüchern der UdSSR und der Bundesrepublik Deutschland' in Gerd R. Ueberschär and Wolfram Wette (eds.), *'Unternehmen Barbarossa'. Der deutsche Überfall auf die Sowjetunion 1941* (Paderborn, 1984) pp.49–65.

15 John Erickson, *The Road to Stalingrad. Stalin's War with Germany. Volume I* (London, 1975).

16 For his major works on 1941 see: David M. Glantz, *Barbarossa Derailed. The Battle for Smolensk 10 July–10 September 1941. Volume I. The German Advance, the Encirclement Battle, and the First and Second Soviet Counteroffensives, 10 July–24 August 1941* (Solihull, 2010); David M. Glantz, *Barbarossa Derailed. The Battle for Smolensk 10 July–10 September 1941. Volume II. The German Offensives on the Flanks and the Third Soviet Counteroffensive, 25 August–10 September 1941* (Solihull, 2011); David M. Glantz, *Barbarossa. Hitler's Invasion of Russia 1941* (Stroud, 2001); David M. Glantz, *The Battle for Smolensk: 7 July–10 September 1941* (Privately published by David M. Glantz, 2001).

17 Further studies by Alexander Hill, Evan Mawdsley, Jonathan M. House, Chris Bellamy, Walter S. Dunn, Jakob W. Kipp and Rodric Braithwaite underscoring the Soviet aptitude for resistance have helped establish a high benchmark for scholarship on the eastern front. Nevertheless, it is notable that these authors all tend to favour Russian-language source material.

18 As Erickson accurately determined, the bitter disputes within the German high command stemmed, at least in part, from the vigorous Soviet countermoves, which 'spelt admission that the blitzkrieg had been bludgeoned to a pause by Timoshenko and by Kirponos, each in his own way'. Erickson, *The Road to Stalingrad*, p.196.

19 There are too many such memoirs to cite here, but among the best known in English are: Guy Sajer, *The Forgotten Soldier* (New York, 1990); Günther K. Koschorrek, *Blood Red Snow. The Memoirs of a German Soldier on the Eastern Front* (London, 2002); Gottlob Herbert Bidermann, *In Deadly Combat. A German Soldier's Memoir of the Eastern Front* (Lawrence, KS, 2000). There has been some debate about the authenticity of the aforementioned work by Guy Sajer. I believe the most convincing case has been advanced by Douglas E. Nash who argues that the book should be accepted in spite of its minor inconsistencies. Submissions on the debate can be accessed online at www.members.shaw.ca/grossdeutschland/sajer.htm. Further discussion can found in the 'Letters to the Editor' of *The Professional Bulletin of Army History*, Fall 1997 and Spring 1998. See also the 'Letters to the Editor' in *The Journal of Military History*, Vol. 62, No.1 (January 1998) pp.242–246.

20 This was the subject of a recent study; see: Ronald Smelser and Edward J. Davies II, *The Myth of the Eastern Front. The Nazi–Soviet War in American Popular Culture* (Cambridge, 2008).

21 For more on this see my discussion in Stahel, *Operation Barbarossa and Germany's Defeat in the East*, pp.25–29.

22 For an introduction see: David M. Glantz, 'Forgotten Battles' in The Military Book Club (ed.), *Slaughterhouse. The Encyclopedia of the Eastern Front* (New York, 2002) pp.471–496. For a more detailed look at the forgotten battles in 1941 see: David M. Glantz, *Forgotten Battles of the German–Soviet War (1941–1945). Volume I The Summer–Fall Campaign (22 June–4 December 1941)* (Privately published by David M. Glantz, 1999).

23 At the start of Operation Barbarossa Panzer Groups 2 and 3 were roughly equal in strength, but during the course of August Panzer Group 3 had to give up a corps to aid Army Group North.

24 Halder was very dismissive of Leningrad's strategic importance and later declared that Hitler's preferences, including this and the diversion of forces to the south, had led Germany to catastrophe. Christian Hartmann, *Halder Generalstabschef Hitlers 1938–1942* (Munich, 1991) p.284.

25 For this study I have adopted Arabic ordinals for referring to divisions, Roman numerals for corps and spelled-out ordinals for armies.

26 Although the designation 'panzer corps' was only uniformly adopted in the summer of 1942 I have used it throughout my study to differentiate easily between motorized corps and infantry corps. Although a technical inaccuracy, it is interesting to note that the war diary of Panzer Group 2 makes the same distinction. The XXIV Army Corps (mot.) was not redesignated a panzer corps until 21 June 1942, but even as early as the summer of 1941 the diary always refers to the XXIV Panzer Corps.

27 Werner Haupt, *Kiew. Die grösste Kesselschlacht der Geschichte* (Dorheim, 1980).

28 These losses occurred between 1 September and 26 September; see: Franz Halder, *Kriegstagebuch: Tägliche Aufzeichnungen des Chefs des Generalstabes des Heeres 1939–1942. Band III. Der Russlandfeldzug bis zum Marsch auf Stalingrad (22.6.1941–24.9.1942)*, (eds.) Hans-Adolf Jacobsen and Alfred Philippi (Stuttgart, 1964) pp.213 and 260 (3 and 30 September 1941). Hereafter cited as: Halder, KTB III.

29 This is a Russian word, which refers to the biannual difficulties caused by heavy rains or melting snow in Russia, Belarus and the Ukraine. The *rasputitsa* may be directly translated as 'quagmire season'.

30 Elke Fröhlich (ed.), *Die Tagebücher von Joseph Goebbels. Teil II Diktate 1941–1945, Band 1 Juli–September 1941* (Munich, 1996) p.398 (11 September 1941).

1 The bulldog, the eagle and the bear

1 Max Hastings, *Bomber Command* (London, 1993) p.116.

2 Overy, *Why the Allies Won*, p.108.

3 Martin Kitchen, *A World in Flames. A Short History of the Second World War in Europe and Asia 1939–1945* (London, 1990) p.128.

4 Richard Overy, 'Statistics' in I. C. B. Dear and M. R. D. Foot (eds.), *The Oxford Companion to the Second World War* (Oxford, 1995) p.1060.

5 Kitchen, *A World in Flames*, p.129; Hastings, *Bomber Command*, pp.108–109.

6 R. A. C. Parker, *Struggle for Survival. The History of the Second World War* (Oxford, 1989) p.151. The World War II defence scientist Professor Pat Blackett concluded in 1941 that losses of highly trained British airmen were roughly equal to the number of German civilians killed over the course of the year. Hastings, *Bomber Command*, p.111.

7 Overy, *Why the Allies Won*, p.112.

8 Hastings, *Bomber Command*, pp.120–121; Kitchen, *A World in Flames*, pp.129–130.

9 John Keegan, *The Second World War* (New York, 1989) pp.321 and 327.

10 Ibid., pp.321–324.

11 Ian Kershaw, *Hitler 1936–1945. Nemesis* (London, 2001) p.366.

12 Keegan, *The Second World War*, pp.160 and 171.

13 Ibid., pp.328–329.

14 Martin Kitchen, *Rommel's Desert War. Waging World War II in North Africa, 1941–1943* (Cambridge, 2009) pp.118–119; Kitchen, *A World in Flames*, pp.92–93.

15 Kitchen, *A World in Flames*, p.94.
16 Marc Milner, 'Atlantic, Battle of the' in Dear and Foot (eds.), *The Oxford Companion to the Second World War*, p.63.
17 Overy, *Why the Allies Won*, p.31.
18 Milner, 'Atlantic, Battle of the', p.65.
19 Ibid., p.65.
20 Bernd Stegemann, 'Operation Crusader' in Militärgeschichtliches Forschungsamt (ed.), *Germany and the Second World War. Volume III. The Mediterranean, South-East Europe and North Africa 1939–1941* (Oxford, 1995) pp.725–726. My thanks to Dr Craig Stockings at the Australian Defence Forces Academy for providing me with information on Italian forces in North Africa.
21 Ernst Klink, 'Die militärische Konzeption des Krieges gegen die Sowjetunion' in Militärgeschichtliches Forschungsamt (ed.), *Das Deutsche Reich und der Zweite Weltkrieg. Band 4. Der angriff auf die Sowjetunion* (Stuttgart, 1983) pp.186–187.
22 Ian Kershaw, *Fateful Choices. Ten Decisions that Changed the World, 1940–1941* (New York, 2007) chapter 7: 'Washington, DC, Summer–Autumn 1941. Roosevelt Decides to Wage Undeclared War'.
23 Hubert P. van Tuyll, *Feeding the Bear. American Aid to the Soviet Union, 1941–1945* (Westport, CT, 1989) p.4.
24 George C. Herring Jr, *Aid to Russia 1941–1946: Strategy, Diplomacy, the Origins of the Cold War* (New York, 1973) p.6.
25 Kershaw, *Fateful Choices*, p.304.
26 Ibid., p.303.
27 Herring, *Aid to Russia 1941–1946*, p.9.
28 Ibid., p.7.
29 Ibid., p.10.
30 Van Tuyll, *Feeding the Bear*, p.4; Kershaw, *Fateful Choices*, p.305.
31 Alexander Hill, 'British Lend-Lease Aid and the Soviet War Effort, June 1941–June 1942', *The Journal of Military History*, Vol. 71, No. 3 (July 2007) p.779.
32 Kershaw, *Fateful Choices*, p.305.
33 Van Tuyll, *Feeding the Bear*, p.5.
34 Kershaw, *Fateful Choices*, pp.305–306.
35 Herring, *Aid to Russia 1941–1946*, p.12.
36 Kershaw, *Fateful Choices*, pp.307–308.
37 Ministry of Foreign Affairs of the USSR (ed.), *Stalin's Correspondence with Churchill, Attlee, Roosevelt and Truman 1941–1945* (New York, 1958) pp.17–18, Document 8 (received 15 August 1941).
38 Evan Mawdsley, *Thunder in the East. The Nazi–Soviet War 1941–1945* (London, 2005) p.191; Rolf-Dieter Müller, *Der letzte deutsche Krieg 1939–1945* (Stuttgart, 2005) p.105.

39 Herring, *Aid to Russia 1941–1946*, pp.19–20.
40 Kershaw, *Fateful Choices*, pp.309–310.
41 See research by Alexander Hill, 'British Lend-Lease Tanks and the Battle for Moscow, November–December 1941 – Revisited', *Journal of Slavic Military Studies*, Vol. 22, No. 4 (November 2009) pp.574–587; Alexander Hill, 'British "Lend-Lease" Tanks and the Battle for Moscow, November–December 1941 – a Research Note', *Journal of Slavic Military Studies*, Vol. 19, No. 2 (June 2006) pp.289–294; Hill, 'British Lend-Lease Aid and the Soviet War Effort, June 1941–June 1942'.
42 Hill, 'British Lend-Lease Aid and the Soviet War Effort, June 1941–June 1942', pp.788 and 792.
43 Van Tuyll, *Feeding the Bear*, p.52.
44 Kershaw, *Fateful Choices*, pp.312–313.
45 Robert Dallek, *Franklin D. Roosevelt and the American Foreign Policy* (Oxford, 1995) p.288.
46 Kershaw, *Fateful Choices*, pp.328–330.
47 This thesis is greatly expanded upon in my preceding study: Stahel, *Operation Barbarossa and Germany's Defeat in the East.*
48 The precise figure given is 27.8 per cent. Chris Bellamy, *Absolute War. Soviet Russia in the Second World War* (New York, 2007) pp.473 and 476; Jacques Sapir, 'The Economics of War in the Soviet Union during World War II' in Ian Kershaw and Moshe Lewin (eds.), *Stalinism and Nazism. Dictatorships in Comparison* (Cambridge, 2003) p.216.
49 G. F. Krivosheev (ed.), *Soviet Casualties and Combat Losses in the Twentieth Century* (London, 1997) p.94.
50 David M. Glantz and Jonathan House, *When Titans Clashed. How the Red Army Stopped Hitler* (Lawrence, KS, 1995) p.301.
51 Walter S. Dunn Jr, *Stalin's Keys to Victory. The Rebirth of the Red Army in WWII* (Mechanicsburg, PA, 2006) p.91. Jacques Sapir cites the lower figure of 17,500. Sapir, 'The Economics of War in the Soviet Union during World War II', p.217.
52 Lyons (ed.), *The Russian Version of the Second World War*, p.30.
53 By the time of the German invasion the Red Army had suffered the loss of an estimated 75,000–80,000 officers with some 30,000 imprisoned or executed. Specifically, this included 3 of 5 marshals, all 11 deputy defence commissars, all commanders of the military districts, 14 of 16 army commanders, 60 of 67 corps commanders and 136 of 199 divisional commanders. Glantz and House, *When Titans Clashed*, p.11.
54 Lieutenant-General Ivan Boldin wrote that the orders he received in June 1941 'gave my non-existent assault group one combat order after another, without being in the least interested in whether they reached me or not, and without worrying if they were realistic or not in view of the situation that had arisen on the Western Front'. According to Boldin, the reaction of field commanders

was calculated to ensure that Moscow would be convinced that drastic steps were being taken to halt the German advance. As cited in: Bernd Bonwetsch, 'The Purge of the Military and the Red Army's Operational Capability during the Great Patriotic War' in Bernd Wegner (ed.), *From Peace to War. Germany, Soviet Russia and the World, 1939–1941* (Oxford, 1997) p.411.

55 Glantz, *Barbarossa*, pp.62–63.

56 Roger R. Reese, *Stalin's Reluctant Soldiers. A Social History of the Red Army 1925–1941* (Lawrence, KS, 1996) p.188.

57 As cited in: Richard Overy, *Russia's War* (London, 1997) p.33.

58 Otherwise referred to as 'deep battle', this concept arose in the 1920s and 1930s from reforms to the Soviet operational art as emphasized by Mikhail Frunze, Vladimir Triandafillov and Mikhail Tukhachevsky. The emphasis was first on breaking through the enemy front (tactical deep battle) and then on using uncommitted reserves to achieve wide-ranging strategic depth in the enemy's rear (deep battle operations).

59 A report from 15 June 1941 stated that of the great mass of T-26s and BT models, 29 per cent were in need of capital repair and 44 per cent of lesser maintenance, making a total of 73 per cent. David M. Glantz, *Stumbling Colossus. The Red Army on the Eve of World War* (Lawrence, KS, 1998) pp.117–118.

60 Ibid., pp.116–118.

61 Ibid., pp.110–116.

62 Ibid., pp.187–193. See also: John Erickson, *The Soviet High Command. A Military-Political History 1918–1941* (London, 1962) p.583.

63 Reese, *Stalin's Reluctant Soldiers*, p.199.

64 Catherine Merridale, *Ivan's War. Life and Death in the Red Army, 1939–1945* (New York, 2006) p.89.

65 John Barber and Mark Harrison, *The Soviet Home Front 1941–1945. A Social and Economic History of the USSR in World War II* (London, 1991) p.60.

66 Mikhail M. Gorinov, 'Muscovites' Moods, 22 June 1941 to May 1942' in Robert Thurston and Bernd Bonwetsch (eds.), *The People's War. Responses to World War II in the Soviet Union* (Chicago, 2000) p.131.

67 As cited in: Albert Axell, *Russia's Heroes 1941–45* (New York, 2001) p.1.

68 Ibid.

69 Gennadi Bordiugov, 'The Popular Mood in the Unoccupied Soviet Union: Continuity and Change during the War' in Thurston and Bonwetsch (eds.), *The People's War*, p.68.

70 Alexander Werth, *Russia at War 1941–1945* (New York, 1964) p.xvi.

71 Even Tsar Alexander I's imperial manifesto appealing for a patriotic war against Napoleon was not without precedent in Russian history and harked back to the so-called Time of Troubles two hundred years before when

Russian society was roused to prevent a Polish prince from ascending to the throne. Dominic Lieven, *Russia against Napoleon. The Battle for Europe, 1807 to 1814* (London, 2010) p.217.

72 Barber and Harrison, *The Soviet Home Front 1941–1945*, p.68.

73 Mark von Hagen, 'Soviet Soldiers and Officers on the Eve of the German Invasion: Towards a Description of Social Psychology and Political Attitudes' in Thurston and Bonwetsch (eds.), *The People's War*, p.200.

74 For a more detailed look at these problems see Part II of my preceding volume, *Operation Barbarossa and Germany's Defeat in the East.*

75 Robert Thurston, 'Cauldrons of Loyalty and Betrayal: Soviet Soldiers' Behavior, 1941 and 1945' in Thurston and Bonwetsch (eds.), *The People's War*, p.236, see also footnote 7.

76 Ibid., p.235 and footnote 2.

77 Christian Streit, *Keine Kameraden: Die Wehrmacht und die sowjetischen Kriegsgefangenen 1941–1945* (Bonn, 1997) p.83. The remaining 900,000 Soviet POWs no doubt included a percentage of deserters, but German military files do not report this as a mass phenomenon.

78 Thurston, 'Cauldrons of Loyalty and Betrayal', p.239.

79 Christian Hartmann, *Wehrmacht im Ostkrieg. Front und militärisches Hinterland 1941/42* (Munich, 2010) pp.259–267; Axell, *Russia's Heroes, 1941–45*, chapter 2: 'The Hero Fortress'; Harrison E. Salisbury, *The Unknown War* (London, 1978) chapter 3: 'Bravery at Brest'. See also the first-hand accounts provided in: Robert Kershaw, *War without Garlands. Operation Barbarossa 1941/42* (New York, 2000) pp.47–51, 59–60, 65–67 and 78–79; and Constantine Pleshakov, *Stalin's Folly. The Tragic First Ten Days of WWII on the Eastern Front* (New York, 2005) pp.238–245.

80 Anatoli G. Chor'kov, 'The Red Army during the Initial Phase of the Great Patriotic War' in Bernd Wegner (ed.), *From Peace to War. Germany, Soviet Russia and the World, 1939–1941* (Oxford, 1997) pp.424–425.

81 Thurston, 'Cauldrons of Loyalty and Betrayal', p.241.

82 Mark Harrison, '"Barbarossa". The Soviet Response, 1941' in Wegner (ed.), *From Peace to War*, p.446.

83 Glantz, *Stumbling Colossus*, p.30.

84 David M. Glantz, *Colossus Reborn. The Red Army at War, 1941–1943* (Lawrence, KS, 2005) p.378.

85 Marius Broekmeyer, *Stalin, the Russians, and their War 1941–1945* (London, 2004) p.169.

86 Ibid., p.168.

87 Soviet penal battalions formally began in the summer of 1942, but the fronts more than likely operated 'disciplinary battalions' (the pre-war variant) in 1941. My thanks to David Glantz for his assistance on this matter.

88 Broekmeyer, *Stalin, the Russians, and their War 1941–1945*, pp.170–179.

89 For more on the mass murders perpetrated within the Soviet state before the war see: Timothy Snyder, *Bloodlands. Europe between Hitler and Stalin* (New York, 2010) chapters 1–3.

90 The Soviet occupations of eastern Poland, the Baltic States, Bessarabia and Northern Bukovina led to numerous officially sanctioned war crimes. While there is also certainly plenty of evidence of war crimes by members of the Red Army between June 1941 and May 1945, especially during the march across East Prussia in 1944–1945, there is no evidence to suggest that this was part of a state-sponsored campaign (although one can say certain excesses were tolerated) similar to Nazi Germany's war of annihilation in the Soviet Union.

91 Merridale, *Ivan's War*, p.125.

92 Overy, *Russia's War*, pp.79–80; Alexander Hill, *The Great Patriotic War of the Soviet Union, 1941–45. A Documentary Reader* (Abingdon and New York, 2009) pp.49–50.

93 Glantz and House, *When Titans Clashed*, pp.67–68.

94 Glantz, *Colossus Reborn*, p.538.

95 Glantz and House, *When Titans Clashed*, pp.68–70. It must be remembered that German and Soviet armies cannot be directly compared in terms of size, organization or quality.

96 Dunn, *Stalin's Keys to Victory*, p.10. See also: Walter S. Dunn Jr, *Hitler's Nemesis. The Red Army, 1930–45* (Mechanicsburg, PA, 2009) chapter 3: 'Wartime Mobilization'.

97 Ibid., pp.91 and 93.

98 Glantz, *Colossus Reborn*, p.247; David M. Glantz, 'Introduction: Prelude to Barbarossa. The Red Army in 1941' in David M. Glantz (ed.), *The Initial Period of War on the Eastern Front 22 June–August 1941* (London, 1993) p.33. See also: Merridale, *Ivan's War*, p.103.

99 Mark Harrison, *Soviet Planning in Peace and War 1938–1945* (Cambridge, 2002) p.92.

100 Colonel-General Ewald von Kleist commented after the war: '[The Soviet] equipment was very good even in 1941, especially the tanks. Their artillery was excellent, and also most of the infantry weapons – their rifles were more modern than ours, and had a more rapid rate of fire.' As cited in: Basil Liddell Hart, *The Other Side of the Hill* (London, 1999) p.330. See also: Erhard Raus, 'Russian Combat Methods in World War II' in Peter G. Tsouras (ed.), *Fighting in Hell. The German Ordeal on the Eastern Front* (New York, 1998) pp.35–36 (one should note that Raus's name is incorrectly spelled Rauss in this title); R. Koch-Erpach, '4th Panzer Division's Crossing of the Dnepr River and the Advance to Roslavl' in Glantz (ed.), *The Initial Period of War on the Eastern Front*, p.404.

101 In addition the Soviets began producing the T-60 light tank in 1941, which had a crew of two, a 20mm gun, 15–35mm armour and a total weight of just 6.4 tons. Dunn Jr., *Hitler's Nemesis*, p.119.
102 Jacob Kipp, 'Overview Phase 1: to 20 July 1941' in Glantz (ed.), *The Initial Period of War on the Eastern Front*, p.371. See also: Glantz, *Colossus Reborn*, p.307.
103 Von Hardesty, *Red Phoenix. The Rise of Soviet Air Power 1941–1945* (Washington, DC, 1982) p.170. In an open letter to factory workers early in the war Stalin remarked that the Il-2 *Shturmovik* was 'as essential to the Red Army as air and bread'.
104 Harrison, '"Barbarossa". The Soviet Response, 1941', p.439.
105 Jacob W. Kipp, 'Barbarossa, Soviet Covering Forces and the Initial Period of War: Military History and Airland Battle' (Foreign Military Studies Office, Fort Leavenworth, 1989) pp.7–8, available at http://fmso.leavenworth.army.mil/fmsopubs/issues/barbaros.htm.
106 Barber and Harrison, *The Soviet Home Front 1941–1945*, p.127.
107 Glantz and House, *When Titans Clashed*, p.71.
108 Harrison, *Soviet Planning in Peace and War 1938–1945*, p.73.
109 Alec Nove, 'Soviet Peasantry in World War II' in Susan J. Linz (ed.), *The Impact of World War II on the Soviet Union* (Totowa, NJ, 1985) pp.81–82.
110 Glantz and House, *When Titans Clashed*, pp.71–72.
111 As cited in: Barber and Harrison, *The Soviet Home Front 1941–1945*, p.131.
112 Harrison, *Soviet Planning in Peace and War 1938–1945*, p.78.
113 Overy, *Why the Allies Won*, p.184.
114 Bellamy, *Absolute War*, p.220.
115 Harrison, *Soviet Planning in Peace and War 1938–1945*, p.78.
116 Barber and Harrison, *The Soviet Home Front 1941–1945*, p.130.
117 Werth, *Russia at War 1941–1945*, p.216.
118 For the best study of the human dimension of the evacuation see: Rebecca Manley, *To the Tashkent Station. Evacuation and Survival in the Soviet Union at War* (Ithaca, NY, 2009).
119 Ibid., p.219. Soviet wartime reports claim that most evacuated factories were operational again in six to eight weeks, but according to John Barber and Mark Harrison this must be seen as a minimum. Barber and Harrison, *The Soviet Home Front 1941–1945*, p.139.
120 M. R. D. Foot, 'USSR' in Dear and Foot (eds.), *The Oxford Companion to the Second World War*, Table 7: 'Production of New Weapons', p.1231.
121 '"Barbarossa". The Soviet Response, 1941', p.440.
122 Overy, *Russia's War*, Table I: 'Soviet and German Wartime Production 1941–45', p.155.
123 Foot, 'USSR', Table 7: 'Production of New Weapons', p.1231.

124 Overy, *Russia's War*, Table I: 'Soviet and German Wartime Production 1941–45', p.155.
125 Sapir, 'The Economics of War in the Soviet Union during World War II', p.232.
126 The success of the large-scale Soviet offensives from the summer of 1943 onwards was largely made possible by the quantity of American trucks supplied under the Lend-Lease programme.
127 For problems of German standardization see: Overy, *Why the Allies Won*, p.217.
128 Dunn, *Stalin's Keys to Victory*, pp.25–26.
129 For a detailed look at the remarkable expansion of the Soviet economy in the interwar years see: R. W. Davies, Mark Harrison and S. G. Wheatcroft (eds.), *The Economic Transformation of the Soviet Union, 1913–1945* (Cambridge, 1994).
130 Harrison, *Soviet Planning in Peace and War 1938–1945*, p.86.
131 Harrison, '"Barbarossa". The Soviet Response, 1941', p.441.
132 Barber and Harrison, *The Soviet Home Front 1941–1945*, p.127; Harrison, *Soviet Planning in Peace and War 1938–1945*, p.72. Walter Dunn suggests a far lower figure, claiming that millions of people fled German occupation and that only about 60 million remained in the occupied zone. Dunn, *Hitler's Nemesis*, p.42.
133 Barber and Harrison, *The Soviet Home Front 1941–1945*, pp.157 and 186–187.
134 Harrison, *Soviet Planning in Peace and War 1938–1945*, p.91; Barber and Harrison, *The Soviet Home Front 1941–1945*, p.141.
135 Barber and Harrison, *The Soviet Home Front 1941–1945*, p.160.
136 In 1942 the defence and heavy industries counted 40–50 per cent of their workers as under twenty-five years of age. Ibid., pp.175–176.
137 Overy, *Why the Allies Won*, pp.188–189.
138 Ibid., p.187; Overy, *Russia's War*, p.80.
139 Barber and Harrison, *The Soviet Home Front 1941–1945*, p.220.
140 In 1944 N. A. Bulganin was also inducted as a member. Hill, *The Great Patriotic War of the Soviet Union*, p.271.
141 Rodric Braithwaite, *Moscow 1941. A City and its People at War* (New York, 2006) p.84.
142 Harrison, *Soviet Planning in Peace and War 1938–1945*, p.94.
143 Erickson, *The Road to Stalingrad*, p.136.
144 Glantz, *Barbarossa*, pp.59–60.
145 Ibid., pp.61–62; Glantz and House, *When Titans Clashed*, p.63.
146 Glantz, *Barbarossa*, p.64.
147 Ibid., pp.64–65; Glantz and House, *When Titans Clashed*, pp.65–66.

148 Glantz, *Barbarossa*, p.62.

149 Krivosheev gives the figure of 3,137,673 irrecoverable losses. Krivosheev (ed.), *Soviet Casualties and Combat Losses in the Twentieth Century*, p.94.

150 Cynthia Simmons and Nina Perlina, *Writing the Siege of Leningrad. Women's Diaries, Memoirs, and Documentary Prose* (Pittsburgh, 2002) p.98.

151 For more on this see: Glantz, *Stumbling Colossus*, pp.60–62; Dunn, *Stalin's Keys to Victory*, p.16.

2 Germany's defeat in the east

1 The concept of a 'railway advance' came from German experiences in Russia during 1918 when the absence of resistance enabled German soldiers simply to ride the Russian railways from one station to the next, capturing towns and soldiers. See: John Keegan, *The First World War* (New York, 2000) p.382.

2 Alan S. Milward, *The German Economy at War* (London, 1965).

3 Richard Overy, 'Hitler's War Plans and the German Economy' in Robert Boyce and Esmonde M. Robertson (eds.), *Path to War. New Essays on the Origins of the Second World War* (London, 1989) pp.96–127.

4 See Müller's contributions in Militärgeschichtliches Forschungsamt (ed.), *Das Deutsche Reich und der Zweite Weltkrieg. Band.5/1. Organisation und Mobilisierung des deutschen Machtbereichs. Erster Halbband: Kriegsverwaltung, Wirtschaft und Personelle Ressourcen 1939–1941* (Stuttgart, 1988).

5 Adam Tooze, *The Wages of Destruction. The Making and Breaking of the Nazi Economy* (London, 2006) p.667.

6 These are published in: Rolf Wagenführ, *Die deutsche Industrie im Kriege, 1939 bis 1945* (Berlin, 1954).

7 Tooze, *The Wages of Destruction*, p.667.

8 Gerhard Schreiber, 'Mussolini's "Non-Belligerence"' in Militärgeschichtliches Forschungsamt (ed.), *Germany and the Second World War. Volume III*, p.29.

9 Werner Abelshauser, 'Germany: Guns, Butter, and Economic Miracles' in Mark Harrison (ed.), *The Economics of World War II. Six Great Powers in International Comparison* (Cambridge, 2000) p.156.

10 Tooze, *The Wages of Destruction*, chapter 13: 'Preparing for Two Wars at Once'.

11 Rolf-Dieter Müller, 'The Victor's Hubris: Germany Loses its Lead in Armaments after the French Campaign' in Militärgeschichtliches Forschungsamt (ed.), *Germany and the Second World War. Volume V/I.*

Organization and Mobilization of the German Sphere of Power (Oxford, 2000) p.564.

12 During the period October 1940–April 1941 the year-on-year increase in weapons and armaments for the army was 54 per cent, aircraft for the Luftwaffe increased by 40 per cent and the navy's U-boat production tripled. Tooze, *The Wages of Destruction*, p.435.

13 Ibid., p.411.

14 Schreiber, 'Mussolini's "Non-Belligerence"', pp.25–27.

15 Mark Mazower, *Hitler's Empire. Nazi Rule in Occupied Europe* (London, 2009) p.271.

16 For a good discussion of Germany's fuel shortages in the east during 1941 see: Joel Hayward, *Stopped at Stalingrad. The Luftwaffe and Hitler's Defeat in the East, 1942–1943* (Lawrence, KS, 1998) pp.5–12.

17 Tooze, *The Wages of Destruction*, p.412.

18 Ibid., pp.413–414.

19 Roderick Kedward, 'France' in I. C. B. Dear and M. R. D. Foot (eds.), *The Oxford Companion to the Second World War* (Oxford, 1995) p.393.

20 Schreiber, 'Mussolini's "Non-Belligerence"', p.29.

21 Tooze, *The Wages of Destruction*, pp.415–418.

22 Only in Norway and Denmark, two of the smallest economies in the German sphere of control, did growth remain steady. Ibid., p.420.

23 Mazower, *Hitler's Empire*, p.272. For the role of Europe in Hitler's plans for empire see: Michael Burleigh, *The Third Reich. A New History* (London, 2001) pp.425–426.

24 Alex J. Kay, *Exploitation, Resettlement, Mass Murder. Political and Economic Planning for German Occupation Policy in the Soviet Union, 1940–1941* (Oxford, 2006) pp.41–42, see also footnote 85.

25 Numerous reports of the SD make reference to this and in November 1940 one stated that the concern of the population was being 'unanimously stressed'. See: Kay, *Exploitation, Resettlement, Mass Murder*, pp.49–50.

26 Franz Halder, *Kriegstagebuch: Tägliche Aufzeichnungen des Chefs des Generalstabes des Heeres 1939–1942. Band II. Von der geplanten Landung in England bis zum Beginn des Ostfeldzuges (1.7.1940–21.6.1941)*, (ed.) Hans-Adolf Jacobsen (Stuttgart, 1963) p.240 (23 December 1940).

27 Tooze, *The Wages of Destruction*, p.419.

28 Mark Mazower, *Inside Hitler's Greece. The Experience of Occupation 1941–1944* (New Haven, 2001) chapter 3: 'The Famine'.

29 Rolf-Dieter Müller, 'From Economic Alliance to a War of Colonial Exploitation' in Militärgeschichtliches Forschungsamt (ed.), *Germany and the Second World War. Volume IV*, p.187.

30 Tooze, *The Wages of Destruction*, p.437.

31 Bernhard R. Kroener, 'Squaring the Circle: Blitzkrieg Strategy and the Manpower Shortage, 1939–1942' in Wilhelm Deist (ed.), *The German Military in the Age of Total War* (Leamington Spa, 1985) pp.295–296.
32 Bernhard R. Kroener, 'The "Frozen Blitzkrieg": German Strategic Planning against the Soviet Union and the Causes of its Failure' in Bernd Wegner (ed.), *From Peace to War. Germany, Soviet Russia and the World, 1939–1941* (Oxford, 1997) pp.142–143.
33 Müller, 'From Economic Alliance to a War of Colonial Exploitation', pp.200–201.
34 Rudolf Steiger, *Armour Tactics in the Second World War. Panzer Army Campaigns of 1939–41 in German War Diaries* (Oxford, 1991) p.127.
35 Omer Bartov, *Hitler's Army. Soldiers, Nazis, and War in the Third Reich* (Oxford, 1992) chapter 1: 'The Demodernization of the Front'.
36 Alan S. Milward, *War, Economy and Society 1939–1945* (Berkeley, CA, 1979) pp.79–80.
37 Müller, 'From Economic Alliance to a War of Colonial Exploitation', p.218.
38 Tooze, *The Wages of Destruction*, p.435.
39 This was also a point that Todt was wary of when cuts were being made in munitions output during September 1940. Müller, 'From Economic Alliance to a War of Colonial Exploitation', p.202.
40 Max Domarus, *Hitler. Speeches and Proclamations 1932–1945. The Chronicle of a Dictatorship. Volume IV. The Years 1941 to 1945* (Wauconda, IL, 2004) p.2494 (3 October 1941).
41 See Müller, 'From Economic Alliance to a War of Colonial Exploitation', p.217, Table I.III.2: 'Armament Production by the Great Powers, 1940–1941'. See also: Rolf-Dieter Müller, 'The Crippling of Armaments Production' in Militärgeschichtliches Forschungsamt (ed.), *Germany and the Second World War. Volume V/I*, p.608, Table II.V.4: 'Armament Production by the Great Powers, 1940–1941'.
42 Abelshauser, 'Germany: Guns, Butter, and Economic Miracles', p.155. Although the Volkswagen plant at Wolfsburg was eventually adapted for military manufacture only one-fifth of its capacity was utilized for production. Even then only a few thousand vehicles were produced, which the army accepted, but didn't regard highly. Most of the production at the plant concerned items such as camp stoves for the army or military issue foot warmers. See Overy, *Why the Allies Won*, p.202.
43 Müller, 'From Economic Alliance to a War of Colonial Exploitation', p.188; Abelshauser, 'Germany: Guns, Butter, and Economic Miracles', p.156.
44 Overy, *Why the Allies Won*, p.202.
45 Albert Speer, *Inside the Third Reich* (London, 1971) p.259. For more on Hitler's building plans see: Mazower, *Hitler's Empire*, pp.124–126.

46 Overy, *Why the Allies Won*, p.206.
47 Tooze, *The Wages of Destruction*, p.423; Müller, 'From Economic Alliance to a War of Colonial Exploitation', p.193.
48 Müller, 'From Economic Alliance to a War of Colonial Exploitation', pp.203–206.
49 Georg Thomas, *Geschichte der deutsch Wehr- und Rüstungswirtschaft (1918–1943/45)*, (ed.) Wolfgang Birkenfeld (Boppard am Rhein, 1966) pp.436–437.
50 As cited in: Müller, 'From Economic Alliance to a War of Colonial Exploitation', pp.209–210 and 212.
51 Hugh R. Trevor-Roper (ed.), *Hitler's War Directives 1939–1945* (London, 1964) p.130 (11 June 1941).
52 Ibid., p.137 (14 July 1941).
53 Thousands of trucks were seized from the civilian economy or purchased from allied or neutral countries, yet many of these were older model vehicles and few were suited to the demands of a campaign in the east.
54 Kroener, 'The "Frozen Blitzkrieg"', p.144.
55 Müller, 'From Economic Alliance to a War of Colonial Exploitation', p.220.
56 Burleigh, *The Third Reich*, pp.491–492.
57 Domarus, *Hitler*, pp.2509–2510 (8 November 1941).
58 Tooze, *The Wages of Destruction*, pp.447–449.
59 Thomas, *Geschichte der deutsch Wehr- und Rüstungswirtschaft (1918–1943/45)*, p.467.
60 Milward, *War, Economy and Society 1939–1945*, p.57.
61 Hardesty, *Red Phoenix*, p.63. Peter I (the Great) made a similar deduction upon facing the invading Swedish army of Charles XII in 1708. William C. Fuller Jr, *Strategy and Power in Russia 1600–1914* (New York, 1992) pp.80–83.
62 Glantz, *Barbarossa*, p.68.
63 As cited in: Liddell Hart, *The Other Side of the Hill*, p.265.
64 Finland and Spain never formally joined the Axis.
65 H. F. Hinsley, 'British Intelligence and Barbarossa' in John Erickson and David Dilks (eds.), *Barbarossa. The Axis and the Allies* (Edinburgh, 1998) p.72; Andreas Hillgruber, *Hitlers Strategie. Politik und Kriegführung 1940–1941* (Bonn, 1993) pp.444, footnote 93, and 558.
66 As cited in: Sönke Neitzel, *Tapping Hitler's Generals. Transcripts of Secret Conversations, 1942–45* (St Paul, MN, 2007) p.112, Document 44 (14–17 October 1944).
67 William Shirer, *The Rise and Fall of the Third Reich* (New York, 1960) p.1119. References to 'Russia' and 'the Russians' are common throughout a large selection of the primary source literature and have been maintained in this study in all direct quotations. I, however, prefer to refer to 'the Soviet Union' since the country was an amalgamation of many different ethnic and

national groups; exceptions are only made when the matter refers to a specific national group.

68 Distances are worked out along the north–south lines of the respective army groups or 'as the crow flies'; thus, real distances were somewhat longer in practice.

69 Mawdsley, *Thunder in the East*, pp.75–76.

70 Bellamy, *Absolute War*, p.181.

71 Glantz, *Stumbling Colossus*, pp.116–118.

72 For a good overview of the opening border battles in Army Group South's sector see: David M. Glantz, 'The Border Battles on the Lutsk–Rovno Axis: 22 June–1 July 1941' in David M. Glantz (ed.), *The Initial Period of War on the Eastern Front 22 June–August 1941* (London, 1997) pp.248–288.

73 Victor J. Kamenir, *The Bloody Triangle. The Defeat of Soviet Armor in the Ukraine, June 1941* (Minneapolis, 2008) p.144.

74 Ibid., p.147.

75 Glantz and House, *When Titans Clashed*, p.54.

76 *True to Type. A Selection from Letters and Diaries of German Soldiers and Civilians Collected on the Soviet–German Front* (London, n.d.) p.20 (26 June 1941). This book makes no reference to its editor or date of publication.

77 Karl Wilhelm Thilo, 'A Perspective from the Army High Command (OKH)' in Glantz (ed.), *The Initial Period of War on the Eastern Front*, p.298 (26 June 1941).

78 Ingeborg Ochsenknecht, '*Als ob der Schnee alles zudeckte*'. *Eine Krankenschwester erinnert sich an ihren Kriegseinsatz an der Ostfront* (Berlin, 2005) p.68.

79 David M. Glantz, *Atlas and Operational Summary. The Border Battles 22 June–1 July 1941* (Privately published by David M. Glantz, 2003) p.27.

80 Braithwaite, *Moscow 1941*, pp.77–78.

81 As cited in: Kamenir, *The Bloody Triangle*, p.141.

82 Halder, KTB III, p.16 (26 June 1941).

83 As cited in: Liddell Hart, *The Other Side of the Hill*, p.330.

84 H.C. Robbins Landon and Sebastian Leitner (eds.), *Diary of a German Soldier* (London, 1963) p.78 (7 July 1941).

85 Peter Bamm, *The Invisible Flag* (New York, 1958) p.43.

86 Heinz Guderian, 'III Panzer Corps Operations' in Glantz (ed.), *The Initial Period of War on the Eastern Front*, p.311.

87 Ibid. See also: Kamenir, *The Bloody Triangle*, p.245.

88 See, for example: Klaus J. Arnold, *Die Wehrmacht und die Besatzungspolitik in den besetzten Gebieten der Sowjetunion. Kriegführung und Radikalisierung im 'Unternehmen Barbarossa'* (Berlin, 2005).

89 See: Omer Bartov, *The Eastern Front, 1941–45. German Troops and the Barbarisation of Warfare* (London, 1985).

90 *True to Type*, p.21 (27 July 1941).

91 Landon and Leitner (eds.), *Diary of a German Soldier*, p.78 (7 July 1941).

92 Hannes Heer, 'How Amorality Became Normality. Reflections on the Mentality of German Soldiers on the Eastern Front' in Hannes Heer and Klaus Naumann (eds.), *War of Extermination. The German Military in World War II 1941–1944* (New York and Oxford, 2006) pp.329–344.

93 Christiane Sahm, *Verzweiflung und Glaube. Briefe aus dem Krieg 1939–1942* (Munich, 2007) p.41 (2 July 1941).

94 Konrad Elmshäuser and Jan Lokers (eds.), *'Man muß hier nur hart sein'. Kriegsbriefe und Bilder einer Familie (1934–1945)* (Bremen, 1999) p.86. (Hans-Albert Giese's calendar entries from 22 June to 13 September 1941 are recorded without specific dates.)

95 Willi Kubik, *Erinnerungen eines Panzerschützen 1941–1945. Tagebuchaufzeichnung eines Panzerschützen der Pz.Aufkl.Abt. 13 im Russlandfeldzug* (Würzburg, 2004) p.25 (30 June 1941).

96 Department of the US Army (ed.), *German Tank Maintenance in World War II* (Washington, DC, 1988) pp.2–3.

97 'KTB der Oberquartiermeisterabteilung der 1st Panzer-Armee 2.5.41–31.10.41', BA-MA RH 21–1/347, p.15 (3 July 1941).

98 Department of the US Army (ed.), *German Tank Maintenance in World War II*, p.44.

99 'Kriegstagebuch des Panzerarmee-Oberkdos.1 Band II 22.6.41–31.8.41', BA-MA RH 21–1/50, fol.39 (5 July 1941).

100 Rundstedt's letter is cited in: Johannes Hürter, *Hitlers Heerführer. Die deutschen Oberbefehlshaber im Krieg gegen die Sowjetunion 1941/42* (Munich, 2006) p.290, footnote 47.

101 Mawdsley, *Thunder in the East*, p.77.

102 Emphasis in the original. Thilo, 'A Perspective from the Army High Command (OKH)', pp.301–302 (8 July 1941).

103 In spite of such orders an appeal was made to Air Fleet 4 requesting that most of its tactical support be put at the disposal of the attack on Kiev and not the encirclement of Soviet forces. Klink, 'The Conduct of Operations', p.562.

104 As cited in: ibid., pp.562–563.

105 Halder, KTB III, p.60 (10 July 1941).

106 Not to be confused with the Western Bug River (commonly referred to as simply the Bug River) which formed part of the border between the German and Soviet forces until 22 June 1941.

107 Halder, KTB III, p.61 (10 July 1941).

108 Ibid., p.62 (10 July 1941).

109 As cited in: Klink, 'The Conduct of Operations', p.565.

110 Ibid. Such a deferral of command responsibility is in line with the German concept of '*Auftragstaktik*'.

111 Mawdsley, *Thunder in the East*, p.78.

112 Robert Kirchubel, *Operation Barbarossa 1941 (1): Army Group South* (Oxford, 2003) p.45.

113 Ibid., pp.57–58.

114 For a first-rate perspective on the problems of city fighting in Barbarossa see: Adrian Wettstein, 'Operation "Barbarossa" und Stadtkampf', *Militärgeschichtliche Zeitschrift*, Vol. 66 (2007) pp.21–44; Adrian Wettstein, 'Urban Warfare Doctrine on the Eastern Front' in Alex J. Kay, Jeff Rutherford and David Stahel (eds.), *Nazi Policy on the Eastern Front, 1941: Total War, Genocide and Radicalization* (forthcoming).

115 According to Heinz Magenheimer, 'A German leadership that would have been prepared to take political as well as military action in order to gain the goodwill of the population and future allies could have brought about Stalin's downfall.' Heinz Magenheimer, *Hitler's War. Germany's Key Strategic Decisions 1940–1945* (London, 1999) p.116.

116 According to German command reports and intelligence estimates around 90 per cent of the population exhibited a friendly disposition. Alex Alexiev, 'Soviet Nationals in German Wartime Service, 1941–1945' in Antonio Munoz (ed.), *Soviet Nationals in German Wartime Service 1941–1945* (n.p., 2007) p.13.

117 Karel C. Berkhoff, *Harvest of Despair. Life and Death in Ukraine under Nazi Rule* (Cambridge, MA, 2004) pp.20–21.

118 Antony Beevor and Luba Vinogradova (eds.), *A Writer at War. Vasily Grossman with the Red Army 1941–1945* (New York, 2005) p.38.

119 Bidermann, *In Deadly Combat*, p.43.

120 Helmut Günther, *Hot Motors, Cold Feet. A Memoir of Service with the Motorcycle Battalion of SS-Division 'Reich' 1940–1941* (Winnipeg, 2004) p.150.

121 Erich Kern, *Dance of Death* (New York, 1951) p.34.

122 For German pre-war economic planning and occupation policies see: Kay, *Exploitation, Resettlement, Mass Murder.*

123 Alex J. Kay, '"The Purpose of the Russian Campaign is the Decimation of the Slavic Population by Thirty Million": the Radicalisation of German Food Policy in Early 1941' in Kay *et al.* (eds.), *Nazi Policy on the Eastern Front, 1941.*

124 According to Hitler, 'Even when at first it appears easier to secure the military assistance of the subjugated peoples, it is wrong. They will inevitably turn against us some day. Therefore only the German should be armed, not the Slav, not the Czech, not the Cossack, not the Ukrainian.' Alexiev, 'Soviet Nationals in German Wartime Service, 1941–1945', p.30.

125 In many ways Hitler's perceived missed opportunity in 1941 echoes a similar, though equally ahistorical, missed opportunity in France's 1812

invasion of Russia. Criticisms of Napoleon's decision not to proclaim the emancipation of the serfs, and thereby attempt to shatter the very fabric of Russian society, take no account of Napoleon's far more limited war aims, nor the adverse bearing such a radical step would have had on the endurance of France's aristocratic alliances.

126 Kern, *Dance of Death*, p.45.

127 KTB OKW, Vol. II, p.560 (8 August 1941).

128 Rundstedt's letter is cited in: Hürter, *Hitlers Heerführer*, p.292; LH 15/4/40, 'The Germans in Russia', see the file entitled 'Von Rundstedt writes home' p.2 (12 August 1941).

129 Bamm, *The Invisible Flag*, pp.34–35.

130 *True to Type*, p.107 (2 August 1941).

131 Alois Scheuer, *Briefe aus Russland. Feldpostbriefe des Gefreiten Alois Scheuer 1941–1942* (St Ingbert, 2000) p.26 (26 July 1941).

132 Kern, *Dance of Death*, p.20.

133 Klink, 'The Conduct of Operations', p.560.

134 Bidermann, *In Deadly Combat*, pp.25 and 27.

135 Williamson Murray and Allan R. Millett, *A War to be Won. Fighting the Second World War* (Cambridge, MA, 2000) p.126.

136 *True to Type*, p.21 (8 August 1941).

137 'KTB der Oberquartiermeisterabteilung der 1st Panzer-Armee 2.5.41–31.10.41', BA-MA RH 21–1/347, p.26 (28 July 1941). For more on the problems of the *Grosstransportraum* see: Ferdinand Prinz von der Leyen, *Rückblick zum Mauerwald. Vier Kriegsjahre im OKH* (Munich, 1965) pp.19–20.

138 Curzio Malaparte, *The Volga Rises in Europe* (Edinburgh, 2000) p.54 (7 July 1941).

139 Halder, KTB III, p.167 (10 August 1941).

140 Halder, KTB III, p.145 (2 August 1941).

141 Martin Gareis, *Kampf und Ende der Fränkisch-Sudetendeutschen 98. Infanterie-Division* (Eggolsheim, 1956) p.103.

142 Halder, KTB III, p.172 (11 August 1941).

143 Walter Bähr and Hans Bähr (eds.), *Kriegsbriefe Gefallener Studenten, 1939–1945* (Tübingen and Stuttgart, 1952) pp.414–415 (3 August 1941).

144 *True to Type*, p.9 (10 August 1941).

145 Landon and Leitner (eds.), *Diary of a German Soldier*, p.90 (4 August 1941).

146 Hermann Plocher, *The German Air Force versus Russia, 1941* (New York, 1965) p.51.

147 For some examples from the Ukraine see: Artem Drabkin (ed.), *The Red Air Force at War. Barbarossa and the Retreat to Moscow. Recollections of Fighter Pilots on the Eastern Front* (Barnsley, 2007) pp.67–69.

148 Kamenir, *The Bloody Triangle*, p.228.

149 James S. Corum, *Wolfram von Richthofen. Master of the German Air War* (Lawrence, KS, 2008) pp.265–267.
150 Plocher, *The German Air Force versus Russia, 1941*, p.65.
151 Kubik, *Erinnerungen eines Panzerschützen 1941–1945*, p.69 (21 August 1941).
152 Glantz, *Stumbling Colossus*, p.187.
153 Between July and December 1941 the Soviet Union produced some 5,173 modern fighters, easily surpassing the Luftwaffe's 1,619 fighters. Richard Overy, *The Air War 1939–1945* (London, 1980) p.49.
154 Glantz, *Stumbling Colossus*, p.187.
155 Hardesty, *Red Phoenix*, p.59.
156 As cited in: Liddell Hart, *The Other Side of the Hill*, p.266.
157 Emphasis in the original. Berkhoff, *Harvest of Despair*, pp.17–18.
158 Ibid., pp.18–24.
159 For a background to Romania's involvement in the war against the Soviet Union see: Dennis Deletant, 'German–Romanian Relations, 1941–1945' in Jonathan Adelman (ed.), *Hitler and his Allies in World War II* (New York, 2007) pp.166–176.
160 For Hungary's desire for war between Germany and the Soviet Union see: Attila Pok, 'German–Hungarian Relations, 1941–1945' in Adelman (ed.), *Hitler and his Allies in World War II*, pp.156–158; Miklós Szinai and László Szúcs (eds.), *The Confidential Papers of Admiral Horthy* (Budapest, 1965) pp.179–182, Document 42.
161 For Slovakia's path to war see: Mark Axworthy, *Axis Slovakia. Hitler's Slavic Wedge 1938–1945* (New York, 2002) chapter 2: 'The Axis Straight Jacket Tightens: Slovakia Groomed for War, 1939–1941'.
162 For Italy's decision to join the war see: Brian R. Sullivan, 'The Path Marked out by History: the German–Italian Alliance, 1939–1943' in Adelman (ed.), *Hitler and his Allies in World War II*, pp.116–132.
163 Dennis Deletant, *Hitler's Forgotten Ally. Ion Antonescu and his Regime, Romania 1940–1944* (London, 2006) pp.81–82 and 116–120.
164 Richard L. DiNardo, *Germany and the Axis Powers. From Coalition to Collapse* (Lawrence, KS, 2005) p.122.
165 Ibid., p.124. Halder, KTB III, pp.217–218 (9 September 1941).
166 Walter Görlitz (ed.), *The Memoirs of Field-Marshal Keitel. Chief of the German High Command, 1938–1945* (New York, 1966) p.157.
167 For an assessment of the Romanian army from the Chief of Staff of the German army mission to Romania, Colonel Arthur Hauffe, see: Deletant, *Hitler's Forgotten Ally*, p.77.
168 Mark Axworthy, Cornel Scafes and Cristian Craciunoiu, *Third Axis Fourth Ally. Romanian Armed Forces in the European War, 1941–1945* (London, 1995) pp.49–51.

169 Rolf-Dieter Müller, *An der Seite der Wehrmacht. Hitlers ausländische Helfer beim 'Kreuzzug gegen den Bolschewismus' 1941–1945* (Berlin, 2007) pp.42 and 101.
170 For Germany's failure in this regard see: Richard L. DiNardo, 'The Dysfunctional Coalition: the Axis Powers and the Eastern Front in World War II', *Journal of Military History*, Vol. 60, No. 4 (October 1996) pp.718–720.
171 Görlitz (ed.), *The Memoirs of Field-Marshal Keitel*, p.159.
172 Glantz, *Barbarossa*, pp.125–127; Earl F. Ziemke and Magna E. Bauer, *Moscow to Stalingrad: Decision in the East* (New York, 1988) pp.32–33.
173 Order published in Werner Haupt, *Army Group South. The Wehrmacht in Russia 1941–1945* (Atglen, PA, 1998) pp.46–47.
174 Ibid., p.47.
175 '11.Pz.Div. KTB Abt. Ia vom 1.5.41–21.10.41', BA-MA RH 27–11/16, fol.107 (17 August 1941).
176 Franz Halder, KTB III, p.202 (28 August 1941).
177 'KTB der Oberquartiermeisterabteilung der 1st Panzer-Armee 2.5.41–31.10.41', BA-MA RH 21–1/347, p.35 (20 August 1941).
178 For one unvarnished account of Germany's dire circumstances see the diary of Ulrich von Hassell, *Vom Andern Deutschland* (Freiburg, 1946). For the English translation see: Ulrich von Hassell, *The von Hassell Diaries 1938–1944* (London, 1948).

3 The road to Kiev

1 Viktor Anfilov, 'Zhukov' in Harold Shukman (ed.), *Stalin's Generals* (London, 1993) pp.348–349.
2 Erickson, *The Road to Stalingrad*, pp.177–178; G. K. Zhukov, *The Memoirs of Marshal Zhukov* (London, 1971) pp.286–289.
3 Glantz, *Barbarossa*, pp.85–86.
4 Erickson, *The Road to Stalingrad*, p.178. See also: Otto Preston Chaney, *Zhukov* (Norman, OK, 1996) pp.121–122.
5 Anfilov, 'Zhukov', p.349.
6 For the details of the meeting see: Stahel, *Operation Barbarossa and Germany's Defeat in the East*, chapter 10: 'Showdown'.
7 Emphasis in the original. As cited in: Liddell Hart, *The Other Side of the Hill*, p.275.
8 Ibid., p.276; LH 15/4/40, 'The Germans in Russia': see the untitled essay from Blumentritt pp.11–12. Whatever Kluge's personal feelings he was also without a command between the dissolution of the Fourth Panzer Army in late July and the reconstitution of the Fourth Army, of which Kluge assumed

command on 27 August 1941. This suggests a contrasting explanation for Kluge's absence and may indicate Blumentritt had his own axe to grind with his former commander.

9 'Kriegstagebuch Nr.1 (Band August 1941) des Oberkommandos der Heeresgruppe Mitte', BA-MA RH 19-II/386, p.375 (24 August 1941).
10 Heinz Guderian, *Panzer Leader* (New York, 1996) p.202.
11 Franz Halder, *Hitler als Feldherr* (Munich, 1949) p.43.
12 Fedor von Bock, *Generalfeldmarschall Fedor von Bock. The War Diary 1939–1945*, (ed.) Klaus Gerbet (Munich, 1996) p.292 (24 August 1941). Hereafter references for Bock's diary will be cited as Bock, *War Diary.*
13 Albrecht Kesselring, *The Memoirs of Field-Marshal Kesselring* (London, 1988) p.98.
14 Heusinger's letter as cited in: Georg Meyer, *Adolf Heusinger. Dienst eines deutschen Soldaten 1915 bis 1964* (Berlin, 2001) p.158 (27 August 1941).
15 Rochus Misch, *Der letzte Zeuge. Ich war Hitlers Telefonist, Kurier und Leibwächter* (Munich, 2009) p.133.
16 Heusinger's letter as cited in: Meyer, *Adolf Heusinger*, p.158 (27 August 1941).
17 Walter Warlimont, *Im Hauptquartier der deutschen Wehrmacht 1939 bis 1945. Band I. September 1939–November 1942* (Koblenz, 1990) p.205. English translation: Walter Warlimont, *Inside Hitler's Headquarters, 1939–1945* (New York, 1964) p.191.
18 Jürgen Löffler, *Walter von Brauchitsch (1881–1948)* (Frankfurt am Main, 2001) p.250.
19 KTB OKW, Vol. II, pp.1063–1068, Document 100 (22 August 1941).
20 Warlimont, *Im Hauptquartier der deutschen Wehrmacht 1939 bis 1945*, p.205; Warlimont, *Inside Hitler's Headquarters, 1939–1945*, pp.191–192.
21 Hildegard von Kotze (ed.), *Heeresadjutant bei Hitler 1938–1943. Aufzeichnungen des Majors Engel* (Stuttgart, 1974) pp.110–111 (21 August 1941). Engel's book, although presented in the form of a diary, was in fact written after the war from his personal notes.
22 Glantz, *The Battle for Smolensk*, p.62.
23 Bock, *War Diary*, p.287 (19 August 1941).
24 Glantz, *The Battle for Smolensk*, p.62.
25 Bock, *War Diary*, p.287 (19–20 August 1941).
26 '3rd Pz. Gr. KTB 25.5.41–31.8.41', BA-MA Microfilm 59054, fol.227 (21 August 1941). 'Kriegstagebuch Nr.3 der 7.Panzer-Division Führungsabteilung 1.6.1941–9.5.1942', BA-MA RH 27–7/46, fol.104 (21 August 1941).
27 Bock, *War Diary*, p.288 (21 August 1941).
28 As cited in: A. Eremenko, *The Arduous Beginning* (Honolulu, 2004) pp.198–199.

29 Ibid., p.199.
30 Horst Slesina, *Soldaten gegen Tod und Teufel. Unser Kampf in der Sowjetunion. Eine soldatische Deutung* (Düsseldorf, 1943) pp.267–269.
31 See my discussion in: Stahel, *Operation Barbarossa and Germany's Defeat in the East*, pp.390–392.
32 'Tagesmeldungen der Heersgruppe Mitte vom 6.8.41 bis 26.8.41', BA-MA RH 19 II/130, fol.18 (8 August 1941).
33 'KTB Nr.1 Panzergruppe 2 Bd.II vom 22.7.1941 bis 20.8.41', BA-MA RH 21–2/928, fol.186 (8 August 1941).
34 'Tagesmeldungen der Heersgruppe Mitte vom 6.8.41 bis 26.8.41', BA-MA RH 19 II/130, fol.27 (9 August 1941).
35 'Kriegstagebuch 4.Panzer-Divison Führungsabtl. 26.5.41–31.3.42', BA-MA RH 27–4/10, p.103 (11 August 1941).
36 'KTB Nr.1 Panzergruppe 2 Bd.II vom 22.7.1941 bis 20.8.41', BA-MA RH 21–2/928, fol.215 (11 August 1941).
37 Ibid., fol.237 (13 August 1941).
38 Bock, *War Diary*, p.279 (10 August 1941).
39 'Kriegstagebuch 4.Panzer-Divison Führungsabtl. 26.5.41–31.3.42', BA-MA RH 27–4/10, p.109 (14 August 1941).
40 Glantz, *Barbarossa*, p.86.
41 Erickson, *The Road to Stalingrad*, p.199.
42 Ibid., pp.199–200.
43 Ibid., p.200.
44 Geoffrey P. Megargee, *Inside Hitler's High Command* (Lawrence, KS, 2000) p.122.
45 Peter Bor, *Gespräche mit Halder* (Wiesbaden, 1950) p.86.
46 'KTB 3rd Pz. Div. I.b 19.5.41–6.2.42', BA-MA RH 27–3/218. This war diary has no folio stamped page numbers so references must be located using the date (18 August 1941).
47 'KTB Nr.1 Panzergruppe 2 Bd.II vom 22.7.1941 bis 20.8.41', BA-MA RH 21–2/928, fol.296 (19 August 1941).
48 'Kriegstagebuch 4.Panzer-Divison Führungsabtl. 26.5.41–31.3.42', BA-MA RH 27–4/10, p.115 (20 August 1941).
49 Bock, *War Diary*, p.287 (20 August 1941).
50 Johannes Hürter (ed.), *Ein deutscher General an der Ostfront. Die Briefe und Tagebücher des Gotthard Heinrici 1941/42* (Erfurt, 2001) p.75 (19 August 1941). Bock's diary from 20 August records 78,000 Soviet POWs from the battles at Gomel and Krichev. Bock, *War Diary*, p.287 (20 August 1941).
51 Guderian, *Panzer Leader*, p.196.
52 'Kriegstagesbuch Ia. 14.Inf.Div. (mot) vom 25.5.41–1.10.41', BA-MA RH 26–14/10, fols.69–70 and 74 (20 July 1941); Hermann Hoth,

Panzer-Operationen. Die Panzergruppe 3 und der operative Gedanke der deutschen Führung Sommer 1941 (Heidelberg, 1956) p.99.

53 Glantz, *The Battle for Smolensk*, p.64.

54 Halder, KTB III, p.196 (25 August 1941).

55 Bock, *War Diary*, p.294 (26 August 1941).

56 Glantz, *The Battle for Smolensk*, p.65.

57 As cited in: Liddell Hart, *The Other Side of the Hill*, p.272.

58 Nicolaus von Below, *Als Hitlers Adjutant 1937–45* (Mainz, 1999) p.292.

59 Ibid.

60 Bock, *War Diary*, pp.292–293 (25 August 1941).

61 Kesselring, *The Memoirs of Field-Marshal Kesselring*, p.98.

62 Hürter (ed.), *Ein deutscher General an der Ostfront*, pp.76–77 (23 August and 1 September 1941).

63 As cited in: Neitzel, *Tapping Hitler's Generals*, p.32.

64 Bähr and Bähr (eds.), *Kriegsbriefe Gefallener Studenten, 1939–1945*, p.160 (26 August 1941).

65 Landon and Leitner (eds.), *Diary of a German Soldier*, p.100 (1 September 1941).

66 The Soviet Fortieth Army had been newly organized in late August and was in fact separated from the rest of the South-Western Front by the Briansk Front's Twenty-First Army.

67 Guderian, *Panzer Leader*, p.202.

68 Two weeks into Operation Barbarossa the formations of Kluge's Fourth Army were transferred to Second Army and the Fourth Army was redesignated Fourth Panzer Army. This new command was given control of Panzer Groups 2 and 3; however, the panzer commanders, particularly Guderian, resisted the move and it was to prove an ineffectual arrangement. Ultimately Fourth Panzer Army was terminated at the end of July. On 22 August Kluge's Fourth Army was reinstated between the Ninth and the Second Armies, taking over formations that had previously been commanded by Guderian and Weichs.

69 Guderian had supplied this argument himself when on 23 August he had argued against the southern operation and claimed that the units of Vietinghoff's corps would have to travel between 470 and 560 kilometres to join the operation. 'Kriegstagebuch Nr.1 Panzergruppe 2 Band II vom 21.8.1941 bis 31.10.41', BA-MA RH 21–2/931, fol.22 (23 August 1941).

70 Ibid., fol.36 (24 August 1941).

71 Guderian, *Panzer Leader*, pp.202–203.

72 Emphasis in the original. 'Kriegstagebuch Nr.1 Panzergruppe 2 Band II vom 21.8.1941 bis 31.10.41', BA-MA RH 21–2/931, fol.22 (23 August 1941).

73 Steiger, *Armour Tactics in the Second World War*, p.127.

74 'Kriegstagebuch Nr.1 Panzergruppe 2 Band II vom 21.8.1941 bis 31.10.41', BA-MA RH 21–2/931, fol.17 (22 August 1941).

75 Alan Clark, *Barbarossa. The Russian–German Conflict 1941–1945* (London, 1996) pp.129–130.

76 The German war diaries sometimes record wide discrepancies in figures for combat-ready tanks, probably stemming from differing definitions of what constituted 'combat ready'. On the day before these figures were reported (21 August), the same war diary reported that the 3rd and 4th Panzer Divisions were at only 15 per cent of their starting strength. 'Kriegstagebuch Nr.1 Panzergruppe 2 Band II vom 21.8.1941 bis 31.10.41', BA-MA RH 21–2/931, fols.9 and 17 (21 and 22 August 1941).

77 Ibid., fol.17 (22 August 1941).

78 Ibid., fol.18 (22 August 1941).

79 For the most comprehensive set of maps detailing the developments in the Ukraine during the summer of 1941 see: David M. Glantz, *Atlas of the Battle for Kiev Part I. Penetrating the Stalin Line and the Uman' Encirclement 2 July–9 August 1941* (Privately published by David M. Glantz, 2005); David M. Glantz, *Atlas of the Battle for Kiev Part II. The German Advance to the Dnepr River, 9–26 August 1941* (Privately published by David M. Glantz, 2005); David M. Glantz, *Atlas of the Battle for Kiev Part III. The Encirclement and Destruction of the Southwestern Front, 25 August–26 September 1941* (Privately published by David M. Glantz, 2005).

80 Haupt, *Army Group South*, p.63.

81 For a more detailed look at the problems of city fighting in Dnepropetrovsk see: Wettstein, 'Operation "Barbarossa" und Stadtkampf', pp.21–44; Wettstein, 'Urban Warfare Doctrine on the Eastern Front'.

82 Eberhard von Mackensen, *Vom Bug zum Kaukasus. Das III. Panzerkorps im Feldzug gegen Sowjetrußland 1941/42* (Neckargemünd, 1967) p.28.

83 'KTB der Oberquartiermeisterabteilung der 1st Panzer-Armee 2.5.41–31.10.41', BA-MA RH 21–1/347, p.42 (6 September 1941). This figure appears extremely high and seems unlikely to be correct, unless it includes large stocks of captured Soviet shells. In any case it seems clear that the munition consumption at the bridgehead was exceptionally high.

84 Wettstein, 'Operation "Barbarossa" und Stadtkampf', p.40.

85 'KTB der Oberquartiermeisterabteilung der 1st Panzer-Armee 2.5.41–31.10.41', BA-MA RH 21–1/347, p.37 (24 August 1941).

86 Ibid. (25 August 1941).

87 Klaus Schüler, 'The Eastern Campaign as a Transportation and Supply Problem' in Bernd Wegner (ed.), *From Peace to War. Germany, Soviet Russia and the World, 1939–1941* (Oxford, 1997) p.213, footnote 6.

88 'KTB der Oberquartiermeisterabteilung der 1st Panzer-Armee 2.5.41–31.10.41', BA-MA RH 21–1/347, p.38 (25 August 1941).
89 'Heersgruppe Süd Kriegstagebuch II. Teil Band 3, 16 Aug.–15 Sept. 1941', BA-MA RH 19-I/254, fol.102 and 111 (26 and 27 August 1941).
90 Halder, KTB III, p.198 (26 August 1941).
91 'Heersgruppe Süd Kriegstagebuch II. Teil Band 3, 16 Aug.–15 Sept. 1941', BA-MA RH 19-I/254, fol. 84 (25 August 1941).
92 Ibid., fol.85 (25 August 1941).
93 J. P. Stern, *Hitler. The Führer and the People* (Berkeley, CA, 1992) chapter 7: 'Hitler's Ideology of the Will'.
94 Halder wrote this in his preface to General Erhard Raus's post-war memoir, originally published by the US Army Historical Department and reproduced in: Peter G. Tsouras (ed.), *Panzers on the Eastern Front. General Erhard Raus and his Panzer Divisions in Russia 1941–1945* (London, 2002) p.9.
95 Guderian, *Panzer Leader*, p.204.
96 'Kriegstagebuch Nr.1 Panzergruppe 2 Band II vom 21.8.1941 bis 31.10.41', BA-MA RH 21–2/931, fol.42 (25 August 1941).
97 Glantz, *Barbarossa*, p.87.
98 Erickson, *The Road to Stalingrad*, p.201.
99 'Kriegstagebuch 4.Panzer-Division Führungsabtl. 26.5.41–31.3.42', BA-MA RH 27–4/10, p.120 (25 August 1941).
100 'Kriegstagebuch Nr.2 XXXXVII.Pz.Korps. Ia 25.5.1941–22.9.1941', BA-MA RH 24–47/2 (25 August 1941). This war diary has no folio stamped page numbers so references must be located using the date.
101 Guderian, *Panzer Leader*, p.204.
102 'Kriegstagebuch Nr.1 Panzergruppe 2 Band II vom 21.8.1941 bis 31.10.41', BA-MA RH 21–2/931, fol.42 (25 August 1941).
103 For a tactical account of this action see: Paul Carell (aka Paul Karl Schmidt), *Hitler's War on Russia. The Story of the German Defeat in the East* (London, 1964) pp.114–115. Schmidt served in the German Foreign Ministry during the war and directed Nazi propaganda. He was also an *Obersturmbannführer* in the SS. His post-war historical writings enjoyed a wide readership, but reflect many of the problematic conclusions common to former Nazis.
104 'KTB 3rd Pz. Div. vom 16.8.40 bis 18.9.41', BA-MA RH 27–3/14, p.191 (26 August 1941).
105 As cited in: Steven H. Newton, *Hitler's Commander. Field Marshal Walther Model – Hitler's Favorite General* (Cambridge, MA, 2006) p.138.
106 Guderian, *Panzer Leader*, p.204.
107 Halder, KTB III, p.200 (27 August 1941).

108 'Kriegstagebuch Nr.1 Panzergruppe 2 Band II vom 21.8.1941 bis 31.10.41', BA-MA RH 21–2/931, fol.60 (27 August 1941).
109 Ibid., fol.53 (27 August 1941).
110 'Kriegstagebuch 4.Panzer-Divison Führungsabtl. 26.5.41–31.3.42', BA-MA RH 27–4/10, pp.124–125 (28 and 29 August 1941).
111 'KTB 3rd Pz. Div. I.b 19.5.41–6.2.42', BA-MA RH 27–3/218 (27 August 1941).
112 'Kriegstagebuch Nr.2 XXXXVII.Pz.Korps. Ia 25.5.1941–22.9.1941', BA-MA RH 24–47/2 (28 August 1941).
113 '18.Panzer Division, Abt.Ia KTB Teil II vom 21.8.–29.9.41', BA-MA RH 27–18/21, p.7 (28 August 1941). This war diary has different page numbers at the top and bottom of the documents; my references refer to those at the top.
114 'Kriegstagebuch Nr.1 Panzergruppe 2 Band II vom 21.8.1941 bis 31.10.41', BA-MA RH 21–2/931, fol.53 (27 August 1941). See also: Halder, KTB III, p.199 (27 August 1941).
115 Although it was no larger part of Guderian's panzer group, Halder's average figure includes the tanks from the XXXXVI Panzer Corps.
116 Halder, KTB III, p.202 (28 August 1941).
117 New production between June and August 1941 equalled 815 armoured fighting vehicles, but Hitler held these back in anticipation of new operations following the success of Barbarossa. Rolf-Dieter Müller, 'The Failure of the Economic "Blitzkrieg Strategy"' in Militärgeschichtliches Forschungsamt (ed.), *Germany and the Second World War. Volume IV*, p.1127.
118 'Kriegstagebuch Nr.1 Panzergruppe 2 Band II vom 21.8.1941 bis 31.10.41', BA-MA RH 21–2/931, fol.57 (27 August 1941).
119 Guderian, *Panzer Leader*, p.206. The account in Guderian's memoir incorrectly suggests that all discussions up to and including the dispatch of a communiqué to the OKH took place in his absence. Paulus apparently had come to his conclusions after speaking with Guderian's Chief of Staff, Colonel Kurt Freiherr von Liebenstein. The panzer group's war diary makes clear that Guderian himself spoke with Paulus and agreed to contact the OKH.
120 Bock, *War Diary*, pp.294–295 (27 August 1941).
121 Halder, KTB III, pp.200–201 (27 August 1941). Bock, *War Diary*, pp.294–295 (27 August 1941).
122 'Kriegstagebuch Nr.1 Panzergruppe 2 Band II vom 21.8.1941 bis 31.10.41', BA-MA RH 21–2/931, fol.61 (27 August 1941).
123 Guderian, *Panzer Leader*, p.207.
124 'Kriegstagebuch Nr.1 Panzergruppe 2 Band II vom 21.8.1941 bis 31.10.41', BA-MA RH 21–2/931, fols.59–60 (27 August 1941).

125 Bock, *War Diary*, p.297 (29 August 1941).
126 Ibid., p.298 (30 August 1941).
127 Guderian, *Panzer Leader*, p.208.
128 Halder, KTB III, p.180 (15 August 1941).
129 Glantz, *The Battle for Smolensk*, pp.62 and 67–76.
130 'Kriegstagebuch Nr.1 (Band August 1941) des Oberkommandos der Heeresgruppe Mitte' BA-MA RH 19-II/386, p.381 (25 August 1941).
131 Hermann Geyer, *Das IX. Armeekorps im Ostfeldzug 1941* (Neckargemünd, 1969) p.122.
132 Günther Blumentritt, 'Moscow' in William Richardson and Seymour Freidin (eds.), *The Fatal Decisions* (London, 1956) pp.51–52.
133 Bock, *War Diary*, p.292 (25 August 1941).
134 Ibid., p.293 (26 August 1941).
135 'Kriegstagebuch Nr.1 (Band August 1941) des Oberkommandos der Heeresgruppe Mitte' BA-MA RH 19-II/386, p.376 (24 August 1941).
136 Bähr and Bähr (eds.), *Kriegsbriefe Gefallener Studenten, 1939–1945*, pp.110–111 (18 August 1941).
137 Kern, *Dance of Death*, p.50. Many German battlefield accounts give an impression of Soviet soldiers that tends to reflect the dehumanizing depictions of Nazi propaganda. Yet such accounts may also be a result of the trauma associated with such memories and the desire to distance oneself from involvement in an otherwise barbarous action. In that sense Nazi propaganda not only offered 'explanations' for Soviet actions, but also provided coping strategies for the wholesale killing that was often demanded in the east.
138 There are certainly many examples of ill-equipped Red Army formations in the summer of 1941. To cite just one example, a German soldier's letter from 26 August recorded the testimony of Soviet POWs who claimed their units were suffering from a shortage of weapons, which meant they were being sent into battle unarmed, with instructions to pick up the rifles of their fallen comrades. Elmshäuser and Lokers (eds.), *'Man muß hier nur hart sein'*, p.127 (26 August 1941).
139 Ibid., p.122 (17 August 1941).
140 Better known as the battle of Königgrätz, this was the decisive battle of the Austro-Prussian War in 1866.
141 As cited in: Clark, *Barbarossa*, pp.138–139.
142 On 28 August Halder recorded in his diary that only 24 per cent of the tanks in 7th Panzer Division were combat ready. Halder, KTB III, p.203 (28 August 1941).
143 'Kriegstagebuch Nr.1 (Band August 1941) des Oberkommandos der Heeresgruppe Mitte' BA-MA RH 19-II/386, p.389 (27 August 1941).
144 This constituted two infantry divisions marching up from the south.

145 'Kriegstagebuch Nr.1 (Band August 1941) des Oberkommandos der Heeresgruppe Mitte' BA-MA RH 19-II/386, pp.380 and 393–394 (25 and 28 August 1941).
146 Ibid., pp.393 and 395 (28 August 1941).
147 Bock, *War Diary*, p.295 (28 August 1941).
148 Halder, KTB III, p.220 (10 September 1941).
149 Solomon Perel, *Europa Europa* (New York, 1997) p.36.
150 Scheuer, *Briefe aus Russland*, p.35 (25 August 1941).
151 Halder, KTB III, p.202 (28 August 1941).
152 Ibid., p.199 (26 August 1941).
153 Kroener, 'The "Frozen Blitzkrieg"', p.145. See also: Kroener, 'Squaring the Circle,' pp.282–335.
154 Bernhard R. Kroener, 'The Winter Crisis of 1941–1942: the Distribution of Scarcity or Steps towards a More Rational Management of Personnel' in Militärgeschichtliches Forschungsamt (ed.), *Germany and the Second World War. Volume V/I*, pp.1014–1018.
155 Stephen G. Fritz, *Frontsoldaten. The German Soldier in World War II* (Lexington, KY, 1995) p.62.
156 Department of the US Army (ed.), *Effects of Climate on Combat in European Russia* (Washington, DC, 1952) p.60.
157 As cited in: James Lucas, *War of the Eastern Front 1941–1945. The German Soldier in Russia* (London, 1980) p.74.
158 Elmshäuser and Lokers (eds.), '*Man muß hier nur hart sein*', pp.90 and 102 (5 and 17 July 1941).
159 Hans Pichler, *Truppenarzt und Zeitzeuge. Mit der 4. SS-Polizei-Division an vorderster Front* (Dresden, 2006) p.98 (5 September 1941).
160 Günther, *Hot Motors, Cold Feet*, p.184.
161 Department of the US Army (ed.), *Effects of Climate on Combat in European Russia*, p.42.
162 Hürter (ed.), *Ein deutscher General an der Ostfront*, p.87 (19 September 1941).
163 Günther, *Hot Motors, Cold Feet*, p.183.
164 Department of the US Army (ed.), *Effects of Climate on Combat in European Russia*, p.42.
165 Martin Humburg, *Das Gesicht des Krieges. Feldpostbriefe von Wehrmachtssoldaten aus der Sowjetunion 1941–1944* (Wiesbaden, 1998) p.158 (5 October 1941).
166 Horst Fuchs Richardson (ed.), *Sieg Heil! War Letters of Tank Gunner Karl Fuchs 1937–1941* (Hamden, CT, 1987) p.122 (3 August 1941).
167 Lucas, *War of the Eastern Front 1941–1945*, p.74.
168 Scheuer, *Briefe aus Russland*, pp.23 and 26 (7 and 26 July 1941).

169 Department of the US Army (ed.), *Effects of Climate on Combat in European Russia*, pp.42.
170 Bidermann, *In Deadly Combat*, pp.48–49.
171 Elmshäuser and Lokers (eds.), '*Man muß hier nur hart sein*', p.92 (12 July 1941).
172 Kern, *Dance of Death*, p.71.
173 Humburg, *Das Gesicht des Krieges*, p.158 (8 August 1941).
174 Department of the US Army (ed.), *Effects of Climate on Combat in European Russia*, p.60.
175 One soldier's letter described the laborious method of cleaning his combat jacket. First he said he had to pick out the lice (he counted thirty-seven 'thick and fat' specimens), then he began a three-stage cleaning process whereby the dirt was removed first with a knife, then with a wire-brush and finally by washing. Harry Mielert, *Russische Erde. Kriegsbriefe aus Russland* (Stuttgart, 1950) p.16 (22 September 1941).
176 Seaton, *The Battle for Moscow*, p.73.
177 Scheuer, *Briefe aus Russland*, p.24 (16 July 1941).
178 Gareis, *Kampf und Ende der Fränkisch-Sudetendeutschen 98. Infanterie-Division*, pp.128–129.

4 War in the Ukraine

1 Commanded by General Giovanni Messe the CSIR consisted of three semi-motorized divisions, a cavalry group and a black-shirt legion numbering 60,900 men with 5,500 vehicles and 4,600 horses. Ciro Paoletti, *A Military History of Italy* (Westport, CT, 2008) p.176. On the performance of the Italian army in the east see: Brian R. Sullivan, 'The Italian Soldier in Combat, June 1940–September 1943: Myths, Realities and Explanations' in Paul Addison and Angus Calder (eds.), *A Time to Kill. The Soldier's Experience of War in the West 1939–1945* (London, 1997) pp.177–205.
2 It was not the first time that substantial Italian forces had been committed to a campaign in Russia. During the 1812 campaign, Napoleon's stepson, Eugène de Beauharnais, commanded the largely Italian IV Corps, which fought at the pivotal battles of Borodino (7 September) and Maloiaroslavets (24 October).
3 Henrik Eberle and Matthias Uhl (eds.), *The Hitler Book. The Secret Dossier Prepared for Stalin from the Interrogations of Hitler's Personal Aides* (New York, 2005) pp.74–75. See also: Domarus, *Hitler*, pp.2472–2473. On the relative combat value of the CSIR in 1941 see the discussion in Thomas Schlemmer (ed.), *Die Italiener an der Ostfront 1942/43. Dokumente zu Mussolinis Krieg gegen die Sowjetunion* (Munich, 2005) pp.15–17.

4 Sullivan, 'The Path Marked out by History', pp.131–132.
5 Görlitz (ed.), *The Memoirs of Field-Marshal Keitel*, p.160. See also: MacGregor Knox, *Hitler's Italian Allies. Royal Armed Forces, Fascist Regime, and the War of 1940–1943* (Cambridge, 2009) p.115.
6 Below, *Als Hitlers Adjutant 1937–45*, p.288.
7 Hassell, *Vom Andern Deutschland*, p.223 (20 September 1941); Hassell, *The von Hassell Diaries 1938–1944*, pp.193 (20 September 1941).
8 Hassell, *Vom Andern Deutschland*, p.224 (20 September 1941); Hassell, *The von Hassell Diaries 1938–1944*, p.194 (20 September 1941).
9 Alexander Dallin, *Odessa, 1941–1944. A Case Study of Soviet Territory under Foreign Rule* (Oxford, 1998) p.38.
10 Trevor-Roper (ed.), *Hitler's Table Talk, 1941–1944*, p.32 (17–18 September 1941).
11 Albert Axell, *Stalin's War. Through the Eyes of his Commanders* (London, 1997) p.153.
12 Axworthy *et al.*, *Third Axis Fourth Ally*, p.52.
13 Mark Axworthy, 'Peasant Scapegoat to Industrial Slaughter: the Romanian Soldier at the Siege of Odessa' in Addison and Calder (eds.), *A Time to Kill*, p.227.
14 Mihai Tone Filipescu, *Reluctant Axis. The Romanian Army in Russia 1941–1944* (Chapultepeq, 2006) p.26.
15 Soviet losses in the same period are thought to have been about 60,000 men. Axworthy *et al.*, *Third Axis Fourth Ally*, pp.55–58.
16 Axworthy, 'Peasant Scapegoat to Industrial Slaughter', p.227.
17 The Soviet naval base of Hanko on the southern coast of Finland was blockaded by mines and defended by almost 23,000 Soviet troops along the narrow peninsula linking it to the mainland. It was only evacuated in early December 1941. Across the Gulf of Finland the siege of Tallinn lasted from mid-July until 28 August and ended with the capture of 20,000 Soviet POWs. The monumental siege of Leningrad was only just getting underway in early September. Further south the siege of the Soviet fortress at Brest lasted from the first day of the war until the last few defenders were killed in late July. Mogilev on the Dnepr was the site of another desperate siege in July, which like those of Odessa and Leningrad eventually earned the city the Soviet Union's exulted distinction of 'Hero City'. Kiev was also under siege from the second week of July and repulsed a number of costly German assaults until its eventual fall on 19 September.
18 Axworthy *et al.*, *Third Axis Fourth Ally*, p.59.
19 Halder, KTB III, pp.217–218 (9 September 1941).
20 'Kriegstagebuch des Panzerarmee-Oberkdos.1 Band III 1.9.41–31.10.41', BA-MA RH 21–1/51, fol.10 (6 September 1941).

21 Jürgen Förster, 'The Decisions of the Tripartite Pact States' in Militärgeschichtliches Forschungsamt (ed.), *Germany and the Second World War. Volume IV*, pp.1029–1030.
22 Axworthy, *Axis Slovakia*, pp.103–116.
23 Förster, 'The Decisions of the Tripartite Pact States', p.1036.
24 'Heersgruppe Süd Kriegstagebuch II. Teil Band 3, 16 Aug.–15 Sept. 1941', BA-MA RH 19-I/254, fols.111 and 123 (28 and 29 August 1941).
25 'Kriegstagebuch des Panzerarmee-Oberkdos.1 Band III 1.9.41–31.10.41', BA-MA RH 21–1/51, fol.10 (6 September 1941).
26 Mackensen, *Vom Bug zum Kaukasus*, p.29.
27 'Kriegstagebuch des Panzerarmee-Oberkdos.1 Band II 22.6.41–31.8.41', BA-MA RH 21–1/50, fol.203 (31 August 1941).
28 Wettstein, 'Urban Warfare Doctrine on the Eastern Front'.
29 'Kriegstagebuch des Panzerarmee-Oberkdos.1 Band III 1.9.41–31.10.41', BA-MA RH 21–1/51, fol.3 (2 September 1941).
30 Bähr and Bähr (eds.), *Kriegsbriefe Gefallener Studenten, 1939–1945*, pp.60–61 (early September 1941).
31 'Kriegstagebuch des Panzerarmee-Oberkdos.1 Band III 1.9.41–31.10.41', BA-MA RH 21–1/51, fol.4 (3 September 1941).
32 Wettstein, 'Urban Warfare Doctrine on the Eastern Front'.
33 Helmut Schiebel, *Einen besser'n findst Du nicht. Der Krieg im Osten 1941–1945. Ein Zeitzeuge erzählt* (Leoni am Starnberger See, 1991) p.54 (25 August 1941).
34 Mackensen, *Vom Bug zum Kaukasus*, p.28.
35 Schiebel, *Einen besser'n findst Du nicht*, p.63 (27 August 1941).
36 'Kriegstagebuch des Panzerarmee-Oberkdos.1 Band III 1.9.41–31.10.41', BA-MA RH 21–1/51, fol.9 (5 September 1941).
37 'KTB der Oberquartiermeisterabteilung der 1st Panzer-Armee 2.5.41–31.10.41', BA-MA RH 21–1/347, p.39 (29 August 1941).
38 'Kriegstagebuch des Panzerarmee-Oberkdos.1 Band II 22.6.41–31.8.41', BA-MA RH 21–1/50, fol.202 (30 August 1941).
39 Emphasis in the original. 'Heersgruppe Süd Kriegstagebuch II. Teil Band 3, 16 Aug.–15 Sept. 1941', BA-MA RH 19-I/254, fol.128 (29 August 1941).
40 Glantz, *Atlas of the Battle for Kiev Part III*, p.12, see also map 28; Halder, KTB III, p.209 (31 August 1941).
41 'KTB der Oberquartiermeisterabteilung der 1st Panzer-Armee 2.5.41–31.10.41', BA-MA RH 21–1/347, p.40 (1 September 1941).
42 Kroener, 'The "Frozen Blitzkrieg"', p.147.
43 Bähr and Bähr (eds.), *Kriegsbriefe Gefallener Studenten, 1939–1945*, pp.111–112 (2 September 1941).
44 By mid-September 1941 some eight hundred death sentences had been pronounced on members of the Wehrmacht, the majority for desertion.

Fröhlich (ed.), *Die Tagebücher von Joseph Goebbels, Teil II Band 1*, p.444 (18 September 1941).

45 Bidermann, *In Deadly Combat*, p.40.

46 Ingo Stader (ed.), *Ihr daheim und wir hier draußen. Ein Briefwechsel zwischen Ostfront und Heimat Juni 1941–März 1943* (Cologne, 2006) p.31 (3 September 1941).

47 Konrad H. Jarausch and Klaus J. Arnold (eds.), *'Das stille Sterben . . .' Feldpostbriefe von Konrad Jarausch aus Polen und Russland 1939–1942* (Munich, 2008) pp.300–301 (30 August 1941).

48 'Heersgruppe Süd Kriegstagebuch II. Teil Band 3, 16 Aug.–15 Sept. 1941', BA-MA RH 19-I/254, fol.147 (1 September 1941).

49 Bock, *War Diary*, p.298 (30 August 1941).

50 'Kriegstagebuch Nr.1 Panzergruppe 2 Band II vom 21.8.1941 bis 31.10.41', BA-MA RH 21–2/931, fol.94 (31 August 1941); see also: Guderian, *Panzer Leader*, p.208.

51 'Kriegstagebuch Nr.1 Panzergruppe 2 Band II vom 21.8.1941 bis 31.10.41', BA-MA RH 21–2/931, fol.94 (31 August 1941).

52 As cited in: Kenneth Macksey, *Guderian. Panzer General* (London, 1975) p.151.

53 Bock, *War Diary*, p.298 (31 August 1941).

54 'Kriegstagebuch Nr.1 (Band August 1941) des Oberkommandos der Heeresgruppe Mitte', BA-MA RH 19-II/386, p.409 (31 August 1941).

55 Halder, KTB III, p.208 (31 August 1941).

56 As cited in: Macksey, *Guderian*, p.151.

57 Halder, KTB III, p.209 (31 August 1941).

58 'Kriegstagebuch Nr.1 (Band August 1941) des Oberkommandos der Heeresgruppe Mitte', BA-MA RH 19-II/386, p.392 (27 August 1941).

59 'Kriegstagebuch Nr.1 Panzergruppe 2 Band II vom 21.8.1941 bis 31.10.41', BA-MA RH 21–2/931, fol.84 (30 August 1941).

60 Ibid., fol.92 (31 August 1941); see also: Hans-Joachim Röll, *Oberleutnant Albert Blaich. Als Panzerkommandant in Ost und West* (Würzburg, 2009) p.95.

61 The 3rd Panzer Division started the war with 198 tanks and the 4th Panzer Division with 169 tanks.

62 'Kriegstagebuch Nr.1 (Band August 1941) des Oberkommandos der Heeresgruppe Mitte', BA-MA RH 19-II/386, p.415 (31 August 1941). This was made possible by the arrival of the 255th Infantry Division behind the front of Ninth Army. 'Kriegstagebuch Nr.1 Panzergruppe 2 Band II vom 21.8.1941 bis 31.10.41', BA-MA RH 21–2/931, fol.98 (31 August 1941).

63 Warlimont, *Im Hauptquartier der deutschen Wehrmacht 1939 bis 1945*, p.205; Warlimont, *Inside Hitler's Headquarters, 1939–1945*, p.191.

64 Halder, KTB III, pp.206–207 (30 August 1941).
65 Ibid., p.207 (30 August 1941).
66 Bock, *War Diary*, p.299 (31 August 1941).
67 Ibid., p.297 (30 August 1941).
68 Ibid., p.299 (31 August 1941).
69 Halder, KTB III, p.208 (31 August 1941).
70 Bock, *War Diary*, pp.301–302 (2 September 1941).
71 Halder, KTB III, p.209 (31 August 1941).
72 The name was given on 19 September. Klaus Reinhardt, *Moscow – the Turning Point. The Failure of Hitler's Strategy in the Winter of 1941–42* (Oxford, 1992) p.60.
73 Walther Lammers (ed.), *'Fahrtberichte' aus der Zeit des deutsch-sowjetischen Krieges 1941. Protokolle des Begleitoffiziers des Kommandierenden Generals LIII. Armeekorps* (Boppard am Rhein, 1988) p.80 (3 September 1941).
74 Pichler, *Truppenarzt und Zeitzeuge*, p.94 (22 August 1941).
75 *True to Type*, pp.26–27 (2 and 5 September 1941).
76 Glantz, *The Battle for Smolensk*, pp.74–76.
77 Bock, *War Diary*, p.301 (2 September 1941). This English translation mistakenly refers to the Ninth Army instead of the Fourth Army. Thanks to Robert Kirchubel for taking the time out of his own busy research schedule at the German military archive to confirm this discrepancy for me.
78 Bock, *War Diary*, p.302 (2 September 1941).
79 Halder, KTB III, p.211 (2 September 1941).
80 Geyer, *Das IX. Armeekorps im Ostfeldzug 1941*, pp.122–125.
81 Halder, KTB III, p.220 (10 September 1941); Burkhart Müller-Hillebrand, *Das Heer 1933–1945. Band III. Der Zweifrontenkrieg. Das Heer vom Beginn des Feldzuges gegen die Sowjetunion bis zum Kriegsende* (Frankfurt am Main, 1969) p.19.
82 Geyer, *Das IX. Armeekorps im Ostfeldzug 1941*, p.126.
83 Franz A. P. Frisch in association with Wilbur D. Jones Jr, *Condemned to Live. A Panzer Artilleryman's Five-Front War* (Shippensburg, PA, 2000) pp.74–77.
84 Ibid., p.78.
85 Ortwin Buchbender and Reinhold Sterz (eds.), *Das andere Gesicht des Krieges. Deutsche Feldpostbriefe 1939–1945* (Munich, 1982) pp.79–80 (2 September 1941).
86 Heusinger's letter as cited in: Meyer, *Adolf Heusinger*, p.159 (3 September 1941).
87 Halder, KTB III, p.214 (5 September 1941).
88 Erhard Raus and Steven H. Newton (ed.), *Panzer Operations. The Eastern Front Memoir of General Raus, 1941–1945* (Cambridge, MA, 2005) p.77.
89 Geyer, *Das IX. Armeekorps im Ostfeldzug 1941*, p.129.

90 Müller-Hillebrand, *Das Heer 1933–1945. Band III*, p.22.
91 Glantz, *The Battle for Smolensk*, p.82.
92 Reese, *Stalin's Reluctant Soldiers*, p.198.
93 Jacob W. Kipp, 'Barbarossa and the Crisis of Successive Operations: the Smolensk Engagements, July 10–August 7, 1941' in Joseph Wieczynski (ed.), *Operation Barbarossa. The German Attack on the Soviet Union, June 1941* (Salt Lake City, 1993) pp.117 and 150.
94 Glantz, *The Battle for Smolensk*, p.92.
95 Bellamy, *Absolute War*, p.247.
96 Glantz, *The Battle for Smolensk*, p.82. The four Soviet divisions were the 100th, 127th, 153rd and 161st. These divisions were respectively renamed as the 1st, 2nd, 3rd and 4th Guards Divisions. Glantz, *Colossus Reborn*, p.181.
97 Bock, *War Diary*, p.302 (3 September 1941).
98 Glantz, *The Battle for Smolensk*, pp.82–84; Glantz, *Barbarossa*, pp.91–92.
99 Robert Kirchubel, *Hitler's Panzer's Armies on the Eastern Front* (Barnsley, 2009) p.74.
100 Halder, KTB III, p.199 (26 August 1941).
101 Horst Boog, 'The German Air Force' in Militärgeschichtliches Forschungsamt (ed.), *Germany and the Second World War. Volume IV*, p.364.
102 Overy, *The Air War 1939–1945*, p.49.
103 Bryan I. Fugate and Lev Dvoretsky, *Thunder on the Dnepr. Zhukov–Stalin and the Defeat of Hitler's Blitzkrieg* (Novato, CA, 1997) pp.245–246. Although this book lacks adequate footnoting, it seems these figures come from Soviet-era publications and therefore represent, at best, high-end estimates. While not offering any figures on losses, German military files confirm that Soviet aerial attacks during this period were particularly heavy and destructive.
104 '18.Panzer Division, Abt.Ia KTB Teil II vom 21.8.-29.9.41', BA-MA RH 27–18/21, p.9 (30 August 1941).
105 'Kriegstagebuch Nr.2 XXXXVII.Pz.Korps. Ia 25.5.1941–22.9.1941', BA-MA RH 24–47/2 (30 August 1941).
106 Eremenko, *The Arduous Beginning*, p.218.
107 KTB OKW, Vol. II, p.601 (30 August 1941).
108 Ibid., p.602 (31 August 1941).
109 Christer Bergström, *Barbarossa – the Air Battle: July–December 1941* (Hersham, 2007) pp.68–69.
110 John Weal, *More Bf 109 Aces of the Russian Front* (Oxford, 2007) p.22.
111 Glantz, *Colossus Reborn*, p.323.
112 Bellamy, *Absolute War*, p.244.

113 Walter Schwabedissen, *The Russian Air Force in the Eyes of the German Commanders* (New York, 1960) pp.139–141; Bob Carruthers (ed.), *The Wehrmacht, Last Witnesses. First-Hand Accounts from the Survivors of Hitler's Armed Forces* (London, 2010) p.128.

114 Kern, *Dance of Death*, p.83. According to Hans Rudel, 'We are frequently subjected to raids by small aircraft at night with the object of disturbing our sleep and interrupting our supplies. Their evident successes are generally few... It is less a normal method of warfare than an attempt to fray our nerves.' Hans Ulrich Rudel, *Stuka Pilot* (New York, 1979) p.18.

115 Elmshäuser and Lokers (eds.), *'Man muß hier nur hart sein'*, p.104. (Hans-Albert Giese's calendar entries from 22 June to 13 September 1941 are recorded without specific dates.)

116 'Kriegstagebuch Nr.1 Panzergruppe 2 Band II vom 21.8.1941 bis 31.10.41', BA-MA RH 21–2/931, fol.62 (27 August 1941).

117 'Kriegstagebuch Nr.2 XXXXVII.Pz.Korps. Ia 25.5.1941–22.9.1941', BA-MA RH 24–47/2 (30 August 1941).

118 Glantz, *The Battle for Smolensk*, pp.84–86.

119 'Kriegstagebuch Nr.2 XXXXVII.Pz.Korps. Ia 25.5.1941–22.9.1941', BA-MA RH 24–47/2 (31 August 1941).

120 '18.Panzer Division, Abt.Ia KTB Teil II vom 21.8.-29.9.41', BA-MA RH 27–18/21, p.13 (1 September 1941).

121 'Kriegstagebuch Nr.1 Panzergruppe 2 Band II vom 21.8.1941 bis 31.10.41', BA-MA RH 21–2/931, fol.107 (1 September 1941).

122 Steiger, *Armour Tactics in the Second World War*, pp.79–80.

123 Ibid., p.54.

124 Bock, *War Diary*, p.301 (2 September 1941).

125 Guderian, *Panzer Leader*, p.209.

126 Ibid., p.210.

127 Bock, *War Diary*, p.301 (2 September 1941).

128 Ibid., p.302 (2 September 1941); 'Kriegstagebuch Nr.1 Panzergruppe 2 Band II vom 21.8.1941 bis 31.10.41', BA-MA RH 21–2/931, fol.112 (2 September 1941).

129 'Kriegstagebuch Nr.1 Panzergruppe 2 Band II vom 21.8.1941 bis 31.10.41', BA-MA RH 21–2/931, fol.78 (29 August 1941).

130 'Kriegstagebuch Nr.1 (Band August 1941) des Oberkommandos der Heeresgruppe Mitte', BA-MA RH 19-II/386, p.401 (29 August 1941). The expression quoted is only an English approximation of the phrasing used by Halder. In German Halder stated, 'Wenn jemand scharf an der Wand entlang streift, ist es nicht zu verwundern, dass ihn dabei Kalk auf den Kopf fällt.'

131 Halder, KTB III, p.207 (31 August 1941).

132 Ibid., p.212 (2 September 1941).

133 As cited in: Macksey, *Guderian*, p.151.

134 Guderian, *Panzer Leader*, p.210. See also: Clark, *Barbarossa*, pp.140–141; Seaton, *The Battle for Moscow*, p.53.

135 Halder, KTB III, pp.213–214 (4 September 1941).

136 'Kriegstagebuch Nr.1 Panzergruppe 2 Band II vom 21.8.1941 bis 31.10.41', BA-MA RH 21–2/931, fol.129 (4 September 1941).

137 Ibid., fols.131–133 (4 September 1941).

138 Bock, *War Diary*, pp.303–304 (4 September 1941).

139 'Kriegstagebuch Nr.1 Panzergruppe 2 Band II vom 21.8.1941 bis 31.10.41', BA-MA RH 21–2/931, fol.133 (5 September 1941).

140 Halder, KTB III, p.214 (4 September 1941).

141 Ibid.

142 Guderian, *Panzer Leader*, p.212.

143 As cited in: Macksey, *Guderian*, p.152.

144 Guderian, *Panzer Leader*, p.212.

145 'Kriegstagebuch Nr.1 Panzergruppe 2 Band II vom 21.8.1941 bis 31.10.41', BA-MA RH 21–2/931, fol.135 (4 September 1941).

5 Ominous horizons

1 Glantz, *Barbarossa*, p.126.

2 Erickson, *The Road to Stalingrad*, p.202; Geoffrey Roberts, *Stalin's Wars. From World War to Cold War, 1939–1953* (New Haven, 2006) p.101.

3 Viktor Anfilov, 'Budenny' in Shukman (ed.), *Stalin's Generals*, p.63.

4 Erickson, *The Road to Stalingrad*, p.206.

5 Ibid.

6 Glantz, *The Battle for Smolensk*, p.91.

7 Glantz, *Barbarossa*, p.128. See also: Geoffrey Jukes, 'Vasilevsky' in Shukman (ed.), *Stalin's Generals*, p.279.

8 Glantz, *Barbarossa*, p.128. See also: Roberts, *Stalin's Wars*, p.101.

9 Trevor-Roper (ed.), *Hitler's War Directives 1939–1945*, p.152 (6 September 1941).

10 Ibid., pp.153–154 (6 September 1941).

11 These two divisions had been employed in the Balkan campaign and had therefore been in need of thorough overhauls and partial re-equipping, rendering them unavailable for Operation Barbarossa.

12 Bock, *War Diary*, pp.307 (7 September 1941).

13 Jürgen Kleindienst (ed.), *Sei tausendmal gegrüßt. Briefwechsel Irene und Ernst Guicking 1937–1945* (Berlin, 2001). Accompanying this book is a CD Rom with some 1,600 letters, mostly unpublished in the book. The quoted letter appears only on the CD Rom and can be located by its date (25 August 1941).

14 Hans Pichler, *Truppenarzt und Zeitzeuge*, p.98 (1 September 1941).
15 Kleindienst (ed.), *Sei tausendmal gegrüßt*, CD Rom (2 September 1941).
16 Perel, *Europa Europa*, p.42.
17 Fröhlich (ed.), *Die Tagebücher von Joseph Goebbels, Teil II Band 1*, p.316 (27 August 1941).
18 'Gen.v.Waldau, Chef Fü St Lw Persönl. Tagebuch, Auszugeweise', BA-MA RL 200/17, p.73 (9 September 1941).
19 As the Chief of the Army General Staff Halder was responsible not only for the planning of operations, but also for ensuring their feasibility. The prodigious faults and oversights inherent to Operation Barbarossa were by no means his alone, but he was the man entrusted with its overall viability and co-ordinated the efforts of all the major departments of the army. Barbarossa's failure was first and foremost a failure of the German General Staff, which Halder headed. For a detailed assessment of Halder's pivotal role in the planning stages of Operation Barbarossa see: Stahel, *Operation Barbarossa and Germany's Defeat in the East*, Part I.
20 As cited in: Clark, *Barbarossa*, p.147. After the war Halder erroneously sought to emphasize the army's prescience in the matter by claiming that Brauchitsch had already approached Hitler about winter equipment in the planning stages of the campaign. Having been tersely rebuffed by Hitler, Halder claims that he and Brauchitsch tried again in July, but again to no avail. Bor, *Gespräche mit Halder*, p.198.
21 Hans Meier-Welcker, *Aufzeichnungen eines Generalstabsoffiziers 1939–1942* (Freiburg, 1982) p.131 (6 September 1941).
22 *Daily Mail* (11 August 1941). Reproduced in: Janusz Piekalkiewicz, *Moscow 1941. The Frozen Offensive* (London, 1981) p.60.
23 Bergström, *Barbarossa – the Air Battle*, pp.79–80; John Erickson and Ljubica Erickson, *Hitler versus Stalin. The Second World War on the Eastern Front in Photographs* (London, 2004) p.54.
24 At the same time the Soviets were receiving their first shipments of American-built Curtiss Tomahawks, which most Soviet pilots agreed were superior fighters compared with the British Hurricanes. George Mellinger, *Soviet Lend-Lease Fighter Aces of World War 2* (Oxford, 2006) pp.23–24.
25 It was here that the first references to Anglo-American war materiel on the eastern front appear in German sources. Fröhlich (ed.), *Die Tagebücher von Joseph Goebbels, Teil II Band 1*, p. 414 (14 September 1941). Interestingly, the Finnish air force also contained Hurricane fighters supplied by the British during the Winter War against the Soviet Union. See: Corum, *Wolfram von Richthofen*, p.402, footnote 3.
26 Mail Online, 'Stalin's British Heroes' (14 May 2009), available at www.dailymail.co.uk/news/article-1181390. See also: Hugh Morgan, *Soviet*

Aces of World War 2 (Madrid, 1999) pp.54–56; Martin Gilbert, *The Second World War. A Complete History* (London, 2009) p.234.

27 Max Hastings, *Finest Years: Churchill as Warlord 1940–45* (London, 2009) pp.152–154.

28 From John Colville's diary as cited by: David Carlton, *Churchill and the Soviet Union* (New York, 2000) p.84.

29 Knowing that he was asking a great deal of Churchill, Stalin concluded his letter: 'I realise that this message will cause Your Excellency some vexation. But that cannot be helped. Experience has taught me to face up to reality, no matter how unpleasant it may be, and not to shrink from telling the truth, no matter how unpleasant.' Ministry of Foreign Affairs of the USSR (ed.), *Stalin's Correspondence with Churchill, Attlee, Roosevelt and Truman 1941–1945*, pp.20–22, Document 10 (3 September 1941).

30 Churchill had already had a heated confrontation with the Soviet ambassador, Ivan Maisky, over the issue of a second front in 1941. Ivan Maisky, *Memoirs of a Soviet Ambassador. The War 1939–43* (London, 1967) pp.190–191.

31 Ministry of Foreign Affairs of the USSR (ed.), *Stalin's Correspondence with Churchill, Attlee, Roosevelt and Truman 1941–1945*, p.22, Document 11 (6 September 1941).

32 Martin Kitchen, *British Policy towards the Soviet Union during the Second World War* (London, 1986) pp.74–75.

33 Overy, *Why the Allies Won*, p.332.

34 Tuyll, *Feeding the Bear*, pp.23 and 52.

35 Fröhlich (ed.), *Die Tagebücher von Joseph Goebbels, Teil II Band 1*, pp.310–311 (26 August 1941).

36 Paul Kemp, *Convoy! Drama in Arctic Waters* (London, 1993) pp.16–18; Richard Woodman, *Arctic Convoys 1941–1945* (Barnsley, 2007) pp.36–37.

37 Hill, 'British Lend-Lease Aid and the Soviet War Effort, June 1941–June 1942', p.781.

38 Bock, *War Diary*, p.305 (5 September 1941).

39 'Kriegstagebuch Nr.1 Panzergruppe 2 Band II vom 21.8.1941 bis 31.10.41', BA-MA RH 21–2/931, fol.150 (6 September 1941); ibid., pp.305–306 (6 September 1941).

40 Bock, *War Diary*, p.306 (6 September 1941).

41 Eremenko, *The Arduous Beginning*, pp.224–225.

42 'Kriegstagebuch Nr.2 XXXXVII.Pz.Korps. Ia 25.5.1941–22.9.1941', BA-MA RH 24–47/2 (5 September 1941).

43 Malaparte, *The Volga Rises in Europe*, p.157 (September 1941).

44 'The Germans in Russia', LH 15/4/40. See the file entitled 'Von Rundstedt writes home', p.2 (4 September 1941).

45 Ibid. (5 September 1941).
46 'Kriegstagebuch Nr.2 XXXXVII.Pz.Korps. Ia 25.5.1941–22.9.1941', BA-MA RH 24–47/2 (6 September 1941).
47 '18.Panzer Division, Abt.Ia KTB Teil II vom 21.8.–29.9.41', BA-MA RH 27–18/21, pp.25 and 27 (7 September 1941).
48 Ibid., p.28 (7 September 1941).
49 Emphasis in the original. Ibid., p.29 (7 September 1941). The division was not cut off in the classical sense (i.e. surrounded); rather it is meant that the road conditions did not allow it to move back.
50 Bock, *War Diary*, pp.304 and 306–307 (5 and 7 September 1941).
51 Halder, KTB III, p.217 (9 September 1941).
52 Martin van Creveld, *Supplying War. Logistics from Wallenstein to Patton* (Cambridge, 1984) pp.152–153.
53 'Kriegstagebuch der O.Qu.-Abt. Pz. A.O.K.2 von 21.6.41 bis 31.3.42', BA-MA RH 21–2/819, fol.212 (4 September 1941).
54 'Kriegstagebuch Nr.1 Panzergruppe 2 Band II vom 21.8.1941 bis 31.10.41', BA-MA RH 21–2/931, fol.176 (9 September 1941).
55 'KTB 3rd Pz. Div. I.b 19.5.41–6.2.42', BA-MA RH 27–3/218 (4, 7 and 10 September 1941).
56 Guderian, *Panzer Leader*, p.214.
57 'Kriegstagebuch Nr.1 Panzergruppe 2 Band II vom 21.8.1941 bis 31.10.41', BA-MA RH 21–2/931, fol.183 (10 September 1941).
58 Ibid., fol.192 (11 September 1941). See also: Guderian, *Panzer Leader*, pp.215–216.
59 Fröhlich (ed.), *Die Tagebücher von Joseph Goebbels, Teil II Band 1*, p.409 (13 September 1941).
60 Rudolf Steiger, *Armour Tactics in the Second World War*, p.122.
61 Bidermann, *In Deadly Combat*, p.46.
62 'Kriegstagebuch Nr.1 Panzergruppe 2 Band II vom 21.8.1941 bis 31.10.41', BA-MA RH 21–2/931, fol.164 (8 September 1941).
63 Klaus Schüler, *Logistik im Russlandfeldzug. Die Rolle der Eisenbahn bei Planung, Vorbereitung und Durchführung des deutschen Angriffs auf die Sowjetunion bis zur Krise vor Moskau im Winter 1941/42* (Frankfurt am Main, 1987) pp.198–199; Van Creveld, *Supplying War*, pp.164.
64 Schüler, 'The Eastern Campaign as a Transportation and Supply Problem', pp.209–210; Department of the US Army (ed.), *German Tank Maintenance in World War II*, p.2.
65 Fröhlich (ed.), *Die Tagebücher von Joseph Goebbels, Teil II Band 1*, p.375 (8 September 1941).
66 Steiger, *Armour Tactics in the Second World War*, p.117.
67 Ibid.

68 Rolf-Dieter Müller, 'The Failure of the Economic "Blitzkrieg Strategy"', p.1127.
69 Von der Leyen, *Rückblick zum Mauerwald*, p.29.
70 Guderian, *Panzer Leader*, p.216.
71 Kroener, 'The "Frozen Blitzkrieg"', p.147.
72 George Blau, *The Campaign against Russia (1940–1942)* (Washington, 1955) pp.72–73.
73 Theo Schulte, *The German Army and Nazi Policies in Occupied Russia* (Oxford, 1989) p.109.
74 Jeffrey Rutherford, 'The Radicalization of German Occupation Policies: *Wirtschaftsstab Ost* and the 121st Infantry Division in Pavlovsk, 1941' in Alex J. Kay, Jeff Rutherford and David Stahel (eds.), *Nazi Policy on the Eastern Front, 1941: Total War, Genocide and Radicalization* (forthcoming); Norbert Kunz, 'Das Beispiel Charkow: Eine Stadtbevölkerung als Opfer der deutschen Hungerstrategie 1941/42' in Christian Hartmann, Johannes Hürter and Ulrike Jureit (eds.), *Verbrechen der Wehrmacht. Bilanz einer Debatte* (Munich, 2005) pp.136–144.
75 Helmut Pabst, *The Outermost Frontier. A German Soldier in the Russian Campaign* (London, 1957) pp.18–19 and 39.
76 Jarausch and Arnold (eds.), '*Das stille Sterben . . .*', p.311 (16 September 1941).
77 Richard J. Evans, *The Third Reich at War. How the Nazis Led Germany from Conquest to Disaster* (London, 2009) p.193.
78 Fröhlich (ed.), *Die Tagebücher von Joseph Goebbels, Teil II Band 1*, p.398 (11 September 1941).
79 See my discussion in Stahel, *Operation Barbarossa and Germany's Defeat in the East*, p.437.
80 Hitler remained there from 9 May to 6 June 1940.
81 During the war Hitler was to spend more than eight hundred days at the Wolf's Lair between the start of Operation Barbarossa and his final departure on 20 November 1944. On the problems of conducting the war from the Wolf's Lair see: Megargee, *Inside Hitler's High Command*, pp.148–149.
82 Mazower, *Hitler's Empire*, pp.227–231.
83 Kershaw, *Hitler 1936–1945*, p.420.
84 Heinrich Breloer (ed.), *Mein Tagebuch. Geschichten vom Überleben 1939–1947* (Cologne, 1984) p.63 (6 July 1941).
85 As cited in: Robert Kershaw, *War without Garlands*, p.175.
86 Emphasis in the original. Heinz Boberach (ed.), *Meldungen aus dem Reich. Die geheimen Lageberichte des Sicherheitsdienstes der SS 1938–1945*, Volume VII (Berlin, 1984) p.2609, Document 208 (1–4 August 1941).

87 Anne Nelson, *Red Orchestra. The Story of the Berlin Underground and the Circle of Friends who Resisted Hitler* (New York, 2009) chapter 8: 'Other Worlds 1941'.
88 As cited in: Kershaw, *Hitler 1936–1945*, p.423.
89 Ibid.
90 Boberach (ed.), *Meldungen aus dem Reich*, Volume 8, p.2738. Document 218 (8 September 1941).
91 Ibid., p.2745, Document 219 (11 September 1941).
92 Ibid., p.2746, Document 219 (11 September 1941).
93 Fröhlich (ed.), *Die Tagebücher von Joseph Goebbels, Teil II Band 1*, p.404 (12 September 1941).
94 Ibid., pp.327–328 (29 August 1941).
95 Ibid., p.362 (5 September 1941).
96 For a useful overview of the content and focus of German propaganda for Operation Barbarossa see: Wolfram Wette, 'Die propagandistische Begleitmusik zum deutschen Überfall auf die Sowjetunion an 22. Juni 1941' in Gerd R. Ueberschär and Wolfram Wette (eds.), *'Unternehmen Barbarossa'. Der deutsche Überfall auf die Sowjetunion 1941* (Paderborn, 1984) pp.111–129.
97 Marlis Steinert, *Hitlers Krieg und die Deutschen. Stimmung und Haltung der deutschen Bevölkerung im Zweiten Weltkrieg* (Düsseldorf and Vienna, 1970) pp.209–213.
98 Fröhlich (ed.), *Die Tagebücher von Joseph Goebbels, Teil II Band 1*, p.384 (9 September 1941).
99 As cited in: Piekalkiewicz, *Moscow 1941*, p.49. For more on Swiss public opinion in relation to Operation Barbarossa see: Daniel Bourgeois, 'Operation "Barbarossa" and Switzerland' in Bernd Wegner (ed.), *From Peace to War. Germany, Soviet Russia and the World, 1939–1941* (Oxford, 1997) pp.597–600.
100 Fröhlich (ed.), *Die Tagebücher von Joseph Goebbels, Teil II Band 1*, p.392 (10 September 1941).
101 Ibid., p.406 (12 September 1941).
102 Ibid., p.410 (13 September 1941).
103 Elmshäuser and Lokers (eds.), *'Man muß hier nur hart sein'*, p.90 (5 July 1941).
104 Karl Reddemann (ed.), *Zwischen Front und Heimat. Der Briefwechsel des münsterischen Ehepaares Agnes und Albert Neuhaus 1940–1944* (Münster, 1996) p.288 (20 August 1941).
105 As cited in: Kershaw, *War without Garlands*, p.175.
106 Anne Nelson concluded that, 'By the end of 1941 the circles [of resistance] had spread and multiplied in many directions. There was never a way to

count their members, since no roster could be kept for security's sake. But the groups extended to the medical profession, the military, academia, and the arts. Politically, they were made up of Conservatives, Communists, Social Democrats and former Nazis . . . Their activities were concentrated in a few neighbourhoods in central Berlin, but their contacts extended across the country.' Nelson, *Red Orchestra*, pp.219–220.

107 Elke Fröhlich (ed.), *Die Tagebücher von Joseph Goebbels, Teil I Aufzeichnungen 1923–1941, Band 9 Dezember 1940–Juli 1941* (Munich, 1998) p.377 (16 June 1941).

108 For an insightful look at the Wehrmacht's perception of the Soviet Union see: Jürgen Förster, 'Zum Russlandbild der Militärs 1941–1945' in Hans-Erich Volkmann (ed.), *Das Russlandbild im Dritten Reich* (Cologne, 1994) pp.141–163.

109 Jürgen Förster, 'Motivation and Indoctrination in the Wehrmacht, 1933–45' in Paul Addison and Angus Calder (eds.), *A Time to Kill. The Soldier's Experience of War in the West 1939–1945* (London, 1997) pp.263–273.

110 For evidence of the indoctrination of the rank and file see: Bartov, *Hitler's Army*; Fritz, *Frontsoldaten*, chapter 8: 'Trying to Change the World'. For the view of the Soviet enemy within the high command of the Wehrmacht see: Hürter, *Hitlers Heerführer*; Andreas Hillgruber, 'The German Military Leaders' View of Russia Prior to the Attack on the Soviet Union' in Wegner (ed.), *From Peace to War*, pp.169–185; Jürgen Förster, 'New Wine in Old Skins? The Wehrmacht and the War of "Weltanschauungen", 1941' in Wilhelm Deist (ed.), *The German Military in the Age of Total War* (Leamington Spa, 1985) pp.304–322.

111 Bartov, *The Eastern Front*, p.83.

112 Landon and Leitner (eds.), *Diary of a German Soldier*, p.75 (4 July 1941).

113 Fuchs Richardson (ed.), *Sieg Heil!*, p.116 (5 July 1941).

114 Ibid., p.122 (3 August 1941).

115 Hans Becker, *Devil on my Shoulder* (London, 1957) p.22.

116 Ibid.

117 Examples are particularly found in studies on German occupation policies because rear area troops typically had more contact with the population. There is an enormous amount of literature in this area, much of it available only in German. For the most recent and complete listing see the third edition of Rolf-Dieter Müller and Gerd R. Ueberschär, *Hitler's War in the East 1941–1945. A Critical Assessment* (Oxford, 2009) Parts C and D. The best general studies are: Dieter Pohl, *Die Herrschaft der Wehrmacht: Deutsche Militärbesatzung und einheimische Bevölkerung in der Sowjetunion 1941–1944* (Munich, 2008); Kay, *Exploitation, Resettlement, Mass Murder*; Geoffrey P. Megargee, *War of Annihilation. Combat and Genocide on the Eastern Front 1941* (Lanham, MD, 2006). On the role of the Wehrmacht in

the war of annihilation see the range of opinions and studies in: Christian Hartmann, Johannes Hürter and Ulrike Jureit (eds.), *Verbrechen der Wehrmacht. Bilanz einer Debatte* (Munich, 2005); Hannes Heer and Klaus Naumann (eds.), *War of Extermination. The German Military in World War II 1941–1944* (New York and Oxford, 2006). On the German occupation in Belorussia see: Christian Gerlach, *Kalkulierte Morde. Die deutsche Wirtschafts- und Vernichtungspolitik in Weißrussland 1941 bis 1944* (Hamburg, 2000). On the German occupation in the Ukraine see: Berkhoff, *Harvest of Despair*; Wendy Lower, *Nazi Empire-Building and the Holocaust in Ukraine* (Chapel Hill, NC, 2005). On the German occupation in Russia see: Schulte, *The German Army and Nazi Policies in Occupied Russia*.

118 For the most recent overview of the criminal orders see: Felix Römer, 'The Wehrmacht in the War of Ideologies: the Army and Hitler's Criminal Orders on the Eastern Front' in Kay *et al.* (eds.), *Nazi Policy on the Eastern Front, 1941*.

119 Erhard Moritz (ed.), *Fall Barbarossa. Dokumente zur Vorbereitung der faschistischen Wehrmacht auf die Aggression gegen die Sowjetunion (1940/41)* (Berlin, 1970) p.321, Document 97.

120 Ibid., p.321, Document 100. For the most comprehensive study on the commissar order see: Felix Römer, *Der Kommissarbefehl: Wehrmacht und NS-Verbrechen an der Ostfront 1941/42* (Paderborn, 2008).

121 For an overview of the planning for the war of annihilation see: Jürgen Förster, 'Operation Barbarossa as a War of Conquest and Annihilation' in Militärgeschichtliches Forschungsamt (eds.), *Germany and the Second World War. Volume IV*, pp.481–521.

122 Geyer, *Das IX. Armeekorps im Ostfeldzug 1941*, p.126.

123 Stader (ed.), *Ihr daheim und wir hier draußen*, p.31 (3 September 1941).

124 Kern, *Dance of Death*, p.40.

125 Pichler, *Truppenarzt und Zeitzeuge*, p.94 (19 August 1941).

126 As cited in: Clark, *Barbarossa*, p.146.

127 As cited in: ibid., p.146.

128 Pichler, *Truppenarzt und Zeitzeuge*, p.101 (16 September 1941); see also: Kern, *Dance of Death*, p.50.

129 Bergström, *Barbarossa – the Air Battle*, p.69.

130 As cited in: Axell, *Stalin's War*, p.85.

131 *True to Type*, p.20 (15 July 1941); see also: Landon and Leitner (eds.), *Diary of a German Soldier*, p.99 (25 August 1941); Guderian, *Panzer Leader*, p.218.

132 Wolf-Dieter Mohrmann (ed.), *Der Krieg hier ist hart und grausam! Feldpostbriefe an den Osnabrücker Regierungspräsidenten 1941–1944* (Osnabrück, 1984) p.42 (19 August 1941).

133 As cited in: Liddell Hart, *The Other Side of the Hill*, p.265.

134 Van Creveld, *Supplying War*, pp.164.
135 Malaparte, *The Volga Rises in Europe*, pp.158–159 (September 1941).
136 'Gen.v.Waldau, Chef Fü St Lw Persönl. Tagebuch, Auszugeweise', BA-MA RL 200/17, p.73 (11 September 1941).
137 Malaparte, *The Volga Rises in Europe*, p.158 (September 1941).
138 Van Creveld, *Supplying War*, p.165.
139 In the bridgehead there were, however, no German tanks, only one regiment of the SS *Wiking* Division, the 60th Motorized Infantry Division and the 198th Infantry Division.
140 There is no explanation in the panzer group's war diary for why Kleist himself was not present.
141 'Kriegstagebuch des Panzerarmee-Oberkdos.1 Band III 1.9.41–31.10.41', BA-MA RH 21–1/51, fols.14–15 (8 September 1941).
142 Ibid., fol.12 (6 September 1941).
143 Ibid., fol.17 (8 September 1941).
144 Ibid., fols.15–16 (8 September 1941).
145 'Heersgruppe Süd Kriegstagebuch II. Teil Band 3, 16 Aug.–15 Sept. 1941', BA-MA RH 19-I/254, fols.176 and 187 (5 and 6 September 1941).
146 In December 1708 Romny had served as the winter headquarters for King Charles XII of Sweden during his failed campaign against Peter the Great.
147 Without disclosing his source Werner Haupt's study of Army Group South suggests Kleist attacked out of the Kremenchug bridgehead with the lower figure of 331 panzers; see: Werner Haupt, *Army Group South*, p.65.
148 'Kriegstagebuch des Panzerarmee-Oberkdos.1 Band III 1.9.41–31.10.41', BA-MA RH 21–1/51, fol.16 (8 September 1941).
149 This was the SS Regiment *Leibstandarte Adolf Hitler* (later reorganized into the 1st SS Division).
150 'Kriegstagebuch des Panzerarmee-Oberkdos.1 Band III 1.9.41–31.10.41', BA-MA RH 21–1/51, fols.16–17 (8 September 1941).
151 'Heersgruppe Süd Kriegstagebuch II. Teil Band 3, 16 Aug.–15 Sept. 1941', BA-MA RH 19-I/254, fol.199 (8 September 1941).
152 Ibid.
153 Halder, KTB III, p.217 (8 September 1941).
154 Whether Halder's opinion on the matter had changed in light of the clear strategic irrelevance of the bridgehead is unknown.
155 'Kriegstagebuch des Panzerarmee-Oberkdos.1 Band III 1.9.41–31.10.41', BA-MA RH 21–1/51, fols.21–22 (10 September 1941).
156 For the best overviews into the planning stages of Operation Barbarossa see: Ernst Klink, 'The Military Concept of the War against the Soviet Union' in Militärgeschichtliches Forschungsamt (ed.), *Germany and the Second World War. Volume IV*; Barry Leach, *German Strategy against Russia 1939–1941* (Oxford, 1973).

157 Carl von Clausewitz was a Prussian officer, military historian and theorist. He fought in the Napoleonic wars, but is most famous for his unfinished study *Vom Kriege*, which has become a standard text in assessing the character of war.

158 Carl von Clausewitz, *On War*, (eds.) Michael Howard and Peter Paret (New York, 1993) Book 7, chapter 4: 'The Diminishing Force of the Attack'.

159 See the quote by Major-General Walther Nehring as cited in: Bartov, *Hitler's Army*, p.20.

6 The battle of Kiev

1 Halder, KTB III, p.215 (5 September 1941).

2 'Heersgruppe Süd Kriegstagebuch II. Teil Band 3, 16 Aug.–15 Sept. 1941', BA-MA RH 19-I/254, fol.193 (7 September 1941). The war diary also listed seven divisions from Weichs's Second Army that would have to be transferred back to Bock's control. Yet they never in fact came under Rundstedt's authority.

3 Bock's diary incorrectly spells his name 'Grolmann'.

4 Bock, *War Diary*, p.307 (7 September 1941).

5 KTB OKW, Volume II, pp.1034–1035, Document 80 (23 July 1941).

6 Bock, *War Diary*, p.309 (10 September 1941). Brauchitsch had never been particularly strong in his role as Commander-in-Chief of the Army and the demands of the eastern campaign as well as the failed standoff with Hitler reduced his standing even further. By September Brauchitsch did not exude much self-confidence and professionally he preferred to refer decisions to Hitler or leave them to the relevant field commander. Not surprisingly, disparaging views of Brauchitsch were soon widely shared within both the OKW and the OKH. Fröhlich (ed.), *Die Tagebücher von Joseph Goebbels, Teil II Band 1*, pp.378–379 (8 September 1941); Heidemarie Gräfin Schall-Riaucour, *Aufstand und Gehorsam. Offizierstum und Generalstab im Umbruch. Leben und Wirken von Generaloberst Franz Halder Generalstabchef 1938–1942* (Wiesbaden, 1972) p.167 (28/29 July 1941). See also: Brian Bond, 'Brauchitsch' in Correlli Barnett (ed.), *Hitler's Generals* (London, 1989) pp.93–94.

7 Bock, *War Diary*, p.309 (10 September 1941).

8 Ibid., p.310 (11 September 1941).

9 Ibid., p.311 (13 September 1941). The day before (12 September) Halder had expressed criticism of Bock's attempt to avoid an encirclement at Viaz'ma, but maintained it was 'the only option'. Halder, KTB III, p.224 (12 September 1941).

10 Bock, *War Diary*, pp.311–312 (14 September 1941).

11 Gilbert, *The Second World War*, p.232.

12 Perel, *Europa Europa*, p.42.
13 Buchbender and Sterz (eds.), *Das andere Gesicht des Krieges*, p.80 (14 September 1941).
14 Glantz, *The Battle for Smolensk*, p.91.
15 Guderian, *Panzer Leader*, p.213.
16 By 10 September Eremenko noted there was a 60 kilometre gap between his Briansk Front and Kirponos's South-Western Front. Eremenko, *The Arduous Beginning*, p.226.
17 Bock, *War Diary*, p.308 (9 September 1941).
18 Although the town was under German control small pockets of resistance had to be eliminated over the course of the day. 'Kriegstagebuch Nr.1 Panzergruppe 2 Band II vom 21.8.1941 bis 31.10.41', BA-MA RH 21–2/931, fol.183 (10 September 1941). See also: Guderian, *Panzer Leader*, p.215.
19 'KTB 3rd Pz. Div. I.b 19.5.41–6.2.42', BA-MA RH 27–3/218 (10 September 1941).
20 Guderian, *Panzer Leader*, p.215.
21 'KTB 3rd Pz. Div. I.b 19.5.41–6.2.42', BA-MA RH 27–3/218 (11 and 13 September 1941).
22 Guderian, *Panzer Leader*, p.215.
23 'Kriegstagebuch 4.Panzer-Divison Führungsabtl. 26.5.41–31.3.42', BA-MA RH 27–4/10, pp.151 and 154–155 (9 and 10 September 1941).
24 '18.Panzer Division, Abt.Ia KTB Teil II vom 21.8.–29.9.41', BA-MA RH 27–18/21, pp.6–8 (10, 11 and 12 September 1941).
25 As part of a reorganization of command structures effective from 9 September, Panzer Group 2's three corps consisted of XXIV Panzer Corps (3rd Panzer Division, 4th Panzer Division, 10th Motorized Infantry Division and *Das Reich*), XXXXVI Panzer Corps (17th Panzer Division and the SS Infantry Regiment *Grossdeutschland*) and XXXXVII Panzer Corps (18th Panzer Division and the 29th Motorized Infantry Division). 'Kriegstagebuch der O.Qu.-Abt. Pz. A.O.K.2 von 21.6.41 bis 31.3.42', BA-MA RH 21–2/819, fol.206 (9 September 1941).
26 'Kriegstagebuch Nr.2 XXXXVII.Pz.Korps. Ia 25.5.1941–22.9.1941', BA-MA RH 24–47/2 (13 September 1941).
27 Bock, *War Diary*, p.308 (8 September 1941). For the local impact of Soviet aerial attacks in this time see: Walther Lammers (ed.), *'Fahrtberichte' aus der Zeit des deutsch-sowjetischen Krieges 1941*, p.83 (10 September 1941).
28 Halder, KTB III, p.220 (10 September 1941).
29 Bock, *War Diary*, p.310 (11 September 1941).
30 '3rd Pz. Gr. KTB Nr.2 1.9.41–31.10.41', BA-MA Microfilm 59060 (10 September 1941). This diary is recorded in the reference books of the BA-MA as missing. It did in fact survive the war and exists on microfilm. The

microfilm can be misleading as it consists of countless handwritten notes and combat reports from units in Panzer Group 3. Only towards the end of the microfilm does the Ia war diary for Panzer Group 3 begin. The diary has no folio stamped page numbers so references must be located using the date.

31 Bock, *War Diary*, p.310 (12 September 1941).
32 Slesina, *Soldaten gegen Tod und Teufel*, pp.278–280.
33 Hürter (ed.), *Ein deutscher General an der Ostfront*, p.77 (11 September 1941).
34 Glantz, *Barbarossa*, p.130.
35 Ibid., p.128.
36 Ibid., p.130; Glantz, *Atlas of the Battle for Kiev Part III*, p.13.
37 Roberts, *Stalin's Wars*, p.101.
38 Erickson, *The Road to Stalingrad*, pp.207–208. Speaking to Kirponos, Budenny had expressed confidence that his request would be granted. Viktor Anfilov, 'Budenny', p.63.
39 Erickson, *The Road to Stalingrad*, p.208.
40 Bellamy, *Absolute War*, p.260.
41 Bock, *War Diary*, p.309 (10 September 1941).
42 Ibid., p.310 (11 September 1941).
43 Halder, KTB III, p.220 (10 September 1941).
44 Fröhlich (ed.), *Die Tagebücher von Joseph Goebbels, Teil II Band 1*, p.401 (12 September 1941).
45 Bock, *War Diary*, p.310 (12 September 1941); Halder, KTB III, p.224 (12 September 1941).
46 'Kriegstagebuch Nr.1 Panzergruppe 2 Band II vom 21.8.1941 bis 31.10.41', BA-MA RH 21–2/931, fol.198 (12 September 1941).
47 The German *Kampfgruppe* was an ad hoc, combined arms formation that was typically organized for a specific purpose. A *Kampfgruppe* often took the name of its commanding officer or parent division.
48 'Kriegstagebuch Nr.1 Panzergruppe 2 Band II vom 21.8.1941 bis 31.10.41', BA-MA RH 21–2/931, fol.198 (12 September 1941); Newton, *Hitler's Commander*, pp.141–142.
49 'Kriegstagebuch der O.Qu.-Abt. Pz. A.O.K.2 von 21.6.41 bis 31.3.42', BA-MA RH 21–2/819, fol.204 (11 September 1941); see also: Bock, *War Diary*, p.310 (11 September 1941).
50 Hube lost his left arm in World War I, but remained an extremely active commander who would go on to fight at Stalingrad and in Italy. Before his death in April 1944 he was awarded the Knight's Cross with Oak Leaves and Swords by Hitler.
51 'Kriegstagebuch des Panzerarmee-Oberkdos.1 Band III 1.9.41–31.10.41', BA-MA RH 21–1/51, fol.26 (12 September 1941).

52 Ibid. (12 September 1941).
53 Halder, KTB III, p.218 (10 September 1941).
54 Glantz, *Atlas of the Battle for Kiev Part III*, map 91.
55 'Kriegstagebuch des Panzerarmee-Oberkdos.1 Band III 1.9.41–31.10.41', BA-MA RH 21–1/51, fol.26 (12 September 1941).
56 Ibid., fol.28 (13 September 1941).
57 Emphasis in the original. 'The Germans in Russia', LH 15/4/40. See the file entitled 'Von Rundstedt writes home', p.2 (12 September 1941).
58 Bock, *War Diary*, p.311 (13 September 1941).
59 'Kriegstagebuch Nr.1 Panzergruppe 2 Band II vom 21.8.1941 bis 31.10.41', BA-MA RH 21–2/931, fols.204–206 (13 September 1941).
60 Bock, *War Diary*, p.311 (12 September 1941).
61 Guderian, *Panzer Leader*, p.216.
62 'Kriegstagebuch des Panzerarmee-Oberkdos.1 Band III 1.9.41–31.10.41', BA-MA RH 21–1/51, fols.28–30 (13 September 1941).
63 Carell, *Hitler's War on Russia*, p.123.
64 'Kriegstagebuch des Panzerarmee-Oberkdos.1 Band III 1.9.41–31.10.41', BA-MA RH 21–1/51, fols.29–30 (13 September 1941); see also: Carell, *Hitler's War on Russia*.
65 Halder, KTB III, p.224 (12 September 1941).
66 Ibid., p.230 (13 September 1941); Guderian, *Panzer Leader*, p.218.
67 Bock, *War Diary*, p.310 (12 September 1941).
68 'Kriegstagebuch des Panzerarmee-Oberkdos.1 Band III 1.9.41–31.10.41', BA-MA RH 21–1/51, fol.28 (13 September 1941).
69 Halder, KTB III, p.215 (5 September 1941).
70 Viktor Anfilov, 'Timoshenko' in Shukman (ed.), *Stalin's Generals*, pp.248–249.
71 Glantz, *Barbarossa*, pp.94–95.
72 Erickson, *The Road to Stalingrad*, p.208.
73 Glantz, *Barbarossa*, p.131.
74 Ministry of Foreign Affairs of the USSR (ed.), *Stalin's Correspondence with Churchill, Attlee, Roosevelt and Truman 1941–1945*, p.24, Document 12 (13 September 1941).
75 Ibid., Document 12 (13 September 1941).
76 Interestingly, while Churchill certainly did not warm to the idea, he did not entirely rule out the prospect of a British force operating on the eastern front. In his reply to Stalin, Churchill referred only to potential British action in Norway and, more vaguely, in the south assisting a belligerent Turkey. A second letter to Stalin addressed the matter more directly. Churchill wrote, 'If we can clear our western flank in Libya of the enemy, we shall have considerable forces, both air and army, to cooperate upon the southern flank of the Russian front.' Ibid., p.27, Document 14 (21 September 1941). In the

event the only substantive Allied force deployed to the Soviet Union during the war came in 1944 when the United States air force abortively attempted to operate a system of airbases in the Ukraine. For an excellent study of this operation see: Mark J. Conversino, *Fighting with the Soviets. The Failure of Operation Frantic 1944–1945* (Lawrence, KS, 1997).

77 Bock, *War Diary*, p.312 (14 September 1941).

78 Halder, KTB III, p.231 (14 September 1941).

79 Guderian, *Panzer Leader*, pp.216–218.

80 '18.Panzer Division, Abt.Ia KTB Teil II vom 21.8.-29.9.41', BA-MA RH 27–18/21, p.8 (14–18 September 1941).

81 Guderian, *Panzer Leader*, p.218.

82 Kleindienst (ed.), *Sei tausendmal gegrüßt*, CD Rom (13 September 1941).

83 Guderian, *Panzer Leader*, p.218.

84 Liddell Hart, *The Other Side of the Hill*, p.265.

85 Gerd R. Ueberschär, 'Das Scheitern des Unternehmens "Barbarossa". Der deutsch-sowjetische Krieg vom Überfall bis zur Wende vor Moskau im Winter 1941/42' in Gerd R. Ueberschär and Wolfram Wette (eds.), *'Unternehmen Barbarossa' Der deutsche Überfall auf die Sowjetunion 1941* (Paderborn, 1984) p.165.

86 Fröhlich (ed.), *Die Tagebücher von Joseph Goebbels, Teil II Band 1*, pp.363–364 (5 September 1941).

87 Von der Leyen, *Rückblick zum Mauerwald*, p.37.

88 KTB OKW, Volume II, p.1022, Document 72 (15 July 1941).

89 Müller, 'The Failure of the Economic "Blitzkrieg Strategy"', p.1134.

90 Guderian, *Panzer Leader*, p.218; see also: Halder, KTB III, p.230 (14 September 1941).

91 Carell, *Hitler's War on Russia*, p.124.

92 Max Kuhnert, *Will We See Tomorrow? A German Cavalryman at War, 1939–1942* (London, 1993) p.96.

93 Ibid.

94 Model's success stemmed from his talent for organization and command, but was also a result of his sheer ruthlessness. As Hitler himself commented in 1942, 'I trust that man to do it. But I wouldn't want to serve under him.' Carlo D'este, 'Model' in Barnett (ed.), *Hitler's Generals*, p.323.

95 The detachment consisted of only one Mark III tank, a command panzer with radio and a collection of overland vehicles. Altogether there were just two officers and forty-five men. Haupt, *Kiew*, p.106.

96 Carell, *Hitler's War on Russia*, pp.124–126; Haupt, *Army Group Centre*, p.74.

97 'KTB 3rd Pz. Div. vom 16.8.40 bis 18.9.41', BA-MA RH 27–3/14, p.228 (13 September 1941). Tannenberg was the name given to the decisive battle won by Germany in August 1914 against Russia.

98 '9.Pz.Div. KTB Ia vom 19.5.1941 bis 22.1.1942', BA-MA RH 27–9/4, fol.101 (15 September 1941); 'Kriegstagebuch Nr.1 Panzergruppe 2 Band II vom 21.8.1941 bis 31.10.41', BA-MA RH 21–2/931, fol.220 (15 September 1941); KTB OKW, Volume II, p.636 (15 September 1941).

99 Halder, KTB III, p.233 (15 September 1941).

100 Bock, *War Diary*, p.313 (15 September 1941).

101 Ibid. (15 September 1941).

102 Glantz and House, *When Titans Clashed*, p.77.

103 Fröhlich (ed.), *Die Tagebücher von Joseph Goebbels, Teil II Band 1*, p.432 (17 September 1941).

104 Ibid., p.430 (16 September 1941).

105 Adolf Heusinger, *Befehl im Widerstreit. Schicksalsstunden der deutschen Armee 1923–1945* (Tübingen, 1957) pp.132–135.

106 During September 1941 estimates suggest that the Germans, together with their local accomplices, killed between 136,000 and 137,000 Jews in the Ukraine alone. Alexander Kruglov, 'Jewish Losses in Ukraine, 1941–1944' in Ray Brandon and Wendy Lower (eds.), *The Shoah in Ukraine. History, Testimony, Memorialization* (Bloomington, IN, 2008) p.275.

107 For the best introductions to the mass killing of Jews in the east see: Christopher R. Browning and Jürgen Matthäus, *The Origins of the Final Solution. The Evolution of Nazi Jewish Policy, September 1939–March 1942* (London, 2005); Peter Longerich, *The Unwritten Order. Hitler's Role in the Final Solution* (Stroud, 2005); Raul Hilberg, *The Destruction of the European Jews* (New York, 1985).

108 Just over 10 million Soviet soldiers were killed during the course of World War II, whereas the total number of Soviet citizens who died in the conflict (civil and military) approaches 27 million. For the Red Army's losses see: Glantz and House, *When Titans Clashed*, p.292. For the total figure of Soviet war dead see: Krivosheev (ed.), *Soviet Casualties and Combat Losses in the Twentieth Century*, p.83. See also: John Erickson, 'Soviet War Losses. Calculations and Controversies' in John Erickson and David Dilks (eds.), *Barbarossa. The Axis and the Allies* (Edinburgh, 1998) pp.255–277.

109 Kay, '"The Purpose of the Russian Campaign is the Decimation of the Slavic Population by Thirty Million"'.

110 Trevor-Roper (ed.), *Hitler's Table Talk, 1941–1944*, pp.32–33 (17–18 September 1941).

111 Georgi Kniazev, a civilian in Leningrad, noted in his diary on 21 September, 'The newspapers are full of reports of German atrocities. If they were assembled systematically, you couldn't compile a more terrifying account.' Ales Adamovich and Daniil Granin, *Leningrad under Siege. First-Hand Accounts of the Ordeal* (Barnsley, 2007) p.63. See also: Martin Gilbert, *The*

Holocaust. The Jewish Tragedy (London, 1986) p.186; Evans, *The Third Reich at War*, p.192.

112 Leonidas E. Hill (ed.), *Die Weizsäcker-Papiere 1933–1950* (Frankfurt am Main, 1974) pp.269 (15 September 1941).

113 Martin Humburg, *Das Gesicht des Krieges*, p.122 (19 September 1941).

114 Ibid. (28 September 1941).

115 Hürter (ed.), *Ein deutscher General an der Ostfront*, p.83 (15 September 1941).

116 As cited in: James Lucas, *Das Reich. The Military Role of the 2nd SS Division* (London, 1991) pp.67–68.

117 Ibid.

118 Halder, KTB III, p.236 (17 September 1941).

119 Geyer, *Das IX. Armeekorps im Ostfeldzug 1941*, p.125.

120 'Kriegstagebuch Nr.1 Panzergruppe 2 Band II vom 21.8.1941 bis 31.10.41', BA-MA RH 21–2/931, fol.220 (15 September 1941).

121 Eremenko, *The Arduous Beginning*, pp.225–226.

122 Halder, KTB III, p.235 (16 September 1941).

123 Kleindienst (ed.), *Sei tausendmal gegrüßt*, CD Rom (9 September 1941).

124 Buchbender and Sterz (ed.), *Das andere Gesicht des Krieges*, p.80 (19 September 1941).

125 Fröhlich (ed.), *Die Tagebücher von Joseph Goebbels, Teil II Band 1*, p.419 (15 September 1941).

126 Jarausch and Arnold (eds.), '*Das stille Sterben . . .*', p.318 (23 September 1941).

127 Hans Schäufler (ed.), *Knight's Cross Panzers. The German 35th Panzer Regiment in WWII* (Mechanicsburg, PA, 2010) p.117.

128 Humburg, *Das Gesicht des Krieges*, p.122 (15 August 1941).

129 Jarausch and Arnold (eds.), '*Das stille Sterben . . .*', p.316 (21 September 1941).

130 *True to Type*, p.107 (8 September 1941).

131 Halder, KTB III, p.223 (12 September 1941).

132 The Fieseler Fi-156 *Storch* was a small, light and highly manoeuvrable plane, serving throughout the war as both a liaison and reconnaissance aircraft.

133 Erich von Manstein, *Lost Victories* (Novato, CA, 1958) p.205. See also: Domarus, *Hitler*, p.2481.

134 Colonel-General Werner von Fritsch was not senior to Schobert at the time of his death. Fritsch, Brauchitsch's predecessor as the Commander-in-Chief of the Army (1 February 1934 to 4 February 1938), retired from the army after trumped-up charges of homosexuality orchestrated by Himmler. He was cleared by a special court of inquiry, but not reinstated. On 12 August 1938 he was made an honorary colonel of his old 12th Artillery Regiment,

which he led until his death in the Polish campaign on 22 September 1939. See: Robert O'Neill, 'Fritsch, Beck and the Führer' in Barnett (ed.), *Hitler's Generals*, pp.35 and 40. Thanks also to Dr Adrian Wettstein for his assistance on this matter.

135 Fröhlich (ed.), *Die Tagebücher von Joseph Goebbels, Teil II Band 1*, p.418 (14 September 1941). By contrast General Heinrici gave a somewhat different picture of Schobert. On 13 September he wrote, 'Schobert was no clever man, but very ambitious, vain and besides that brave.' Hürter (ed.), *Ein deutscher General an der Ostfront*, p.83 (13 September 1941).

136 Boberach (ed.), *Meldungen aus dem Reich*, Volume VIII, p.2772, Document 221 (18 September 1941).

137 Hürter (ed.), *Ein deutscher General an der Ostfront*, pp.74–75 (18 August 1941).

138 Guderian, *Panzer Leader*, p.206.

139 Ibid., p.204.

140 Walter Görlitz, *Paulus and Stalingrad* (London, 1963) p.139.

141 Alex Alexiev, 'Soviet Nationals in German Wartime Service, 1941–1945', pp.29–30.

142 Reddemann (ed.), *Zwischen Front und Heimat*, p.297 (31 August 1941).

143 Fröhlich (ed.), *Die Tagebücher von Joseph Goebbels, Teil II Band 1*, p.401 (12 September 1941).

144 Rolf-Dieter Müller, *An der Seite der Wehrmacht*, p.207.

7 Slaughter in the Ukraine

1 'Heersgruppe Süd Kriegstagebuch II.Teil Band 4, 16 Sept.–5 Okt. 1941', BA-MA RH 19-I/73, fol.4 (17 September 1941).

2 Even without having directly contravened Stalin's orders General Dmitri Pavlov, the commander of the Soviet Western Front at the start of Operation Barbarossa, was executed in July on Stalin's order for the disaster which befell his front. Pavlov was at least correct when he stated in his defence, 'I am not a traitor. The defeat of the forces I commanded took place for reasons beyond my control.' Kirponos might evoke the same defence, but defying Stalin's direct orders would certainly have made his case far less tenable. Mawdsley, *Thunder in the East*, p.62.

3 'Heersgruppe Süd Kriegstagebuch II.Teil Band 4, 16 Sept.–5 Okt. 1941', BA-MA RH 19-I/73, fols.4–5 (17 September 1941).

4 Hürter (ed.), *Ein deutscher General an der Ostfront*, p.84 (15 September 1941).

5 'Heersgruppe Süd Kriegstagebuch II.Teil Band 4, 16 Sept.–5 Okt. 1941', BA-MA RH 19-I/73, fol.4 (17 September 1941).

6 Halder, KTB III, p.231 (14 September 1941).
7 Ibid., p.234 (16 September 1941).
8 Bergström, *Barbarossa – the Air Battle*, p.69.
9 Plocher, *The German Air Force versus Russia, 1941*, p.130.
10 Kesselring, *The Memoirs of Field-Marshal Kesselring*, p.94.
11 Plocher, *The German Air Force versus Russia, 1941*, p.130.
12 Kesselring, *The Memoirs of Field-Marshal Kesselring*, p.94.
13 As cited in: Horst Boog, 'The Luftwaffe' in Militärgeschichtliches Forschungsamt (ed.), *Germany and the Second World War*, p.784.
14 Bergström, *Barbarossa – the Air Battle*, p.70.
15 Plocher, *The German Air Force versus Russia, 1941*, pp.131–132. See also: Boog, 'The Luftwaffe', p.784.
16 As cited in: Kershaw, *War without Garlands*, p.159.
17 Plocher, *The German Air Force versus Russia, 1941*, p.132.
18 Halder, KTB III, p.225 (12 September 1941).
19 Fröhlich (ed.), *Die Tagebücher von Joseph Goebbels, Teil II Band 1*, p.318 (28 August 1941).
20 Kesselring, *The Memoirs of Field-Marshal Kesselring*, p.93.
21 David Irving, *The Rise and Fall of the Luftwaffe. The Life of Erhard Milch* (London, 1973) p.131.
22 Williamson Murray, *The Luftwaffe 1933–45. Strategy for Defeat* (Washington, 1996) pp.94–96.
23 Figures do not include the month of November.
24 Murray, *The Luftwaffe 1933–45*, p. 93, table XVII: German Losses, All Causes – 1941. In addition to the damage done to aircraft, the inexperience of aircrew increased the number of instances of friendly fire. Lucas, *Das Reich*, p.66.
25 Figures for the average monthly crew strengths are calculated for the period 22 June–1 November 1941.
26 Murray, *The Luftwaffe 1933–45*, p. 89, table XIII: Crew and Aircraft Losses on the Eastern Front.
27 Halder, KTB III, p.231 (14 September 1941).
28 Müller-Hillebrand, *Das Heer 1933–1945. Band III*, p.205. Reproduced in: Bryan I. Fugate, *Operation Barbarossa. Strategy and Tactics on the Eastern Front, 1941* (Novato, CA, 1984) p.349.
29 Guderian, *Panzer Leader*, p.219.
30 Department of the US Army (ed.), *German Tank Maintenance in World War II*, pp.2–3.
31 After being wounded in the early phase of Operation Barbarossa, Arnim returned to command the 17th Panzer Division on 15 September, replacing the aforementioned Wilhelm Ritter von Thoma.

32 Halder, KTB III, p.231 (14 September 1941).
33 'Kriegstagebuch des Panzerarmee-Oberkdos.1 Band III 1.9.41–31.10.41', BA-MA RH 21–1/51, fol.42 (17 September 1941).
34 Halder, KTB III, p.235 (17 September 1941).
35 '9.Pz.Div. KTB Ia vom 19.5.1941 bis 22.1.1942', BA-MA RH 27–9/4, fol.107 (17 September 1941).
36 'Heersgruppe Süd Kriegstagebuch II.Teil Band 4, 16 Sept.–5 Okt. 1941', BA-MA RH 19-I/73, fol.22 (17 September 1941).
37 Glantz, *Atlas of the Battle for Kiev Part III*, map 137.
38 Erickson, *The Road to Stalingrad*, p.209.
39 The Psel River runs north–south passing through Sumy in the north of the Ukraine and running into the Dnepr River just east of Kremenchug.
40 Anfilov, 'Timoshenko', p.249.
41 Erickson, *The Road to Stalingrad*, p.209.
42 Glantz, *Barbarossa*, p.131.
43 This was an SS rank equivalent to a major in the German army.
44 Eberle and Uhl (eds.), *The Hitler Book*, p.77.
45 Ibid.
46 Bock, *War Diary*, p.312 (14 September 1941).
47 Halder, KTB III, p.232 (15 September 1941).
48 Bock, *War Diary*, p.313 (15 September 1941).
49 '3rd Pz. Gr. KTB Nr.2 1.9.41–31.10.41', BA-MA Microfilm 59060 (9 September 1941).
50 As Basil Liddell Hart observed in relation to German plans against the Soviet Union in 1941, 'The issue in Russia depended less on strategy and tactics than on space, logistics, and mechanics. Although some of the operational decisions were of great importance they did not count so much as mechanical deficiency in conjunction with excess of space, and their effect has to be measured in relation to these basic factors.' Basil Liddell Hart, *History of the Second World War* (London, 1970) p.163.
51 Bock, *War Diary*, p.313 (16 September 1941).
52 '3rd Pz. Gr. KTB Nr.2 1.9.41–31.10.41', BA-MA Microfilm 59060 (9 and 18 September 1941).
53 'KTB 3rd Pz. Div. I.b 19.5.41–6.2.42', BA-MA RH 27–3/218 (15 September 1941).
54 The 4th Panzer Division also made note of its 'very strained' fuel supply. 'Kriegstagebuch 4.Panzer-Divison Führungsabtl. 26.5.41–31.3.42', BA-MA RH 27–4/10, p.167 (16 September 1941).
55 'Kriegstagebuch der O.Qu.-Abt. Pz. A.O.K.2 von 21.6.41 bis 31.3.42', BA-MA RH 21–2/819, fol.199 (16 September 1941).
56 'Kriegstagebuch Nr.2 XXXXVII.Pz.Korps. Ia 25.5.1941–22.9.1941', BA-MA RH 24–47/2 (18 September 1941).

57 The large numbers of Ford trucks in the Soviet Union were not yet the result of Lend-Lease aid, but rather of the establishment of a large factory built under contract by Ford engineers brought over from the USA during the early 1930s.
58 Bidermann, *In Deadly Combat*, p.46.
59 Ibid.
60 'Kriegstagebuch Nr.1 Panzergruppe 2 Band II vom 21.8.1941 bis 31.10.41', BA-MA RH 21–2/931, fol.235 (17 September 1941).
61 Ibid.
62 Samuel W. Mitcham Jr, *The Men of Barbarossa. Commanders of the German Invasion of Russia, 1941* (Newbury, 2009) pp.170–171.
63 Guderian, *Panzer Leader*, p.220.
64 'Kriegstagebuch Nr.1 Panzergruppe 2 Band II vom 21.8.1941 bis 31.10.41', BA-MA RH 21–2/931, fol.244 (18 September 1941).
65 Guderian, *Panzer Leader*, pp.220–222.
66 'Kriegstagebuch Nr.1 Panzergruppe 2 Band II vom 21.8.1941 bis 31.10.41', BA-MA RH 21–2/931, fol.245 (18 September 1941).
67 Guderian, *Panzer Leader*, p.222.
68 'Kriegstagebuch 4.Panzer-Divison Führungsabtl. 26.5.41–31.3.42', BA-MA RH 27–4/10, p.170 (18 September 1941).
69 'KTB 3rd Pz. Div. vom 19.9.41 bis 6.2.42', BA-MA RH 27–3/15, p.248 (19 September 1941).
70 'Kriegstagebuch Nr.1 Panzergruppe 2 Band II vom 21.8.1941 bis 31.10.41', BA-MA RH 21–2/931, fol.259 (20 September 1941).
71 'Kriegstagebuch des Panzerarmee-Oberkdos.1 Band III 1.9.41–31.10.41', BA-MA RH 21–1/51, fol.48 (19 September 1941).
72 Hans Bähr and Walter Bähr, *Die Stimme des Menschen. Briefe und Aufzeichnungen aus der ganzen Welt, 1939–1945* (Munich, 1961) p.135 (19 September 1941). See also: Kershaw, *War without Garlands*, p.158.
73 Cathy Porter and Mark Jones, *Moscow in World War II* (London, 1987) p.99.
74 Lucas, *War of the Eastern Front 1941–1945*, p.193.
75 '9.Pz.Div. KTB Ia vom 19.5.1941 bis 22.1.1942', BA-MA RH 27–9/4, fol.109 (19 September 1941); Guderian, *Panzer Leader*, p.222.
76 '9.Pz.Div. KTB Ia vom 19.5.1941 bis 22.1.1942', BA-MA RH 27–9/4, fol.111 (20 September 1941).
77 'Kriegstagebuch XXXXVIII.Pz.Kps. Abt.Ia September 1941', BA-MA RH 24–48/25 (20 September 1941). This war diary has no folio stamped page numbers so references must be located using the date.
78 Kern, *Dance of Death*, pp.56 and 60. See also: von Below, *Als Hitlers Adjutant 1937–45*, p.289.
79 Evans, *The Third Reich at War*, p.192.
80 Landon and Leitner (eds.), *Diary of a German Soldier*, p.107 (20 September 1941).

81 For one overview of the initial German conquest and occupation of Kiev see: Klaus Jochen Arnold, 'Die Eroberung und Behandlung der Stadt Kiew durch die Wehrmacht im September 1941; Zur Radikalisierung der Besatzungspolitik', *Militärgeschichtliche Mitteilungen*, No. 58 (1999) pp.23–63.

82 For tactical details on the siege and conquest of the city see: Haupt, *Army Group South*, pp.77–82; Karl Knoblauch, *Kampf und Untergang der 95. Infanteriedivision. Chronik einer Infanteriedivision von 1939–1945 in Frankreich und an der Ostfront* (Würzburg, 2008) pp.108–115.

83 Halder, KTB III, p.240 (19 September 1941).

84 Haupt, *Kiew*, p.137.

85 Breloer (ed.), *Mein Tagebuch*, pp.98–99 (19 September 1941).

86 Fröhlich (ed.), *Die Tagebücher von Joseph Goebbels, Teil II Band 1*, p.465 (22 September 1941).

87 Wettstein, 'Urban Warfare Doctrine on the Eastern Front'.

88 Klink, 'The Conduct of Operations', p.602; Bellamy, *Absolute War*, p.261.

89 Berkhoff, *Harvest of Despair*, pp.29–30.

90 Klink, 'The Conduct of Operations', p.602.

91 Berkhoff, *Harvest of Despair*, pp.30–31.

92 Klink, 'The Conduct of Operations', p.603.

93 Berkhoff, *Harvest of Despair*, pp.30–31.

94 Klink, 'The Conduct of Operations', p.603.

95 According to Richard J. Evans the city's population had dropped by half from 600,000 to 300,000. Evans, *The Third Reich at War*, p.192.

96 Berkhoff, *Harvest of Despair*, p.31.

97 Ibid., pp.31–32.

98 Bernd Boll and Hans Safrian, 'On the Way to Stalingrad: the 6th Army in 1941–42' in Hannes Heer and Klaus Naumann (eds.), *War of Extermination. The German Military in World War II 1941–1944* (New York and Oxford, 2006) p.254.

99 Ernst Klee, Willi Dressen and Volker Riess (eds.), *'The Good Old Days'. The Holocaust as Seen by its Perpetrators and Bystanders* (Old Saybrook, CT, 1991) pp.66–67. For more first-person accounts of the massacre see: Gilbert, *The Holocaust*, pp.202–205; Richard Rhodes, *Masters of Death. The SS Einsatzgruppen and the Invention of the Holocaust* (New York, 2003) chapter 11: 'Babi Yar'; Hartmut Rüss, 'Kiev/Babij Jar 1941' in Gerd R. Ueberschär (ed.), *Orte des Grauens. Verbrechen im Zweiten Weltkrieg* (Frankfurt am Main, 2003) pp.102–113.

100 Knowledge of what had happened at Babi Yar spread quickly through Kiev. One woman wrote in her diary about the awful details she had heard and then concluded, 'There are more and more such rumours and accounts. They

are too monstrous to believe. But we are forced to believe them, for the shooting of the Jews is a fact. A fact which is starting to drive us insane... I am writing, but my hair is standing on end.' Saul Friedläder, *The Years of Extermination. Nazi Germany and the Jews, 1939–1945* (New York, 2007) p.197.

101 Nor were the Nazis solely responsible for the mass killing of Ukrainian Jews. After the occupation of Odessa by Romanian forces an attack on the military headquarters led to Antonescu ordering the deaths of 18,000 Jews. In the event some 34,000–35,000 Jews were shot or burned to death in the city during October 1941. See Wendy Lower, 'Axis Collaboration, Operation "Barbarossa" and the Holocaust in Ukraine' in Kay *et al.* (eds.), *Nazi Policy on the Eastern Front, 1941*.

102 Although the subject of far less research, it is important to remember that Soviet Roma were also being targeted in the Ukraine. See: Martin Holler, 'Extending the Genocidal Programme: Did Otto Ohlendorf Initiate the Systematic Extermination of Soviet "Gypsies"?' in Kay *et al.* (eds.), *Nazi Policy on the Eastern Front, 1941*.

103 Halder, KTB III, p.239 (19 September 1941).

104 'Heersgruppe Süd Kriegstagebuch II.Teil Band 4, 16 Sept.–5 Okt. 1941', BA-MA RH 19-I/73, fol.43 (19 September 1941).

105 Halder, KTB III, p.240 (19 September 1941).

106 Bergström, *Barbarossa – the Air Battle*, p.70.

107 'Heersgruppe Süd Kriegstagebuch II.Teil Band 4, 16 Sept.–5 Okt. 1941', BA-MA RH 19-I/73, fol.43 (19 September 1941).

108 Landon and Leitner (eds.), *Diary of a German Soldier*, p.106 (19 September 1941).

109 'Kriegstagebuch XXXXVIII.Pz.Kps. Abt.Ia September 1941', BA-MA RH 24–48/25 (19 September 1941).

110 Werner Haupt, *Army Group Centre. The Wehrmacht in Russia 1941–1945* (Atglen, PA, 1998), p.75.

111 Eremenko, *The Arduous Beginning*, pp.233–234.

112 'KTB 3rd Pz. Div. vom 19.9.41 bis 6.2.42', BA-MA RH 27–3/15, p.248 (19 September 1941).

113 Aleksander A. Maslov, *Fallen Soviet Generals. Soviet General Officers Killed in Battle, 1941–1945* (London, 1998) p.28.

114 He would survive his wounds as well as German imprisonment and, despite the Stalinist-era stigma of having been captured, Potapov returned to service in the Red Army after 1945. Mawdsley, *Thunder in the East*, p.80; Haupt, *Army Group Centre*, p.75.

115 Eremenko, *The Arduous Beginning*, p.235.

116 Bähr and Bähr, *Die Stimme des Menschen*, p.135 (19 September 1941).

117 'Kriegstagebuch XXXXVIII.Pz.Kps. Abt.Ia September 1941', BA-MA RH 24-48/25 (20 September 1941).
118 '14.Pz.Div. KTB Ia vom 1.5.1941 bis 15.12.1941', BA-MA RH 27-14/1, fol.139 (17 September 1941).
119 'KTB 3rd Pz. Div. vom 19.9.41 bis 6.2.42', BA-MA RH 27-3/15, p.258 (21 September 1941).
120 Bidermann, *In Deadly Combat*, p.44.
121 Alexander Dallin, Ralph Mavrogordato and Wilhelm Moll, 'Partisan Psychological Warfare and Popular Attitudes' in John A. Armstrong (ed.), *Soviet Partisans in World War II* (Madison, 1964) pp.321–322. See also: Matthew Cooper, *The Phantom War. The German Struggle against Soviet Partisans 1941–1944* (London, 1979) p.43.
122 Hürter, *Hitlers Heerführer*, pp.415–416.
123 According to Solomon Perel's testimony, 'For them [the Germans] it was routine to tear the clothes off men under suspicion and to hang a sign reading; "I was a partisan" around their necks. On the women's chests they'd pin a sign: "I'm a gun moll [*Flintenweib*]." After that, they strung them up on scaffolds set up in the marketplace or by the side of the road. That was intended to intimidate the local population, to keep them from joining the partisans who had begun to organize under the noses of the Germans.' Perel, *Europa Europa*, p.44.
124 Dominic Lieven, *Russia against Napoleon*, p.218.
125 Alexander Hill, *The War behind the Eastern Front. The Soviet Partisan Movement in North-West Russia 1941–1944* (New York, 2006) p.83. Among the more outstanding studies on partisan warfare in the east with a relevance to 1941 see: Ben Shepherd, *War in the Wild East. The German Army and Soviet Partisans* (Cambridge, 2004); Kenneth Slepyan, *Stalin's Guerrillas. Soviet Partisans in World War II* (Lawerence, KS, 2006); Antonio Munoz and Oleg V. Romanko, *Hitler's White Russians. Collaboration, Extermination and Anti-Partisan Warfare in Byelorussia 1941–1944. A Study of White Russian Collaboration and German Occupation Policies* (New York, 2003); John A. Armstrong (ed.), *Soviet Partisans in World War II* (Madison, 1964).
126 Anatoly Golovchansky, Valentin Osipov, Anatoly Prokopenko, Ute Daniel and Jürgen Reulecke (eds.), *'Ich will raus aus diesem Wahnsinn'. Deutsche Briefe von der Ostfront 1941–1945. Aus sowjetischen Archiven* (Hamburg, 1993) p.33 (20 September 1941); Hans Pichler, *Truppenarzt und Zeitzeuge*, p.100 (14 September 1941).
127 Lammers (ed.), *'Fahrtberichte' aus der Zeit des deutsch-sowjetischen Krieges 1941*, p.85 (18 September 1941).
128 Nor was it only in the territories of the Soviet Union that Germany was facing a costly partisan war. Tito's partisans in Yugoslavia were estimated to

number 70,000 in September 1941 and even managed to seize the town of Uzice with its rifle factory. They held it for two months. Gilbert, *The Second World War*, p.236. See also: Fröhlich (ed.), *Die Tagebücher von Joseph Goebbels, Teil II Band 1*, p.324 (29 August 1941).

129 Kuhnert, *Will We See Tomorrow?*, p.100.

130 As cited in: Berkhoff, *Harvest of Despair*, p.12.

131 Ibid., pp.12–13.

132 Ibid., p.13.

133 '14.Pz.Div. KTB Ia vom 1.5.1941 bis 15.12.1941', BA-MA RH 27–14/1, fol.145 (21 September 1941).

134 In jest, the soldiers from the regiment decided to write to Goebbels himself requesting he send them replacement cigarettes. The propaganda minister sent the regiment a personal reply along with 20,000 cigarettes. Fröhlich (ed.), *Die Tagebücher von Joseph Goebbels, Teil II Band 1*, p.405 (12 September 1941).

135 Ibid., p.445 (18 September 1941).

136 Boberach (ed.), *Meldungen aus dem Reich*, Volume VIII, p.2760, Document 220 (15 September 1941).

137 Ibid., Volume VIII, p.2772, Document 221 (18 September 1941).

138 Fröhlich (ed.), *Die Tagebücher von Joseph Goebbels, Teil II Band 1*, pp.445–446 (20 September 1941).

139 Ibid., p.463 (21 September 1941).

140 Mihail Sebastian, *Journal, 1935–1944* (London, 2003) p.413 (21 September 1941).

141 Golovchansky *et al.* (eds.), *'Ich will raus aus diesem Wahnsinn'*, p.34 (21 September 1941).

142 Boberach (ed.), *Meldungen aus dem Reich*, Volume VIII, p.2787, Document 222 (22 September 1941).

143 Goebbels spelled this 'Oesel', but the correct German spelling is Ösel. The island is known today by its Estonian name, 'Saaremaa'.

144 Goebbels spelled this 'Moen', but the correct German spelling is Moon. The island is known today by its Estonian name, 'Muhu'.

145 Fröhlich (ed.), *Die Tagebücher von Joseph Goebbels, Teil II Band 1*, p.470 (22 September 1941). For an overview and map of the German operation to capture the Baltic islands see: Robert Kirchubel, *Operation Barbarossa 1941 (2): Army Group North* (Oxford, 2005) pp.65–67 and 72–73.

146 Emphasis in the original. Humburg, *Das Gesicht des Krieges*, p.125 (24 September 1941).

147 Hürter (ed.), *Ein deutscher General an der Ostfront*, p.88 (24 September 1941).

148 Hassell, *Vom Andern Deutschland*, pp.222–223 (20 September 1941); Hassell, *The von Hassell Diaries 1938–1944*, p.193 (20 September 1941).

149 Hassell, *Vom Andern Deutschland*, p.223 (20 September 1941); Hassell, *The von Hassell Diaries 1938–1944*, p.193 (20 September 1941).
150 Hassell, *Vom Andern Deutschland*, p.227 (no date given, September 1941); Hassell, *The von Hassell Diaries 1938–1944*, p.197 (no date given, September 1941).
151 Malcolm Muggeridge (ed.), *Ciano's Diary 1939–1943* (Kingswood, 1947) p.373 (22 September 1941).

8 Visions of victory

1 Glantz, *Barbarossa*, p.101.
2 Richard Muller, *The German Air War in Russia* (Baltimore, 1992) p.55.
3 Halder, KTB III, pp.178 and 180 (15 August 1941).
4 Ibid., p.145 (2 August 1941).
5 Georg Meyer (ed.), *Generalfeldmarschall Wilhelm Ritter von Leeb. Tagebuchaufzeichnungen und Lagebeurteilungen aus zwei Weltkriegen* (Stuttgart, 1976) p.345 (27 August 1941), hereafter cited as Leeb, KTB.
6 The letter refers to the 'K.d.F.', the 'Kraft durch Freude' (literally the 'Strength through Joy') programme organized by the German Labour Front to provide affordable leisure activities for workers and their families.
7 Reddemann (ed.), *Zwischen Front und Heimat*, p.288 (20 August 1941).
8 Klink, 'The Conduct of Operations', p.641.
9 Leeb, KTB, p.352 (8 September 1941).
10 For more on Finland's military and political calculations in the war against the Soviet Union see: Olli Vehviläinen, *Finland in the Second World War. Between Germany and Russia* (New York, 2002) pp.93–96.
11 As cited in: Jones, *Leningrad*, p.37.
12 As cited in: Hürter, *Hitlers Heerführer*, p.296.
13 Ibid.
14 Ibid.
15 For example see: Samuel W. Mitcham, *Hitler's Field Marshals and their Battles* (Chatham, 1988) p.141.
16 As cited in: Liddell Hart, *The Other Side of the Hill*, p.278.
17 See: Jones, *Leningrad*, chapter 2: 'The Biggest Bag of Shit in the Army'.
18 Keegan, *The Second World War*, p.197.
19 Adamovich and Granin, *Leningrad under Siege*, p.60.
20 As cited in: David M. Glantz, *The Battle for Leningrad, 1941–1944* (Lawrence, KS, 2002) p.75; Chaney, *Zhukov*, p.147.
21 See the excellent discussion in: Clark, *Barbarossa*, pp.126–127.
22 As cited in: Jones, *Leningrad*, p.39; Kershaw, *War without Garlands*, p.125.

23 William Lubbeck with David B. Hurt, *At Leningrad's Gates. The Story of a Soldier with Army Group North* (Philadelphia, 2006) p.102.
24 Leeb, KTB, p.360 (20 September 1941).
25 Ibid., p.353 (11 September 1941).
26 As cited in: Jones, *Leningrad*, p.39; Kershaw, *War without Garlands*, p.125.
27 Jörg Ganzenmüller, *Das belagerte Leningrad 1941–1944. Die Strategien von Angreifern und Verteidigern* (Paderborn, 2005) I. 'Die Belagerung als Vernichtungsstrategie'.
28 Halder, KTB III, p.239 (18 September 1941).
29 Fröhlich (ed.), *Die Tagebücher von Joseph Goebbels, Teil II Band 1*, p.389 (10 September 1941).
30 As cited in: Jones, *Leningrad*, p.40.
31 Harrison E. Salisbury, *The 900 Days. The Siege of Leningrad* (New York, 1985) pp.289–291.
32 Simmons and Perlina, *Writing the Siege of Leningrad*, p.24. See also the diary of Georgi Zim reproduced in: Lektorat Antjeleetz and Barbara Wenner (eds.), *Blockade. Leningrad 1941–1945. Dokumente und Essays von Russen und Deutschen* (Hamburg, 1992) p.59 (21 September 1941).
33 Reddemann (ed.), *Zwischen Front und Heimat*, p.311 (16 September 1941).
34 Humburg, *Das Gesicht des Krieges*, p.123 (10 September 1941).
35 Domarus, *Hitler*, p.2483 (29 September 1941).
36 As cited in: Jones, *Leningrad*, p.129.
37 Ibid., p.38.
38 Hans Röttiger, 'XXXXI Panzer Corps during the Battle of Moscow in 1941 as a Component of Panzer Group 3' in Steven H. Newton (ed.), *German Battle Tactics on the Russian Front 1941–1945* (Atglen, PA, 1994) p.16.
39 Halder, KTB III, p.224 (12 September 1941).
40 Clark, *Barbarossa*, p.123.
41 From a starting strength of 231 tanks on 22 June 1941.
42 'KTB Nr.1 der 12. Panzer-Division Heft 1 25.5.–30.9.41', BA-MA RH 27–12/2, fol.128 (13 September 1941); see also: fols.136 and 140 (15 and 17 September 1941).
43 Leeb, KTB, p.353 (11 September 1941).
44 Trevor-Roper (ed.), *Hitler's War Directives 1939–1945*, p.154 (6 September 1941).
45 Glantz, *The Battle for Leningrad, 1941–1944*, p.83.
46 Halder, KTB III, p.231 (14 September 1941).
47 Bismarck was only a temporary divisional commander, taking over from Lieutenant-General Horst Stumpff on 10 September and handing command of the division over to Major-General Wilhelm Ritter von Thoma on 14 October 1941. Andris J. Kursietis, *The Wehrmacht at War 1939–1945. The Units and*

Commanders of the German Ground Forces during World War II (Soesterberg, 1999) p.103.

48 'Gen.Kdo.LVII.Pz.Korps KTB Nr.1 vom 15.2.41–31.10.41', BA-MA RH 24–57/2, fols.210–211 (8 September 1941).

49 Ibid., fol.239 (22 September 1941).

50 '20.Pz.Div. KTB vom 15.8.41 bis 20.10.41 Band Ia', BA-MA RH 27–20/25, fol.93 (20 September 1941). The war diary for Panzer Group 4 claimed that before the march south began the 20th Panzer Division had 'over twenty serviceable tanks'. See: 'Anlage zum KTB Panzer Gruppe 4: 20.9.41–14.10.41', BA-MA RH 21–4/34, fol.121 (22 September 1941).

51 Ibid., fol.90 (19 September 1941).

52 The 3rd Motorized Infantry Division was not quite so well equipped, with two of its regiments having been fitted out with French trucks.

53 Bock, *War Diary*, p.314 (17 September 1941).

54 As cited in: Michael Jones, *The Retreat. Hitler's First Defeat* (London, 2009) p.28.

55 Ibid; Walter Chales de Beaulieu, *Generaloberst Erich Hoepner. Militärisches Porträt eines Panzer-Führers* (Neckargemünd, 1969) pp.193–194.

56 Halder, KTB III, p.236 (17 September 1941).

57 Bock, *War Diary*, p.315 (20 September 1941).

58 Halder, KTB III, p.53 (8 July 1941). Hitler did, however, make an exception to his rule in July, releasing a total of eighty-five tanks after Halder pleaded 'the urgent needs of the front'. See: ibid., p.54 (8 July 1941).

59 Ibid., p.233 (15 September 1941).

60 Müller, 'The Failure of the Economic "Blitzkrieg Strategy"', p.1127.

61 Klink, 'The Military Concept of the War against the Soviet Union', p.318.

62 Halder, KTB III, p.242 (20 September 1941).

63 Ibid., p.233 (15 September 1941).

64 Halder, *Hitler als Feldherr*, p.43.

65 The diary of Georgi Zim is reproduced in: Antjeleetz and Wenner (eds.), *Blockade*, p.59 (22 September 1941).

66 Glantz, *Barbarossa*, p.132; Bellamy, *Absolute War*, p.261.

67 'Kriegstagebuch des Panzerarmee-Oberkdos.1 Band III 1.9.41–31.10.41', BA-MA RH 21–1/51, fol.55 (21 September 1941).

68 The period for these figures extends from 25 August to 21 September. 'Kriegstagebuch Nr.1 Panzergruppe 2 Band II vom 21.8.1941 bis 31.10.41', BA-MA RH 21–2/931, fol.275 (22 September 1941).

69 'KTB Nr.2 der 125.Inf.Div. (Abt.Ia) 22.6.1941–15.12.1941', BA-MA RH 26–125/3, p.324 (21 September 1941).

70 'Kriegstagebuch des Panzerarmee-Oberkdos.1 Band III 1.9.41–31.10.41', BA-MA RH 21–1/51, fol.55 (21 September 1941); see also: 'Kriegstagebuch

XXXXVIII.Pz.Kps. Abt.Ia September 1941', BA-MA RH 24–48/25 (21 September 1941).

71 'KTB Nr.7 Generalkommando XI.A.K. Führungsabteilung 19.8.41–31.12.41', BA-MA RH 24–11/38, fol.75 (21 September 1941). It certainly did not help that Neuling's infantry regiments were not outfitted with any machine gun companies until November 1941 and the division also lacked a tank destroyer battalion until December. See: Samuel W. Mitcham Jr, *German Order of Battle. Volume I. 1st–290th Infantry Divisions in WWII* (Mechanicsburg, PA, 2007) p.284.

72 Ibid., fol.76 (21 September 1941).

73 'KTB Nr.2 der 125.Inf.Div. (Abt.Ia) 22.6.1941–15.12.1941', BA-MA RH 26–125/3, p.322 (21 September 1941).

74 *True to Type*, p.22 (23 September 1941).

75 Ingo Stader (ed.), *Ihr daheim und wir hier draußen*, p.34 (23/24 September 1941).

76 'KTB Nr.2 der 125.Inf.Div. (Abt.Ia) 22.6.1941–15.12.1941', BA-MA RH 26–125/3, p.330 (22 September 1941).

77 Ibid., p.324 (22 September 1941).

78 Ibid., pp.332 and 338 (23 September 1941).

79 'KTB Nr.7 Generalkommando XI.A.K. Führungsabteilung 19.8.41–31.12.41', BA-MA RH 24–11/38, fol.82 (23 September 1941).

80 Ibid., fols.82 and 84 (22 and 23 September 1941).

81 Denysivka is a small town about 12 kilometres to the north-west of Orzhitsa.

82 Both regiments belonged to the 125th Infantry Division.

83 The Orzhitsa is a small river of the same name as the town.

84 'KTB Nr.2 der 125.Inf.Div. (Abt.Ia) 22.6.1941–15.12.1941', BA-MA RH 26–125/3, pp.342–344 (25 September 1941).

85 As cited in: Christopher Ailsby, *Images of Barbarossa. The German Invasion of Russia, 1941* (Shepperton, 2001) p.115.

86 Landon and Leitner (eds.), *Diary of a German Soldier*, p.107 (20 September 1941).

87 Guderian, *Panzer Leader*, p.222.

88 '9.Pz.Div. KTB Ia vom 19.5.1941 bis 22.1.1942', BA-MA RH 27–9/4, fol.113 (21 September 1941).

89 Becker, *Devil on my Shoulder*, pp.26–29.

90 Kuhnert, *Will We See Tomorrow?*, p.97.

91 As cited in: Kershaw, *War without Garlands*, p.162; Haupt, *Kiew*, p.145.

92 Reinhardt, *Moscow – the Turning Point*, p.59.

93 Halder, KTB III, p.249 (24 September 1941).

94 Bock, *War Diary*, p.317 (24 September 1941).

95 Guderian, *Panzer Leader*, pp.224–225.

96 Bock, *War Diary*, p.317 (24 September 1941).
97 Ibid. (24 September 1941).
98 Ibid., p.316 (22 September 1941).
99 Ibid., p.317 (23 September 1941).
100 Ibid., pp.317–318 (24 September 1941).
101 Ibid., p.318 (25 September 1941). The Spanish 'Blue' Division consisted of volunteers from Franco's Falangist movement and remained on the eastern front until October 1943. For the best English-language study of the 'Blue' Division (soon designated the 250th Infantry Division) see: Gerald R. Kleinfeld and Lewis A. Tambs, *Hitler's Spanish Legion. The Blue Division in Russia* (St Petersburg, FL, 2005). In Spanish see: Xavier Moreno Juliá, *La División Azul: Sangre española en Rusia, 1941–1945* (Barcelona, 2005).
102 'Kriegstagebuch Nr.1 Panzergruppe 2 Band II vom 21.8.1941 bis 31.10.41', BA-MA RH 21–2/931, fol.249 (19 September 1941).
103 Ibid., fols.258–259 (20 September 1941).
104 'Kriegstagebuch Nr.2 XXXXVII.Pz.Korps. Ia 25.5.1941–22.9.1941', BA-MA RH 24–47/2 (20 September 1941).
105 Guderian, *Panzer Leader*, p.225.
106 'Kriegstagebuch 4.Panzer-Divison Führungsabtl. 26.5.41–31.3.42', BA-MA RH 27–4/10, pp.177 and 179 (22 September 1941).
107 David Garden and Kenneth Andrew (eds.), *The War Diaries of a Panzer Soldier. Erich Hager with the 17th Panzer Division on the Russian Front 1941–1945* (Atglen, PA, 2010) pp.51–52 (22 September 1941).
108 Guderian, *Panzer Leader*, p.225.
109 Chales de Beaulieu, *Generaloberst Erich Hoepner*, p.192.
110 Trevor-Roper (ed.), *Hitler's Table Talk, 1941–1944*, p.41 (25 September 1941).
111 On 23 May 1945 in a secretly recorded lecture given by Lieutenant-General Ferdinand Heim to his fellow high-ranking German POWs at Trent Park in England, Heim addressed the question of Germany's loss in the war. 'Could the war have been won at all, even if no military mistakes had been made? My opinion is: no. From 1941 onwards at the latest it was just as much lost as the Great War because the political aims bore no relation whatsoever to Germany's military and economic possibilities.' Neitzel, *Tapping Hitler's Generals*, p.159, Document 82 (23 May 1945).
112 'The Germans in Russia', LH 15/4/40. See the file entitled 'Von Rundstedt writes home' p.2 (22 September 1941).
113 Buchbender and Sterz (eds.), *Das andere Gesicht des Krieges*, p.81 (22 September 1941).
114 Winston S. Churchill, *The Second World War*, Abridged Edition (London, 1959) p.462.

115 As cited in: Kershaw, *War without Garlands*, p.161.

116 Ibid., p.160.

117 Fröhlich (ed.), *Die Tagebücher von Joseph Goebbels, Teil II Band 1*, p.517 (30 September 1941).

118 Haupt, *Kiew*, p.127.

119 The level of suspicion tended to increase with the length of time a man had remained behind German lines.

120 Domarus, *Hitler*, p.2481 (24 September 1941).

121 'Kriegstagebuch des Panzerarmee-Oberkdos.1 Band III 1.9.41–31.10.41', BA-MA RH 21–1/51, fol.61 (24 September 1941).

122 'Kriegstagebuch Nr.1 Panzergruppe 2 Band II vom 21.8.1941 bis 31.10.41', BA-MA RH 21–2/931, fol.283 (23 September 1941).

123 'Kriegstagebuch des Panzerarmee-Oberkdos.1 Band III 1.9.41–31.10.41', BA-MA RH 21–1/51, fols.65–66 (25 September 1941).

124 Fröhlich (ed.), *Die Tagebücher von Joseph Goebbels, Teil II Band 1*, p.502 (27 September 1941).

125 Ibid., p.507 (28 September 1941). See also: KTB OKW, Volume II, p.661 (26 September 1941); 'Heersgruppe Süd Kriegstagebuch II.Teil Band 4, 16 Sept.–5 Okt. 1941', BA-MA RH 19-I/73, fol.132 (26 September 1941).

126 Keegan, *The Second World War*, p.196; Murray and Millett, *A War to be Won*, p.130; Gerhard Weinberg, *A World at Arms. A Global History of World War II* (Cambridge, 1994) p.272; Kitchen, *A World in Flames*, p.81; Müller, *Der letzte deutsche Krieg 1939–1945*, p.110. The figure also appears in the memoirs of the German generals who took part. See: Guderian, *Panzer Leader*, p.225; Kesselring, *The Memoirs of Field-Marshal Kesselring*, p.94.

127 Glantz, *Barbarossa*, p.132; Krivosheev (ed.), *Soviet Casualties and Combat Losses in the Twentieth Century*, p.114; Roberts, *Stalin's Wars*, p.102. Chris Bellamy cites slightly different figures. He claims the Soviet South-Western Front lost 585,598 men. Bellamy, *Absolute War*, p.262.

128 Fröhlich (ed.), *Die Tagebücher von Joseph Goebbels, Teil II Band 1*, p.514 (29 September 1941).

129 For my study of the panzer groups in the battle of Kiev I have dated Guderian's involvement from 25 August and Kleist's from 12 September.

9 The calm before the storm

1 Fröhlich (ed.), *Die Tagebücher von Joseph Goebbels, Teil II Band 1*, p.481 (24 September 1941).

2 Ibid. (24 September 1941).

3 Halder, KTB III, p.246 (23 September 1941).

4 As cited in: Jones, *The Retreat*, p.27. See also: Hürter, *Hitlers Heerführer*, p.295, footnote 81.

5 Boberach (ed.), *Meldungen aus dem Reich*, Volume VIII, p.2795, Document 223 (25 September 1941).

6 Ibid., Volume VIII, p.2809, Document 224 (29 September 1941).

7 Fröhlich (ed.), *Die Tagebücher von Joseph Goebbels, Teil II Band 1*, p.505 (27 September 1941).

8 Kleindienst (ed.), *Sei tausendmal gegrüßt*, CD Rom (29 September 1941).

9 The 11th Panzer Division was under the direction of Reichenau's Sixth Army, but it played no role in the last two weeks of the battle.

10 As cited in: Jones, *The Retreat*, p.27. Schönbeck was interviewed in Guido Knopp's documentary 'Die Wehrmacht – Eine Bilanz' (2007), episode 2: 'Wende des Krieges'.

11 Boberach (ed.), *Meldungen aus dem Reich*, Volume VIII, p.2809, Document 224 (29 September 1941).

12 Since the 1980s there have been a handful of historians who have attempted to ameliorate Germany's guilt in this matter by erroneously arguing that shortages and the harsh conditions in the east simply prevented the best efforts of the army to provide for the Soviet POWs. Klaus J. Arnold is the latest and currently the most prominent advocate of such fallacious views.

13 Schulte, *The German Army and Nazi Policies in Occupied Russia*, p.180.

14 Christian Streit, 'Soviet Prisoners of War in the Hands of the Wehrmacht' in Hannes Heer and Klaus Naumann (eds.), *War of Extermination. The German Military in World War II 1941–1944* (Oxford, 2006) p.81; Schulte, *The German Army and Nazi Policies in Occupied Russia*, p.203.

15 Siegfried Knappe with Ted Brusaw, *Soldat. Reflections of a German Soldier, 1936–1949* (New York, 1992) pp.220–222.

16 Bartov, *The Eastern Front, 1941–45*, p.114.

17 Edmund Blandford (ed.), *Under Hitler's Banner. Serving the Third Reich* (Edison, NJ, 2001) p.127.

18 Kuhnert, *Will We See Tomorrow?*, p.99.

19 Christian Streit, 'Partisans – Resistance – Prisoners of War' in Joseph Wieczynski (ed.), *Operation Barbarossa. The German Attack on the Soviet Union June 22, 1941* (Salt Lake City, 1993) p.272.

20 Streit, *Keine Kameraden*, p.154.

21 Nikolai I. Obryn'ba, *Red Partisan. The Memoir of a Soviet Resistance Fighter on the Eastern Front* (Washington, DC, 2007) pp.28–30.

22 Neitzel, *Tapping Hitler's Generals*, p.189, Document 103 (27–28 August 1944).

23 Streit, 'Partisans – Resistance – Prisoners of War', p.272.

24 Schulte, *The German Army and Nazi Policies in Occupied Russia*, p.195.

25 Streit, 'Soviet Prisoners of War in the Hands of the Wehrmacht', pp.81–82.
26 Muggeridge (ed.), *Ciano's Diary 1939–1943*, p.402 (24 November 1941).
27 Gerald Reitlinger, *The House Built on Sand. The Conflicts of German Policy in Russia 1939–45* (London, 1960) p.104.
28 Schulte, *The German Army and Nazi Policies in Occupied Russia*, p.195.
29 Neitzel, *Tapping Hitler's Generals*, p.189, Document 103 (27–28 August 1944).
30 Streit, *Keine Kameraden*, p.153.
31 'KTB Nr.2 der 125.Inf.Div. (Abt.Ia) 22.6.1941–15.12.1941', BA-MA RH 26–125/3, p.342 (25 September 1941).
32 '14.Pz.Div. KTB Ia vom 1.5.1941 bis 15.12.1941', BA-MA RH 27–14/1, fol.146 (23 September 1941).
33 Overy, *Russia's War*, p.87; Knappe with Brusaw, *Soldat*, p.225.
34 Steiger, *Armour Tactics in the Second World War*, p.93.
35 The German report is cited in: Thurston, 'Cauldrons of Loyalty and Betrayal: Soviet Soldiers' Behavior, 1941 and 1945', p.239.
36 Glantz, *Barbarossa*, p.132; Beevor and Vinogradova (eds.), *A Writer at War*, p.36.
37 It should be noted that Blumentritt originally wrote this as part of an essay on *Kesselschlachten* (encirclement battles) for the British historian Basil Liddell Hart. Blumentritt wrote in English and my quotation corrected one very awkward construction, but otherwise it appears as it was written. 'The Germans in Russia', LH 15/4/40. See the essay entitled '*Kesselschlachten*', p.2.
38 Nor would it be the last time that Vlasov would find himself behind German lines, but on the next occasion in July 1942 he was captured and soon agreed to work with the Germans. He eventually led the so-called Russian Liberation Army, but after the war he was hanged by the Soviets. Catherine Andreyev, 'Vlasov' in Shukman (ed.), *Stalin's Generals*, p.304.
39 Erickson, *The Road to Stalingrad*, p.210.
40 Overmans, *Deutsche militärische Verluste im Zweiten Weltkrieg*, pp.277–278.
41 The Eleventh Army fighting on the Black Sea coast and the German forces in Finland would also constitute a part of the figure.
42 Kuhnert, *Will We See Tomorrow?*, p.98.
43 As cited in: Kershaw, *War without Garlands*, p.162.
44 'Verlustmeldungen 5.7.1941–25.3.1942', BA-MA RH 21–2/757, fols.10 and 14 (31 August and 5 October 1941).
45 Lucas, *Das Reich*, p.69.
46 *Sturmbannführer* was a rank of the SS equivalent to major in the German Army.
47 As cited in: Kershaw, *War without Garlands*, p.175.

48 Trevor-Roper (ed.), *Hitler's Table Talk, 1941–1944*, p.40 (25 September 1941).
49 Halder, KTB III, p.266 (4 October 1941).
50 Ibid., p.254 (26 September 1941).
51 Stader (ed.), *Ihr daheim und wir hier draußen*, pp.48–49 (27 September 1941).
52 Gilbert, *The Second World War*, p.236.
53 Halder's diary refers first to the 291st Infantry Division and then the 99th Light Division, but neither of these would ultimately be sent to Serbia. Halder, KTB III, pp.247 and 249 (23 and 25 September 1941).
54 Ibid., p.275 (9 October 1941).
55 Ibid. (9 October 1941).
56 Ibid., p.247 (23 September 1941).
57 Trevor-Roper (ed.), *Hitler's War Directives 1939–1945*, p.156 (22 September 1941).
58 'Kriegstagebuch Nr.1 Panzergruppe 2 Band II vom 21.8.1941 bis 31.10.41', BA-MA RH 21-2/931, fols.314–315 (26 September 1941).
59 Carl Wagener, *Moskau 1941. Der Angriff auf die russische Hauptstadt* (Dorheim, 1985) p.41. Although the shipment of American supplies to the Soviet Union was extremely limited before the First Protocol was agreed (1 October 1941), a total of 1,575 tons of trucks and other vehicles were sent via the Atlantic and Pacific routes. Robert Huhn Jones, *The Roads to Russia. United States Lend-Lease to the Soviet Union* (Norman, OK, 1969) appendix A, table 1, p.272.
60 Mawdsley, *Thunder in the East*, p.191.
61 Gilbert, *The Second World War*, p.240.
62 Having read the German reports pertaining to Operation Typhoon Churchill is said to have asked his head of intelligence, 'Are you warning the Russians of the developing concentrations?' He then added, 'Show me the last five messages you have sent . . . ' Ibid., p.239.
63 DiNardo, *Germany and the Axis Powers*, p.123.
64 Müller, *An der Seite der Wehrmacht*, p.42.
65 Cecil D. Eby, *Hungary at War. Civilians and Soldiers in World War II* (University Park, PA, 1998) p.26.
66 Vehviläinen, *Finland in the Second World War*, p.96.
67 DiNardo, *Germany and the Axis Powers*, pp.107–108.
68 Müller, *An der Seite der Wehrmacht*, p.32.
69 Vehviläinen, *Finland in the Second World War*, p.96.
70 Before being transferred to Kleist's Panzer Group 1 the corps had already been involved in some fighting as part of Schobert's Eleventh Army.
71 For maps and details of the Petrikovka operation see: Patrick Cloutier, *Regio Esercito. The Italian Royal Army in Mussolini's Wars 1935–1943* (Lexington,

KY, 2010) pp.94–95; Schlemmer (ed.), *Die Italiener an der Ostfront 1942/43*, pp.18–19.

72 Muggeridge (ed.), *Ciano's Diary 1939–1943*, p.377 (30 September 1941).

73 DiNardo, *Germany and the Axis Powers*, p.128.

74 Axworthy *et al.*, *Third Axis Fourth Ally*, pp.71–72.

75 For more on these battles see: Klink, 'The Conduct of Operations', pp.607 and 611–613; Manstein, *Lost Victories*, chapter 9: 'The Crimean Campaign'; Glantz, *Barbarossa*, pp.155–157.

76 Axworthy, 'Peasant Scapegoat to Industrial Slaughter', p.227.

77 Axworthy *et al.*, *Third Axis Fourth Ally*, p.67.

78 Lieven, *Russia against Napoleon*, p.250.

79 Sebastian, *Journal, 1935–1944*, p.410 (14 September 1941).

80 Halder, KTB III, p.237 (17 September 1941).

81 Röttiger, 'XXXXI Panzer Corps during the Battle of Moscow in 1941 as a Component of Panzer Group 3', p.16.

82 Esebeck had replaced the aforementioned Major-General Ludwig Crüwell.

83 '11.Pz.Div. KTB Abt. Ia vom 1.5.41–21.10.41', BA-MA RH 27–11/16, fol.131 (19–26 September 1941).

84 Glantz, *Atlas of the Battle for Kiev Part III*, map 171; Glantz, David M., *Atlas of the Battle of Moscow. The Defensive Phase: 1 October–5 December 1941* (Privately published by David M. Glantz, 1997) map 6.

85 Chales de Beaulieu, *Generaloberst Erich Hoepner*, p.192.

86 'Kriegstagebuch 19.Panzer-Division Abt.Ib für die Zeit vom 1.6.1941–31.12.1942', BA-MA RH 27–19/23 (22 September 1941). This war diary has no folio stamped page numbers so references must be located using the date.

87 'Anlage zum KTB Panzer Gruppe 4: 20.9.41–14.10.41', BA-MA RH 21–4/34, fols.120–121 (22 September 1941).

88 'Gen.Kdo.LVII.Pz.Korps KTB Nr.1 vom 15.2.41–31.10.41', BA-MA RH 24–57-2, fol.244 (28 September 1941).

89 'Anlage zum KTB Panzer Gruppe 4: 20.9.41–14.10.41', BA-MA RH 21–4/34, fols.112–113 (28 September 1941).

90 'Gen.Kdo.LVII.Pz.Korps KTB Nr.1 vom 15.2.41–31.10.41', BA-MA RH 24–57-2, fol.245 (29 September 1941).

91 As stated earlier, different files give contrasting figures for the strength of the division's panzer regiment. Accordingly the 20th Panzer Division fielded between twenty and forty tanks *before* its transfer south began. See respectively: 'Anlage zum KTB Panzer Gruppe 4: 20.9.41–14.10.41', BA-MA RH 21–4/34, fol.121 (22 September 1941); '20.Pz.Div. KTB vom 15.8.41 bis 20.10.41 Band Ia.', BA-MA RH 27–20/25, fol.93 (20 September 1941).

92 'Anlage zum KTB Panzer Gruppe 4: 20.9.41–14.10.41', BA-MA RH 21-4/34, fol.120 (22 September 1941).
93 Müller-Hillebrand, *Das Heer 1933–1945. Band III*, p.205.
94 'Anlage zum KTB Panzer Gruppe 4: 20.9.41–14.10.41', BA-MA RH 21-4/34, fols.118–119 (22 September 1941).
95 Ibid., fols.112–113 (28 September 1941).
96 Ibid.
97 Bock, *War Diary*, p.320 (29 September 1941).
98 For Typhoon Schaal's corps was to take over command of the 14th Motorized Infantry Division, the 7th Panzer Division, the 129th Infantry Division and the 6th Panzer Division.
99 'Kriegstagebuch Nr.7 des Kdos. Der 1.Panzer-Div. 20.9.41–12.4.42', BA-MA 27-1/58, fol.7 (20 September 1941).
100 Röttiger, 'XXXXI Panzer Corps during the Battle of Moscow in 1941 as a Component of Panzer Group 3', p.16.
101 Halder, KTB III, p.237 (17 September 1941).
102 Italics in the original. Röttiger, 'XXXXI Panzer Corps during the Battle of Moscow in 1941 as a Component of Panzer Group 3', pp.16–17.
103 Reddemann (ed.), *Zwischen Front und Heimat*, pp.317–318 (22 September–9 October 1941). The war diary of the 20th Panzer Division claimed that in the opinion of the commanding officer (Colonel von Bismarck) the 'exceedingly high' loss of trucks was due mainly to the deficient training of his drivers and their officers. This, he stated, was responsible for no less than 80 per cent of all damage caused to his vehicles. '20.Pz.Div. KTB vom 15.8.41 bis 20.10.41 Band Ia.', BA-MA RH 27-20/25, fol.100 (27 September 1941).
104 Reddemann (ed.), *Zuischen Front und Heimat*, pp.320 and 323 (22 September–9 October 1941).
105 'Kriegstagebuch Nr.1 Panzergruppe 2 Band II vom 21.8.1941 bis 31.10.41', BA-MA RH 21-2/931, fols.322–323 (27 September 1941). The totals reported in this file are slightly different, but the addition of the figures is sometimes in error.
106 Müller-Hillebrand, *Das Heer 1933–1945. Band III*, p.205.
107 'Kriegstagebuch Nr.1 Panzergruppe 2 Band II vom 21.8.1941 bis 31.10.41', BA-MA RH 21-2/931, fols.323 and 327–328 (27–28 September 1941).
108 'Anlagen zum Kriegstagebuch Tagesmeldungen Bd.I 1.9–31.10.41', BA-MA RH 21-3/70, fol.65 (4 October 1941).
109 Müller-Hillebrand, *Das Heer 1933–1945. Band III*, p.205.
110 '3rd Pz. Gr. KTB Nr.2 1.9.41–31.10.41', BA-MA Microfilm 59060 (19 September 1941).

111 Ibid. (7 September 1941).

112 '20.Pz.Div. KTB vom 15.8.41 bis 20.10.41 Band Ia.', BA-MA RH 27–20/25, fol.101 (27 September 1941).

113 As one study noted, 'In general, a few weeks after a new shipment of tanks arrived at the Russian front, most of the vehicles were deadlined and many became a total loss, simply because parts whose installation would have required only a few hours were missing.' Department of the US Army (ed.), *German Tank Maintenance in World War II*, p.43.

114 Müller-Hillebrand, *Das Heer 1933–1945. Band III*, p.205.

115 Müller, 'The Failure of the Economic "Blitzkrieg Strategy"', p.1129.

116 Guderian, *Panzer Leader*, p.227.

117 'Kriegstagebuch Nr.1 Panzergruppe 2 Band II vom 21.8.1941 bis 31.10.41', BA-MA RH 21–2/931, fols.322–323 (27 September 1941).

118 Ferdinand Maria von Senger und Etterlin, *German Tanks of World War II. The Complete Illustrated History of German Armoured Fighting Vehicles 1926–1945* (Harrisburg, PA, 1969) p.30.

119 Kesselring, *The Memoirs of Field-Marshal Kesselring*, p.95.

120 Muller, *The German Air War in Russia*, p.58.

121 'Interrogations IV Liddell Hart', LH 15/15/149. See file entitled 'Talk with Rundstedt 26 October 1941'. See also: Liddell Hart, *The Other Side of the Hill*, p.279.

122 'Interrogations IV Liddell Hart', LH 15/15/149: 'Conversation with Lieut. Gen. Siewert.'

123 Halder, KTB III, p.222 (11 September 1941).

124 Ibid., p.237 (17 September 1941).

125 Ibid., p.242 (20 September 1941).

126 Ibid., p.245 (22 September 1941).

127 Ibid., p.257 (28 September 1941).

128 Ibid., p.259 (29 September 1941); Klaus Schüler, *Logistik im Russlandfeldzug*, p.408.

129 Emphasis in the original. 'Kriegstagebuch Nr.1 Panzergruppe 2 Band II vom 21.8.1941 bis 31.10.41', BA-MA RH 21–2/931, fol.319 (27 September 1941).

130 Ibid., p.157.

131 'Kriegstagebuch 4.Panzer-Divison Führungsabtl. 26.5.41–31.3.42', BA-MA RH 27–4/10, p.188 (2 October 1941).

132 Röttiger, 'XXXXI Panzer Corps during the Battle of Moscow in 1941 as a Component of Panzer Group 3', p.17.

133 Müller, 'The Failure of the Economic "Blitzkrieg Strategy"', p.1130.

134 Van Creveld, *Supplying War*, pp.170–171.

135 As cited in: Macksey, *Guderian*, p.153.

136 'The Germans in Russia', LH 15/4/40. See the untitled essay from Blumentritt, p.7.
137 Müller, 'The Failure of the Economic "Blitzkrieg Strategy"', p.1131.
138 '3rd Pz. Gr. KTB Nr.2 1.9.41–31.10.41', BA-MA Microfilm 59060 (13 and 29 September 1941).
139 Kuhnert, *Will We See Tomorrow?*, p.99.

10 Moscow in the crosshairs

1 Perel, *Europa Europa*, p.42.
2 As cited in: Kershaw, *War without Garlands*, p.176.
3 Landon and Leitner (eds.), *Diary of a German Soldier*, p.108 (28 September 1941).
4 Ibid., p.108 (26 September 1941); see also: Henry Metelmann, *Through Hell for Hitler* (Havertown, PA, 2005) p.35.
5 Lammers (ed.), *'Fahrtberichte' aus der Zeit des deutsch-sowjetischen Krieges 1941*, p.94 (24 September 1941).
6 'Anlage zum KTB Panzer Gruppe 4: 20.9.41–14.10.41', BA-MA RH 21–4/34, fol.122 (15 September 1941).
7 'Kriegstagebuch 19.Panzer-Division Abt.Ib für die Zeit vom 1.6.1941–31.12.1942', BA-MA RH 27–19/23 (2 October 1941).
8 Scheuer, *Briefe aus Russland*, p.41 (24 September 1941).
9 Humburg, *Das Gesicht des Krieges*, p.123 (10 and 19 September 1941).
10 Franz and Leopold Schober, *Briefe von der Front. Feldpostbriefe 1939–1945*, (ed.) Michael Hans Salvesberger (Gösing am Wagram, 1997) p.127.
11 Landon and Leitner (eds.), *Diary of a German Soldier*, p.109 (29 September 1941).
12 'The Germans in Russia', LH 15/4/40. See the file entitled 'Von Rundstedt writes home', p.2 (30 September 1941).
13 Halder, KTB III, p.263 (1 October 1941).
14 Fröhlich (ed.), *Die Tagebücher von Joseph Goebbels, Teil II Band 1*, p.506 (27 September 1941).
15 The Siegfried Line was a system of defensive structures stretching some 630 kilometres in length along Germany's western border. It was built in the 1930s in part as a response to the French Maginot Line.
16 *Völkischer Beobachter* (30 September 1941). Reproduced in: Piekalkiewicz, *Moscow 1941*, pp.65–66.
17 Wolfram Wette, *The Wehrmacht. History, Myth, Reality* (Cambridge, 2006) chapter 1: 'Perceptions of Russia, the Soviet Union, and Bolshevism as Enemies'.
18 Glantz, *Barbarossa*, p.68; Mawdsley, *Thunder in the East*, pp.112–113.

19 Guderian, *Panzer Leader*, pp.226–227 and 229.
20 Seaton, *The Battle for Moscow*, pp.75–76.
21 '9.Pz.Div. KTB Ia vom 19.5.1941 bis 22.1.1942', BA-MA RH 27–9/4, fol.123 (28 September 1941).
22 Guderian, *Panzer Leader*, pp.226–227.
23 Bock, *War Diary*, p.320 (1 October 1941).
24 *True to Type*, p.23 (1 October 1941).
25 'Kriegstagebuch Nr.1 Panzergruppe 2 Band II vom 21.8.1941 bis 31.10.41', BA-MA RH 21–2/931, fols.344–346 (30 September 1941).
26 Halder, KTB III, p.263 (1 October 1941).
27 Ulrich de Maizière, *In der Pflicht. Lebensbericht eines deutschen Soldaten im 20. Jahrhundert* (Bielefeld, 1989) p.70.
28 Dunn, *Hitler's Nemesis*, p.45.
29 The war diary stated that Bock commanded nine panzer divisions on 22 June, but in fact it was just eight. The subsequent totals have all been adjusted accordingly.
30 Typically a light artillery battery contained about four guns, while a heavy battery had around three guns, making a theorical total of 3,700 guns. Yet batteries equipped with non-German weapons (of which there were many) often had fewer guns and by early October combat losses would suggest that the figure could not have been more than 3,000. Thanks to Dr Adrian Wettstein for his expert advice on this matter.
31 'Kriegstagebuch Nr.1 (Band Oktober 1941) des Oberkommandos der Heeresgruppe Mitte', BA-MA RH 19-II/411, fols.525–526 (2 October 1941).
32 Actually my earlier estimates for Panzer Groups 2 (400), 3 (350) and 4 (780) coincidently equalled exactly 1,530, but this figure did not include Knobelsdorff's 19th Panzer Division because it was not assigned to any of the panzer groups, but held in the army group reserve. The only available figure for the panzer strength of this division stems from the period *before* its transfer to the south. At that time Knobelsdorff's panzer regiment numbered some sixty-five tanks. 'Anlage zum KTB Panzer Gruppe 4: 20.9.41–14.10.41', BA-MA RH 21–4/34, fols.118–119 (22 September 1941).
33 On 22 June 1941 the panzer divisions subsequently assigned to Bock for Operation Typhoon had the following panzer strengths. 1st Panzer Division = 154; 3rd Panzer Division = 198; 4th Panzer Division = 169; 6th Panzer Division = 254; 7th Panzer Division = 299; 9th Panzer Division = 157; 10th Panzer Division = 206; 11th Panzer Division = 175; 17th Panzer Division = 180; 18th Panzer Division = 200; 19th Panzer Division = 239; 20th Panzer Division = 245. Müller-Hillebrand, *Das Heer 1933–1945. Band III*, p.205.
34 'Kriegstagebuch Nr.1 (Band Oktober 1941) des Oberkommandos der Heeresgruppe Mitte', BA-MA RH 19-II/411, fol.526 (2 October 1941).

35 Chales de Beaulieu, *Generaloberst Erich Hoepner*, pp.191–192.
36 'Anlage zum KTB Panzer Gruppe 4: 20.9.41–14.10.41', BA-MA RH 21–4/34, fol.122 (15 September 1941).
37 Konev replaced Timoshenko on 10 September after the latter was sent to take over command of the South-Western Direction.
38 Having been removed from command of the South-Western Direction on 10 September Budenny replaced Zhukov as head of the Reserve Front. At the same time Zhukov was sent to take command of the Leningrad Front.
39 Glantz, *Barbarossa*, pp.141–143.
40 Dunn, *Hitler's Nemesis*, p.29.
41 Glantz, *Barbarossa*, pp.141–142 and 144; Erickson, *The Road to Stalingrad*, p.214.
42 Kleindienst (ed.), *Sei tausendmal gegrüßt*, CD Rom (29 September 1941).
43 Ibid. (30 September 1941).
44 Scheuer, *Briefe aus Russland*, p.42 (28 September 1941).
45 Breloer (ed.), *Mein Tagebuch*, p.99 (27 September 1941).
46 'Kriegstagebuch Nr.1 (Band Oktober 1941) des Oberkommandos der Heeresgruppe Mitte', BA-MA RH 19-II/411, fol.529 (2 October 1941).
47 Pabst, *The Outermost Frontier*, p.29.
48 Heinrich Haape with Dennis Henshaw, *Moscow Tram Stop. A Doctor's Experiences with the German Spearhead in Russia* (London, 1957) p.120.

Conclusion

1 KTB OKW, Volume II, p.693 (11 October 1941); Günther Blumentritt, *Von Rundstedt. The Soldier and the Man* (London, 1952) p.111.
2 Mawdsley, *Thunder in the East*, p.89.
3 Glantz, *Barbarossa*, p.153.
4 Mawdsley, *Thunder in the East*, p.74.
5 Jones, *The Retreat*, p.27.
6 As cited in: Nagorski, *The Greatest Battle*, p.161.
7 Roberts, *Stalin's Wars*, p.100.
8 Eremenko, *The Arduous Beginning*, p.235.
9 Robert M. Citino, *The German Way of War. From the Thirty Years' War to the Third Reich* (Lawrence, KS, 2005) p.173. As Citino stated (p.159), 'Other kingdoms and other armies might coolly add up the odds, deciding on a course of action based on a head- or gun-count of the enemy, the terrain, or the overall strategic situation. The Prussian officer was expected to attack. As Frederick the Great had stated on numerous occasions, the Prussian army always attacked, even when the odds seemed to be against it. The Great Elector at Fehrbellin, Frederick at Kolin, L'Estocq at Eylau: the history of the Prussian army is studded with these events.'

10 Halder, KTB III, p.229 (13 September 1941).

11 Schall-Riaucour, *Aufstand und Gehorsam*, p.172 (2 October 1941).

12 'Interrogations V Liddell Hart', LH 9/24/94–104. The document began with Brauchitsch's opening assertion: 'As the last Commander-in-Chief of the German army prior to the command being taken over by Adolf Hitler in December 1941 and in agreement with several generals of the former army, I feel myself bound to bear witness before the International Court of Justice at Nuremberg for the whole German army . . . The declaration has been completed from memory without any official documents.'

13 As cited in: Axell, *Stalin's War*, p.89. Two minor corrections were made to the English in this quotation, neither of which altered the meaning in any way.

14 Glantz, *The Battle for Smolensk*, pp.66–82.

15 See Evan Mawdsley's review in the *English Historical Review*, Vol. 75, No. 514 (June 2010) p.776.

16 Overmans, *Deutsche militärische Verluste im Zweiten Weltkrieg*, pp.277–278.

17 Malaparte, *The Volga Rises in Europe*, p.159 (September 1941).

BIBLIOGRAPHY

Archives

Bundesarchiv-Militärarchiv, Freiburg im Breisgau (BA-MA)

Army Group South

RH 19-I/254 'Heersgruppe Süd Kriegstagebuch II. Teil Band 3, 16 Aug.–15 Sept. 41'

RH 19-I/73 'Heersgruppe Süd Kriegstagebuch II. Teil Band 4, 16 Sept.–5 Okt. 1941'

Panzer Group 1

RH 21–1/50 'Kriegstagebuch des Panzerarmee-Oberkdos.1 Band II 22.6.41–31.8.41'

RH 21–1/51 'Kriegstagebuch des Panzerarmee-Oberkdos.1 Band III 1.9.41–31.10.41'

RH 21–1/347 'KTB der Oberquartiermeisterabteilung der 1st Panzer-Armee 2.5.41–31.10.41'

RH 24–11/38 'KTB Nr.7 Generalkommando XI.A.K. Führungsabteilung 19.8.41–31.12.41'

RH 24–48/25 'Kriegstagebuch XXXXVIII.Pz.Kps. Abt.Ia September 1941'

RH 26–125/3 'KTB Nr.2 der 125.Inf.Div. (Abt.Ia) 22.6.1941–15.12.1941'

RH 27–9/4 '9.Pz.Div. KTB Ia vom 19.5.1941 bis 22.1.1942'

RH 27–11/16 '11.Pz.Div. KTB Abt. Ia vom 1.5.41–21.10.41'

RH 27–14/1 '14.Pz.Div. KTB Ia vom 1.5.1941 bis 15.12.1941'

Army Group Centre

RH 19-II/130 'Tagesmeldungen der Heersgruppe Mitte vom 6.8.41 bis 26.8.41'

RH 19-II/386 'Kriegstagebuch Nr.1 (Band August 1941) des Oberkommandos der Heeresgruppe Mitte'

RH 19-II/411 'Kriegstagebuch Nr.1 (Band Oktober 1941) des Oberkommandos der Heeresgruppe Mitte'

Panzer Group 2

RH 21–2/757 'Verlustmeldungen 5.7.1941–25.3.1942'

RH 21–2/819 'Kriegstagebuch der O.Qu.-Abt. Pz. A.O.K.2 von 21.6.41 bis 31.3.42'

RH 21–2/928 'KTB Nr.1 Panzergruppe 2 Bd.II vom 22.7.1941 bis 20.8.41'

RH 21–2/931 'Kriegstagebuch Nr.1 Panzergruppe 2 Band II vom 21.8.1941 bis 31.10.41'

RH 24–47/2 'Kriegstagebuch Nr.2 XXXXVII.Pz.Korps. Ia 25.5.1941–22.9.1941'

RH 27–3/14 'KTB 3rd Pz. Div. vom 16.8.40 bis 18.9.41'

RH 27–3/15 'KTB 3rd Pz. Div. vom 19.9.41 bis 6.2.42'

RH 27–3/218 'KTB 3rd Pz. Div. I.b 19.5.41–6.2.42'

RH 27–4/10 'Kriegstagebuch 4.Panzer-Divison Führungsabtl. 26.5.41–31.3.42'

RH 27–18/21 '18.Panzer Division, Abt.Ia KTB Teil II vom 21.8.–29.9.41'

Panzer Group 3

Microfilm 59054 '3rd Pz. Gr. KTB 25.5.41–31.8.41'

Microfilm 59060 '3rd Pz. Gr. KTB Nr.2 1.9.41–31.10.41'

RH 24–57/2 'Gen.Kdo.LVII.Pz.Korps KTB Nr.1 vom 15.2.41–31.10.41'

RH 26–14/10 'Kriegstagesbuch Ia. 14.Inf.Div. (mot) vom 25.5.41–1.10.41'

RH 27–7/46 'Kriegstagebuch Nr.3 der 7.Panzer-Division Führungsabteilung 1.6.1941–9.5.1942'

RH 27–20/25 '20.Pz.Div. KTB vom 15.8.41 bis 20.10.41 Band Ia'

Panzer Group 4

RH 21–3/70 'Anlagen zum Kriegstagebuch Tagesmeldungen Bd.I 1.9–31.10.41'

RH 21–4/34 'Anlage zum KTB Panzer Gruppe 4: 20.9.41–14.10.41'

27–1/58 'Kriegstagebuch Nr.7 des Kdos. Der 1.Panzer-Div. 20.9.41–12.4.42'

RH 27–19/23 'Kriegstagebuch 19.Panzer-Division Abt.Ib für die Zeit vom 1.6.1941–31.12.1942'

Sixteenth Army

RH 27–12/2 'KTB Nr.1 der 12. Panzer-Division Heft 1 25.5.–30.9.41'

Luftwaffe

RL 200/17 'Gen.v.Waldau, Chef Fü St Lw Persönl. Tagebuch, Auszugeweise'

Liddell Hart Centre for Military Archives (LH)

LH 9/24/94–104 'Interrogations V Liddell Hart'
LH 15/4/40 'The Germans in Russia'
LH 15/15/149 'Interrogations IV Liddell Hart'

Primary and Secondary Sources

Abelshauser, Werner, 'Germany: Guns, Butter, and Economic Miracles' in Mark Harrison (ed.), *The Economics of World War II. Six Great Powers in International Comparison* (Cambridge, 2000) pp.122–176.

Adamovich, Ales and Daniil Granin, *Leningrad under Siege. First-hand Accounts of the Ordeal* (Barnsley, 2007).

Ailsby, Christopher, *Images of Barbarossa. The German Invasion of Russia, 1941* (Shepperton, 2001).

Alexiev, Alex, 'Soviet Nationals in German Wartime Service, 1941–1945' in Antonio Munoz (ed.), *Soviet Nationals in German Wartime Service 1941–1945* (n.p., 2007) pp.5–44.

Andreyev, Catherine, 'Vlasov' in Harold Shukman (ed.), *Stalin's Generals* (London, 1993) pp.301–311.

Anfilov, Viktor, 'Budenny' in Harold Shukman (ed.), *Stalin's Generals* (London, 1993) pp.57–65.

'Timoshenko' in Harold Shukman (ed.), *Stalin's Generals* (London, 1993) pp.239–253.

'Zhukov' in Harold Shukman (ed.), *Stalin's Generals* (London, 1993) pp.343–360.

Antjeleetz, Lektorat and Barbara Wenner (eds.), *Blockade. Leningrad 1941–1945. Dokumente und Essays von Russen und Deutschen* (Hamburg, 1992).

Armstrong, John A. (ed.), *Soviet Partisans in World War II* (Madison, 1964).

Arnold, Klaus Jochen, 'Die Eroberung und Behandlung der Stadt Kiew durch die Wehrmacht im September 1941; Zur Radikalisierung der Besatzungspolitik', *Militärgeschichtliche Mitteilungen*, No. 58 (1999) pp.23–63.

Die Wehrmacht und die Besatzungspolitik in den besetzten Gebieten der Sowjetunion. Kriegführung und Radikalisierung im 'Unternehmen Barbarossa' (Berlin, 2005).

Axell, Albert, *Russia's Heroes 1941–45* (New York, 2001).

Stalin's War. Through the Eyes of his Commanders (London, 1997).

Axworthy, Mark, *Axis Slovakia. Hitler's Slavic Wedge 1938–1945* (New York, 2002).

'Peasant Scapegoat to Industrial Slaughter: the Romanian Soldier at the Siege of Odessa' in Paul Addison and Angus Calder (eds.), *A Time to Kill. The Soldier's Experience of War in the West 1939–1945* (London, 1997) pp.221–232.

Axworthy, Mark, Cornel Scafes and Cristian Craciunoiu, *Third Axis Fourth Ally. Romanian Armed Forces in the European War, 1941–1945* (London, 1995).

Bähr, Hans and Walter Bähr, *Die Stimme des Menschen. Briefe und Aufzeichnungen aus der ganzen Welt*, 1939–1945 (Munich, 1961).

Bähr, Walter and Hans Bähr (eds.), *Kriegsbriefe Gefallener Studenten, 1939–1945* (Tübingen and Stuttgart, 1952).

Bamm, Peter, *The Invisible Flag* (New York, 1958).

Barber, John and Mark Harrison, *The Soviet Home Front 1941–1945. A Social and Economic History of the USSR in World War II* (London, 1991).

Bartov, Omer, *The Eastern Front, 1941–45. German Troops and the Barbarisation of Warfare* (London, 1985).

Hitler's Army. Soldiers, Nazis, and War in the Third Reich (Oxford, 1992).

Becker, Hans, *Devil on my Shoulder* (London, 1957).

Beevor, Antony and Luba Vinogradova (eds.), *A Writer at War. Vasily Grossman with the Red Army 1941–1945* (New York, 2005).

Bellamy, Chris, *Absolute War. Soviet Russia in the Second World War* (New York, 2007).

Below, Nicolaus von, *Als Hitlers Adjutant 1937–45* (Mainz, 1999).

Bergström, Christer, *Barbarossa – the Air Battle: July–December 1941* (Hersham, 2007).

Berkhoff, Karel C., *Harvest of Despair. Life and Death in Ukraine under Nazi Rule* (Cambridge, MA, 2004).

Bidermann, Gottlob Herbert, *In Deadly Combat. A German Soldier's Memoir of the Eastern Front* (Lawrence, KS, 2000).

Blandford, Edmund (ed.), *Under Hitler's Banner. Serving the Third Reich* (Edison, NJ, 2001).

Blau, George, *The Campaign against Russia (1940–1942)* (Washington, 1955).

Blumentritt, Günther, 'Moscow' in William Richardson and Seymour Freidin (eds.), *The Fatal Decisions* (London, 1956) pp.29–75.

Von Rundstedt. The Soldier and the Man (London, 1952).

Boberach, Heinz (ed.), *Meldungen aus dem Reich. Die geheimen Lageberichte des Sicherheitsdienstes der SS 1938–1945*. Volumes VII and VIII (Berlin, 1984).

Bock, Fedor von, *Generalfeldmarschall Fedor von Bock. The War Diary 1939–1945*, (ed.) Klaus Gerbet (Munich, 1996).

Boll, Bernd and Hans Safrian, 'On the Way to Stalingrad: The 6th Army in 1941–42' in Hannes Heer and Klaus Naumann (eds.), *War of Extermination. The German Military in World War II 1941–1944* (New York and Oxford, 2006) pp.237–271.

Bond, Brian, 'Brauchitsch' in Correlli Barnett (ed.), *Hitler's Generals* (London, 1989) pp.75–99.

Bonwetsch, Bernd, 'The Purge of the Military and the Red Army's Operational Capability during the Great Patriotic War' in Bernd Wegner (ed.), *From Peace to War. Germany, Soviet Russia and the World, 1939–1941* (Oxford, 1997) pp.395–414.

Boog, Horst, 'The German Air Force' in Militärgeschichtliches Forschungsamt (ed.), *Germany and the Second World War. Volume IV. The Attack on the Soviet Union* (Oxford, 1998) pp.326–385.

'The Luftwaffe' in Militärgeschichtliches Forschungsamt (ed.), *Germany and the Second World War. Volume IV. The Attack on the Soviet Union* (Oxford, 1998) pp.763–832.

Bor, Peter, *Gespräche mit Halder* (Wiesbaden, 1950).

Bordiugov, Gennadi, 'The Popular Mood in the Unoccupied Soviet Union: Continuity and Change during the War' in Robert Thurston and Bernd Bonwetsch (eds.), *The People's War. Responses to World War II in the Soviet Union* (Chicago, 2000) pp.54–70.

Bourgeois, Daniel, 'Operation "Barbarossa" and Switzerland' in Bernd Wegner (ed.), *From Peace to War. Germany, Soviet Russia and the World, 1939–1941* (Oxford, 1997) pp.593–610.

Braithwaite, Rodric, *Moscow 1941. A City and its People at War* (New York, 2006).

Breloer, Heinrich (ed.), *Mein Tagebuch. Geschichten vom Überleben 1939–1947* (Cologne, 1984).

Broekmeyer, Marius, *Stalin, the Russians, and their War 1941–1945* (London, 2004).

Browning, Christopher R. and Jürgen Matthäus, *The Origins of the Final Solution. The Evolution of Nazi Jewish Policy, September 1939–March 1942* (London, 2005).

Buchbender, Ortwin and Reinhold Sterz (eds.), *Das andere Gesicht des Krieges. Deutsche Feldpostbriefe 1939–1945* (Munich, 1982).

Burleigh, Michael, *The Third Reich. A New History* (London, 2001).

Carell, Paul, *Hitler's War on Russia. The Story of the German Defeat in the East* (London, 1964).

Carlton, David, *Churchill and the Soviet Union* (New York, 2000).

Carruthers, Bob (ed.), *The Wehrmacht. Last Witnesses. First-Hand Accounts from the Survivors of Hitler's Armed Forces* (London, 2010).

Chales de Beaulieu, Walter, *Generaloberst Erich Hoepner. Militärisches Porträt eines Panzer-Führers* (Neckargemünd, 1969).

Chaney, Otto Preston, *Zhukov* (Norman, OK, 1996).

Chor'kov, Anatoli G., 'The Red Army during the Initial Phase of the Great Patriotic War' in Bernd Wegner (ed.), *From Peace to War. Germany, Soviet Russia and the World, 1939–1941* (Oxford, 1997) pp.415–429.

Churchill, Winston S., *The Second World War*, abridged edition (London, 1959).

Citino, Robert M., *Death of the Wehrmacht. The German Campaigns of 1942* (Lawrence, KS, 2007).

The German Way of War. From the Thirty Years' War to the Third Reich (Lawrence, 2005).

Clark, Alan, *Barbarossa. The Russian–German Conflict 1941–1945* (London, 1996).

Clausewitz, Carl von, *On War*, (eds.) Michael Howard and Peter Patet (New York, 1993).

Cloutier, Patrick, *Regio Esercito. The Italian Royal Army in Mussolini's Wars 1935–1943* (Lexington, KY, 2010).

Conversino, Mark J., *Fighting with the Soviets. The Failure of Operation Frantic 1944–1945* (Lawrence, KS, 1997).

Cooper, Matthew, *The Phantom War. The German Struggle against Soviet Partisans 1941–1944* (London, 1979).

Corum, James S., *Wolfram von Richthofen. Master of the German Air War* (Lawrence, KS, 2008).

Creveld, Martin van, *Supplying War. Logistics from Wallenstein to Patton* (Cambridge, 1984).

Dallek, Robert, *Franklin D. Roosevelt and the American Foreign Policy* (Oxford, 1995).

Dallin, Alexander, *Odessa, 1941–1944. A Case Study of Soviet Territory under Foreign Rule* (Oxford, 1998).

Dallin, Alexander, Ralph Mavrogordato and Wilhelm Moll, 'Partisan Psychological Warfare and Popular Attitudes' in John A. Armstrong (ed.), *Soviet Partisans in World War II* (Madison, 1964) pp.197–337.

Davies, R. W., Mark Harrison and S. G. Wheatcroft (eds.), *The Economic Transformation of the Soviet Union, 1913–1945* (Cambridge, 1994).

Deletant, Dennis, 'German–Romanian Relations,1941–1945' in Jonathan Adelman (ed.), *Hitler and his Allies in World War II* (New York, 2007) pp.166–185.

Hitler's Forgotten Ally. Ion Antonescu and his Regime, Romania 1940–1944 (London, 2006).

de Maizière, Ulrich, *In der Pflicht. Lebensbericht eines deutschen Soldaten im 20. Jahrhundert* (Bielefeld, 1989).

Department of the US Army (ed.), *Effects of Climate on Combat in European Russia* (Washington, DC, 1952).

(ed.), *German Tank Maintenance in World War II* (Washington DC, 1988).

D'este, Carlo, 'Model' in Correlli Barnett (ed.), *Hitler's Generals* (London, 1998) pp.319–333.

DiNardo, Richard L., 'The Dysfunctional Coalition: the Axis Powers and the Eastern Front in World War II', *The Journal of Military History*, Vol. 60, No. 4 (October 1996) pp.711–730.

Germany and the Axis Powers. From Coalition to Collapse (Lawrence, KS, 2005).

Domarus, Max, *Hitler. Speeches and Proclamations 1932–1945. The Chronicle of a Dictatorship. Volume IV. The Years 1941 to 1945* (Wauconda, IL, 2004).

Drabkin, Artem (ed.), *The Red Air Force at War. Barbarossa and the Retreat to Moscow. Recollections of Fighter Pilots on the Eastern Front* (Barnsley, 2007).

Dunn, Walter S., Jr, *Hitler's Nemesis. The Red Army, 1930–45* (Mechanicsburg, PA, 2009).

Stalin's Keys to Victory. The Rebirth of the Red Army in WWI (Mechanicsburg, PA, 2006).

Eberle, Henrik and Matthias Uhl (eds.), *The Hitler Book. The Secret Dossier Prepared for Stalin from the Interrogations of Hitler's Personal Aides* (New York, 2005).

Eby, Cecil D., *Hungary at War. Civilians and Soldiers in World War II* (University Park, PA, 1998).

Elmshäuser, Konrad and Jan Lokers (eds.), *'Man muß hier nur hart sein'. Kriegsbriefe und Bilder einer Familie (1934–1945)* (Bremen, 1999).

Eremenko, A., *The Arduous Beginning* (Honolulu, 2004).

Erickson, John, *The Road to Stalingrad. Stalin's War with Germany. Volume I* (London, 1975).

The Soviet High Command. A Military-Political History 1918–1941 (London, 1962).

'Soviet War Losses. Calculations and Controversies' in John Erickson and David Dilks (eds.), *Barbarossa. The Axis and the Allies* (Edinburgh, 1998) pp.255–277.

Erickson, John and Ljubica Erickson, *Hitler versus Stalin. The Second World War on the Eastern Front in Photographs* (London, 2004).

Evans, Richard J., *The Third Reich at War. How the Nazis Led Germany from Conquest to Disaster* (London, 2009).

Filipescu, Mihai Tone, *Reluctant Axis. The Romanian Army in Russia 1941–1944* (Chapultepeq, 2006).

Foot, M. R. D., 'USSR' in I. C. B. Dear and M. R. D. Foot (eds.), *The Oxford Companion to the Second World War* (Oxford, 1995) pp.1207–1243.

Förster, Jürgen, 'The Decisions of the Tripartite Pact States' in Militärgeschichtliches Forschungsamt (ed.), *Germany and the Second World War. Volume IV. The Attack on the Soviet Union* (Oxford, 1998) pp.1021–1048.

'Motivation and Indoctrination in the Wehrmacht,1933–45' in Paul Addison and Angus Calder (eds.), *A Time to Kill. The Soldier's Experience of War in the West 1939–1945* (London, 1997) pp.263–273.

'New Wine in Old Skins? The Wehrmacht and the War of "Weltanschauungen", 1941' in Wilhelm Deist (ed.), *The German Military in the Age of Total War* (Leamington Spa, 1985) pp.304–322.

'Operation Barbarossa as a War of Conquest and Annihilation' in Militärgeschichtliches Forschungsamt (eds.), *Germany and the Second World War. Volume IV. The Attack on the Soviet Union* (Oxford, 1998) pp.481–521.

'Zum Russlandbild der Militärs 1941–1945' in Hans-Erich Volkmann (ed.), *Das Russlandbild im Dritten Reich* (Cologne, 1994) pp.141–163.

Friedläder, Saul, *The Years of Extermination. Nazi Germany and the Jews, 1939–1945* (New York, 2007).

Frieser, Karl-Heinz, *Blitzkrieg-Legende. Der Westfeldzug 1940* (Munich, 1996). English translation: Karl-Heinz Frieser, *The Blitzkrieg Legend. The 1940 Campaign in the West* (Annapolis, 2005).

Frisch, Franz A. P with Wilbur D. Jones Jr, *Condemned to Live. A Panzer Artilleryman's Five-Front War* (Shippensburg, PA, 2000).

Fritz, Stephen G., *Frontsoldaten. The German Soldier in World War II* (Lexington, KY, 1995).

Fröhlich, Elke (ed.), *Die Tagebücher von Joseph Goebbels, Teil I Aufzeichnungen 1923–1941, Band 9 Dezember 1940–Juli 1941* (Munich, 1998).

(ed.), *Die Tagebücher von Joseph Goebbels, Teil II Diktate 1941–1945, Band 1 Juli–September 1941* (Munich, 1996).

Fuchs Richardson, Horst (ed.), *Sieg Heil! War Letters of Tank Gunner Karl Fuchs 1937–1941* (Hamden, CT, 1987).

Fugate, Bryan I., *Operation Barbarossa. Strategy and Tactics on the Eastern Front, 1941* (Novato, CA, 1984).

Fugate, Bryan I. and Lev Dvoretsky, *Thunder on the Dnepr. Zhukov–Stalin and the Defeat of Hitler's Blitzkrieg* (Novato, CA, 1997).

Fuller, William C., Jr, *Strategy and Power in Russia 1600–1914* (New York, 1992).

Ganzenmüller, Jörg, *Das belagerte Leningrad 1941–1944. Die Strategien von Angreifern und Verteidigern* (Paderborn, 2005).

Garden, David and Kenneth Andrew (eds.), *The War Diaries of a Panzer Soldier. Erich Hager with the 17th Panzer Division on the Russian Front 1941–1945* (Atglen, PA, 2010).

Gareis, Martin, *Kampf und Ende der Fränkisch-Sudetendeutschen 98. Infanterie-Division* (Eggolsheim, 1956).

Gerlach, Christian, *Kalkulierte Morde. Die deutsche Wirtschafts- und Vernichtungspolitik in Weißrussland 1941 bis 1944* (Hamburg, 2000).

Geyer, Hermann, *Das IX. Armeekorps im Ostfeldzug 1941* (Neckargemünd, 1969).

Gilbert, Martin, *The Holocaust. The Jewish Tragedy* (London, 1986).

The Second World War. A Complete History (London, 2009).

Glantz, David M., *Atlas of the Battle for Kiev Part I. Penetrating the Stalin Line and the Uman' Encirclement 2 July–9 August 1941* (Privately published by David M. Glantz, 2005).

Atlas of the Battle for Kiev Part II. The German Advance to the Dnepr River, 9–26 August 1941 (Privately published by David M. Glantz, 2005).

Atlas of the Battle for Kiev Part III. The Encirclement and Destruction of the Southwestern Front, 25 August–26 September 1941 (Privately published by David M. Glantz, 2005).

Atlas of the Battle of Moscow. The Defensive Phase: 1 October–5 December 1941 (Privately published by David M. Glantz, 1997).

Atlas of the Battle of Smolensk (Privately published by David M. Glantz, 2001).

Atlas and Operational Summary. The Border Battles 22 June–1 July 1941 (Privately published by David M. Glantz, 2003).

Barbarossa. Hitler's Invasion of Russia 1941 (Stroud, 2001).

Barbarossa Derailed. The Battle for Smolensk 10 July–10 September 1941. Volume I. The German Advance, the Encirclement Battle, and the First and Second Soviet Counteroffensives, 10 July–24 August 1941 (Solihull, 2010).

Barbarossa Derailed. The Battle for Smolensk 10 July–10 September 1941. Volume II. The German Offensives on the Flanks and the Third Soviet Counteroffensive, 25 August–10 September 1941 (Solihull, 2011).

The Battle for Leningrad, 1941–1944 (Lawrence, KS, 2002).

The Battle for Smolensk: 7 July–10 September 1941 (Privately published by David M. Glantz, 2001).

'The Border Battles on the Lutsk–Rovno Axis: 22 June–1 July 1941' in David M. Glantz (ed.), *The Initial Period of War on the Eastern Front 22 June–August 1941* (London, 1997) pp.248–288.

Colossus Reborn. The Red Army at War, 1941–1943 (Lawrence, 2005).

'Forgotten Battles' in The Military Book Club (ed.), *Slaughterhouse. The Encyclopedia of the Eastern Front* (New York, 2002) pp.471–496.

Forgotten Battles of the German–Soviet War (1941–1945). Volume I. The Summer–Fall Campaign (22 June–4 December 1941) (Privately published by David M. Glantz, 1999).

'Introduction: Prelude to Barbarossa. The Red Army in 1941' in David M. Glantz (ed.), *The Initial Period of War on the Eastern Front 22 June–August 1941* (London, 1993) pp.1–39.

Stumbling Colossus. The Red Army on the Eve of World War (Lawrence, KS, 1998).

Glantz, David M. and Jonathan House, *When Titans Clashed. How the Red Army Stopped Hitler* (Lawrence, KS, 1995).

Golovchansky, Anatoly, Valentin Osipov, Anatoly Prokopenko, Ute Daniel and Jürgen Reulecke (eds.), *'Ich will raus aus diesem Wahnsinn'. Deutsche Briefe von der Ostfront 1941–1945. Aus sowjetischen Archiven* (Hamburg, 1993).

Gorinov, Mikhail M., 'Muscovites' Moods, 22 June 1941 to May 1942' in Robert Thurston and Bernd Bonwetsch (eds.), *The People's War. Responses to World War II in the Soviet Union* (Chicago, 2000) pp.108–134.

Görlitz, Walter, *Paulus and Stalingrad* (London, 1963).

Görlitz, Walter (ed.), *The Memoirs of Field-Marshal Keitel. Chief of the German High Command, 1938–1945* (New York, 1966).

Guderian, Heinz, 'III Panzer Corps Operations' in David M. Glantz (ed.), *The Initial Period of War on the Eastern Front 22 June–August 1941* (London, 1997) pp.308–316.

Panzer Leader (New York, 1996).

Günther, Helmut, *Hot Motors, Cold Feet. A Memoir of Service with the Motorcycle Battalion of SS-Division 'Reich' 1940–1941* (Winnipeg, 2004).

Haape, Heinrich with Dennis Henshaw, *Moscow Tram Stop. A Doctor's Experiences with the German Spearhead in Russia* (London, 1957).

Hagen, Mark von, 'Soviet Soldiers and Officers on the Eve of the German Invasion: Towards a Description of Social Psychology and Political Attitudes' in Robert Thurston and Bernd Bonwetsch (eds.), *The People's War. Responses to World War II in the Soviet Union* (Chicago, 2000) pp.187–210.

Halder, Franz, *Hitler als Feldherr* (Munich, 1949).

Kriegstagebuch: Tägliche Aufzeichnungen des Chefs des Generalstabes des Heeres 1939–1942. Band II. Von der geplanten Landung in England bis zum Beginn des Ostfeldzuges (1.7.1940–21.6.1941), (ed.) Hans-Adolf Jacobsen (Stuttgart, 1963).

Kriegstagebuch: Tägliche Aufzeichnungen des Chefs des Generalstabes des Heeres 1939–1942. Band III. Der Russlandfeldzug bis zum Marsch auf Stalingrad (22.6.1941–24.9.1942), (ed.) Hans-Adolf Jacobsen and Alfred Philippi (Stuttgart, 1964).

Hardesty, Von, *Red Phoenix. The Rise of Soviet Air Power 1941–1945* (Washington, DC, 1982).

Harrison, Mark, '"Barbarossa". The Soviet Response, 1941' in Bernd Wegner (ed.), *From Peace to War. Germany, Soviet Russia and the World, 1939–1941* (Oxford, 1997) pp.431–448.

Soviet Planning in Peace and War 1938–1945 (Cambridge, 2002).

Hartmann, Christian, *Halder Generalstabschef Hitlers 1938–1942* (Munich, 1991).

Wehrmacht im Ostkrieg. Front und militärisches Hinterland 1941/42 (Munich, 2010).

Hartmann, Christian, Johannes Hürter and Ulrike Jureit (eds.), *Verbrechen der Wehrmacht. Bilanz einer Debatte* (Munich, 2005).

Hassell, Ulrich von, *Vom Andern Deutschland* (Freiburg, 1946). English translation: Ulrich von Hassell, *The von Hassell Diaries 1938–1944* (London, 1948).

Hastings, Max, *Bomber Command* (London, 1993).

Finest Years: Churchill as Warlord 1940–45 (London, 2009).

Haupt, Werner, *Army Group Centre. The Wehrmacht in Russia 1941–1945* (Atglen, PA, 1997).

Army Group South. The Wehrmacht in Russia 1941–1945 (Atglen, PA, 1998).

Kiew. Die grösste Kesselschlacht der Geschichte (Dorheim, 1980).

Hayward, Joel, *Stopped at Stalingrad. The Luftwaffe and Hitler's Defeat in the East, 1942–1943* (Lawrence, KS, 1998).

Heer, Hannes, 'How Amorality Became Normality. Reflections on the Mentality of German Soldiers on the Eastern Front' in Hannes Heer and Klaus Naumann (eds.), *War of Extermination. The German Military in World War II 1941–1944* (New York and Oxford, 2006) pp.329–344.

Heer, Hannes and Klaus Naumann (eds.), *War of Extermination. The German Military in World War II 1941–1944* (New York and Oxford, 2006).

Herring, George C., Jr, *Aid to Russia 1941–1946. Strategy, Diplomacy, the Origins of the Cold War* (New York, 1973).

Heusinger, Adolf, *Befehl im Widerstreit. Schicksalsstunden der deutschen Armee 1923–1945* (Tübingen, 1957).

Hilberg, Raul, *The Destruction of the European Jews* (New York, 1985).

Hill, Alexander, 'British Lend-Lease Aid and the Soviet War Effort, June 1941–June 1942', *Journal of Military History*, Vol. 71, No. 3 (July 2007) pp.773–808.

'British "Lend-Lease" Tanks and the Battle for Moscow, November–December 1941 – a Research Note', *Journal of Slavic Military Studies*, Vol. 19, No. 2 (June 2006) pp.289–294.

'British Lend-Lease Tanks and the Battle for Moscow, November–December 1941 – Revisited', *Journal of Slavic Military Studies*, Vol. 22, No. 4 (November 2009) pp.574–587.

The Great Patriotic War of the Soviet Union, 1941–45. A Documentary Reader (Abingdon and New York, 2009).

The War behind the Eastern Front. The Soviet Partisan Movement in North-West Russia 1941–1944 (New York, 2006).

Hill, Leonidas E. (ed.), *Die Weizsäcker-Papiere 1933–1950* (Frankfurt am Main, 1974).

Hillgruber, Andreas, 'The German Military Leaders' View of Russia Prior to the Attack on the Soviet Union' in Bernd Wegner (ed.), *From Peace to War. Germany, Soviet Russia and the World, 1939–1941* (Oxford, 1997) pp.169–185.

Hitlers Strategie. Politik und Kriegführung 1940–1941 (Bonn, 1993).

Hinsley, H. F., 'British Intelligence and Barbarossa' in John Erickson and David Dilks (eds.), *Barbarossa. The Axis and the Allies* (Edinburgh, 1998) pp.43–75.

Holler, Martin, 'Extending the Genocidal Programme: Did Otto Ohlendorf Initiate the Systematic Extermination of Soviet "Gypsies"?' in Alex J. Kay, Jeff Rutherford and David Stahel (eds.), *Nazi Policy on the Eastern Front, 1941. Total War, Genocide and Radicalization* (forthcoming).

Hoth, Hermann, *Panzer-Operationen. Die Panzergruppe 3 und der operative Gedanke der deutschen Führung Sommer 1941* (Heidelberg, 1956).
Humburg, Martin, *Das Gesicht des Krieges. Feldpostbriefe von Wehrmachtssoldaten aus der Sowjetunion 1941–1944* (Wiesbaden, 1998).
Hürter, Johannes, *Hitlers Heerführer. Die deutschen Oberbefehlshaber im Krieg gegen die Sowjetunion 1941/42* (Munich, 2006).
Hürter, Johannes (ed.), *Ein deutscher General an der Ostfront. Die Briefe und Tagebücher des Gotthard Heinrici 1941/42* (Erfurt, 2001).
Irving, David, *The Rise and Fall of the Luftwaffe. The Life of Erhard Milch* (London, 1973).
Jacobsen, Hans-Adolf (ed.), *Kriegstagebuch des Oberkommandos der Wehrmacht (Wehrmachtführungsstab). Band I/1. 1. August 1940–31. Dezember 1941. Band I/2. 1. August 1940–31. Dezember 1941* (Munich, 1982).
Jarausch, Konrad H. and Klaus J. Arnold (eds.), *'Das stille Sterben...' Feldpostbriefe von Konrad Jarausch aus Polen und Russland 1939–1942* (Munich, 2008).
Jones, Michael, *Leningrad. State of Siege* (London, 2008).
The Retreat. Hitler's First Defeat (London, 2009).
Jones, Robert Huhn, *The Roads to Russia. United States Lend-Lease to the Soviet Union* (Norman, OK, 1969).
Jukes, Geoffrey, 'Vasilevsky' in Harold Shukman (ed.), *Stalin's Generals* (London, 1993) pp.275–285.
Juliá, Xavier Moreno, *La División Azul: Sangre española en Rusia, 1941–1945* (Barcelona, 2005).
Kamenir, Victor J., *The Bloody Triangle. The Defeat of Soviet Armor in the Ukraine, June 1941* (Minneapolis, 2008).
Kay, Alex J., *Exploitation, Resettlement, Mass Murder. Political and Economic Planning for German Occupation Policy in the Soviet Union, 1940–1941* (Oxford, 2006).
'"The Purpose of the Russian Campaign is the Decimation of the Slavic Population by Thirty Million": the Radicalisation of German Food Policy in Early 1941' in Kay *et al.* (eds.), *Nazi Policy on the Eastern Front, 1941*.
Kedward, Roderick, 'France' in I. C. B. Dear and M. R. D. Foot (eds.), *The Oxford Companion to the Second World War* (Oxford, 1995) pp.391–408.
Keegan, John, *Barbarossa. Invasion of Russia 1941* (New York, 1971).
The First World War (New York, 2000).
The Second World War (New York, 1989).
Kemp, Paul, *Convoy! Drama in Arctic Waters* (London, 1993).
Kern, Erich, *Dance of Death* (New York, 1951).

Kershaw, Ian, *Fateful Choices. Ten Decisions that Changed the World, 1940–1941* (New York, 2007).

Hitler 1936–1945. Nemesis (London, 2001).

Kershaw, Robert, *War without Garlands. Operation Barbarossa 1941/42* (New York, 2000).

Kesselring, Albrecht, *The Memoirs of Field-Marshal Kesselring* (London, 1988).

Kipp, Jacob W., 'Barbarossa and the Crisis of Successive Operations: the Smolensk Engagements, July 10–August 7, 1941' in Joseph Wieczynski (ed.), *Operation Barbarossa. The German Attack on the Soviet Union, June 1941* (Salt Lake City, 1993) pp.113–150.

'Barbarossa, Soviet Covering Forces and the Initial Period of War: Military History and Airland Battle' 'Foreign Military Studies Office' (Fort Leavenworth, 1989), available at http://fmso.leavenworth.army.mil/fmsopubs/issues/barbaros.htm.

'Overview Phase 1: to 20 July 1941' in David M. Glantz (ed.), *The Initial Period of War on the Eastern Front 22 June–August 1941* (London, 1997) pp.354–379.

Kirchubel, Robert, *Hitler's Panzer's Armies on the Eastern Front* (Barnsley, 2009).

Operation Barbarossa 1941 (1): Army Group South (Oxford, 2003).

Operation Barbarossa 1941 (2): Army Group North (Oxford, 2005).

Kitchen, Martin, *British Policy towards the Soviet Union during the Second World War* (London, 1986).

Rommel's Desert War. Waging World War II in North Africa, 1941–1943 (Cambridge, 2009).

A World in Flames. A Short History of the Second World War in Europe and Asia 1939–1945 (London, 1990).

Klee, Ernst, Willi Dressen and Volker Riess (eds.), *'The Good Old Days'. The Holocaust as Seen by its Perpetrators and Bystanders* (Old Saybrook, CT, 1991).

Kleindienst, Jürgen (ed.), *Sei tausendmal gegrüßt. Briefwechsel Irene und Ernst Guicking 1937–1945* (Berlin, 2001).

Kleinfeld, Gerald R. and Lewis A. Tambs, *Hitler's Spanish Legion. The Blue Division in Russia* (St Petersburg, FL, 2005).

Klink, Ernst, 'English Translation: Ernst Klink, The Military Concept of the War against the Soviet Union' in Militärgeschichtliches Forschungsamt (ed.), *Germany and the Second World War. Volume IV. The Attack on the Soviet Union* (Oxford, 1998) pp.225–385.

'Die militärische Konzeption des Krieges gegen die Sowjetunion' in Militärgeschichtliches Forschungsamt (ed.), *Das Deutsche Reich und der*

Zweite Weltkrieg. Band 4. Der Angriff auf die Sowjetunion (Stuttgart, 1983) pp. 186–187.

'Die Operationsführung', in Militärgeschichtliches Forschungsamt (ed.), *Das Deutsche Reich und der Zweite Weltkrieg. Band IV. Der Angriff auf die Sowjetunion* (Stuttgart, 1983) pp.451–652. English translation: Ernst Klink, 'The Conduct of Operations' in Militärgeschichtliches Forschungsamt (ed.), *Germany and the Second World War. Volume IV. The Attack on the Soviet Union* (Oxford, 1998) pp.525–763.

Knappe, Siegfried with Ted Brusaw, *Soldat. Reflections of a German Soldier, 1936–1949* (New York, 1992).

Knoblauch, Karl, *Kampf und Untergang der 95. Infanteriedivision. Chronik einer Infanteriedivision von 1939–1945 in Frankreich und an der Ostfront* (Würzburg, 2008).

Knopp, Guido, 'Die Wehrmacht – Eine Bilanz', documentary (2007).

Knox, MacGregor, *Hitler's Italian Allies. Royal Armed Forces, Fascist Regime, and the War of 1940–1943* (Cambridge, 2009).

Koch-Erpach, R., '4th Panzer Division's Crossing of the Dnepr River and the Advance to Roslavl' in David M. Glantz (ed.), *The Initial Period of War on the Eastern Front 22 June–August 1941* (London, 1997) pp.403–404.

Koschorrek, Günther K., *Blood Red Snow. The Memoirs of a German Soldier on the Eastern Front* (London, 2002).

Kotze, Hildegard von (ed.), *Heeresadjutant bei Hitler 1938–1943. Aufzeichnungen des Majors Engel* (Stuttgart, 1974).

Krivosheev, G. F. (ed.), *Soviet Casualties and Combat Losses in the Twentieth Century* (London, 1997).

Kroener, Bernhard R., 'The "Frozen *Blitzkrieg*": German Strategic Planning against the Soviet Union and the Causes of its Failure' in Bernd Wegner (ed.), *From Peace to War. Germany, Soviet Russia and the World, 1939–1941* (Oxford, 1997) pp.135–149.

'Squaring the Circle: Blitzkrieg Strategy and the Manpower Shortage, 1939–1942' in Wilhelm Deist (ed.), *The German Military in the Age of Total War* (Leamington Spa, 1985) pp.282–303.

'The Winter Crisis of 1941–1942: the Distribution of Scarcity or Steps towards a More Rational Management of Personnel' in Militärgeschichtliches Forschungsamt (ed.), *Germany and the Second World War. Volume V/I. Organization and Mobilization of the German Sphere of Power* (Oxford, 2000) pp.1001–1127.

Kruglov, Alexander, 'Jewish Losses in Ukraine, 1941–1944' in Ray Brandon and Wendy Lower (eds.), *The Shoah in Ukraine. History, Testimony, Memorialization* (Bloomington, IN, 2008) pp.272–290.

Kubik, Willi, *Erinnerungen eines Panzerschützen 1941–1945. Tagebuchaufzeichnung eines Panzerschützen der Pz.Aufkl.Abt. 13 im Russlandfeldzug* (Würzburg, 2004).

Kuhnert, Max, *Will We See Tomorrow? A German Cavalryman at War, 1939–1942* (London, 1993).

Kunz, Norbert, 'Das Beispiel Charkow: Eine Stadtbevölkerung als Opfer der deutschen Hungerstrategie 1941/42' in Christian Hartmann, Johannes Hürter and Ulrike Jureit (eds.), *Verbrechen der Wehrmacht. Bilanz einer Debatte* (Munich, 2005) pp.136–144.

Kursietis, Andris J., *The Wehrmacht at War 1939–1945. The Units and Commanders of the German Ground Forces during World War II* (Soesterberg, 1999).

Lammers, Walther (ed.), *'Fahrtberichte' aus der Zeit des deutschsowjetischen Krieges 1941. Protokolle des Begleitoffiziers des Kommandierenden Generals LIII. Armeekorps* (Boppard am Rhein, 1988).

Landon, H. C. Robbins and Sebastian Leitner (eds.), *Diary of a German Soldier* (London, 1963).

Leach, Barry, *German Strategy against Russia 1939–1941* (Oxford, 1973).

Leyen, Ferdinand Prinz von der, *Rückblick zum Mauerwald. Vier Kriegsjahre im OKH* (Munich, 1965).

Liddell Hart, Basil, *History of the Second World War* (London, 1970).

The Other Side of the Hill (London, 1999).

Lieven, Dominic, *Russia against Napoleon. The Battle for Europe, 1807 to 1814* (London, 2010).

Löffler, Jürgen, *Walter von Brauchitsch (1881–1948)* (Frankfurt am Main, 2001).

Longerich, Peter, *The Unwritten Order. Hitler's Role in the Final Solution* (Stroud, 2005).

Lower, Wendy, 'Axis Collaboration, Operation "Barbarossa" and the Holocaust in Ukraine' in Alex J. Kay, Jeff Rutherford and David Stahel (eds.), *Nazi Policy on the Eastern Front, 1941. Total War, Genocide and Radicalization* (forthcoming).

Nazi Empire-Building and the Holocaust in Ukraine (Chapel Hill, NC, 2005).

Lubbeck, William with David B. Hurt, *At Leningrad's Gates. The Story of a Soldier with Army Group North* (Philadelphia, 2006).

Lucas, James, *Das Reich. The Military Role of the 2nd SS Division* (London, 1991).

War of the Eastern Front 1941–1945. The German Soldier in Russia (London, 1980).

Lyons, Graham (ed.), *The Russian Version of the Second World War. The History of the War as Taught to Soviet Schoolchildren* (New York, 1976).

Mackensen, Eberhard von, *Vom Bug zum Kaukasus. Das III. Panzerkorps im Feldzug gegen Sowjetrußland 1941/42* (Neckargemünd, 1967).

Macksey, Kenneth, *Guderian. Panzer General* (London, 1975).

Magenheimer, Heinz, *Hitler's War. Germany's Key Strategic Decisions 1940–1945* (London, 1999).

Mail Online, 'Stalin's British Heroes' (14 May 2009), available at www.dailymail.co.uk/news/article-1181390.

Maisky, Ivan, *Memoirs of a Soviet Ambassador. The War 1939–43* (London, 1967).

Malaparte, Curzio, *The Volga Rises in Europe* (Edinburgh, 2000).

Manley, Rebecca, *To the Tashkent Station. Evacuation and Survival in the Soviet Union at War* (Ithaca, NY, 2009).

Manstein, Erich von, *Lost Victories* (Novato, CA, 1958).

Maslov, Aleksander A., *Fallen Soviet Generals. Soviet General Officers Killed in Battle, 1941–1945* (London, 1998).

Mawdsley, Evan, *Thunder in the East. The Nazi–Soviet War 1941–1945* (London, 2005).

Mazower, Mark, *Hitler's Empire. Nazi Rule in Occupied Europe* (London, 2009).

Inside Hitler's Greece. The Experience of Occupation 1941–1944 (New Haven, 2001).

Megargee, Geoffrey P., *Inside Hitler's High Command* (Lawrence, KS, 2000).

War of Annihilation. Combat and Genocide on the Eastern Front 1941 (Lanham, MD, 2006).

Meier-Welcker, Hans, *Aufzeichnungen eines Generalstabsoffiziers 1939–1942* (Freiburg, 1982).

Mellinger, George, *Soviet Lend-Lease Fighter Aces of World War 2* (Oxford, 2006).

Merridale, Catherine, *Ivan's War. Life and Death in the Red Army, 1939–1945* (New York, 2006).

Metelmann, Henry, *Through Hell for Hitler* (Havertown, PA, 2005).

Meyer, Georg, *Adolf Heusinger. Dienst eines deutschen Soldaten 1915 bis 1964* (Berlin, 2001).

Meyer, Georg (ed.), *Generalfeldmarschall Wilhelm Ritter von Leeb. Tagebuchaufzeichnungen und Lagebeurteilungen aus zwei Weltkriegen* (Stuttgart, 1976).

Mielert, Harry, *Russische Erde. Kriegsbriefe aus Russland* (Stuttgart, 1950).

Milner, Marc, 'Atlantic, Battle of the' in I. C. B. Dear and M. R. D. Foot (eds.), *The Oxford Companion to the Second World War* (Oxford, 1995) pp.62–69.

Milward, Alan S., *The German Economy at War* (London, 1965).

War, Economy and Society 1939–1945 (Berkeley, CA, 1979).

Ministry of Foreign Affairs of the USSR (ed.), *Stalin's Correspondence with Churchill, Attlee, Roosevelt and Truman 1941–1945* (New York, 1958).

Misch, Rochus, *Der letzte Zeuge. Ich war Hitlers Telefonist, Kurier und Leibwächter* (Munich, 2009).

Mitcham, Samuel W., Jr, *German Order of Battle. Volume I. 1st–290th Infantry Divisions in WWII* (Mechanicsburg, PA, 2007).

Hitler's Field Marshals and their Battles (Chatham, 1988).

The Men of Barbarossa. Commanders of the German Invasion of Russia, 1941 (Newbury, 2009).

Mohrmann, Wolf-Dieter (ed.), *Der Krieg hier ist hart und grausam! Feldpostbriefe an den Osnabrücker Regierungspräsidenten 1941–1944* (Osnabrück, 1984).

Morgan, Hugh, *Soviet Aces of World War 2* (Madrid, 1999).

Moritz, Erhard (ed.), *Fall Barbarossa. Dokumente zur Vorbereitung der faschistischen Wehrmacht auf die Aggression gegen die Sowjetunion (1940/41)* (Berlin, 1970).

Mosier, John, *Deathride. Hitler vs. Stalin: the Eastern Front, 1941–1945* (New York, 2010).

Muggeridge, Malcolm (ed.), *Ciano's Diary 1939–1943* (Kingswood, 1947).

Muller, Richard, *The German Air War in Russia* (Baltimore, 1992).

Müller, Rolf-Dieter, 'The Crippling of Armaments Production' in Militärgeschichtliches Forschungsamt (ed.), *Germany and the Second World War. Volume V/I. Organization and Mobilization of the German Sphere of Power* (Oxford, 2000) pp.604–640.

'From Economic Alliance to a War of Colonial Exploitation' in Militärgeschichtliches Forschungsamt (ed.), *Germany and the Second World War. Volume IV. The Attack on the Soviet Union* (Oxford, 1998) pp.118–224.

'The Failure of the Economic "Blitzkrieg Strategy"' in Militärgeschichtliches Forschungsamt (ed.), *Germany and the Second World War. Volume IV. The Attack on the Soviet Union* (Oxford, 1998) pp.1081–1188.

Der letzte deutsche Krieg 1939–1945 (Stuttgart, 2005).

An der Seite der Wehrmacht. Hitlers ausländische Helfer beim 'Kreuzzug gegen den Bolschewismus' 1941–1945 (Berlin, 2007).

'The Victor's Hubris: Germany Loses its Lead in Armaments after the French Campaign' in Militärgeschichtliches Forschungsamt (ed.), *Germany and the Second World War. Volume V/I. Organization and Mobilization of the German Sphere of Power* (Oxford, 2000) pp.564–721.

Müller, Rolf-Dieter and Gerd R. Ueberschär, *Hitler's War in the East 1941–1945. A Critical Assessment* (Oxford, 2009).

Müller-Hillebrand, Burkhart, *Das Heer 1933–1945. Band III. Der Zweifrontenkrieg. Das Heer vom Beginn des Feldzuges gegen die Sowjetunion bis zum Kriegsende* (Frankfurt am Main, 1969).

Munoz, Antonio and Oleg V. Romanko, *Hitler's White Russians. Collaboration, Extermination and Anti-Partisan Warfare in Byelorussia 1941–1944. A Study of White Russian Collaboration and German Occupation Policies* (New York, 2003).

Murray, Williamson, *The Luftwaffe 1933–45. Strategy for Defeat* (Washington, DC, 1996).

Murray, Williamson and Allan R. Millett, *A War to be Won. Fighting the Second World War* (Cambridge, MA, 2000).

Nagorski, Andrew, *The Greatest Battle. Stalin, Hitler, and the Desperate Struggle for Moscow that Changed the Course of World War II* (New York, 2007).

'Stalin's Tipping Point', *Newsweek* (US edition, 10 September 2007) p.44.

Neitzel, Sönke, *Tapping Hitler's Generals. Transcripts of Secret Conversations, 1942–45* (St Paul, MN, 2007).

Nelson, Anne, *Red Orchestra. The Story of the Berlin Underground and the Circle of Friends who Resisted Hitler* (New York, 2009).

Newton, Steven H., *Hitler's Commander. Field Marshal Walther Model – Hitler's Favorite General* (Cambridge, MA, 2006).

Nolte, Hans-Heinrich, 'Die erste Phase des Zweiten Weltkrieges und der deutsche Überfall auf die Sowjetunion in Schulbüchern der UdSSR und der Bundesrepublik Deutschland' in Gerd R. Ueberschär and Wolfram Wette (eds.), *'Unternehmen Barbarossa'. Der deutsche Überfall auf die Sowjetunion 1941* (Paderborn, 1984) pp.49–65.

Nove, Alec, 'Soviet Peasantry in World War II' in Susan J. Linz (ed.), *The Impact of World War II on the Soviet Union* (Totowa, NJ, 1985) pp.77–90.

Obryn'ba, Nikolai I., *Red Partisan. The Memoir of a Soviet Resistance Fighter on the Eastern Front* (Washington, DC, 2007).

Ochsenknecht, Ingeborg, *'Als ob der Schnee alles zudeckte'. Eine Krankenschwester erinnert sich an ihren Kriegseinsatz an der Ostfront* (Berlin, 2005).

O'Neill, Robert, 'Fritsch, Beck and the Führer' in Correlli Barnett (ed.), *Hitler's Generals* (London, 1989) pp.19–41.

Overmans, Rüdiger, *Deutsche militärische Verluste im Zweiten Weltkrieg* (Munich, 2000).

Overy, Richard, *The Air War 1939–1945* (London, 1980).

'Hitler's War Plans and the German Economy' in Robert Boyce and Esmonde M. Robertson (eds.), *Path to War. New Essays on the Origins of the Second World War* (London, 1989) pp.96–127.

Russia's War (London, 1997).

'Statistics' in I. C. B. Dear and M. R. D. Foot (eds.), *The Oxford Companion to the Second World War* (Oxford, 1995) pp.1059–1062.

Why the Allies Won (New York, 1996).

Pabst, Helmut, *The Outermost Frontier. A German Soldier in the Russian Campaign* (London, 1957).

Paoletti, Ciro, *A Military History of Italy* (Westport, CT, 2008).

Parker, R. A. C., *Struggle for Survival. The History of the Second World War* (Oxford, 1989).

Perel, Solomon, *Europa Europa* (New York, 1997).

Pichler, Hans, *Truppenarzt und Zeitzeuge. Mit der 4. SS-Polizei-Division an vorderster Front* (Dresden, 2006).

Piekalkiewicz, Janusz, *Moscow 1941. The Frozen Offensive* (London, 1981).

Pleshakov, Constantine, *Stalin's Folly. The Tragic First Ten Days of WWII on the Eastern Front* (New York, 2005).

Plocher, Hermann, *The German Air Force versus Russia, 1941* (New York, 1965).

Pohl, Dieter, *Die Herrschaft der Wehrmacht: Deutsche Militärbesatzung und einheimische Bevölkerung in der Sowjetunion 1941–1944* (Munich, 2008).

Pok, Attila, 'German–Hungarian Relations,1941–1945' in Jonathan Adelman (ed.), *Hitler and his Allies in World War II* (New York, 2007) pp.152–165.

Porter, Cathy and Mark Jones, *Moscow in World War II* (London, 1987).

Raus, Erhard, 'Russian Combat Methods in World War II' in Peter G. Tsouras (ed.), *Fighting in Hell. The German Ordeal on the Eastern Front* (New York, 1998) pp.13–153.

Raus, Erhard and Steven H. Newton, *Panzer Operations. The Eastern Front Memoir of General Raus, 1941–1945*, compiled and translated by Steven H. Newton (Cambridge, MA, 2005).

Reddemann, Karl (ed.), *Zwischen Front und Heimat. Der Briefwechsel des münsterischen Ehepaares Agnes und Albert Neuhaus 1940–1944* (Münster, 1996).

Reese, Roger R., *Stalin's Reluctant Soldiers. A Social History of the Red Army 1925–1941* (Lawrence, KS, 1996).

Reinhardt, Klaus, *Moscow – the Turning Point. The Failure of Hitler's Strategy in the Winter of 1941–42* (Oxford, 1992).
Reitlinger, Gerald, *The House Built on Sand. The Conflicts of German Policy in Russia 1939–45* (London, 1960).
Rhodes, Richard, *Masters of Death. The SS Einsatzgruppen and the Invention of the Holocaust* (New York, 2003).
Roberts, Geoffrey, *Stalin's Wars. From World War to Cold War, 1939–1953* (New Haven, 2006).
Röll, Hans-Joachim, *Oberleutnant Albert Blaich. Als Panzerkommandant in Ost und West* (Würzburg, 2009).
Römer, Felix, *Der Kommissarbefehl: Wehrmacht und NS-Verbrechen an der Ostfront 1941/42* (Paderborn, 2008).
'The Wehrmacht in the War of Ideologies: the Army and Hitler's Criminal Orders on the Eastern Front' in Alex J. Kay, Jeff Rutherford and David Stahel (eds.), *Nazi Policy on the Eastern Front, 1941. Total War, Genocide and Radicalization* (forthcoming).
Röttiger, Hans, 'XXXXI Panzer Corps during the Battle of Moscow in 1941 as a Component of Panzer Group 3' in Steven H. Newton (ed.), *German Battle Tactics on the Russian Front 1941–1945* (Atglen, PA, 1994) pp.13–54.
Rudel, Hans Ulrich, *Stuka Pilot* (New York, 1979).
Rüss, Hartmut, 'Kiev/Babij Jar 1941' in Gerd R. Ueberschär (ed.), *Orte des Grauens. Verbrechen im Zweiten Weltkrieg* (Frankfurt am Main, 2003) pp.102–113.
Rutherford, Jeffrey, 'The Radicalization of German Occupation Policies: *Wirtschaftsstab Ost* and the 121st Infantry Division in Pavlovsk, 1941' in Alex J. Kay, Jeff Rutherford and David Stahel (eds.), *Nazi Policy on the Eastern Front 1941. Total War, Genocide and Radicalization* (forthcoming).
Sahm, Christiane, *Verzweiflung und Glaube. Briefe aus dem Krieg 1939–1942* (Munich, 2007).
Sajer, Guy, *The Forgotten Soldier* (New York, 1990).
Salisbury, Harrison E., *The 900 Days. The Siege of Leningrad* (New York, 1985).
The Unknown War (London, 1978).
Sapir, Jacques, 'The Economics of War in the Soviet Union during World War II' in Ian Kershaw and Moshe Lewin (eds.), *Stalinism and Nazism. Dictatorships in Comparison* (Cambridge, 2003) pp.208–236.
Schall-Riaucour, Heidemarie Gräfin, *Aufstand und Gehorsam. Offizierstum und Generalstab im Umbruch. Leben und Wirken von Generalobberst Franz Halder Generalstabchef 1938–1942* (Wiesbaden, 1972).

Schäufler, Hans (ed.), *Knight's Cross Panzers. The German 35th Panzer Regiment in WWII* (Mechanicsburg, PA, 2010).

Scheuer, Alois, *Briefe aus Russland. Feldpostbriefe des Gefreiten Alois Scheuer 1941–1942* (St Ingbert, 2000).

Schiebel, Helmut, *Einen besser'n findst Du nicht. Der Krieg im Osten 1941–1945. Ein Zeitzeuge erzählt* (Leoni am Starnberger See, 1991).

Schlemmer, Thomas (ed.), *Die Italiener an der Ostfront 1942/43. Dokumente zu Mussolinis Krieg gegen die Sowjetunion* (Munich, 2005).

Schober, Franz and Leopold, *Briefe von der Front. Feldpostbriefe 1939–1945*, (ed.) Michael Hans, Salvesberger (Gösing am Wagram, 1997).

Schreiber, Gerhard, 'Mussolini's "Non-Belligerence"' in Militärgeschichtliches Forschungsamt (ed.), *Germany and the Second World War. Volume III. The Mediterranean, South-East Europe and North Africa 1939–1941* (Oxford, 1995) pp.8–98.

Schüler, Klaus, 'The Eastern Campaign as a Transportation and Supply Problem' in Bernd Wegner (ed.), *From Peace to War. Germany, Soviet Russia and the World, 1939–1941* (Oxford, 1997) pp.205–222.

Logistik im Russlandfeldzug. Die Rolle der Eisenbahn bei Planung, Vorbereitung und Durchführung des deutschen Angriffs auf die Sowjetunion bis zur Krise vor Moskau im Winter 1941/42 (Frankfurt am Main, 1987).

Schulte, Theo, *The German Army and Nazi Policies in Occupied Russia* (Oxford, 1989).

Schwabedissen, Walter, *The Russian Air Force in the Eyes of the German Commanders* (New York, 1960).

Seaton, Albert, *The Battle for Moscow* (New York, 1993).

Sebastian, Mihail, *Journal, 1935–1944* (London, 2003).

Senger und Etterlin, Ferdinand Maria von, *German Tanks of World War II. The Complete Illustrated History of German Armoured Fighting Vehicles 1926–1945* (Harrisburg, PA, 1969).

Shepherd, Ben, *War in the Wild East. The German Army and Soviet Partisans* (Cambridge, 2004).

Shirer, William, *The Rise and Fall of the Third Reich* (New York, 1960).

Simmons, Cynthia and Nina Perlina, *Writing the Siege of Leningrad. Women's Diaries, Memoirs, and Documentary Prose* (Pittsburgh, 2002).

Slepyan, Kenneth, *Stalin's Guerrillas. Soviet Partisans in World War II* (Lawrence, KS, 2006).

Slesina, Horst, *Soldaten gegen Tod und Teufel. Unser Kampf in der Sowjetunion. Eine soldatische Deutung* (Düsseldorf, 1943).

Smelser, Ronald and Edward J. Davies II, *The Myth of the Eastern Front. The Nazi–Soviet War in American Popular Culture* (Cambridge, 2008).

Snyder, Timothy, *Bloodlands. Europe between Hitler and Stalin* (New York, 2010).

Speer, Albert, *Inside the Third Reich* (London, 1971).

Stader, Ingo (ed.), *Ihr daheim und wir hier draußen. Ein Briefwechsel zwischen Ostfront und Heimat Juni 1941–März 1943* (Cologne, 2006).

Stahel, David, *Operation Barbarossa and Germany's Defeat in the East* (Cambridge, 2009).

'Radicalizing Warfare: the German Command and the Failure of Operation Barbarossa' in Alex J. Kay, Jeff Rutherford and David Stahel (eds.), *Nazi Policy on the Eastern Front, 1941: Total War, Genocide and Radicalization* (forthcoming).

Stegemann, Bernd, 'Operation Crusader' in Militärgeschichtliches Forschungsamt (ed.), *Germany and the Second World War. Volume III. The Mediterranean, South-East Europe and North Africa 1939–1941* (Oxford, 1995) pp.725–754.

Steiger, Rudolf, *Armour Tactics in the Second World War. Panzer Army Campaigns of 1939–41 in German War Diaries* (Oxford, 1991).

Steinert, Marlis, *Hitlers Krieg und die Deutschen. Stimmung und Haltung der deutschen Bevölkerung im Zweiten Weltkrieg* (Düsseldorf and Vienna, 1970).

Stern, J. P., *Hitler. The Führer and the People* (Berkeley, CA, 1992).

Stolfi, R. H. S., *Hitler's Panzers East. World War II Reinterpreted* (Norman, OK, 1993).

Streit, Christian, *Keine Kameraden: Die Wehrmacht und die sowjetischen Kriegsgefangenen 1941–1945* (Bonn, 1997).

'Partisans – Resistance – Prisoners of War' in Joseph Wieczynski (ed.), *Operation Barbarossa. The German Attack on the Soviet Union June 22, 1941* (Salt Lake City, 1993) pp.260–275.

'Soviet Prisoners of War in the Hands of the Wehrmacht' in Hannes Heer and Klaus Naumann (eds.), *War of Extermination. The German Military in World War II 1941–1944* (Oxford, 2006) pp.80–91.

Sullivan, Brian R., 'The Italian Soldier in Combat, June 1940–September 1943: Myths, Realities and Explanations' in Paul Addison and Angus Calder (eds.), *A Time to Kill. The Soldier's Experience of War in the West 1939–1945* (London, 1997) pp.177–205.

'The Path Marked out by History: the German–Italian Alliance, 1939–1943' in Jonathan Adelman (ed.), *Hitler and his Allies in World War II* (New York, 2007) pp.116–151.

Szinai, Miklós and László Szűcs (eds.), *The Confidential Papers of Admiral Horthy* (Budapest, 1965).

Thilo, Karl Wilhelm, 'A Perspective from the Army High Command (OKH)' in David M. Glantz (ed.), *The Initial Period of War on the Eastern Front 22 June–August 1941* (London, 1997) pp.290–307.

Thomas, Georg, *Geschichte der deutsch Wehr- und Rüstungswirtschaft (1918–1943/45)*, (ed.) Wolfgang Birkenfeld (Boppard am Rhein, 1966).

Thurston, Robert, 'Cauldrons of Loyalty and Betrayal: Soviet Soldiers' Behavior, 1941 and 1945' in Robert Thurston and Bernd Bonwetsch (eds.), *The People's War. Responses to World War II in the Soviet Union* (Chicago, 2000) pp.235–257.

Tooze, Adam, *The Wages of Destruction. The Making and Breaking of the Nazi Economy* (London, 2006).

Trevor-Roper, Hugh R. (ed.), *Hitler's Table Talk, 1941–1944. His Private Conversations* (London, 2000).

(ed.), *Hitler's War Directives 1939–1945* (London, 1964).

True to Type. A Selection from Letters and Diaries of German Soldiers and Civilians Collected on the Soviet–German Front (London, n.d.).

Tsouras, Peter G. (ed.), *Panzers on the Eastern Front. General Erhard Raus and his Panzer Divisions in Russia 1941–1945* (London, 2002).

Turney, Alfred W., *Disaster at Moscow. Von Bock's Campaigns 1941–1942* (Albuquerque, 1970).

Tuyll, Hubert P. van, *Feeding the Bear. American Aid to the Soviet Union, 1941–1945* (Westport, CT, 1989).

Ueberschär, Gerd R., 'Das Scheitern des Unternehmens "Barbarossa". Der deutsch-sowjetische Krieg vom Überfall bis zur Wende vor Moskau im Winter 1941/42' in Gerd R. Ueberschär and Wolfram Wette (eds.), *'Unternehmen Barbarossa'. Der deutsche Überfall auf die Sowjetunion 1941* (Paderborn, 1984) pp.141–172.

Vehviläinen, Olli, *Finland in the Second World War. Between Germany and Russia* (New York, 2002).

Wagener, Carl, *Moskau 1941. Der Angriff auf die russische Hauptstadt* (Dorheim, 1985).

Wagenführ, Rolf, *Die deutsche Industrie im Kriege, 1939 bis 1945* (Berlin, 1954).

Warlimont, Walter, *Im Hauptquartier der deutschen Wehrmacht 1939 bis 1945. Band I. September 1939–November 1942* (Koblenz, 1990). English translation: Walter Warlimont, *Inside Hitler's Headquarters, 1939–1945* (New York, 1964).

Weal, John, *More Bf 109 Aces of the Russian Front* (Oxford, 2007).

Weinberg, Gerhard, *A World at Arms. A Global History of World War II* (Cambridge, 1994).

Werth, Alexander, *Russia at War 1941–1945* (New York, 1964).
Wette, Wolfram, 'Die propagandistische Begleitmusik zum deutschen Überfall auf die Sowjetunion an 22. Juni 1941' in Gerd R. Ueberschär and Wolfram Wette (eds.), *'Unternehmen Barbarossa'. Der deutsche Überfall auf die Sowjetunion 1941* (Paderborn, 1984) pp.111–129.
The Wehrmacht. History, Myth, Reality (Cambridge, 2006).
Wettstein, Adrian, 'Operation "Barbarossa" und Stadtkampf', *Militärgeschichtliche Zeitschrift*, Vol. 66 (2007) pp.21–44.
'Urban Warfare Doctrine on the Eastern Front' in Alex J. Kay, Jeff Rutherford and David Stahel (eds.), *Nazi Policy on the Eastern Front, 1941: Total War, Genocide and Radicalization* (forthcoming).
Woodman, Richard, *Arctic Convoys 1941–1945* (Barnsley, 2007).
Zhukov, G. K., *The Memoirs of Marshal Zhukov* (London, 1971).
Ziemke, Earl F. and Magna E. Bauer, *Moscow to Stalingrad: Decision in the East* (New York, 1988).

INDEX

CPSIA information can be obtained at www.ICGtesting.com
Printed in the USA
LVOW072039250313

325984LV00001B/1/P

9 781107 014596